THE TEARS
OF THE
RAJAS

THE TEARS OF THE RAJAS

Mutiny, Money and Marriage in India 1805–1905

FERDINAND MOUNT

**SIMON &
SCHUSTER**

London · New York · Sydney · Toronto · New Delhi

A CBS COMPANY

First published in Great Britain by Simon & Schuster UK Ltd, 2015
A CBS COMPANY

1 3 5 7 9 10 8 6 4 2

Simon & Schuster UK Ltd
1st Floor
222 Gray's Inn Road
London WC1X 8HB

www.simonandschuster.co.uk

Simon & Schuster Australia, Sydney
Simon & Schuster India, New Delhi

A CIP catalogue record for this book
is available from the British Library

Hardback ISBN: 978-1-4711-2945-2
eBook ISBN: 978-1-4711-2947-6

Typeset by M Rules
Printed and bound by CPI Group (UK) Ltd, Croydon, CR0 4YY

For Mary and Pankaj

'India had been won by the sword and must be retained by the sword.'

Sir John Kaye, *History of the Indian Mutiny*,
Vol I, p 146

'The conquest of the earth, which mostly means the taking it away from those who have a different complexion or slightly flatter noses than ourselves, is not a pretty thing when you look into it too much. What redeems it is the idea only. An idea at the back of it; not a sentimental pretence but an idea; and an unselfish belief in the idea – something you can set up, and bow down before, and offer a sacrifice to ...'

Joseph Conrad, *Heart of Darkness,* Chapter 1

'Not that any of them *like* us much.'

John Low to John Russell Colvin,
July 23, 1838

'I worry about the nightingales
Now that spring has come:
The hunter pitches camp
Right outside the garden.'

Khwaja Haidar Ali Atish (1777–1847)

CONTENTS

CONTENTS

INTRODUCTION

Aunt Ursie and the elephants

A ll I have from my grandmother are the two elephants. They are carved out of ebony and though they are less than two feet high, each is as heavy as a five-year-old child. The tusks have long gone from both of them, either fallen out of the sockets or removed for the ivory, if they were ivory, which they probably were. That is a curious thing if you think about it – the imitation tusk carved out of the real one. They must have had little ivory toenails as well, but there are none left now in the tiny niches for them. The flaps of their ears have fallen off, too, which is a pity because it would be nice to pinch and fondle them as the *mahouts* do. Along their backs the warp of time has prised the blocks of ebony apart a little, so you can see how they were put together. Only the little bead eyes are intact, so absurdly small compared to the rest of the body. They seem to peer out with a rheumy suspicious gaze.

I used to ride on the elephants when I was a child and they were in my grandmother's house. My father said he had ridden on them in his grandfather's house when he was my age. It was that great-grandfather of mine, Malcolm Low, who had brought the elephants back from India in 1874 when he was invalided out of the Indian Civil Service. My own children tried to ride on them, too, but none of them stuck on for long. The same thing with my grand-children. Four generations of us sliding off and now and then getting hurt when the elephant fell over and bruised our toes. The trouble is that elephants don't have a saddleback like a horse, which is why you need a howdah, unless you ride them well forward, just behind the ears, as the sahibs used to and the Indians do, and even then, with our elephants, you slide over the bony forehead because they are really not quite big enough for even a child to ride.

I remember how disappointed I was when I slid off, because I had just read, or had read to me, the story 'Toomai of the Elephants' in *The Jungle Book*, and there was an illustration of little Toomai lying flat out on Kala Nag's back so that no swinging branch can sweep him off as they go crashing through the jungle to the secret place where the elephants gather for their wonderful dance which very few men have ever seen.

The story, like other great children's stories, is the adventure of a child on his own in a hidden world unknown to grown-ups. But it is also a parable of liberation. For Kala Nag, like some of the other elephants dancing and trumpeting in the jungle, is really an escaped beast of burden, who normally has a leg-chain shackling him to a post. He remembers pushing a gun stuck in the mud before the Afghan War of 1842 with a big leather pad on his forehead. On the march into Upper India he had carried 12 cwt of tents. He had been hoisted on a steam crane to be shipped to Africa where he had carried a mortar on his back to the war in Abyssinia. Then he had been taken to Burma to haul big baulks of teak in the timberyards at Moulmein. Elephants were the heavy hauliers of Empire.

Long before Kipling's day, the elephant was adored by the British in India. In a country which was perennially strange and potentially hostile, the elephant sometimes seemed like the only reliable ally.[1] Perhaps the British unconsciously identified themselves with the huge animals that were so essential to them both in peace and war. For the British, too, seemed clumsy in their strength and would lash out when they were maddened.[2]

The ebony elephants were not the only feature of my childhood which came back from India. There was also my great-aunt Ursie, my grandmother's elder sister. The two sisters were only a year apart, but while my grandmother was born in South Kensington after Malcolm had come home, Ida Mary Ursula Low was born at Pachmarhi while he was still Commissioner of the Nerbudda Districts. Pachmarhi was and still is a delightful hill station, 'the Queen of the Satpura Mountains'. It was a miniature Simla, where the officials of the Central Provinces retired in the hot season to recover their health, write up their voluminous reports, delight in the streams and waterfalls, marvel at the ancient cave paintings and bag the occasional tiger. This was the picturesque paradise that Aunt Ursie knew only as a baby. For she came to England with the ebony elephants, still only half their size.

There was, alas, nothing picturesque about Aunt Ursie. She was the classic maiden aunt. You might have found her in the pages of E.M. Forster, either peering inside an Indian cave or pouring tea in a Surrey rectory. She looked not unlike Miss Marple as played by Joan Hickson and she wore tweed in various shades of oatmeal and beige. She was tactless, either by nature or because living on her own had made her insensitive to others, or a bit of both. While benign in her intentions, after only a short visit to any of her three nephews,

she got on everyone's nerves. She asked probing questions on subjects which none of them wanted to talk about, such as divorce or
German rearmament. Her great-nieces called her The Aunt.

At first she had a flat in South Kensington, in Wetherby Gardens,
near her parents. She was especially close to her father, whom she
accompanied on his genealogical rambles, notably the one to establish whether his mother Augusta Shakespear was descended from the
poet (she was not). Later on, she hung out in residential hotels in the
same quarter, tending, according to my father, to select those where
gruesome murders had recently occurred and the rates were accordingly competitive. Her last residence was called the Milton Court
Hotel. I used to go and have tea with her there in the quiet and
stuffy lounge and wondered how soon I could leave after I had had
my quota of cucumber and Marmite sandwiches.

Like many another person living on her own, she took up all sorts
of religious and philosophical pursuits. She attended lectures on
theosophy and spiritualism, making notes afterwards. It may have
been for some reason connected with these pursuits, or perhaps
from a more down-to-earth fear, that she left unusual instructions in
her will for the disposal of her body (she died in 1963 at the age of
88, having been delicate all her life). She wished to be cremated at
Putney Vale crematorium where her parents were buried and 'to
have my ashes scattered to the four winds', thoughtfully adding that
'should my death be at an inconvenient distance from a crematorium
then I wish my body to be buried wherever I may die' – which in
practice might have been more inconvenient, something not uncommon in her life, for while protesting that she did not wish to be a
trouble, Aunt Ursie's arrangements often turned out to contain some
hidden snag. But what caught my eye was her further addendum,
that 'in any case I wish that careful and thorough means should be
taken by a doctor to ensure that my life is extinct'. I have no idea
what inspired this stern caveat. Had there been an outbreak of people
being buried alive in South Kensington?

She wrote a novel, which was not published. It was a society novel, about love and marriage among the genteel classes, and nobody in the family has ever read it, as far as I know, because what could The Aunt know about love? But she wrote another book, which was published, in 1936, by the distinguished house of John Murray. The book was called *Fifty Years with John Company: from the letters of General Sir John Low of Clatto, Fife, 1822–1858*. It had 436 pages and 12 black-and-white illustrations and cost 16 shillings, and it was reviewed, quite kindly, in *The Times* and elsewhere. The book was mockingly referred to in the family as 'Low Company', and my father and his two brothers had copies on their shelves, but I doubt if any of them was ever opened. Aunt Ursie could have written *War and Peace*, and we still wouldn't have read it.

But it wasn't just because of The Aunt that the book remained among the Great Unread. The truth is that for my parents' generation, and for mine too I think, the subject of the British Empire in India was unmentionable. The memory of it was a huge embarrassment, a chapter in our island story that we wanted to skip. We brushed it away with jokes about pigsticking and memsahibs. I have always been irritated by the phrase 'we just didn't want to know' but it does describe our feelings on this subject. Even before the Union Jack had been hauled down in 1947, India had been more or less erased from our conversation. We were still fascinated by events in other parts of the Empire which remained British but we didn't much care what went on in India, either before or after independence.

We have been energetic in writing about the misdeeds and misfortunes of other peoples, but we have kept rather quiet about our own. During the years after India simultaneously won her independence and was partitioned with such appalling slaughter, there was a remarkable reluctance back in Britain to think or write about the whole imperial experience. If the subject was raised at all, we told ourselves that the whole thing had had remarkably little impact on us, that it had barely left a scratch on our souls.

It was not until 1966 when Paul Scott published the first volume of what became his Raj Quartet, *The Jewel in the Crown* (which was to be taken as the title for the whole famous ITV series), that the all-but two centuries of British rule began to seem a subject worth recreating. And even Scott concentrated on the concluding years of the Raj, from 1942 onwards, with only some detours back to the 1900s. He did not explore the earlier, wilder years, before the Raj was usually known by that name. The horrific events of the Indian Mutiny of 1857 – the most traumatic event of the entire nineteenth century for the British nation – remained untouched by serious modern writers until J.G. Farrell's *The Siege of Krishnapur* came out in 1973. Krishnapur is a fictional town but the siege is closely based on the terrible events at Cawnpore and Lucknow and draws on the many unsparing accounts published soon after by survivors. For the Victorians took the horrors full on. We were until recently more squeamish.

Nearly half a century after Aunt Ursie's death, when I began to plan our first visit to India, I still had no thought of picking up her book. Our daughter Mary and her husband, the Indian writer Pankaj Mishra, were eager for us to take the trip. They volunteered to take us in hand and show us around. With infinite kindness, they planned the itinerary, booked the tickets and the hotels, and gave us some books to read – John Keay's *Into India*, Sam Miller's *Delhi*, *In Light of India* by Octavio Paz, a good life of Gandhi whose author's name I have forgotten, novels and stories by R.K. Narayan, Amit Chaudhuri and Kamila Shamsie. But of course no Aunt Ursie.

Then, a few weeks before we were due to fly out to Delhi, I opened the *Sunday Times* and read the headline **By Jingo, PM's family killed for the Empire**. The strapline offered a gloss to this crude screamer: *Rediscovered letters reveal with bloody relish how David Cameron's ancestors helped put down the Indian Mutiny.* The peg on which this story was flung was that David Cameron had the previous week made a goodwill trip to India, his first visit as Prime Minister, in the hope of forging new trade links with the emerging economic superpower and of burying unhappy past history. 'He did not', the

Sunday Times told us, 'mention his own family's part in that history. It has now emerged that his great-great-grandfather was a British cavalryman who mercilessly helped suppress the Indian Mutiny. William Low left behind accounts of how he slew natives with his sabre and almost lost a hand and an ear in combat. He also participated in a mass hanging of civilians that would probably be interpreted as a war crime by modern standards.' (*Sunday Times*, August 1, 2010)

The report went on to list other atrocities committed by William and his brother Robert, the sons of General Sir John Low, none other than the Low of Aunt Ursie's book. 'William' was in fact William Malcolm, always known by his second name, and he was not a cavalryman but a civil servant who had picked up a sabre when the Mutiny broke out (thus conforming to the iron rule that a newspaper report on a subject you know anything about always has something wrong with it). Malcolm was Aunt Ursie's father and my great-grandfather. And he was David Cameron's ancestor, too, because Cameron's mother Mary is my first cousin.

The *Sunday Times* opined that if all this had been known before Cameron went to Delhi, it could have caused embarrassment. In the event, the story was reprinted in the Indian newspapers, but public outrage was conspicuous by its absence. Such atrocious tales are not exactly news to most Indians, and the country has long ago moved on from unhappy far-off things.

But I hadn't. I found the report startling and disorienting. It upset my long-established view of things in general and of my grandmother's family in particular. If I thought of them at all, I thought of them as rather dull, a little too pious for my taste, the epitome of Lowland Scots of their class and era. I remembered my grandmother as a rather forbidding grey-haired old lady, who did, however, unbend to me, though not to my girl cousins, and showed me where to find the wild strawberries in the cracks between the paving stones. My father remembered his grandfather Malcolm as a sweet old gentleman who was frightened of his well-born wife. I had not thought of any of them as mass murderers. Malcolm Low recorded proudly in his entry in *Who's Who* that he had 'received special letter conveying thanks of Her Majesty for services in the field during the Indian Mutiny'. He did not specify exactly what kind of services they had been, nor I imagine had Her Majesty.

Where, I wondered, had this news story come from? Halfway through the story the reporters helpfully revealed their source: a genealogist called Nick Barratt who had worked for the BBC's highly successful programme *Who Do You Think You Are?*

But where had Mr Barratt got his stuff? Again, the reporters were helpful. It all came out of 'letters from William uncovered last week in a book in the British Library'. A book in the British Library? Well, all books are in the British Library. That's what it's there for. So not exactly 'rediscovered' or 'uncovered' then. Rather, just sitting there waiting to be read. But what was this book? It couldn't be . . .

It was. I hurried to my bookshelves and located *Fifty Years with John Company* in the same spot where it had been sitting unopened for 40 years. One of the book's many virtues, I immediately discovered, is that it has a first-rate index at the back. In no time at all, I had located every quotation, every fact cited in the *Sunday Times* report. Aunt Ursie was the sole source for the whole story.

I thought how wonderful it was that this woman, so disregarded and unloved for most of her life, should have risen from the grave like this to hit the headlines, if only briefly, on two continents. If in a different way from the one she feared, she had not been properly buried after all.

That was only my first thought. I then and there resolved to read every line of her forgotten work, to make up for the years of neglect and to immerse myself in this part of our history, my history, over which I had so carelessly skipped.

I had not expected to enjoy the task nearly as much as I did. To my surprise, Ursula Low (it is high time to liberate her from aunt-dom) writes with a light and easy swing. She knows the background, both the Indian end and the Scottish end; she is clued up on the politics of the British government and the East India Company, and she remembers several of the participants as they were in life. Occasionally there is a wry aside or a gentle sad reflection. She does not ink in all the horrors – not from a maidenly shrinking but because she sticks closely to her task of recounting the ups and downs of one Fifeshire family in India. She does not overegg the undertaking or claim too much for it, but what she succeeds in doing, and succeeds beautifully, is to evoke the rise, the heyday and the fading of a whole civilization. I use the word civilization neutrally to denote a complex human society; for its proceedings were both civil and uncivil, being in parts greedy and brutal, in other parts decent and dedicated in an unobtrusive way. What she misses out is how strung up with doubt most of them were, perhaps because she did not suffer much from doubt herself. I was not prepared for the ferocity, but I was not prepared for the doubt either.

I do not mean merely the ordinary human doubts that everyone has, about health and money and promotion and getting married and whether the children are all right. The Lows had those doubts in profusion most of the time, and Ursula tells us about them. What I mean above and beyond all that is the nagging doubt about what they were doing in India at all, whether they should have come to this vast bewildering subcontinent and how long they should stay, and what ultimately this distant straggling Empire was *for* and how long it would last and whether it deserved to last.

Did Britain really need to keep up a standing army of over 150,000 men in India, one of the largest European-style armies anywhere in the world at the time? British goods had penetrated every quarter of the globe, Scotsmen had built railways and founded great trading houses in Latin America, Russia and other parts of Asia, without needing to establish a formal empire. Looking at the alarming deficits which kept on appearing in the accounts of the Indian Empire, Governors-General and Cabinet Ministers could be forgiven for wondering whether it was really a burden rather than a bonanza. And the Company's officers who had to carry out the economies to make the books balance could do the dire sums too.

Those doubts dwelled deep inside them and did not always come to the surface. Only the sanest of them understood that the best way to stay sane was to let those doubts breathe, to air them in talk and in letters, both public and private, so that they did not lurk at the back of the mind as an unspeakable and disabling dread. And the sanest of them all was John Low.

He took an active part in deposing three kings, each of them rulers over a territory and population the magnitude of a middle-sized European state. He deprived a fourth raja, perhaps the grandest of them all, of a large portion of his kingdom. He survived three shattering mutinies. Yet at no time do you have the feeling that he was spurred on by a sense of imperial mission. He wanted, if possible, to do his duty, that was all. But what exactly was his duty? That too was shadowed in doubt and mired in misgiving.

How strange it all was, yet how natural it seemed most of the time to those who were part of it. From the day in 1771 that Robert Low set out from Leith to take up his commission in the Madras Army, to the day in 1909 when his grandson Robert Cunliffe Low came home in glory as the general who relieved Chitral to take up his last appointment as Keeper of the Crown Jewels in the Tower of London, there were never less than 20, sometimes twice as many, of the extended family in India – the Lows, the Shakespears and Thackerays, all knotted together by marriage and regiment and patronage.

All over India they were busily engaged, for none of them was ever idle – the Lows were not Lowland Scots for nothing. They fought and collected taxes and dispensed justice and scolded mahara-jahs and married and gave birth and died, from Madras and the Deccan in the South to the foothills of the Himalayas and the Hindu Kush, from the deserts of Rajasthan to the swamps of east Bengal.

How thinly spread they were, like the Empire they served. In some parts, you could travel for a hundred miles without seeing a

British soldier. John Low wrote to his mother when he was the British Resident in the city of Jaipur: 'The only European society I have is the Doctor, who belongs to the station and who lives with me. He is a Scotchman of the name of Simpson, very well disposed and particularly kind and attentive to his patients. The nearest place where any Europeans reside is Nuseerabad, which is about 90 miles off.'[3] He had five years of this solitude, with no other company but his cello and his flute.

In their solitude they wrote: letters, diaries, memoirs of the great events they had endured and helped to shape, and memoranda to their masters in Calcutta complaining about their instructions or their pay and conditions or explaining what the situation was really like on the ground. The public letters were preserved in the India Office archives, and the personal letters were treasured either by the writers, who often made copies of them, or by the recipients, for the letters were all they had to remind them of the parents and the children they had not seen for years and might never see again. There is a wonderful ease and intimacy about these letters. They read as though they are written by a friend who has just gone across the Firth to Edinburgh for a few weeks.

For three or four generations they followed the rites of passage without complaint or rancour, as though no other way of life was imaginable: leaving the farm or manse aged 16 at the latest (the great Sir John Malcolm was commanding native troops at the age of 15), the long passage round the Cape, the arrival at Madras or Calcutta, the letters of recommendation, the balls and race meetings, then the lonely years in camp or cantonment, the flirtations in the hill stations in the hot months, the violent headlong campaigns across country in the cold months, the marriage in the garrison church, the children sprawling on the bungalow lawn for a cruelly short time before they were sent off, sometimes as young as two or three but at any rate by the age of six or seven, to be schooled at 'home', in most cases not to be seen again until they came out at 16 or 17 to repeat the whole cycle. These huge to-ings and fro-ings seem to us as inexplicable and unendurable as the migrations of the salmon or the swallow. How did they endure the long separations, so often ending not in reunion but in death from malaria, cholera or diseases of the kidneys or liver, or shipwreck on the passage to or from India, the careers becalmed while antique and unfit officers refused to make way, and the blank gazes and casual mockery of their fellow countrymen if they survived long enough to come home and lay their bones in Norwood or Cheltenham? And the peril of it all, not only to their lives but to their immortal souls, about which they cared a great deal.

I do not set out with glib intentions, and I hope to honour them all as fully as they deserve, but we cannot leave out the horrors, not even when they are so close to home, perhaps especially not then.

It seemed somehow the proper thing, not so much to attempt their biographies in the ordinary sense but rather to try to recreate their Life-Times, to show something of what they went through, by means of letters (their own and other people's), by eyewitness accounts, by public documents and histories, and by pictures, too, for you would be mad to venture into India with your eyes shut. So this is not a biography, or even a group biography, it is more a collection of India tales, a Human Jungle Book. At times in this narrative, John Low and his family will be off-stage, not even direct witnesses of the events that were shaping their lives. At most other times, they will be in the thick of it. But at all times, they will have felt the vibrations, for in India the air was full of noises, and though it might take a month to hear the news from Java or the Himalayas, and though they were scattered over such huge distances, ultimately the British in India stood or fell together.

A note on spelling: As every writer on nineteenth-century India has found, it is impossible to be consistent; one can only hope to be understood. Like most of my predecessors, I have followed the practice of using the old spellings for well-known names of places: Bombay, Calcutta, Oudh, Poona, rather than Mumbai, Kolkata,

Avadh, Pune. With lesser-known names, I have tended to use the modern spelling rather than the 'ow's and 'ee's and 'ah's the Victorians went in for: thus Karauli rather than Kerowlee, 'Peshwa' rather than 'Peishwah'. Here too, I have made exceptions in favour of the familiar, 'suttee' rather than 'sati', for example. This sometimes leads to conflict with the quotations from letters and documents, but I think it makes easier reading. At least I shall be more consistent than the British were then. John Low sometimes spells 'Maratha' three different ways in a single letter.

I

LOW COUNTRY

From the top of Clatto Hill you can see the Paps of Fife, those twin rounded peaks that dominate the scene. They were volcanoes once and they have polite names, too, East and West Lomond, but I prefer to say that my grandmother came from beyond the Paps of Fife. To the north, the River Eden runs through the placid vale past the Old Course at St Andrews, for the golfer the Garden of Eden, and out into the North Sea. Further to the north, you can see the broad waters of the Firth of Tay; to the south lies the Firth of Forth and on the other side, Edinburgh – I first glimpsed the Paps in one of those heart-stopping views you get when you look to the right as you are walking in Edinburgh through the New Town towards Charlotte Square. It is a quiet, gentle country, for which the Scots word 'douce' might have been invented. In August, the fields are a pale gold, but even then there is a greenish shiver to the corn, long after the English Midlands are brown stubble. The landscape may be douce, but the climate is not.

These days you can walk into Edinburgh's Waverley Station and be across the water in Fife in 20 minutes (or drive over the newish road bridge). At the time I am thinking of, though, there is no railway, no bridge across the Forth until the river narrows at Stirling and no bridge across the Tay below Perth. Fife is a peninsula surrounded

by seawater on three sides and cut off on the fourth by the grim barrier of the Ochil Hills. It is on its own, a kingdom, and the Lows of
Clatto were Fifeshire born and bred if ever a family was.

The rest of Scotland, let alone England, was to them then a blur,
dimly perceived and rarely visited. They gossiped and danced with
their neighbours and usually ended up marrying them – the
Bethunes of Blebo, the Foulises of Cairnie, the Deases of Hilton, the
Fetteses (the William Fettes who founded the school was John Low's
uncle by marriage) – some of their little estates within walking distance, others no more than a carriage ride away. Now and then a
partner would be picked up at the Assembly Rooms in Edinburgh,
but for the most part it had the appearance of a closed society, at ease
with itself, with no need to venture outside the kingdom. But it
wasn't like that, not at all.

For a century and more, their plans and hopes and disappoint-
ments were all centred elsewhere. It was as though this broad tongue
of land licking the North Sea was one gigantic airstrip with flights all
running to the same destination. Life for the Lows seemed to hold
no other serious possibility. It was not as if there was nothing else
happening in Fife, or that the county was especially impoverished by
Scottish standards, or that there were no local opportunities. The
burns in the steep 'dens', as the valleys are called, held flax mills and
jute mills, and there were linen factories in Dunfermline, the town
the Lows originally came from. The coalfields were opening in west
Fife. Soon Charlie Nairn would be starting up his great floorcloth
works which was to make Kirkcaldy the linoleum capital of the
world. A lad of parts could always ride down to Queensferry and go
across to Edinburgh to become a Writer to the Signet, or a Minister
of the Kirk or an apothecary surgeon. But these alternatives held no
enchantment to the Lows. In their dreams the East Wind from the
cold sea whispered one word and one word only – India.

Robert Low heard it first. He was loafing on a lawyer's stool in
Edinburgh when in 1771 he heard the call and upped and offed to
join the Madras Army. After only 11 years he returned a captain with

a comfortable fortune – a deliciously speedy rate of return which was to offer misleading encouragement to his children and grandchildren. He had piled up enough to buy the estate of Clatto, a couple of miles to the east of Cupar, to demolish the old house that stood there and to build his own tall boxy house of Fifeshire sandstone. He had 'shaken the pagoda tree', as the saying went, and the fruit had come down copiously. The saying refers to the gold and silver coins called pagodas, which were the currency in southern India at the time when Robert was scooping them up.

How had he done it? Certainly not by saving his pay. In his little book *The Thackerays in India*, Sir William Hunter records that the nominal salaries of the servants of the East India Company 'scarcely yielded a subsistence. These meagre stipends, which they looked on as retainers rather than as pay, they augmented sometimes a hundredfold by private trade and by presents from natives.'[1] William Makepeace Thackeray, the novelist's grandfather, made his money by supplying bullocks and elephants (at 1,600 rupees each) for the Company's troops, by killing tigers for payment by the local villagers and rajas, by taking a cut on the land tax paid in cowrie shells to Dacca and by commissions on the supply of lime and timber and pretty much anything else the Company needed.[2] For an officer in the Company's Army like Robert Low, the opportunities for graft were no less appetizing. An army needed bullocks and elephants, and soldiers needed tents and uniforms, horses needed forage, the troops needed to be fed and watered – on all these contracts an enterprising officer could reckon to assemble a sum which would dwarf his actual pay. Out of his mountain of cowrie shells, Thackeray senior built himself a delightful house in the classical taste, with its pediments and porticoes picked out in raspberry and cream, which still stands in a banana grove in the Calcutta suburb of Alipore (there is a plaque inside to mark the novelist being born there). Captain Robert Low went home to Fife. The two families were to mingle and marry in the next generation, and their children were to people the residencies and cantonments

of India from Ceylon to the Himalayas for the whole of the nineteenth century.

We must never forget that the fortunes of both the Thackerays and
Lows were made in the easy days when John Company (as the East
India Company was personalized, imitating the Dutch who had
called their East Indies Company by the same name) did not care
how his servants made their pile, so long as the trade went on flowing and the profits were still luscious enough to satisfy the
shareholders and the Court of Directors back in Leadenhall Street.
After Pitt's India Act (1784) and the impeachment of Warren
Hastings, the colonels and tax collectors were no longer able to
chisel their commissions out of the natives for their own personal
benefit. Now it was the Government that scooped the pool. All his
time as Governor-General (1786–94), Lord Cornwallis had struggled
to stamp out the lucrative private trades between the Company's servants and native merchants. 'Dubashism' – from 'do bhasha', one
who speaks with two tongues – was nothing other than corruption.[3]
The old easy relations between the races were now regarded as per-
nicious. In 1793 people of mixed race were banned from
government service. Social apartheid followed on from commercial
separation. Company officers no longer lived with their native *bibis*,
no longer accompanied their men to the cockfight and the nautch
dancing. The historian C.A. Bayly argues that 'the disappearance of
the "corrupt" Company official trading on his own account may not
have been the victory that early Victorians claimed it was.'[4] The
Indian economy seemed to lose some of its mysterious buoyancy and
flexibility. What is clear is that the new policy deprived the
Company's British servants, both civil and military, of the nice little
earners they had become accustomed to. A new spectre haunted the
Company's officers to add to cholera, dysentery and death in battle:
debt.

Undaunted by these changed circumstances or, more probably,
not properly aware of them, Robert Low's three sons, John being
the eldest, all went out to India and spent much of their adult life

there. Three of Robert's daughters married Fifeshire neighbours
who then rose to become colonels or generals in the Army in India.
In the next generation, John Low's four sons all served in the Bengal
Cavalry or the Indian Civil Service. His eldest daughter married the
Chief Magistrate in Delhi, the son of the British Resident at the
Mughal's court. Only the unmarried daughters stayed behind in
Fife.

Even Robert Low's youngest and only unmarried daughter,
Georgina, had her place in the scheme of Empire. For as soon as her
brother John's children could walk a few steps, they were sent back
from Lucknow where they had been born, in order to be raised and
schooled at 'home'. Georgina was to be their mother throughout the
rest of their childhood, except for the four years in the 1840s that
John and his wife spent on leave at Clatto.[5]

Poor Georgina, so pretty and lively when she was young (how she
revelled in George IV's richly comic but triumphal visit to
Edinburgh in 1822), so strict and joyless in her middle years, especially after her first bout of cancer and her refuge in relentless
religious observance. The Sundays at Clatto became memorably
grim for the young Lows when Georgina was in charge: church
service twice at least, no books other than the Lord's word, no
games, no music, no toys and, worst of all, no jam on their bread. All
the enthusiasm that had once gone into gossip and dancing now
went into policing the Sabbath and making sure that the Low children learnt their French irregular verbs.

Georgina took the side of the strictest sects in the theological
quarrels which broke out across Scotland in those years. The quarrels
divided families, much as Suez and the Iraq war were to in our own
time. The preachers and the preached-at were not uniformly dour
and religiose, though. In some respects, North Britain, as the more
Anglo Scots called it, was a more unbuttoned place then than the
South. Scholars have found that there was little discouragement to
illegitimacy in rural Scotland and that 'previous unchasteness with
another individual does not form a very serious bar to marriage'.

One minister in Banffshire reported that 'Notwithstanding all our preaching and teaching, this sin is not seen in its true light. In fact it is thought very little of – scarcely thought a sin at all, just a mistake, rather annoying and hard when the father does not take with the child and pay for it.'[6] In the letters that survive between the Lows (apart from Georgina), the normal ups and downs of life – drinking too much, marriages coming unstuck – are taken on the chin, and remarked on with candour and rueful humour.

Some Fifeshire worthies went rather further. David Low – a close neighbour if not a close relation – was the Episcopalian Minister at Pittenweem, on Fife's pretty south-east coast, the so-called 'East Neuk'. He was nominally also Bishop of Ross, Moray, Argyll and the Isles, although there is scant record of his visiting his far-flung diocese. What seems to have interested him more was the Beggar's Benison, a dining club dedicated to the erotic, which was centred on the neighbouring fishing port of Anstruther. The club's curious name derives from the tale that King James V of Scotland was carried across a stream by a buxom beggar lass who hoisted her skirts to wade through the stream. The King, who was on his way to Dreel Castle at Anstruther, gave her a gold sovereign, and in return she blessed him with the words:

> 'May your purse naer be loom
> And your horn aye in bloom.'

The members of the Benison met twice a year, on St Andrew's Day and at Candlemas, compared their erect horns and masturbated together, surrounded by erotic tableware in the shape of penises and vulvas, occasionally egged on by the presence of a naked local girl hired for the occasion. These lubricious proceedings continued for more than a century, until they were toned down and eventually extinguished by Victorian propriety. Even Bishop Low was finally driven to ask for his name to be expunged from the Benison's records, but the malicious secretary, who was also the town clerk of

Anstruther, insisted on minuting this request to all other members, thus further publicizing the Bishop's long-standing membership.

An equally unlikely member of the Benison was Robert Low's best friend and neighbour Hugh Cleghorn, Professor of Civil History at St Andrews and one of the most remarkable men of the Scottish Enlightenment. As a young man, Cleghorn had toured Europe as tutor to the young Earl of Home. While in Switzerland, he became friends with the Comte de Meuron, a dodgy character who was proprietor of a mercenary regiment that had been hired by the Dutch to guard Colombo and the other Dutch strongholds in Ceylon. When war broke out, Cleghorn was taken on by the British government as in effect a spy, much as English dons were recruited to MI6 in World War Two. He proposed to Henry Dundas, the chief government minister in Scotland, that if they could 'turn' de Meuron and his regiment, Ceylon could be won for Britain, without, in Cleghorn's words, 'great effusion of blood'.

Unlike most such cunning short cuts in history, this one came off brilliantly. De Meuron was already discontented with his Dutch pay-masters and readily agreed to switch sides. Britain assumed control over the island quite bloodlessly. Cleghorn and de Meuron entered Colombo in triumph. It was an extraordinary episode in the history of Empire, and one which could only fire the younger Lows with the belief that great things awaited anyone who went out East.

Scarcely less extraordinary is the fact that this pillar of the university should have accepted membership of the Benison before he left Fife (his 'diploma' is still among the Cleghorn Papers at St Andrews). When he returned to Fife, he found to his surprise that his two sons Peter and John had been proposed for the club 'unknown to me'. He readily forked out the six guineas required for membership and for-warded the diplomas to the boys, both by then in India, with the caution 'keep them out of female sight'. Peter and John were great friends of the next generation of Lows and in each other's company the whole time when they were in Scotland. When Robert Low died in 1825, Hugh Cleghorn wrote to Peter:

'I received your most affectionate letter yesterday while passing through St Andrews to attend the funeral of Mr Low. I have lost a friend with whom I lived for half a century in the most kind and confidential habits without one moment of coolness or reserve. He was eminently good-tempered without a particle of selfishness; he was warm in his friendships without any bitterness in his enmities.'[7]

It is hard to resist the thought that the Cleghorns and the Lows must now and then, after a dram or two, have exchanged the odd aside about the Benison.[8] It is inconceivable that Robert Low's youngest son Henry could have stayed away. Henry was ten years younger than John, and in his early twenties he was a Writer to the Signet in Edinburgh, in theory at least. In practice he spent most of his time drinking, and playing golf and making big bets on himself. For the one club that the Lows indubitably did belong to was the Royal and Ancient Golf Club (then called the Society of St Andrews Golfers), the most famous club of its sort in the world. Captain Robert Low was captain of the club in 1784, but it was Henry who was the star. He won the club's Gold Medal three times, in 1821, 1823 and 1824, and in 1826–7 became Captain of the Honourable Company of Edinburgh Golfers, while still in his twenties. Not content with having occupied the most famous office in the game, he became Secretary of the Honourable Company the following year.

Henry always played for high stakes. Five pounds was his standard bet. However, it was not his gambling on the links but his partnership in the Fife Bank which undid him. The bank's crash in 1825 hit the whole family hard, but it hit Henry hardest. He was declared bankrupt and fled to Australia in the spring of 1830. There he managed an estate, but that went bankrupt, too. By 1833 he had turned up in India working for a firm of solicitors in Calcutta and writing home to his mother: 'I am unwilling to give up all hope of retrieving myself without a struggle.' His brother John, who was moving quietly up the military ladder the while, wrote hopefully of him at this time: 'he lives most quietly and does not seem to have the least disposition to extravagance.' If only he could stick with it, 'the profession he has chosen is one in which there is no risk of losing money.' Henry came to stay with John and his family in Lucknow, and John wrote home to his mother: 'For several days past Henry has been an inmate of our house. I fully believe that he is determined to be industrious and strictly economical. In the latter respect his management has been quite extraordinary; he seems to have nothing now of that over-sanguine feeling from which many of his former misfortunes proceeded.'[9]

John pressed the Governor-General, Lord William Bentinck, to appoint 'my poor brother' as Assistant Secretary to the Lottery Committee: 'he has had a very superior education and much subsequent practice in business of various kinds'.[10] Alas, it was feared that Henry's practice had been of the wrong kind, and his expertise in matters of chance failed to secure him even this modest sinecure.

He began to speculate again, with no better luck, and he was declared bankrupt once more. As the *History of The Royal & Ancient* remarks: 'It can safely be said of him that he is the only triple medal winner of the St Andrews Society to have been declared bankrupt in three different continents.'[11] John's brother-in-law William Dick bumped into him in Calcutta and told John: 'there is a strong family likeness; his manners are mild and gentlemanly with a melancholy cast, which however lessened as he engaged in conversation.'[12]

Like a doomed character from a Conrad novel, Henry plunged further east, retreating deeper into the jungle. His last refuge was Burma, then not yet under British rule. Among the mass of papers at Clatto, there was a single sheet from the *Bengal Hurkaru (hurkaru* means 'messenger' or 'spy') of September 17, 1855. Why was this preserved? Well, the first column headed 'A Few Facts from Pegu' records that Major Phayre and his suite had crossed the British boundary on their way to Ava. At Malun, the first large town beyond the boundary, 'they were received by the Governor of the district, apparently a Scotchman, who with the national ability has risen high in the service of the Burmese court.' Had Henry made good at last? If so, it was not to be for long, because the only other record of him is a brief notice in another family paper: 'Henry Malcolm Low, died April 5th, at Mendi Pegu, unmarried.'[13] I like to think of Henry, with his melancholy courtesy, possibly by this stage dressed in Burmese robes, receiving Major Phayre and his weary party, enquiring perhaps as he helps them out of their palanquins or off their elephants whether by any chance they might know who had won the gold medal at St Andrews last summer.

While Henry had gone to St Andrews to play golf, drink and gamble, John went there to study. He was not yet 14 when he rode his pony into town to enroll at the university as a Bejant, or first-year student, to polish his mathematics, Latin, French and history before setting out on a military career. He wore the famous scarlet gown for only a single academic year,[14] which meant that he was only 15 when he set off for India, his father having secured him a Madras cadetship on the nomination of Mr John Hudleston MP, a director of the East India Company. How swiftly life moved on then. The shadow of mortality discouraged dawdling.

All the same, it must have been a wrench to leave St Andrews and home at Clatto so soon, even for someone possessed of as much natural fortitude as John. Life had been sweet there. For all their Presbyterian roots, the Lows were a gossipy, easy-going lot. There was rough shooting on the hill, and fish to be caught in the tumbling burns, birdies to be savoured on the Old Course (the only course there was at the time) and no shortage of congenial neighbours to call on. For Robert Low, their existence must have come close to the dreams with which he had consoled himself all the time he was chiselling commissions from the natives on the barren plateaus of the Deccan. Now it was John's turn.

Before he left Fife to take ship for Madras, he had his portrait painted. The Minister in the next-door village of Pitlessie had a brilliant son, three years older than John, who had left Fife at the age of 14 and enrolled at the Trustees Academy in Edinburgh. Five years later, the ambitious young David Wilkie returned home, in order to earn enough money from painting portraits of the local gentry to finance the next leg of his ascent, the move to London. At Clatto, he painted three of them, for £5 each, the equivalent of one of Henry's golf bets. The most attractive is his three-quarter-length of Catherine, the eldest Low daughter and the beauty of the family, in a white Empire gown and a red velvet shawl with a Clatto-ish landscape in the background. In 2007, the picture was sold by Christie's in New York for $32,200. Catherine was engaged to be married at the time to Colonel William Deas of Hilton, who was twice her age and looks it in Wilkie's portait, a battered florid gent in a Madras Army uniform that also looks as if its best days are gone.

Again and again, we shall find both in Scotland and India this pattern of middle-aged Army officers taking brides who were only 18 or 19, after a courtship as brief as a mayfly's. Time was so agonizingly short, whether in a hill station or at the Assembly Rooms. If the chance was missed, one or other of you would be gone away and the chance would never come again. In its way, marriage in the Indian Army was based on an acquaintance as brief as an arranged marriage among the Indians themselves. John Low's own marriage was to follow this headlong pattern more than 20 years later.

Catherine was skittish and was indulged all her life, as the family beauty often is, moving effortlessly from flirtatiousness to hypochondria as she grew older. She and William were married in the drawing room at Clatto just before John left for India. She wore a scarlet riding habit to go away in and rode off with her husband for their honeymoon on Loch Leven. Rather oddly, bride and groom were accompanied by John, perhaps because she might not see him again. In fact, she very nearly didn't because he fell into the loch and almost drowned while the happy couple were canoodling out of sight.

John's own portrait shows him dressed in a blue coat and frilled shirt with a bunch of seals dangling from his buff waistcoat. In the background a burst of gunfire advertises his future calling. His expression is rather memorable: watchful, a little uneasy, with a touch of that melancholy that Henry had. Like Catherine, in fact like most of the Lows, he has a long downward-curling, tremulous upper lip which makes him look as if he might be on the verge of tears. A misleading impression. John was far from insensitive, but he was stoical. Perhaps he was partly trying to look grown-up for Mr Wilkie.[15] For the next 38 years, his mother had only his portrait and his letters to keep his memory alive. John never saw his father again and by the time he returned to Clatto in 1843, his mother was dying.

The voyage out to India took four months, give or take a week, a length of time which was barely to alter for the next 30 years and more. By the time John landed in Madras, the East India Company had been persuaded to modernize the training of its cadets, or 'griffins' as the new arrivals were known (the 'griffs' were mercilessly teased and the victims of endless practical jokes). Instead of being thrown raw into cantonments where they might succumb to drink or despair or dysentery before they had found their feet, they were now dispatched to be 'seasoned', and given a proper military education in the cadet college which had recently been removed to the fort of Tripassur, about 15 miles outside Madras. There, according to the regulations laid down by the Commander-in-Chief at Fort St George, the 'gentleman cadets' were to be subjected to a rigorous and healthy regime. They were to be rigged out in close-fitting scarlet jackets with yellow cuffs and collar, three rows of white metal buttons, a round black hat with cockade and red feather, white linen waistcoats and pantaloons, and half-boots with side-arms and a bayonet.[16] They were to rise at daybreak, breakfast at 7 or 8am according to the season, dine at 2pm, sup at 8pm, and retire to rest immediately after, with lights out and lock-up at 9pm. No spirituous liquor, wine or beer was to be admitted to the fort. Apart from training in drill, military manoeuvres and the use of firearms, the cadets were to study the Hindustani language. The more industrious cadets such as John Low were also expected to acquire a good knowledge of Persian, which was the language employed at native courts. There was not to be much fun at Tripassur. 'Except on occasion of taking some manly exercise, such as playing cricket, fives or other games, no cadet shall appear out of his quarters, otherwise than dressed in the prescribed uniform. The habit of lounging from quarter to quarter in a white waistcoat is expressly forbid.'[17]

All of which sounds spick and spanking, if forbidding. The reality of Tripassur was different. The truth was that the place had turned out to be a hellhole. The C-in-C himself, Sir John Cradock, had drawn attention to 'the very unhealthy situation at Tripassur'. 'My own observations upon the persons whom I see occasionally arrive from thence whose altered appearance and emaciated figure all proclaim too just a foundation for apprehension'.[18] The superintending officer was at the moment seriously indisposed and his assistant had just been obliged to resign for health reasons. Even the doctor whom Cradock appointed to lead a committee of inquiry into conditions at Tripassur pleaded that he was too ill to go.

The Committee reported to Cradock that the fort was situated in a treeless plain, exposed to the cruel heat of summer and the full force of the monsoon. The barracks where the cadets lived lay below the level of the surrounding paddy fields and the large tanks which irrigated the fields. As a result, the cadets' quarters were chilly and damp when the north-east wind was blowing and intolerable in the hot weather, for 'the naked paddyfield surface, when the water is all evaporated, is baked nearly to the hardness of stone.' In the hot season, the cadets preferred to sleep outdoors and caught the cold, early-morning winds from the hills. The Committee tried cutting drains to dry out the quarters, but because they were so low-lying, this only let the water run in from the paddy fields instead of out. Several cadets had died of liver complaints and dysentery, one or two exacerbated by 'their own imprudence' – that is, by drinking arrack or toddy in defiance of the regulations. The only answer was to abandon Tripassur and find another site for the cadet college.[19] But by then John Low, as hardy a Scot as ever

came out of Fife, had finished his training and on July 17, 1805, had
been appointed a lieutenant in the 1st Madras Native Infantry. He
had survived Tripassur. He could survive anything. He was on his
way.

II

MASSACRE IN A FIVES COURT

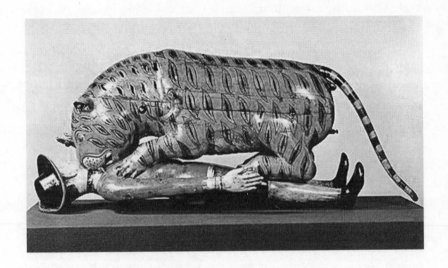

'We are resolved to fight and kill our officers. Rivers of blood shall flow and heaps of dead be carried out.'

[Rustam Ali Shah, *Madras Secret Proceedings*, vol 25, f4312, Hoover, p 101]

John had every reason to be proud of the regiment he had joined. The 1st Battalion of the 1st Madras Native Infantry was the oldest in the service of the East India Company. No other battalion of native troops anywhere in the country had a higher reputation. It had first distinguished itself against Hyder Ali, the ruler of Mysore, in the 1760s. The battalion was then nearly destroyed in Colonel Baillie's catastrophic defeat of 1780, but rose magnificently to do great things in the next Mysore Campaign of the 1790s, which culminated in the British victory at Seringapatam. Hyder's son, Tipu Sultan, 'the Tiger of Mysore', died in that fierce battle, defending his fort and his people with his sabre in his hand. The deeds of the 1st at Seringapatam had earned it a reputation as tigerish as Tipu's.

At the end of the eighteenth century, the outright British possessions in India were still largely confined to the hinterlands of the three towns known as Presidencies: Calcutta, Bombay and Madras. Beyond and around these territories lay a hundred princely states varying from major kingdoms with large armies to petty chiefdoms with a dozen muskets, often divided by race, religion and old grievances against their neighbours. Many of them were already under the thumb of the British, and paying for British-commanded troops to protect them, although still independent in theory. The commercial life of the subcontinent spilled across the porous borders of these states, leading to fresh opportunities for the East India Company's traders and fresh challenges for its armies, whose prime mission was, after all, to protect that trade.

Robert Clive's decisive victories at Arcot (1751) and Plassey (1757) had established British dominance over the Carnatic (the long coastal region around Madras) and Bengal, the heartland of the emerging Empire. Now victory at Seringapatam had brought in the central southern state of Mysore. Richard Wellesley, the rapacious little Governor-General, began to dream of extending British rule to the western coasts, so that eventually the three sprawling pink blotches on the map might bleed into one glorious Empire covering the entire subcontinent and extinguishing the lingering claims of the French to the mastery of India. In the next big push, the 1st Battalion of the 1st Madras Native Infantry could expect to be a spearhead.

Yet within a year of John Low joining it, two thirds of the battalion had erupted in bloody mutiny. Their European officers had been murdered in their sleep and the sepoys, innocent and guilty alike, had been gunned down in their hundreds by the British. (The native troops were known as sepoys from 'sipahi', the Persian word for army.) The colours of the battalion had been ceremonially burnt on the parade ground and the remnants of the battalion had been disbanded in disgrace. It was the greatest shock to British power in India yet seen. And, in a curious way, that victory over Tipu had been the start of it.

Tipu was first and foremost a soldier. He had been educated in tactics by the French mercenaries employed by his father, who had risen from the ranks to become first Commander-in-Chief and then de facto ruler of Mysore. Tipu himself was short and fat with big eyes. In his time he had sent Colonel Baillie packing and forced the ferocious Sir Hector Munro to retreat. He built ports along the Kerala shore and dams along the rivers. He also constructed what are said to be the world's first rockets for military purposes. He wrote poetry and spoke Urdu, Persian and Arabic. He was a devout Muslim ruling a Hindu kingdom, but he was broad-minded enough to build a church for the French colony – though he later destroyed dozens of other churches and there are claims, disputed, that he forcibly converted thousands of Indian Catholics to Islam. He was also notorious for the atrocities he committed in his frequent wars with other Indian principalities.

His enduring hatred, however, was against the East India Company, whose armies he fought for 20 years until his death in battle. Tipu's Tiger, that amazing life-size toy of carved and painted wood which has delighted generations in the V&A, is trampling on a prostrate European in the uniform of the Honourable Company. Tipu was a formidable opponent, and when his body was found in the ruins of his palace (the Tiger was found there, too), Colonel Arthur Wellesley, the Governor-General's soon to be world-famous younger brother, took the precaution of feeling his pulse to make sure that he was dead.

As is so often the way, none of Tipu's sons was a patch on him. All the same, they posed a problem to the British, one which was to become familiar over the course of the ensuing century: what to do with the kings they had deposed, their wives and their children? The only solution, which appeared to combine compassion with security, was to lock them up in the nearest fort and lull their resentments with generous pensions and a numerous retinue.

Accordingly, Tipu's 12 sons and eight daughters were banged up in one of the strongest and most beautiful forts of southern India, the fort of Vellore, about 90 miles from Madras and 16 miles from Arcot, the scene of one of Clive's greatest triumphs and, by 1800, the site of a cantonment of British cavalry. Never before in their conquest of India had the British locked an entire royal lineage into a fortress prison.[1] Vellore Fort had a garrison composed of the 69th Regiment and of John Low's own 1st Battalion the 1st Madras Native Infantry. As everywhere else in British India, British troops were vastly out-numbered by native forces: 383 to 1,500, not to mention the several thousand followers of the Mysore Princes who had taken up resi-dence in the fort and in the surrounding town.[2]

Tipu's family were held in the palace within the fort, which also contained a beautiful Hindu temple, the Jalakantesvara Temple. This temple was famous for some of the greatest stone carving in the country, but it had long been abandoned and was now used as an arsenal for ammunition and other supplies, and was known to the British as the Great Pagoda. There was also a mosque to serve the largely Muslim garrison, as well as barracks for two thousand sepoys. The accommodation needed to be roomy because Tipu's courtiers and camp followers poured in to assist the exiled sons in their pleas-ures, inflame their resentments and tickle up their dreams of a comeback. The British officer responsible for both their security and their welfare, Lieutenant-Colonel Thomas Marriott, had a low opinion of his charges; he claimed that they spent their long days quarrelling with one another, committing sodomy and incest (often with their mothers-in-law) and frittering away their generous allowances of 25,000 rupees per annum per prince. He had infiltrated into the Palace a number of *hurkaru*, or spies, but these spies seem to have been a waste of pagodas.

All this was tolerable, if expensive, from the British point of view. What was not tolerable to the authorities were the sloppiness and the erratic dress codes of the native troops who were guarding the princes. Commanding officers just landed from Europe were driven mad by the lack of soldierly trim everywhere in the Madras Army. Uniform was meant, after all, to be uniform. Sir John Cradock had already stepped in to remove the cadets from Tripassur, after he noticed the pale faces and shrunken features of officers recently returned from that plague spot. Now his inquisitorial eye swivelled to focus on the turn-out of his troops. New regulations were issued. Para 10 of Section 11 ran:

> It is ordered by the Regulation that a native soldier shall not mark his face to denote his caste, or wear earrings when dressed in his uniform; and it is further directed that at all parades, and upon all duties, every soldier of the battalion shall be clean shaven on the chin. It is directed also that uniformity shall, as far as it is practicable, be preserved in regard to the quantity and shape of the hair on the upper lip.[3]

At the same time, new turbans were to be issued to the native troops. To their horror, these bore an unholy resemblance to the rounded caps worn by European troops and by the East Indian drummers, a contemptible lot. The new cap had a feather in it and a cockade made either of pigskin, abhorrent to the Muslims, or of cow-leather, abhorrent to the Hindus. During April, May and June 1806, the new turbans were sent out along with the new regulations. To Indian eyes, they scarcely looked like turbans at all, but like the *topis* worn by the English infidels. Even while the turbans were still being made up, the sepoys were already suffering relentless teasing from the Princes' hangers-on that they were being turned into feringhees and would lose touch with their castes if they wore these *hats*.

The Commandant at Vellore, Colonel St John Fancourt, reported the furious protests to Madras. General Cradock could see nothing wrong with the regulations or the turbans, nor could his adjutant and his general staff, which was not surprising because they themselves had designed them before Cradock had arrived in India. Cradock was the son of the Archbishop of Dublin. He had spent most of his earlier military career suppressing native dissent, first in Ireland, then in the West Indies and in Egypt. He may not have known much about India, but he knew about discipline and he knew about authority. Colonel Fancourt was informed that 'the Commander-in-Chief finds it his duty to check, by the most decided resolution, the symptoms of insubordination.'4 A detachment of the 19th Dragoons was to be sent to Vellore to round up the dissidents and take them for trial in Madras. Colonel Fancourt pleaded for delay. His Excellency saw no reason to resile from the orders he had given. Orders were orders, just as uniform was meant to be uniform. So 21 privates, half of them Muslims, half of them Hindus, were tried at Fort St George, the military HQ and seat of Government in Madras. On June 29, 1806, they were sentenced to receive 500 lashes each. Two of them got 900 lashes and were discharged from the service as 'turbulent and unworthy subjects'.

Undeterred, the sepoys continued their protests. Lieutenant-Colonel James Brunton, an experienced officer, then the Military Auditor-General, pleaded for the order to be rescinded because objections to the turban were almost universal and were widely feared to be only a prelude to forcible conversion en masse to Christianity. In India, Brunton warned, 'many things of serious moment have originated in trifles'.5

This fear lies at the root of so much that was to follow at Vellore, and elsewhere in India, throughout the nineteenth century. To the officers of the East India Company and its Army, the fear seemed quite misplaced, absurd even. They had no such intention and never had had. They had permitted Portuguese and Danish missionaries to circulate in their territories, nothing more.

Sir John Cradock professed himself bewildered by the rumour. There were no British missionaries in the Peninsula, and 'from the almost complete absence of religious establishments in the interior of the country, from the habits of life prevalent among military men, it is a melancholy truth that so infrequent are the religious observances of officers doing duty with the Battalions that the sepoys have not until very recently discovered the nature of the religion professed by the English.'[6] It was indeed the lament of those members of the Court of Directors who belonged to the rising school of evangelicals and who did wish to convert the natives that 'At Vellore, or near it, I believe there was not one Chaplain or missionary'.[7]

The reality was that, at this era, the British in India were not at all devout. Lieutenant John Blakiston remembered in the 1820s that 'when I first arrived in India there was a general disregard of religion among the European part of the population.' Few of them attended divine worship. 'Many of the elder inhabitants among the English, who ought to have set a better example, used to assemble at each other's houses to pass the leisure hours afforded by the Sabbath in playing at billiards or cards, when considerable sums were won and lost.'[8] There were then few churches (Blakiston, like other engineers in the Company's service, was later to build several himself), and the Company's chaplains 'were in general less calculated to lead the stray sheep into the field than to drive them out of it'. They swore and drank and gambled with their messmates. One chaplain, on being asked to tiffin and a rubber of whist, excused himself by saying that 'he had a d——d soldier to bury'.[9]

All the same, in the Madras Presidency, even if not in northern India, there were plenty of black Christians to be seen. They were often of mixed race, having followed the religion of their white fathers, or they were low-grade servants of the Empire: messengers, bottle-washers, laundrymen. The one thing a high-caste sepoy dreaded most of all was to be degraded into such company. The Christian Church in South India had very ancient origins. The Apostle Thomas, Doubting Thomas, was said to have been martyred on the mount outside Madras. There were unimpeachable remains of Christian buildings dating back to the second and third centuries AD. But for all its antiquity, the Christian faith had never made much headway among the higher social classes. Its only chance of a great leap forward was for the Europeans to use their military strength to impose their faith. Such a thing was of course not unprecedented in Indian history. Tipu was certainly not the first Muslim ruler to embark on a wave of forced conversions, including all those Catholics. Why should the Europeans not retaliate in kind?

This fear seemed entirely rational to the Indians. Most Europeans never understood the force of it. This yawning gap in perceptions was to worsen over the course of the nineteenth century, often with tragic consequences. It seemed to Hindus and Muslims alike, the religious observances of both being such an intrinsic part of daily life, that it would be only natural for the new superior power to impose its sacred as well as its secular values upon those they had conquered. Worse still, evidence for this fear appeared to be building up as a new generation of Evangelical Englishmen came out to govern the country, cherishing the secret and sometimes not-so-secret hope that, in due course, the Indians would be brought to see the truth of Jesus Christ, even though it would still be wrong to use force to impose the true faith. The Evangelicals had their supporters in the Company's Court of Directors, so perhaps, in the long run, the fear did not seem quite so fanciful.

By now, Cradock was past worrying about such high matters. His priority was to cover his back. The only way was to consult the Governor-General. If Lord William Bentinck thought it sensible to climb down, then he was ready to do so. What was clear was that only Lord William could get him out of what he now recognized was an awful hole.

If Lord William had been a wise and seasoned pro, the sort of man you would fondly imagine in such an august post, no doubt that is what he would have done. Bentinck was not that sort of man. For a start, he was only 31 years old and he had come out to India to make money. Although he was the younger son of the Duke of Portland, the family estate was deeply in debt and he had to scratch his own living. His father had wangled him the Madras post and his aim was to hang on there for ten years, save £100,000 and then be promoted to the more lucrative governorship of Bengal. Later apologists have tried to depict him as a forward-thinking idealist who was unlucky and unfairly treated. There is something in that. But he was also inexperienced, insecure, impatient and obsessed with unthought-through schemes of reform. He looks like the classic accident waiting to happen.

For a start, he hadn't bothered to read the new regulations, which were 'not my department'. He had not been consulted about the protesters' courts-martial, and nobody had told him how deeply the troops resented the turbans. The new regulations had not been highlighted in red, as was the normal practice[10] and 'so far as Colonel Brunton's warning was concerned, His Lordship remarked that the health of that officer had long been so bad, that his nerves were gone, and that he suffered from great despondency'.[11] But, having got this far, it 'would be impossible to recede without committing the discipline of the army'.

This passing the buck and rubbishing the opposition all came later. What Bentinck actually did at the time, on July 4, 1806, was to issue an order basically saying that the whole business had been exaggerated. There had, after all, been a Court of Inquiry held at Vellore on May 14, composed of three of the four lieutenant-colonels stationed there: Forbes commanding the 1st Battalion 1st (John Low's commanding officer), McKerras commanding the 2nd Battalion 23rd, and Marriott of the 1st Battalion 5th, whose men guarded the Mysore Princes and who had his quarters inside the Palace. This worthy trio had quizzed the native officers and none of them had objected to the new turban or claimed that it was an offence to their religious principles.

The native officers were unlikely to object. Only the week before, the order had come from Madras for the court-martial and severe punishment of the privates who had objected. The native officers would be mad to land themselves in the same trouble, or worse.

That thought did not occur to Lord William, who had little grasp of other people's thought processes. He decreed, therefore, that in these circumstances 'the alternative of yielding to the "clamor" arising from an unfounded prejudice should, if possible, be avoided.'[12]

What none of the three colonels, and certainly not Lord William, grasped was that by now the evidence of the native officers was irredeemably tainted. They had already held numerous secret meetings, at which they had first pledged themselves to resist these ghastly innovations to the bitter end, and then formed a detailed plan to overpower and kill all the European officers and men in the fort. By mid-June, the majority of the native officers of John Low's battalion at Vellore were in on the plot, and they were in daily communication with the retainers of Tipu's sons, who were only a few yards' stroll away in the Palace, with nothing to do all day but dream of being restored to their former glories.

According to later reports, gathered in *Secret Sundries*, the intelligence reports sent up to Government House, some of the native officers were in touch, not merely with native officers in other local garrisons, but with distant feudal chieftains on the Deccan plateau, with Maratha princes to the north and west, with the deposed rulers of Hyderabad and even with the French at their remaining Indian toehold of Pondicherry. How extensive and detailed these contacts were is hard to establish, but the general intention behind them is clear enough. The rising at Vellore was to be the signal for a general uprising which would spread in a huge wave across India and eventually expel the British, just as the fakirs who had mysteriously appeared on the streets of Vellore were prophesying in their ballads and puppet shows. If the rebels could hold out for a week at Vellore, the British would simply be too overstretched to contain the wave of rebellions as they swept across the subcontinent.

On June 17, Mustapha Beg, a private of the 1st Battalion, went to his commanding officer, Colonel Forbes, and gave him a complete rundown on the intentions of the would-be mutineers. Instead of quietly making further enquiries, the Colonel sent for his native officers again. They all protested their innocence and ignorance of any such plot, and once more swore that they were perfectly happy to wear the new turban. This Mustapha Beg, they said, was a well-known madman previously imprisoned for drunkenness, and they urged the Colonel to have him blown away from a gun. The Colonel was not prepared to dispatch Mustapha Beg that far, but he did put him in irons and have him locked up.[13]

Even this was not the final warning. Two or three weeks later,[14] a Eurasian woman came to the Commandant of the fort, Colonel Fancourt of the 34th, and told him that everything Mustapha Beg had said was true. Mrs Burke she was called and she had come primarily to claim the prize money that she said was due to her late husband. Colonel Fancourt immediately conceived the notion that she was a loose woman (she already had a reputation as a trouble-maker), most likely now being passed from one NCO to the next. He sent her away and dismissed her warning as the gossip of the ser-geants' mess, which had floated up from the bazaar.[15]

Now two of the four colonels at Vellore had received clear and detailed intelligence of the plot, not to mention Colonel Brunton's warning at roughly the same moment, the end of June, which had gone straight to the C-in-C. All the warnings had been brushed aside on personal grounds: Brunton because he was said to have had a nervous breakdown, Mustapha Beg because he was mad and Mrs Burke because she was a whore. Nobody wanted to contemplate the awful possibility that the warnings might be reliable.[16]

Nothing was done to reinforce the European troops at Vellore. Inside the fort no extra precautions were taken. On Wednesday July 9, one of Tipu's daughters was to be married, and a merry, colourful throng poured in over the drawbridge, through the main entrance with its four mighty gates, across the parade ground and into the Palace. If the guests seemed excited and noisy, the watching British officers put it down to the wedding spirit, their bonhomie enhanced by the prospect of seeing their confined royal relatives and patrons once again. Nobody seems to have imagined that the wedding guests might be reinforcements in disguise.

Apart from the wedding, the population of the fort that night was swollen because the next day there was a 'field day', an exercise in firing practice which was held once or twice a month. To save delays, all the sepoys taking part were allowed to sleep inside the fort instead of in the native town and to draw six rounds of ball cartridges each; this meant not only that on the night of July 9 the sepoys would outnumber the European troops in the fort by three to one, they would also be armed.[17]

The Assistant Surgeon John Dean had dined with his commanding officer, Colonel McKerras, and 'on crossing the parade to my house, found more than usual gaiety in the Palace. The Mahal was lighted up, and the sound of music gave every appearance of mirth and gaiety and I little dreamt that the hand I had so recently shaken, warm with friendship, would in a few short hours be cold as death, near the spot where I then stood.'[18]

The field officer that night was Captain Miller of the 1st/23rd Native Infantry. Captain Miller did not feel like getting up in the small hours, so he claimed to be 'indisposed' and deputed his duties to his *subahdar*, the commissioned native officer ranking below a British lieutenant. That gentleman did not see why he should have a worse night's sleep than his superior officer, so he was 'indisposed', too, and ordered his junior, the *jemadar*, who was called Kassim Khan, of the 1st/1st, to deputize for him. It so happened that Kassim was one of the leaders of the whole conspiracy. It was not surprising, therefore, that at the appropriate hour, shortly after midnight, he returned a report of 'All Correct'.

The Colonel's lady, Amelia Fancourt, tells the story of what happened next. Her narrative is preserved on two yellowing sheets in the British Library, amongst the collection of Warren Hastings letters in what used to be the India Office Library. There is no better account of the terror and bloodshed of those dark first hours of July 10, 1806.[19]

Amelia and her husband St John were living with their two children, Charles aged two and a baby girl, in the Commandant's quarters just to the left of the main gate and looking out over the parade ground. You must imagine this as a huge arena. A few yards away beyond the Fancourts' house was the Main Guard, the security centre of the whole place. On the far side of the parade ground was the sprawling Palace where Tipu's sons were celebrating their sister's wedding, with the European barracks to its right and behind them the sepoy barracks which housed six companies, the greater part of John Low's battalion. To the left of the Palace were the flagstaff and the powder magazine. To the right was the Hindu temple, now commandeered as the garrison arsenal. All around were the great old purple-brown ramparts with cavalier turrets sticking out at intervals. And outside the ramparts was the broad and glassy moat, filled with crocodiles. This is how Amelia tells the story:

> Colonel Fancourt and I retired to rest at ten o'clock. About the hour of two on Thursday morning we were awakened at the same instant by a loud firing. We both got out of bed and Col. F— went to the window of his writing room which he opened and called aloud and repeatedly to know the cause of the disturbance, to which he received no reply but by a rapid continuation of the firing by numberless sepoys assembled at the main guard ... I looked at my husband. I saw him pale as ashes. I said, 'Good God! What is the matter, St John?' To which he replied 'Go into your room, Amelia.' I did so for I saw him so agitated I did not think it right to repeat my question at that moment. I heard him two minutes after leaving the writing room and go out of the house.

It was the worst moment of his life. The moment he heard the firing he knew everything was lost. He had been wrong, unforgivably, pig-headedly, tragically wrong. What Mustapha Beg had told

Forbes was the plain, ghastly truth. And if only he had listened to Mrs Burke and not let her wheedling Indian-Irish brogue and her slatternly appearance put him off. Those wretched turbans – well, he had at least pleaded for delay, but that stuck-up martinet Cradock was not a big enough man to climb down. How easy it would have been, as late as yesterday, to have whistled up the cavalry from Arcot. As soon as they rumbled over the drawbridge, the plot would have been scotched. Now it was all over. His men were being butchered in the Main Guard. Soon it would be his turn, and Amelia's and the children. Once they had started, they would not stop until every white man in the fort was dead.

Between 2 and 3am, the moon rose, and the sepoys rose with it. At 2.30am, the sentry at the Main Guard called out to Corporal Piercy saying that a shot or two had been fired somewhere near the barracks where the 69th lay sleeping. Piercy had no time to answer. Within seconds, the sepoys on the guard rushed on the Englishmen and murdered every one of them except Corporal Piercy and a couple of others. Piercy lay doggo, played dead. Squinting through the door of the Main Guard, he could see the sepoys rushing across the parade ground to the 69th barracks.[20]

> After my husband left the house I believe he returned again though I imagine just for a moment. I certainly heard the door of his writing room tried very soon after the firing at the main guard but after he had quitted me. I bolted the door and if it was him he could not enter – when I heard the door attempted I called out 'Is it you, St John?' to which I received no answer, but if it was he quitted the house again immediately.

It was not St John. He had gone straight down in his dressing gown to the front door. 'Don't go out, sir, for your dear life's sake,' the guard had cried. 'Never mind,' Fancourt replied, and he walked out on the parade ground shouting, 'Fall in!' and he was shot down a few yards from his front door.[21] He lay there dying, very slowly, in his dressing gown, while the sepoys of the 1st directed volley after volley into the European barracks. Many of the 69th were killed as they lay naked on their cots. Others had struggled to their feet and were killed putting on their breeches. The sick men in the hospital wing were brought out on to the parade and slaughtered in rows in front of the Palace gates.

Now the retainers of the princes began to slip out of the Palace and fraternize with the sepoys. Tipu's third son, Mu'izz-ud-din, gave the mutineers the symbolic betel nut to cement their alliance and promised them amazing rewards once the great dynasty was restored. He told the sepoys not to kill the white women, for after the Englishmen had been destroyed, the bravest of the rebels could take the women for their wives (the nightmare of every upstanding Englishman).[22]

Then one of Mu'izz-ud-din's servants brought out the famous flag of Mysore, with its tiger stripes, and the flag was hoisted from the flagstaff on the ramparts. It was a flag of the old pattern, green stripes on a red field with a sun in the centre, and it was said to have been purchased at the sale of the booty which the British had looted from Tipu's Palace seven years earlier.[23]

The Princes' followers could come and go without hindrance now that their guards had been slaughtered. Colonel Marriott, their guardian, was penned up in his house inside the Palace with several lieutenants who had taken refuge there. As the sepoys peppered his windows, Marriott and his party retreated from room to room, then scuttled down the back steps into the basement unobserved and waited for – well, who knew what they were waiting for, but they had no intention of venturing out of the house until it was all over.[24] As they crouched there shuddering, they heard the sepoys outside the next-door house calling, 'Come out, Nawab, come out, Nawab, there is no fear.' The next-door house was occupied by Fateh Hyder Ali, the eldest of the four princes of Mysore and heir presumptive to the throne.

Fateh Hyder Ali lacked the courage of his father or the grand-father after whom he was named, and he did not come out, any more than Colonel Marriott did. For the sons of Tipu Sultan might like to play with the dream of restoration, but they did not fancy the bloody reality. There is no evidence that any of them played the slightest active part in the fighting. They stayed indoors to survive that day. Which was all that Amelia Fancourt could hope for, too.

> I bolted all the doors in my room. I brought my children into it. I fell on my knees and fervently prayed that Col. F's endeavour to bring peace to the Garrison might be crowned with success and his life spared through the mercy of God! I dressed and cautiously opened the hall door and felt my way to the lower end to look where they were firing *most* . . . As I stood at the lower end of the hall which was quite open to the verandah – a figure approached me. It was so dark I could only see the Red Coat by the light of the firing at the Barracks. I was dreadfully frightened expecting to be murdered and having left the children in my bedroom. I had, however, the courage to ask who was this and the answer I received was 'Madam, I am an officer.' I then said 'But who are you?' to which the Gentleman replied, 'I am an officer of the Main Guard.' I enquired what was the matter – he said it was a mutiny – that *every* European had already been murdered on Guard *but* himself and that we should *all* be murdered. I made no reply but walked away to the room where my babes and female servant were. The officer went out of the opposite door of the hall where we had spoken together and never got downstairs for he was butchered most cruelly in Col. F's dressing room. I have since heard his name Lt O'Reilly of the 1st.

This encounter with the ghostly redcoat were the only words Amelia exchanged with a fellow countryman during her ordeal. O'Reilly was in charge of all those troops of the 1st who were on duty: four native officers, nine *havildars* (the rough equivalent of a sergeant) and 251 rank and file. How sparse the European officers were in the native regiments, not merely in Vellore but across India.

Now O'Reilly was gone. Colonel McKerras, who commanded the 2nd/23rd, lay dead in the middle of the parade ground. A few yards away, Colonel Fancourt lay in mortal agony. Captain Miller of the 1st, the one who had refused to cut short his sleep, was sleeping the long sleep now. As were almost all the officers and half the men of the 69th. The first massacre of the night was mostly done within an hour.

Colonel Marriott was still penned up in his basement, listening to the sepoys' fruitless appeal to the sons of Tipu. The fourth colonel at Vellore, Lieutenant-Colonel Forbes, commanding officer to John Low and that infamous 1st battalion, which had done its share of the murdering, where was he? He was the only colonel who had quarters outside the fort. When the shooting broke out, he made several vain efforts to get inside the walls. Then he joined forces with his adjutant, Lieutenant Ewing. How this came about is put with some delicacy in Wilson's *History of the Madras Army*: Ewing 'assembled several European stragglers, and making his way out of the fort, he joined Forbes. These two officers, accompanied by a number of unarmed men belonging to the 1st battalion, then took possession of the principal hill fort, where they remained until after the dispersion of the mutineers.' In other words, they legged it and lay low.[25]

If Colonel Marriott's behaviour seems less than heroic, what are we to think of Colonel Forbes? He had been fooled by his native officers not once but twice, first when he believed their protestations that no, sahib, there was no objection at all to the turbans, and secondly when they told him Mustapha Beg was mad. Now all hell had broken loose and Colonel Forbes had scampered to the hill fort at the other end of the town where he could still hear the firing as the remnants of his battalion were finished off. What's more, he appears to have made no attempt to send for help from Arcot, or anywhere else.[26]

I at this moment gave all for lost. I opened my dressing table drawer and took out my husband's miniature which I tied on and

hid under my Habit shirt, determined to *lose* that *but* in Death. I
had secured his watch some time before, to ascertain the hour. I
had *hardly* secured this *much* valued resemblance of my husband
before I heard a loud noise in the hall adjoining my bedroom. I
moved softly to the door and looking through the keyhole discovered two sepoys knocking a chest of drawers in pieces – I was
struck with horror, knowing their next visit would be to my
apartment. My children and their female servant were at this time
lying on the mat just before the door which opened into the back
verandah which at the commencement of the Mutiny seemed
the safest place. As shots were fired at the windows we were
obliged to move as far as possible from them.

I whispered to my Ayah that the sepoys were in the hall and
told her to move from the door. She took the children under my
bed and begged me to go there also. I had no time to reply for the
door we had just left was at that instant burst open. I got under the
bed and was no sooner there than several shots were fired into the
room but altho' the door was open nobody entered. The children
were screaming with terror at the fire and I expected our last
hour was come but willing to make any effort to save my babes I
got from my hiding place. I flew into the small adjoining room off
the back staircase. I opened the window from which I only saw
two horsekeepers. I returned instantly to my bedroom and desiring my Ayah to take my little babe in her arms, I took Charles St
John in my own and opening the door off the back stairs ran
down them as quick as I could.

When we got to the bottom we found several sepoys on
guard at the back of the house. I showed them my babes and
told my Ayah to inform them they might take all we had if they
would spare our lives. One of them desired us to sit down in the
stable with the horses. Another looked very surly but did not
prevent our going there. Whilst we stood in the stable I told my
Ayah I had my husband's watch and requested she would hide it
for me. She dug up some earth with her fingers and threw it

over the watch and put two or three chatties [small clay pots] upon it.

We had not been seated for five minutes before we were ordered by a third sepoy. He told us to go into the fowl house which had a bamboo front to it and in consequence we were quite exposed to view until the same man brought us an old mat which we made use of by placing it before the door to hide ourselves and afterwards the same sepoy brought my little boy baby a loaf of bread to satisfy his hunger. Here I suppose we sat about three hours in the greatest agony of mind endeavouring to quiet my dear Charles whom I found it very difficult to pacify – he was so alarmed by the constant firing and cried sadly to go out several times. I saw the sepoys from my concealment taking out immense loads of our goods on their backs, tied up in table cloths and sheets.[27]

The only active British resistance was now led by a small party of eight survivors who had bumped into each other earlier at the house of the adjutant, Lieutenant Ewing of the 1st, but unlike Ewing, they did not later choose to slip out of the fort to join Colonel Forbes. They consisted at first of Ewing and two surgeons, Mr Jones and his assistant Mr Dean, with four other subalterns and the redoubtable Sergeant Brady of the 69th.[28] After crouching in Ewing's house, just to the right of the Palace gates, for nearly four hours, from 3.30 to just after 7am, they made a run for it and managed to gain the European barracks where they found a large number of men dead and wounded and 'the remainder quite disheartened'. The officers rallied them and they knocked out the windows at the rear of the barracks and managed to scramble up on to the ramparts under a fierce fire of musketry. From there they gained control of a bastion and then fought their way along the ramparts until they reached the main gateway. A sepoy fired at Dean and knocked his cap off. Dean recognized him as a man from his own battalion whom he had often treated in hospital. 'I exclaimed, almost involuntarily "What! Adam

Khan!" My cap off he instantly recognized me and cried "Doctor Sayeb, Doctor Sayeb, forgive me, forgive me!"'[29]

By this time, all the officers in the party had fallen and they had run out of cartridges. As they passed the Paymaster's House, they saw that the Pay Office had been broken open and ransacked, and bags of rupees were lying about the rampart. Dean suggested that they use the smaller rupee coins as bullets, and he soon heard a sergeant who had killed an insurgent with this high-value ammo calling out, 'I'll trouble you for change out of that' – the only recorded joke of the night.

Now only the gallant surgeons, Jones and Dean, and Sergeant Brady remained standing to lead the assault on the magazine, but it had already been burst open by the insurgents.[30] Only loose powder was left. On the way back from this fruitless sally, two men of the 69th managed to tear down the Mysore flag under heavy fire, both from inside the fort and from the native town, or *pettah*, beyond the moat which was well within range of the southern face of the ramparts where the flagstaff was. By now Dean and his party were firing pieces of gravel because the rupees took too long to load.

The pitiful remnants of the British garrison still held the rampart over the main gateway. There they waited. They had not a single cartridge between them. All they had to fight with was their bayonets. The dauntless surgeons inflicted enough damage to leave plenty of repair work for them to perform later. Below the ramparts the crocodiles were preparing to pick up stragglers.

At this moment, in an incident recorded only in Dean's account, some of the non-commissioned officers came to him and said that they were now without any officers, their numbers were greatly reduced, they had no ammunition left and no provisions, and the sepoys also had possession of the hill fort (they pointed out their red jackets on the skyline). They considered their case hopeless and saw no chance of relief. The only way to save the lives of those who were left would be to make the best terms they could.

This could have been a crucial turning point. If the Europeans had

surrendered, resistance in the fort would have ended, and the news
would have been all over southern India in a twinkling. Fort after
fort, garrison after garrison would have risen against the British.
Dean was having none of it. He told the despairing NCOs that several officers lived outside the fort and would have given information
to the cantonment at Arcot, they still held the main gateway and,
anyway, who would they surrender to? He pulled off the mattress he
had laid over the corpse of his friend Willison, and asked the NCOs
what could be expected but similar treatment from men who had
committed such dreadful excesses? He just about managed to hold
them off from surrendering, and persuaded them 'that we must keep
possession to the last extremity'.[31]

In the fowl house Amelia and Charles and the baby girl crouched
in the chickenshit listening to the guns and the rattle of the bamboo
screen and the mad clucking of the hens, as the sun climbed over the
eastern ramparts and began to dry the blood on the bodies.

I hoped for the arrival of the 19th Dragoons from Arcot. The few
lines Col. F. wrote in his room was most probably intended to be
sent express to Col. Gillespie (he was that morning coming to
spend a few days with us) but whether Col. F. had the means of
sending off his dispatches or not I was quite ignorant. Still, however, I thought the news must reach Col. Gillespie on the road by
one means or another and hearing a tremendous firing at the
gates strengthened my hopes that the Regiment was arrived.

She was surely right about those few lines that Colonel Fancourt
had penned before he went out being an urgent appeal to Colonel
Gillespie to bring help from Arcot in the shape of the 19th
Dragoons. The great cavalry barracks at Arcot was only 16 miles
from Vellore, and there was no other European regiment for miles.
She was right, too, alas, in doubting whether her husband had been
able to send off his message. The scrap of paper was still crumpled in
St John's hand as he lay semi-conscious on the parade.

Her one comfort was that Colonel Gillespie was coming anyway to Vellore that morning to spend a few days with them. He had arranged to dine with the Fancourts the night before, but had sent word that the mail had just arrived at Arcot and he had to deal with all the matters arising, so would they excuse him if he came to breakfast the next morning. Surely, surely, someone would meet him on the road and tell him the dreadful news.

Rollo Gillespie and St John Fancourt were old friends. They had met first when they were both fighting in the West Indies ten years earlier. They had been delighted to meet again when Gillespie had exchanged into the 19th Light Dragoons with another colonel who did not wish to serve so far afield. Gillespie, by contrast, had his reasons for wishing to go as far east as possible, plenty of them.

The great historian of the Army, Sir John Fortescue, in his little sketches of great commanders, *A Gallant Company*, says of Gillespie: 'Reviewing his career again, I still think him the bravest man who ever wore the King's uniform.' 'Brave' doesn't cover the half of it. Robert Rollo Gillespie was the most impetuous, umbrageous, impatient, ruthless and unstoppable soldier there ever was. He was the epitome of Wellington's dictum that what a great commander in battle must have above everything else was *dash*. Gillespie's tiny frame pulsed with a ferocity that welled up in a nanosecond at the faintest provoking. His red hair crackled with energy. He was in your face before you were out of your chair. His life was not so much a military career as a series of uncontrolled explosions.

Like many of the feistiest British commanders, he was an Ulster Scot by birth: born in the little town of Comber, Co. Down, in 1766, educated at a private school and with a vicar at Newmarket. He had been intended for Cambridge but, judging his own temperament correctly, became a cornet in the Dragoons instead, contracting, almost en passant and with characteristic haste, a clandestine marriage with a girl called Annabell whom he had met three weeks earlier in the deanery at Clogher.

Almost immediately he found himself on trial for murder. He

had acted as second in a duel for an officer called Mackenzie who had quarrelled with William Barrington, brother to the well-known lawyer Sir Jonah Barrington. The duel took place on the Barrington estate, in a meadow by the banks of the River Barrow, Co. Carlow. Mackenzie and Barrington each fired twice and missed both times. Sir Jonah then suggested that the two principals should become reconciled. Gillespie, who was smarting under a stream of insults from William, objected furiously to this idea. He drew a handkerchief from his pocket and challenged William to fight him instead. They squared up and Gillespie shot Barrington through the heart, while Barrington's ball only dented a button on Gillespie's jacket.[32] It is hard to dissent from Sir Jonah's furious outburst: 'Will it be believed that in a civilized country, when both contestants are satisfied, one of the principals should be slain by a *second*?'[33]

Gillespie was tried at the spring assizes at Maryborough in 1788. No less than ten members of the jury were military officers. He was acquitted in triumph and speedily took ship for the West Indies to join his fellow Dragoons in suppressing the rebellion in Haiti. He was deputed to demand the surrender of Port au Prince and swam ashore bearing a flag of truce in his hand and his sword in his mouth, the sea around him being peppered with bullets.

He then returned to Ireland on leave. While waiting at Cork for his ship back to the West Indies, he went to the theatre. Noticing that his neighbour, a heavy-built man with a large nose, refused to stand and remove his hat during the playing of the National Anthem, he seized the big man's nose so hard that he broke it. On hearing of this fracas, the big man's fiancée broke off their engagement. In a steaming rage at this double humiliation, the big man obtained a warrant against Rollo for assault and battery. Rollo went into hiding. In order to board his ship without being arrested, he put on a bonnet and shawl and borrowed a baby from a helpful fellow passenger.[34] With his slender stature, he had no trouble passing as a woman. The story is typical: the instant and implacable umbrage, the fierce loyalty to the Crown, the surprising muscular strength and the ability to improvise at a moment's notice.

Back in San Domingo, he set about the rebels with such vigour that eight republican hitmen were sent to his house. He killed six of them with his sword alone amid a hail of bullets, one of which passed through his auburn hair and severed his temporal artery. He was found in a dead faint on his bed, with blood streaming from his temple and the dead hitmen scattered down the stairs.

This exploit made Gillespie celebrated in the West Indies and beyond. Years later, at a court levee, when he was presented to George III, the King remarked with royal surprise: 'Eh, eh, what, what, is this the little man that killed the brigands?'[35] As soon as he got back to England, Rollo was in trouble again. A fellow Dragoon, Major Allen Cameron, a bad hat who had been prosecuted for mutiny and sedition, alleged that Gillespie had been claiming allowances for officers and men in his regiment beyond the actual numbers under his command – in short, claiming expenses for men who did not exist, the oldest scam in the book. There was no alternative to a court martial, at which a stream of high-ranking witnesses came forward to vouch for Gillespie's courage, generosity and good character. If he had overdone the allowances now and then, it was only because, as the Quartermaster said, 'Lieutenant-Colonel Gillespie acted to the soldiers under his command like a tender parent to his children.'[36] Once again he was acquitted in triumph (the deplorable Cameron was discharged from the Army).

All the same, in his short life Rollo had already been tried for murder, prosecuted for assault and court-martialled for corruption, not to mention abandoning Annabell. Next time he might not get off. It was time for a change of air. Like so many hot-blooded chancers, he could begin again in India.

The air had never seemed sweeter as he rode out from Arcot towards Vellore just after dawn on the morning of July 10, 1806. A leisurely amble of 16 miles would work up an appetite for breakfast with his old friends. There was nothing like the morning ride in the hot season: the bullock carts creaking along the road, the heavy dew still lying under the trees, the green parrots squawking in the palm groves, the buffalo wallowing in the muddy shallows, the sky already blue as it would be all day but the air still fresh.

It was a deliciously tranquil scene. Anyone who moved at all moved at that graceful walking pace which makes the Indian countryside such a restful place to be. So it was with some surprise that he saw a trooper on a horse coming towards him at a feverish gallop.

Major Coates of the 69th Regiment had quarters outside the fort. He was responsible for perimeter security and he had posted a guard consisting of a sergeant, two corporals and 12 privates, a rather modest detachment for such a huge fort (a mile in circumference), considering that only three of the privates were to be posted as sentries at any one time.[37] When the firing broke out, Major Coates and some men of the 23rd first tried to get into the fort.[38] But, ironically, the security was too good. The main gate had four redoubtable doors. The mutineers in their excitement had neglected to pull up the drawbridge and had left open the first two gates. But the two inner gates were no less robust: massive full-height wooden doors with huge iron bolts and locks. They would have to be blown open. So Coates turned round and sent one of his officers who had been trying to get into the fort, Captain Stevenson of the 23rd, with an urgent message for Colonel Gillespie at Arcot.

That had been an hour and a half ago. It was now 7am[39] as Captain Stevenson came out of a cloud of dust and gave Gillespie the news. Within minutes Gillespie was galloping back to Arcot to whistle up a squadron of his own 19th Dragoons plus a troop of the 7th Cavalry, throwing out orders for the rest of the cavalry and the galloper guns to follow, leaving only a security detachment to guard the barracks.

Gillespie was soon well ahead of the rest of his troop. By 8.30am, he was outside Vellore Fort. Sergeant Brady, standing on the rampart over the main gate, saw the little figure coming like the clappers up the Arcot road and cried out: 'If Colonel Gillespie be alive, that is he, and God Almighty has sent him from the West Indies to save our lives in the East.'[40] The cavalry had arrived and Gillespie was at the head of them.

There were still two massive gates to be breached and Gillespie and the advance guard had nothing but their own muskets and pistols. Instantly Gillespie perceived that the outer of the two gates was more or less shielded from the mutineers' fire by the inner gate and he shouted this to the little band on the ramparts. They had not a cartridge between them and were repelling the sepoys with their bayonets alone. But they did have a rope and Sergeant Brady let down a couple of men who quickly unbolted the outer gate from the inside.

Just as quickly, Gillespie grabbed the rope himself and climbed up to the rampart to egg on the surgeons and the gallant few who were now the only Europeans in the fort still holding out. But egg on and fire his pistol down at the insurgents on the parade ground was all he could do, until he spotted that the battery on the next turret was only lightly held by the insurgents and could be taken at the point of the bayonet. He led a charge along the rampart and quickly overpowered the sepoys and took their three guns, but this was little use as there was no ammunition left in the battery either.[41]

Meanwhile the mutineers were massing in their hundreds in front of the Palace preparing to take total control of the fort. The resistance was surely all but over.

Then at last the galloper guns came up the Arcot road with the rest of the Dragoons. With them came Lieutenant John Blakiston, who gives us the most vivid account of the final desperate moments of the whole morning. Blakiston had been ordered up from Madras to superintend various building works to be carried on at the three central barracks of the Madras Army. He had been having a pleasant time wandering from one cantonment to the next, repairing a rampart here, designing a new court of justice there, for military engineers in India were expected to turn their hand to anything. At Arcot in particular, the cavalry officers, many of them old comrades of his, had welcomed him to their mess. He had been over at Vellore a day or two earlier, and it was only because he had been summoned back to Arcot to inspect some of his works that he escaped being murdered in his cot.

Blakiston heard about the mutiny only after Gillespie had already set out for Vellore, but he had an unquenchable thirst for action, and he caught up with the main body of the 19th on their gallop and arrived at the fort at exactly the same time as the regiment's guns were approaching the gates.

Gillespie was shouting down from the rampart, ordering the artillery sergeant to blow open the gate, but 'observing that he did not appear to know how to go to work, I ventured to give an opinion, when Colonel Gillespie immediately put the guns under my orders. I immediately directed the sergeant to load without shot, intending to run the muzzle of the gun up to the gate and make use of it as a petard, but finding that it was already loaded and with shot, I told him to discharge the piece and that he might as well lay it for the bolt, pointing with my sword to where I thought it was [the bolt being on the inside of the gate and so invisible to Blakiston]. He did so and the gate flew open.'

Gillespie slithered back down the rope and formed up the few loyal survivors on the parade – Dean thinks there were 'no more than fifty or sixty able to act'. He gave the word 'Forward' and with Dean and Brady advanced towards the Palace, with nothing but their bayonets to disperse the sepoys. (Dean says, 'I do not believe there was one musket loaded with ball cartridge.') For a few minutes the sepoys returned a tremendous fire from the pagoda and from the Palace railings. These 'smart and well-directed volleys' killed and wounded a great number, but then Gillespie directed the foot soldiers off to the right, to give space for the cavalry to charge. Soon the sepoys were falling back, running in swarms to get away through the sally port.[42]

For most of the sepoys there was to be no escape. On the bare slope outside the fort, the southern glacis in military jargon, they were cut down in their hundreds by another detachment of the 19th which had been sent round to intercept. Those who managed to crawl on slithered into the moat where the crocodiles were by now on full alert.

In the whirl of the onslaught, Gillespie was knocked down and flattened by a Dragoon's horse riding over him. He broke his wrist, but he was up in a flash. On they charged. The first thing they saw was the body of Colonel McKerras in the middle of the parade ground. Then they passed over the stiffening bodies of the European sick, lying in their hospital clothing in the rows where they lay, having been brought out to be butchered in front of the Palace gates. Blakiston saw, too, the body of Colonel Fancourt, very near death now. He had been lying there for four or five hours.

Though John Blakiston was to perform several other feats of daring and brilliance, he certainly deserves to be remembered as the man who blew open the gate at Vellore. But he deserves to be remembered for something else, too.

Both inside and outside the fort, the slaughter was furious, the revenge inexorable. That is the sort of language which the military historians deploy to describe the unspeakable horror of war at close quarters. Sir John Kaye in his marvellous *History of the Indian Mutiny* says, for example, that 'the retribution was terrible, and just'.[43] Wilson's *History of the Madras Army* tells us baldly that 'about 350 sepoys were killed'.[44] Blakiston says that 'upwards of 800 bodies were carried out of the fort, besides those who were killed after they escaped through the sally port.'[45]

What Blakiston also tells us, and what the official reports do not tell us, is exactly how it was that hundreds of those sepoys died:

For my own part, I must say that nothing like pity entered my breast during that day. Upwards of a hundred sepoys, who had sought refuge in the palace, were brought out, and, by Colonel Gillespie's order, placed under a wall and fired at with canister-shot[46] from the guns till they were all dispatched. Even this

appalling sight I could look upon, I may almost say, with composure. It was an act of summary justice, and in every respect a most
proper one, yet, at this distance of time[47] I find it a difficult matter
to approve the deed, or to account for the feeling under which I
then viewed it.

Those hundred-plus sepoys were prisoners of war. By our standards, what Blakiston observed was a war crime. Nor should it be
supposed that Blakiston was more of an onlooker than a participant.
Captain Charles Marriott, the colonel's brother who shared his lodg-
ings, saw Blakiston charging into the temple and seeking out sepoys
who had taken refuge there and running them through.

Blakiston was not the only witness to report this massacre.
Lieutenant Keighley of the 19th Dragoons observed the methods of
his commanding officer from close quarters:

> Colonel Gillespie immediately took prompt and decisive action.
> The Princes being all secured, he removed them to separate places,
> putting them in charge of the Dragoons, two men in the room
> with each and four outside the doors. Such sepoys as were taken
> at that time were about forty in number; these he ordered to be
> tied to each other and being near the fives court, the guard of the
> 19th loaded with grape and fired on them at the distance of about
> thirty yards. Twenty more who were secured soon after shared a
> similar fate.[48]

This shows greater deliberation in the process. There are fewer
victims, and they are fired on with grape not canister shot, but they
are rounded up, tied together and taken to a separate place of execution: the fives court.

I had not been aware that Vellore boasted such an English thing as
a fives court. But now that I look closer at the plan of the fort, I see
it. There it is, in the bottom right-hand corner, a little oblong
attached to the mighty bulk of the temple. And, in truth, it is not so

very surprising that the garrison should have a court, for this was the heyday of fives, or handball as it was still sometimes known. Every reputable public school – Eton, Harrow, Winchester, Rugby – had its own variant of knocking a ball against a wall with your gloved bunch of fives. John Low learnt the game as a cadet at Tripassur where cricket and fives were prescribed to relieve the unhealthy air. Later on, he played the game with zest during the times he was stationed at Vellore. Twenty years later, he wrote from Jaipur in a gloomy mood to his sister Susan, 'That robust health which I enjoyed when you were at Vellore, such as permitted of cricket & fives playing is gone for ever! – at least as long as my fate condemns me to live in Hindoostan.'[49] There was no spot in the fort that he knew better than the fives court.

It was not until 1870 that the details of the massacre were finally fleshed out. In his *Narrative of Historical Events connected with the 69th Regiment,* W.F. Butler tells us:

> Between the great pagoda and the eastern rampart there was situated a large oblong court in which the English soldiers had been accustomed to exercise at the game of 'fives' when the rays of the sun grew less intense.
>
> Into this court, the mutineers, to the number of three hundred, were now placed; they filled almost the entire space between the walls, and the dense dark mass reaching to the extremity of the flag-way had around it, upon three sides, lofty walls; and upon the fourth a wall less lofty but more impassable, a living wall of steel from the centre of which protruded the muzzles of the galloper guns.
>
> The order given to the dismounted troops, who stood around these guns, was one apparently easy of fulfillment; it was to fire until the living crowd became a heap of dead; but it is said that half an hour afterward there were arms moving and a few bodies writhing amidst the confused shapeless mass of black corpses which lay four and five deep upon the flagged floor of the blood-saturated fives court.[50]

This startling passage occurs in a book intended to celebrate the glorious deeds of the 69th. Butler is not a wholly reliable writer. The numbers are certainly exaggerated. A fives court could scarcely hold 300 men, even if packed together. He also justified Gillespie's vengeance by claiming that 'nearly all the ladies, women and children in the fort and cantonments were shot down or butchered in cold blood', which did not happen.[51] But in general Butler's report carries conviction.

It is also supported by another eyewitness account of the massacre, which I have not seen referred to elsewhere. This was written 35 years later by the heroic Assistant Surgeon John Dean and it is to be found in the *United Service Magazine* for January 1841.[52] After fighting so bravely on the ramparts, Dean had returned to his house to see what damage the sepoys had done. He washed and changed his clothes and then mounted his horse and went again to the parade.

I found that the prisoners had been removed from the Palace and placed under the gallery wall of the fives court, where some preparations were going on to execute them.

At that moment Dean was called away to attend on a major called Armstrong, who was lying about half a mile away, but he turned out to be dead when the surgeon arrived. Dean then galloped back to the fort:

The preparations for the execution were now complete – the galloper guns having been brought into the fort, and within a few paces of the mutinous sepoys, who were now about to be punished for the enormities they had so recently committed.

Gillespie had deputed his fellow officer, Lieutenant-Colonel Kennedy, who came up with the main body of the Dragoons, to supervise the executions (to judge by the dateline of his dispatch to Cradock, he was himself dictating to a Captain Wilson at that moment, because of his broken wrist). When they saw Dean, some of the native officers who had been herded into the fives court called out to him, saying that they belonged to the 1st Regiment, not the 23rd, which was then thought to be responsible for all the killing. Dean confirmed that they did not belong to the 23rd, and Kennedy had them taken away.

> I think there must have been sixty men when the guns were opened upon them, loaded with grape; and, after a few rounds, all appeared to have been killed. In the afternoon, the party of sepoys who had left the fort in the early part of the morning, to take possession of the hill fort, were brought down and were placed over the bodies of those who had been killed, and the same example was made of them.

When they got to the hill fort, this second batch had found to their chagrin that Colonel Forbes and his band were already in control there. They instantly pretended to be innocent refugees, but their muskets were still smoking and they were taken back down to the fives court to be killed, several hours after the mutiny had been utterly extinguished.

Dean's account, which is a punctilious one, confirms Keighley's estimate of about 60 men in the first batch and a further batch later killed on top of them. It confirms, too, the deliberate and purposeful nature of the killing. Dean has time to gallop half a mile, check up on Major Armstrong and still get back before the shooting has started. And in soberer terms, he echoes, too, Butler's more lurid description of the sepoys packed into the fives court and the two galloper guns which had blown open the main gate now blowing the men apart from close range.

What Dean also makes clear is that only the vaguest attempt was made to select the guilty. He admits that it was soon discovered that 'the 23rd were not the originators of this unhappy affair but that the 1st regiment had been the mainspring of everything.' The treacherous

Kassim confessed as much to Colonel Forbes and Lieutenant Coombes after the mutiny.[53] The native officers who had escaped the fives court, with many others of both regiments, were court-martialled and executed or imprisoned. Conversely, many quite innocent sepoys were mown down in the fives court: 'I was desired by Colonel Gillespie to find if possible the native cookboy who had joined us [and fought bravely alongside them]. I searched every prison in vain. He survived all the fighting part of it; but with many others equally undeserving was put to death in the general row; for to call out "Here is a sepoy!" was enough.' Inside the Palace, concubines and dancing girls were cut down along with servants who may have had nothing to do with the plot at all.

Another thing Dean tells us is that shortly after Gillespie had been hauled up on to the rampart by the drag rope, they met the wounded Captain Barrow on the cavalier bastion with Mrs Barrow and their three young children. Barrow could move no further and on leaving him Gillespie said: 'By the Sacred God! I'll revenge you!' And he did.

Gillespie's revenge sent a shudder through southern India. A year later, an *arz*, or petition, from 11 native officers stationed at Hyderabad asserted that 'three portions [I think this means three-quarters] of the native troops were ignorant of the intention to mutiny and were faithful to their duty' and warned that 'If another insurrection should occur in the army, all the men will be united in the sentiment and action, in consequence of Colonel Gillespie's undistinguishing vengeance.'[54]

Seldom can a fine historian have been so wholly mistaken as Sir John Kaye when he declares in his *History of the Indian Mutiny*[55] that Gillespie 'would not soil his victory with any cruel reprisals'.

It could have been worse still. The Dragoons' blood was up and, now that they had spilled so much of other people's, they were eager to press on into the Palace and finish the business by killing the Princes and their retinues, to eliminate the threat of Tipu's cubs for ever. Had the tiger stripes not been seen flying from the flagstaff? Anyone could see that this was a deep-laid plot to obliterate British rule in India and the Princes must be in it up to their necks.

The British authorities made the most exhaustive efforts after the mutiny to get at the truth about the role played by the Princes. In the course of three separate official inquiries, they were repeatedly interviewed, as was Mustapha Beg, but the whole question remained infuriatingly cloudy. The most we can say is that the Princes were informed about the plot and invited to become its patrons, but there seems little likelihood that they took any sort of active lead. They showed no wish to risk their cushioned luxury and were happy to wait on events.

Ever since the mutiny of 1806, historians, first the British and more recently the Indian, have sought to isolate a single predominant cause for the Mutiny at Vellore. Was it the scheming of the Princes, or the turban and the ornaments of caste, the so-called 'joys' (from *joia*, the Portuguese for jewel), or the threat of the missionaries, or the accumulated hardships of the sepoys' conditions of service – the inadequate pay, often months in arrears, the inequalities between the native and the European troops and the casual insults of the European officers? But need we search for a single cause? Is it not enough to say, as with so many violent explosions in human life, that a whole lot of things came together and feelings boiled over into events so terrible that both sides were, to misquote Clive of India, surprised by their own immoderation?

At the last horrible gasp of the proceedings, about 10.30am, Colonel Marriott emerges blinking from his basement and makes a stand. It is the only stand he takes in the whole story, but it is a crucial one.[56]

Gillespie himself is all for going on and finishing the job. To say that he is not a man for half-measures would be a heroic understatement. Undeterred, Marriott makes his case. The Princes are under his guard, which incidentally is his justification for staying inside the Palace throughout the fighting. It would be a personal dereliction of duty if he were to allow them to be cut down unarmed, to say nothing of their women and children and their hundreds of retainers. Such an atrocity would be long remembered to the discredit of Britain. Far better to take them all prisoner and send them somewhere a long way from Mysore where they will no longer offer a potential focus for insurrection. Secretly, Marriott is highly dubious about the innocence of his charges (his doubts emerge later, at the inquiries, and cause a sensation) but, both at the time and later, he is firmly opposed to killing them. And he persuades Gillespie to stay his hand.

At first Bentinck refused to remove the Princes. But then he caved in, largely to protect his own reputation. For his new defence was that the mutiny had been primarily not a protest about the turbans, for which he could be blamed, but a plot to restore the Mysore dynasty, which was not his fault. There was weeping and shrieking from the women in the Palace as the Princes were carried away in 13 palanquins, but no more was heard from them after that. They disappear from our story.

By about 11am it was all over. The King's standard of the 23rd regiment flew from the flagstaff again, and the work of towing away the pile of corpses which filled the parade and spilled out of the barracks and hung over the ramparts began. The whole thing had lasted just over eight hours. The news of the terrible mutiny and of its prompt and terrible suppression spread within days across southern India and far beyond. It was a huge boost to British power. The brutality of that suppression was what made it so impressive. It is often, and plausibly, argued that the example that had been made at Vellore ensured that there was no serious mutiny by the native troops anywhere in the Madras Presidency over the next decades and that the south remained relatively peaceful throughout 1857.

Although the memory of Vellore was eclipsed by the Great Mutiny, its resonance was still enough to inspire 'Gillespie', a ballad by Sir Henry Newbolt, first published in his collection *The Island Race* in 1898. Though it may not quite have the tingle of 'There's a desperate hush in the Close tonight' or 'Drake's Drum', the stuff still stirs. And I cannot resist reprinting some of it:

Riding at dawn, riding alone,
Gillespie left the town behind;
Before he turned by the Westward road
A horseman crossed him, staggering blind.

'The Devil's abroad in false Vellore,
The Devil that stabs by night,' he said,
'Women and children, rank and file,
Dying and dead, dying and dead.'

In fact, there were no women and children dying and dead. There were only two recorded exceptions to this. Mrs Potter's child was shot through the knee accidentally. Lieutenant Ely's daughter was murdered alongside him, but this appears to have been a personal revenge killing, the Elys being mistaken for the intended victims in the darkness.[57] Nor, as far as we can tell, had any white women been sexually assaulted in this, or any other mutiny in India, contrary to the propaganda put about back home after every outbreak of violence. This nightmare was so potent that the authorities went to exhaustive lengths to prove that no such outrages had occurred.[58]

'Trumpeter, sound for the Light Dragoons,
Sound to saddle and spur,' he said;
'He that is ready may ride with me,
And he that can may ride ahead.'

Fierce and fain, fierce and fain,
Behind him went the troopers grim,
They rode as ride the Light Dragoons
But never a man could ride with him.

Alone he came to false Vellore,
The walls were lined, the gates were barred;

Alone he walked where the bullets bit,
And called above to the Sergeant's Guard.

'Sergeant, Sergeant, over the gate,
Where are your officers all?' he said;
Heavily came the Sergeant's voice,
'There are two living and forty dead.'

'A rope, a rope,' Gillespie cried:
They bound their belts to serve his need.
There was not a rebel behind the wall
But laid his barrel and drew his bead.

There was not a rebel among them all
But pulled his trigger and cursed his aim,
For lightly swung and rightly swung
Over the gate Gillespie came.

He dressed the line, he led the charge,
They swept the wall like a stream in spate,
And roaring over the roar they heard
The galloper guns that burst the gate.

The belt chain is a myth, but otherwise Newbolt follows the course of events more or less accurately. His version is of course hugely sanitized, and the casualty figure for the British officers is exaggerated. There were not 40 of them inside the fort; the true figure for European officers killed was 15, with 115 European NCOs and men dead. It was the sepoys who died in such enormous numbers.[59] The troops from Arcot had negligible losses – one trooper killed and three wounded – all because of Gillespie's dash. But it is the dash that Newbolt captures so vividly; the image of the light, almost weightless figure swinging on the rope is unforgettable. Gillespie was born to be balladed.

What the ballad does not record is how the dead bodies were carried out of the fort on carts and then the sepoys were burnt together in deep holes about a mile and a half away, while the European dead received individual burial in the cemetery beyond the drawbridge. Separate, even in death; in fact, especially in death. Nor does Newbolt say anything about the massacre in the fives court, despite his enthusiasm for manly sports. In most respects, conditions in that early morning at Vellore pretty much paralleled the circumstances described in Newbolt's most famous poem 'Vitaï Lampada':

> The sand of the desert is sodden red,
> Red with the wreck of a square that broke;
> The Gatling's jammed and the Colonel dead
> And the regiment blind with dust and smoke.

Killing batches of unarmed men tied together does not, I think, quite correspond with the exhortation in the concluding line:

> 'Play up! play up! and play the game!'

The reckoning was an appalling one, not only in terms of blood but of the degree of disloyalty among the sepoys. Of the 1,700 native troops stationed at Vellore that night, 879 were dead or missing, 378 were confined for mutiny and 516 were considered implicated but not confined.[60] In the 1st Battalion of the 1st Madras Native Infantry, one soldier and only one was accounted innocent. This was Mustapha Beg, who was rewarded for the intelligence which Colonel Forbes had pooh-poohed with an award of 2,000 pagodas and a *subahdar*'s pension.[61]

For the leaders of the mutiny the ultimate punishment was reserved, and in deliciously varied forms. In India as in mediaeval Europe, considerable importance was attached to the method of execution. So it was that, of the worst offenders in the disloyal battalions, eight were sentenced to the low-grade fate of hanging, five were to be shot by firing parties drawn from their own battalions, and six, the elite, were to be 'blown away from guns'.[62] Never before in the history of the Madras Army had so many sepoys been executed as the result of a formal court-martial.[63]

This last punishment deserves a little explaining. Some say that the British inherited it from the Mughal rulers, others that the British devised it themselves. By 1800 the procedure had become standard practice. What happened was that the regiment was drawn up on parade and the condemned man was led forward, strapped to the mouth of the cannon and blown to pieces at the word of command. The most notorious recorded early instance of this punishment was inflicted by Sir Hector Munro in suppressing a mutiny in Bengal in 1764. He ordered no less than 24 rebellious sepoys to be blown away, and when the rest of his native battalion made as if to rebel, he ordered them to ground their arms and threatened to shoot the lot of them.[64] Blowing away remained a popular and effective method of suppressing dissent. Even condemned men preferred it to being hanged like a dog. We have seen how the native officers urged Colonel Forbes to have the treacherous Mustapha Beg blown away. Mountstuart Elphinstone, the Governor of Bombay, described by the military historian Philip Mason as one of the most humane, kindly and farsighted men ever to govern India, remarked that this mode of execution 'contains two valuable elements of capital punishment: it is painless to the criminal and terrible to the beholder'.[65] Blowings away drew huge crowds, apart from the members of the regiment summoned to witness the execution. The blackened head of the victim often shot high in the air and came down amongst the crowd. The firing party would find their uniforms and sun helmets spotted with sticky particles of flesh.

But what of the European commanders whose actions had provoked the ghastly chain of events at Vellore? Had they not been guilty of pig-headedness, negligence or downright stupidity? It was not until February 1807 that official reports of the mutiny reached London, and it was nearly a year after the mutiny, in April 1807, that the Court of Directors in London came to their conclusions, and they were damning. Sir John Cradock was stripped of his command and sent home in a fury – his fury made all the worse because the Company refused to pay his passage home, costing him a total of £3,500 for his family and servants.[66]

Lord William Bentinck had shown many of the same failings as Cradock. Certainly the Court of Directors thought so. Bentinck was sent home, too, and when he remonstrated against his treatment, the Court repeated their critique with knobs on, regretting that 'greater care and caution had not been exercised in examining into the real sentiments and dispositions of the sepoys before measures of severity were adopted to enforce the order respecting the use of the new turban'.[67]

Colonel Forbes escaped with a reprimand, for his failure to pay close attention to the warning of Mustapha Beg. 'Col. Forbes's conduct upon that occasion proceeded from the same laxity of system which there is reason to suppose predominated at Vellore for a considerable period before the unfortunate mine was sprung.' Colonel Fancourt, too, would have been reprimanded if he had lived; he had disregarded Mrs Burke's information 'for reasons the most frivolous'.[68]

What about John Low? Where has he been throughout all these terrible events? Why have we not heard a single word about him? It is an odd thing to choose a protagonist who is so utterly absent from the proceedings. If he wasn't at Vellore at all, why have we followed the whole bloody affair, hour by hour, sometimes minute by minute, in such excruciating detail?

The answer is that John Low was not at Vellore that night. He was miles away in one of the two detached sections of the 1st Battalion 1st MNI. Of the 401 men of the 1st/1st on detachment that night, every single one was accounted exempt from guilt. Because they were detached from the native adjutant who was at Vellore, they heard nothing of the new turban, nothing of the new regulations, for it was through the adjutant that all such instructions came. John was either at Chandragiri, about 40 miles from Vellore, or at Chittoor, no more than 20 miles away. There was no prospect of his being called up from either station that terrible morning. Nobody in his right mind would summon more native troops, for they would be liable only to strengthen the mutineers. The European cavalry at Arcot were the only hope. So at Chittoor and Chandragiri alike, the morning of July 10 dawned like any other morning in the hot season, blue and fresh – and utterly peaceful. The cocks crew, the dogs barked, the bullocks wallowed in the muddy shallows, the kites dipped and planed overhead. Nothing happened.[69]

Because he was not at Vellore, John Low lived.

It took only a week for the C–in–C to sweep away all the nonsense about the turbans and the moustaches and ornaments (the new regulations were rescinded on July 17). It took rather longer to decide what to do with the shattered remnants of the 1st Battalion which were no longer sustainable as a separate military unit. It was not until January 14, 1807, that the whole of the 1st and 23rd regiments were ordered to be 'struck off the list of the army'. The surviving European officers and the sepoys who had not rebelled, if only because they had not been at Vellore, were re-formed into the 24th Madras Native Infantry.

John Low was still only 18 years old, and he had been a lieutenant for 18 months. He had not fired a shot in anger, or had a shot fired at him. Yet more than half his battalion were dead or discharged in ignominy. The colonel and the adjutant had fled. The battalion had now been disbanded in disgrace. John Low's entry in the *Dictionary of National Biography* speaks of 'the loyal men and the officers (Low included)' being re-formed into the new regiment, but this gives a picture which is quite misleading. None of the European officers or European troops dreamed of rebelling. As for the native troops, it was not really a question of some men struggling with their consciences and staying loyal to the Company whose salt they had taken, while others went over to Tipu's sons. It was simply a question of whether you happened to be stationed at Vellore and were swept up into the mutiny or whether you were at Chittoor or Chandragiri where nothing was happening.

This was the terrible thing. Because John Low knew perfectly well that, if his company had been at Vellore, they would have risen with the same ferocity and slit his throat with just as little compunction. His men would have been just as offended by the new regulations if they had heard about them, would have loathed the new turban just as fiercely if they had been forced to wear it; they had no less reason to fear that they would, sooner or later, be forcibly converted to the white man's faith; they had the same grouses about pay and allowances. At seven rupees a month, the pay of the sepoy was not much more than half that of a European private in one of the King's regiments, and less than Tipu Sultan had paid. Moreover, the sepoys' pay was often months in arrears, while the Company made a point of paying its British troops on time.[70] These anxieties about money and status were just as gnawing as the fears about the breach of their religious purity or the longing to restore the dynasty of Tipu.

It is a myth that there was only one great mutiny in India under British rule, one single aberration from the peaceful onward flow of the British Raj. As C.A. Bayly points out, 'armed revolt was endemic in all parts of early colonial India.'[71] Ranajit Guha tells us in *Elementary Aspects of Peasant Insurgency in Colonial India* that, at a simple count, there were 110 uprisings between 1783 and 1900 – roughly the years during which the Lows were in India. Apart from the recurring military mutinies, in the cities there were repeated riots against the new house taxes, which spilled out into the countryside. Nor were these revolts necessarily futile. On the contrary, the authorities often adjusted the terms of service or the revenue assessments as a result. Only in 1857 did the entire British Empire seem on the verge of toppling. But the sense of grievance among the Company's thousands of native soldiers never ceased to be a lurking danger.[72]

We must not ignore this consciousness of a relative inferiority, which was sharpening all the time, as more and more callow young European cadets were coming out to officer native regiments and usurping the functions and perks that had once been reserved for native officers. As British rule spread across southern India, there was less and less chance of employment with native princes. The Company's service might now be the least bad way of providing for your family and your old age. But it was odd to speak so blithely of 'loyalty', when all that could be observed was a mixture of fear, prudence and conformity to the mood of the moment.

John could not remain ignorant of any horrific detail from that night. He may well have been summoned to Vellore on September 23 to watch the sentences of death carried out on the ringleaders on the western glacis of the fort behind the Palace. Some of his 'loyal' sepoys were needed to form the firing party for those of their comrades who were to be shot.[73] And the blowing away from guns demanded a big audience if it was to have the full educative effect noted by Mountstuart Elphinstone. It is a relief to know that, according to Colonel George Harcourt of the 12th regiment, 'the painful duty was performed without a single failure or accident'.[74]

Nor was John in much danger of forgetting what had happened. Five years later, in the expedition to capture the Dutch East Indies, he served alongside Gillespie and Blakiston, the heroes of the night. Later on, he was himself stationed at Vellore. Every day as he walked across the causeway into or out of the fort, he passed the English cemetery where his brother officers were buried near the tall memorial to the mutiny. And in the cool of the early evening, he would have a game of fives, with the sun dipping over the back wall of the court and the curious kites planing overhead.[75]

Again and again, the same resentments boiling into murderous plots. Again and again, the same grim lessons to be learnt. And if anything is clear from all his words and actions over his 50 years in India, it is clear that John Low learnt those lessons and had them by heart by the time he was 18 years old.

The first lesson for any commander in India was never to ignore warnings of disaffection. You were never as secure as you thought you were. First-class intelligence was the only guarantee of safety.

The second lesson was that, as soon as there was the slightest hint of trouble, an adequate supply of European troops must be rushed to the scene.

To avoid trouble it was of the highest importance never to give even the appearance of interfering with native custom and religious ceremony, was the third lesson.

Fourth, the old allegiances to deposed or decayed ruling dynasties were not obliterated but merely sleeping. They could be reawakened with devastating effect at the drop of a turban.

Finally, there was Gillespie's lesson – it was Wellington's lesson, too. When it was necessary to act, it was essential to act decisively, ruthlessly and, above all, *immediately*.

If Gillespie had been half an hour later at Vellore or five minutes slower to storm the fort, the place would have fallen decisively to the rebels, and every other citadel in the Presidency would have joined in. Even after Gillespie's prompt and brutal suppression, for weeks afterwards minor uprisings broke out at intervals in towns and at forts within a radius of 50 miles and more. Gillespie had saved Vellore, perhaps he had saved the Presidency.

John never ceased to be intensely conscious of how fragile the whole enterprise was. There were one or two others who felt this fragility, too – Elphinstone, Sir Henry Lawrence, Sir Thomas Munro, not many more. By all means, show a calm and dignified front, radiate confidence and assurance both to your own men and to the natives. But you must never, ever fool yourself.

The Court of Directors in their gratitude presented Rollo Gillespie with 7,000 pagodas and Sergeant Brady with 800 pagodas. Amelia Fancourt was granted an annuity of £100, so long as she continued a widow (which she did all her long life), and her two children were each to receive an allowance of £25 per annum until they were grown up. Perhaps we should conclude this melancholy narrative with the conclusion of her own:

At last I heard distinctly the horses of the 19th on the drawbridge, and huzza repeated aloud; then I hoped everything, and presently after heard them enter the fort. An officer rode in and called for me by name, but I could not answer or move; again I heard my name repeated, and saw an officer in a red jacket I thought looked like my husband. I sprang forward to meet him; it was Mr Maclean. I called for my husband; he told me he was alive. Colonel Gillespie and Mr Maclean then joined us, and both gave me the same assurance. They took me up stairs and placed me on a chair, giving me wine and water to drink. When the agitation of my mind was calmed, they told me Colonel Fancourt was wounded, though not dangerously, and that he must be kept quiet. About an hour after I was told by the surgeon of the 69th [the gallant Mr Jones, now returned to his day job of saving people rather than bayoneting them] my husband was in danger but that worse wounds had been cured; they were flesh wounds and the balls had not lodged. Hope still made me think he would recover. I would not even ask to see him, thinking the sight of me might agitate him so much. Alas! I found too late there was no hope from the first; he breathed his last about four o'clock the same evening. Thank God he died easily; his death was happy. I am fully satisfied, for he lived religiously and met his death in the faithful discharge of his duty.

The final words of Amelia's account are reproduced on the memorial to St John and herself in Christ Church, at Cheltenham, where she died on January 7, 1852, aged 75.

III

THE WHITE MUTINY

It was an inglorious start to a military career. The first shots that John Low's battalion had fired with deadly intent since his arrival in India had been aimed at their mutinous comrades. He had been baptized by firing squad.

What came next was, if anything, even more inglorious, still more bizarre, and very nearly as bloody. Even the description of it will sound improbable, almost as though the facts had somehow been turned upside down in transmission. Three years later, it was not the Indian sepoys but their European commanders who mutinied almost to a man.

Out of 1,300 officers commanding native troops in the Madras Presidency, 90 per cent refused to obey the orders of their superior officers. Only 150, most of them lieutenant-colonels and above, signed the test of loyalty imposed by the Governor, Sir George Barlow. The rest locked up their colonels, broke open the nearest Treasury and took out thousands of pagodas to pay their native troops, whom they then marched off wherever the fancy took them. From the beginning of July to the middle of September 1809, the whole of southern India was in a state of lawlessness – hysterical, exhilarating, terrifying anarchy. When Lieutenant-Colonel John Malcolm was sent to quell one of the worst outbreaks at Masulipatam, on the north-east coast of the Presidency, he reported back to Barlow on July 5 that he was 'satisfied there was not a single corps in the Company's army from Cape Comorin to Ganjam which was not pledged to rise against Government, and that no commanding officer had any real control over his regiment or battalion'.[1] And the officers of what was left of John Low's disgraced battalion, now renamed the 1st of the 24th, were as hot for mutiny as the rest of them.

Nothing on this scale had ever happened before in the British armed services, not even at Spithead or the Nore in the 1790s.[2] Never before and never since had a mutiny by British officers swept through an entire army. The mutiny of the Madras Officers in 1809 remains a unique event.

Yet the affair has remained strangely obscured, glossed over if not actually omitted in most histories of the British Empire and the Indian Army. Philip Mason, in his compendious history of the Indian Army, *A Matter of Honour,* allots a mere nine lines to the whole business out of 570 pages.[3] Sir John Kaye, in his six-volume history of the Great Mutiny of 1857, gives it only half a page, commenting in an offhand way: 'How the mutiny of the officers grew out of the mutiny of the men of the Coast Army, it would not be difficult to show; but the chapter of Indian history which includes the former need not be rewritten here.'[4]

Why not? The two mutinies offer valuable parallels and warnings for the Great Mutiny. Certainly at the time the Establishment back in London did not consider either mutiny to be a minor tiff which it was better to gloss over and forget. The fat volume of documents published by the House of Commons a year later[5] brings together every scrap of paper, every letter and memo that might conceivably help to explain this bewildering and catastrophic chain of events.[6]

So why was there a White Mutiny? Why on earth did the hand-picked guardians of the new master race in India turn on their commanders and plunge the bottom half of the country into giddy internal strife? What exactly happened, and why did it happen?

There was not one but two British armies in India. There was the King's Army, those of His Majesty's Regiments which had been seconded to India for a period – anything from a few months to 20 years – but which could sooner or later be expected to be posted to another station, in the West Indies, say, as Rollo Gillespie and Sergeant Brady and St John Fancourt had all been, or to the European battlefields, where Sir Arthur Wellesley, fresh from his triumphs in southern India, was at that moment fighting his way up through Spain and Portugal, or to a home station in Britain and Ireland, where Sir John Cradock had won his spurs. All these men were King's officers. And then there was the army of the East India Company, which was raised in India, trained in India, fought in India and could look for no such transfer this side of the grave.[7]

In all three British regions, or Presidencies as they were called – Madras, Bombay and Bengal (with its HQ at Calcutta, the undisputed capital of British India) – not only did the Company's Army soon come to outnumber the King's Regiments, the Company's Army was soon predominantly made up of Indian troops. Realizing that it could never attract or afford to pay nearly enough British troops to police its ever-expanding domain, the Company had gone on to recruit thousands of sepoys to its own army.

British rule depended on the fidelity of the sepoys, and on that alone. And that fidelity could be earned and kept only if the British officers who commanded the native regiments were up to the job.[8] The discontent of the native officers was one of the leading causes, perhaps the leading cause of the mutiny at Vellore. The chief conspirators, men like Sheikh Adam and the nicely named Sheikh Nutter, had often served previously in the army of Tipu Sultan or at his court. They had taken fresh service with the British because after Tipu's defeat there was no other game in town, but they had become convinced that their lot in life had become unhappier as a result.

On the European side, the growing corps of young British officers in the native infantry and cavalry were growing disillusioned, too.

Once they had found their feet in India, they began to look around them. They did not much like what they saw. There was no denying that they were widely seen as inferior to the officers in the King's Regiments, in their social origins, in their seniority, in their prospects and in their pay. Most of them arrived in India without a penny and soon fell into debt. A subaltern on arrival had to find between 1,500 and 1,800 rupees for equipment and uniform. He would need to borrow this money and then insure his life as security for the debt. Even if he did not drink or gamble, his debt was likely to have doubled by the time he became a captain, up to six or seven thousand rupees – £35–40,000 in today's money. He was unlikely to be able to clear his debts until and unless he became a major, which might be years off, because promotion was so slow.[9] Looking back after the Great Mutiny, Sir George Otto Trevelyan reflected that 'In old days, it was no uncommon thing for men of advanced life and high standing in the Service to be tormented with debts contracted during their first 18 months in the country. With minds of a certain class, to have "turned your lac" – that is, to owe ten thousand pounds – was conventionally supposed to be a subject of mutual congratulation.'[10] The less insouciant John Low was plagued with debt for more than half his time in India.[11]

Grimmer still, an officer who joined the Company's Army at the end of the eighteenth century had little reason to hope that he would ever see England or his family again. The annual returns of the Bengal Army showed that between 1796 and 1820 only 201 officers lived to retire to Europe on pension, while 1,243 were killed or died on service.[12] Officers in the King's service, by contrast, would come and, if their health held, usually go back to Britain. In the Company's Army in those early days, you could expect to lay your bones in India or, with alarming frequency, be buried at sea on the voyage home.[13]

The officers of the Coast Army had another source of grievance, too. Not only were they reckoned lower than the King's officers, they also were reckoned inferior to the armies of Bombay and

Bengal. Socially, the 'Mulls', as the Madras Army were known (after 'mulmull', a kind of muslin in which the Company had traded), ranked below the 'Ducks' of Bombay and the 'Qui-Hyes', the nickname for the Bengal Army, after the custom of shouting 'Koi hai?' meaning 'is anybody there?' when summoning servants. The sepoys of Bengal were said to be taller and tended to come from higher castes. The small dark men of the south claimed to be hardier, but, then as now, size mattered.[14]

There was an economic gulf as well. The officers of Bombay and Bengal were entitled to higher pay and allowances. The south was poorer country, in general. The wastelands of the Deccan plateau were no match for the fertile black earth of Oudh. George Buchan, the Chief Secretary to the Government of Madras, had made the position brutally clear to Malcolm a year before the officers' mutiny, when he heard the officers were preparing a petition demanding the same allowances as the Bengal officers:

> Such a measure is quite impossible, as it would entail such an insupportable burden on the finances of this Government as to make it at once better to renounce the country to any power that would take it.[15]

The Court of Directors was adamant. Bengal was settled first, in Calcutta it possessed the capital and seat of Government, and it was richer. Men took service with the Honourable Company 'perfectly aware of these inequalities, and are therefore not entitled to expect that they should be afterwards removed'. In the present state of the finances of the Company, a general equalization of allowances and emoluments was utterly out of the question. The 'inferior Presidencies', as the Directors unashamedly called them, would have to stay inferior.[16]

The British Empire in India was the creation of merchants and it was still at heart a commercial enterprise, which had to operate at a profit and respond to the ups and downs of the market. Behind the

epaulettes and the jingle of the harness, the levees and the balls at
Government House, lay the hard calculus of the City of London. So
it's a delusion to portray one Governor or Commander-in-Chief as
more penny-pinching than another. The retrenchment that had
begun under Lord Cornwallis continued under Barlow's stopgap
regime (1805–07) and was now being pursued with equal rigour by
Lord Minto, who had finally arrived to take over, and by Barlow
himself in Madras, where he had been sent to succeed Bentinck as
Governor as a consolation prize for not being made permanent in
the top job.[17]

This was not just a temporary squeeze but a permanent constric-
tion on the finances of Empire. Could the books be balanced and a
healthy profit returned to shareholders without unfairly squeezing
the civil and military servants of Empire and/or the Indian tillers of
the soil? Far-sighted members of the imperial elite, such as Charles
Metcalfe and Mountstuart Elphinstone, were already in the first
decades of the nineteenth century beginning to see symptoms of that
malady which modern historians have described as 'imperial over-
stretch'.

From the beginning of 1807, if not from an earlier date, a spirit of
discontent was fermenting among the Madras officers.[18] These were
the men who had to bear the heat of the hot season and the alarms
of the night, as they had at Vellore. What did they have to look forward to? Mounting debts, the contempt of the King's officers, and
ever-receding prospects of promotion, not to mention the likelihood
of an early grave on foreign soil. Coming over the horizon was a
wave of austerity measures imposed at London's unappeasable behest.

In such circumstances, it would have taken outstanding leadership
to prevent trouble. What the officers needed was a wise and persua-
sive Governor and a seasoned and patient Commander-in-Chief.
They had neither. In fact, it would have been hard to imagine two
men more ill-suited to rub along either with each other or with the
1,300 officers under their command than Sir George Barlow and
Lieutenant-General Hay Macdowall.

Many officers in the Coast Army liked the sound of Barlow. He was a lifer, for one thing. Just as so many of them had done themselves, he had come out to India at the age of 15 as a 'writer' (clerk) and worked his way up from modest origins (his father had been a mercer in Covent Garden). He learnt the native languages and the intricacies of the revenue, especially the newly fashionable system of settling taxes directly with the peasant cultivator, the *ryotwar*, rather than through grasping and corrupt middlemen. He knew Oudh and Bihar intimately. He looked just the ticket. John Malcolm wrote on hearing of his appointment: 'He comes like an angel of light among the heroes of Madras.'[19]

John Malcolm was too far away to be aware just how unpopular Sir George had become during his temporary kingship in Calcutta. Major Wilson in his *History of the Madras Army* is usually a charitable judge of men, but when it comes to Barlow, he is unable to restrain himself:

> During the time Sir George Barlow filled the office of Governor-General, he not only failed to obtain the deference and respect due to his station, but made himself highly obnoxious by his despotic conduct in official matters and his cold and repulsive manners in private life.[20]

In other words, he was both a pipsqueak and a martinet. Most observers at the time held Barlow personally responsible for what was to bring to Madras 'a season of unprecedented private misery, and unexampled public peril and alarm'.

In Hay Macdowall, Sir George had a Commander-in-Chief who was just as disastrous but in a quite different way: hot-headed and hot-tempered where Barlow was frigid; vain and umbrageous where Barlow was the inhuman bureaucrat; a trigger-happy Hotspur to Barlow's Widmerpool. To get some idea of Macdowall, you need look no further than Raeburn's full-length portrait of him.[21] Never was a 'swagger portrait' better so described.

The first reform that tickled up the existing resentments was the affair of the bazaar duties. From time immemorial, it was said – well, for a decade or two anyway – officers commanding districts and stations all over India had been entitled to take a cut on the goods sold in the military bazaars which straggled along the back of cantonments, where everybody did their shopping. This had been a nice earner to supplement those wretched salaries.

The Court now pronounced that levying such duties was contrary to the Articles of War and 'has an evident tendency to make the soldiers discontented with their officers, by feeling themselves taxed for the benefit of those who command them'. Worse still, 'the amount of the collections in military bazaars has always depended, principally, on the extension of spirituous liquors to the troops.'[22] Not only were the officers exploiting the poor sepoys and their families, they were encouraging them to drink – something which particularly horrified the Court, where strong Evangelical tendencies were taking hold.

Sir George was not personally responsible for this puritanical retrenchment. It was an order from London to all three Presidencies, and it applied to the Royal officers as well as to the Company's. In July 1807, the bazaar duties were duly abolished.

The next scam to be tidied up by the retrenchers and reformers was the so-called 'tent contract'. This was a bit of business left behind by Sir John Cradock, who could not observe any established practice in his army without wishing to reform it. Under the existing system, which was only five years old (it had begun in 1802), the CO of a regiment held the contract for everything required to fit it out for movement in the field – tents, carts, bullocks, drivers and labourers etc.[23]

The allowance did not vary. In peace or war it was the same. When nothing much was happening, the CO could carve himself a pretty slice of the allowance. At all times, there was a temptation for him to economize on the welfare and efficiency of his troops.

Abolish the tent contract, said Colonel Munro, the

Quartermaster-General, in his report to Cradock (June 1807). Abolish it, agreed Cradock. Abolish it, said Government in Madras and Supreme Government in Calcutta. And so, nearly a year later, in May 1808 (these things always took time) the tent contract, too, was abolished.[24] Cradock had already been recalled the previous September and so was no longer there to see his brainchild born.

By now Hay Macdowall was in post, and he was already in a steaming rage. What had first detonated his umbrage was not a matter of the welfare of the officers. It was, characteristically, a question of his own pay and perquisites. Previous Commanders-in-Chief had always enjoyed an *ex officio* seat on the Governor's Council, with a handsome additional allowance to go with it. But Bentinck had been driven to distraction by Cradock's high-handed and devious behaviour, which had helped to cause the Mutiny at Vellore and for which he himself was being blamed. The Governor believed that the C-in-C should be more clearly subordinate to the civil power (as he would be in England), and he appealed to the Court of Directors to curb the excessive power of the military in India. The Court had responded by removing the C-in-C's automatic right to a seat in Council.[25]

Macdowall was unaware when he took the job that he would be the first C-in-C not to have either the seat or the allowances. When he found out, he was apoplectic. First, he said he would resign unless the position was rectified. Then he said he would go to Europe in person to complain. Finally, he wrote a letter. It took the usual six months for the letter to reach the Court. The Court decided that it had been wrong, and in November 1808 wrote to Lord Minto instructing him to give the General his seat back.

But long before the Court's dispatch was received in Madras, Hay Macdowall was on the rampage, and he soon gathered a noisy and indignant following throughout the Coast Army for his campaign against what he called 'these disgusting measures'.[26] On Christmas Eve, he reviewed the Madras European regiment at Masulipatam. He told them that they had been overlooked and neglected in their remote station. They had been left to rot in the wilderness and it was the Government's fault.[27] In early January, he forwarded to the Court of Directors the officers' petition complaining that 'the inalienable rights of the Army' had been violated, implausibly praising its 'studied moderation'. He followed this up on January 15 with a letter of resignation as C-in-C, declaring that he could not 'tamely submit to see the exalted station disgraced in my person, nor can I be answerable to the Army if I do not resist so uncommon a deviation which deprives it of a representative in Council.'

Then he took ship for England, firing off reprimands and protests in all directions. Barlow tried to recall Macdowall's ship, the *Lady Jane Dundas*, in order to dismiss him. The fleet was not yet out of sight across the bay. Guns were fired from the fort, but the signal was either not heard or misread. Barlow flew into an even greater fury, announcing that though Hay Macdowall had set sail, he had not yet officially resigned. He was now therefore sacked.

To this final peevish blast, Hay Macdowall was destined to make no reply. For the *Lady Jane Dundas,* along with three other ships in the Company's service, was lost with all hands in a hurricane off Table Bay seven weeks later. Hay Macdowall's torch was finally dowsed. By a strange coincidence, his portrait in the Cape Town gallery hangs only a few miles ashore of his bones.

Instead of pausing to reflect that his greatest enemy had now disappeared from the scene and it might be possible to begin mending his fences with the Army, Sir George in his feverish pet cast around for someone else to punish. Major Thomas Boles was the Deputy Adjutant-General. His signature appeared on Macdowall's parting sally, but only as a formality because all such orders had to be transmitted through the Adjutant. Boles's superior, Colonel Capper, had gone to Europe. In fact, he too went down with the *Lady Jane Dundas.* Barlow suspended both Boles and Capper. This was worse than an injustice. It was a ghastly blunder, giving the unmistakable impression that Barlow was now at war with the whole Coast Army.[28]

Not unnaturally, Major Boles protested that he had done nothing wrong and refused to apologize. In no time, yet another petition was circulating through the cantonments, this time addressed to the Governor-General in Calcutta, demanding that Barlow be sacked.

This was demanding money with menaces. It was not just a protest, it was an ultimatum. But Barlow had one last chance to ward off the gathering stormclouds. The petition had not in fact been circulated very widely, and he could well have pretended that he had never seen the text of the document. But his blood was up. Someone had to be punished. On May 1, 1809, he had half a dozen colonels and another half-dozen majors and captains suspended or removed from their commands.[29]

Finally, provoked and inflamed where they could have been assuaged and ignored, the officers of the Madras Army broke into open mutiny. This was no overnight flouncing out: it had taken three years of petitions suppressed, of grievances overruled or aggravated, of officers sacked for daring to protest, and finally a Commander-in-Chief going off the deep end, alas, in every sense.

The mutiny spread across virtually all the garrisons and cantonments where the native regiments of the Madras Army were stationed: from Masulipatam and Samulcottah and Ellore in the north-east to Tanjore, Quilon and Cochin in the south, at Madras on the east coast and Goa on the west, through Seringapatam and Chittledroog in the middle and over the borders of the Presidency into Hyderabad, where the Company had so-called 'subsidiary' troops in the service of the Nizam stationed at Jalna and at Hyderabad itself. The King's Regiments played no part (although there was sympathy for the mutineers in plenty of Royal messes), but many of the Company's European regiments joined in with a will.

The first outbreak took place within a European regiment, the first division Madras, which was stationed at Masulipatam. These were the very men to whom Hay Macdowall had delivered his inflammatory farewell address on Christmas Eve, telling them that they had been left to rot in a backwater.[30] Macdowall's remarks could not help having an impact, and the new commanding officer had been warned to expect trouble. Colonel James Innes, well-known to be not the sharpest knife in the box, arrived in a mood to detect 'sedition in every word and mutiny in every gesture'.[31] On his first evening (May 7), he was invited to dine in the mess. There were several strangers present, and after dinner the usual series of toasts was drunk. A lieutenant called Forbes, seconded by Lieutenant Maitland, the Quartermaster, proposed that they should drink to 'The Friends of the Army'. Innes smelled sedition. Did not 'Friends of the Army' mean 'Enemies of the Government' and, in particular, 'Enemies of Sir George Barlow'? So he objected. Could they not drink to 'The Madras Army' instead? No, they bloody well could not and would not. So the Colonel left the room in a huff. As he closed the door behind him, he could hear the defiant drinking of the toast 'The Friends of the Army' – followed by loud and prolonged huzzas, which he imagined, not unnaturally, to be aimed at him personally.[32] Innes later discovered that the seditious toast was drunk no less than nine times that night, suggesting high levels of intoxication of all sorts.[33]

The next day it got worse. Innes summoned the two lieutenants and demanded that they apologize for their conduct. Both of them refused. The Colonel reported the matter to HQ. Back came an order dated May 17, received May 22 (giving some idea how long it took to get an order out to a place like Masulipatam): Maitland was to be sacked as quartermaster, and Forbes was sent off to the notorious plague spot of Condapilly, 54 miles away, where there was not a single European. Any more such irregular conduct, and they would be court-martialled.[34]

That was not the end of it. By sheer bad luck, at this very moment, Admiral Drury, the naval commander at Madras, ran short of European troops to serve as marines on his coast squadron. Under recent regulations, King's soldiers were no longer to be detached for such purposes except in an emergency, which this was not, so the Government lighted on the 1st Madras European regiment to fill the complement that Drury desired – 100 men and three officers. This was the last thing anyone in Masulipatam wanted, service at sea being even more dangerous and unhealthy than service on land.

The frigates were already steaming up the coast to collect the men. On June 2 a further order arrived, directing the hapless Maitland to embark as officer-in-charge of these unwilling marines and, in a further sideswipe, Forbes was told to ready himself for a transfer to Penang in the Straits Settlements, which was, if anything, even more unhealthy and certainly a great deal more remote than Condapilly.[35] This was both personal and collective victimization. To the more paranoid officers, it looked sinisterly like a prelude to the disbanding of the regiment.

Whatever the motives, the officers were all united. The day after the distasteful order was received, they formed themselves into a committee to oppose *by force* the embarkation of the men who were to serve as marines. Fresh orders then came for two more parties of marines to be supplied (you sense here, as again and again in the history of the British in India, the desperate and recurring shortage of European manpower). Their worst suspicions were confirmed.

On June 24 the dreaded ships arrived – a frigate and a sloop. A deputation of officers went to Innes and begged Innes to suspend the embarkation until they had referred their protest to HQ. No dice. On the contrary, he told them that he intended to ask the frigate captain to land a party of troops to help him hustle the men on to the ship. He was prepared to use the Artillery and the King's Regiment stationed at Masulipatam, the 59th Foot, to compel the men to go aboard – which meant at bayonet point if they would not go voluntarily.

At 1pm the next day, he instructed the Adjutant to warn the unwilling marines to be ready to embark at 6pm. Tumult broke out across the barracks. At 3pm, Major Joseph Storey of the 1st/19th Native Infantry, the officer next in seniority to the Colonel, led a posse to Innes's bungalow, demanding he recall his orders. Innes refused.

'Unless you give way, sir,' said Storey, 'I shall be compelled to place you under arrest for the safety of the garrison.'

'What, you place me under arrest, sir?' cried Innes. 'I can place *you* in arrest and all the officers of the garrison.'

He could not. The men were with Storey. Innes was confined in his bungalow under armed guard. The embarkation orders were cancelled. Major Storey wrote to Madras explaining what he had done. He also wrote urgent messages to the disaffected officers in other garrisons, appealing for their support. Joseph Storey was the first white mutineer.

The officers at Masulipatam had formed a committee. So had the officers at most other stations in the Coast Army. These committees now began to pledge each other to support their brother officers to the last drop of their blood. At Secunderabad, Jalna and Ellore, plans were speedily formed to march to the aid of the Masulipatam offi-cers, if they were attacked by Government forces.[36]

These committees of officers were something new and intensely alarming to the authorities. They appeared to be fraternities in which all were equal, rather than the usual vertical military hierarchy where power ran strictly from top to bottom. In some cases, the leadership of the committee rotated at intervals, to avoid any sort of hierarchy forming. Worried Government men detected a sinister resemblance to the committees which the seamen had formed in the mutinies at Spithead and the Nore in the 1790s.[37] Colonel Henry Davis, com-manding the loyal forces at Mysore, compared them to the Committee of Public Safety in the French Revolution.[38] It was also said that the committees modelled themselves on that subversive home-grown institution, the London Corresponding Society, some of whose members had been arrested and tried for treason.[39]

Such terrifying organizations with their demands for 'our birthright as a soldier' were subversive of all discipline and could only urge each other on to more extreme acts of mutiny. On June 15, John Malcolm wrote to HQ, 'It is impossible to convey to men who are calm and think rationally any idea of the state of the Army.

All respectable men in it appear to suffer a set of mad-headed boys to take the lead.'[40] Clearly some senior officer of stature had to be sent to Masulipatam. Colonel John Malcolm was a brave and genial soldier, affable to everybody, of huge experience gathered since he had come out from Scotland at the age of 14 and commanded native troops a year later. For a long time, he had been warning that the Company's officers had a raw deal which was getting rawer. He had a wide correspondence with officers of all ranks. If anyone knew what was really going on, it was John Malcolm. He happened to be in Madras.

So on July 1, the day that the unnerving news of Innes's detention reached HQ, Sir George summoned Malcolm to his garden house in the pleasant suburbs of Madras. It was agreed that he should set sail the next day.[41] On July 4 he landed at Masulipatam, where he found the garrison 'in a state of bold and open mutiny'. He tried to reason with them. Over and over they said the same thing: they would not return to their allegiances until their grievances were remedied. Four hours later, Malcolm was still pleading with them not to seal their own destruction. All they would concede was that they would delay their march on Hyderabad out of deference to him – 'he was the only officer of rank in India they would have admitted into the garrison at all.'

The only other thing Malcolm achieved that night was to order the sentries removed from the wretched Colonel Innes's bungalow, thus signalling his release from arrest.[42]

Then came the ordeal of dinner in the mess. Another large party, with several strangers present. And after dinner, again the toasts, including the one to 'The Friends of the Army', with glasses raised three times three. Malcolm, emollient as ever, said he was sure that this toast included most men, both in India and England, and he drank it happily.

He was not out of the woods yet. Some officer at table began singing a sea shanty. Nobody is quite sure which it was, but the song kept on referring to 'the common cause'. The flushed young officers caught at the phrase and insisted that the whole party should rise to drink to 'the common cause'. For a moment, Malcolm was flummoxed. Any fool could spot the sedition in the phrase. After a delay that was scarcely perceptible, he rose, filled his glass to the brim and in a loud baritone proclaimed an amendment: 'The Common Cause of Our Country'. Everyone drank with enthusiasm, and as Malcolm went off to bed his own health was proposed and drunk with zest, three times three. 'Thus closed,' he wrote in his journal that night, 'the most anxious day of my life'.[43]

All next day he pleaded with Major Storey and the other officers:

You will be deserted by your brethren when Government is compelled to declare you in rebellion. And see how wretched are your means, how unconnected your plans. If you had double the numbers, do you really think that after the chain of discipline is once broken, and you are commanded by committees and everybody thinks he possesses the right to question the authority of his superior, that it will be possible to oppose the organized army?

He appealed to their hearts, too, as well as their heads: 'I have been in this Army since I was twelve years of age; and such is my regard for my brother officers that I would give my life to see the present unfortunate dispute happily adjusted, but if any circumstances whatever lead you to rise in rebellion against your King and Country, then I must stand in the opposite rank. And as to that Ultimatum,' he concluded, slapping the paper which had come from Hyderabad and was lying upon the table, 'I declare to God, I would not serve a Government one hour that could yield to such degrading demands.'[44]

It was a magnificent performance. No officer in India was more eloquent than John Malcolm when he was stirred. But the officers did not budge. If he would not give them any assurances (and he could not), then they would cease to recognize his authority. All that he could claim to be gaining was time. He wrote off to Sir George, urging conciliation, restoration and amnesty for the rebels.

Barlow had changed his mind, or perhaps was now definitively revealing what he had thought all along, but had not disclosed in his two talks with Malcolm. He wrote back on July 12 that he did not believe in forgiveness or conciliation. In fact he had always thought that Malcolm was wrong to be so soft on the mutineers.

It had been either a huge misunderstanding or a huge deception. Malcolm, good-hearted and trusting to a fault, could not quite believe it. If only he could talk face to face with Barlow again and tell him how desperate the situation was at Masulipatam and the other stations from which friends wrote to him, then surely Barlow would see reason. So on July 22, he stepped into his palanquin again and set off for Madras, which he reached four days later. He saw at once that he was out in the cold – and nobody in India could be colder than Sir George Barlow. He closed his doors against Colonel Malcolm for ever.

On the same day that Malcolm returned to Madras, Barlow showed just how he was going to play it from here on in. He had become convinced that the only way to bring the Army to its senses was to compel every European officer to sign a Declaration of Loyalty. The text was issued on July 26 and it ran:

> We, the undersigned officers of the Honourable Company's Service, do, in the most solemn manner, declare upon our word of honour as British Officers, that we will obey the orders, and support the authority of the Governor in Council of Fort St George, agreeably to the tenor of the Commissions which we hold from that Government.[45]

The loyalty test appeared at first to be a humiliating failure. Only 150 officers out of 1,300 agreed to sign the declaration, demonstrating the huge scale of the mutiny. But the sting of the loyalty test lay in the follow-up to it. Any officer who declined to sign was to be removed to any station he chose on the sea coast, to live there and draw his allowances until it was possible for him to be re-employed.

Separate the officers from the men, Barlow reasoned, and the mutiny would fizzle out. The officers might provide the verbal bombast, but it was the sepoys who provided the firepower, and the sepoys had no interest in this fight.

At this point, what happened began to vary widely from station to station. In some stations, the rebellious officers consented, quite docilely, to be separated from their troops and to decamp to the sea coast, either under armed guard of the King's troops, or under their own steam. This happened at Madras itself. Almost all the officers of the native cavalry and infantry regiments who had been assembled at the racecourse there did not agree to sign, but the non-signers did agree to be sent off to the coast.[46]

At other stations, Hyderabad, for example, the mutineers did not go quietly. Two days after Malcolm had first set off for Masulipatam, Barlow had ordered one of the battalions stationed at Hyderabad to march away to Goa, with the idea of splitting up the sepoys and weakening the mutineers.[47] This order provoked open resistance. On July 21, the Hyderabad Committee presented their CO, Colonel Montresor, with an ultimatum: the restoration of all suspended or sacked officers, the trial of Colonel Innes, and the sacking of every officer on Barlow's staff who had influenced his decisions and, just for good measure, a general amnesty.[48]

What they got instead was the loyalty test. And, to persuade them to sign it, they got Barry Close. If there was any field officer as loved and admired as John Malcolm, it was Barry Close. But his high reputation did not bring him any better luck at Hyderabad than Malcolm had had at Masulipatam. Worse luck if anything, because when he went out on parade at the big cantonment at Secunderabad, just outside Hyderabad (these days the two cities are contiguous), to persuade the 16th Native Infantry to sign the loyalty test, he found the men beginning to prime and load their weapons as he began to plead with them. He left the parade ground in a hurry and went straight to Colonel Montresor's bungalow, where he relinquished his command. The next day, the Committee sent him a note accusing *him* of acting in a manner 'subversive of the discipline they are anxious to maintain', and directing him 'to leave the place in the course of this day, lest more unpleasant decisive measures should be necessary'. Seldom has a more gallant officer beat a more embarrassing retreat. Letters intercepted by Barlow's spies indicate that the men of the 16th were quite ready to arrest Close and possibly fire on him if he had not scurried off.[49]

After locking up the colonel and then chasing him off the station, the next move for the more determined mutineers was to march off and join forces with other rebellious garrisons. They needed to pay and feed their sepoys to keep them loyal. So in station after station the mutineer officers took to armed robbery. They went to the nearest Treasury, overpowered the guards, broke open the chests and took whatever they found inside. Captain Patterson marched his troops out from Samulcottah and emptied the Treasury at Cocanada, ten miles away, removing 342,539 rupees from a quavering paymaster. For good measure, as he passed through Rajahmundry on their way to join the rebels at Maṣulipatam, Patterson took possession of the post office and seized the mail. At Chicacole, the 1st Battalion of the 25th Regiment – the renamed remnant of one of the battalions that had mutinied at Vellore – looted the treasure at their own HQ, while another detachment went on to Vizagapatam and scooped up 550,000 rupees there.[50]

Ellore was a sizeable cantonment north of Masulipatam which had been suspected of disaffection for some time. Here was stationed the 1st Battalion of the 24th Native Infantry – John Low's regiment – which had been disbanded in disgrace after Vellore and then renumbered. The first task of Lieutenant-Colonel Robert Fletcher on taking over the battalion had been to ascertain whether his officers were as disaffected as reports had claimed. They were, every man of them. Given half a chance, they would march their troops out of barracks to join the local centre of rebellion at Masulipatam. Fletcher set out to follow the recommended procedure. If the British officers refused to sign the declaration (and they all did), he intended to remove them from their commands and manage the regiment through the native officers who were thought to be perfectly loyal.

The difficulty, here as elsewhere, was to communicate the plan to the native officers without alerting the Europeans. And in this Fletcher failed. The native adjutant, through whom the order had to pass, instantly betrayed the plan to the European adjutant. In a flash, the tables were turned. It was Colonel Fletcher who was seized and placed in confinement. On August 5, once they had secured him, Captain James Sadler assumed command. That same night, Sadler sent off a note to General Pater, the head of the Northern Division:

> In consequence of the Native Adjutant having told the European Adjutant, that it was Colonel Fletcher's intention, if the officers of the battalion would not agree with him in what he had to acquaint them, to seize all the officers (ensigns excepted) and send them to Masulipatam, I have conceived it necessary, at the request of the officers, to place him under restraint, for fear of any unpleasant circumstance taking place.[51]

How high-toned and cocky they sound, these mutinous officers. After all, from the point of view of Colonel Fletcher and Sir George Barlow, it was the mutineers who were the 'unpleasant circumstance'.

So it seemed that, for the first and last time in his 50 years of service to the East India Company, John Low had joined a mutiny – a most extraordinary and unexpected departure from his otherwise impeccable path of duty. He never spoke of the business. Nor did any of his brother officers. There are a hundred personal accounts of the Great Mutiny – everyone from the subaltern to the General had a story to tell, including their womenfolk, and they are still being republished today under such stirring titles as *Under Deadly Fire* and *Ladies of Lucknow*. There is not a single first-hand account by a White Mutineer. Certainly not a word from John Low.

All this was unnerving enough, but not quite as unnerving or peculiar as what happened at Jalna, in the old Hyderabad domain at the furthest northern reach of the Presidency. Everywhere else, either the rebellious officers had locked up the loyal colonel, or the loyal colonel had managed to detach the rebellious officers and send them off to stew on the coast. Only at Jalna do we find a different, third turn of events: the colonel puts himself at the head of the mutineers and marches them off in the direction of Madras.

Colonel John Doveton of the 8th Native Cavalry was brave as anything when charging the enemy. But in dealings with his fellow officers he tended to find himself hesitant and perplexed. On July 5, his officers from Berar came in deputation to him with an address to the Governor-General, warning Lord Minto not to lay a finger on the mutinous officers at Masulipatam, or there would be hell to pay.[52] What was Doveton to do? He did not dare attempt to arrest his entire corps of officers. He would not tamely resign and leave them to run amok across the country. He chose a third option, which may seem odder and more personally perilous than the other two. He could not beat them, so he would join them. He himself would lead the troops southwards. He went further: he addressed the native officers in the vernacular on the parade ground, earnestly exhorting them to follow their European officers.

On August 14, they all set off together with Doveton at their head. They had gone about 30 miles when news came that the mutineers at Secunderabad – the ones who had threatened Barry Close's life – had surrendered and signed the test (perhaps his appeal to their loyalty had finally sunk in). After a night of dithering, Doveton decided that to go on would be to lead his troops to certain destruction. They must go back to Jalna. They obeyed, boiling with rage that the officers at Secunderabad had let them down. Colonel Doveton had led the mutinous excursion, now he led the humiliating retreat. An in-and-out performer, to say the least.

Yet at least Doveton could say that no blood had been spilt under his command. This was not true of the last and most passionate and pig-headed centre of mutiny, Seringapatam, nor could the fort's commandant, Lieutenant-Colonel John Bell of the Madras Artillery, offer any such justification for his actions. Bell was torn in much the same way as Doveton. He was a man of the Madras Army, he felt the grievances of his officers, he wanted to avoid bloodshed and he wanted to save his own skin, not necessarily in that order.

To weaken the garrison at Seringapatam, the C-in-C had ordered two of its detachments, the Artillery and the 2nd Battalion of the 19th, to move to Bangalore where there would be two King's Regiments to keep an eye on them. The 'Board of Officers', as they styled themselves, rejected this order and counter-ordered that not a man was to leave the fort, which amounted to mutiny.[53]

Three days later, Colonel Henry Davis arrived to administer the loyalty test, rather like a district medical officer arriving to dispense a life-saving vaccine. He invited the officers to meet him at noon the next day. Nobody showed up. Two hours later, several officers appeared at his lodging. Had he orders to separate them from their men? No, he had not, and please would they sign the declaration. They said nothing, and then said could they take it away and study it. More time passed. It was a very hot afternoon. Davis started writing a dispatch to Madras: 'I remain in a state of uncertainty with regard to my own situation, whether I am at this moment (2pm) a prisoner or not.' Then at 3.15pm he received an order from Bell that he was not to leave the fort, and there was no point his getting into his palanquin because he would not be allowed to pass the gates. Impasse, literally.

Then at 6.30pm 'a deputation from the Committee of Public Safety waited upon me to assure me that it was entirely a mistake my being detained, and that the guard at my house was intended as a honorary guard only &c. &c.'[54] You can almost hear Davis spitting out the words, for certainly the Board of Officers was behaving more like Robespierre than the Chairman of the Board of the Honourable Company.

The whole of that day, the drawbridges of the fort had been kept raised and the garrison had been under arms. Bell had issued explicit orders that fire was to be opened on any armed body of men seen coming along the road from Bangalore and Mysore or crossing the bridge.[55] To get rid of any possible opposition within the fort, Bell then sent away to Bangalore the small detachment of Royal troops stationed there – thus accomplishing the very reverse of Barlow's intention to weaken the native troops inside. In a bloodcurdling threat, he told Lieutenant Adamson, who was commanding at Bangalore, not to venture near the neighbouring town of Mysore, because 'Mysore would be in ashes in a few days'.

In short, Bell and his 'Board' had effectively declared UDI. They were in open and unabashed mutiny; although Bell, alone of all the officers there, had already signed the declaration. Well then, said Colonel Davis, why don't you abandon the mutineers and come to Mysore? No, Bell said, he would stay in the fort as long as he could be of any service. Bell's next 'service' was to invite the rebellious native regiments at Chittledroog, numbering about 1,120 officers and men, to come and join him in the fort. The Chittledroog troops left their barracks with enthusiasm and set out for Seringapatam.

Upon the scene now comes Lieutenant-Colonel Samuel Gibbs of HM 59th Regiment. If there was any battle commander in India to match Rollo Gillespie, it was Samuel Gibbs. Not yet 40, Gibbs had already made a name for himself in Canada, Corsica, the Low Countries, the West Indies and South Africa – reminding us yet again what a global conflict Britain was engaged in. Now he was dispatched by Barlow to surround Seringapatam. He had a large force of Dragoons, Cavalry, Infantry and Artillery, and his first object was to cut off the Chittledroog troops. Once they reached the fort, the rebellion would acquire a critical mass which would be hard to dislodge. He sent a body of Mysore Horse to intercept, under Rama Row, a native officer. Rama Row caught up with the Chittledroog force about 30 miles from Mysore. There was an inconclusive parley. The next day, at about 10am, the Mysore Horse attacked and were easily fended off. But Gibbs heard the firing, and at 11am he sent off heavier forces – a squadron of Dragoons and the light infantry of his own 59th. They had some trouble finding their enemy and kept tumbling into the nullahs, the deep ditches which scored the terrain. An officer of the 59th was ordered to advance carrying a white flag. The flag was either not seen or misunderstood. The officer was fired on and slightly wounded. Gibbs then ordered his Dragoons to attack the startled sepoys from Chittledroog who believed that the European troops were their friends. When they discovered their mistake, they broke and fled for the safety of the fort, pursued by the Dragoons, who cut them down with their usual brutal efficiency.

The official tally was nine dead and 281 missing, but most of the missing were thought to be killed. A realistic estimate might be around 300 dead. The British had no casualties to speak of.

Colonel Bell made only futile efforts to intervene on behalf of the unfortunate men from Chittledroog. But there was no doubt whose side he was on. There was a feeble sortie from the fort, led by Lieutenant Munro, against the British camp, but Munro and his men fled back to the fort as soon as they were fired on. Bell also ordered a heavy cannonade from the battlements. But the only effect was to force Gibbs to shift his camp to a safer distance, with the loss of four horses and an unlucky grasscutter.

There were then more parleys, more flags of truce, but the decisive factor as at Jalna was the news that the mutineers at Secunderabad had submitted and signed the test and were advising the Seringapatam garrison to do the same. On August 22, Bell forwarded to Davis the signatures of all 54 Company officers within the fort. He pleaded that the sepoys should not be dishonoured by being disarmed. But Davis, no doubt still smarting from his maltreatment, insisted that they should all pile their arms inside the fort and march out in unconditional surrender.

So the great White Mutiny came to its inglorious end. And several hundred sepoys lay dead in the ditches of Seringapatam, gunned down by Dragoons who were supposed to be their comrades-in-arms. The sepoys had never had any quarrel with the Honourable

Company. In marching, they were simply obeying the commands of their discontented officers.

The sepoys had every reason to be indignant. They are the unseen and unheard masses in this weird jerky saga. Their voices have largely vanished from the records. With one exception: Major James Hazlewood of the 1st/24th was dispatched to Ellore 'to tranquillise the minds and restore the subordination of the troops under his command'. He reported on August 20 that all the officers present and on detachment had now signed the pledge.[56] He added, however, that the native officers told him that 'they were not aware of any fault they had committed; that it was not possible for them to decide who the commanding officer was, but according to the usage of the service they obeyed those orders delivered to them by the European Adjutant.'

They were especially miffed because Colonel Fletcher, when he was being arrested, had made 'some reproaches upon the battalion in allusion to the unfortunate catastrophe at Vellore'. Something, one imagines, along the lines of 'you bloody native officers never change – once a mutineer, always a mutineer.'

Major Hazlewood adds, not without a touch of smugness, a PS that 'in justice to Colonel Fletcher I ought to state that the alleged reproaches appear to have been made in the heat of passion, immediately subsequent to the arrest and upon seeing himself deserted by the men under his legitimate command.'[57] Or, in other words, just as they were manhandling him into his bungalow and putting the guard on him.[58]

Anyway, if Major Hazlewood was to be trusted at all, John Low must have signed the Declaration of Loyalty, too, along with the rest of the subalterns, because Hazlewood states, beyond any possibility of misunderstanding, that he has 'the signature of all the officers present and detached in the district belonging to the 1st/24th.' *All*. And he gives their names: 'Lieutenants W. Stone, J. McIntosh, G.M. Stuart, G. Ogilvie, R. Jenkins, E. Burges.'[59]

John Low was not there. He was not with his regiment at Ellore or anywhere in the district. He was not one of the hot-brained young subalterns working each other up into an indignant frenzy in the officers' mess when the White Mutiny broke out, and he was not there when it ended either.

Once again he had managed to avoid the catastrophe. If he had been at Vellore, he would have been murdered. If he had been at Ellore, he would have been court-martialled or cashiered. Cashiering was an unpleasant enough fate – to be dismissed from the service, to have your epaulettes torn off on the parade ground and your sword broken, to lose all the money you had paid in to secure your commission, above all, to lose your vocation and to see all the years you had sweated in the service of the Company rendered worthless and tarnished for ever – that was something to be dreaded.

But where was he? His regiment had been reconstituted only recently. His service had been much too brief for him to be allowed to go back to Scotland on leave. Perhaps he was away sick. Almost every young subaltern fell ill at some time or other during his Indian service, especially in the south. Sickness seemed like the most likely explanation.

Then by chance, looking through the letters that John Low wrote nearly ten years later, I came across what can only be described as a job application with CV attached. Datelined Bangalore, June 23, 1817, and addressed to his future patron, none other than John Malcolm, by now a Brigadier, he writes, 'Ever since the beginning of 1809 when at Colonel Close's recommendation I went up to Poonah as a surveyor . . .'[60]

John Low was several hundred miles away, busy with chain and primitive theodolite, charting the roads and rivers and hills of the Deccan, an apprentice in that enormous work which the British thought so crucial, of reducing the vast, unruly subcontinent to a reliable map. And, crucially for him, Poona was only a few miles east of Bombay. It lay outside the Madras Presidency, and those who worked there or thereabouts had no call to be signing or not signing Declarations of Loyalty. Here and there in the messes of the Bombay

Army, there was some sympathy for the rebellious officers of Madras. One or two sly toasts were drunk on nights when the Colonel was not dining in. But there was no rebellion.

How were those who had been involved to be dealt with? They still awaited their fate, lounging about in the coast stations, still simmering with resentment, overdoing the arrack, waiting for the decision of the Governor-General.

It was not until September 11 that Lord Minto landed at Madras. He had intended to leave Calcutta much earlier, in July, but he had been assured by Barlow that the agitation was rapidly subsiding – which showed how little Sir George really understood about the state of mind of the Company's officers. Only on August 5, alarmed by the news of the mutiny at Masulipatam, did Minto cross the surf. Not for the first time in the Bay of Bengal, the ship was blown back by bad weather, and he took over a month to make the shortish crossing.[61]

It is tempting to wonder whether, if he had got there sooner, his mild and agreeable temper might have calmed the temper of the Madras officers. Perhaps, given more time and a less confrontational attitude from the Governor, the mutinies at the worst centres might never have got so bad. As it was, Lord Minto arrived after it was all over, and was thus enabled to play the part for which nature had so thoughtfully equipped him, that of the *deus ex machina* at the end of a Greek drama descending from the clouds to settle human imbroglios with effortless ease.

There had to be a general amnesty. That much was clear. With 1,150 Company officers out of 1,300 having initially refused the loyalty test, oblivion was the only policy. But someone had to be punished for these criminal and desperate acts which had paralysed the whole of southern India. Examples had to be made.

Inside a fortnight, on September 25, Minto produced a General Order naming three officers – Colonel John Doveton, Major Joseph Storey and Colonel John Bell – to be tried forthwith by court-martial and 18 others to be given the choice between a court-martial and

dismissal from the service. The other 1,300 officers in the Madras
Army, loyal and mutinous alike, were forgiven and restored to their
former rank and pay.

This singling out of 21 lieutenant-colonels, majors and captains
was unfair. At all stations, it had been the impassioned young lieutenants and ensigns who had made the running and pushed their
reluctant superiors into criminal acts. John Malcolm had, for example, immediately formed the view that Storey was a weak character,
entirely under the influence of 'mad-headed young men'. Still, leaders are supposed to lead, and if they do not, then they must expect
to be held to account.

In this extraordinary affair, nothing is more extraordinary than the
outcome of these three courts-martial. In all three cases, the C-in-C
had demanded the death penalty. Nothing surprising in that. If you
flip through William Hough's catalogue of Indian courts-martial
between 1801 and 1821, you will find the death penalty frequently
demanded and quite often inflicted in cases of mutiny or violent
conduct towards an officer.[62]

However, the Madras officers received no such extreme penalty.
Doveton was found not guilty and acquitted of all charges 'in the
most full and honourable manner'. Storey was found guilty and sentenced to be cashiered, but the Court sent a letter to the C-in-C
recommending mercy. Bell was found guilty, too, and sentenced to
be cashiered and declared for ever unworthy to serve the Company
in any military capacity whatsoever.[63]

The juries at these courts-martial were composed of nine officers
belonging to Native Infantry regiments and nine belonging to the
King's service. They simply refused to sentence their blood brothers
to death or, in Doveton's case, to anything at all. They appeared, too,
quite unfussed by the glaring difference between the treatment meted
out to black mutineers (at Vellore, for example) and white ones.

Even the equable Lord Minto was roused to fury. He wrote to his
wife back in England that the sentences had been 'very soft'. If
anyone was going to exercise clemency, it ought to be the Governor-

General himself. The C-in-C, General Gowdie, was apoplectic. He demanded that the juries reconsider their 'erroneous' verdicts. The juries reconsidered. They found no reason to alter their verdicts. The mutiny might have been quelled, but the mutinous spirit lingered on.

As for the other 18 culprits or scapegoats, 14 of them accepted dismissal without trial (six of these first opted to stand trial, then thought better of it). Only three of them, all from the Seringapatam garrison, elected to stand trial. One officer, Captain John Turner, he who had seized the 11,000 pagodas from the Treasury at Seringapatam, died in October before he could be tried.[64]

The White Mutiny has one further surprise in store for us. It is true that John Bell never saw service with the Company again. Nor did Captain Aiskill and Captain McIntosh, who had commanded the luckless native detachments from Chittledroog. There was a lot of blood on their hands. The same applied to Captain James Patterson, who had seized those thousands of pagodas from the Treasury at Cocanada and spread violence and fear through that countryside.[65] But the other 17 officers were all restored and re-employed by the Company, some sooner, some later, and, what's more, most of them were promoted, some quite stratospherically. Thirteen of them rose to become lieutenant-colonels at least. No less than seven of these went on to become generals. Captain James Lushington, whom we last saw riding out of Jalna alongside Colonel Doveton on their way to terrorise Madras, not only became a lieutenant-general, he was made a director of the East India Company and was three times chairman of the Court as Sir James Lushington, not to mention sitting as a Tory MP for three different constituencies. Thirty years later, John Low was writing to him as an old friend, lamenting the crazy decision to invade Afghanistan.[66] Doveton himself was knighted, too, after his heroic leadership in the third and final war against the Marathas.[67] Never were there more remarkable resurrections from mutinous pasts. Captain Bligh of the *Bounty* did go on to become Governor of New South Wales in later life, but he was being mutinied *against*.

Captain James Sadler, John Low's superior officer, cocky Captain Sadler who had arrested and confined their Colonel, was among those restored. He was to die in action, fighting in the last battle against the Marathas. If he had lived, he might have become a general, too.

These amazing re-employments of men who had been drummed out of the service only a year or two earlier tell us something about what happened subsequently to the East India Company and its armies. One of the officers' main complaints had been that the top jobs were reserved for the King's officers, who received much faster promotion. And the Court of Directors had already accepted the justice of this complaint. Back in their letter of June 12, 1807, they had stressed the injustice of the King's officers being preferred to the Company's officers, 'particularly in situations where the superior local knowledge of the latter, and their acquaintance with the manners, customs and prejudices of the natives pointed them out as the fittest to be employed.'[68]

There was more in this critique than simply establishing fairness between the two armies. It followed from such an analysis that the wisest way to govern India must be, to a great extent, through the officers of the Company's Army. Not only did that army form the overwhelming majority of British troops in India, it was through the European officers in those native armies that the British had the most intimate and continuous contact with the natives. These officers could not be treated like hired hands, subject to the arbitrary whim of the Court and the Governor. They must be involved and interwoven in the governance of the country. Hence the decision to reverse the foolish instruction to deny the C-in-C his automatic seat on Council. If only Hay Macdowall had had the patience to wait to be proved right.

Twice in three years, the Governor in Madras had refused to listen to the voice of the Army – first over the turbans and the joys and now over pay and promotions. As a result, a thousand of their own men, Company men, lay dead on the parade ground of Vellore and in the ditches of Seringapatam. Even the merchants of Leadenhall Street eventually worked it out for themselves. You could not govern Madras – or any other part of India – the way Sir George Barlow governed it. And after interminable to-ings and fro-ings and endless votes, Sir George was sacked. First, Bentinck and Cradock, now Macdowall and Barlow. Not exactly a brilliant record of leadership selection.

So when the Court came to think about it, the complaints of the Madras officers had not been so crazy and jacobinical. The Court began to glimpse, dimly perhaps at first, that the British Empire in India, like the Roman Empire and the Ottoman Empire before it, was at bottom a military empire which depended for its survival on native troops led by an imperial military fraternity. The sensible thing was to admit this military fraternity into a share in the governing of it, and to educate its officers in humane and liberal principles.[69] There must be colleges to tutor the Empire's servants, and so Haileybury and Addiscombe came into being.

Over the next 40 years in India, we see something new: the gradual emergence of grizzled Company colonels into positions of *political* power. Men who had spent their youth under canvas or in cantonment alongside their sepoys, men who had served as military officers and Residents at native courts and had come to know the charms and weaknesses of rajas and nawabs, these were the new rulers of India: men like John Malcolm, Barry Close and Thomas Munro, the three Lawrence brothers, Henry, John and George, and William Sleeman, James Outram – and John Low.

Look at some of them in the engravings and first photographs taken of them in their heyday. How unkempt they are, how wild and shaggy. They have spent a thousand nights under canvas, their complexions are distempered by bouts of dysentery and malaria and every kind of insect fever; they have unmistakably been through it. How unlike they are to the dashing aristocrats who carved out the Empire in the eighteenth century or the smooth bureaucrats who administered it in the early twentieth. They did not just govern India, they lived it.

These men were not romantics (although their deeds might some-times be spectacular). Rather, they prided themselves on an unblinking realism and an undeceived understanding of the limits of imperial pretension.

They were usually of middle-class origin, the sons of farmers or clergymen or merchants in Ulster or the Scottish lowlands. They came out to serve in the Company's Army in their mid-teens, rose to command a battalion and then either went on to command armies or transferred into the political service to become Residents at the native courts, at Poona, or Mysore or Hyderabad or Lucknow, and even to become Governor of Bombay or the Punjab and, in the case of Sir John Lawrence, Governor-General of India.

It was these men who were principally responsible for suppressing the bandits who made life hell for the peasants – the *pindaris*, the thugs, the dacoits – for bringing an end to the burning of widows on their husbands' pyres, for introducing new crops and new methods of cultivation, for trying (but more often failing) to make taxes fairer and more supportable. But more than any of these reforms, their principal virtue was their sense of limit, their unwillingness to push things too far. Time and again, their endeavours were interrupted or harassed, not by the Indians themselves but by the ignorant and impatient aristocrats sent out from Britain to govern them. This is the story of John Low and his kind.

What they governed was still an empire of white men over black men, and one that relied on harsh and swift, though seldom arbitrary, punishment to keep the peace. It is at least arguable that over the next 50 years India was less badly governed than it had been before. In retrospect, although there were plenty of minor wars still being fought and plenty of small mutinies to be suppressed, that era did deserve its popular soubriquet of the 'The Golden Calm'.

When the calm broke, it was because the grizzled colonels were no longer being listened to, and the lessons they had taken decades to learn had been forgotten.

IV

LORD MINTO TAKES A TRIP

'From what I have lately heard from Bengal, Lord Minto's character is more of a smooth and cautious than a bold and enterprising one, and he will be satisfied with preserving what we have.'[1]

So wrote John Malcolm to his friend Barry Close at Poona on November 1, 1807, soon after Lord Minto had arrived in Calcutta as Governor-General.

The ever-trusting Malcolm could not have been more wrong. On the very day that he wrote these soothing words, Minto was writing to the President of the Board of Control back in London – the job Minto had held himself only a few months earlier – to boast of his expedition to capture the Dutch Navy off the far-away coast of Java. In almost every line that Minto wrote or uttered during the six years he was Governor-General you sense a boyish enthusiasm for fresh conquests. He was in his mid-fifties when he arrived in India, but his head was still spinning with dreams of imperial fame.

What a curious character Sir Gilbert Elliot, later first Earl of Minto, was: always beguiling, incurably devious, sometimes acute and playful, almost camp in his manner. All his life, he possessed three conspicuous qualities: high liberal principles, buckets of charm and a recurring shortage of cash. His father managed to scrape enough money together to have him educated in Paris, at the prompting of the philosopher David Hume. There he met the pockmarked, irresistible Comte de Mirabeau, the John the Baptist of the French Revolution, and they became great friends. Not a usual start for a minor Scots landowner. And it was in the role of an avant-garde liberal that the young Gilbert first hit the political headlines. As a 30-year-old MP, he broke with Lord North's government and came out for American independence. With this spectacular volte-face, he became a friend of Edmund Burke and Charles James Fox. Burke flattered him and egged him on: 'You *must* be less modest. You must be all that you can be, and you can be everything.'[2]

In truth, for all his charming self-deprecation, Gilbert had a pretty good conceit of himself. When the war with France broke out, he had no hesitation in accepting the conspicuous post of Civil Commissioner at Dunkirk, should the siege of that port in September 1792 be successful. It was not, but a couple of weeks later, the siege of Toulon looked as if it would be. As he already had his pads on, Elliot was appointed Commissioner there instead, and sailed off to watch Admiral Hood complete his blockade of the French fleet in support of Louis XVII, the eight-year-old son of the guillotined King.

Unfortunately, a surly young artillery captain called Napoleon Bonaparte passed through the French camp, escorting a supply convoy from Avignon to Nice. And after he began to cannonade the fleets from the heights behind Toulon, Hood's fleet had to make a run for it, leaving hundreds of Royalists to have their heads cut off. This was Napoleon's first triumph, and, rather less widely advertised, Gilbert's first humiliation.

The second humiliation was not long in following. Just as it had seemed the obvious thing to transfer Gilbert from Dunkirk to Toulon, so now it seemed natural to move him on to the next big thing in the Med: the assistance of the Corsican rebels against the French. A cocky young captain called Horatio Nelson took Bastia on

May 21, 1794 – it was the action in which Nelson lost an eye. And Gilbert became the island's Viceroy.[3]

A glorious moment for Gilbert, in theory. From then on, things went downhill, rather quickly. The Corsicans did not care for the British, and the British despised the Corsicans. Anna Maria Elliot, in her only appearance overseas at her husband's side, spoke for her nation: 'All that Nature has done for the Island is lovely and all that Man has added filthy.' Like the citizens of Toulon, the Corsicans began to realize that the British were more interested in naval bases than in popular sovereignty.

Gilbert, alas, failed to display grace under pressure. He became prickly and suspicious. He dissolved Parliament and exiled Pasquale Paoli, the charismatic Corsican leader, to England. As inevitably as the sun rose over the impenetrable maquis of the island, a guerrilla movement developed (indeed, the Corsican guerrillas have some claim to be the first maquis, or macchia – 'darsi alla macchia' means to become a fugitive, to take to the hills). Bonaparte's army in Leghorn was ready to attack. The Viceroy still had not grasped the consequences of his intemperate actions. Back in London, Pitt and Dundas had. For the second time, Gilbert was ordered to pack his bags. After an adventurous voyage home in which he and Nelson were pursued by a Spanish squadron, Sir Gilbert was consoled by a peerage.

Lord Minto turned out to be a wily man of business, even if he had been a headstrong Viceroy, and Pitt found him useful in the Upper House. But beneath his debonair exterior his resentments burned. Three times he had been pumped up by the promise of greatness. Dunkirk had come to nothing. That was not his fault. In Toulon he had not displayed the diplomacy that might have been expected of him. In Corsica he had been a disaster: intolerant, panicky and paranoid.

You might have thought that his record made him the least likely man to be resurrected a decade later in the most glittering viceregal role of all: Governor-General of Bengal. But the British Establishment has never been shy of rewarding failure. In the intervening years

Gilbert had kept his head down and become a utility team player. Pitt and Grenville offered him the Presidency of the Board of Control (the political overlord of the Honourable Company). From there it was only a short hop to Bengal, after the Court's Directors had vetoed the first suggested candidate.

What they did not know was Lord Minto's secret: that he was going out to avenge all those past humiliations, and that he intended to turn the Indian Ocean into a British sea. He kept up his mild front: 'it has been fortunate for me that my ambition has always been temperate and never could interfere with what I thought my public duty or disturb my private tranquility and comfort.'[4]

But this was a façade. He was out for glory and he was out for gold, too. He did admit that he was 'not at all insensible to the attractions of power or the private conveniences of office'. According to the diarist Joseph Farington, he managed to pile up £245,000 during his years as Governor-General, an enormous sum and probably an exaggeration. As for his family, he left his wife and daughters at home, but the frigate *Modeste* that took him to India was to be captained by his son George. And when he got there, another son, John, was to be his private secretary.

The moment he arrived, temptation was put directly his way. Plans for the conquest of Java, Goa and Macao were laid in front of him. For the moment, he had to put them aside. For one thing, as he told the ever-eager Admiral Pellew, the Directors of the Honourable Company had made it brutally clear that economy was '*indispensable* both for the permanent restoration of our finances and for avoiding present distress or embarrassment at our Treasury'.

There was another, no less crucial dampener on any such eastern adventures: 'a positive prohibition of any expedition to Java and other places eastward of India was transmitted to the Indian Government when Lord Castlereagh, at present War Minister, was Secretary of State for the Colonial and War Departments, and also President of the Board of Control.'

What Castlereagh said went. He was the supreme driving force in the British Government and perhaps the greatest (if by no means the most popular) war minister in British history. Governors-General could act on their initiative when they had no specific instructions; in emergencies, they could act before they had approval from London, because that approval might be a year or more in coming. However, they could not act in defiance of explicit instructions.

Castlereagh's veto on action to the east did not say anything about initiatives to the west or the north, though. Minto's predecessors, Sir John Shore and Sir George Barlow, had never lost much sleep over the threat from Afghanistan or Persia. These weak and divided kingdoms might dream of invading the rich plains of Hindustan, but they lacked the will and the wherewithal. New arrivals from England were less nonchalant. As Sir John Kaye said of Lord Minto, 'the inexperience of English statesmen suddenly transplanted to a new sphere of action, often sees in the most ordinary political phenomena strange and alarming portents.'[5]

Within a year of his arrival, Lord Minto launched a flurry of ambitious embassies in these other directions. To Tehran, he dispatched for the second time John Malcolm, with instructions to detach Persia from her new and worrying closeness to Napoleon, and persuade her to revive the alliance with Britain which he had negotiated on his first mission five years earlier and which might also act as a bulwark against any future threat from Russia. To Lahore, he sent Charles Metcalfe, himself a future Governor-General, then only 23 years old but born and bred in the Calcutta elite, to inveigle Ranjit Singh, ruler of the Punjab, into a close affiliation with Britain, again in the hope of warding off the Russians. To Kabul, he sent the learned and subtle Mountstuart Elphinstone, like Malcolm a master of several Oriental languages.

The long-term effect of these probes was not to be measured in the scant and fleeting treaties they generated. For all his supposed modesty, Minto had played the first moves in the Great Game, that deadly and interminable obsession which was to leave so many British bones whitening in the deserts and mountain passes of

Central Asia over the next two centuries. It was a game that Minto's successors were to find irresistible.

Having fanned out British influence to the north-west quadrant, Minto then turned to the south, to the huge spaces of the Indian Ocean and the scattered islands that gave their owners command over it. In 1809, he sent a task force to the remote Mascarene Islands, the best known of them being Mauritius and Réunion, or the Isle de France and the Isle de Bourbon, as they were then known. There was a decent military justification for this expedition. Ever since the war had broken out, the attacks of French men-of-war and privateers based in those islands had preyed on the trade of the Honourable Company, which had been deterred only by the expense from sending ships.[6]

Even the tightwads in London agreed that the financial position was now improving, and Dundas gave him the go-ahead. By the time Minto received approval from London, all the Mascarene Islands were already in British hands. The year before, he had jumped the gun in the same way by sending a series of smaller expeditions against the Dutch possessions in the Moluccas, the famous Spice Islands, then the unique source of nutmeg and mace and celebrated, too, for cloves, peppers and birds of paradise. It did not take long to overwhelm the little Dutch forts scattered through the islands.[7] To the Court of Directors, Minto justified all these far-flung excursions on strictly defensive grounds. As long as Napoleon roamed the globe, every flank had to be secured. This excuse for expansion persisted long after the little Corsican was safely penned up on Saint Helena, to be gawped at by the English on their way to and from India. For, as Sir John Kaye remarked, 'in the plenitude of our national self-love, we encouraged the conviction that Great Britain had conquered the entire continent of Hindostan by a series of purely defensive measures.'[8]

Minto was in ecstasy. He had wiped out the Company's deficit and he had swept the French out of the Indian Ocean, and all on his own initiative without waiting for approval from Leadenhall Street.

The memories of Toulon and Corsica had been erased. At the age of 59, he was a made man.

There still remained Castlereagh's veto on Java, an infinitely more formidable proposition, with a population of five million people. But then an absurd and quite unforeseeable event in London changed the situation. Castlereagh and Canning, War Minister and Foreign Secretary respectively, became caught up in one of those personal quarrels which seem trivial and inexplicable to everyone else, and which tend to break out among politicians who have been getting on each other's nerves for years. Canning wanted more troops sent to Portugal; Castlereagh sent them to the Low Countries instead. Canning threatened to resign unless Castlereagh was removed. The ailing Prime Minister, the Duke of Portland, agreed, but did not inform Castlereagh that he was for the chop. Castlereagh discovered the secret agreement and challenged Canning to a duel.

Shortly after dawn on a sunny September morning (September 21, 1809), the two men met on Putney Heath. Canning had never fired a pistol in his life and missed by yards. Castlereagh wounded Canning in the thigh. General public outrage at the childish behaviour of great men followed. Both great men felt honour-bound to resign their posts.

The Castlereagh veto was now non-operative. There was an opening and Minto did not wait to be given permission to jump through it. Britain set out to conquer the Dutch East Indies, because of a half-cock duel between two hot-tempered ministers, and John Low got his first serious experience of combat, a rather more serious experience than the proceedings on Putney Heath.

Minto had been dreaming about Java for years. Even before his ships had sailed off to take Mauritius, he warned his wife Anna Maria: 'I have still one object more, in the event of a prosperous issue to the present enterprise, which will fill up the whole scheme of my warlike purposes, and which will purge the Eastern side of the globe of every hostile or rival European establishment.'[9] A year later, His Lordship had more precise, and more startling, news for Anna Maria:

'we are now in the agony of preparation for Java; and I will whisper in your ear that I am going there myself, not to command the army, but to see all the political work done to my mind. "Modeste" is to be my stage coach.'[10]

The ship might be modest by name, but his sailing in it certainly was not. For a Governor-General to accompany a military expedition was highly unusual. He tried to reassure his wife by giving a list of reasons. For one thing, it would be a family party. His son George would be captaining the ship. His third son, John, who was a clerk in Calcutta, would act as his private secretary, and their kinsman Captain William Taylor would be his military secretary. The political justification was that the Governor-General had to be on the spot, so that the military commanders should not have to wait several months for further orders to settle the future of the Dutch East Indies.

The real reason was that he was intoxicated with the project. There was only one other man in the East who dreamed of it more feverishly: the young Thomas Raffles, then aged 28. Raffles was a humble clerk from Leadenhall Street who had used every scrap of influence to get himself out East, where he had networked and beavered his way up to become Secretary to the Governor of Penang. Raffles yearned to expand the Eastern frontiers of the Empire beyond the straggle of settlement down the west coast of the Malay peninsula.

In the summer of 1810, he brought a memo to Lord Minto. Java, he claimed, could be taken with ease. The Dutch were slack and degenerate as well as tyrannical slave masters. The native chiefs had become semi-independent powers and could easily be conciliated. Java was the rice granary of the East, and bursting with pepper, cotton, tobacco and indigo. Java was central, too, as the crown jewel of the Dutch Empire, from which other, no less valuable jewels dangled, such as Sumatra and Sumatra's offshore islands of Bangka and Billiton.

Raffles spoke boldly of annexing the whole lot. At this stage,

Minto spoke more cautiously, only of capturing Batavia, the capital. He was right to show a certain caution in public. Instructions finally reached him from London on January 15, 1811, by which time his preparations for Java were far advanced. And those instructions could not have been clearer.

The Secret Committee of the Court of Directors gave whole-hearted approval for driving the enemy from their settlements in Java and everywhere else in the Eastern seas. But – and it was a huge but:

> It is by no means our wish or that of His Majesty's Government that they [the islands] should be permanently occupied as British colonies, and that observation applies, not only to the unhealthiness of Batavia but to the general inexpediency of expanding our military establishments. We merely wish to expel the enemy from all their settlements in those seas, to destroy all the forts, batteries and works of defence . . . wishing to leave possession of those settlements to the occupation of the natives.[11]

Get the French out, and then get out yourself. Nothing could be clearer. And nothing could be clearer than Lord Minto's determination to disobey those orders. He fired back a letter by the Indian equivalent of return of post, on January 22. He protested that he was but anticipating the wishes of the Honourable Committee and of HM Government, but – and it was another huge but – he persisted in his intention 'to form such an establishment as may afford to the British government all the commercial advantages of the island'. This could only mean imitating the Dutch monopoly of trade in pretty much everything Java was rich in – teak, coffee, indigo, sugar, rice, opium and tin. Such a degree of control would have entailed a sizeable bureaucracy and a sizeable military presence to protect the business (Raffles sent Minto a full list of all the Dutch civil and military officers on Java – it ran to a dozen pages).

Lord Minto had another objection to the Company's limitations on his actions, one which he called 'forcible, if not decisive'. If the

British totally abandoned the island, they would be leaving the European colony to 'the rude sway and yet more to the vindictive power of the Malay princes who have had too much cause to harbour deep resentments against the Dutch'. The 'total and sudden extermination' of the civilized inhabitants of the island would be a calamity. The Honourable Company would have blood on its hands.

Thus Lord Minto gave notice that he intended to exercise the two main functions of a colonial power – commercial exploitation and protection of the inhabitants – and he could only venture the hope that, as circumstances changed, the Secret Committee would come round to his way of thinking. This was unabashed insubordination, but as usual news of it would reach Leadenhall Street months after the invasion was launched. By the time Leadenhall Street's riposte reached him, the fighting would be over.

The two most prominent Malay chiefs, the Sushunan of Solo (also known as Surakarta) in the hinterland, and the Sultan in the beautiful palace at Yogyakarta on the south coast, had lived in grumbling proximity with the Dutch settlers for two centuries, without either side coming to much harm in the occasional skirmish. Yet now keeping these two forces apart was to become the moral justification for a totally unauthorized annexation of the island. It is hard to think of a more dishonest rationale in British history until Sir Anthony Eden announced that he was occupying the Suez Canal in order to separate Israel and Egypt in a war which he had himself colluded in starting.

Minto gleefully reported his response to Raffles, informing him that 'I have already stated my reasons for considering the modification of all their orders.'[12] Raffles and Minto were instant soulmates. After their first meeting, Raffles wrote to his brother:

On the mention of Java his Lordship cast a look of such scrutiny, anticipation and kindness upon me, as I shall never forget.

'Yes,' he said, 'Java is an interesting island. I shall be happy to receive any information you can give me concerning it.'[13]

Raffles wrote this account of their meeting some time later. And some of his critics have accused him of claiming that he had planted the idea of Java in Minto's head. But surely the point of the recollection is rather different: Minto had recognized a potential henchman for his grand project, and he was signing him up.[14]

They were off and running. On April 18, 1811, the expeditionary force sailed from Madras, under the command of Sir Samuel Auchmuty, an American loyalist of Fifeshire stock (of course) who had served for years in India and Egypt. There were nearly 12,000 men sailing, including the largest number of native Indian troops ever to go on an expedition overseas. Minto's best troops were only just back from Mauritius in time, and he had to draw regiments in from Bombay and Ceylon to make up the numbers. There was, as always, a shortage of officers. Captains and lieutenants were plucked from local Madras Native Infantry regiments to serve in the King's Regiments. These extra officers were volunteers, young men who jumped at the chance of action and glory. To take part in the great Peninsular War against Napoleon was out of their reach, but here at least was the chance to drive Boney out of the Indian Ocean and become a part of history, rather than plod on through the repetitious routine of life in the cantonments.

Lieutenant John Low, now aged 22, was one of them. For two years he had been working for Colonel Barry Close over in Poona, surveying roads, counting tents and bullocks, and drawing up intelligence reports on the local *pindaris* – everything except actually fighting. In February 1811, he was transferred back to his disgraced and renamed regiment, the 1st Battalion of the 24th Native Infantry, but a month later, he joined the task force that was assembling at Madras.

There he was posted to the 59th Regiment under the command of none other than Colonel Samuel Gibbs. The other assault brigade was under the command of Rollo Gillespie. The two men selected for the sharp end were the fiercest and bravest battle commanders in India.[15] It no doubt escaped attention at the time that between them they were also responsible for the deaths of 1,000 of their own side's troops during the suppression of those two regrettable mutinies.

It was quite an armada that set out from Madras: four battleships led by Commodore Broughton on *Illustrious* (the naval C-in-C, Rear-Admiral Stopford in *Scipion,* was to join them at Batavia), 14 frigates (including *Modeste* bearing the precious cargo of the Governor-General and his suite), seven sloops, eight cruisers, 57 transports and several gunboats, amounting to 100 sail in all.[16] By the time they got to the assembly point of Malacca, 1,200 men were sick and a further 1,500 were laid low by the time they actually landed at Batavia[17], a sadly typical rate of attrition in tropical expeditions.

Lord Minto in his comfortable cabin on *Modeste,* with his two sons and Captain Taylor to wait on him, never ceased to be in high spirits. He protested to Anna Maria that 'it is not matter of taste or choice, but of duty, or rather of necessity, that I am going to friskify in this manner, although I confess, since it is right, that I never engaged in any affair with greater interest or pleasure.'[18]

Also friskifying on board the *Modeste* was Lord Minto's pet, his fellow countryman, the poet-surgeon John Leyden. Born only a few miles from the Minto estate on the River Teviot, as a child Leyden worked as a shepherd on his parents' farm. From these rustic origins (he was mocked for his strong Teviotdale accent), he made the most amazing progress, teaching himself half a dozen languages and studying medicine and philosophy in Edinburgh. The charm of his conversation eclipsed even his linguistic powers. In no time, he was friends with all the literati, including Sir Walter Scott, for whom he contributed several poems to *The Border Minstrelsy.*

Then the lure of colonial adventure overcame him and William Dundas wangled him the post of Assistant Surgeon at Madras, though his medical education was little better than his poetry, which was terrible. Within a month or two, Leyden sailed on to Penang, where he wrote a survey of the languages and literature of the Indo-Chinese nations and became a friend of Raffles and of His Lordship. In his spare time, he translated the Gospels into various Asian tongues.

Leyden was, above all, one of the champion talkers in human history. Lord Minto had taken him on board, partly to provide the mission with its bard, to gild a grubby commercial grab with the spirit of poesy, but also because he was bewitched by Leyden's company. However, after two months at sea, he was beginning to wonder:

> I do not believe that so great a reader was ever so great a talker before ... [a] feature of his conversation is a shrill, piercing and at the same time grating voice. A frigate is not near large enough to place the ear at the proper point of hearing. If he had been at Babel he would infallibly have learned all the languages there, but in the end they must all have merged in the *Tividale How* [Teviotdale twang], for not a creature would have *spoken* but himself.[19]

At Malacca, this gay company, more like a salon in Charlotte Square than a military command and control centre, were greeted by Raffles, now officially Secretary to the Governor-General, and by the station commandant, William Farquhar, an old colonial hand whom Raffles spent much of his time trying to elbow aside, partly because he was embarrassed by Farquhar's native wife. Raffles's young interpreter, Abdullah bin Abdul Kadir, recorded the meeting years later. He was amazed by the unpretentious appearance of the Governor-General: 'He had passed middle age. His body was thin, his manner mild, his face gentle. I should not have supposed him capable of lifting even a twenty-five pound weight, so fragile was his build. I noticed that he wore a tunic of black cloth, black trousers and nothing else worthy of mention.'[20] These impressions were misleading. As the cannon roared and the cavalry pranced and the band played to welcome His Majesty's vicar in Asia, Lord Minto was in heaven.

He fled Government House (too stuffy in every sense) and relaxed with his son George in a bungalow on the hill which had an open verandah fronting the sea: 'It is in the verandah that George and I are at present writing love letters to our absent wives. We swallow the breeze fresh from the sea, and the climate is entirely disarmed.' In front lay the harbour roads, with all the fleet and a string of small islands. Beyond were distant mountains and somewhere amongst them Mount Ophir where they were still mining gold.[21] Even in his most romantic flights, Minto never quite lost sight of the commercial prospects.

After breakfast, Lord M accepted gifts from the local princes: a baby orang-utan from the Raja of Pontjanak, five slave boys and two girls from a Raja of Bali. Minto immediately emancipated the lot of them. 'The boys will probably grow into very good servants. The girls will puzzle me most. I have some thought of baking them in a pie against the Queen's birthday.'[22] His plans for the orang-utan are not recorded.

Soon it was June 4, the birthday of mad old King George, and Lord M celebrated by 'a levee in the forenoon, a great dinner to all mankind, and a ball in the evening to all womankind'. He escaped during the first dance and took refuge up in the bungalow 'out of earshot of the fiddlers'. This eve-of-battle ball in Malacca was not quite on the scale of the Duchess of Richmond's affair before Waterloo, although Gilbert tells Anna Maria that the daughters of Malay-Dutch marriages 'dress, dance and flirt very much as well-educated young women do in Europe with the advantage of being intensely and beautifully brown. You are *lily-fair* compared with the fairest of the Batavo-Malaya fair sex. My fidelity, you see, is put to the test'[23] – a fidelity which was doubted by the London gossips. The report of the ball in the *Calcutta Gazette* [August 8, 1811] implies that these beauties must have been hard fought over, reckoning that there were only 20 ladies among the 150 persons present.

Lord Minto lost no opportunity to display the liberal credentials of the expedition. After his levee, he released all the government's slaves at Malacca, presenting each with a certificate of his freedom and four dollars to help him make a fresh start (though the fresh start would most probably be in their old jobs). Better still, he came across some instruments of torture which were still preserved in Government House. He had the wooden ones (the racks and crosses on which prisoners had been broken) burnt in front of the magistrate's windows. The iron articles – the thumb-screws, arm-cuffs and leg-irons – he ordered the executioner himself to collect up and row them out to sea and sink them in deep water.[24] These instruments had long been disused, as Minto himself admits, but it was the thought that counted.

Also on the expedition was John Blakiston who had blown open the gates at Vellore and who Gillespie thought was a useful man to have around. It was Blakiston whom he selected to accompany the expedition's chief engineer, Lieutenant-Colonel Colin Mackenzie, on the reconnaissance in the *Phoenix* to choose a suitable landing spot on Java.

Mackenzie was as remarkable an upwardly mobile Scot as John Leyden, but rather more practical and down-to-earth. He was born at Stornaway on the Isle of Lewis, the son of a Gaelic-speaking postmaster, and had made his own way to India in the 1780s. Now 58, this gaunt, ascetic Hebridean had surveyed most of India. His ingenuity and courage had won Arthur Wellesley's admiration at the siege of Seringapatam. Of all the colourful crew concerned in the invasion of Java, Colin Mackenzie has the best title to be called a serious man.

The two men splashed ashore at the beach of Chilinching, about 12 miles to the east of Batavia, the nucleus of today's Jakarta. They had decided to dress in rough seamen's clothes to be less conspicuous, though at 6ft 2ins with his sailor's trousers only reaching to his knees, the tiny islanders could have seen Mackenzie coming a mile off. They walked nonchalantly to the village, through palm groves and foraging chickens, too nonchalantly as it turned out, because they tumbled through a swamp and fell into the path of a large party of French or Dutch soldiers, they could not tell which (there were still detachments of both on the island, for the French take-over had happened only the year before). Blakiston and Mackenzie ran for their lives, pursued by a fusillade, the Lieutenant being much impressed by the Colonel 'taking at least three yards at a stride' and outpacing their pursuers. When they reached the shore, still with the bullets whistling around them, they found that marines had shifted the boats out of range and they had to splash through the shallows. Again, Mackenzie's physique and stamina were impressive: 'In reaching the boats, the Colonel's height was again of considerable use to him, for while I was compelled to swim some distance, he strode along, like Gulliver among the Lilliputian fleet.'[25]

Despite this nasty scrape, they decided, after trying other beaches, that Chilinching was the best. There was a good road to Batavia and another to Fort Cornelis, the stronghold on the fate of which the whole campaign was likely to stand or fall. Chilinching was also in effect an island. There was a canal on one side of the village and a river on the other, protecting the invading army from the enemy during the tricky business of getting nearly 10,000 men ashore.

The first man ashore on this flat marshy coastline was no soldier or sailor. It was the unstoppable John Leyden, dressed as a pirate in a costume raided from the ship's dressing-up box for their Saturday-night plays. He wore a fez with a tassel and brandished a cutlass in one hand and a pistol in the other as he scampered along the swampy shore. There, as Captain Taylor drily observed in his journal, 'he bore the brunt of the attack which came from a flock of barn-door fowls, headed by an aggressive rooster.'[26] For on the beach at Chilinching, in the words of the old song, 'there ain't nobody here but us chickens'.

There was hard fighting to come on Java and many men were to die. Yet the absurdity of the first landing seems to say something about the whole expedition. Though much heroism was to be displayed, the conquest of Java never quite manages to resound in our ears like D-Day or Iwo Jima. The story seems to belong better in a bad poem by John Leyden.

The comic opera continued as the great men of the expedition came ashore. Blakiston noted that as the Governor-General's boat hit the beach, Lord Minto jumped out of it, 'eager to be among the foremost', and found himself plunged up to his waist in water. General Auchmuty, who was in a boat alongside, was carried ashore on the back of a sailor. Blakiston reflected but did not say that 'this is the difference between an old soldier and an old fool'.[27]

They stumbled up the beach in the steamy afternoon of August 4 to find a run-down village inhabited by Chinese families who brought out their coconuts, onions and cabbages for sale to the invaders, as well as their scrawny ducks and hens. Coffee was served steaming hot from wayside stalls. The Chinese were happy to serve anybody. It was like expecting Omaha Beach and finding a North London farmers' market.

Lord Minto was charmed by the scene. He took a ride with the General and declared that 'the country is like Chinese paper on a wall'. The only battle they saw was between two of the Dutch Paymaster-General's farmyard cocks.[28]

The enemy had withdrawn, which was just as well for the British, for the advantage of Chilinching was also its great drawback. To reach Batavia they had to cross the river, and the enemy had destroyed the only bridge. The indispensable Blakiston was put aboard the *Leda* and landed at the mouth of the river after dark, to see if it was possible to ford the tidebar. It wasn't. Blakiston and his party stuck in the black mud and they had to cling to fishing stakes to avoid being swallowed in the morass. They staggered back to the *Leda* black from head to foot. After washing and giving their clothes to be dried in the galley, Blakiston and the other scouts lay naked wrapped in the flags which had been spread out on the Captain's cabin. They were awakened from this picturesque rest by a huge fire upstream in the city.

As they stood on deck wrapped in their flags watching the blaze, their nostrils were filled by the most deliciously scented smoke. The enemy had blown up the main spice warehouses to prevent them falling into British hands. While inhaling the exquisite perfume,

Blakiston reflected sourly on the loss of the vast hoard of pepper and sugar and cloves and nutmeg which might have made their fortune.

The following morning, they tiptoed into the city of Batavia – and found it empty of troops and nearly deserted.

It would have been easy enough for the French to make life hell for the invaders as they stumbled through the swamps. But the new French commander, General Janssens, who had just succeeded the much more fearsome General Daendels, both of them Dutchmen in Napoleon's service, had taken his huge but motley army, reckoned to be about 17,000 strong, up the road to the great fort of Meester Cornelis (named after an old schoolteacher who had lived there years earlier). In downtown Batavia, only a few locals were to be seen dragging off burst and smouldering bags from the burning spice stores. Captain William Taylor wrote, 'I do not exaggerate when I say that the streets were covered with coffee and pepper as with gravel, and in other places quantities of sugar.'[29] There is a nice irony about the invaders crunching the riches of the East underfoot in their advance.

Auchmuty's aides routed out the city's mayor, a Mynheer Hillebrink, who reluctantly took supper with the British officers. Mayor Hillebrink was jumpy throughout the meal and tried to escape when he heard firing outside. He was clearly forewarned that a party of Frenchmen were stealing back into the city centre. Gillespie leapt up from the table and led a sally out through the west gate and surprised the intruders from the flank and chased them off easily enough. Still, it was an eerie, unquiet night. The main square of Batavia, surrounded by its dignified Dutch colonial mansions, was crammed with sleepless soldiers lying beside their muskets. Above them the August night was sticky with the scent of burnt pepper and coffee, and beneath them the grains of sugar lay thick as snow, coating their white breeches and red coats.

At 4am on August 10, Gillespie set off from the French Commandant's quarters where he had slept. Before he and his staff officers mounted their horses, they tossed back cups of the heavy black Java coffee which the Commandant's servant handed them. The coffee was poisoned, and Gillespie and every man on his staff were immediately seized with the most violent pains and vomiting. They set off into the interior retching uncontrollably as they jogged along. The servant escaped with his life only because their minds were fixed on the battle to come. His punishment was to be made to drink his own coffee.[30]

They had set off in the delicious cool before dawn, passing the 'very superb' Dutch mansions, all now deserted, for the gentlemen of Batavia had fled. By daybreak they had reached the pleasant pepper plantations and villas of Weltevreden ('well-contented' in Dutch). It was a model new town, with a healthier climate than low-lying Batavia, built by Governor-General Herman Willem Daendels, who was one of those indefatigable tyrant-modernizers. He also built the great post road from one end of Java to the other, which was to prove so helpful to the British. And here at Weltevreden the expedition met its first serious resistance.

As they approached the enemy cantonments, the British saw blue lights and rockets going up, but they found the huts and the parade ground deserted. The French had taken up a strong position in the pepper plantations beyond the little town. Some 3–4,000 of them, including most of their better European troops, were concealed behind a long barricade of felled trees (an *abattis* in military jargon), and they opened fire with four horse artillery guns as soon as the left column of the British came within range. The British guns – one 12-pounder and two six-pounders – responded with vim. But the battle was won, like so many in India, by the poor bloody infantry clambering through scrub, over ditches and in and out of pepper vines, to get round the end of the enemy's line. On the right flank, Lieutenant John Low had his first taste of action. It lacked the glamour and exhilaration of a cavalry charge or a *coup de main* up and over the battlements. It was sweaty, serious work.[31]

Gillespie was keen to press on and pursue the fleeing French all the way to Fort Cornelis. After two hours of hard fighting, the General thought the men needed a breather, he preferred to spy out the land, and ordered the impetuous Gillespie to hold his men back. As it was, the enemy had lost several hundred of their best men. Their commander, General Alberti, who had survived three campaigns in Spain and had come to India with Janssens, was badly wounded, and along with General Jumel only just escaped back to Cornelis.

Even so, the French should have been safe against assault with 13,000 men inside a fort defended by substantial stone redoubts every two hundred yards. But their commanders had less than total confidence in their men, who were a hotchpotch of French, Dutch, Javanese, Molucca and Celebes islanders. Language difficulties abounded. The newly arrived French officers were also unfamiliar with the uniforms. Alberti got shot when he charged into the British lines and, mistaking the green jackets for a Dutch regiment, shouted '*Suivez-moi*' to them.[32] Jumel's superior, General Janssens, had been previously taken prisoner after the Battle of Blueberg when he was Governor of the Cape. On returning to France, Napoleon had said to him, 'Remember, sir, a French general does not allow himself to be captured twice.' Now here he was being summoned by Minto to parley, which he had refused. The battle preparations of this amiable but ineffectual French commander do not suggest any confidence that the same fate would not befall him again. After all, he wasn't even French.

The British knew none of this. All that their scouts could see, peering through the pepper vines, were the walls of Cornelis. It was a daunting place: a parallelogram, about a mile and a half long and half a mile across at its widest point, lying between the Great Batavia River and the Slokan Canal, with ditches connecting them at each end. Attacking either the front or the rear would be suicidal. On the west side, the river banks were steep and slithery. Hopeless to try and cross under fire from the batteries above. The only chance was from the east, where there was one redoubt, which they called Number Three, built by itself on the near side of the canal to command the rising ground. If this isolated fort could be taken before the enemy destroyed the little bamboo bridge over the canal, there was a chance – not a very good one – of being able to pour through the breach in the line. The cautious Auchmuty thought it vital to knock the enemy about a bit before launching an attack. Over the next week, working parties crept through the pepper grounds, setting up batteries. At first there was a strange quiet, as though the French were unaware of the sweating British engineers fetching their guns and digging their protective trenches no more than two hundred yards away.

Then the enemy seemed to wake up. The first sign was a sudden gurgle of water at midnight as the French tried to flood their ditches. Then by day they could see the French artillerymen reinforcing the battlements of their redoubts and placing their guns *en barbette,* on platforms, so that they could poke over the top and fire down. Just before daybreak on August 22, the enemy launched a surprise attack, carrying bagfuls of nails to spike the British guns, which were now in place. John Low's working party from the 59th had some fierce hand-to-hand fighting to winkle them out of the batteries. The siege of Cornelis had begun with the French besieging the British, which was not in the script at all. The British lost 100 men that day. In the confusion and carnage, Lieutenant Macleod was shot dead by one of his own side who failed to recognize his uniform. The British had their own confusions and cock-ups.

Now mutual bombardment began and went on relentlessly. The British could not be sure how much damage they were doing inside the fort, but every day they themselves were losing men to grapeshot and to the terrible heat of the Javan August. Worse still, they were losing cover from the enemy and shelter from the sun. The enemy shells stripped the branches of the pepper vines, and the mortars knocked down the trees and poles that supported the vines. When the British arrived, the delicate betel plantations had looked to them like hopfields in Kent. Now they were pulped into muddy scrub. Time was running out. Gillespie was as impatient to move as he had ever been in his impatient life.[33]

Soon after midnight, in the small hours of August 26, Gillespie set off, guided by a Dutch deserter who led them on a long detour across ravines and betel forests. Gillespie had with him Captain William Thorn, who was later to write the story of the expedition and Gillespie's biography, the indispensable Blakiston and William Taylor, now eager for his next battle. Behind them came the second column, commanded by Samuel Gibbs, with John Low in one of the grenade companies.

They blundered through the darkness, came to a crossroads where the Dutch deserter stammered and could not make up his mind when Gillespie hissed at him, but Captain Dickson of the Madras Cavalry remembered the right road, and they stumbled on until they came out through the pepper grounds and could see the black outline of the redoubts of Cornelis against the night sky, which was just beginning to lighten.

It was this moment that an aide de camp whispered to Gillespie that Gibbs's column was not up with them, indeed was not to be seen or heard of, though they had sent scouts back down the path. 'It was an awful moment! One of those pauses of distressful anxiety, which can be better conceived than described; and can be felt only in all its force by a soul engaged in a great undertaking, on the success or failure of which depend the lives of thousands, and the honor and credit of a whole army.'[34]

William Thorn did not exaggerate. Standing there in the dewy pepper grounds with the smell of the artillery in his nostrils and what was unmistakably dawn coming up behind him, Rollo Gillespie had another of those decisions which seemed to come to him not once or twice in a lifetime but every time he went into battle. If he waited ten minutes, they would be plainly visible, the surprise would all be gone, and they would be as easy to knock off as the ducks on the beach. But without Gibbs and the Grenadiers of the 59th and the 14th and the 78th, what chance did he have of blasting his way into Number Three redoubt and on into the great fortress?

In his usual nanosecond, Gillespie decided to go for it. Gibbs's lot would hear the firing and crash their way through the jungle soon enough.

They were already drenched in sweat and aching-tired. Blakiston had been up for several nights on end repairing the batteries, and he kept on sinking to the ground and falling asleep whenever the advance halted. He would have been left behind if a trooper had not stumbled over him in the dark. From then on, he kept a man beside him to prod him when the silent march resumed. They stole on so quietly that they reached the first enemy sentry posts without being detected. The sentry challenged the head of Gillespie's column, and some British officer grunted 'Patrouille' in his best French accent. Then Gillespie shouted 'Forward' and the 60-odd French picquet had time only for a few odd shots before they were overwhelmed by British bayonets. None of them lived to reload.

The pale dawn sky exploded in blue flares, and the artillery in Number Three and Four redoubts opened up on them, but the grapeshot passed over their heads. More bayonets, more stifled cries as they thundered over the fragile bridge (still not destroyed) and on to the redoubts. Now the British were falling in numbers on both sides of the dark canal.

The last and crucial redoubt was Number Two, only 200 yards to the right of Number Three. Once that had been captured, the British would control the whole south-eastern quadrant of the fort and they would be able to pour through along its entire length. But Number Two was a mini-arsenal, packed with enemy troops, field guns and ammunition. This was the grim heart of the battle.

At this tense, decisive moment, Colonel Gibbs's column came streaming across the bamboo bridge, and began clambering up through the fraises, the classic palisades of pointed sticks. Luckily, here at Cornelis they offered poor protection to the defenders because they were driven into the ground so far apart that a man could force his way through them.

Up in the redoubt, the fighting was intense, savage, point blank. In the confined space of Number Two, about 80 yards square, there were several hundred men on both sides tossing grenades and thrusting bayonets at the nearest target. It was one of the hottest fights ever fought. But it was also one of the shortest. Within ten minutes, 20 at most, Gibbs and Gillespie had gained control of the redoubt. There was no doubt who had won, and the British began rounding up prisoners. Then they caught their breath and shook each other by the hand and gave three knackered cheers for the victory.

It was at this moment that the powder magazine blew up. Or rather, was blown up. Two French captains named Muller and Osman, enraged by the British cheers, had fired the powder store. They themselves died in the explosion, as they knew they would. So did dozens of soldiers on both sides, most of the survivors being mangled horribly. Blakiston was there:

> The shock raised me several feet in the air, and then threw me down on my face almost deprived of sense and breath. The first thought that suggested itself to me, on recovering my ideas, was that I had been killed, and was then suffering for my sins in the infernal regions; and it was some time before the cloud of dust and sulphur would permit me to recognize any object that could lead me to suppose that I was still an inhabitant of this terrestrial globe; while the shower of stones, dirt and timber, which kept descending from their vertical flight, caused me to expect that, if I were still in the land of the living, I should not long continue so. As soon as the atmosphere had cleared, so as to admit of our looking around us, it was truly melancholy to see the shattered remains of our brave companions bestrewing the ground in all directions.[35]

Alongside him up into the air went John Low, his white breeches spattered with the dust and dirt of the redoubt, his nostrils full of sulphur and his eardrums blasted into a momentary total deafness.

The explosion was heard on board the British ships miles out at sea, but neither Thorn nor Blakiston recalled hearing any noise themselves. Lord Minto heard it, too, lying sleepless in bed in his commandeered villa at Weltevreden, dreading the outcome of the day on which depended his whole unauthorized odyssey.[36]

Blakiston says that he and Colonel Gibbs were the only men present in the redoubt who were not killed or seriously injured. All
three captains of the grenade companies lay dead there, including
Captain Olphert, John Low's superior officer.

John himself did not have such a lucky landing as Gibbs and
Blakiston. He is listed among the wounded. He can have been in
action for no more than a quarter of an hour before he was blown
sky high. But they were the 15 minutes that counted, the fragile
margin between a glorious and emphatic victory and a long gruelling
action that could have gone either way. For the British were
exhausted by the long night hike through the jungle and depleted by
heat and fever and dysentery and the artillery barrage. They mustered
at best 8,000 men against the 17,000 under Janssens's command in
the best-defended fort in the Eastern Seas.

Those men of the 59th who were still standing followed their
battalion commander, Alexander Macleod from the Isle of Skye,
out of the redoubt. Deafened, crack-ribbed but still going, John
Low went on with his temporary comrades as they assaulted
General Janssens's artillery park. The French cavalry were drawn up
to the right of the guns to protect them. They thought about
charging, but then thought better of it when the 59th started firing
at them, and they wheeled and cantered off down the rat runs out
of the fort which General Jumel had thoughtfully pointed out
before the battle, like an air stewardess indicating the exits before
take-off.

Macleod, himself carrying a wound from the fighting in Number
Two redoubt, led his men on along the line of redoubts, past
Number Four until they reached the small brick fort of Cornelis in
the heart of the compound. There, the demoralized remnants of the
garrison made a last stand in the shelter of the barracks. But this, too,
crumbled under a shower of grapeshot as the British brought the
enemy's own captured guns to bear.

Then they all skeltered out of the impregnable stronghold down
the emergency exits, French, Dutch, Javanese, Molucca and

Celebese Islanders, the whole ragbag army. As soon as they got outside the fort, the fugitives were cut down in their hundreds by the
waiting British cavalry or taken prisoner in their thousands. A total
of 5,000 prisoners were taken in the operation, including three generals, 34 colonels, 70 captains and 150 lieutenants. As for the dead,
General Auchmuty reported that about 1,000 men had been found
buried inside the fort and that 'multitudes have been cut down in the
retreat, the rivers are choaked [sic] up with dead, and the huts and
woods were filled with the wounded who have since expired.'[37]
Gillespie had been weak and faint from fever before he started. Now
he collapsed into the adoring arms of Captain Thorn, but he was up
again with a toss of his russet hair and personally took a brigadier
prisoner and several colonels.

So far the attack had been entirely on foot, because the paths
through the jungle were too narrow for cavalry and the jingle of
harness would have given them away. Now was the time to be up
and after the enemy before they had a chance of regrouping.
Gillespie had a horse cut loose from an enemy gun carriage and
leapt into the saddle, shouting to Lieutenant Hanson, the Assistant
Quartermaster-General, 'Bring up Roarer!' Hanson had whistled
up the Colonel's charger before Gillespie was out of the fort, and
he remembered ever after giving the feverish little coppernob a leg
up into Roarer's saddle and watching Gillespie gallop off down the
south road towards Janssens's hillside villa of Buitenzorg – 'Without
care' in Dutch, a name and thought borrowed from Frederick the
Great's pleasure palace of Sans Souci at Potsdam. But the Dutch
were neither carefree nor well contented any more. Those thousands of them who had taken service with the French were running
for their lives.

Gibbs and the 59th were at the head of the demonic pursuit of
General Janssens, who had to swim across the Slokan Canal to get
away. The chase went on for weeks, the length of the island, with
here and there a skirmish and a desperate stand until Janssens finally
surrendered and was made prisoner. He was sent back on parole to

France. Much to his surprise, Napoleon forgave him for being taken prisoner a second time.

At dawn the next morning, Lord Minto went again to Cornelis to 'take a peep' at the battlefield. 'A field of battle seen in cold blood the day after,' he told his wife, 'is a horrid spectacle.' Besides the 'objects' scattered along the road and over a wide plain, there was 'a crowded, accumulated scene of slaughter and destruction, collected together in a small space within each of the many redoubts that had been taken from the enemy. In one of them [he means Number Two redoubt] the dead more mangled than can be described were the conquerors themselves. They were the Grenadiers of two English regiments and of course the finest men of the army.'[38] Although ready enough to dwell on the ghastly sight, Lord Minto does not betray any tremor of guilt for it.

On the contrary. A week later, he wrote in high excitement to the Secret Committee, announcing that he had taken possession of Java in the name of the Honourable Company: 'I shall on first sight seem to have departed from the tenor of your Honourable Committee's instructions, by keeping possession instead of dismantling and evacuating the island.' The country was so much richer and 'the destructive field of massacre and ruin, to which the disarming of the colony and arming the natives must have led' too extensive and shocking to be contemplated.[39]

A month later, he wrote to Robert Dundas, the President of the Board of Control, in even more forthright terms: 'I think we ought to make it an English colony as soon as we can by the introduction of English colonists, English capital and, therefore, an English interest.'[40]

He had selected as Lieutenant-Governor to do this great work none other than Tom Raffles, soon to emerge from his chrysalis and spread his wings as Stamford Raffles, Stamford being his second and more resonant name.

Yet Minto was not so deluded as to think that he had persuaded the Directors. He tacitly admitted that it remained uncertain whether the British would retain the island when he told a merchant of Batavia just before he left Java: 'While we are here, let us do as much good as we can.'[41]

The fear that the island might be returned to the Dutch at the end of the war with Napoleon led him into an unsavoury thought which he did not shrink from expressing to Dundas: 'All that I fear is the general peace.'[42] The longer that Bonaparte went on fighting, the better the chance of entrenching British rule so that the conquest became irreversible. Raffles shared these unseemly sentiments. When Napoleon escaped from Elba, he wrote: 'The reappearance of Buonaparte has, for all its horrors, shed one consoling ray on the sacred Isle; and Java may yet be permanently English.'[43] The colonial appetite could twist even quite rational minds into semi-treasonous channels.

Minto's most immediate anxiety was that he might not receive the praise due for the conquest. It was, after all, primarily due to him that the French had been chased out of the Indian Ocean. 'Java, therefore, so far as credit is concerned, is as much my own as the French islands; for the plan was formed, and the resolution taken, and the preparations made, and the service would have been performed, precisely as it has, on my own judgment and at my own risk.'[44] None the less, he began to brood that 'I cannot help suspecting that an attempt has been made by Ministers to cloke [sic] themselves in my feathers.'[45] And from London there came only silence – an indifferent, ominous silence.

On Java, though, Minto's name was up in lights, literally. Raffles knew how to repay a patron. The day before His Lordship sailed off back to Calcutta, the Lieutenant-Governor gave a grand dinner in his honour, with fireworks. The avenue through the garden of Government House was illuminated, and at the far end there was a temple blazoned with the simple word MINTO.[46]

Among his other gifts of boundless energy and limitless ambition, Raffles was a master of the limelight. He founded the *Java Government Gazette* to broadcast the beneficence of the new regime.

A year after the battle at Cornelis, the *Gazette* carried a glowing account of the anniversary feast to celebrate the victory and the dawn of British power in Java. Gillespie, now a major-general, presided: 'the toasts of the General were as rapid as his movements in the field.' There were 14 toasts, culminating in three times three to Lord Minto, to absent friends, to General Gillespie, the hero of Cornelis, and of course to the Lieutenant-Governor. It was one of the last times that the two little redheads sat so amicably together. 'The heat of the engagement,' the *Gazette* went on to report, 'was suspended by a song composed for the occasion' by Lieutenant, now Captain Hanson of the 14th Madras Native Infantry, who had given the leg-up to the fainting Gillespie on his beloved Roarer.

'The Fall of Cornelis' was sung that night to the popular tune of 'The Saucy Arethusa', the rollicking shanty which was to be included in Sir Henry Wood's 'Fantasia on British Sea Songs' and until recently was still belted out at the last night of the Proms. At 14 verses and choruses, Hanson's song is even longer than Newbolt's ballad on Gillespie at Vellore, and it has to be admitted that the Assistant Quartermaster was rather less accomplished as a versifier. It is unusual, though, to find a quite detailed account in verse of a battle by someone who was actually there. Two stanzas describe John Low's share in the action:

> But gallant Gibbs appeared in sight,
> With boys well tuned for desperate fight,
> Whose double quick from left to right
> Soon brought them to Cornelis.
> Gillespie cheered, and on they flew,
> And Gibbs, he dashed at battery two,
> While brave Macleod led on his corps,
> Amidst the thundering cannon's roar.
> *Chorus:* Amidst the thundering cannon's roar
>   Within the proud Cornelis.

And now what dreadful scene we view!
A mine is sprung from Number Two,
And mangled bodies upward flew,
Within the proud Cornelis.
Alas! What horrors thicken round,
Our brave companions strew the ground,
And future ages long shall tell,
How many a gallant soldier fell.
Chorus: How many a gallant soldier fell,
    Within the proud Cornelis.[47]

General Auchmuty had returned to India soon after Janssens had reluctantly signed the articles of surrender on September 17, 1811. With him went the dispatches telling the world of his great triumph, and the bulk of the troops who had won it went too – including John Low and the other officers who had been detached from their regiments for this special operation. Lieutenant Low carried with him a few cracked ribs, a couple of impaired eardrums and his copy of an order published by Colonel Macleod 'expressive of his satisfaction with my conduct during the period I had been attached to the regiment under his command'.[48]

Gillespie stayed behind with the modest number of troops thought sufficient to hold the island, notable among them Alexander Macleod and the 59th, with whom John had fought so furiously after their late start. The 59th and its successor regiments to this day carry JAVA among their battle orders, though they may have long forgotten when and why they were there.

V

THE TIN MEN

At Cornelis, it had been said that 'Gillespie was everywhere'. And in the following months, he was everywhere on the entire island. For Raffles used Gillespie's troops, especially Macleod and the 59th, relentlessly and repeatedly as his attack dogs. Charitable biographers of Raffles (and there have been many) have arranged their narrative to suggest that Raffles was only responding to threats and challenges from the native rajas which had to be met. In truth, his actions look more like a proactive and purposeful campaign to impose British dominion, not just on Java but throughout the Eastern Seas. His ultimate aim was to create an Empire as great as the Dutch, covering more or less the territory of present-day Indonesia. He was fuelled in equal measure by the lust for glory and by commercial greed. He cherished also a desire, both selfless and selfish, to celebrate, record, and appropriate the cultural riches of Java and her neighbours. Raffles wanted to be lord of all he surveyed, and he wanted to survey it all.

Over the next year, Raffles launched three forays which between them made his intentions unmistakable. In those intentions he was heartily backed all the way by his beloved patron. It was at Minto's urging, in fact, that he wrote a bunch of sycophantic letters to the native rajas of the region, assuring them of British goodwill and support against the Dutch, and dangling before them some permanent alliance.

To the Sultan of Palembang in north-east Sumatra he wrote several times. In particular, he must have wished in later years that he had never written the two letters dated December 10 and December 15, 1810, still more that he had never sent copies of them to Lord Minto in his bundle for the Governor-General dispatched on January 31, 1811.[1] There they damningly are, in the old India Office Library, which preserves instances of English perfidy as scrupulously as it preserves everything else.

In the first letter, Raffles told the Sultan in forceful terms: 'I lose no time in dispatching this letter to put Your Majesty on guard against the evil machinations of the Dutch, a nation that is desirous of enriching themselves from the property of Your Majesty, as it has done with that of every Prince of the East with whom it has had connection.' There was only one course of action: 'I would recommend to Your Majesty to drive them out from your Country at once, but if Your Majesty has reasons for not doing so and is desirous of the friendship and assistance of the English, let Your Majesty inform me thereof . . . for I have power over many ships and if I think proper to do it, I can drive the Dutch out even were they 10,000 in number.'[2]

Why Palembang? What lay behind Raffles's threats and promises? Sultan Badruddin claimed descent both from the Prophet and from the old Hindu kings of Java. He ruled over a sprawling hinterland of swamp and jungle, much of it uninhabited, and though it did contain teak forests and plantations of rice and pepper and indigo, these alone would not have attracted such assiduous attention from Raffles. What the Sultan was also lord of were the two sizeable offshore islands at the mouth of the Musi River: Bangka and Billiton.

Raffles had written to Minto that 'Bangka may be considered as an immense tin mine'.[3] He had not exaggerated. Cassiterite, the primary ore of tin, spurts to the surface out of the long granite ridge of Eastern Sumatra and is found there in greater abundance than in any other single spot in the world. Billiton, its slightly smaller neighbour, has huge deposits of iron ore as well as of cassiterite. The muddy streams of both islands had been panned for a century or more by the locals, recently under organized direction by Chinese merchants. Billiton was China's largest source of steel. These lovely islands in the Eastern Seas, with their wind-tossed palms and white beaches, were as much cauldrons of the Industrial Revolution as the valleys of South Wales and Northern England. From the first, Raffles had been determined to get his hands on them. Ditto Minto. Before His Lordship had left Java in October 1811, he minuted to the Bengal Secret Committee, under 'Miscellaneous': 'Palembang is to be occupied as soon as possible ... With regard to Banca and the tin, the Lieutenant-Governor knows my sentiments.'[4]

At first the Sultan showed no sign of responding to Raffles's menacing overtures. His Majesty seemed happy enough with his long-standing attachment to the Dutch. Then came news of the fall of Batavia. Immediately the Sultan saw this as a golden opportunity to drive the Dutch out and reclaim his own sovereignty. He would do as Raffles advised, but he would not put himself under the thumb of the British instead. The miserable Dutch compound across the River Musi from the Sultan's palace was cleared, and two dozen Dutchmen and one Dutch woman plus their 60-odd native servants were sent downstream in an open boat. By the time the boat reached the sea, it was carrying 86 corpses.[5]

The news of the massacre reached Batavia three months later, at the beginning of January 1812. Officially, Raffles expressed horror at this vile deed. Unofficially, he was delighted. The massacre was the perfect pretext for invading Palembang and getting rid of the Sultan. He wrote to Minto that 'We evidently, I think, must break with him, block up his river which we can do with three or four cruisers, and establish ourselves on Banca.'[6] With unabashed callousness, he wrote again to his patron, declaring that 'I am inclined to contemplate the present state of affairs [viz, the 86 corpses] as fortunate for the eventual security of our interests in that quarter.'[7]

In other words, the Sultan had done exactly what Raffles had asked him to do: get rid of the Dutch. And for doing it, now he himself was to be got rid of. Without any sanction at all from London for invading Sumatra – a territory the size of England – Raffles dispatched Gillespie and Macleod with several hundred men and 11 ships to depose Badruddin and replace him with his more pliable brother. But, above all, 'the possession of Banca is to be the *sine qua non*'; whether it was obtained by a treaty 'or by the mere act of settling there'.[8]

It was an eerie voyage they had in the dark, rowing up the muggy river after a violent thunderstorm, but the operation turned out to be unopposed. The Sultan had fled his bloodsoaked palace. His grateful brother Adipati was dumped on the throne in his stead, happy enough to 'cede to His Majesty the King of Great Britain and the Honourable the East India Company, in full and unlimited sovereignty, the islands of Banca and Billiton' – not that he had much choice.

Bangka was to be renamed Duke of York Island in honour of Gillespie's ultimate boss. And Muntok, the little capital of the island, what else could that be called but Minto?

Naturally the new Sultan had to have a proper coronation. At 9.30am on May 14, the day chosen for the auspicious new moon, Prince Adipati landed at the Palace steps where he was received by Colonel Macleod and escorted to the great hall. There he was greeted by Gillespie who sat him down on a crimson velvet couch, from which he was conducted to the throne under a canopy of yellow silk – to listen to a recital of his brother's crimes read out in Malay. Captain Thorn thought that this affected Adipati greatly, for he was 'observed to wipe his eyes several times during the recital'.[9] One can think of other reasons he might be weeping.

Then Colonel Gillespie physically plumped poor Adipati upon the throne and a royal salute was fired. The British standard, which had been flying over the palace during what Thorn delicately calls 'the Interregnum', was lowered and the Sultan's colours raised instead. Nothing could have made it clearer that the new Sultan was to rule solely by the grace of the British. In his flight, the old Sultan had managed to have his treasure buried in some secret place and had had the diggers put to death to keep the secret. As if Bangka were not enough, there was a clause in the treaty stipulating that when the treasure was unearthed, half of it should be surrendered to the British.

Simple souls like Captain Thorn, who had accompanied Gillespie upriver, found the enthronement of the new Sultan 'very striking and impressive' and 'a brilliant display of that magnanimity for which the British character is celebrated through the whole Eastern world'. The rest of us may find the whole episode a breathtaking display of ruthless and cynical calculation. Raffles had posed as a sincere friend of the Sultan and an eternal enemy of the Dutch. Now he had toppled the Sultan, posing as the friend and avenger of the Dutch settlers. But who cared? He had Bangka and Billiton.

Raffles had the tin, and he also had a big toehold on Sumatra. He was Lieutenant-Governor of Java and ruler of the Spice Islands. There remained only the largest island of them all, that vast, mountainous wilderness full of pirates and headhunters, and said to contain limitless untapped reserves of iron, copper, gold and diamonds: Borneo.

Raffles had a friend from Malacca, called Alexander Hare. This dissolute wanderer might have stumbled out of a Conrad novel. He was a Lord Jim without the good intentions (the novel is said to be partly set off and on the shores of Bangka). Hare had started life working in the docks at Lisbon, had drifted to Calcutta where he married a 14-year-old dancer called Dishta. When Raffles met him in Malacca, he already had a houseful of under-age girls of various races and was running trading ships into Banjarmasin, the capital of southern Borneo, where he claimed to be on calling terms with the Sultan.

General Daendels had pulled all the Dutch officials out of Borneo in 1809.[10] Alexander Hare was just the man to step in as the British

Resident. In no time, Hare had accepted Raffles's offer. He had also been presented by the Sultan with 1,400 square miles of the Sultan's swampy domain. It was strictly against the Company's rules to accept such a personal fiefdom, but Raffles was delighted.[11] Unfortunately, there was no money to go with the estate. Hare started making sizeable demands on the Batavia Treasury to build himself a Residence, which he insisted had to be on stilts and taller than the tallest tree in the jungle. The natives had mostly fled, so Hare also indented for some convicts to do the building. Raffles sent convicts, many of them arrested for some trifling offence against public order. Then Hare demanded women so that he could breed more settlers. He preferred women 'of loose morals', he said. Raffles sent loose women, these too picked up on the streets of Batavia for petty theft or vagrancy. The women's first duty, it turned out, was to satisfy the huge sexual appetite of the Resident. Raffles was, in effect, servicing a private slave trade, and on a considerable scale.

At the same time, he was issuing noble proclamations about the abolition of the slave trade and the reform of land taxation to end the oppression of the peasants. He appeared to see no contradiction between these fine sentiments and the nightmare of sex and serfdom that he was helping to hatch in the swamps of southern Borneo. When Hare was finally kicked out by the returning Dutch, they forced him to tot up the number of his wretched slaves. There were 907 men, 462 women and 123 children crouching in his filthy huts. These figures did not include the hundreds who had already died or fled into the jungle. If Hare had not yet plunged as deep into evil as Conrad's Mr Kurtz, it was only because he did not stay there long enough. Hare's hideous reign in Borneo came to be known to Dutch historians as 'De Bandjermasinsche Afschuwelijkheid', or 'the Banjarmasin Enormity'. British historians preferred to ignore the shameful episode altogether. In his two-volume The History of Java, Raffles never mentions Banjarmasin.

In any case, his attention was now focused on establishing thoroughgoing dominion over the island of Java itself. He needed to

bring to heel the Sultan of Mataram and conquer his stronghold of
Yogyakarta, the most illustrious royal city on Java and the most beautiful, with its magnificent palace compound in which nestled the
delicious Taman Sari, the Water Palace, with its rippling pools and
dribbling stone serpents. Raffles wanted a pretext for assaulting this
formidable and magical place, known as the Kraton. He found one
in October 1811, when he intercepted a rather dawdling correspondence between the Sultan and the neighbouring potentate, the
Sushunan of Solo, in which these two effete rajas discussed the
unlikely possibility of rising together and throwing the British off the
island.[12]

Once again Gillespie was dispatched, this time at the head of a
weary detachment of the 59th – minus John Low, by now recuperating back in Madras. Raffles came, too (imitating Lord Minto's
example), and they set themselves up in the little Dutch fort opposite the Kraton, where the new British Resident, the stern and
scholarly Scot, John Crawfurd, now lived. After some fruitless par-
leying, the British began firing from the Dutch fort, and the Kraton
returned fire; thus, as Thorn puts it, 'presenting the singular spectacle of two contiguous forts, belonging to nations situated at opposite
extremes of the globe, bombarding each other.'[13]

For a second time, Macleod and the 59th were late for the battle.
They had once again lost touch with Gillespie's column. The messengers sent out to make contact had failed to turn up (one had been
murdered on the road). As at Cornelis, when the 59th did arrive,
they made up for lost time. They were soon swarming across the
Kraton ditch on their bamboo ladders. The ladders turned out to be
too short to scale the high palace walls. So some of the sepoys
climbed the walls upon one another's shoulders until they could
wriggle through the embrasures. Then the grenadiers blew open
the gates and the sepoys let down the drawbridge from the inside to
allow the rest of Macleod's column to thunder across into the Crown
Prince's Palace. The Javanese never forgot how the British infantry
advanced, heads lowered like charging bulls. They smashed through

gate after gate. At the end of it all, three hours later, the Javanese lay dead in their thousands everywhere, on the ramparts, in the bastions, in heaps under every gateway. The British had 23 men killed. According to Major Thorn as he now was:

> the handful of brave troops engaged, being less than one thousand firelocks, defeating upwards of seventeen thousand men, well appointed, and obstinately bent on defending the Crattan to the last; together with the discipline of the troops in the execution, will render this act conspicuous in the annals of our Military History. The word was 'Death or Victory!' ... Such was the effect of this elevated sentiment, which pervaded all orders, that not a man attempted to leave his ranks, or to go after plunder.[14]

The reality was not quite like that. And we know that it wasn't, because, for once, we have an eyewitness report from the other side. One of the Sultan's half-brothers, Arya Panular, wrote a minute-by-minute account, in verse, of the defence and fall of the Kraton. This sophisticated, wry, rather courageous observer feared the British, but he also admired them for their skills in war. And when the whole bloody business was over, he appears to have given a copy of his account on tree-bark paper to the British Resident, John Crawfurd, whom he particularly liked. From Crawfurd the manu-script made its way to the British Museum, along with a heap of other looted Javanese manuscripts and treasures.[15]

From Panular's account, it is clear that the Sultan had not expected an outright attack on the Kraton, let alone formed any serious inten-tion of sending an army against the British. General Daendels had gone no further a couple of years earlier than bombarding the com-pound – quite enough to show who ultimately was boss. Gillespie's all-out attack had reduced the Javanese to catatonic panic. Their artillery were poorly trained and poorly paid. The snipers posted on the Kraton battlements mostly fled as soon as the grapeshot hurtled over them. Hurrying to the inner royal sanctum, Panular found the

Sultan moaning and weeping surrounded by his female bodyguards in their war-dress. These Amazons were a picturesque feature of the Yogya Court, but the Sultan does not seem to have thought of sending them or any other troops up to the Crown Prince's residence, which was the part of the Kraton most heavily under attack. How could such an effete HQ have masterminded any sort of effective counter-attack, let alone succeeded in expelling the British from the island? Raffles and Gillespie must have thought so, too, or they would not have attacked a garrison of 17,000 men with scarcely a thousand troops of their own.

The most conspicuous figure in the Sultan's chamber was one of the Sultan's sons, Mangkudiningrat, who had decided to become a devout Islamist (like most Javanese Muslims then and now, the court was generally rather easy-going in its devotions). He had changed his name to Muhammad Abubakar, and kept on claiming to be about to make the pilgrimage to Mecca but never actually set off. When Abubakar heard the firing from the Dutch fort, he declared that this was the beginning of a Holy War and went off to put on his pilgrim's white robes and white turban. Everyone else was wearing brown batik, so when he appeared on the battlements he made a perfect target for the snipers across the square. A few minutes later, he came rushing into the Sultan's quarters with a bullet through his turban. It was suggested that he should change into something less conspicuous. A full set of battledress was brought. Abubakar put on the hat and the jacket, but refused to change into the short breeches in the presence of the Sultan and the female bodyguards.

Meanwhile, the Amazons had been sitting around chanting 'there is no God but Allah', and the Sultan kept asking all the other princes what to do next, but could not make up his mind to take any of their advice. Shells began falling on the inner palace. The Crown Prince's Palace was captured by the enemy. The Crown Prince fled to the inner Kraton but found the doors bolted against him. Other princes fled out of the Kraton and melted into the countryside, where they were sure of a welcome, for in its dozy way the regime was not unpopular with the people.

The British had been looking everywhere for the Crown Prince. He was their prime candidate to replace the Sultan on the throne, although they already had a spare quisling in the shape of another royal brother, Pakualam, who was already sitting in the Dutch fort dressed in the uniform of a British cavalryman. The Crown Prince now surrendered to Gillespie, who then returned to crush the last resistance. In a skirmish outside the palace mosque, Gillespie was wounded in the left arm and, maddened by the pain, he indulged in one of his manic fits of retaliation and ordered his riflemen to mow down a huddle of by now defenceless defenders.

The Crown Prince was taken to the Dutch fort. Panular gives a marvellous description of the quisling Pakualam and the Crown Prince sitting in the hall, while in another room Raffles and Crawfurd argue about which of the two princes is to be plonked on the throne of Yogyakarta. The two pretenders are seated side by side, separated by the empty chairs just vacated by Raffles and Crawfurd: 'Neither utters a word, but in a haughty manner studiously ignore each other, staring straight ahead like women with new co-wives who have just been abandoned by their menfolk.'[16]

Panular then reconstructs the argument between Raffles and Crawfurd (or perhaps Crawfurd told him later how it went). Raffles opts for Pakualam who is obviously reliable and pliant; Crawfurd says no, if you want the kingdom to remain quiet, you must choose the Crown Prince, he is the legitimate heir, he had been declared regent by General Daendels only 18 months earlier (December 3, 1810), he is the one the people will expect and recognize as their sovereign. Raffles accepts the logic of this.[17]

There then followed a grisly ceremony. The British forces and the Javanese were all summoned to witness the enthronement. Raffles embraced the new Sultan, and the confused older princes paid homage, kissing their nephew's knees as was the custom. They were even more confused when Crawfurd forced their necks down, one after the other, and compelled them to kiss Raffles's knees, too. Nothing like this had ever happened before in 200 years of Dutch rule. To the Javanese, with their exquisite sense of protocol and minute gradations of ceremony, what made it even worse was that Raffles was only a Lieutenant-Governor, in their eyes a mere lackey at the court of the great Lord Minto. The grasp of a meaty Scotch hand round the back of their necks felt like a redhot brand of humiliation.[18]

Meanwhile, the British had been looting. The princesses and the concubines had been stripped of their bangles and necklaces (though not of their virtue – as usual with the British, plunder trumped sex). The redcoats kicked down doors, smashed open chests and cabinets, clambered down wells and dug up floors in the frenzied search for treasure. Far from attempting to stop the looting, the senior officers had their personal pillagers, much as the rich today have their personal shoppers. Gillespie's private share was reckoned at £15,000 in coin, gold and jewellery – something like £500,000 in modern money. Seldom can a decent man have told a bigger lie than Major Thorn when he claimed that 'not a man attempted to leave his ranks or go after plunder'. But then he was only echoing the dispatch of his Commanding Officer, in which Gillespie claimed that 'no part of the property was either pillaged or molested'.[19]

Raffles wrote to Lord Minto on June 25, five days after the triumph, 'A more splendid event than the fall of the proud and haughty Court of Djocja never graced the annals of any country, and Java will long have reason to remember with gratitude the events of the 20th June.'[20]

There were, however, difficulties about the loot. At first Raffles declared that 'The Craton having fallen by assault, it was impracticable for Government to cover the expenses of the Undertaking. Consequently the whole Plunder became Prize to the Army.' And the loot 'could not have fallen into better hands. They richly deserved what they got.' Far from plunder being something to be ashamed of, it was the legitimate reward (as it had been regarded in the eighteenth century and before). Yet Raffles later thought that 'in the immediate distribution, they took more upon themselves than was justifiable.'[21] Not because looting was wrong but because Government had a right to and a desperate need of its proper share. For the government of Java was skint, and Raffles needed every ill-gotten penny he could lay his hands on.

For the first 12 months of British occupation, he had budgeted for a surplus of three-quarters of a million Spanish dollars. The actual result had been an embarrassing loss. Britain and the USA were now at war, and so the American ships had not called at Batavia to buy their coffee, the Javanese were not smoking enough opium, and even the tin from Bangka was not yet providing the expected 'tin' (it is a symbol of the mineral's glorious future through the nineteenth century that it was just about now that 'tin' became the slang word for cash). Minto had claimed that 'Java will supply resources at the least for its own expense.'[22] Raffles had claimed the same. The Court of Directors had not believed them. Even after the conquest of Batavia, they had been unconvinced: 'We are so strongly imbued in this country with the inexpediency of extend-ing our Colonial possessions in India that we shall be very unwilling to depart from the line of policy.'[23] They never did. The only things they were itching to change were the Governor-General and his Lieutenant-Governor.

An excuse was not long in coming. Gillespie had always resented that Raffles should have been preferred to him as Lieutenant-Governor. He had done all the fighting, while Raffles was a mere onlooker, literally so at the siege of the Kraton when he had his front-row seat in the Dutch fort. The two little redheads were des-tined to quarrel violently from the moment that Raffles questioned Gillespie's share of the plunder. The danger to Raffles multiplied when Gillespie returned to India and launched what amounted to a one-man impeachment campaign, primarily on the grounds of a dodgy speculation in land around Buitenzorg, where Raffles had taken up residence in Daendels's old villa.

If his Eastern Empire had been making a profit, such peccadilloes could have been forgiven. But the losses were mounting. His patron Lord Minto had been recalled six months early. Minto's successor, a rather ferocious Ulsterman called Lord Moira, seemed immune to the romance of the East. Moira's principal object in India was to clear the Company's debts and his own. Sir Thomas Metcalfe, a director of the Company, wrote from India House to his son Charles: 'You will find Lord Moira a highminded man *open to flattery* and totally careless in money matters. His debts in this country are enormous and I think his intended stile of living in Calcutta will not admit of any saving out of his salary.'

Lord Moira was, however, determined that nobody but himself should be allowed to waste the Company's money. He immediately identified Java as 'a drain'.[24]

Worse still, Raffles was now dreaming of extending the British presence as far as the Philippines, and even to Japan, because, as he told the Batavian Society of Arts and Sciences, the Japanese were a nervous, vigorous people 'just like us'. The Governor of Penang, William Petrie, a sceptical old India hand, dismissed these ideas as 'altogether chimerical and impracticable'. So did Lord Moira.[25] Raffles was obviously going a little mad.

The Honourable Company had had enough. On May 5, 1815, the Court of Directors complained to Moira that he had not done enough to prevent the occupation of Java from continuing to be a drain on the finances of the British Government. Whatever the results of the current investigations into the charges against Mr Raffles, 'we are of the opinion that his continuance on the Government of Java would be highly inexpedient.' Moira needed no prodding. No one in India was happier to see Raffles leave Java.[26]

In any case, his whole empire in the East was vanishing into smoke. In August the year before, Castlereagh, back in power again, had signed the treaty by which Java and her dependencies were to be given back to the Dutch. A copy of the treaty reached Raffles on November 3, 1815, by the same vessel which brought news of

Napoleon's defeat at Waterloo. The unseemly hope that had flared
when the Emperor escaped from Elba was finally doused.[27]

Raffles had personal grief, too. His wife Olivia had died the year
before (November 26, 1814). Lord Minto had died in June that
year, not before he had also suffered a personal loss, his son William
dying from consumption at Madras shortly after Minto returned to
India.

The marks which the two confederates had made on the map
were swiftly rubbed out. Duke of York Island became Bangka again,
and Minto Town reverted to Muntok. The tin mines went from
strength to strength under Dutch control. The Billiton Mining
Company was incorporated at the Hague in 1860 and, after passing
through various hands, eventually merged in 2001 with the
Australian mining giant Broken Hill Proprietary to form BHP
Billiton, today the largest mining group in the world.

On the islands of Bangka and Billiton, there are still local labourers panning the turquoise waste ponds under the palm trees by
methods that have not changed much since the days of Raffles and
Gillespie. They scavenge and dredge, enduring the same dangers of
being drowned or buried alive in their scrabble for the dark specks of
cassiterite. It is reckoned that 100–150 miners on Bangka die in
industrial accidents each year.[28] For a century and more, the tin
went into the tin cans that we all lived out of. Today much of it goes
into solder for mobile phones, which might have pleased the loqua-
cious Stamford Raffles.

On his way home, he made the usual stop-off at Saint Helena.
That island might seem like the end of the world to the exiled
Napoleon, but for the British in India it was a breezy station to
recover your health in. Raffles met Napoleon taking a walk on the
lawns of Longwood. He described the Emperor as 'a heavy, clumsy-
looking man, moving with a very awkward gait, and reminding us of
a citizen lounging in the tea-gardens about London of a Sunday
after noon'.[29] As is the way of powerful and ex-powerful men,
Napoleon rapped out a series of questions about Java and Raffles's

role in its conquest. Afterwards, Raffles wrote to none other than Alexander Hare: 'Believe me, Hare, the man is a monster, who has none of those feelings of the heart which constitute the real man.'[30] Which could be said of Hare himself, though Raffles still refused to see it. And in a smaller compass, Raffles himself was not without his Napoleonic side: the same urge to conquest, the same gift for publicity, the same trumpeted claims to be sweeping away the old abuses in the states he conquered, the same indifference to the human costs. When he was later sidelined in the insalubrious station of Bencoolen on the far side of Sumatra, Raffles did like to compare his plight to that of the exiled Bonaparte. Though he was in 'the most wretched place I ever beheld', he asserted that 'they say that I am a spirit that will never allow the East to be quiet and that this second Elba in which I am placed is not secure enough.'[31]

Another trait they shared was the unashamed looting in the name of culture. The British Museum and the British Library owe much of their Javanese collections to Raffles and Crawfurd and the indefatigable Colin Mackenzie. All over the island, Mackenzie crawled through mud and vines and banyan branches, up overgrown hillsides and across treacherous torrents to unearth the Hindu and Buddhist monuments of old Java. He surveyed the temples of Prambanan and Borobudur. The latter is the largest Buddhist monument in the world (and is today a UNESCO World Heritage Site). Neither he nor Raffles *discovered* anything much. The natives always knew that the monuments were there, and the Dutch engineers had explored quite a few of them first. But the new (if temporary) masters of the islands did reveal their amazing sculptures to the world. They drew and catalogued them, and housed them in museums, in Batavia as well as in London. Raffles's two-volume *History of Java* relied a lot on borrowings from other scholars. He and Crawfurd 'borrowed' a shameful quantity of the sculptures and the manuscripts, too.

Nor was Lord Minto forgotten in the share-out. Raffles had shipped off to Calcutta a six-foot, tenth-century, inscribed stone weighing three or four tons. Minto in his thank-you letter promised 'to mount this Javan rock upon our Minto craigs, that it may tell eastern tales of us, long after our heads lie under other stones.'[32] For two centuries the 'Minto Stone' has gathered moss by the banks of the Teviot.

Some of the Dutch settlers were bemused by the restless energy of Raffles and his collaborators. What was the purpose of all this fossicking for old stones, this slashing away at the tangled vines, when you could sit and look at the sea with a pipe and a glass of rum? But Raffles had a vision of himself in the eyes of posterity: 'The Dutch colonists accuse us of folly; and the only answer I can make is that I am ambitious of the title of Bitara in after days.' Bitara/Batara was the royal title taken by the old Majapahit Emperors who ruled Java up to the sixteenth century. In reclaiming the island's pre-Islamic heritage, Raffles was aiming as high as it was possible to aim.[33]

Even after his dismissal and his dismal years in Bencoolen where three of his four children died, he bobbed up at the last, as he had prophesied, to become co-founder of Singapore with William Farquhar, whom once again he managed to elbow out of the limelight. After his death in 1825, his second wife Sophia managed, by writing an airbrushed life of him and by ceaseless lobbying, to erase most of his earlier failures. He stands today immemorial in marble both on the waterfront at Singapore and in Westminster Abbey, one of the great manufactured heroes of British history, a man like Dr Livingstone and Lawrence of Arabia whose achievements are better viewed from a distance. The Raffles Hotel is still Singapore's finest and claims the longest bar in the world.

On his return to India, Gillespie was promoted Major-General and sent to command the key station of Meerut, north of Delhi. Almost immediately he was dispatched further north to repel the advancing Gurkhas. The Raja of Nepal had taken advantage of Minto's preoccupation with the Eastern Seas to advance into disputed territory. A vast army – four divisions, 30,000 men – was put together to push the Gurkhas back into Nepal. The Raja had little more than a third of that number.[34] Gillespie's division was sent up to

Dehra Dun, in the foothills. They found the charming hill town of
Dehra unoccupied. The Gurkha forces had retired to the fort of
Kalunga, 600 feet above the town and surrounded by jungle. There
were not more than 600 Gurkhas inside the stone fortress, but the
position was worth several thousand men. The first British attempt
to take it failed miserably. At his camp lower down the valley on the
banks of the upper Yamuna River, here a babbling torrent, Gillespie
summed up the situation in typically dramatic terms:

> Here I am, with as stiff and strong a position as ever I saw, gar-
> risoned by men who are fighting *pro aris et focis* [for hearth and
> altar] in my front, and who have decidedly formed the resolution
> to dispute the fort as long as a man is alive. The fort stands on the
> summit on an almost inaccessible mountain, and covered with
> impenetrable jungle; the only approach is commanded and stiffly
> stockaded. It will be a tough job to take it; but by the first prox-
> imo I think I shall have it, *sub auspice deo* [with the grace of God]![35]

We must not assume from this flamboyant, Latin-larded declaration that Gillespie charged bull-headed at Kalunga. He prepared the
attack carefully, insisted on strict silence and the passing of orders
from front to rear by whispering, on not stopping to reload but
relying on the bayonet, and on pausing to catch breath before the
final assault. 'In ambuscade, coolness' was what turned out to be his
last battle order.

The plan was for four columns to attack simultaneously from the
flanks two hours after a prearranged signal: five minutes silence and
then five gunshots. At 7am on October 31, the five shots were fired.
At 9am, Gillespie's column prepared to assault the main gate, but
there was no sign of the other columns. He sent messages. There
came no reply. The messages did not get through. The other
columns were stuck in the jungle, hopelessly lost. As at Vellore, as at
Cornelis, Gillespie had to decide in a moment: to wait for the others
or to go it alone.

He went it alone, of course. They were within 25 yards of the stone walls. He turned to a young lieutenant called Charles Pratt Kennedy, a horse gunner and a fellow Ulsterman from Co. Down, and said: 'Now, Charles, now for the honour of Down.'

But this time his men refused to follow him. He yelled at them, cursed them, waved his sword at them. But it was no use. Gillespie's men had followed him everywhere, through the waters of Haiti, over the gate at Vellore, into the redoubts at Cornelis, up the dark river of Palembang, through the gates of Yogyakarta. But now they wouldn't come. The attack was suicidal. Not more than four men out of 150 in the assault column followed him. The rest broke and ran down the hill.

The tiny figure stumbled on upwards, a little plumper than he had been when he started on these suicide missions, his russet hair a little thinner. For a moment he was silhouetted against the mountains and the blue sky. Then he fell, shot through the heart, in the main gateway. Charles Kennedy dragged his body back down to the town.

Afterwards, Gillespie was accused by everyone from the Governor-General downwards of being too impetuous, even of disobeying orders. He should have waited, he should have first reduced Kalunga by an artillery barrage, as Lord Moira had stipulated. But if his men had followed him, he might well have pulled it off, and there would have been no such recriminations. Failure was, as ever, friendless. Charles Kennedy survived to become celebrated as the founder of Simla, where he was political agent to the Hill States. Nearly half a century later, he was still presiding over the resort rather as Beau Nash had presided over the Assembly Rooms at Bath.

In the valley below Kalunga, two obelisks still commemorate the British and the Gurkha dead, for it was a great Gurkha victory, the single action which firmed up their reputation as dauntless fighters. Gillespie's body was taken down to Meerut in a barrel of rum – the standard preservative – and buried there under another monument. For all his criticisms, Lord Moira also had a cenotaph erected to him in Calcutta. But Gillespie's most spectacular memorial is in his home town of Comber, Co. Down: a colossal stone pillar, Comber's answer to Nelson's columns in Dublin and London. The column bears the names of Gillespie's serial victories and his one fatal defeat: Port-au-Prince, Vellore, Batavia, Cornelis, Palembang, Djocjocarta and Kalunga. Below are carved the slightly improved last words: 'One shot more for the honour of Down.'

Samuel Gibbs was sent off in the other direction, across the Atlantic to fight the Americans. There, he was second in command to Sir Edward Pakenham, whose sister was married to the Duke of Wellington. The Iron Duke was fond of his brother-in-law and said of him in one of his finely calibrated judgements: 'Pakenham may not be the brightest genius, but my partiality for him does not lead me astray when I tell you that he is one of the best we have.'[36]

The British attack on New Orleans, on January 8, 1815, failed miserably. Both Pakenham and Gibbs were killed by grapeshot from the Americans' makeshift barricades, commanded by Colonel Andrew Jackson. Like the victory of the Gurkhas, the American triumph became a patriotic legend, and it propelled Stonewall Jackson to the Presidency. Again, the British defeat was blamed on poor preparation, notably by the Colonel of the Essex Foot who failed to bring the ladders and fascines (bundles of sticks) required to pass across the swamps and ditches of the Delta.

The bodies of Pakenham and Gibbs were carried back to Britain in rum barrels, too. They were commemorated by Richard Westmacott in a joint memorial in St Paul's Cathedral. The two men stand side by side, with half-smiles on their faces and Gibbs's hand resting lightly on Pakenham's shoulder, both looking as though nothing in life had ever gone wrong for them.

By coincidence, just the other side of the South Door, there is one more memorial to Rollo Gillespie (his fifth), this one by Francis Chantrey, the other great sculptor of imperial heroes. The little man is gazing upwards to some unseen fortress with his battle plans in his hands. He too looks pretty serene and unmarked by life.

The nation was not ungrateful. We cherish our losers if they die in battle. Gillespie and Gibbs were both knighted in the New Year's Honours of 1815; Gillespie had already been dead two months, Gibbs was to die a week later. In St Paul's they are reunited. Only the width of a door separates them. They are as close together as they were in the blood, smoke and stench of Number Two redoubt at Fort Cornelis.

So it was all gone; this insubstantial pageant faded utterly.[37] Those five years of British rule, from 1811 until Java was handed back to the Dutch in 1816, have been erased from the popular memory, as have the 10,000-odd Javanese who died in the wars launched by Minto and Raffles. The Minto Stone still stands proud on the banks of the Teviot, despite recent efforts by the Indonesians to reclaim it for the National Museum in Jakarta first created by Raffles two centuries ago. But how many people now remember exactly how it got there? The names of the ancient Javanese kings inscribed on the stone will be better remembered than the imperial ambitions of Lord Minto.

Everything returned to what it had been, and John Low returned to soldiering.

VI

THE MUTTON AND
THE BARONET

Mingled with the relief at being alive and only the occasional rib-ache to remind him of Fort Cornelis, John must have had a faint feeling of anti-climax on returning to his regiment at the end of 1811. He had, after all, taken part in a famous victory, and the rest of the 1st Battalion 24th Native Infantry had not. If anyone gave the 1st/24th a thought at all, it was of the battalion in which both the officers and the sepoys were incurably mutinous. All the same, they were thought reliable enough to be bundled up into the Field Force that was being put together under Colonel William Dowse to subdue the southern Maratha country – roughly the lower western half of the Deccan, a wild, mountainous region where the rivers rose to flow eastward into the plains and out into the Indian Ocean.

This task force was quite a big affair. By August 1812, about 6,000 men were assembled at Bellary, the centre of the districts that the Nizam of Hyderabad had ceded to the British Crown. From Bellary, it was only a short traverse across the Toombudra River (today Tungabhadra) in the picturesque basket boats, woven out of local willow, and they were into the beginning of the Maratha territory, the heartland of the fierce little warriors who only a few years earlier had ruled most of India.

The country they were crossing into was notoriously desolate and lawless – desolate mostly because it was so lawless. Property ownership was fragile. Growing any sort of crop was scarcely worth the seed. As soon as the crop was harvested, the local nomadic hordes, the so-called *pindaris*, would descend and commandeer the lot. Famines swept the country year after year, and the local chiefs amused themselves by stealing each other's land. Nominally owing fealty to the Peshwa, the supreme ruler of the Marathas, in his fortress in Poona, most of them had long ceased to pay him either their respect or their taxes, let alone render him the military service that was due. This was a feudal system in a state of decay that looked terminal.

Lieutenant John Blakiston, who rode through the district with Arthur Wellesley in 1803, gives a horrific description of the consequences on the ground:

> From the time we quitted Poonah all signs of cultivation ceased. The villages were mostly deserted, such of the inhabitants as remained were exposed to all the horrors of famine. These forlorn wretches, of whom some, perhaps, had refused to migrate from an obstinate attachment to the soil of their birth, while others had lingered in hope till they had not strength to move, might be seen hovering round their dismantled dwellings in different degrees of exhaustion.[1]

Returning to camp one night, Blakiston loses his way and stops at one of these forlorn villages to ask the route:

> The moon had just risen, and showed me a group of famished wretches, seated under the walls of the village, surrounded by the mortal remains of those who, happily for them, had already preceded their comrades in the agonies of death. As I approached, packs of jackals, preying on the wasted bodies of the latter, even before the eyes of the helpless survivors, ran howling at the sound

of my horse's feet . . . while the vulture, rising reluctantly from his bloody banquet, flapped his broad wings in anger, and joined the wild chorus with discordant cries.[2]

The theoretical overlord of this blighted region was the Raja of Satara, but he had long given up effective control to the Peshwa and retired into dignified obscurity. The Peshwas are traditionally described as hereditary Prime Ministers, but that makes the set-up sound more ordered and constitutional than it was. A better parallel would be with the modern dynasties of strong men who have ruled Arab states in modern times, such as the Assad family in Syria. The trouble was that most of the Peshwas were not strong enough. Peshwa Baji Rao II (1775–1851) wasn't up to the weight of his grandfather, Baji Rao I. By the age of 25, he had been forced to flee Poona and take refuge with the British in Bombay. Under the Treaty of Bassein of 1802, the British agreed to reinstate him in return for the right to station British troops on his territory, under the stern eye of the British Resident, the formidable Barry Close who had negotiated the treaty (and who had given John Low his first serious job as a surveyor).

The Peshwa was now a British puppet and had to endure the scorn and disregard of both his rivals and his subordinate landowners. When Holkar and Sindia attacked him a year later, it was the punch and dash of British troops under the young Arthur Wellesley that defeated them at the bloody Battle of Assaye. It seemed clear to the British that only their own troops would be capable of restoring order and prosperity to the Peshwa's southern hill country. By 1812 it seemed even clearer. Hence Colonel Dowse and his Field Force.

John Low was still a lieutenant and only 23, but as soon as he joined the Field Force, he was plucked out, probably on the recommendation of Barry Close who had seen him at work in the Quartermaster's Department at Poona, and was appointed as Brigade-Major to Colonel Dowse. Then as now, this confusing title describes the chief of staff in a brigade. He is deliberately lower in rank than the

half-colonels who command the combat battalions. He has direct
responsibility for the brigade's intelligence operations – John was a
qualified Persian interpreter and had already drawn up some reports
on the various local chiefs when he was at Poona. But the Brigade-
Major, fatefully for John, also has the mundane responsibility of
overseeing the Admin and Quartermaster's Departments. Complaints
flow up through him, advice and instructions come down from him
on every conceivable subject, including the quality of the food served
to the men. Especially the food.

If John was pleased to be moving off into the field again, Major Sir
Charles Burdett, Bt., was in a state of high exhilaration. After 20
years in India, he was riding out at the head of his first command, the
1st Battalion, His Majesty's 56th Regiment, the West Essex Foot,
popularly known as the Pompadours from the pink-purple facings of
their uniform, that being Madame de Pompadour's favourite colour.[3]
They had left their invalids behind in Bellary, and as they marched
out of camp, he looked with pride on 'between 11 and 1200 strong
and in the highest degree healthy men'. In his eyes, it was some of
the finest King's troops anywhere in India whom he watched taking
turns to cross the Toombudra in the wicker coracles.

Alas, the high spirits of the regiment did not last long. Nor did Sir
Charles's. After only a couple of months, his exhilaration had
mutated into a baleful gloom. The business of bringing the local
chiefs back into a state of obedience and compliance with their obli-
gations to the Peshwa went easily enough. Skirmishes were rare and
casualties at the hands of the *pindaris* even rarer.

What was demoralizing the Pompadours and reducing their
strength, both physical and numerical, was sickness. From their
arrival at Gudduk with its temples and mosques (modern Gadag) on
September 28, to the end of the year and beyond, the regiment's
hospital lists swelled at a terrifying rate. By December, no less than
471 of the effective strength of 1,147 men were in hospital, and 13
of those had died in that month alone. The lists hovered at around
500 for the first six months of 1813, and each month more men

died: 11 in January, 7 in February, 15 in March, 13 in April, 26 in May, 25 in June. As a result, the effective strength of the regiment had been reduced to 951. Mr Fallowfield, the regimental surgeon, in his report of January 12, had broken down the causes of recent admissions to hospital: 138 had venereal disease, 108 had dysentery, 10 had fever, 6 liver complaints, 14 ulcers, and 8 were suffering from the after-effects of being flogged.

All armies are vulnerable to venereal disease, and British soldiers in the Deccan were more vulnerable than most, taking their pleasure where they could find it from the whores of the bazaar. The complaint was certainly not confined to the common soldiery. The elegant Mountstuart Elphinstone, as a 21-year-old travelling through the Deccan, had suffered agonies with the clap on top of a nagging bowel complaint and the Malabar Itch, a maddening skin eruption. Typically, he quoted Homer to describe the agonies he suffered while he was rubbing in mercury and sulphur to cure his complaints: *duo moira tanelegeos thanatoio* – I endure the long, stretched-out pains of death. He did, however, record in his journal that 'I erectate comfortably enough considering' (on rereading the passage, he overwrote 'vegetate' instead). And a month later reported with regret from Hyderabad that 'A whore whom I am going to keep was to come to be looked at but did not.' The younger staff at the Residency there had all had a dose. Henry Russell wrote to his brother Charles, who was recovering at the coast from a nasty go, that 'Bailey has proved himself, and has communicated the fashionable disease to his girl.' A week later, Henry got it, too.[4]

But the condition of the Pompadours was no joke. At this rate, they would cease to be a fighting force at all. The hot-tempered baronet was in a state of furious despair. He cast around for a suitable something or someone to blame. On February 17 he found it. The Quartermaster brought to his tent part of the mutton which was to be issued to the men. The Quartermaster thought the meat was bad, 'having little or no fat on the kidneys'. What did Sir Charles think? Sir Charles thought it was bad too, very bad, grossly inferior to the meat that was issued to the growing numbers of his men who were in hospital. He sent the meat back to the Provisions Department and dispatched his adjutant, Mr Mallett, to complain to the Commissary, Captain Josiah Stewart, but Captain Stewart was out.

Burdett simmered. Three days later, after the next issue of mutton, he reported to John Low that he had sent back the entire consignment of mutton, all 300 sides of it. They were now at Tiggidy Camp on their way to Goa – we must remember that throughout this whole imbroglio the regiment was on the move, moving across wild and inhospitable country where meat of any sort was hard to come by. The arrival of a field force like Colonel Dowse's in the backwoods was a mixed blessing to the locals. On the one hand, it brought a welcome flow of rupees into desolate regions. Trade in the bazaars picked up, especially for the vast quantities of meat consumed by European regiments. The merchants had to scour the barren hills for whatever miserable animals could be found to satisfy the huge appetites of the feringhee and to carry their enormous baggage. On the other hand, prices for grain and oil were likely to go up to intolerable levels until the military cavalcade had passed on its way.[5]

Captain Stewart said that the mutton was good enough and the best he could get, but to mollify Sir Charles, he would serve beef instead.

Sir Charles was not mollified. He assembled a regimental committee under a Major Grant to examine the meat. The committee compared it with the mutton bought at the same price intended for the hospital. They obediently came to the conclusion that 'it is very inferior in quantity and quality, as much from its lean and thin state it did not appear to be sufficient or capable of affording the requisite nutriment for the soldiers' mess, although it does not appear to be tainted or otherwise unwholesome.'

John retorted the same day: 'it is impossible to judge fairly of meat after it has been taken to different parts of the camp exposed to the weather.' In future, complaints must be stated before removing the meat from the Provisions Department. One does not like to think of those huge flyblown slabs being carted to and fro between the tents, and soldiers, many of them about to go down with dysentery, being required to poke their noses into the stringy joints. And it was all bound to get worse. Stewart pointed out to Low the next day that 'from the increasing heat, it may soon be expected that the sheep will get still more lean', and that Sir Charles would keep on complaining and throwing out the meat.

He did. Ten days later, he again rejected the whole of the mutton issued to his men. On March 4, Colonel Dowse himself had a look at the meat and found no good cause for rejecting it. But he set up his own committee under Lieutenant-Colonel Dalrymple to make a more thorough inspection.

The Dalrymple Committee, as obedient to Dowse as the Grant Committee had been to Burdett, recorded that in their opinion the mutton killed that morning was 'equally good if not better than what is generally served to European troops on field service'.

Armed with this favourable verdict, John began a counter-attack. Sir Charles, he wrote on March 14, 'had acted with indiscretion in rejecting indiscriminately the whole of the meat as unfit'. Such a proceeding would naturally tend to render the other Europeans in camp dissatisfied with their meat. Sir Charles had also 'unnecessarily cast imputations on the conduct of public officers'.

Burdett wrote back furiously the same day: 'I am not aware of having acted hastily or with any want of discretion.' And he demanded to see the Dalrymple Report. No, that 'would not be expedient for an officer in Sir Charles's position', riposted John on March 22 in a magnificent bureaucrat's put-down. By now the Field Force had finally reached Goa, but they might as well have been in Moscow for all the notice the dramatis personae took of that charming Portuguese enclave. Mutton was the only subject on their mind.

On March 30, Sir Charles went one step too far. In his letter to John, he launched an unforgivable accusation: 'many of the deaths and much of the sickness in the 56th Regiment proceeds from the bad quality of the meat.' And he said it twice. He was in effect accusing Captain Stewart and the Commissariat – and by extension Colonel Dowse and John Low – of something close to manslaughter.

Later that day, Dowse instructed John to place Burdett under arrest and to issue a charge sheet for which the phrase 'throwing the book at him' might have been invented:

> Major Sir Charles Burdett of HM 56th Regiment placed in arrest by order of Lt-Col Dowse charged with conduct unbecoming, disrespectful and insubordinate in having on 30 March 1813 addressed a letter to the Major of Brigade to the Force, conveying indecent insinuations against the conduct of a superior officer . . . arraigning in terms highly improper the public orders of the Commanding Officer approving the proceedings of a committee assembled under his authority and falsely imputing many of the deaths and much of the sickness which has unhappily occurred in HM 56th Regiment to the bad quality of the meat issued to the men; conveying thereby an unwarrantable and unfounded charge against the conduct of the Commissariat Department in Camp – the whole tending to excite discontent and disaffection and being therefore to the prejudice of good order and military discipline . . .

Sir Charles had his sword removed along with his command of the 56th, not to mention the handsome extra allowances he had continued to receive as the Commanding Officer *in absentia* of Poonamallee, a station just outside Madras. His resentment burned hotter and hotter whilst he sat in his tent awaiting the court-martial which was to follow.[6]

He had to wait a very long time. The Field Force slogged on through the fiery heat of a Deccan summer and on through the following winter, but in a camp in these backwoods it was never practicable to stage the court-martial of a commanding officer with the requisite number of senior officers to judge him. By October, even Colonel Dowse was feeling some qualms. Perhaps Burdett could be induced to climb down and acknowledge his error. No, he could not. He refused either to apologize or to withdraw the notorious letter of March 30.[7] He wanted justice, not forgiveness.

Then early in 1814, the Field Force was broken up, having fulfilled its mission, and soon afterwards the health of Colonel Dowse himself broke down. He died at Goa on June 27, 1814 amid general lamentation, the ultimate casualty of an expedition which had suffered a mortality rate appalling even by the standards of south India.[8]

All this further delayed Sir Charles's case coming to court. And it was not until 10.30am on July 19, 1814, that the court-martial opened at Fort St George, a full 16 months after Sir Charles had been arrested, and a year and a half after the first sheep's carcase had been flung back at the Provisions Department. The court-martial was presided over by Major-General Hare, and among its members was the distinguished Dutch officer Baron Tuyll, whose commissariat John Low was later to be in charge of.[9]

The court-martial was a shambles – the only appropriate word for a huge fuss about a pile of slaughtered sheep. Not only was the instigator of the charge, William Dowse, lately deceased, most of the prosecution witnesses were stationed far away and unavailable. And even after the intolerable delay, the Judge-Advocate had to begin by admitting that, 'being only furnished with instructions to carry on the prosecution at a late hour yesterday, I have not been able to give that full consideration to all the circumstances of the case which I could have wished.' In other words, he hadn't read the papers. The Judge-Advocate had to ask the Court to allow John Low to remain in court and help examine the witnesses.

Thus John was in effect both the solicitor preparing the case, the assistant prosecutor and the principal witness. He hadn't a chance. He was up against a vengeful and energetic baronet who had had 16 months of incarceration to prepare his defence and who had rounded up a flock of supporters from the Pompadours. The proceedings of the court-martial occupy 233 folio pages, most of which are taken up with Burdett's defence, which at times is as vivid and grandiloquent as Burke's impeachment of Warren Hastings. Only it's all about rotten mutton.

Sir Charles kicks off with a riproaring run of witnesses from the ranks of the 56th, every one of them prepared to swear blind that the meat was uneatable. Sergeant Michael Cunningham, for example: 'I frequently saw the men after a day's march throw away the mutton as they could not eat it, it was so bad. I heard several of them say it would rot them.' Or Sergeant Miller and Sergeant-Major Richard Smith: they had both been cooped up in the fort at Seringapatam during the White Mutiny and the meat had been a great deal better there. Or John Bateman, a former butcher: 'it was not fit for any Christian in the world to eat.' Or the two privates who recalled the day when the entire contents of the mess were thrown into a nullah because it was so revolting. In these testimonies from Other Ranks, we hear, as so rarely, the voices of the men who took the orders rather than giving them. And the accumulated weight of their testimony must have left its mark on General Hare and his colleagues.

Then Burdett turns his fire on Captain Stewart: 'The Commissary received orders from Lt-Col Dowse to oblige the contractors to furnish the best meat they could procure, orders which he disobeyed, because it will be proved in evidence that far superior meat could be bought in the bazaar from the retail butcher at a cheaper rate than the price allowed by government.'

Captain Stewart had been culpably negligent, 'seldom if ever attending the serving out of provisions but trusting the duty of the commissariat to be performed by the Contractor with whom and the Quartermaster there might be a secret understanding'. So Stewart was not only negligent but probably corrupt as well. And his idleness left the way open to a variety of abuses: 'the meat was very rarely changed and when it was the Men got little or no better in lieu of it, and even the rank raw-boned old goats which are to be had in the country for three or four annas a piece on all occasions formed a considerable proportion of what they received.' It really was a ghastly pass they had come to, when in the most literal sense it was impossible to tell the sheep from the goats.

How could Dalrymple's Committee judge meat that 'was piled up in 300 half carcases selected, picked and packed by the servants of the Commissariat', when they examined only two or three of the sheep sides lying on top of the heap? How could meat be called wholesome which was mostly skin and bone from animals which in a few days or perhaps a few hours would, if not killed by the butcher, die a natural death?

Sir Charles only wishes that 'Mr Commissary Stewart and those who coincide with him in opinion had nothing but Commissariat mutton to feed upon for the sixteen months I have been in arrest; and they would perhaps by this time have learnt a little more humanity and consideration for their fellow soldiers.' A glancing, probably unintended allusion here to the fact that none of the officers ate the same meat as the men. Burdett could have pointed out that none of the officers in the Field Force had died on the service, suggesting that the relative quality of the diet might, after all, have something to do with the mortality rate.

All that Sir Charles's grand philippic lacked was some exhibits of the bad mutton. But he made up for this absence with a lurid word picture: 'there was not the slightest appearance or trace of fat on any part of them; their carcases could be seen through them, their kidneys hung down by a piece of skin; they were entirely void of flesh and substance and consequently so soft and flabby that by pressing the legs and shoulders, you could grasp and feel the entire bone.'

Having thus brought the Courtroom to the verge of vomiting, Sir Charles raised his tone: 'Is this, Gentlemen, proper food to give the brave English soldier who has been fighting the battles of Europe for twenty years?' How could he have forgiven himself if, as their Commanding Officer, he had not pursued every possible avenue to protect their health and secure their proper nutriment?[10]

Major-General Hare and his colleagues took only a few hours to reach their verdict. On Wednesday August 3, 1814, the prisoner was found not guilty and was 'most fully and honourably acquitted'. On the Friday he was released from arrest and his sword was returned to him.

Now it was Captain Josiah Stewart who was boiling with indignation. He had been accused of corruption and negligence as well as manslaughter. By finding Sir Charles innocent, the court-martial had implicitly endorsed those accusations. To add insult to this injury, Stewart had got to Madras too late to address the Court. He had not only been told that the Court was now closed but received a severe reprimand from Major-General Hare for failing to turn up in time. This was a monstrous injustice, not only to himself but to the whole Commissariat and to the memory of the late Colonel Dowse.

There had to be another inquiry, this time to rescue the reputation, not just of the Commissariat, but of the Army in general. And so, two months later, on October 4, 1814, yet another inquiry into the rotten-or-not-rotten meat opened under the Presidency of an even more senior officer, one who helped to clear up the mess at the end of the White Mutiny, General Pater. This fourth committee ran into November and was an even more massive affair, occupying no less than 633 folio pages of the records.[11] But this time the balance of the evidence was stacked the other way.

For one thing, John Low was now beautifully prepared. In the Pater Inquiry, he managed to steer the emphasis away from the mutton to the provable causes of the terrible sickness and mortality within the 56th.

'One great cause,' he argued, 'was that the venereal disease had prevailed to a great extent before the Regiment left Bellary and that a great number of men who had been affected with the complaint and who might have done well in garrison were very much injured in their constitutions by being much exposed to wet the first six weeks of the march, particularly to their laying on the wet ground.'

It wasn't the meat that was rotten, it was the men.

Then 'there was about 150 young recruits who joined the day we left Bellary and who were therefore not seasoned to the climate, particularly the heavy dews at night'. The worst factor was 'the great quantity of Arrack which was made in the villages all round the camp and which the men procured in spite of all endeavour to prevention.' In other words, the causes were endemic in the damp conditions and in the imprudent habits of the younger men – just as they had been for the unseasoned cadets back in Tripassur.

John Low had personally posted sentries on the roads leading out of camp and put guards on the grog shops to control the sale of the fierce coconut-flower spirit. The grog merchants had to produce notes signed off by officers before they were permitted to sell. But apart from the legitimate stuff, there was bad arrack coming in from Goa. This 'Pariah Arrack', what we would call bootleg hooch, was intercepted and destroyed whenever possible, and its imbibers punished. During the period of the Dowse Field Force there were endless floggings and 74 courts-martial for drunkenness. But still the stuff kept getting in, and the men kept getting out. John remembered several instances of grass-cutters bringing in arrack concealed in bundles of hay. And the private soldiers would sneak out to the villages, sink a skinful and sleep it off in the ditch. There was no stopping them. Even Sir Charles had admitted that 'if I had tried to stop all Pariah Arrack, I might have had a court-martial perpetually sitting and might have done nothing but flog.'

So this was the reality of Sir Charles's 'between 11 and 1200 strong and in the highest degree healthy men' who had set out from Bellary in August 1812. Many of them were already infected with VD, and most of them were half-blind with dubious firewater long before they reached the treacherous damps of the high country, where, to make matters worse, they found themselves without tents or bedding because the bullock contractor had failed.

The Pater Inquiry found little difficulty in coming to the conclusion for which it had been programmed. Captain Stewart and the Commissariat were vindicated on every charge and praised for their efficiency and devotion to duty. As for the mutton, Pater was quite clear: 'Animal provisions issued to the European troops were on no occasion during the service of a quality which could have conduced to the sickness and mortality which prevailed in HM 56th Regiment.' The causes were the arrack, the venereal disease and the loss of bedding, plus the failure of the men to report themselves sick when they were first taken ill.

Just like the Grant and Dalrymple Committees, the court-martial and the Pater Inquiry had come to utterly opposite conclusions, leaving all concerned free to feel vindicated by one or the other.

The whole business had now consumed 1,000 pages of best India Office folio paper. But even this was not the end of the freakish story. For Sir Charles Burdett persisted in feeling cruelly done by. He now put in a claim for the payment of the allowances which had been withdrawn from him during the 16 months he had been under arrest. These totted up to the useful sum of 1,801 pagodas or 720 pounds 15 shillings and tenpence – roughly £40,000 in today's money.[12]

The claim reached Fort St George the following year. His Excellency contented himself with observing that such a claim was 'entirely novel', because the allowances in question had already been drawn, 'under competent authority', by other officers while Sir Charles was under arrest. Such a claim would set an unsettling precedent; anyone acquitted at a court-martial would be led to try it on and the civil authorities would be under pressure to scrutinize the independent decisions of military tribunals. So the Governor ducked the decision[13] and referred it on to the Directors in Leadenhall Street. Nearly three years later, the Directors came up with a frosty No: 'We have attentively considered the case and we can perceive no reason whatever for granting any compensation to Sir Charles Burdett'.[14] Again Burdett appealed, this time to HRH the Duke of York, the C-in-C of the whole Army. The Duke was moved enough to invite the Directors to take into consideration the hard circumstances of the case. The Court of Directors were unmoved. In fact, they 'cannot refrain from adding that the conduct of Lieutenant-Colonel Dowse in arresting Sir Charles Burdett was

THE MUTTON AND THE BARONET 171

strictly proper'. In other words, they thought that Burdett should never have been acquitted.

Even this didn't slow up the indignant baronet. There is a final weary note in the file: 'Since September 1820 the application of Sir Charles Burdett has been frequently renewed. The last official proceeding upon it bears the date of 12 March 1834.' But the answer was always the same: no compensation. For two decades, long after he had retired in 1821, Burdett continued to insist that he was being denied his deserts. He died at Colombo, unmarried, in 1839.

Did he ever have a point? Could the lack of nutrition in the thin and stringy meat have fatally weakened the resistance of the troops to their other ailments? But the 1st battalion were not the only Pompadours to suffer. A year later, the 2nd battalion lost 329 NCOs and men to sickness while in camp on manoeuvres.[15] European troops in India were catastrophically vulnerable, whatever the quality of the meat. From our vantage point two centuries later, all we can see is a long column of shivering men soaked to the skin, half of them with the clap, most of them stultified by arrack, stumbling on through the monsoon into the barren ravines of the Deccan. If we want to know what service in the Madras Army could be like at its worst, we have only to look at the saga of the baronet and the mutton. As the French say, *revenons à ces moutons*.

VII

THE PESHWA'S LAST SIGH

John Low was becalmed. He did not like it where he was and he did not know where he should try to go next. After 12 years in India he was still a lieutenant in the Commissariat at Bangalore, haggling with bullock contractors, counting tents and uniforms and inspecting scrawny sides of mutton to prevent another Burdett Affair. At his age, Arthur Wellesley had already been a colonel commanding troops in battle. Promotion in the Company's Army came at the pace of a three-legged cow. There was no leapfrogging except by influence, and all John's obvious contacts were now out of play.[1]

As a last throw, John wrote to someone he did not know at all well but who was a man whose warmth and curiosity about you made you feel he had known you for ever. Sir John Malcolm had just returned to India from England, where he had been knighted and lionized after his dashing mission to Persia (to which country he had introduced the potato, sometimes known there as 'Malcolm's plum').[2]

John confessed to Malcolm that, ever since he went up to Poona, 'I have been very desirous of being employed in some situation not in the common walks of the service' – something in the political line, as a Resident or being attached to some native prince, with all the advantages that such service might bring him. He was painfully

aware that he had done nothing much to signal him out for recommendation. 'Although I have been 12 years in India, yet I cannot
claim to have performed any service of importance.' When his contacts dropped off one by one, 'I conceived that all my prospects of
advancement in those lines of service for which I was most ambitious
were entirely at an end.' And he settled for a plodder's life on the
Commissariat, 'under the impression that promotion in it would be
much more rapid than it has proved to be.'

Depressed subalterns fanning themselves from the heat of a tropical June must have been writing such last-chance letters from all
over southern India. Most of them probably never got an answer. But
this one did. Only nine days later Malcolm replied from Madras in
his large sprawling hand, as oversized and impulsive as the rest of
him: 'My dear Sir, I have neither forgot nor lost sight of you. I have
rejoiced in your past progress and shall if I can promote your further
prospects.' Better still, 'I mean to go to Bangalore and I shall be there
on the 11th. We shall then talk over everything quietly and make an
arrangement if possible.' The letter was dated the 2nd, so it was only
a couple of days before the great Sir John would be with him. What
luck, what timing.

What a career John Malcolm had enjoyed – and enjoyed is the
word, because a rumbustious enjoyment was part of everything he
did. At the age of 15, 'Boy Malcolm', as he was long known, was an
ensign commanding sepoys on a mission to escort English prisoners
surrendered by Tipu Sultan under the Treaty of 1784. Since then, he
had led three missions to Persia and had written *A History of Persia*
which became the standard work for several generations. In his careless youth, Boy Malcolm had gambled his pay away and took years to
pay off his debts. He had suppressed two mutinies, one by his own
sepoys at Hyderabad, the other the White Mutiny, although he had
a long propaganda tussle with Sir George Barlow as to whose tactics
were ultimately responsible for the Madras officers seeing sense. He
had charmed and bargained with every native prince in south India;
the Nizam and the Peshwa each regarded him as their best friend,

and so did every sepoy, spy and stallholder. More importantly, each incoming Governor-General came instantly to rely on him. When any sticky business was bubbling up, famously the cry went 'Send Malcolm!'

The new Governor-General was no exception. There was trouble brewing in the Deccan, and when John Malcolm docked at Madras, he had scarcely time to get dressed for dinner – in fact he forgot to put on his epaulettes[3] – before Lord Moira had appointed him his agent in the Deccan and Brigadier in the force assembled down there. Which was why Malcolm was just setting off from Madras to Bangalore, then as now the chief town in Mysore, when he wrote to John.

The whole region was familiar ground to Malcolm. He had been Resident in Mysore ten years earlier. As he rode to Arcot along the bank of the river, he wrote to his wife (by now he had five children – he did nothing by halves):

> it brought a thousand associations to my mind. There was pride in the recollection of having come past and galloped over the same ground with the Duke of Wellington thirteen years ago; and there was something better and more delightful than any emotion which pride can give in having travelled it with you ten years ago.[4]

As he came over the border into the Mysore country: 'I was welcomed with horns and tom-toms, dancing girls, tax collectors, peasants and bazaar-men; in short, by high and low of every description. My vanity was not a little tickled to hear "Malcolm-Sahib" in every tongue.' Surrounded by his fan club, he rode in his palanquin into Bangalore, where he scooped up John Low as an Afghan rider scoops a head off a pole.

A week later, they were in Hyderabad, where Boy Malcolm had begun his diplomatic career. There the 48-year-old, no longer boyish but plump and stately, put up at the Resident's superb mansion. Though a little mildewed and neglected, this is still the finest British Residency in India, with its magnificent portico and Oriental gardens running down to the River Musi. The whole complex, built at the Nizam's expense, with its Mughal pavilions and classical follies, was described mockingly by Mountstuart Elphinstone as 'laid out partly in the taste of Islington & partly in that of Hindostan'. In fact, it was a happy fusion of East and West, embodying the happy if clandestine and short-lived marriage between the Resident who rebuilt it, James Kirkpatrick, and his enchanting Indian sweetheart and eventual wife, Khair un-Nissa.

The political situation was less happy. The Nizam ruled under British sufferance, entangled in a series of those degrading deals which left him drained of ultimate power but free to enjoy all of life's luxuries. Rarely has the moral change brought about by such a relationship been better described than in Malcolm's letter to his wife recording his reunion with his old friend Mah Laqa Bai Chanda, the celebrated dancing girl and poet who had dedicated her collection of verse, her *Divan,* to him when they last knew one another:

I had received several trays of fruit from this lady; she had also sent me her picture, with expressions of regard that were meant, she said, to revive pleasing recollections. The Court of Hyderabad is altered and the dance and the song no longer prevail. A moody, melancholy sovereign, degraded and dejected nobles, and the impoverished retainers of a fallen Court, offer no field for the genius of Chandah; but even yet, changed as she is by eighteen years, she maintains considerable influence, and has the lion's share of all that is spent in dissipation ... She commands the principal sets of dancing-girls, and, now that her bloom is past (she is above sixty), is the first monopolist in the market of beauty at the capital. She danced and she sang for upwards of an hour, but – I know not how it is – the fine tones, the fine acting, the faint, the recovery, the melancholy, the intoxication which she exhibited in turns, as she chanted her Hindostanee and Persian odes, did not

charm me as they were wont. After all, eighteen years do make
some difference in the appearance and feelings both of man and
woman.[5]

Thirty years later, John Low himself was to occupy this grand
Residency, and he too had to witness – and himself to engineer –
painful scenes. But this first sight of a great princely court in decline
was then a new experience to him. No less memorable was the
contrast between the decadent splendour of the Nizam's palace and
the wretched condition of his dominions. Malcolm certainly was
under no illusions: 'the people are a broken and oppressed race. I am,
indeed, disposed to believe that no country was ever more miserably
governed. What indeed can be expected when the Prince (the
Nizam) is a melancholy madman, and the Prime Minister
(Chundoo-lal) a low Hindoo who owes his power to the support of
our Government, and pays the price of subservience to our resident
for continuance in office? Where power is without pride there can
be no motive for good government.'[6]

Yet this was the very combination which Malcolm himself had
helped to shore up and administer over so many years in different
Indian principalities: the depressed and debauched prince, the servile
(and usually corrupt) minister, the wretched overtaxed peasants and
the British Resident who masked his ultimate power under a façade
of exquisite courtesy. It was the system that John Low too was so
brilliantly to operate, to question and eventually to undermine.[7]

On they rode to Poona, where the real business of the mission lay.
All at once, the sluggish routines of the Nizam's court were
exchanged for a long-distance ride of barely credible vigour.
Sometimes on horseback, sometimes in his palanquin, Malcolm and
his ADCs covered the entire distance of 364 miles in three days,
stopping only for a few minutes twice each day to eat a piece of
bread and to drink a cup of milk. The four bearers carrying the covered litter must have had aching shoulders as well as blistered feet.
For the last stage, they rode on wiry little Maratha horses sent to

meet them at the Peshwa's frontier, and they galloped 64 miles in eight hours.

Why the hurry? If the Peshwa, like the Nizam, was now little better than a toothless puppet, what was the cause of this anxiety? Why was such a great army massing on the safe ground of Hyderabad under Sir Thomas Hislop? Why was John Malcolm dashing at such a headlong gallop from one princely capital to another?

To gain any understanding of the long and perplexing story of the downfall of the Maratha Empire, any notion of Western military superiority must be discarded. Cocky young British officers certainly did entertain such notions. Back in 1803, John Malcolm had himself written to his C-in-C, the redoubtable Lord Lake, asserting that the 'British arms would meet with little opposition from even the combined efforts of the weak and discordant branches of the Maratha Empire, and one short campaign would for ever dissipate the terror with which the Indian politicians in England are accustomed to contemplate the power of the Mahratta nation.'[8] One wonders if Lord Lake ever reminded him of that 'one short campaign' after the bloody battles of Assaye and Argaum in the southern Maratha country and the battles Lake himself fought in the northern Maratha territories reaching into Hindustan, at Delhi, Agra and Laswari. Arthur Wellesley himself had fallen for the common delusion that the Marathas would be a pushover.[9] Wellesley had the grace, after the battle, to write to John Malcolm conceding that 'Their infantry is the best I have ever seen in India, excepting our own . . . I assure you that their fire was so heavy that I much doubted at one time whether I should be able to induce our troops to advance, and all agree that the battle was the fiercest that has ever been seen in India.'[10] Even after Waterloo, he stuck to the opinion that he had never been in a hotter fight than at Assaye.

As for the Battle of Argaum, Arthur managed to prevent three entire battalions of sepoys from running from the field only by forcing them to lie down (not his own trick but a good one, because it reduced their target profile while making it harder for them to keep on running). It was of Argaum that he first uttered a version of his famous words at Waterloo: 'If I had not been there, I am convinced we should have lost the day.'[11]

So why were the Maratha infantry – and their artillery, too – so much more formidable than the British had expected?[12] If the Maratha were worthy opponents, so the line went, it was only because they were officered by French and Scottish and German mercenaries. Men like General Benoit de Boigne who commanded Mahadji Sindia's army, de Boigne's successor General Perron, Colonel Hugh Sutherland, Colonel Pohlman and a dozen others.

It's a mistake, though, to imagine that the European officers taught the Maratha troops everything they knew. Long before the European officers trickled into their ranks at every level from private soldier to force commander, Maratha armies were drilling and performing complex manoeuvres, which they executed on the battlefield as well as any European regiment. They were never simply ragbag collections of *pindaris* and other nomad bands, whose only skills were in irregular guerrilla warfare. Massed infantry and organized artillery barrages were employed by the great Maratha warlord Shivaji Bhonsle (1627–80), whose equestrian statue still welcomes new arrivals at Bombay's Gateway to India and after whom the railway station and the airport are now named. For modern Hindu nationalists, Shivaji is a more stirring icon than Gandhi.[13]

Eighteenth-century Maratha infantry used both flintlocks and matchlocks, but they enjoyed a technological advantage, not because of the ignition system of their muskets but because their matchlocks had superior range and velocity. Their smaller bore and thicker barrels enabled them to use proportionally larger powder charges; hence the greater muzzle velocity and longer range, possibly greater accuracy, too,[14] of the handmade *jezail*, the long-barrelled musket which Conan Doyle tells us wounded Dr Watson in the Battle of Malwand and which Kipling tells us is so deadly:

A scrummage in a border station
A canter down some dark defile
Two thousand pounds of education
Drops to a ten-rupee jezail.

A generation after the Maratha wars, the *jezail* was still outgun-
ning the British musket, in the defiles of the Khyber and across the
plains of Afghanistan.

The Maratha artillery had its reasons for feeling superior, too. By
the first quarter of the eighteenth century, Marathas were using pre-
bagged powder charges for their cannons, so much quicker and less
dangerous than ladling in the powder as the Europeans still did.[15]
Their big guns benefited from centuries of local experience in cast-
ing temple ornaments. Maratha field pieces were cast in local
foundries, notably at Mathura near Agra, and many of them were
much lighter and more durable than European guns, because they
consisted of an inner hexagonal iron tube within a brass sleeve. Also
they were often cast in sections, to be reassembled on the battlefield – easier for carrying over hills or across rivers swollen by the
monsoon. These 'pre-fab' guns were fully operational in Maratha
armies as early as 1586. A Venetian traveller saw them in action:
'Though they were made in pieces the guns worked marvellously
well.'[16]

The Marathas had all these advantages – infinite superiority in
available manpower, a high level of military training and discipline,
and actual technological superiority in musketry and gunnery.[17] So
why did they lose? What happened in 1803 was that, as war between
Sindia and the British loomed, there was a mass exodus from his
ranks of all the European officers, not just the British ones. Sindia's
C-in-C, General Perron, discharged them all in August 1803, or
thereabouts, with a good grace and a certificate of good conduct for
what were delicately described as 'Political Reasons'. Over they all
came: Captain James Skinner, the legendary founder of Skinner's
Horse and builder of Skinner's Church in Delhi, Captain Stuart, little

George Carnegie, who wrote to his mother 'I had done my duty to my country in leaving poor Dowlet Row [Daulat Rao Sindia] when he most wanted my services ... I did not feel myself authorised (even in this just and necessary War!!!) to assist personally in the destruction of an Army, in which almost every individual was known to me.'[18] For the British, national allegiance and racial solidarity trumped military engagement. During the second week of August, Sindia's command structure began to evaporate. In Carnegie's brigade alone, there were eight battalions commanded by Britons or the sons of Britons who he said were all desperate to leave. Then the Governor-General, Richard Wellesley, Arthur's brother, rubbed it in at the end of the month by issuing a grand proclamation requiring all British subjects serving Sindia or the Raja of Bihar to relinquish their service and to report to British depots where they would be taken into the service of the Honourable Company on terms just as good as those they had received from native princes. Another proclamation issued simultaneously in Marathi made the same offer to native NCOs and sepoys.[19]

The military damage to the cause of Sindia was shattering. It was precisely because the British officers could leave only at the last possible moment that their defection (to use a modern anachronism) was so crippling. It was impossible to train a new cadre of battle commanders within a month (Wellesley's proclamation was published on August 29, 1803; the Battle of Assaye took place on September 23).

The loss of European officers was particularly calamitous for an infantry battle of that date, because the commanders, up to and including generals such as Lake and Arthur Wellesley, physically led their troops into battle. The infantry would not march on steadily towards the guns unless they saw their commanders out there in front of them. Sindia's cavalry and artillery performed very creditably in the battles that were to come, as did the defenders of his fortresses, but the infantry did not muster the almost incredible steadfastness needed to carry on walking forwards when they saw their comrades falling beside them.

Wellesley could make this handsome offer – in effect, a lifetime bribe – because he had the financial might of the East India Company behind him. The EIC's shares were a kind of global reserve currency – which native princes often held large blocks of. General Perron had a huge holding, estimated at £280,000.[20] The Company could raise cash on the money markets of the world without difficulty, so long as its own finances were thought to be in reasonable shape.

The Directors of the Company were in a constant fret about losing their AAA status and kept pressing Governors-General to be more economical. The politicians at the Board of Control were equally anxious that the Company should not forfeit its prime credit rating and have to pay more for its money. In the last resort, though, the Company could always raise the money to meet an emergency.

By contrast, the Indian rajas, though ruling over huge territories and commanding extensive natural resources and limitless manpower, were often desperately short of cash. The worst managed among them were about as credit-worthy as Greece today. When it came to an auction, ultimately the EIC could always outbid the native powers, or – which happened all too often – the native powers beggared themselves by trying to compete.

It was only when the East India Company lost its prime credit rating, as it did during Lord Auckland's disastrous Afghan War, that Britain could be made to sue for peace. For even the East India Company was not invulnerable; it was not a sovereign government issuing its own currency. And the British Government refused to bail out the Company, preferring in extremis to take it over and abolish it, as it did after the Great Mutiny of 1857. It is all too easy to write Indian history in terms of treaties and bayonets, but we must never forget the financial pressures that are weighing hard on individuals and governments most of the time. For the British, it was a tale of heat and debt.

If the rulers of the Maratha confederacy were to survive against the relentless encroachments of the British, they too had to manage

Ursula Low in the 1930s.

Captain Robert Low, returning nabob and builder of Clatto. Perhaps by David Wilkie.

Georgina Low: 'no jam on Sundays'. The book in her lap is probably devotional.

John Low, aged 15, by David Wilkie, aged 18 – 'the £5 portrait', 1804.

'Our Padre', by Captain George Francklin Atkinson, from *Curry and Rice*, 1859. Note the abandoned card table in the inner room.

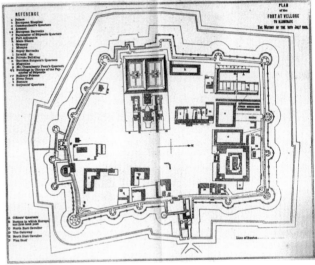

Plan of Vellore Fort at the time of the mutiny. The fives court is the little penthouse attached to the temple in the lower right corner. The Fancourts' quarters are just behind the main gate at the bottom.

The Jalakantesvara Temple, Vellore, 1816, with the fives court attached to its right. Several redcoats are watching the game from the gallery.

Blowing away from guns. The crowd of onlookers, both civil and military, would usually have been much larger.

Rollo Gillespie, by George Chinnery.

Sir George Barlow, by unknown artist: the ultimate bureaucrat.

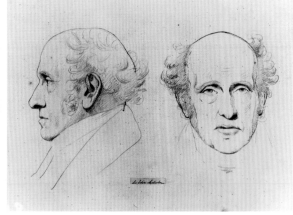

Lieutenant-General Hay Macdowall, by Sir Henry Raeburn: the ultimate swagger portrait.

Sir John Malcolm, two drawings by Francis Chantrey.

Lord Minto, by James Atkinson.

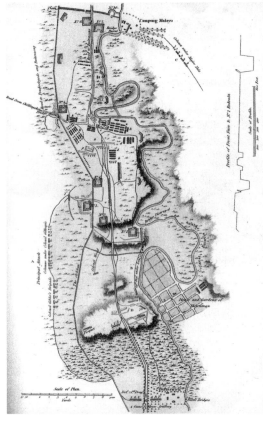

Plan of Fort Cornelis, from
Thorn's *Conquest of Java*.

Colonel Colin Mackenzie, with his native
assistants on the survey of India, by Thomas
Hickey.

Sir Stamford Raffles in his pomp, by G.F.
Joseph, about 1817.

The Peshwa is persuaded to sign the Treaty of Bassein. Unknown artist of the Company School.

Mountstuart Elphinstone, engraving after Henry William Pickersgill.

The British Residency at Hyderabad, at the time of John Low's first visit in 1817, by Robert Melville Grindlay.

The Palace of the Peshwas and Parvati Hill, where the Peshwa watched the Battle of Kirkee through his telescope and had his last sight of Poona, watercolour by Lieutenant G. Rowley.

Ghazi-ud-din Haidar entertains Lord and Lady Moira and the John Talbot Shakespears, Lucknow, 1814.

The monument to John Talbot Shakespear and his wife Amelia (Emily, née Thackeray), South Park Street Cemetery, Calcutta.

Thackeray House, Alipore, Calcutta, where the novelist was born.

A Hunting Procession near the Stone Bridge, Lucknow, 1820.

Nasir-ud-din Haidar at dinner with a British official and his lady, Company School, early 1830s. Traditionally said to show Lord and Lady William Bentinck on their visit to Lucknow in 1831, but Bentinck was elderly by then and looked it. More likely on grounds of age and hairstyle to depict John and Augusta Low, possibly at the banquet for the King's annual coronation.

Nasir-ud-din goes duck-shooting. From the illustrated edition of the scandalous *Private Life of an Eastern King.*

Partridge-fighting, from the same source. Nasir-ud-din is in European dress and surrounded by his European cronies, including the Barber of Lucknow, George Derusett, and the King's landscape gardener, John Rose Brandon.

their domestic finances prudently, and they had to act together, as reliable and loyal confederates. Almost without exception, they were incapable of doing either of these things. Which I suppose is not surprising, since they had inherited no such traditions.

If the Peshwa of Poona, or the Sindia at Gwalior, or the Holkar at Indore, or the Bhonsle of Nagpur looked back at their fathers and forefathers, what did they see? Not much but treachery, murder, especially fratricide, slaphappy extravagance and debauchery, only tempered by equally extravagant religious observances. It is hard when reading the records of these dynasties not to assume the prim and melancholy tones of the British Resident sitting in his handsome Residency down the road (usually built for him at the Raja's expense) and receiving yet more shocking reports from his numerous spies at the Palace.[21]

By the end of the eighteenth century, Maratha princes still ruled over a great swathe of central and southern India, but there was a decided end-of-the-line feeling in the air. The heir of the Sindias, Daulat Rao, Mahadji's great-nephew (1779–1827), was only 14 when Mahadji died in 1796, and he immediately fell into the clutches of a ghastly character, Sharzarao Ghatge, who had originally been sent to Sindia's court as a spy by the Peshwa's minister, the serpentine Nana Fadnavis.

Ghatge got the boy to marry his beautiful daughter and led him into a course of excess which raised eyebrows even at a Maratha court. Drunk most of the time, Ghatge had more or less exhausted his sexual powers and had recourse to 'provocatives' such as stewed goat's flesh and dishes of female white ants to revive his flagging powers. He and the Maharaja shared their favourite dancing girls and amused themselves by having men of rank or wealth who had fallen out of favour capriciously put to death, sometimes blowing them into the air fastened to rockets made of small tree trunks.[22]

More damaging to his kingdom was Daulat Rao's total incapacity for finance.[23] His opposite number at Poona, the Peshwa Baji Rao II, was a little older, 21, when he ascended the throne in the same year.

Baji Rao's background was even less promising than Daulat Rao's. His immediate predecessor, Madhavrao, had died falling from a balustrade into a marble basin below; nobody knew for sure whether he had simply lost his balance or thrown himself in a delirium or whether someone had pushed him.[24] After all, Madhavrao's father, the Peshwa before him, had been murdered by palace guards acting on the orders of his uncle, Baji Rao's father, a remarkably nasty piece of work who was then locked up in prison, where he died on the orders of the real power in the kingdom, the cadaverous vizier Nana Fadnavis, who, apart from being twice as cunning as the rest of them, had accumulated a fortune that dwarfed the wealth of his supposed master.

This unlovely crowd was scarcely likely to improve Baji Rao's character. And indeed it did not. Brought up in a prison, bewildered, lonely and suspicious, this fair, plumpish youth turned out to be the worst possible choice. The best that Sir James Mackintosh could find to say of him when he was about 30 was that 'no lady's hands, fresh from the toilet and the bath, could be more nicely clean than his uncovered feet'.[25] According to the British, Baji Rao became 'a disgusting mixture of superstitious and dissolute manners'. The time that he spared from his religious devotions and his women he devoted to a series of intrigues which almost always blew up in his face; his only constant purpose was to get hold of Nana's huge wealth and to keep the rapacious Sindia out of Poona. He betrayed everyone, including the British, so frequently that it was safer to assume that he would do the opposite of what he promised.

Hundreds of miles away in Calcutta, Richard Wellesley waited and waited for the Peshwa to make such a catastrophic error that control of his kingdom would plop softly into British hands. And it was not long before just such an opportunity, unmissable, delicious and almost painless, presented itself.

Baji Rao unintentionally provoked the neighbouring house of Holkar, now settled at Indore, into a fight. He managed to capture one of the Holkar brothers and had him dragged about the palace yard tied to the feet of an elephant, and then had him finished off. Baji Rao and his generals watched this charming spectacle from a terrace, possibly the same one that the last Peshwa had fallen to his death from.[26]

This was not simply a disgusting act. It was terminally foolish. If there was one thing in life that the remaining Holkar brother, Yashwant Rao, was now determined on, it was to destroy Baji Rao once and for all. The Maratha princes bore less resemblance to a confederacy than they did to a sack of rabid ferrets.

If it had been a British battle, we would have heard a good deal more about the terrific Battle of Poona on October 25, 1802, the day of Diwali. Baji Rao and his allies lost 5,000 men and were scattered in all directions. This was supposed to be the Peshwa's great battle, fought as it was under the wall of his capital. But the Peshwa was nowhere to be seen. He had left his Palace that morning full of confidence, with every intention of being there at the kill. Then the noise of the firing frightened him, and he ran for it.

He himself and a few thousand followers fled out into the Konkan, the coastal strip south of Poona. The rest of his troops liked the prospect of battle no better than their prince and retired back within the walls of Poona almost before a shot was fired.

The same day, the Peshwa asked for safety and protection from the Governor of Bombay, Jonathan Duncan, who responded with joyful alacrity. On December 1, by a roundabout route the Peshwa reached the Port of Mhar, where Captain Kennedy and *HMS Herculean* were ready to ferry him out of harm's way. They landed him on December 6 at the old Portuguese sea fort of Bassein (today Vasai), only a few miles north of Bombay and safely under British control. Inland, the British Resident, Barry Close, was tracking his route, and the stocky, inconspicuous Ulsterman was on hand at Bassein to offer him a deal. On December 31, he finally gave in. With Close at his elbow, he signed what became known, and by the Marathas cursed, as the Treaty of Bassein.

Its terms were as uncompromising as even Baji Rao knew they

would be. He was to be reinstalled as Peshwa but at a steep price. A British force of 6,000 troops was to be permanently stationed at Poona. Territory yielding the considerable annual revenue of 2.6 million rupees was to be ceded to the Company to pay for these troops. The Peshwa was not to have relations with any other native or European power without the knowledge and consent of the British. No alliances and no wars unless the British approved. In terms of external power, Baji Rao was now an impotent puppet, and his pretensions to be the sovereign overlord of all the Marathas were at an end.

Up in Calcutta, Wellesley was delighted. Before the treaty was signed, he had told the Secret Committee of the Court of Directors (December 24, 1802) that 'In my judgment, the confusion now prevailing among the Mahratta powers cannot terminate in any event unfavourable to the security of the Hon Company or its allies.' Not everyone was so ecstatic. James Kirkpatrick, the Resident at Hyderabad, told Wellesley bluntly that his actions would only succeed in uniting the Marathas in a great 'hostile conspiracy' against the British. Charles Grant, the high-minded Evangelical chairman of the East India Company, said of the Treaty of Bassein: 'We are chargeable with all the guilt of it, the bloodshed, miseries and devastations which it has occasioned.'[27]

Unfortunately for Wellesley, the President of the Board of Control at that moment happened to be that notorious sceptic, Lord Castlereagh. He wrote as soon as he could, pointing out that it was well known how all the other Maratha chiefs would hate this sort of subsidiary alliance which could be founded only on force. And 'so long as we are forcing, and not inviting this alliance, however for the time it may give a lustre to our authority, [it] can only embark us in difficulties from which it may be embarrassing to recede.'[28]

Castlereagh, as so often, was right but unpopular. By the time his secret letter reached Wellesley (it was not written until March 4, 1804), British forces under Wellesley had won the battles of Assaye and Argaum, and Lake had won the battles of Aligarh and Delhi and

Laswari. All these encounters had been provoked by the enduring hatred that was generated by the Treaty of Bassein.

Barry Close was made a baronet for his role in imposing the Treaty of Bassein. Then in 1810 Sir Barry went home and Mountstuart Elphinstone, aged 24, who had been Close's assistant back in 1803, succeeded him as British Resident.

Poor Peshwa! In Barry Close he had endured a pleasant but remorseless gaoler whose vigilance never let up for a minute. Close had forged the Peshwa's chains down to the last shackle, and he was alert to the slightest rattling of them. If Baji Rao sent out a *vakeel* (agent) to open communication with any other native prince, Close knew about it within the hour.

Close was almost lackadaisical compared with Elphinstone. From 1811 until his final downfall six years later, the wretched Baji Rao was in the hands of one of the most formidable, talented and eccentric colonial servants in history.

Mountstuart Elphinstone looked as if an evening breeze would blow him off his verandah. Although he was just under six foot, his stoop and his pale oval face made him seem a frailer man. His expression was sweet and mild, though his eyes would gleam when he was excited. He was an ascetic and a solitary. In his warm and diverting letters written in a flowing scrawl, he would speak teasingly of 'philandering' with Calcutta ladies, and of his weakness for dancing girls, even theoretically of marriage, but he seems never to have become deeply attached to any woman (perhaps the damage done by his early sexual adventures put him off). Nor did he much care for drink. He would occasionally take a weak port and water. He thought it preposterous to lie down to sleep on a bed, preferring merely to rest his head on his hands and go to sleep with his elbows on the table. He would shake himself out of his chair at 4am to read something by Sophocles or Anacreon, or some of the classic Persian poets, such as Hafiz and Sa'adi. He had few if any religious beliefs, and he was sternly opposed to the introduction of Christian missionaries into India. Back in England, Elphinstone caused public consternation when he professed a partiality for Pontius Pilate. The first duty of the Governor of Judaea was to maintain peace, and hence what he did was right.[29]

When John Low was staying with Elphinstone in Bombay, they took daily tête-à-tête walks together. John soon came to worship the Governor: 'I had such an admiration of Mr Elphinstone's mind & conversation that I used to strive to the utmost of my power to store up all his opinions of public men and public measures (sometimes writing down his words)', and as a result he kept a more vivid recollection of Elphinstone's remarks than of any other man he ever met.[30]

In some ways Elphinstone was farsighted, even visionary. Far from believing that education was a dangerous thing for Indians – as John Malcolm did – he believed that education was the remedy for all the ills of Indian society[31] and that after the natives had been improved by good laws and education, 'we should gradually admit them into all civil services, reserving to ourselves the military power and political control.' But that would not be the end of it. 'I do not mean to say this could go on without the press in time becoming free and the people politicians but that period would be remote, and after our expulsion, which of course would soon follow, we should leave behind a people capable of maintaining the institutions which we had formed.'[32] In 1826, a date by which British power had only just been consolidated over the whole territory of modern India, Elphinstone was already foreseeing the end of Empire – indeed, taking it for granted.

Yet in his land taxation – the central task facing any Indian administration – he was cautious and conservative, preferring to preserve the power of the landlords rather than trust too wholeheartedly in the virtue of the peasants. And crucially his officers assessed the taxable capacity of both peasant and landlord too high, and too inflexibly, taking little account of bad harvests.[33] When Elphinstone eventually left India in 1827, he was widely praised as one of the greatest of Indian statesmen. But the peasants of the Deccan did not have much to thank him for. The great Sir Bartle Frere told the Bombay Council that in many districts 'frequently as much as two-thirds of the land was waste. Villages almost deserted were frequently to be met with.'[34] Elphinstone applied himself diligently to agriculture, as he did to everything. But it is to be doubted how much he really understood of the subject – or rather whether he was simply in the grip of his masters in the East India Company who pitched their demands higher and higher, to pay for these large armies which they saw as indispensable to retaining British power.

In truth, the British were in a permanent dither about how best to raise the revenue on which their Raj depended. They began with, and never really lost, a sentimental attachment to the idea of Indian village life. As Sir Charles Metcalfe famously put it: 'The village communities are little republics, having nearly everything they want within themselves, and almost independent of any foreign relations. They seem to last where nothing else does. Dynasty after dynasty tumbles down. Revolution succeeds to revolution. Hindoo, Patan, Mughal, Mahratta, Sikh, English, are all masters in turn, but the village communities remain the same.'[35] This view was not confined to British proconsuls. Karl Marx shared it too.[36]

But at the same time, the British also dreamed of modernizing the country, of letting the bracing gusts of capitalism blow through the backwoods of their empire. Property rights needed to be entrenched in the British fashion. Creditors ought to be able to seize land in satisfaction of unpaid debts. The consequence was that the moneylenders, the hated *banias*, began to grab the revenue rights over thousands of acres, to such an extent, especially when Lord Richard Wellesley was Governor-General, that conscience-stricken British officials began to fear that 'in the landed property of the country, a very extensive and melancholy revolution has been effected.'[37]

Yet even this upheaval was not quite what it looked like because what were mostly changing hands were the rights to collect the revenue, not the actual dominion over the tilling of the land itself. By and large, beneath the often hectic market in those rights, the same sort of people were ploughing, sowing and reaping. The *banias* didn't like getting their feet muddy and for the most part stayed in the towns.

The trouble was that the immensely complex pattern of land-holding in India was not really like anything else the British had encountered, though they liked to compare it to the feudal system in their own Middle Ages. Only about a tenth of even the poorest peasants were landless serfs. Most of the rest had land rights of various sorts over a few acres. And even the rights which were whirling around mostly ended up with different members of the existing families. It was almost impossible to make neat class distinctions between landlord, tenant and labourer, because many a cultivator might be a labourer in one place, and a tenant or even a proprietor in another, or all three. This overlapping hotch-potch made it fiendishly difficult to set a reasonable tax rate.

This difficulty was compounded in areas where large tracts of land were tax exempt, *inam* as it was called – having been granted to some court favourite or for the upkeep of a temple or a mosque. Elphinstone reckoned that in some of his districts 40 or 50 per cent of the acreage was *inam* – which meant that the rest of the district had to shoulder a crippling revenue burden. The brightest British minds were continually experimenting with new systems for collecting the revenue; in the north, they swept away half the big landowners, the *taluqdars*, and collected the revenue direct from the peasants; they tried temporary settlements, and they tried permanent settlements.

But again and again the same harsh tendencies broke the surface when the British needed extra rupees to fight a war and when the peasants' ability to pay was cruelly undermined by drought, or famine or banditry – or by a change in the water table which might turn fertile country into a salty wasteland.[38]

Elphinstone was subject to recurring melancholy, which he kept at bay by riding an elephant through the night to look at waterfalls and ruined temples. Even so, 'my own world is often overhung with gloom, peopled with dismal phantoms. Even the most pleasing pictures of my imagination lead to melancholy by holding out prospects of fame, felicity and perfection – perhaps never found together by anyone, and certainly unattainable to me; and this at once takes away all interest from the pleasure within my reach, and saddens me with the idea of my own mediocrity.'[39]

His happiest moments in life had probably been riding at Wellesley's side as political agent in the great battles of 1803 (John Malcolm had been slated for this role but had fallen ill and had never got over the disappointment). Elphinstone found to his delight that he was impervious to danger. At Argaum, he and Arthur took part in the cavalry charge: 'The balls knocked up the dust under our horses' feet. I had no narrow escapes this time; and I felt quite unconcerned, never winced, nor cared how near the shot came about the worst time. And all the while I was at pains to see how the people looked, and every gentleman seemed at ease as much as if he were riding a-hunting.'[40]

Someone who was so insouciant in combat was scarcely likely to admire a character like the Peshwa, who hadn't even joined the battle. And to say that Elphinstone did not admire Baji Rao is a heroic understatement. I cannot resist quoting at length from the famous dispatch in which he sums up the Peshwa's character with a laconic panache worthy of Gibbon or Tacitus:

> The character of His Highness the Peshwa has always perplexed those who have been interested in discovering his sentiments or calculating on his conduct ... This is partly owing to the inconsistency of many of his inclinations with his ruling passion of fear, and partly to his deep dissimulation which enables him to conceal his real feelings and intentions, and to display others which are foreign to his mind. If he were less deficient in courage, he would be ambitious, imperious, inflexible and persevering; and his active propensities would probably overcome his love of ease and pleasure ...

As in all the best character sketches, Elphinstone does admit that
the Peshwa has some good points, too:

> To balance his vices, it must be admitted that the Peshwa is by no
> means deficient in abilities; that he is scrupulously just in pecu-
> niary transactions; humane when not actuated by fear or revenge;
> frugal but not parsimonious in his expenses; and at once courte-
> ous and dignified in his manners.

The trouble was that these good points were not made effective by
any sustained attention to public business:

> He is a slave to superstition: half his life is spent in fasts, prayers and
> pilgrimages. A large portion of his revenue is consumed in magi-
> cal practices, and his life is disturbed by his attention to prodigies
> and omens. His superstition imposes no restraint upon his pleas-
> ures, and the greater part of his time that is not occupied by
> religion is devoted to vicious indulgences. Though he affects great
> purity in his own person, scarcely a day passes that he does not
> spend some hours with his favourites in large assemblies of
> women, when he enjoys the coarsest buffoonery, and witnesses
> most disgusting scenes of debauchery.[41]

Notice here how Elphinstone brackets Baji Rao's religious
devotions with his sexual licence. To the puritanical sceptic, both
were equally abominable distractions from the real business of
life, which was attending to business. The contempt that springs
off the page did not, however, tempt Elphinstone to slacken his
guard. On the contrary, it was because the Peshwa was such a low
twister that he had to be watched every moment of the day and
night. All British Residents spent thousands of rupees on intelligence; they expected to be kept fully up to date with court gossip,
with the chatter of the bazaars and with all the manoeuvres of
local bandits and rival rajas. But nobody in the history of the

British Empire can have spent more on his spies than Mountstuart Elphinstone.

His spymaster, Captain James Grant, kept a careful list of all their informants and the sums paid to them. There are 174 names and the total rewards and pensions paid came to 312,500 rupees.[42]

Elphinstone had his eyes and ears everywhere – servants, pimps, whores, messengers, ministers. He may have had reason to be disgusted by the Peshwa's carry-on, but his obsessive snooping has its creepy side, too. No wonder the Peshwa used to complain that the Resident always knew what he had just had for dinner.

The knowledge of how intensely he was watched never stopped Baji Rao from repeatedly undertaking plans to break out from his humiliating dependency. Secret messages from him were repeatedly intercepted, to Holkar, to Sindia, to the Raja of Berar, the Nizam of Hyderabad. Again and again, Baji Rao had to be reminded of the terms of the Treaty of Bassein. Elphinstone enforced every clause with brutal pedantry.[43] Despite all these warnings and dressings-down, Elphinstone never believed for a second that the Peshwa had given up his ambition to regain his independence and his supremacy among the Maratha princes. Throughout the early months of 1817, the British Residents at all the Maratha courts were hearing the buzz of a fresh alliance against the British brewing among their princes.

When these reports reached Mission Control in Calcutta, they found the Governor-General in belligerent and expansive mood. Gone was the dour bean-counter who had been so keen to see the back of Stamford Raffles a couple of years earlier. Lord Moira, now upgraded to the Marquess of Hastings, had blossomed, if that is the word, into an imperial commander of Wellesley-like ambitions. He assembled not one but two grand armies, one in the north of 44,000 men and an even larger one in the Deccan, of over 70,000 men.

These huge armies were officially designed to launch a huge push against the *pindaris*. If banditry could be stamped out across central India, then it would be easier to collect revenue from farmers who would no longer be too scared to cultivate their land. That was a legitimate objective, and one calculated to satisfy the anxious accountants back in Leadenhall Street. But the confederate rajas could be forgiven for thinking that Lord Hastings's overriding intention was to come after them and to extinguish their independence once and for all.

If they had read Hastings's secret dispatches to Elphinstone of April 7 and May 17, 1817, they would have had no doubt that this was indeed Hastings's intention: 'The Peshwa must be considered to have placed himself in the condition of a public enemy of the British government.' If he did not comply with the British demands, Elphinstone was authorized to declare a state of war and direct the troops to attack His Highness's forces and reduce his territory. Baji Rao was to promise once again to renounce all connections with the other Maratha powers and formally to recognize the complete dissolution of the Maratha confederacy and any action implying that he was still the head of it. And if he refused, he was to be deposed and sent into exile somewhere a long way away. 'It would be hazardous to the new settlement to suffer a person as skilled in the art of intrigue to remain in any fort of the Dominions of the State of Poona or their vicinity.'[44]

Baji Rao protested to Elphinstone that he had no such bad intentions. Speaking in Marathi, he insisted: 'Remember that I have been connected with you from my childhood. How can you believe that with all this load of obligation to your government, I should ever have a design to make war against you. My whole body, from my head to my feet, has been nourished by the salt of the English.' He would be mad to wage war against them. Had he not witnessed the crushing defeat, time after time, of the great Maratha chiefs Holkar and Sindia? They had been forced to make peace at great sacrifice of territory and treasure. Where, he asked, were his own regular troops, his guns and his infantry?[45]

These last questions, intended rhetorically, were a mistake, because Elphinstone knew perfectly well where they were. Speaking in

Hindustani (though he understood Marathi well enough), Elphinstone riposted:

> The evidence of warlike preparation in your territories is not wanting. It is notorious that all your Jagirdars [landowning feudal lords] have been recruiting, so as to fill up their quotas for future service. Your cavalry and infantry have been increased in numbers and constantly exercised. The forts have been put into repair and fully garrisoned. Guns have been brought into the city and also teams of bullocks for moving them with an army.

And who else could these preparations be directed against but the British Government?

As a last resort, Baji Rao pleaded his own notorious cowardice: 'You are greatly misinformed. As to going to war, the idea is absurd. It is well-known that I have such a horror of the sound of guns, that whenever salutes are fired, they are not allowed to take place till after I have passed the batteries to a considerable distance.'[46] Then he hurriedly called for a silver tray of betel nut and spices and perfumes, the presentation of which, along with the usual compliments, signalled the conclusion of the interview.

Two months later, on June 18, 1817, after a lot more protesting and grumbling, Baji Rao signed a fresh treaty, the Treaty of Poona, which has been deservedly forgotten, both because it was a rehash of the Treaty of Bassein and because none of the parties believed that the Peshwa would stick to the terms for a minute longer than he had to.

Such was the stand-off when John Malcolm finally reached Poona on August 4 with John Low at his side. Malcolm was delighted to see his old friend Mountstuart.[47] The Peshwa was in camp 70 miles away (like other Maratha chiefs, his court was incurably nomadic). He had also expressed an earnest desire to see Malcolm, to unbosom his griefs. Malcolm, as always confident in his powers, was convinced that he could cheer him up. 'I am one of his earliest friends –

used to laugh with me as well as talk politics, and gave him a beautiful Arabian mare, of which he was very fond.'[48]

Malcolm had first met the Peshwa at the same time as Elphinstone, though he had not seen him for six years. The two Johns galloped eagerly over the high passes to the beautiful valley of Sitara, to the Peshwa's palace of Mahanlee where they found an immense tent full of grain and vegetables and fruit spread out for them. The next morning, they went in to see the Peshwa, whom Malcolm found looking careworn and disconsolate and obviously in need of emotional support. 'He was delighted to have an opportunity of unburdening his heart to one in whom he had such confidence. I had an interview of three hours and a half – what passed is *secret and political*, but the result was satisfactory.'[49]

Satisfactory to whom? The Peshwa had, not for the first time, managed to persuade the bluff and trusting soldier that his heart was in the right place and that he had been led astray by evil counsellors.

When Malcolm got back to Poona, he told Elphinstone that he was sure that this time the Peshwa was quite sincere in his protestations. Elphinstone refused to believe a word of it. He detailed to Sir John all the preparations for war that his spies had detected, all the secret traffic between Poona and the other Maratha capitals. The Peshwa was not now, not ever, to be trusted further than you could throw him, and the Governor-General had already determined that in all probability he would have to be thrown a very long way. John Low, hovering at his master's elbow as a good ADC should, was receiving a master class in the hardest and ever-recurring question in diplomacy: when to trust in the good faith of a third party who shares none of your own beliefs or ambitions.[50]

For the moment, though, it was Malcolm who was calling the shots in the region. He was Political Agent to the Governor-General as well as the Commander of the Third Division of the Army of the Deccan. His was likely to be the deciding influence both on the Governor-General and on the Army C-in-C, Sir Thomas Hislop. And it was quite clearly on Malcolm's recommendation that the

Fourth Division of the Army under Brigadier-General Lionel Smith was ordered to move out from Poona to the north, where it was thought to be more urgently needed.[51]

It was a mistake, with ghastly consequences, not least for the Peshwa himself, who had concluded, not unreasonably, that this was a brilliant opportunity for him to show himself a true leader of his people. As soon as Brigadier Smith and his troops had gone, the Peshwa returned to the city of Poona and immediately began preparations to attack the small remaining British garrison. By the end of October, he had 18,000 horsemen, 8,100 foot and 14 guns assembled outside Poona.[52] Brigadier Smith's division was hurriedly recalled, but too late to discourage the Peshwa, who had now taken the step, both unprecedented and bold for him, of actually joining his troops in person. It was not until November 13 that Smith reached the outskirts of Poona, and by then the decisive battle had been fought.

Just after finishing lunch, on the afternoon of November 5, Elphinstone was standing on the terrace of his Residency, a delightful bungalow known as the Sangam, surrounded by gardens full of almond, fig, apple and peach trees. The Sangam also possessed a vineyard, a stud of 40-odd Arabian and Persian horses, several elephants for state occasions, and a ruined pagoda where widows now and then could not be dissuaded from committing suttee. In the distance cornfields ran away to a range of low hills, with the city of Poona to the east. On that hot afternoon, the Resident and his assistant, the 28-year-old James Grant-Duff, could see that the hills were already covered with a mass of infantry and along all the dusty lanes streams of horsemen were trotting towards them.[53]

Almost without warning the clouds broke, and the rain and the thunder came down, and up the avenue of the Residency came a breathless, dripping messenger from the Peshwa, shouting, 'It is war!'

Elphinstone turned to Grant-Duff and said, 'I think we had better go in and tell the ladies to finish their wine.'[54]

The three women and their three children were placed in palanquins and sent on ahead with the Resident's escort, while

Elphinstone himself jumped on his horse and splashed across the river, just in time to escape being taken prisoner. That night he wrote to the Governor of Bombay. 'I beg you will excuse this scrawl, but all my writing implements, with everything I have except the clothes on my back, form part of the blaze of the Residency, which is now smoking in sight.'[55]

It was a dismal departure. There are few rewards in politics for being proved right.

But the Peshwa's triumph was short-lived, the glory of a single afternoon. The British had withdrawn their forces out of their cantonments, which seemed incapable of being defended, and moved away from Poona a few miles and camped outside a village called Kirkee. There in the late afternoon they were attacked by the great swirling sea of the Peshwa's army.

It is not a battle which has attracted huge attention because it was an inconclusive sort of victory. After a couple of hours, the Peshwa's troops were beaten off, and at eight o'clock Elphinstone agreed that the troops should return to camp. The British had 86 killed and wounded, the enemy plenty more. Neither the losses nor the ferocity of the battle seemed to entitle it to be called anything more than a sharp skirmish.

Yet Kirkee turned out to be decisive. The British had established control of Poona, and as soon as Brigadier Smith and other reinforcements came up, they never looked likely to lose it. The Peshwa could have brushed aside Kirkee as a mere preliminary skirmish and concentrated his forces (which were perhaps five times as large as the British) around Poona. He had a week's window of opportunity before Smith's return. But he did not. He withdrew them to a prudent distance.

Baji Rao himself had been at a prudent distance throughout Kirkee. He watched the battle through a telescope from an adjoining hill, the legendary Parvati Hill, with its temples dedicated to and by former Peshwas. As he took his final look back down at the city before he shut up the telescope and followed his retreating troops, he

was seeing the last he was ever to see of Poona, the equivalent of the
Moor's last sigh as he took his final look at the fabulous city of
Granada.

So the British moved back in under the leadership of Mountstuart
Elphinstone, no longer a mere adviser but the effective governor of
the Peshwa's kingdom. Elphinstone's bungalow was utterly torched,
his orchards blackened in the blaze, his great library which had
gained him the reputation of a necromancer in the bazaars completely destroyed. The natural, the only place he could conduct his
business from was the Peshwa's great wooden palace (itself to be
torched 20 years later but accidentally). And it was from there that he
wrote in his diary of March 17, 1818:

> I am lodged at the Palace, and am now seated in the Peshwa's
> closet, where our first conversations about the Jageerdars took
> place ... The Peshwa's great hall is now my reception room, and
> the place where we used to meet below is the dining-room. Poona
> when approached is unchanged in appearance; but the destruction
> of all our houses destroys every feeling of quiet and home, and the
> absence of Hindoo government occasions a void that alters the
> effect of everything. Our respect for the place is gone and the
> change is melancholy. How must the natives feel this when even
> we feel it![56]

The Peshwa still had his large army, of 15,000–20,000 men, but
from now on he was essentially on the run. It was in the running that
the Peshwa at last earns some title to our respect. It was one of the
great manhunts of history. For seven months, the length and breadth
of Maharashtra, Baji Rao ducked and dodged, and sometimes fought
and sometimes completely disappeared, so that another force had to
be whistled up to look for him. At the Battle of Coregaon, he actually led his troops on the battlefield, but mostly he led them in flight.
Colonel Valentine Blacker's history of the campaign reports that 'his
flight seemed restricted within a magic circle from which he

appeared never to be emancipated.'[57] He fled twice to the north, and twice to the south, sometimes marching hundreds of miles to reach a spot near where his forces had been defeated only a month or two earlier. Sometimes he had 10,000 men and more with him, sometimes fewer; angry young men in the villages flocked to his banner, then stole away from his camp when they saw the hard road ahead and a miserable end to the venture. But there is something strange and admirable about those months on the run. Even when the fox was run to earth, the hounds had to pause for breath. And what a suitable end this was to an empire which had originally been based on irregular horsemen roaming the wild country. The Marathas began as nomads and they ended as nomads.

But we must leave the elusive Peshwa in order to catch up with John Malcolm and his ADC. Malcolm was not a man for regrets, and as he and John Low trotted out from Poona to take up his command of the 3rd Division, I doubt whether he wondered much about what a mess he might be leaving behind.

Besides, it was such a jolly party that was trotting with him. There was John Low, who was by now almost in love with his boss, and wrote home to his mother about the great man all the time. With the party rode John's old ally in the Great Mutton War, Captain Josiah Stewart, now released like John from the tedious routines of the Commissariat in his role as Malcolm's political assistant.[58] Malcolm also had with him several guests who had come along for the ride, sons of noblemen and governors who looked forward to some good hunting, a little sketching, perhaps even a battle, for Malcolm was an irresistible piper to the young. They waded across the streams of the Nizam's dominions, while Malcolm himself splashed through them on the back of an elephant, shooting quails, hunting foxes, rabbits, anything that moved, sometimes jumping on a horse to make up time and cantering on ahead with John Low as his only companion.

Now and then they bumped into other parties of British troops. Once they saw a Bengal corps and the officers came over to pay their respects. Among them was a son of Robert Burns, 'a very fine young man'. This could have been either William Nicol Burns (1791–1872) or James Glencairn Burns (1794–1865), Burns's two surviving sons by Jean Armour, both of whom went out to India and rose to be half-colonels in the Company's Army, for all their father's dislike of imperialism.

Burke and Burns were Malcolm's favourite authors, and he seldom travelled without a volume of Burns's songs. 'We had a grand evening,' he wrote to his wife Charlotte, 'and I made him sing his father's songs.' It is a nice picture, these dust-stained Lowland Scots sitting down round the campfire with the jackals of Hyderabad baying at the moon beyond their tents and listening to the young subaltern singing 'My luve is like a red red rose' or 'Auld lang syne'[59] – though I fancy that the poet would not have cared for Malcolm's mission of suppressing the natives. John Low, too, had been brought up on Burns. His mother's brothers, John and Robert Malcolm (no relation to Sir John, as far as I know – their surname was originally spelled McColme), had had the same schoolteacher in Ayr as the poet and they had learnt French together. Who else spoke so plangently to the exiled Lowlander?

We twa hae paidl'd i' the burn,
Frae morning sun till dine;
But seas between us braid hae roar'd
Sin auld lang syne.

During the last two months of 1817 and the first four months of 1818, the Army of the Deccan was fighting three campaigns simultaneously. By assembling such a vast combined force, Lord Hastings had ensured that every Maratha potentate would feel honour bound to come out and make a show. Only the Sindia failed to turn out his troops, because Hastings, himself commanding the central division of the Grand Army, took him by surprise at Gwalior before he was ready and forced him to sign a crippling treaty.[60]

The last great campaign of November–December 1817 was
against the Holkar. Or rather it was against the Regent of Indore, the
Holkar's favourite wife/concubine, the beautiful Tulsi Bai who had
taken over when her husband became too drunk to govern. After his
early death, Tulsi ruled in the name of her 11-year-old son. She was
said to be cunning but licentious and vindictive and therefore highly
unpopular.[61]

The Regent wanted to make a deal with the British which would
restore her cash flow. But her commanders thought they had done
rather well in the last war, having suffered no great losses and having
inflicted a humiliating retreat on Colonel Monson which had
become emblematic of the fallibility of the British. They suspected
that the Regent intended to sell them out to the British, so on the
same evening, December 19, that the negotiating agents returned
from Malcolm's camp 20 miles along the river, the military commanders seized the Regent and her favourite and confined both of
them. After a hot debate, the next morning they took her out of the
tent and carried her down to the river and, in front of a huge crowd,
cut off her head and threw her body into the river.[62]

This decapitation was not exactly a recipe for a unified command
structure in the battle which was to be fought the following day. On
the other hand, the juvenile Holkar had huge forces at his command.
Colonel Blacker in his memoir of the war claims he had some
45,000 men, with 200 guns.[63]

Malcolm was itching for a fight. Although he had been in India
since he was a teenager, at the age of 48 he had seen little actual military action, and had never commanded troops in the field.[64] He had
missed Assaye, which he keenly regretted, and so was less battle-
hardened than Mountstuart Elphinstone, who was only a civilian.
Even John Low, with his 15 minutes at Fort Cornelis, could be said
to have had more experience at the sharp end. This might well be
Malcolm's last chance, and he was determined to make the most of
it.

As they came over the brow of the hill, they saw the sacred River

Sipra curling away to the north below them. The river is a symbol of purity to Hindus and hundreds of shrines line its banks. The legend is that Lord Shiva went begging for alms using the skull of Lord Brahma as his begging bowl, but found no donors. As his last chance, he went to the home of Vishnu the Preserver, but Vishnu merely showed Shiva his index finger (the equivalent, I think, of the Western two-fingered salute). The enraged Shiva cut Vishnu's fingers with his trident and the blood flowed so profusely that it overflowed the skull and became a stream, and finally a river, the Sipra.

The river had already received a fresh transfusion the day before with the blood of the lovely Tulsi Bai, but there was plenty more to come. Beyond the river and above the ravines which sloped down into it, Malcolm could see the infant Holkar's troops drawn up in line, the infantry in front along the top of the bank with 50 guns pointing straight at him and the hordes of cavalry behind. If Malcolm had any views about military strategy, they amounted pretty much to the one that Arthur Wellesley had taught – and demonstrated – down in the Deccan: 'If the rebels are really in force, let a junction be formed, and then not a moment lost in dashing at them, whatever may be their force.'[65] That always remained the orthodoxy of the British military in India: nothing was more effective than the shock-and-awe effect of charging straight at the enemy before he had time to breathe.[66]

At 10.30am, Malcolm moved forward towards the village of Mehidpur on the near side of the bend of the river. This was to distract attention from the sortie made by the Quartermaster-General Colonel Blacker down to the Sipra to look for a fording place. Blacker discovered that there was only one place to cross and that the bed of the river was so dry there that a considerable body of men could get across the long sand spit in decent formation.[67] So Malcolm went headlong at them, rattling across the shallow bed and the dry sand spit beyond and up the little ravines – and smack into the enemy's guns. Enthused by the prospect of his first proper battle in 30 years of soldiering, the Brigadier took off his hat and waved it in wild encouragement to his men as he galloped forward. Colonel Scott, a disciplinarian of the old school, spurred his horse up to Malcolm's and shouted, 'Oh! Sir John, let us not lose an age of discipline at a time like this.' Momentarily chastened, Malcolm replied meekly, 'I beg your pardon, let us be composed.' And on they rode into a relentless hailstorm of grapeshot.

Pace was the thing. When Malcolm saw one of his sepoy battalions stop and fire as they advanced, he shouted, 'My lads, there is little use in that; I think we had better give them the cold iron.'[68] This, too, was the ancestral British orthodoxy: the bayonet would always beat the bullet – vulgarly handed down to later generations by Corporal Jones in *Dad's Army*, a veteran of Omdurman, in the mantra 'They don't like it up 'em.'

The line swept on, the Holkar's infantry melted away, the guns were taken, and Malcolm's exuberance was limitless. As they swept through the Holkar's batteries to pursue the infantry, he turned to John Low who was riding at his side and cried, 'A man may get a red riband out of this!' To which another ADC, Captain Caulfield of the 5th Bengal Cavalry, retorted, 'I hope to God we may get you *safe* out of this!'[69] At one point Malcolm was so far ahead of the line that he was in danger of being shot by his own men.

For John desperately trying to keep up, this was an intense moment of living. After Malcolm returned to England, he wrote thanking his patron for all his help: 'I shall not easily forget your tall figure upon your tall horse cantering about this day eight years ago at the head of your division, amidst dust and smoke and grapeshot, surrounded by your numerous staff and friends.'[70] That was a noble aspect of war – no less real than the slither and suck of the bayonet in and out of a stranger's guts.

The battle was won, and the Sipra was flowing with more than enough blood to have quenched Lord Shiva's thirst. The cost was heavy on both sides – 3,000 of the enemy had been killed or wounded; the British had lost 800 men. Of the 1,600 men who had taken part in Malcolm's advance 400 were killed or wounded – a cruel casualty rate. Beyond all the official compliments on the victory, there was some sharp criticism of Malcolm's generalship. Lieutenant-Colonel Wilson in his *History of the Madras Army* accepted that Blacker's chosen ford was the only practicable crossing place. But he thought that the Light Artillery had been pushed on too early against superior guns and left exposed too long. The British had been lucky that the enemy had been so lacking in enterprise.[71] I cannot recall Wilson criticizing the manner of any other British *victory* with anything like such severity. Mehidpur was, if you like, 'a bad victory'. Just as well that it was to be Sir John's last as well as his first.[72]

Overjoyed by his first victory in battle, Malcolm forced the usual humiliating treaty on the young Holkar, Mulhar Rao, and his advisers, which was signed on January 6, 1818. This was becoming standard procedure, as one by one the Maratha princes were reduced to a state of humiliating dependency. What was not standard, though, was the way Malcolm personally treated Mulhar Rao.

First he bought back from the prize fund some of Mulhar Rao's captured images and ornaments and restored them to him. When he arrived at Holkar's camp at the end of February, he spoke of 'my young *ward*' and also gave the boy back his beloved baby elephant that 'danced like a dancing girl' and presented him with 'a furiously trotting little Pegu pony'. Malcolm went out hunting with the boy on the pony and the elephant. In no time, the enemies of three months earlier had come to regard Malcolm as their oldest friend. Here was a lesson in the arts of pacification, which John Low appreciated and reported back to his mother[73] with wholehearted admiration. The admiration was reciprocated by Sir John, who was never less than wholehearted. When he returned to Scotland, he paid a visit to John's parents at Clatto and told them that their son 'ranks at the head of my soldier favourites'.[74]

Even after the British had smashed the main army of the infant Holkar, there were bands of freebooters roaming the backwoods to be taken care of. Several months of pacification work lay ahead, and

John Malcolm had no hesitation in putting his young protégé in charge of one of the detachments tasked with clearing up the wild hills of northern Malwa, where the rivers spilled off the edge of the Deccan plateau and flowed down across the plains to meet the Yamuna and eventually the Ganges. These were edgelands. The 2,000 mounted robbers who had been terrorizing the district for half a century would raid the surrounding territories in turn when their rajas were not looking, sometimes pillaging the domains of Holkar or the Sindia, sometimes those of the smaller fry such as the Rajas of Kota and Dewas.[75]

Lieutenant Low had about 3,000 men, consisting of a mixed bag of native infantry, the 3rd Cavalry and a few guns. And his success was magical – perhaps because the robbers had not previously been confronted by an organized force of suppression and/or because they were totally demoralized by Holkar's defeat. Within six weeks, no less than 13 forts were either taken or surrendered, five of them being levelled to the ground by Lowforce. Once the freebooters were dispersed, they soon ran out of supplies and surrendered in small groups, giving up their horses at the same time; many of them meekly settling down to till the land – an unrewarding vocation in those barren foothills. There was one fight, at a fort called Narulla, and after an hour the entire garrison was killed or wounded. The whole operation was more or less a walkover. Lieutenant Low as the Political Assistant to the divisional commander was in charge of negotiations, but in most cases all that he had to negotiate were the terms of the surrender.[76]

But where was the main prize? For months, it looked as if the Peshwa would never be caught. His mazy motions up, down and around the whole territory of the Marathas were so infernally difficult to keep up with. Brigadier-General Smith, who did more of the pursuing than any other commander, confessed a reluctant admiration for Baji Rao in this last phase of his otherwise disastrous reign: 'Not a soul in his camp knows his direction of march till he is in motion himself.'[77] If only he had been as ingenious and indefatigable in governing as he was in flight.

The Peshwa was still at large as the hot weather of 1818 began. All the other Maratha princes, large and small, were now tied down by British treaties and British occupying forces. The only prince left on the loose was their supreme lord – though the nature of that supremacy was as elusive as the man himself.

At the end of March, the Peshwa was encamped on the River Wardha with 20,000 horsemen. Brigadier-General Doveton set out from Jalna at a gallop on April 6 to catch him. The Peshwa retreated and ran slap into Colonel Adams coming the other way at a place called Peepulcote, but somehow once again the Peshwa got away, leaving his camels and his treasure behind. Adams's men were knackered, and Doveton took up the chase. After marching 80 miles in three days, to Omulkair, Doveton's posse were knackered, too, and had outrun their supplies, so that although the Peshwa had passed through the place at 3am that day, he got away once more, leaving a trail of dead and dying bullocks. By the time Doveton resumed the pursuit, the Peshwa was 150 miles away, the far side of the Tapti River and up in the hills round Asirgarh.

By now he had only about 5,000 horsemen and 4,000 infantry with him. The net was at last closing. Doveton was coming up from the south, the 1st/14th and part of the Russell Brigade were coming down from the north. Malcolm had his battalions spread out along the River Nerbudda (today Narmuda) and was bringing troops in from the north-east and the north-west. The Peshwa was as nearly surrounded as was possible in the wild ravines and jungles of these badlands.[78]

Malcolm had determined that Baji Rao must be persuaded to surrender himself. Even now there was no certainty of catching him. The Peshwa had slipped through the British cordon too many times before. He was still capable of running on for months, linking up with the still unconquered Sindia, starting a fresh war, keeping the entire country in uproar. He must be made to understand that his position was hopeless.

Late on May 17, the Peshwa's negotiator, Anand Rao Jeswant,

came into Malcolm's tent. They spent most of the night talking. It was not a happy meeting. Anand Rao began by expressing his master's regrets for the war. Bygones could surely now be bygones, the Peshwa could now return to Poona, everything could now be as it was before and their old friendship could begin again. No, said Sir John, Baji Rao could never return, not even as a nominal sovereign under British guidance.

'But His Highness regards you as his oldest friend. Surely you will not desert him now in his hour of need?'

'That friendship was disregarded when it might have saved,' Sir John returned tartly. 'I warned him of his danger but my advice was thrown away. I shall still, however, rejoice to be the instrument of saving him from total ruin. All opposition is now fruitless. Let him throw himself upon the bounty of the British government, and he will save himself, his family and his adherents, from total destruction.'[79]

The emissary, seeing he was getting nowhere, eventually abandoned this line. Would Sir John come and visit the Peshwa in his camp and they could talk everything over? No, Sir John would not. That would have looked as if he was pleading with the Peshwa, instead of issuing an ultimatum to him. And, in any case, he needed Baji Rao to move quite a bit closer to his camp, because the Peshwa's present position was just inside Sindia's dominions and dangerously close to the fortress of Asirgarh which was still held by Sindia's allies. Malcolm needed to entice him out on to more neutral ground.

The officer whom Sir John chose for the delicate task of persuading the Peshwa to fling himself upon the mercy of the British was Lieutenant John Low of the Madras Army. At the age of 29, he was to bring the Third and final Anglo-Maratha War to a tidy end and fill in the last blank in British dominion over central India. This was his first great career-defining moment.

Malcolm knew from the bitter experience of Sir George Barlow and the White Mutiny what happened if you went on a mission without clear written instructions. The brief he gave John could not be more explicit. He was to find out what sort of condition Baji Rao was in and to hasten him towards Malcolm's camp and keep him away from Asirgarh and Sindia country. The Peshwa's advance to Malcolm's camp 'will place him in a position from which he cannot retreat but as a fugitive'. John was also to tell Baji Rao straight away that he was not empowered to negotiate, except to repeat the terms that Malcolm had already listed to Anand Rao Jeswant: surrender, deposition and exile.[80]

Malcolm wrote to his wife on May 28: 'Look at the date and think of me in a murky jungle, in rather an old tent, with the thermometer above 120 degrees, a terrible land wind blowing; but on the other hand, thank God, I am well, and that the grilling I am undergoing, with many fine fellows, in this part of the world, is likely to terminate the war.'[81]

Captain Low (he had just gone up in the world, as the dignity of his mission demanded) was already trotting up the Rakora Ghat and over 12 or 13 miles of mountainous wasteland. On his march, he fired off a warning letter to Baji Rao to let him know that he was now surrounded and would be attacked immediately unless he came into Malcolm's camp.

'I must warn you distinctly that there is not one moment to lose. God forbid, if your professions really are sincere, that you should neglect this warning and be attacked. What more need I say?'

A grim warning with a hint of melodrama. Not a bad effort for a newly promoted captain.

About 3pm on May 29, John had a message that Baji Rao was ready to see him at a village called Bori. They met on the verandah of a house in the village after a dinner that the Peshwa insisted on serving his British friends.

Baji Rao began with a long speech claiming that the war had arisen 'not from any hostile feelings on my part but by the advice of evil counsellors and by a variety of unlucky misconceptions'. This was nonsense, of course; the only unlucky misconception was Baji Rao's illusion that, once Brigadier Smith's troops had been withdrawn, it would be easy to drive the British out of Poona for good.

John was not one for wasting time in futile argument. 'What Your Highness has said regarding the manner in which the war had been brought on could be very easily refuted, but our time is very precious on account of the advance of our troops. Sir John has shown his true friendship by sending me to meet you and prevent you suffering by the attacks of other forces, if only you will sincerely accept the terms offered.'

'Yes, yes, he is a true friend.'

'Your *Vakeel* has, I hope, distinctly explained that your further residence in the Deccan cannot be permitted.'

The Peshwa looked distraught, on the edge of tears. 'Yes, he did mention the circumstance to me, but I know too much of the greatness and goodness of the Company's government to believe that it could come to any such resolution. I am prepared to lose 10 or 12 annas in the rupee, but I can never believe that the Company would think of taking the whole of my Dominion. To reside anywhere else than Poona would bring eternal disgrace upon me and render my life not worth having. I have many things to say to General Malcolm that will make him think very differently.'

'I will not encourage hopes that cannot be realized.'

John now presses him to fix the next day for the meeting with General Malcolm. But Baji Rao says that it is much too soon, there are so many arrangements to make, but he has no objection to the following day (May 31), provided that the British forces would retire to a proper distance.

'Sir John will meet you anywhere at any hour of the day, but the retirement of our forces is quite unnecessary and Your Highness can have no good reason for requesting it.'

'Oh please, Captain Low, can they not retire one or two marches? Let Sir John remain with his escort at Metawal, but let the remaining body of his force retire one march towards the Nerbudda, let General Doveton recross the Tapti and prevent Colonel Russell from advancing from Charwa, and grant me ten days' cessation if I should not agree to the terms and I will then consent to meet General Malcolm on the 31st May.'

This was a shameless attempt to persuade the British troops to ease their grip, allowing the Peshwa ten days to slip off in any direction he fancied. Captain Low was having none of it.

'These demands are quite unreasonable, and Your Highness making them shows that you are totally insincere. If you do not immediately withdraw these extravagant demands, I will quit Your Highness's camp and you will be immediately attacked by our troops.'

The Peshwa then asked leave to retire to consult with his friends. For the next hour or so, John Low was left alone in the room, while messengers came and went bringing trifling alterations to the Peshwa's extravagant demands. John sat there, outwardly impassive, devoured by uncertainty but fortified by the brutal simplicity of his instructions.

The to-ing and fro-ing eventually exhausted his patience and he demanded that the Peshwa himself return and finish off the conversation. At last, Baji Rao came back into the room, visibly drooping and depressed in spirits.

'I only made those requests to you, Captain Low, on the particular advice of my friends. Your refusing consent to them has greatly disappointed them. It was not through fear of my own safety that I asked you. It is only that my friends would be alarmed if I met Sir John other than at a considerable distance from any body of your troops, who are always suspected, however unjustly, by my men.'

John Low could see how ridiculous this claim was that the fear of treachery was not in his own mind but in that of his followers. The great Peshwa was shaking uncontrollably. Once again John guaranteed his personal safety at the meeting and promised that if he did not agree to the terms he would be allowed sufficient time to rejoin his camp before the British attacked.

'Place your hand on my head, Captain Low.'

John did so.

'And now place your hand on your sword and declare that you will strictly fulfil these promises?'

'I solemnly promise.'

After nearly four hours, the deal was sealed – which did not stop Baji Rao sending a message the next day, again demanding that the troops should be withdrawn at least a day's march during the meeting and that if he did not agree to the terms there should be a cessation of hostilities for eight days. John turned these demands down flat again and repeated the ultimatum. This time the *vakeels* finally returned with the Peshwa's consent to the original terms.[82]

Now the tears of the Peshwa were shed all over again, this time to John Malcolm. They met in a little tent just outside the village of Keiree. The Peshwa was so dejected that to start with he could hardly utter the usual compliments.

'I did not seek the war, Sir John, I did not ask to be treated like an enemy by a government that has been our friend and protector for two generations. I deserve pity, not hatred. My flatterers have turned away from me, my old allies have shrunk from their allegiance, even my family have forgotten the ties of blood. I can turn only to you to take pity on my fallen state.'[83]

There were big tears in his dark eyes. Malcolm, who was never slow to blub himself, was rather moved. But he had to press on:

'There are periods in the lives of men,' he said, 'when great sacrifices are demanded of them. The tribe to which Your Highness belongs has been celebrated in all ages for its courage. Brahmin women have burnt upon the funeral piles of their husbands. Men have thrown themselves from precipices to propitiate the deity for themselves, or to avert misfortune from their families. You are called upon for no such effort. The sacrifice demanded from you is, in fact, only the resignation of a power which you do not possess, and which you can never hope to regain; and your abandonment of a country which has been the scene of your misfortunes. This is all that you sacrifice; and in return you are offered a safe asylum, a liberal provision for yourself and such of the most respectable of your adherents as have been involved in your ruin.'[84]

The Peshwa assented readily, but he was still squirming, still pleading for more time, looking for a chink of light in the gloom. As long as they were talking, the Peshwa felt he had a chance. Could they not meet again for one last meeting? But Sir John was implacable. That evening, he would send Baji Rao the British Government's final terms. He had 24 hours to accept them. Still Baji Rao would not let him go.

'Please, Sir John, I will tell you a secret that nobody must know. I no longer have any power over my troops. Every moment I fear open disobedience, even from my oldest adherents. Only in your presence I am secure of my liberty and life.'[85]

Even this was a pretence. He had already sent most of his property into Asirgarh Fort, which was commanded by a Sindia loyalist. Even now it was hard to be sure that the Peshwa would not make another run for it.

Malcolm's terms were generous: the exile in Benares or any other sacred place in Hindustan that the Governor-General fixed for his residence, that was hard to swallow, but the annual pension that Malcolm promised him – not less than 800,000 rupees per annum, £80,000 and something around £5 million in modern money – that was something to goggle at, and indeed the Governor-General himself goggled at it a good deal when Malcolm reported the promise he had given.

Sir John always remembered June 2, 1818, as the most anxious day he had ever spent (although he had said the same of his stand-off with the White Mutineers of Masulipatam). A little thing could turn the scale in favour of war. The massacre of the Peshwa's army would follow, and that might well provoke one last great fight with Sindia – 'I never had such a task, and I trust that I never shall again,' he told his wife.[86]

No word came. At 6am the next morning, Malcolm and Low set

out for the Peshwa's camp. By 9am, they were at the foothill where the camp was pitched. One of the Peshwa's leading agents was seen galloping towards them and was about to dismount when Malcolm stopped him in his stirrups.

'Is your master coming?'

'Oh, it is an unlucky day,' the horseman groaned.

'It will be an unlucky day for the Peshwa if he is not here within two hours.'

Malcolm sent John Low on ahead to hurry up the meeting, and by 10am, there was the Peshwa, disconsolate, blaming everyone else but himself, but safely in British custody. It was all over.

Then all at once, with that inconstancy of mood which was the despair of everyone who had known him, the Peshwa unaccountably cheered up.

'I am delighted to see you happier,' Malcolm said, and they laughed and joked as they had years before. When Sir John suppressed a mutiny among his followers a week later, the Peshwa called him the saviour of his honour and declared that he would, for the remainder of his days, be guided in everything by the advice of his preserver. The moment the rains stopped, he was ready to set off for Hindustan with no more than four or five hundred of his more respectable followers.[87] Who better to escort him into exile than the man who had brought him into Malcolm's camp, Captain John Low?

On August 15, 1818, John Low took over the guardianship of the last Peshwa, for such he now was. And with many tears shed, the two of them crossed the Nerbudda River and into Hindustan, where troops of the Bengal Army took over the escort duties. John Malcolm said his goodbyes, returning to pursue a long and tetchy argument with the Honourable Company about whether Baji Rao's pension was not indecently large.

The last Anglo–Maratha War was finally finished, and the last piece in the British jigsaw was filled in. Malcolm wrote to Low on his road north in high good humour: 'I am *credulous fool enough* to believe the contest over, at least upon the large scale, and that with the exception of a few Zingarees [gipsy bandits] we shall have a quiet year of it.'[88]

John Low had deposed his first king, but his troubles were only just beginning. He was in effect running a large, slow-moving mobile gaol. Baji Rao's moods switched from one moment to the next: despair, self-pity and indignation could change in a minute to puppyish affection and even gratitude. For the first few weeks, John Low was in mortal terror that he would wake one morning and Baji Rao would have escaped in the night and he, John, would be finished, known for ever as the man who let the Peshwa get away. He wouldn't really feel safe until he had him tucked up the far side of the Yamuna, in the territory between that river and the Ganges known as the Doab. 'Once there,' he wrote to Elphinstone on October 30, 'I shall feel pretty easy respecting his running off – but he may nevertheless be the unseen cause of a good deal of trouble in your quarter long after that.'[89]

In fact, he complained the whole way on their journey north to Hindustan, and John soon acquired the gruff and menacing manners of a professional gaoler, warning that, if Baji Rao tried to keep up any contact with his old retainers in Poona, he would forfeit all his privileges. The plan had originally been to take the ex-Peshwa to Benares. But that city was the pilgrimage centre of the Hindu world. All sorts of trouble might brew if Baji Rao was allowed to become the King Across the Ganges. A less conspicuous station, but also on a sacred river, was settled on: Bithur, a small town just outside Cawnpore. To start with, Baji Rao objected to the Governor-General's choice: the climate was notoriously bad there and, as a good Brahmin, he would have to take his bath in the river every morning, which would certainly injure his health – a complaint which nicely married piety and hypochondria. Hastings dismissed the objection as frivolous.

At the time of his surrender, the Peshwa had about 3–4,000 horsemen and 2–3,000 infantry in his camp, of whom 1,200 were Arab mercenaries. By the time he was settled at Bithur, he had only about

600 horse and 350 foot, besides a flock of camp followers and Brahmin priests. He was a querulous and gloomy prisoner who refused to engage in any serious discussion about his powers over his followers or about anything else much. 'Surely the Governor-General would not degrade me by taking from me what little power I have left.'

Most of Baji Rao's time was spent in religious ceremonies and judging minor cases of thefts and quarrels among his followers. He went on pilgrimages to Mathura and Benares. Suspicious minds feared that these pilgrimages concealed a long-term plan to gather followers for a comeback. But John Low, who saw him the whole time, thought he was too dispirited and disorganized for any such coherent effort. Like most fallen kings, Baji Rao was more pre-occupied with his royal dignity. He urgently appealed to the Governor-General that he might be granted two guns for firing on ceremonial occasions. The Governor-General agreed, provided that the ammunition be kept outside the cantonment. The guns in question had been discarded by the British Army and were so worm-eaten that a man was killed trying to load one of them.

Baji Rao was eager to visit the temples at Cawnpore and to pay his devotions on the banks of the Ganges. But he insisted on a salute of cannon there and would prefer not to go if he could not have one. John had to apply to Calcutta for permission to grant him even this concession, pointing out that Sir John Malcolm had paraded his whole force with flags unfurled and music playing to greet the Peshwa at his camp and denied him a salute only because the guns were loaded with grape at the time. 'I think that, fallen as the con-dition in which Baji Rao is deservedly placed, it is still good policy to keep him in good humour in such little matters, especially as they occur so seldom and cost us so little.'[90]

But the ex-Peshwa still hankered for his lost domains. When Mr Grant, a devious old rascal who was Collector of Customs at Cawnpore, told his aides that he had powerful friends in Calcutta who could restore Baji Rao to part of his old lands in return for 20,000 rupees up front with a larger 'success fee' to follow, Baji Rao jumped at it. John Low was away from Bithur at the time, recovering in Cawnpore from a severe liver complaint. When he discovered the intrigue on his return, he compelled Grant to pay all the money back and told Baji Rao that he had zero chance of ever seeing the Deccan again. But he did not report the affair to the Governor-General, preferring to keep it secret in order not to ruin Grant, who was 70 years old and had respected relatives all over India. This clemency very nearly ruined John's own career. Eleven years later, in 1832, he was still having to justify himself to the then Governor-General, Lord William Bentinck, because poison-pen letters were putting it about that Captain Low had hushed up the business because he was in on the plot or at best was 'of too easy a disposition' for the Residency at Lucknow. Under the stress of these accusations, John told Bentinck that he knew what Iago meant: 'Trifles, light as air, are to the jealous confirmations strong as proofs of holy writ.'[91] Gossip was honeydew for bored and lonely officers in India, but it could drive the victim to drink or suicide, as well as destroy his hope of preferment.

Even if Baji Rao had no hope of ever seeing his homeland again, he did not retreat into solitude. He built a handsome country house at Bithur, as well as temples at Bithur and Benares. He entertained visiting Europeans in style as well as local nobility. He also found time from his devotions to marry five times more during his years at Bithur. His exile was a long one – and thus for the East India Company very costly. He lived by the Ganges for no less than 33 years, dying only in 1851. As Sir John Kaye wryly remarked, 'annuitants are proverbially long-lived.'[92] As Elphinstone had noted, the Peshwa was relatively frugal in his habits. Those 800,000 rupees a year mounted up, so that, laughably, the ex-Peshwa was soon lending the East India Company some of their own money: his indispensable aide, Ramchandra Pant, arranged a loan of 300,000 rupees and two years later a further loan of 300,000 rupees, for which Ramchandra received a handsome commission from the British Government.[93]

The Peshwa's pension was to come back to haunt the East India Company. In fact, in a peculiar way it was indirectly to contribute to the tragic and violent events that precipitated the Company's end.

John Low's tact and consideration were generally agreed to have eased the pangs of the Peshwa's exile. His own solitude was eased by having his younger brother William, a lieutenant in the Madras Army who had also caught John Malcolm's eye, come up to Bithur to serve as his assistant. But a gaoler's life is not an inspiriting one, and ironically it was not Baji Rao's health that was broken by the climate at Bithur but his gaoler's.

John had been at Bithur for three years when he completely collapsed; both his liver and his lungs were badly affected, and he caught any epidemic fever that was going around. Even riding into Cawnpore and back the same day – a distance of only ten miles – completely knocked him out.

So he took the all too well established route to the Cape of Good Hope and on to Saint Helena. It is a curious thought that, while Napoleon was exiled to that island because it was just about the remotest place on earth, for the servants of the British Raj it was a maritime Clapham Junction where ships regularly called and you could get your mail answered and where invalids from India inhaled the reviving sea breezes. John, however, concurred with Napoleon in finding it a dismal spot where there were no decent walks to be had for a bronchial patient, except in the few fields round Longwood. Napoleon had died in May the preceding year, and John felt that the weather might carry him off, too, writing to his mother that 'it has been the wettest season that has ever been known on this island during the recollection of the oldest man.'[94]

He moved back to the Cape, which was better. By January 1823, he was enjoying 'gig exercise', though still too poorly to dine out (in any case, he confessed that he preferred a cup of tea and a book in his bungalow). His letters reflect the uselessness of most treatment of the day: 'I now get on almost entirely without medicine and the only bleeding I have is from leeches, a great change for the better from the large blisters and copious bleedings that I used to have.'[95] By May that year, he thought he was well enough to return to India by stages, stopping off at the Isle de France (Mauritius) where he expected to enjoy the same climate as at the Cape of Good Hope. But when he got off the *Anson* at Port St Louis, he encountered a steamy heat which sent him into such a relapse that he couldn't move for a year. He would have returned to the Cape, but the ship on which he had planned to travel was destroyed in a hurricane. So he moved across to the highlands of Réunion, where he finally managed to get better. And in October 1824 he reached Mangalore. After a full two years on leave, the prospect of returning to Bithur filled him with dread. He delayed the moment by spending four months at Bombay as the guest of Mountstuart Elphinstone, for whom he conceived an affection and veneration equal to his feelings for John Malcolm.[96]

By now he was determined to get away from the Peshwa for good. As he put it to Elphinstone during the hot season of 1825: 'I intend asking Lord Amherst [who had just succeeded Hastings as Governor-General] for some other appointment having heartily tired of watching Rogues, Black and White, on 1500 rupees a month.' If Amherst wouldn't promote him, which he thought likely, 'I shall have a life of total seclusion for a couple of years, so as to save almost all I earn and go home on furlough.'[97]

Saving money and getting home – these were the two things by now that chiefly occupied his thoughts.[98] It was the classic Indian mid-life crisis, one that occupied the mind of many a 37-year-old captain in the Company's service. Debt and homesickness – the two alternating nightmares, the twin jackals barking outside the tent.

Far from clambering towards the solvent uplands of middle age, John was still sinking. He was already in debt to Shotton and Malcolm, the Bombay bankers, and he did not dare to approach them for a further loan because he had no security to offer. Now he turned to Mountstuart Elphinstone: 'I don't know the precise amount of the bills against me here, but all will be more than covered if you will give me a note to your agents desiring them to hold Two Thousand rupees at my disposal.'[99] This loan was to cause John the most exquisite embarrassment. For two years, the 2,000 rupees remained outstanding. And when he finally managed to pay it off, he recalled the agony of a visit to Elphinstone at Bombay when he did not say a word about it because it would look as if he was pleading for an extension if he did. '*I did not forget it, but I could not pay it!*'[100] In the same letter he deplores his 'former extravagance' and laments that 'I have done nothing for the last 10 years but annually get worse as to my ultimate prosperity in money matters.'

In fact, he was not so much extravagant as open-handed. As soon as any cash came his way, he was inclined to send a handsome draft off to his family; 50 pounds to his sister Charlotte on her second marriage;[101] 'some little pocket money' for the feckless Henry, in fact 50 guineas;[102] and regularly over the years £200 or £250 to his mother.[103] John's mother repeatedly urges him not to sacrifice his health to his determination to pay off his debts: 'Dearest John, weigh this matter well, and do not let any consideration of money matters affect you, and if the answer is go to Europe, then I pray you earnestly set off for Europe, and oh! May God grant a happy issue.'[104] Susan Low was full of Scots canniness, but she was full of love, too. She ends a letter to him from Clatto in 1822 (she had not seen him for 17 years): 'Adieu, my dearest John, you are our first thought when we wake and our last before we sleep; what is very extraordinary to me I have never seen you in my dreams, which is a proof we do not dream of the things we think most of.'[105]

His mother's letters tugged him both ways: to return home on the next boat but also to stick it out until he had earned enough to pay off both his debts in India and the heavy mortgages on Clatto.

Suddenly these encumbrances grew a great deal worse. He explained to Elphinstone that his father had run out of money and was obliged in 1824 to sell about two-thirds of the Clatto estate to pay off his debts and leave a small holding round Clatto House for John to inherit and Susan to have the life interest in. When the old

Captain died in 1825, he had even a little money 'which in a unlucky moment he invested in a bank.'[106]

This was the Fife Banking Company. It was set up by 30 or 40 gentlemen in the Cupar neighbourhood to provide working capital for the farmers of the district and later for the fishermen and linen manufacturers of the coast. Alas, the gentlemen of Cupar were all innocents, not least Captain Robert Low. Mr Scott-Moncrieff, the joint agent for the Royal Bank of Scotland in Glasgow, sourly commented: 'I know of none in that quarter that has either money or sense to conduct a bank.'[107]

The condition of all the shares in the Fife Banking Company was that landed property should be placed as security for the value of each share, which, as John Low reflected bitterly, was why 'the said Bank was always considered so *good*! – so it was for those who had money laying in it, for they will all be paid by the sale (if requisite) of some 30 or 40 gentlemen's property.'[108] The country gentlemen were exposed to unlimited liability for the bank's debts. 'The holders of these shares were all then completely taken in – the Cashier was idle or unfit and his Deputy an accomplished villain who contrived to throw dust into the eyes of the proprietors for several years and to rob them of their money.'

John Low speaks with understandable rancour. But historians confirm that this was nothing less than the truth. George Aitken, a local Writer to the Signet, had his hands full with his law business, and Ebenezer Anderson, his deputy and successor, was a small-town Bernie Madoff, who kept his shareholders sweet by declaring juicy dividends of 5 per cent or more, year after year, and never once balanced the books. Worse still, the unreliable Henry Low was an active partner in the bank and abetted Ebenezer in his wilder speculations. In fact, that was the occasion of Henry's first bankruptcy and his flight to Australia.[109]

The bank finally closed its door on December 21, 1825, with £37,000 of notes in issue and £110,000 in deposits. The trustees had Ebenezer Anderson clapped in jail for embezzlement, but his cronies managed to spring him, although some £60,000 was still missing from the bank. Eventually Ebenezer was 'put to the horn' – a picturesque medieval procedure which involved the blowing of a horn at all the Edinburgh markets, and the debtor being declared an outlaw. Ebenezer is believed to have fled to America, leaving John Low to field the liabilities on his father's two shares – which involved a down payment of £4,000 with further heavy calls over the years. If ever there had been any question of John coming home, there wasn't now. 'This unexpected mishap, added to my own former extravagance, will fix me, I fear, for the next 7 or 8 years in India.'[110] Old Hugh Cleghorn believed that the financial catastrophe had accelerated Robert's death, and he understood that Clatto would have to be sold as a consequence.

The only hope of salvation for John lay in promotion, but to have any hope of that he needed to show himself in person at Mission Control in Calcutta. In John's fragile state of health (he still suffered recurring fevers), he did not fancy bumping across country in a series of *daks*. So he took the long way round, sailing on the *Mermaid* from Bombay to Calcutta. And it is from there that he writes to Elphinstone in unabashed joy that he has collared a new job: British Resident at Jaipur.[111]

In his triumph, he cannot resist describing to his old friend the total shambles that he found at the heart of Empire. 'I should not have succeeded had I not been on the spot.' He had to show Mr Secretary Swinton the records of his own office to show him that the three other fancied officers in the Political Department were 'all much junior to me!' including 'Slaughter' Macdonald who was hotly fancied because he had been recommended from home to Lord Amherst.[112] In a section of the letter marked PRIVATE in big letters, John Low describes a running catfight. The Governor-General's supporters complained that they had no assistance at all from the Commander-in-Chief, whose supporters for their part complained of the inefficiency of His Lordship. 'Swinton and Casement are both disliked, and Sir Archibald Campbell absolutely *detested* by both

King's and Company's service.' Sir Edward Paget, the C-in-C, had pretty much given up, 'since he has been in daily expectations of being relieved by Lord Combermere' – which he was. Not that Lord Combermere was thought to be any great shakes. When he was chosen by the Duke of Wellington, someone said: 'But we have always understood that your Grace thought Lord Combermere a fool.' 'So he is and a d–d fool, but he can take Rangoon.'[113]

As for the Governor-General himself, although John was grateful to him for his kindness, he could not help reporting to Elphinstone that 'it is really *quite common* here to mention him as a *mere cipher* in the Government, and people give him all sorts of ludicrous names' – which John thought undeserved, 'though I don't mean to go to the other extreme by saying that I consider him well fitted for his present situation.' John Malcolm could not resist writing to Lord Amherst a few months later to inform him that he was being compared to 'the person who brought the blue flies into the butcher's shop.'[114]

Before setting off for Jaipur, John went back to Bithur to clear up and to take his leave of the Peshwa. It was an unexpectedly touching farewell. They had, after all, been together, off and on, for seven years. John had performed the mechanics of his deposition, had escorted him into exile and had been his chief warder. Yet Baji Rao now saw him as his last friend, the only one who had seen him in the old days. Now as a memento and a token of gratitude, he wanted to give John a ceremonial robe, a *khilat*, worth 4–5,000 rupees.[115] Under Company rules, John had to refuse, but tactfully suggested that his refusal might be delayed until he was permanently appointed to Jaipur.

In return, John had promised a far more modest gift, a mere toy, though it was the must-have toy of the moment: a kaleidoscope. The gadget had been patented by a Scottish inventor, Sir David Brewster, only in 1817, but it had caught on in a flash: within three months, 200,000 kaleidoscopes were sold in London and Paris. John thought it was just the sort of thing that Baji Rao would love, and he had asked his mother to get one. Now four years later, 'I at last had an opportunity of delivering it to him myself, and he was much pleased, not so much at the thing in itself, for he had already seen one, but he is very much attached to me, and finding that my mother even turned her thoughts to him in his downfall was most gratifying, he said, to his feelings.

'He even shed tears, and when taking leave of me he again alluded to it, saying that he had received such kindness from me as he could never forget, and that he prayed the Supreme Being to make me a *Bramin* in the next change in *this world*, and that I should in due time be absorbed in the Deity!!'[116]

As John Low watched the Peshwa playing with his kaleidoscope, he was witnessing the melancholy downside of British rule. Malcolm had seen it on his return to Hyderabad, Elphinstone on his return to Poona. Now John Low was going through the same experience as he left Bithur. This was not the last time he was to experience it.

VIII

AUGUSTA AND JOHN

S he was the eldest of the four children looking out over the blue
water. Augusta Shakespear was two years older than her brother
George and their first cousin William Makepeace Thackeray, who
were both five. Her brother Richmond was a year younger than the
other boys. They were standing at the top of the steps leading down
to the quayside. Out in the middle of the river they could see the
masts of the *Prince Regent*, the East Indiaman that was going to take
them to England. The ship was 953 tons, she had three decks and
was 149 feet long and 38 feet wide, she was due to sail on December
17, 1817, the captain was called Thomas H. Harris and the journey
would take four and a half months. But none of these details can
have much interested Augusta, who was old enough to grasp the terrible fact: that she was about to say goodbye to her parents and she
might never see them again (she didn't). English parents in Calcutta
usually sent their children 'home' when they were younger than
Augusta, too young to have a sense of the years of solitude ahead of
them.

In later life, after he had become famous, William Makepeace
Thackeray wrote that 'boy or man, I have never been able to bear the
sight of people parting from their children.'[1] He recalled, too, that:

In one of the stories by the present writer a man is described tottering 'up the steps of the ghaut', having just parted with his
child, whom he is despatching to England from India. I wrote this,
remembering in long long distant days, such a ghaut, or river-stair,
at Calcutta; and a day when, down those steps, to a boat which
was in waiting, came two children, whose mothers remained on
the shore.[2]

The story is his novel *The Newcomes*, and in fact Thackeray for-
bears to describe the actual parting of Colonel Newcome from his
son Clive because it is too painful. He refers only to the fact of it, and
the father 'in his loneliness rowing back to shore'.[3] Thackeray's
ancestors on both sides were India born and bred. They were all, as
Henry James put it with brutal sharpness in his essay on Thackeray,
'drops in the great bucket of the ravenous, prodigious service'.
Together, his father and grandfathers had experienced 'the huge,
hot, horrible century of English pioneership, the wheel that ground
the dust for a million early graves.'[4]

That was just as true of the Shakespears. They, too, had chiselled
and collected taxes and judged and prospered and sickened and sent
their children back to England, and brought them back again as
soon as they were grown up. John Shakespear, Augusta's grandfather,
came out to India as soon as he had married Mary Talbot Davenport
of Lacock Abbey and enrolled as a Writer in the service of the
Honourable Company. And sitting at the next desk in the office of
Governor Verelst (who had just taken over from Clive of India) he
met another young Writer called William Makepeace Thackeray,
who was to become the novelist's grandfather.[5] They cemented their
friendship when they were again in the same office for two years at
Dacca.

When their children grew up, in that close and limited society,
their children married and mingled so naturally that it was hard to tell
one family from the other. John Talbot Shakespear married Amelia
Thackeray, always known as Emily, and they had nine children. Mary

Anne Shakespear married the Reverend Francis Thackeray and had four children. Richmond Thackeray married the great Calcutta beauty Anne Becher, and had only one child, the novelist, William Makepeace Thackeray Junior, who was accordingly thrown head-long into the society of his cousins, who must have seemed like extensions of his own immediate family, for they all had the same names: there was a William Makepeace Shakespear and an Emily Shakespear and a Charlotte Shakespear and a Richmond Shakespear to match the Thackeray originals.

Up and down the Chowringhee and across the broad lawns of the Maidan, the great green riverside park of the city, the two families romped, coming to rest at the delicious stucco villa in Alipore of Mr Collector Richmond Thackeray or the equally charming mansion of Mr Superintendent of Police, later Judge, John Talbot Shakespear. The heads of the two families were the leaders of the *haute bourgeoisie* of Calcutta. And they lived on a high scale. The *Calcutta Gazette* of 1807 records Richmond Thackeray, then aged 26, and Mountstuart Elphinstone, two years older, giving 'a masqued ball of peculiar splendour' for 300 guests dressed as emperors, dwarves, sailors and babies, dancing to the band of HM 67th Regiment.[6] When Richmond sold up his Calcutta house to take charge of a frontier dis-trict in lower Bengal, the auctioneer's catalogue includes five high-class horses, 'a handsome Europe-built coach lined with yellow cloth', valuable paintings, mirrors and statues, and 'a capital patent Saloon organ'.[7]

John Talbot Shakespear, in his capacity as Superintendent of Police for the whole of Bengal, Bihar and Orissa (a vast area cov-ering much of north-east India), figured no less conspicuously in the pageant of Empire. He accompanied Lord Moira on his tour up the Ganges in the summer of 1814, a spectacular affair on a scarcely credible scale. Emily Shakespear wrote an awestruck account of it in a journal which she kept for her three eldest chil-dren who were already in England.[8] The Governor-General and his wife, Lady Loudoun, who was a grandee in her own right, made their quasi-regal progress in a beautiful green and gold barge, followed by three other barges containing their children and governess, the band, and kitchen and dining facilities. Every now and then they stopped for a tiger hunt or an audience with the local raja, or an excursion on elephants, during which the Moiras scattered largesse to the crowd. George, then three-and-a-half, Richmond aged two and baby Charlotte, six months, crawled in and out of the thrones and banqueting tables (Augusta had been left at home in Calcutta with her nurse). At Lucknow, the boys chortled with delight at the savage animal fights for which the Nawab's court was renowned or notorious: elephants fighting other elephants, tigers being tossed by buffaloes, bulldogs biting dancing bears. At its peak there were reckoned to be 100,000 people accompanying the Governor-General up the river and along its banks.

But the penalties of Empire were as harsh as its rewards were sumptuous. Emily had her ninth and last child, Selina, at the age of 40, and continued to be a leader of Calcutta high jinks. But now it was time to part with another batch of her 'Indian children' – Charlotte, aged seven, and Marianne, a roly-poly four. They never saw their parents again. All her life, Marianne kept the letter which was brought to her on board ship just before she sailed:

My beloved Marianne,

I send you a little parcel because I think it will please you to receive it from your mother. Poor old Ayah has been crying sadly for you both, sweet love. Your mother can think of nothing but her two darling little girls, & would give the world to give you once more a kiss & take her sweet little Marianne once more in her arms . . .

Charlotte will be like a mother to you & I am sure that you sweet girls will never quarrel. Say your prayers every night and morning, never tell an untruth, never be sulky.

I am sure my sweet Marianne will never forget her mother. I

have made you a little tippet & bonnet for your doll, my love, &
send you the little handkerchief you liked so much, & a lock of
my hair. God Almighty bless you, my darling child.

Ever Your affecte. Mother

Emily Shakespear.[9]

On February 5, 1824, Emily gave an entertainment. According
to the *Gazette*, 'all the Beauty and Fashion of our Oriental
Metropolis were assembled last night at Mrs J. Shakespear's Fancy
Dress and Mask Ball in her new and most elegant mansion in Park
Street.' The guests were costumed as pirates and Punch and Judy
and characters out of Sir Walter's *Marmion*. Altogether it was 'a
splendidly antithetical and whimsical' entertainment.[10] But then
came the dreaded hot months and the whole of Calcutta went
down with a fever and Emily never properly recovered. They took
her upriver to Barrackpore – the only remedy then before the days
of hill stations – but the change did her no good, and they brought
her back downstream to the fever city, where she died on
September 28. John Talbot was himself in a bad state of health. He,
too, took a river cruise, but it did him no good either, and he
decided to leave India and recuperate at the Cape, taking his last
child, the five-year-old Selina. From the ship he wrote to his eldest
daughter Emily:

My beloved child,

The *Rose* is standing out to sea and I write by the pilot to bid
you farewell. Little Selina's cot is placed at the bottom of the
cabin, where she sleeps very comfortably.[11]

He did not live to reach the Cape, but a friend of his who was
travelling on the *Rose* said he spoke of his death as certain – 'He
talked of it with the most perfect composure and coolness ... He
told me that he had had his full share of happiness in life and that he
could never have been happy again.' He directed that his wife's

miniature should lie on his heart when his body was committed to the deep, which was on April 13, barely six months after her death.[12]

There is a monument to both of them in that most atmospheric of graveyards anywhere in the world, the South Park Street Cemetery in Calcutta – just across the road from where John and Emily's guests had been 'tripping on the light fantastic toe in Quadrille and Waltz till a late hour'. It is a short round fluted capital, looking like a sandstone pillar box, rather inconspicuous amid the showier obelisks and pyramids and temple tombs, but to me, at any rate, not unmoving. Little Selina survived the journey to join Augusta and her brothers in London – and to outlive them all into the twentieth century.

William Makepeace Thackeray had lost his father the year before he was put aboard the *Prince Regent*. Richmond Thackeray, too, had been suffering from recurring bouts of fever and had been more less confined to bed in Alipore for some time where he eventually died on September 13, 1815, aged only 32 years, 10 months and 33 days, according to his tombstone.[13] He is buried amid the toddy palms and deodars of the now built-over North Park Street Cemetery (Park Street had formerly been called Burial Ground Street). In his will he left £17,000 – a million pounds or more in today's money. Yet it is hard to imagine that he died entirely happy. For three years earlier, in that charming house in Alipore, an episode had happened which seems to have strayed out of a Thackeray novel.

His wife Anne had previously been courted in England by a lieutenant in the Royal Engineers, Lieutenant Henry Carmichael-Smyth, a dashing officer who had fought with Lord Lake in the second Maratha war at Aligarh, Delhi and Laswari. Her grandmother, Mrs Becher, disapproved of the match because Henry was only the younger son of a West End physician. In England, she made Anne promise not to see Henry again, impounded his letters and eventually informed her that, sadly, he had died of a sudden fever. Anne and her sister were then sent off to India to find more suitable husbands, which they both did in no time.[14] Anne landed at Calcutta on February 16, 1810, married Richmond Thackeray in St John's Church on October 13 and gave birth to William Makepeace Junior (a seven-month baby) the following July.

Two years after their marriage, returning from his club one day, Richmond Thackeray said to his wife: 'I have just made the acquaintance of a most delightful and interesting Engineer officer. He only arrived yesterday morning, knows no one, and I have invited him to dine with us tonight so that we can introduce him to our friends.'

The hour of the dinner party arrived, the guests assembled, and the last to come was the stranger. The servant announced in a loud voice, 'Captain Carmichael-Smyth', and in walked Anne's long-lost lover.

What an ordeal the dinner must have been. After what seemed an eternity, Anne and Captain Carmichael-Smyth had a moment to themselves, and in a low trembling voice she exclaimed: 'I was told you had died of a sudden fever.' And with bitter reproach he replied, 'I was informed by your grandmother that you no longer cared for me and had broken our engagement. As a proof, all my letters to you were returned unopened. And when in despair I wrote again and again begging for an interview, you never gave me an answer or a sign.'

After a while the situation became so impossible that Richmond Thackeray had to be informed; apparently, he listened gravely, didn't say much, but was never the same to Anne again.[15]

Far from having died, Henry had been fighting all over the place. He had manned the batteries alongside John Low at Weltevreden and had been wounded in the bombardment before the assault on Fort Cornelis. He had only recently returned from Java. Now he had to leave Calcutta again to resume his duties as Garrison Engineer at Agra.[16] This temporarily relieved the situation, but there was no question of Anne forgetting him. Richmond was barely cold in North Park Street before Anne was promising Henry that she would marry him after 18 months' mourning. They were married at Cawnpore on March 31, 1817 – 18 months and 17 days after she became a widow. It was for that reason that there could be no question of her accompanying her only child on the *Prince Regent*. If she did not take her second chance of marrying Henry, there was no reason to expect that another chance would come. As always in India, one had to move swiftly to survive.[17]

All told, there were 21 children between the ages of one and five on the *Prince Regent*, not an unusual number for a homebound Indiaman. The diaries of adult travellers are full of complaints about 'the uproar of the mob of spoiled children on the quarterdeck'. The notorious William Hickey complained both of their 'horrid screeches' when crying and their 'vociferous mirth' when they were having a good time.

The great event of the voyage was the stop-off at Saint Helena. Thackeray relates that his native servant Lawrence Barlow 'took me a long walk over rocks and hills until we reached a garden, where we saw a man walking. "That is he," said the black man: "That's Bonaparte! He eats three sheep every day and all the little children he can lay hands on."'[18] Augusta and George and Richmond went, too, and gazed on the Emperor stumping about the fields of Longwood.

After the stagecoach dropped the children off in London, Augusta was separated from the boys and sent to Mrs Ludlam's establishment in the North End Road, Fulham, where all the 'Indian' girls in the family were serially dumped. It was a handsome house with two large stone balls on the entrance gate and a decent garden.[19] Mrs Ludlam's is described as 'not a school, but a Home, such as Indian parents paid for highly', concentrating more on dancing and deportment than on academic subjects, with the exception of 'the globes', both terrestrial and celestial – in fact, a rather useful subject, since these nomadic girls were destined to spend so much of their lives travelling the one and staring up at the other from a ship's deck.

Like the keepers of many such establishments, Mrs Ludlam was on a short fuse. Some years later, Augusta's brother John wrote to their younger sister, who had just got married at the age of 19 and was finding it difficult to deal with her servants:

I can therefore only suggest the administering of some of the ferocious slaps which the Ludlam, in days of yore, knew so well how to apply to the checks of her rebellious pupils.[20]

But Augusta was not short of friendly faces. Her elder sister Emily was already at Mrs Ludlam's, so were two half-aunts, daughters of her grandfather Shakespear's second marriage, who were not much older than she was.[21] And when Emily went back to India in 1820, aged 16, she was replaced at Ludlam's by Augusta's younger sisters Charlotte and Marianne,[22] and eventually by the youngest of all, little Selina, the one who had been sleeping in her father's cabin on the *Rose*.[23]

When the Ludlam's slaps became too much, the girls could always take refuge in Southampton Row with their mother's sister, another Charlotte, but always known as Aunt Ritchie. Selina said: 'Dear Aunt Ritchie's house was our *Elysium*, Liberty Hall. Everyone there did as they liked. The elder ones, occasionally William Thackeray with them, got up a good deal of fun and acting.'[24]

He and the Shakespear brothers needed all the laughter they could get. In the autumn of 1817, William and Richmond and George were put into Mr and Mrs Arthur's school at Southampton, 'a school of which our deluded parents had heard a favourable report but which was governed by a horrible little tyrant, who made our young lives so miserable that I remember kneeling by my little bed of a night, and saying "Pray God, I may dream of my mother!"'[25] Elsewhere he exclaims, 'What a dreadful place that private school was: cold, chilblains, bad dinners, not enough victuals, and caning awful!'[26] Even the brutal floggings, the sarcasm of the masters and the casual buggery that he and Richmond later endured at Charterhouse and George at Harrow were not quite as bad as life at the Arthurs'. But at least it was there that he and the Shakespear brothers became friends who would have been lifelong, had both Richmond and George not gone back out to India 12 years later.

For the girls, too, India was the only thinkable destination as soon as they were 16 or 17, although the Shakespear sisters like their brothers no longer had a parent living there, or anywhere. Augusta had left Ludlam's and was living with Aunt Ritchie, when she sat for the fashionable miniaturist Adam Buck, along with her aunt and the rest of the family. She wears the corkscrew curls of the day and looks a little plump – 'a pleasing rather than a strictly pretty face', Ursula Low calls it.[27]

Augusta was 17 when she set off to Gravesend, escorted by two of her uncles and including a harp in her luggage as indication of her musical accomplishment at Mrs Ludlam's. In the passenger list, she appears as 'Miss A. Shakespear, returning to the land of her birth'. The *Asia* left Gravesend on June 10, 1826, and docked in Diamond Harbour, Calcutta, on October 21, four months and 11 days later, not much less than it had taken her mother a generation earlier (the great improvements of the steamship and the short cut overland through Egypt lay in the near future).

In India, Augusta found her sister Emily, her two elder brothers and her widowed aunt Augusta, who had just remarried a comically ugly old Scot called Dr Halliday. She stayed with Aunt Halliday in Calcutta and threw herself into things. From the letter that Augusta wrote to Aunt Ritchie a few months later, you can see what a cheerful, unself-conscious, easy person she was:

> I am sure, my dear Aunt, it will give you great pleasure to hear that I am living with dear Aunt Halliday, who is as kind to me as my dear aunts in England were. Her spirits have suffered severely from her many and great sorrows, and she cannot, even now, bear to hear either of my dear parents mentioned.
>
> My Aunt is a remarkably fine woman and a most sensible and agreeable companion. She is quite one of the best dressers I ever saw and indeed is quite proverbial for it here ... Talking about dress, puts me in mind of a Fancy Ball I was at last week at Mrs Casement's who is famous for her parties.
>
> I was one of a group of eight ladies and eight gentlemen

dressed in the Turkish costume. It caused quite a sensation. The whole staircase was crowded as we went up to see us enter . . .

I ride almost every morning on a beautiful horse of Mrs H. Shakespear's. I think India is one of the most delightful places for a female that can possibly be. I have not experienced any of the miseries of the hot or rainy seasons. The climate ever since I arrived has been one of the most delightful and healthy that can possibly be imagined . . .

Your very affectionate and grateful

Augusta Shakespear[28]

The hot weather came, and Augusta went up into the hills with her sister Emily, married now to William Dick, Judge at Bareilly. For their summer station the Dicks chose a new resort, which also happened to be rather closer to Bareilly than the already booming Simla. It was only four or five years earlier that British officers recuperating or relaxing had begun to settle on the ridges beyond Dehra Dun. Mussoorie, as it came to be called, took its name from the common local shrub, the Mansur (*cororiana nepalensis*), a rather rhododendrous shrub with red flowers, but it took its character from the invalid majors and captains who perched their bungalows along the slopes and saddles with their spectacular views of the whole Himalayan range on one side and the great Ganges–Yamuna plain on the other. The invalids were drawn here also because a military convalescent hospital had just been established further along the ridge, at Landour, which may sound like an Indian name but is alleged to be a corruption of the South Welsh village of Llandowror, just the far side of Carmarthen.

Here came, in the spring of 1828, John Low, worn out in mind, body and spirit. The Residency at Jaipur, which he had manoeuvred so hard to get, was turning out to be a grind. The main problem was the Regent Dowager: 'this fort is at present in the hands of an old woman, and an administration under her orders of five men who surpass all I have before met in the corruptness of their conduct and incapacity for the efficient management of their different Departments,' he wrote to Elphinstone soon after he got there.[29] Things got no better. Eighteen months later, he wrote: 'I am much plagued by an obstinate, perverse, tyrannical old Ranee, who takes precious care that my office shall be no sinecure.'[30] John's only company was the Scottish doctor, who lived with him, 'but I have a good library and my violincello, and what with that and my public business, contrive to pass my time without ennui, tho' I sigh sometimes for a view of my native land and my natural friends, but as I know I must sigh for several years more, I repress such thoughts as much as possible.'[31]

The slog to recover solvency had one dismal consequence which he was now facing up to. He wrote to his sister Susan in the summer of 1827: 'I have now regularly commenced a second time to make my fortune. I begin to think seriously (and I confess that the thought is not an agreeable one) that I shall never marry.' He was already 38. 'I shall be too old when I get home to have it in my power to marry in the way I should like – a man who is both poor and old has but a very low place in a young lady's list of eligibles, and to marry anyone not to my taste in every respect – I don't fancy such a change of situation, and am accordingly under the impression that I shall live and die a bachelor.'[32]

It was in this drained and depressed state that he left Jaipur for the hills. And there everything changed.

> Mussoorie in the Himalaya Mountains
> 6,700 ft. above the level of the sea.
> *28th April*, 1828.

My dearest Mother,

I ascended from the plains to this delightful cool region about ten days ago, and as the heat had very greatly increased before I reached the foot of the hills, you will readily suppose that I enjoyed the translation not a little.

I am sitting in a small-sized tent and the thermometer stands at 71, while the purity and lightness of the air is such that one feels as though the temperature was much lower.

My first scheme was to travel at once into the interior of this interesting country, and to have visited in the course of the next month the place where the Governor resides, but on making two or three experiments I found the fatigue (the hills are often so excessively steep that one is obliged to walk and have the hill poneys [sic] led) brought back the pain in my liver, and having the kind offer of half a friend's house (Captn. Townsend) to live in during the approaching rainy season, I decided to stay here till September.

By that time the weather will be delightfully fair and cold, and I shall take a couple of months ramble in the mountains before descending to the plains, and include a visit of a few days to the Governor, who lives at a place called Simla.[33]

The scenery all around is very beautiful and imposing – to the South there is a clear view of a well-cultivated valley called Doon, and to the East, North and West a succession of stupendous mountains, tumbling over each other as it were in splendid confusion, while the clouds that generally envelop the higher peaks, from frequently changing density and positions, often show the mountains in fantastic and apparently altered situations.

Then the face of the country is covered with verdure of all sorts; we have the oak, the rhododendron, the fir-tree – all unknown to the plains, and many old acquaintances of the vegetable world, equally strangers to me for 23 years – such as the fern bush, the dog-rose, the barbary, the violet, cowslip, etc.[34]

There was another advantage, too. At the other end of the ridge was the bungalow occupied by Mr and Mrs William Dick, and Mrs Dick's sister Augusta. John found Emily Dick 'one of the most accomplished and amiable women in the world.'[35] Or was it simply that she was Augusta's sister?

How easy and natural it must have been. John feeling himself again in the delicious mountain air, walking up the narrow paths between the familiar flowers of his youth, past the friendly bungalows with their brightly painted shutters and their tin roofs shining in the sun and their names so familiar, too: Tipperary, Killarney and Mullingar, Kenilworth, Ivanhoe and Woodstock. There was even a Hampton Court and a Parsonage.[36] And Augusta, too, was a breath of home, so fresh and eager, in bloom every bit as much as the cowslip and the violet.

In February, he wrote to his mother to announce his engagement. By March, he was back at Jaipur, writing to his mother again to reinforce the news of his happiness:

> I am now in almost daily correspondence with Augusta. How I
> wish I could take her to you if it were only for a month to
> establish personal acquaintance. There is something in the
> mildness and cheerfulness of her manners and conversation I am
> confident would greatly please you all.
>
> Let us hope we may all meet at Clatto. I hope to reach the
> hills about the 4th of next month, and to be married on the 8th,
> which is Mrs Dick's birthday.[37]

In fact they were married at Mussoorie on the April 10. He was just 40, she was not quite 20.[38]

They spent their honeymoon at Mussoorie. The honeymoon was as long as the engagement had been short. John lost count of time. He realized that it had been two months since he had written to his mother: 'What makes my silence the more extraordinary is that I have been constantly begged by Augusta to write. She is an agreeable, accomplished, sweet and affectionate companion.'[39] Which is as near as we are likely to get to a confession of overwhelming sexual passion from a starved and lonely major in the Madras Army.

He had recklessly bought a house in Mussoorie, just for the honeymoon, which as usual turned out to be a poor investment: 'I have lost 4,000 rupees by my hill house, for I made it (most foolishly) a splendid mansion. I was most glad to get two-thirds of my house money back in ready cash from Hakeem Mehdee.'[40] This was the once and future Minister at the Court of Lucknow, currently out of favour and in exile but still immensely rich. John was to have many dealings with Hakim Mehdi in the future, but it is interesting to note that not only does he need a native magnate to get him out of a hole but also that Indians, too, are already beginning to delight in the cooler air of places like Mussoorie.

Soon he was writing to his mother again, meandering on various subjects till he closed in on the one she really wanted to hear about:

> I hope you don't forget to give my most affectionate love to Aunt Fettes. The style of my wife's features, high nose and dark hair and eyebrows puts me sometimes a good deal in mind of her.
>
> I will now tell you a piece of news that I trust will be pleasing to you. My dear better-half, if all goes well, will give you a little Indian grandchild about the end of January.[41]

The child, a girl, was born on the January 14, 1830, and was christened Susan Elizabeth after her grandmother by the chaplain at Nasirabad, who happened to be passing through Jaipur on his way to Agra. A few months later, John wrote again to report that 'Little Susan is crowing like a little cock, and is at all times, thank God, in the finest possible health.'[42]

Josiah Stewart, John's old friend from the Mutton Wars and then Malcolm's staff, was leaving the Residency at Gwalior to go to Hyderabad, and John wrote to Malcolm for a helping hand with Lord William Bentinck to secure the succession.[43] Gwalior with its vast fortress and the huge domains of the Sindia dynasty was then regarded as a step up from Jaipur. John had always liked the place and was delighted when he got the job. So it was to Gwalior that Susan Elizabeth Low wrote to her son on August 14, 1831: 'Dearest

John, may all blessings attend you, my dear Augusta, and darling Susan.'

But little Susan had died about two months earlier. The only reference that has survived is from John's reply to his mother a year later: 'Your letter reached me a few days ago, and brought back to our minds many saddening recollections respecting the fate of our beloved infant, but I must not inflict them on you, for I know well that your kind heart must already have been wounded more than I could wish.'[44]

Not the least agony of being separated by such oceans of space and time were the slow reverberations of grief.

At Gwalior, he met the second of the formidable begums who were to cross his path. It is a peculiarity of John's career that all the formidable Indian rulers he crossed swords with, sometimes literally, were women. And the Baiza Bai, the widow of the late ruler, Daulat Rao Sindia, was the most superb, irrepressible, ingenious of the lot. Since Sindia's death in 1827, she had been the Regent, but she had been conspicuous long before that and was to play a lurking, menacing role for another three decades. As a girl, she had been a bold horsewoman, knew how to use both spear and sword, and accompanied Daulat Rao on his campaigns. She fought against the young Arthur Wellesley at Assaye when she was probably about 18. The diarist Fanny Parkes, who met her in exile at Fatehgar, describes how Baiza Bai and her women were all expert judges of horseflesh and laughed at European women for riding side-saddle.

Baiza Bai was also a sophisticated and ruthless woman of business and tucked away a huge fortune at Benares. She would keep her troops in arrears, forcing them to borrow at ruinous rates from the bank she controlled. When the British Government was plotting to sting her for a loan to pay for its wars in Burma, she got in first and put in a request to the amazed Resident, Major Josiah Stewart, our old friend from the Mutton Wars now minus one arm, that the Governor-General should lend *her* a million, which convinced the simple Europeans that she was broke.

She could be courteous and charming, but deep down she was implacably anti-British. Major Stewart and John Low after him, now himself a major, handled her with silken gloves, and she took pleasure in showing John and Augusta around her palaces and sending them fireworks to let off at festivals. She also sent the young Maharaja, Jankoji Sindia, round to pay a visit of condolence after the death of little Susan.[45]

This young Maharaja was the son of a poor farmer, a distant connection of Daulat Rao's who had been selected out of a job lot of relatives to carry on the Sindia line. He turned out violent and unruly, and made no pretence of being polite to Stewart, saying bluntly, 'I have given up any regard for the opinion of people. I don't care what anyone thinks of me.'[46] He deeply resented his adoptive mother and vice versa. When he was 16, Lord William Bentinck passed through Gwalior en route from Simla to Calcutta, and Jankoji took the opportunity to demand that the Governor-General make over the government to him instantly or at least set an early date for hand-over. He offered the startled Bentinck a quarter of his annual revenue if he agreed. When the indignant Lord William refused this bribe, Jankoji asked if he would object if he turned his guns on Baiza Bai one night without calling on the British to help. Lord William, now rather amused by the boy's cheek, did object.

True to his word, after Bentinck had passed on his viceregal way, Jankoji harangued the battalions to join him in a coup against Baiza Bai. The idea was to launch it on the last day of the festival of Muharram while the *tazias*, the portable shrines of bamboo and *papier-mâché*, were being taken into the mosque. Baiza Bai got wind of most things and, being alerted to the plot, ordered that the *tazias* should be processed at dawn to protect the worshippers from the mid-day sun. When the *tazias* passed through the camp before sunrise, the boy and his co-conspirators were still fast asleep.

When John Low left Gwalior, with some regret, after barely a year, he was succeeded by Mark Cavendish, a prickly self-important person who had got used to being treated as a little god in the

Rajput states where there was not the suspicion and rancour against the British that prevailed in the Maratha court of Gwalior. He got off to a surly welcome. Nobody turned out to greet him, nobody saluted him. The locals refused to sell him firewood. The Palace guards shouldered him off the road. Cavendish took umbrage, and began to favour the pretensions of the boy to take over, in the hopes of building a pro-British faction at the durbar.

Bentinck consulted John, who didn't think much of Cavendish. It didn't help that Cavendish had been badmouthing him after succeeding him at Jaipur. He thought that the anti-British feeling that Cavendish reported was 'mainly ascribable to himself in having commenced with finding fault and demanding innovations'. Why make such a fuss about 'salutes from ragamuffin sepoys'? He himself had never been saluted by a sentry either at Jaipur or Gwalior. 'As we have all the substance of power that we require, I think it very unwise to quarrel about these forms.'[47]

In fact, he thought that the British had no right to interfere at all, and he wrote again from Agra[48] to say that 'I fear that my notions do not correspond with Your Lordship's on the grand point regarding the propriety or otherwise of our fixing the period of the Prince's minority.' Daulat Rao on his deathbed had made it clear to Major Stewart that he wanted to leave his wife in complete control. Gwalior was an independent state, and for John that was that. This is the first we hear of his belief in the moral and legal independence of native states, a belief which he held passionately and which was to dominate, and also to plague, the rest of his years in India.

Lord William paid no attention. On the contrary, he encouraged Mr Cavendish to encourage the boy Maharaja, who then launched a second coup against Baiza Bai. Despite her anti-British principles, she fled to the Residency, which was four miles out of town, but was dismayed to discover that Cavendish would not let her into the house and would only pitch a couple of tents on his lawn for her and her women, where they were drenched in a monsoon downpour. The Resident did then allow them to shelter in the Residency, but made it clear that he was keen to hustle her into exile as soon as the rain stopped. Nonplussed for once in her life, Baiza Bai pleaded that 'she had been on terms of most unreserved confidence with Majors Stewart and Low his predecessors. She'd hoped to find the same friend in Mr Cavendish but was grieved that he'd abandoned her in her hour of need.'

Which indeed he had. Into exile Baiza Bai went, to spend more time with her money. Lord William had a royal salute fired at Fort William to greet the new Maharaja. John Low did not hesitate to tell Bentinck later that, in his opinion, it was mostly Cavendish's fault: 'If we had not had any Resident at Gwalior last year, the Byza Baee would never have lost her power.'[49] Mr Cavendish had not meant to interfere, but his actions had given everyone the impression the British Government favoured the boy. This was a pity, he thought, because he had always had considerable respect for the Begum: 'I wish to heavens the ruler here had as much sense in public affairs as the Baee has.'[50]

But Bentinck was delighted by the outcome. He had been sent out to India as a non-interventionist, but like most Governor-Generals he became impatient with the hands-off approach to native rulers. After 1830, he began talking about non-intervention as 'the temporising and unsatisfactory policy hitherto pursued.' In private, he was willing to talk of annexing part or whole of troublesome states such as Jaipur or Gwalior: 'I should be well pleased if [Gwalior] fell into our hands. A Maratha mob and army like that can never be useful, and in adverse times might be a great annoyance.'[51]

Turfing out the Begum was only Stage One of his cunning plan. Suppose, just suppose that Mr Cavendish made the boy a delicate offer to take his troublesome domain off his hands: resign the country to the British Government and enjoy British protection and a handsome pension in perpetuity, paid for out of his own revenues. Such apparently was the burden of the 'demi-official' letter sent by Mr Macnaghten to Mr Cavendish. My source for this is the Superintending Surgeon at Gwalior, John Hope. In his scorching polemic against the British treatment of the province,[52] he claims that this 'mystic document' has disappeared: 'no copy of it can now be found among the archives pertaining to India.' According to Hope, though, Mr Cavendish thought any such suggestion decidedly indelicate 'and his answer threw a damp upon the hopes of the annexationists'.[53] It also threw a damp upon Mr Cavendish's career prospects, for Lord William transferred him to Nagpur where there was no serious business to be done at that time.

In his place, the Governor-General selected Major Sutherland who, though a distinguished cavalry officer, had no experience of political work. So he politely asked Lord William what the policy was to be: intervention or non-intervention. Lord William, who loved a joke, quickly replied: 'Look here, Major,' and His Lordship threw back his head, opened wide his mouth, and placed his thumb and finger together, like a boy about to swallow a sugarplum. Then turning to the astonished Major Sutherland, he said, 'If the Gwalior State *will* fall down your throat, you are not to shut your mouth, as Mr Cavendish did, but swallow it; that is *my* policy.'[54]

I cannot help thinking of another Governor-General's quip 20 years later. In 1851, Lord Dalhousie was to describe the kingdom of Oudh as 'a cherry which will drop into our mouths some day. It has long been ripening.'[55] This notorious declaration of intent was visualized in Satyajit Ray's film *The Chess Players* by a cartoon viceroy plopping a very red cherry into his mouth.

John's stay at Gwalior and its aftermath were marked by his first high-level experience of the rapacity of governors-general. As a humble lieutenant, he had fought to further Lord Minto's dreams of a personal empire in the East. As a captain, he had been the instrument of Lord Hastings's final demolition of the Maratha confederacy. Now as a major he was caught up in Lord William's furtive nibblings at the realm of the Sindias, the most prolific source of opium in all India. And he did not care for it any more than the prickly Mr Cavendish.

John had left Gwalior because he had been promoted again, to the

Residency at Lucknow. It was to be the great experience of his career, but at the outset he was in two minds about it. To William Dick, he wrote that his first impression on receiving the letter offering him the job from Thomas Pakenham, the Governor-General's Secretary, was that 'I would rather have thrown five thousand rupees into the sea than ever have seen it! For I hate the fuss and splendour and vanity of Lucknow.'[56]

But he took the job, mainly on medical advice. To stay in Gwalior was a risk he had no right to take, 'for if ill health were to overtake Augusta, or myself in this feverish place, and still more if a child were to suffer in that way, I should never forgive myself.'

Augusta had been five months pregnant when Susan Elizabeth died. Her second child, Emily, was born at Agra in October when the Lows were on their way to Lucknow, from where John wrote to his sister-in-law, after whom the baby was named: 'Our little girl is a remarkably pretty infant.' They had picked up a corporal's wife at Agra to act as a nanny. She was illiterate and Augusta taught her to read and write. She showed Augusta the first letter she had written to her husband: 'Miss Emily is a grat buty.'[57]

Sadly, after they had reached the supposedly healthier climate of Lucknow, baby Emily began to sicken. John and Augusta had decided to send her home to Scotland. 'I trust that before this day twelve months she will be running about at Clatto.'[58]

But it was too late. In September 1832, John wrote to his sister Georgina. He could not bear to write directly to his mother:

My dearest Georgina,
    My dear wife and I seem fated to suffer deeply in this world of bitter trials. We are again childless. A sweeter-tempered babe never existed than this little angel. She took all the medicines given to her with such patience as could only be expected of a grown-up person, and her little soul fled to a better place so imperceptibly that we were not aware of it till some minutes, I believe, after it was all over.[59]

Such griefs were no less terrible for being so common. William and Emily Dick had already lost four children, and when they left their two remaining children with Emily's double uncle and aunt Francis and Mary Anne (née Shakespear) Thackeray in Cadogan Place, the baby son died of scarlet fever.[60] In the terrible climate of Sumatra, Stamford and Sophia Raffles lost four of their five children. Only their daughter Ella survived, to die at the age of 19.

On May 4, 1833, Augusta gave birth to a third daughter, Charlotte. John took a determinedly optimistic stance:

> The infant is manifestly larger and stronger than either of our lamented lost ones and I would fain hope that, under Providence, our chances are better of preserving her to be a comfort to us to the end of our lives.[61]

This time they were taking no chances, or as few as humanly possible. Within a month of her birth, John was considering how best to get Charlotte out of India. At first he thought that Augusta should take her to Scotland and then herself return to India, but Augusta refused to leave her husband's side, then or at most other times in their long marriage. It was decided that his brother William, who was returning to Europe, should escort 'the dear little pet' and her nurse Mrs Mackenzie on the *Hungerford* when the ship sailed on January 10, 1834.[62]

John and Augusta stayed on in Lucknow to confront the fuss and splendour and vanity with only each other for company.

IX

MIDNIGHT IN LUCKNOW

Nobody quite prepares you for the first sight of Lucknow. Even today, the third courtyard of the Great Imambara is one of the world's greatest spaces. In front of you is the *imambara* itself – the dwelling place of the Imam – with its endless sequence of crinkled arches and pepper-pot domes sheltering what was in its time the largest unsupported vaulted hall in the world. To the right, splayed at an angle so that it faces Mecca, is the Asafi Mosque with its three onion domes and tall twin minarets and a great swirl of shallow steps leading up to it like a fan sweeping the ground in homage, and behind you a procession of huge three-arched gateways, all adorned with the leaping fish, the emblem of the nawabs who built these extraordinary buildings, perhaps the most under-sung architectural marvels anywhere.

Beyond the palaces and temples, there were the gardens. Emily Eden came to Lucknow in 1837 with her sister Fanny. They had come to India as joint hostesses to their stiff and querulous brother George, Lord Auckland, generally regarded as the worst ever Governor-General (though the competition for that title was strong). For reasons of etiquette, Lord Auckland did not feel able to enter the Kingdom of Oudh and bow to the King, but his sisters had a great time at the Residency with John and Augusta. Emily wrote in her letter home:

In the afternoon we went to see the king's yacht, which he had decked out for us, and then his garden. Such a place! The only residence I have coveted in India. Don't you remember where in the 'Arabian Nights,' Zobeide bets her 'garden of delights' against the Caliph's 'palace of pictures'? I am sure this was 'the garden of delights!'

There are four small palaces in it, fitted up in the eastern way, with velvet and gold and marble, with arabesque ceilings, orange trees and roses in all directions, with quantities of wild parroquets of bright colours glancing about. And in one palace there was an immense bath-room of white marble, the arches intersecting each other in all directions, and the marble inlaid with cornelian and bloodstone; and in every corner of the palace there were little fountains; even during the hot winds, they say, it is cool from the quantity of water playing.[1]

Now and then the nawabs and their architecture make us think of Rococo Europe – of pleasure palaces in Bohemia and Bavaria, of Sans Souci and the Grand Trianon. And the nawabs of Lucknow were certainly relentless in their quest for pleasure, but there was another side to them, too.

The ruling dynasty in Lucknow were immigrants from Persia, a tiny Shia minority amongst the Sunni majority, themselves only 12 per cent of the whole population of Oudh who were predominantly Hindus. Nowhere in the Shia world was the martyrdom of Husain commemorated with more passion and anguish than at the Bara Imambara – the world's largest complex of buildings devoted to the cult of Imam Husain. Even today, during the month of Muharram the streets of Lucknow are crowded with live tableaux representing the mutilated, bloody bodies who fell in AD 680 at the Battle of Karbala. The processions are accompanied by men beating themselves with chains, knives and stones to demonstrate their grief for the wounds the martyrs suffered. Some of the flagellants attach razor-blades to the chains, not wishing to be accused of taking the soft option. Husain's tomb is recreated as a portable shrine – a *tazia* – in a hundred different shapes out of papier-mâché, bamboo and silk and glass and precious stones.

The celebration of Muharram was not confined to the Shia minority. Its processions swept up many Hindus. Over the centuries, whether the Imams liked it or not, Hindu tinges had crept into the ceremonies. The British Resident, too, used to distribute rupees to the poor during the period of 'fasting and lament'.[2] The courtesans of Lucknow observed Muharram religiously. Muhammad Hadi Ruswa describes in his bitter-sweet factional novel, *Umrao Jan Ada (Courtesan of Lucknow)*, how every brothel had its shrine decorated with banners, bunting, chandeliers and globes.[3] The courtesan's world was one of elegance and ritual, like most other departments of life in nawabi Lucknow. Successful courtesans had to be able to dance and sing. At night their gardens were full of the scent of jasmine and the soothing smoke of the hookah. Umrao Jan's favoured clients are not only merchants and sultans but *maulvis,* learned clerics, too old to perform but not too old to enjoy the civilized talk and song after preaching their evening sermons.

Lucknow was a city of faith as well as a city of pleasure. Yet its civilization was very recent. Until the late eighteenth century, Lucknow had been a provincial town, nothing compared to the imperial capital of Delhi, and its rulers had been no more than viziers to the Moghul Emperors, as their title of Nawab made clear. When Bishop Reginald Heber came to Lucknow in 1825, Lucknow's most glorious buildings were only 60 years old. In his hymn 'From Greenland's Icy Mountains', Heber laments that:

Every prospect pleases
And only man is vile

A couplet which annoyed Gandhi – and also that:

The heathen in his blindness
Bows down to wood and stone.

Yet Heber was not blind to the achievements of the heathen, and he was greatly struck by the splendour of Lucknow: 'This is in fact the most polished and splendid court at present in India. Poor Delhi has quite fallen into decay.'[4]

Nothing showed this transfer of fame and fortune more vividly than the decision of the ruler of Oudh, Ghazi-ud-din Haidar, to throw off his allegiance to the Mughal Emperor at Delhi. The founder of his dynasty, Sa'adat Ali Khan, had earned his appointment as governor of the province through loyal service to the Emperor. His successors as nawabs had struck their coins with the name of the Great Mughal and carried out all the proper salutations and ceremonies of allegiance. The sovereignty of the Emperor was acknowledged in the Friday-night sermons in the Mosque. Now, one by one, these acknowledgements of inferior status were dropped, and finally in 1819 Ghazi-ud-din decided to have himself crowned as King of Oudh.

Or was it really not he himself who decided, but the British? For the British were mustard-keen to break down the imperial pretensions of the Mughal. They wanted to split the rulers of northern India into isolated fragments, just as they had, ultimately but not without a good deal of grief, managed to split up the Maratha confederacy further south. This was certainly the master plan of the rapacious Lord Hastings.[5]

Ghazi-ud-din was a rather feeble creature. He needed egging on. In his 'Summary of Operations in India', Hastings explained his serpentine technique to the Resident: whenever he saw the Nawab paying ritual homage in the traditional way to a Mughal prince who resided in Lucknow, he was to tell him that he was on his own in making these gestures of deference. The British Government required him to make no such submissions and had itself dropped these servile forms. The Resident was to watch out for any signs of Ghazi-ud-din wishing to emancipate himself, and to encourage him in assuming the kingly title. Which he duly did.

The coronation was celebrated with proper splendour. Ghazi-ud-din was crowned on October 9, 1819. At a cost of a million pounds sterling and accompanied by 400 elephants, Ghazi-ud-din processed through the streets of Lucknow between rows of Oudh and Company troops to the Dargah of Hazrat Abbas, one of the sons of Ali, which was one of the most significant Shia shrines in Lucknow, for it contained relics from the Battle of Karbala. The ruler performed his devotions alone in the inner shrine. Then the procession returned to his palace for a massive breakfast.

Finally came the crowning in the throne room, the *Lal Baradari* (or Great Red Hall, because of its red pillars), where he was crowned by the principal Shia cleric, the Mujtahid, with a strange European-looking crown designed for the occasion, rather like the crown of Charlemagne as worn by the kings on a pack of playing cards. There was a 101-gun salute, and the band played 'God Save the King' – an anthem almost as familiar by then to the nobility of Lucknow as it was to the British Resident and commanding officers of the British regiments who had places of honour throughout the ceremony. Crowning a king was, after all, a British ritual not regularly practised in the Islamic world, indeed scarcely known there.[6] This coronation remained an odd and somewhat bogus business, much mocked by subsequent commentators, who regarded the King as a semi-idiot who was conned into it by the devious British. Irwin in *The Garden of India* calls it 'perhaps the most sterile stroke of the sterile science of diplomacy that was ever conceived'.[7]

One of its oddities was that the anointing appeared to lack any permanent effect, for it had to be repeated every subsequent year, on any day the King happened to fancy. Stranger and murkier still, four years later in 1823, the British Resident took over the crowning from the Mujtahid. The Resident in question, Mordaunt Ricketts, simply reports the fact of the changeover to his government without reporting how or why it happened. Ricketts was just as devious as Lord Hastings – indeed he was later disgraced for corruption on a massive scale – and one can easily imagine him explaining that the coronation would carry so much more weight in the outside world if it were performed by the Chief Representative of the King of England.[8]

Hastings had everything he wanted from the manoeuvre: the new King had broken off allegiance to the Emperor, betokening one more reduction in the scope of that moribund empire, and he was crowned by kind permission of His Britannic Majesty. The beauty of the ceremony being an annual one (unlike any more serious coronation) was that this permission could be withdrawn from one year to the next, and was. In 1822, the Resident declined to attend on grounds that the King had been misgoverning too atrociously to be worthy of crowning. When John Low became Resident, he scuppered the ceremony in 1833 for the same reason. The following year, Low signalled that he was perfectly ready to attend again, but the King was having such a bloodcurdling row with the Queen Mother, his stepmother, that His Majesty did not wish to celebrate the anniversary of his coronation.[9]

Nawabi civilization was at its zenith: poets, musicians and dancers flocked to Lucknow, the black earth of the plains of the Ganges and the Yamuna yielded a rich tribute whenever it was collected efficiently by even half-honest landholders and ministers, and Oudh had its very own King. But this was the very moment at which the real power and independence of the King began to shrink. The heyday of Lucknow was overshadowed by the gradual dominance of the British, and by the prominence of the sole British official on the spot, the Resident.

All this had been quite a time building. For Lucknow, the story began in earnest in 1764 when the ferocious Sir Hector Munro's victory at the Battle of Buxar opened up the Ganges Plain. Never again would the armies of Oudh engage in a serious fight against the British. They were beaten, and they stayed beaten, for nearly a century at any rate. In the same year, the Honourable Company first sent 'Residents' to three major states – Bengal, Hyderabad and Oudh. To begin with, the word 'resident' seemed to have a harmless neighbourly sound.[10]

Yet this purportedly unassuming foreign 'Friend at Court' quickly became, partly by accident, but partly by design, the instrument of inexorable British Imperial expansion. This was not the official agenda. In the words of Pitt's India Act of 1784: 'To pursue schemes of conquest and extension of dominion in India are measures repugnant to the wish, the honour and the policy of the nation.'[11] India House and the British Government, which regulated the Company after the Regulating Act of 1773, rarely ceased to advise caution, prudence and economy. In their experience, fresh territory and fresh involvements with the native states almost always involved fresh expense.

It was the self-appointed mission of successive governors-generals to prove them wrong and to demonstrate that adding to the Indian Empire brought profit as well as power, if allied with rapacity and daring. London might make its preference for non-intervention more or less explicit, but the feisty men on the spot never let up. Not all of them made their game plan quite as plain as Sir George Barlow who, as Vice-President of the Calcutta Council, wrote in 1803:

> It is absolutely necessary that no native State should be left to exist in India, which is not upheld by the British power or the political conduct of which is not under its absolute control.[12]

There were arguments and nuances of view, both official and private, between those who wanted to hurry the process up and those who wanted to slow it down, but the actual thrust of policy remained pretty consistent over the second half of the eighteenth century and first half of the nineteenth. Its most forceful shaper was the Duke of Wellington's brother, Richard Wellesley, Governor-General from 1798 until his 'forward policy' proved a few steps too forward for the Court of Directors and he was recalled in 1805.

Wellesley's methods were simple, brutal and mostly effective. They were also so flagrant as to be notorious.[13] Typically, Wellesley would offer the native ruler a treaty he couldn't refuse: complete protection by a 'subsidiary force' of British troops, subsidiary here in an old meaning of 'relying on subsidy' rather than 'secondary'. These troops

would be paid for by the cession of a huge slice of the ruler's territory to the British. Under the Treaties of 1798–1801, Oudh lost
more than half its territory – all its western lands and great tracts of
the fertile Doab (the area between the Ganges and the Yamuna
rivers), so that it was almost encircled by British India, which of
course meant that there was no practical need for this 'protection' –
the very word makes us think of the protection rackets of modern
mafias, and we are not wrong to think that way. These British
troops – that is, mostly native Indian troops under British officers –
could be used only by permission and direction of the British
Resident. At the same time, the ruler was expected to scale down his
own forces to a tenth of their previous size, now that they were
superfluous to requirements.

Or the ruler could have his arm twisted to pay in cash for the
British protection. This was no better. In fact it was worse. Back in
1798, Wellesley's more celebrated brother Arthur had pointed out
that this forced tribute generally amounted to nearly all the state's
disposable revenue, which was not easy to produce at the stipulated
moment, forcing the ruler into the hands of usurers. The great Sir
Thomas Munro thought that 'the subsidiary system must everywhere run its course and destroy every government which it seeks to
protect.'[14]

The ruler of a rich province like Oudh would be further ham-
strung by the Company's insatiable and irresistible request for huge
loans to pay for its wars in other parts of India. Captain John Paton,
John Low's first assistant, wrote a remarkably frank account of these
forced loans: Lord Moira/Hastings extracted £1 million in
November 1814 to pay for the war against Nepal; then another £1
million in March 1815. By now the Nawab had had enough of
being dunned, and Colonel Baillie, the Resident, after whom the
handsome gateway to the Residency is named, reported to
Government in February 1816: 'I have at length obtained from His
Excellency a direct offer of 50 lacs of rupees [= £500,000] and I
assure you with great truth that this offer has been obtained with a

difficulty which induced me more than once to despair of the smallest success to my labours.' Baillie wanted to make it absolutely clear that he was acting under orders from HQ: the second loan 'was the result of a protracted painful and vexatious negotiation on my part prescribed by Lord Moira [Hastings] which he has thought proper to withhold from the record.'[15] In 1824–5, the Honourable Company extracted a further loan of £1 million to pay for the Burma War.[16]

Then there was the Residency itself, built and paid for by the King. As John and Augusta clattered in through the Baillie Guard from the main street of Lucknow in October 1831, they came into the nearest thing India had to an English country park. The Residency lay at the top of a gentle slope rising from the River Gomti, but it might as well have been a City broker's mansion outside Tunbridge Wells, designed perhaps by Mr Decimus Burton. The architect of the Lucknow Residency is uncertain, but he certainly had access to the best late-Georgian pattern books. The Resident's four-horse barouche would draw up under a tall porte-cochère. The house was square-ish and built of brick and stucco, like most nawabi buildings (Lucknow lacked access to the sandstone and marble quarries enjoyed by Delhi and Agra). Above its classic hooded windows, Italian balustrades ran round the top of the building, later to be somewhat eclipsed by the addition of a domed octagonal tower with its famous flagstaff from which the Union flag fluttered. For practical purposes, the greatest delight of the Residency were the *tykhana*, the high-ceilinged underground rooms where the Resident and his family sought coolth in the hot months, and the garrison sought refuge from the shells during the siege.

The charm of the Residency lies also in the other buildings that dot the 33 acres so generously allotted by Asaf-ud-daula, the Nawab in the late 1770s. There was a strong brick building just to the right of the Baillie Guard to serve as the Resident's Treasury and beyond it a magnificent pilastered banqueting hall, full of silk hangings and chandeliers, where the Resident would entertain the King or the Governor-General, a racquet court, and a little Gothic church, St

Mary's, which might have nestled in some Cotswold combe. Most magical of all, especially in its ruined state today, are the little mosque and the *imambara* beside it, known as the Begum Kothi, the dwelling furnished by Nasir-ud-din for one of his wives who happened to be English.

Emma Walters was the daughter of George Hopkins Walters, a Dragoon officer on half pay who came to Lucknow on the off chance. There he shacked up with, though did not marry, the widow of one English merchant and the daughter of another. They had two daughters. Captain Walters died at Lucknow. Mrs Walters took her two daughters to Cawnpore, some 60 miles away, and there took up with a professional drummer to a party of dancing girls, who also served them as coachman and table waiter. This versatile chancer, called Baksh Ali, told Mrs Walters that her daughters would do better back in Lucknow, where he had connections. Baksh Ali was right. Not only did the King marry Emma, he established the entire family in the Begum Kothi and insisted that Mrs Walters and Baksh Ali should be married according to Mahommedan law – one of the few times that Nasir-ud-din ever made any concession to propriety.[17]

A friend of Fanny Parkes penetrated the *zenana* on the day of the King's coronation in October 1923 (the first one at which the Resident, the dodgy Mr Ricketts, did the crowning) and saw the King's wives and was ravished by his latest darling who had received the name of Tajmahul:

> I never saw anyone so lovely, either black or white. Her features were perfect; and such eyes and eyelashes I never beheld before. She is the favourite queen at present, and has only been married a month or two: her age about fourteen; and such a little creature, with the smallest hands and feet, and the most *timid, modest* look imaginable. You would have been charmed with her, she was so graceful and fawnlike.[18]

By comparison, poor Emma was not much to look at.

The other newly-made queen is nearly *European*, but not a whit fairer than Tajmahul. She is, in my opinion, plain, but is considered by the native ladies very handsome; and she was the king's favourite until he saw Tajmahul.

She was more splendidly dressed than even Tajmahul; her headdress was a coronet of diamonds, with a fine crescent and plume of the same. She is the daughter of an European merchant, and is accomplished for an inhabitant of a *zenana*, as she writes and speaks Persian fluently, as well as Hindustani, and it is said she is teaching the king *English*; though when we spoke to her in English she said she had forgotten it, and could not reply. She was, I fancy, afraid of the old *begum*, as she evidently understood us; and when asked if she liked being in the *zenana*, she shook her head and looked quite melancholy. Jealousy of the new favourite, however, appeared the cause of her discontent as, though they sat on the same couch, they never addressed each other.[19]

Just as Arya Panular had described the two contenders for the throne of Yogyakarta waiting for the decision of Stamford Raffles.

The whole province had been in a far greater disorder just before John arrived. Thomas Maddock, his predecessor, wrote a leaving note to Lord William Bentinck in January 1831, reporting that the roads were beset with thieves and the city with robberies and murders every night: 'During the last cold season hardly a day elapsed that we could not hear at Lucknow the fire of artillery at places which the King's troops were besieging or in engagements between them and the *zemindars* [the landholders who were supposed to collect the revenue]. Now again that the season for operations has arrived, we have hostilities carrying on in the immediate vicinity of the capital.'[20]

Lord William had descended from Calcutta to deliver a rude warning to the King in April that year: 'The conduct of HM's revenue officers was everywhere denounced as oppressive and unjust, their rapacity being exercised with such baneful success as to have brought ruin upon many of his subjects, to have caused the general decline of agriculture, and to have exposed to danger the tranquility of the country.' The British Government could not let this state of things continue. The King must reduce the size of his absurdly large army – 50–60,000 strong, far larger than was sanctioned by the Treaty of 1801. He must make good his repeated assurances of reforming his ways, which would be made easier by the return of the wise old Hakim Mehdi as his minister.

Then came the clincher: if HM disregarded the present warning, 'if he should still neglect to apply a remedy for the existing disorder and misrule, it would then become the bounden duty of the British Government to assume direct management of the Oudh dominions.'

This, Lord William declared, was no empty threat: 'on looking around, HM would perceive that the descendants of those who had persisted in a profligate course of misrule were mere pensioners divested of power and consequence' – for example, the rulers of Murshidabad and Arcot. 'Were the British Government disposed to aggrandise itself, the Oudh Territories encircled by its own, possessing a soil, climate and population unequalled perhaps in any other part of India and the birth-place of a great proportion of its army, would form a most valuable acquisition.'[21] Which of course was precisely the delicious thought that flitted through the mind of every Governor-General. How beautifully Oudh would fill in the gap on the map.

But now was not the moment. Lord William passed on his way through the Upper Provinces, and old Hakim Mehdi returned from exile to clean up the stables. He greeted Major Low warmly as a friend of long standing. 'I had some years ago a slight acquaintance with the present Minister. This he has taken advantage of and represented me to the King as an old and intimate friend. I see no harm likely to result from his having done so but rather the contrary' – though the property deal at Mussoorie with Hakim Mehdi might not stand up to very close scrutiny.[22]

This should have been a close alliance between two sober and prudent operators. For a time, it worked. John wrote hopefully to his brother William: 'This state is positively in a more peaceful and flourishing condition than it has been at any time for the last thirty years.'[23] Hakim (which means physician) Mehdi set about energetically on a doctor's mandate, cutting court and public expenditure and reforming the system of tax-gathering. Within a year, John was writing to Lord William with barely concealed satisfaction to report that 'no open rebellion or public warfare of any kind at present exists in any part of Oudh'; 13 big landowners had made up their quarrels with the Court and were stumping up the revenue; 13,000 of the King's troops had been pensioned off.[24]

As always in Oudh, he exulted too soon. He had not reckoned with the King. Even by the standards of nawabs, Nasir-ud-din Haidar was spoilt, feckless and impatient. He chafed against the restrictions he had inherited, and still more against the restrictions Lord William had now laid upon him. Like other native rulers, he had lost control of foreign policy, being forbidden to communicate with other rulers.[25] The most trivial communications were forbidden, not so much to prevent conspiracies arising as to demonstrate the sole unqualified authority of the Governor-General.

Logically, this could and did also apply to British Residents. They too were forbidden by Calcutta to send 'demi-secret' letters to one another. Calcutta was never to be left out of the loop. Indeed, there was to be no loop. The Residents were to sit in isolation from one another at the rim of the giant web spun by the Governor-General. This was one of the greatest bureaucracies in history, which insisted on the right to authorize the movement of any European from or to a province and to approve or refuse his settlement and employment at a native court. The smallest items of expenditure had to be approved by Calcutta: the building of a new shed, applications for sick leave, indents for saddlery, payments to spies. Long before Lord Cromer used the phrase, Calcutta was 'drowning in paper'. Governors-general worked 18-hour days and retired exhausted and often dying.

By contrast, the Resident's life might be sometimes frustrating, but it was not an unbearably arduous one. As far as internal affairs went, his daily duties were much like those of the British sovereign, as described by Walter Bagehot. He had 'three rights – the right to be consulted, the right to encourage, the right to warn.'[26] But that was all he had. When the King swiftly tired of being told what to do by Hakim Mehdi and dismissed the old man, he did consult the Resident. John Low 'in the most powerful manner placed before His Majesty the extraordinary nature of his proceeding and the probable ruin of his kingdom by reverting to its former sinking condition.'[27] But it didn't do any good at all. Hakim Mehdi was fired, and Oudh sank back into its former disorder, a recurrent state which was serious but never really desperate because, as John Low was to prove, the inherent wealth of the kingdom could always be brought back on stream by an energetic minister like Hakim Mehdi or a brutal but efficient tax collector like Darshan Singh.

Chastened by this experience, John wrote to his mother in September 1832, less than a year after his arrival in Lucknow had seemed adorned with such promise:

> My dearest Mother,
>   I have lately had vexatious duties here owing to the folly of the king, who from a feeling of petty jealousy has dismissed his Prime Minister, and but for a dread of me would have imprisoned him and plundered him of his property. The King is at present in a violent and impotent rage, because I disdained to take an enormous bribe – 25 laks of rupees [£250,000], and to lend my aid to his contemptible complicity. As there will now be an indifferent, if not bad Minister, I shall more labour than I have had hitherto, but I shall get on more smoothly bye and bye, for this silly king has been taught by the late events both to fear and respect me . . .[28]

It was over the siting of the Residency that John and Nasir-ud-din tangled next. The King had informed the previous Resident that members of his durbar found it increasingly irksome that the Palace should be so overlooked by the Residency and its appurtenances. His Majesty had, as it happened, plans to extend the Palace and to join it to the grounds of the Residency. It would be convenient if the Residency were removed elsewhere, and His Majesty had the perfect site in mind.[29]

In the event, nothing happened. This was one more project that Nasir-ud-din lacked the tenacity of purpose to carry though. Again and again, Lieutenant Paton or Major Low would take breakfast with the King and/or his Minister, and the same projects would be discussed: the iron bridge over the Gomti, the new road to Cawnpore, the aviary and the menagerie, the Royal Observatory. And nothing would happen. The parts for the iron bridge stayed in their packing case, the high road to Cawnpore (which would have been so useful for marching troops between the two cantonments) remained a potholed track, beset by brigands. The Royal Observatory was eventually built and still stands today, a pleasant pedimented building which would pass unnoticed in Regent's Park, but even there a cleavage of views emerged: John Low had envisaged that the observatory would pay a key part in the trigono-metric survey that was criss-crossing India – the so-called Great Arc, pioneered by Sir George Everest, running from Cape Comorin to Mussoorie in the Himalayas, where Everest's own lodge still stands.[30] Nasir-ud-din was more anxious that it should forward his astrological researches. Nowhere in Lucknow is the underlying difference in mindsets between the Nawab and the British more vividly displayed than at Tar Wali Kothi – the mansion for observing stars.

The frustrations of a Resident's life at the court of a King like Nasir-ud-din was that, most of the time, it was almost impossible to achieve anything. There were boundary disputes with the surround-ing British provinces, seizures of criminals and bandits escaped from those provinces. All these counted as 'external' matters and came under the Resident. This certainly generated a wearisome quantity of business – there were said to be 50,000 persons out of the 10 million people in Oudh who had the right of appeal to the Resident.[31] But it was not high-flying stuff. John and Augusta had ample time to take their regular evening drive in the Resident's barouche out to Dilkusha and watch the moon rise over the Gomti.

There was, too, the matter of the pay. The Resident's annual salary was 66,000 rupees (roughly £6,600 then, and £400,000 in today's money), which sounds handsome, but so were the expenses – Mordaunt Ricketts's table expenses for the month of October 1824 during which he entertained Bishop Heber were nearly 9,000 rupees. This might be the grandest appointment below the Government of India, as a later Governor-General was to call it, but it was not as much of a money-spinner as it looked. When Bentinck sounded John out on November 1833 on the possibility of being transferred to Rajputana, he begged to stay put, not because the salary in Lucknow was higher but because he had drained his resources in setting himself up there. He was still running to stay in the same place, and he told Bentinck that it would take another three years before he would have saved enough to pay off his father's creditors.[32] He still had £5,500 to stump up. If he went on to Rajputana, he would also have 'the heavy expenses of marching to so distant a place'. Then there would be the inevitable loss on having to buy new equipment, plate and furniture at a dear price there, after having sold his old stuff cheap here, 'especially after all the failure of the agency houses'.

The collapse of these crucial middlemen at Calcutta had sent shockwaves throughout India and the City of London and caused a dreadful shortage of cash. At precisely this moment, Augusta's cousin William Makepeace Thackeray was discovering that he had lost the entire fortune his father had left him – all swallowed up in the collapse of the Calcutta house of Cruttenden & Co. If John Low died in Rajputana, he told Lord William, this would prove an irreparable misfortune to his mother and sister at home and his brother Henry in India, all of whom were entirely dependent on him for their income.

In the 1830s, the Company's servants did not grow rich as they had grown rich in the old days. Unless of course they took the bribes that were still on offer. From the moment John Low arrived in Lucknow, the King never ceased to press money on him. Paton reported in his wonderfully candid 1835 account of relations between the King and the Resident: 'no attempt is left untried to heap favours upon him; and lakhs of rupees, if he would take them, are ever ready to be lavished upon him, and lucrative appointments in the King's service are offered to his friends and relations.'[33]

The Resident's duties were a curious mixture of abstaining and restraining – a mixture which perhaps came naturally to a Lowland Scot. It was not just in matters of personal honesty that he had to hold back. He needed to be fastidious in the deployment of his first and last weapon, which were the regiments sitting in cantonment across the river. And this, one must say, John Low managed beautifully. To watch him in the successive crises of the regime is to watch something of an artist at work.

After leaving the King's bedroom on April 24, 1832, John Low had been accosted by Hakim Mehdi. The King's Minister, then still in favour, gave him a long account of a mutiny by 350 artillerymen two miles east of the city. Worryingly, the artillerymen possessed 13 big guns of varying calibre. The irony was that the mutiny was caused by the King's decision to discharge the men, both to save money and to comply with the Resident's nagging that Nasir-ud-din must reduce the size of his army. Fatally, he had failed to pay them for several months. Nobody had thought that such a smallish body of men would try violence, so nobody had bothered to disarm them. Later on the same day, the mutineers were joined by 700 men from the other side of the city at Musa Bagh (one of the sites the King was pushing for the Residency to be moved to). The mutineers had already announced their intention to bring their guns forward, ready to fire on the city.

In response, Hakim Mehdi had ordered up three battalions of

infantry to positions between the mutineers and the city. Could he rely on the Resident's support?

John Low: Yes, provided you don't push up the infantry too close to the mutineers. What you need to do is send some sensible messengers out to explain to them the folly of what they are doing.

Hakim: Couldn't you send your chokedar (police superintendent)?

JL: No, much better if you settle it without British intervention. So small a body won't attack unless they think they are going to be attacked, especially as they have no bullocks to move the guns.

Nothing happened that night, except for the Musa Bagh mutineers advancing their guns a few yards so as to command the roads into Lucknow.

At 3.30pm the next day there are sounds of firing 'irregular and very slow'. Great alarm in the city. Bazaarmen in the eastern section shut up shops. Labourers desert work. Mothers hide their children.

By 4.30pm – inevitably – a message from the King: please order down troops from the British cantonments to save unnecessary loss of life.

JL: No.

King's messenger: His Majesty thought you would say that. If you won't order down the troops, will you at least go to the Palace and see him?

The Resident immediately proceeds to the Palace in his palanquin, leaving a note updating the British officer commanding the Brigade.

'As I came into the Palace, horsemen brought news that the mutineers had all fled and their guns were now in possession of the King's troops (who had withdrawn behind a bank).'

There were apparently no lives lost – although it later turned out that four or five of the fugitives had drowned in the Gomti, being unable to swim, and an ammunition tumbril had exploded ten minutes after the affair was over and wounded a dozen men. The rumour that the King's infantry had been unwilling to fire turned out to be false. On the contrary, they were impatient to blaze away at the rebels, being kept so long in the sun.

John Low finished the business by urging the King to continue reducing the size of his forces, especially these troublesome artillery-men, but to make sure that they were regularly paid up to date. Also, always to make sure that the cattle were kept separate from the guns.[34]

In the end, the affair turned out to be quite tame, but if the Resident had egged on the King to take a gung-ho approach or had himself sent British troops charging in bull-headed, the casualties would probably have run into hundreds and the King would have hurriedly begun to increase the size of his army again. British power gained by being withheld.

But all the patience, tact and diplomacy in the world would never have been enough to corral the King. Nasir-ud-din Haidar was, quite simply, unmanageable. The word 'dissolute' might have been invented for him. There was something hopelessly dissolved, slack and unpredictable about his character and behaviour. Rarely can two human beings have been more utterly opposite than the King and the resolute, unwavering Resident. Almost from the moment he arrived at Lucknow, John's letters both to Calcutta and to Clatto are full of sighs and lamentations over the latest caper of 'my silly king'. At both destinations, his complaints were sure of a sympathetic hear-ing. Susan Elizabeth Low was tolerant of the foibles of humanity, but she could not abide dishonesty or cruelty. And William Hay Macnaghten, the Secretary to the Governor-General, was twice the stickler and three times the Puritan that John Low ever was. With his obsession with protocol, his flinty ambition and his sinister blue spectacles, Macnaghten began his career in high office as a semi-comic figure, the Efficient Baxter of Government House, and ended it as a tragic and broken one in the Afghan snows.

It was to Macnaghten that John sent his first anguished letters:

For many years past the King of Oudh has been *occasionally* in the habit of getting intoxicated by drinking fermented liquor but

generally speaking without violating public decency. He has however in the course of the past few months indulged in excesses of
that kind to such a degree that I think it my duty to inform the
British Government of the fact.[35]

Three times lately he had been seen reeling about the streets in a
state of complete drunkenness, throwing away large sums of money,
stopping at bazaar shops and 'talking in the most childish manner
with all classes of people'. He was drunk at parties with his royal
uncles, drunk at parties for the British officers from the cantonments. Drunk, above all, at supper parties with his deplorable
favourites. 'His principal favourite for a considerable time has been
a Mr Derusett, who holds the situation of *Barber*.' Never since the
operas of Mozart and Rossini has that word been pronounced with
such thunderous contempt as it was by John Low. Mr Derusett, even
if he had been a miracle of probity, was irremediably jumped up.

Only a few years ago this low fellow had been 'glad to cut any
person's hair for one rupee'. He had wandered into Lucknow in the
winter of 1830–31, looking for any employment he could find. He
happened to do a nice job of curling the hair of the then Resident,
Mr Maddock, and the King, who had lank straight hair and hankered
for ringlets, snapped up his services. Soon Derusett was the master of
the King's revels and much more besides.[36] He was in charge of
hiring and firing the King's tutors and dancers and musicians. At Mr
Derusett's direction, the King's two-masted pinnace, the *Sultan of
Oude*, was fitted out with silken banners and a gilt figurehead,
though it never seems to have sailed more than a few hundred yards
up the Gomti. He tasted the King's wine bottle as a safeguard against
poisoners. He imported a gaggle of brothers, wives, mistresses and
chancers – before skedaddling in 1836 with a sum estimated at
£90,000.

Looked at coolly, George Derusett was probably no better and no
worse than many other favourites who had danced attendance on the
Kings of Oudh – or for that matter on the Prince Regent of

England. Indeed, Nasir-ud-din's carry-on is now and then reminiscent of Prinny's – capricious, so sozzled, so charmed by the pretty and the exotic, and so vindictive against his own nearest and dearest.[37] But there was worse:

> Not only the King's private servants but 18 or 20 Indo-britons [mixed-race] composing the King's English Band had several times seen His Majesty dancing country dances as the partner of Mr Derusett! The latter dressed after some grotesque masquerade fashion and His Majesty attired in the dress of a European lady.

These supper parties would begin at sunset and carry on until 3 or 4am the next morning, with His Majesty led off to bed in a state of complete intoxication, from which he would arise at 3pm. He would then appear in European evening dress and wander about the city purchasing articles of trifling value at the shops. On a recent occasion, he had turfed his *mahout* off his elephant and ridden the beast bareback to a fair out in the country, 'at which a number of prostitutes and a vile tribe of dancing eunuchs belonging to Lucknow were by his command assembled.'

It was well-known in the city that His Majesty had already married some 10 or 20 females of low birth and his panders were scouring the country as far as Cawnpore for any attractive girl with biddable parents. Wives were forcibly separated from their husbands and conscripted into the royal *zenana* either as begums or concubines.[38]

Like most spoiled royalty, Nasir-ud-din had a short attention span. He would soon begin to yawn even when entertained by the most beautiful dancing girl. 'Boppery Bopp, but she wearies me. Is there no other amusement this evening? Let us have a quail fight.'[39]

He had even less patience for public business or, though he professed to love the English, for his English lessons. 'Boppery Bopp, but this is dry work,' he would say, as his tutor made him read out passages from *The Spectator*. 'Let us have a glass of wine.' Even the animal fights for which Lucknow was famous – the crunch of randy elephants' foreheads, the claws of a tiger fastened on the flesh of a buffalo, quails or partridges fighting until one or the other was a bundle of bloody feathers – he wearied of all this, too.

Out of admiration for the English, he professed to be a sportsman, and invited the Resident to go duck-shooting with him out at a lake beyond the Dilkusha Park. Mr Cropley, the King's British librarian, describes the scene:

> The lake was spread out before us shining in the red lurid light of the setting sun. On the side whence we approached, a grassy bank opened round a little bay sloping upward gradually to the summit on which we stood. Round this miniature bay stretched the encampment, the king's tent in the centre – a highly decorated marquee, conspicuous from the crimson lines which ornamented it, and the triangular green flags. The tents for the ladies of the king's household and suite – his wives and their attendants, the female sepoys and bearers, the dancing and singing-girls, and servants – were situated behind the marquee. The resident was to honor the expedition with his presence, and a handsomely-decorated tent had been prepared for him on the right of the king's.[40]

All around were elephants, camels and horses, palanquins and howdahs and barouches galore. The surrounding villages were stripped of food and forage to supply the enormous cavalcade.

Thousands of wild fowl were lured to the lake by corn and rice scattered on the water. The King, kitted out in a European shooting costume, was stationed behind a screen with a hole in it, through which he blazed at the grazing ducks. After the ducks took wing, the attendants gathered up a huge pile of game to prove the King's brilliance, half of the birds pre-slaughtered to swell the count. For three or four days His Majesty adored the sport, though he was not much of a shot. Then the Resident and his party arrived, all of course professional marksmen raised on Scottish moors, and their kill rate was far superior. The King's mood darkened. He demanded other entertainment, hawks versus herons, cheetahs racing after deer. Then these too palled. A thunderstorm deluged the tents. The King decamped for Lucknow without warning, taking his guards and his elite harem with him, leaving behind discarded concubines, disgraced dancing girls and the slower-footed hangers-on to have their tents ripped and plundered by the local villagers who had had enough of the depredations of royal shooting parties. A dozen of the plunderers were later brought back to the King's Palace where their heads were cut off the same day, to add to the bag.[41]

The King tired of everything except his vendetta against his stepmother, the Padsha Begum. She had brought him up, spoilt him rotten and taught him to hate his father, Ghazi-ud-din, as much as she did. One night, John Low reported, 'the King had been reeling home from a supper party at the Prime Minister's in apparent good humour, but on arriving at the Padsha Begum Gate all his bitterness and hostility against that Lady suddenly recurred and he ordered the Gate to be opened and called out to her Attendants that if she would not quit the Palace he would have her pulled out by force. The Gate was forced open by his men with some difficulty and delay amidst the entreaties and cries of the Begum's numerous *vakeels* and female attendants, the noise of which was so great that I was awakened by it out of my sleep at the Residency.'[42]

One cannot help picturing Macnaghten tut-tutting over his blue spectacles as he thought of the blameless slumbers of the Resident and Mrs Low being disturbed by the racket. The King and his plastered cronies tried to break down the inner gate, but it was too strong for them. And in his fury Nasir-ud-din started slapping his followers, before being carted off in his palanquin at two in the morning, swearing that he would never return to the Palace till his mother was removed from it.

The King then began a brief but vicious campaign to eject the Padsha Begum. He had his builders go up on to her roof and

opposite her windows, to pollute her purdah. Then he had his servants throw earthen pots full of urine and offal first into the Palace
and then into the mock tombs she had built in honour of the 12
Imams. The Begum got down on her hands and knees and cleaned
out the tombs herself. Then the King had five ladders put up and
sent up soldiers to begin demolishing the Begum's Palace. The
Begum and her Abyssinian slave girls were starved of food and
water. When they went to the gateway to search for something to
drink, the sepoys threw bricks at them. The Begum's women threw
bricks back, upon which 'these hardhearted unmanly sepoys assembled together and discharged their muskets.'[43] The Begum told
John Low: 'When I observed that these poor thirsty females had
drunk the sherbet of death. In despair I ordered three or four of my
sepoys to fire back.'

Her sepoys were in fact female, but they had their hair coiled up
under their shakos, and European visitors sometimes mistook them
for small men wearing padded coats. They were kitted out like their
male counterparts in white duck trousers with cross-belts and cartridge boxes, musket and bayonet. They were apparently well
trained, and when they fired back, they left as many men, if not
more, to sip the sherbet of death, too. The King's librarian, Mr
Cropley, who heard the firing, thought that altogether 15 or 16 persons had been killed.[44] A few days later, the Padsha Begum was
finally kicked out of the Palace without pension or a place to live in.
And for the next 18 months the King left her dangling without
giving her a single rupee.[45]

Tarikh Badshah Begum was the beloved daughter of Mabashhir
Khan, a seller of almanacs to the nobility of Lucknow. Nawab Saadat
Ali Khan wanted to give her to his son, the heir apparent Ghazi-ud-
din, in a somewhat casual 'dola' ceremony, but the ambitious
almanac-peddler insisted on a proper upper-class wedding. The
couple had only one daughter, and Ghazi-ud-din soon fell in love
with his wife's maidservant, who became pregnant and bore a son,
Nasir-ud-din. The Begum had the girl killed as soon as the boy was

born, and thought of killing him, too, but she became fond of him and brought him up as her own. Not a happy start in life.

The Begum was hot-tempered, grandiose and fond of religious innovations. She devised a 'Chhati' (the sixth) ceremony in honour of the Imam, based on the traditional Indian custom of mother and child taking a bath together six days after birth. She also brought 11 pretty virgins to the Palace and kept them there as symbolic brides of all the Imams save Ali, each of them being given the name of one of the other Imams' wives. These house virgins were known as *achhuti* – too pure to be touched – and the Begum insisted that one of their faces should be the first sight she saw each morning.

These pious rituals were extravagant enough to provoke John Low's distaste, which was nothing to the horror he expressed to Macnaghten when the King began to imitate his stepmother and indeed surpass her. Worse even than the King's debauches with the barber was His Majesty's behaviour during Muharram, 'for which he had devised some new and absurd ceremonies called "Achootas" during which times he abstains from drinking, and devotes himself to superstitious ceremonies ... which invariably end with a grand procession in which His Majesty takes a part dressed in female clothes, sitting in a richly embroidered Palankeen with a doll in his lap which he supposes to represent some newly born prophet or imam. The sums of money thrown away monthly on this new freak of the King's are enormous and all the orthodox musselmen of the City are much shocked by the performance of a ceremony entirely foreign to their religion.'[46]

But not as shocked as the Resident. It would be hard to invent behaviour more calculated to appal John Low, combining as it did superstition, heresy, idolatry and female impersonation. Nor was the procession the end of this charade. On the day of the birth of the Imam, the King would behave like a woman in labour and pretend that he was suffering the pangs of childbirth with the jewel-studded doll in his lap.[47] Six days after the supposed birth, he and the doll performed the usual ceremonial ablutions for mother and child.[48]

Some young men at court began to follow the King's example, acting out female roles and calling themselves Achootas. For weeks the entire court was in drag. Only after the King died did these zealots put off their travesty and return to enjoy family life.

Sharing these tastes for exotic religious ritual as they did, one might have thought the childhood bonds of affection between the King and his stepmother would have, if anything, strengthened when he grew up and succeeded his father. Nothing could be less true. He began to hate her and to mourn the memory of his real mother. He had a tomb built over her grave out in the country graveyard of Jhankar Bagh.[49] Even if he did not know all the circumstances of her death, he must have had his suspicions. Apparently the wily doctor, Hakim Mehdi, who hated the Begum, too, was the first to whisper that she had killed his mother.[50]

Nasir-ud-din had been married first when he was still heir apparent to his father, very respectably, to a granddaughter or possibly a niece of the Emperor of Delhi. This Delhi princess was said to be a beautiful young woman of modest and exemplary character.[51] She had taken one look at her husband and his chaotic, tipsy entourage and had removed herself into a dignified separation at Hussain Bagh, near the mausoleum of the Nawab Asaf-ud-daulah.

Next up was Afzal Mahal, a female attendant at Nasir's court. She was said to be a washerwoman, or at any rate employed somewhere in the household. She too 'had a fair reputation among those who knew her best in a profligate palace', according to Sir William Sleeman, one of John Low's successors as Resident.[52] She had the good sense and prudence to get on well with the fiery Begum, and when she gave birth to a son, Munna Jan, the delighted Begum swept both of them under her wing. Munna Jan became her new love object, to make up for the alienation of her once beloved stepson.

Here the plot really thickens. The Begum looked around for a wet nurse for the baby. Various candidates were summoned. The Begum

liked the look of a girl called Dolaree. The royal physicians pronounced the quality of her milk first-rate and she was hired. Dolaree
had quite a history. She had first been married to Rustom, a groom
in the King's cavalry, but had played the groom false with both a
blacksmith and an elephant driver and produced a son and a daughter, nobody was sure whether by Rustom or the blacksmith or the
elephant driver.

No sooner had Nasir seen Dolaree than he fell hopelessly in love,
'although she seemed very plain and very vulgar to all other eyes.'[53]
And he would not rest until he got his father's approval to marry her,
which he did, in 1826, just before his father died. Nasir continued to
be enraptured by his new queen, on whom he conferred the title
'Queen of the Age' and an estate worth 60,000 rupees a year. Not
content, she prevailed upon the King to declare her son, Kaiwan Jah,
to be his own eldest son and therefore heir apparent. He assured the
British Resident, then Mordaunt Ricketts, that if this were not the
case he would not have spent so many lacs of rupees on the wedding
ceremony. Even Ricketts, who had told a dubious tale or two in his
time, felt compelled to point out that the general impression at
Lucknow was that the boy had been three years old when his mother
was first introduced to the King. This had not the slightest effect.
Nasir-ud-din wrote to the Governor-General to confirm that Kaiwan
Jah was his son and heir. And, as such, he was sent to Cawnpore to
welcome the Commander-in-Chief Lord Combermere in December
1827.

What a strange affair: Lord Combermere, 'that d—d fool', as the
Iron Duke had called him, crossing the Ganges and meeting the
heir to the throne and joining him in the howdah of his elephant
and the cavalcade moving off to a breakfast of champagne and
cherry brandy. The prince was apparently not very prepossessing:
dark, surly, thick-lipped with terrible teeth, his uniform covered
with diamonds and pearls, the surrounding noblemen gorgeous in
red and gold and green and yellow. Lord Combermere, if he considered the question at all, which the Duke of Wellingon's

assessment of him suggests he might not, would have assumed that this surly youth was the heir of a hundred nawabs, when in fact he was the son of a wet nurse and either a groom or a blacksmith or an elephant driver.[54]

Meanwhile, Ghazi told the Resident that the other boy, Munna Jan, was not Nasir-ud-din's son and that he had claimed that he was only to annoy his father and stepmother. Ghazi-ud-din hated the Padsha Begum almost as bitterly as his son was to hate her. Her furious temper had made the old King's life a misery. Her physical assault, as well as her verbal batterings, left his face bleeding and his clothes and beard torn.[55] Nasir-ud-din was no luckier in his latest choice of consort. The Queen of the Age turned out to be a bully, too, and occasionally boxed his ears.[56]

Not surprisingly, the King moved on. In a short space of time, the Queen of the Age was eclipsed by the equally plain Emma Walters and then by the beautiful Taj Mahal. But then he caught sight of one of the Queen of the Age's waiting women, Qudsia. On paying a polite visit to Dolaree's quarters, the King asked for water, and Qudsia brought him a gold cup on a silver tray. She was partly veiled and, with his weakness for horseplay (he loved leapfrog and snowball fights), the King splashed water over her veil. She splashed him back. The King was enchanted. The next day he came again. More mutual splashing. In no time they were married, on December 17, 1831, a few weeks after the Lows had arrived in Lucknow.

Qudsia was handsome, as bad-tempered as the Queen of the Age and outstandingly greedy (she saved 4.4 million rupees out of the money he gave her, and at his death her money formed the bulk of what was left in the Treasury after his reckless extravagance). She is said to have been the only one of his wives who had any real affection for the King, and he for her. But they had bloodcurdling rows, one of which was to prove fatal. Qudsia had now been taught to read and write, but she had still failed to produce an heir. In her fear that she too would be cast aside, she is said to have several times smuggled her ex-husband in female dress into the Palace in the hope that he could make her pregnant, and this was reported to the King. Nasir-ud-din told her in a rage that he had raised her from slavery to the throne and he could just as easily cast her back down again. She fled to her apartments and swallowed arsenic. The King watched over her dying agonies until he could stand no more and ran away to his race-course three miles away, where he crouched in the grandstand until the funeral was over.[57]

She died on August 21, 1834, and the King was inconsolable and would not put off his mourning clothes. After Qudsia's death, it seemed that his caprice took on a darker hue. He became more inclined to strike out in a vicious and cruel manner, which had not originally been part of his make-up. One of his most obsequious favourites was Ghalib Jang, who doubled as Superintendent of Police in Lucknow and Commandant of an infantry brigade. Apart from toadying to the King, Ghalib became much loathed for his willingness to sneak on the peculations of his fellow courtiers, notably the Minister who had replaced Hakim Mehdi, the imbecile but not ill-natured Raushan-ud-daula. Ghalib also had it in for the court tailor, Mucka, whom he suspected of hugely overcharging the King. Picking up one of the silk crowns that Mucka had sent for the King's inspection, Ghalib Jang twirled it on his finger. By accident or design, to prove how flimsy the silk was, Ghalib's finger poked through the top of the hat and Ghalib exclaimed, 'See, there's a hole in Your Majesty's crown!'

This potential allusion to the dodgy circumstances of his acces-sion (his father had locked him up and attempted to replace him with his brother) so enraged the King that he shouted 'Off with his head', had Ghalib's legs fettered, his family incarcerated and his property seized. Later Ghalib was flogged, stoned and jailed, and all the women of his family ordered to be shaved and stripped naked and paraded through the streets. John Low intervened and got these extravagant punishments commuted to exile, under the not-very-tender mercies of his fellow police chief Darshan Singh, being kept in an iron cage for several years.[58]

But the King's chief vendetta continued to be against the Begum. Her latest offence was to refuse to wear mourning for Qudsia. She told her stepson that it was unmanly to be so overcome by grief: 'God has created more beautiful women than her. It is only useless to die for a cheat.'

'If you had a mother's affection for me, you would have put on the mourning dress. But you have none, because you are not my real mother.'[59]

The blood row continued. The position now was that the King had assured John Low, originally through Hakim Mehdi, and then directly in person, that neither of the boys was his son. Both reports were false, the King said, and arose from the same cause, bribery and ambition, and he had posters stuck up proclaiming this throughout the city. The Queen of the Age had paid many lacs of rupees to people at the Court to persuade them to call Kaiwan Jah his son, and the Begum's people had done the same in the case of Munna Jan.[60] But he had ceased to cohabit with Afzal Mahal 24 months before Munna Jan was born.[61] Whoever heard of a 25-month pregnancy?

At the King's request, John Low reported all this to Calcutta, and in due course (December 15, 1832) the Government decided that when the King died they would recognize neither of the boys but instead would crown his old uncle, Muhammad Ali Shah, who was in poor health and 68 years old, but known to be of temperate habits and a prudent disposition, as well as having served, 30 years earlier, as Minister to his father Sa'adat Ali Khan. These instructions to John were kept secret, to prevent intrigue and the risk of poisoning to one or other of the claimants.[62]

After warnings from Residents past and present over nine years, Nasir-ud-din had little reason to believe that Lord William Bentinck's threat would ever be put into effect. He remained equally immune to the Resident's rebukes about his drinking and his antics with Mr Derusett, which were 'bringing disgrace upon the British character as well as upon that of his Majesty'.[63]

What was the King's response? 'Happen what may, I shall continue to amuse myself in my own Palace in whatever way I please, and I will drink, Hip, Hip, Hoora! in company with whomever I please. It is only upon the public affairs of the government of Oudh that I am bound to take the advice of the British government.' Fair enough, the Resident commented ruefully.

Meanwhile, the furious Begum was gathering a sizeable army – 5,000 men plus several assorted field guns. She was signing on hundreds of sepoys, whom the King had lately discharged (just as the Resident had asked him to). Her men were busily digging trenches, while alarmingly the King's troops were saying that they had no desire to fight the Begum because she had custody of the boy Munna Jan. Despite the King publicly disowning him, most people in the city remained under the impression that he was the acknowledged heir, not least because he had been sent out to welcome Lord Combermere (forgivably the public had confused him with the other boy).

Now the King summoned John to see if he could sort out the quarrel, because he himself was completely incapable of negotiating with his ghastly stepmother without bloodshed.

John said that he could not intervene in person but he would send his Chief Munshi – the ceremonial officer who advised the Resident on court ritual and a dozen other things. This particular Munshi was, he said, a person of the utmost tact and probity who had already served the Resident in Hyderabad and Delhi and he would surely calm the aggrieved Begum. The Munshi was called Iltifat Husain Khan and, after he died in office in 1839, John Low wondered to the Governor-General why he had hung on so long in a job which paid so modestly. He was led to 'infer that there exist unknown facilities of making large sums of money with impunity in an office which is so generally, and eagerly sought, though he never figured out what these unknown facilities might be.'[64]

It was a sign of John Low's instinctive modesty that, though he had now been in India for 30 years, he never pretended to understand exactly how the native economy worked. It was a parallel universe which remained a mystery to him, as to other experienced British officers, its robust intricacies largely hidden from view. Indeed, British observers preferred to ignore the far-flung and hugely energetic networks of the merchant community, echoing the famous belief of Sir Charles Metcalfe that the real India lay in the village communities, those 'little republics', which remained unaltered by the rise and fall of dynasties above them, and that the rigidities of class prevented the emergence of anything that could be described as an Indian middle class. Marx and Weber were as convinced of this as the British officials on the spot. But it was the merchant community that made India tick.[65]

The ingenious Munshi was sent off to the Begum with a tactful letter imploring her to disband her troops – once again John Low reserving a direct personal intervention for a later stage, though he had a letter ready to Brigadier Johnstone on the British cantonment, instructing him to have two regiments of infantry in a state of readiness and all the artillery that he could spare. But adding 'Avoid actual hostility entirely at all costs.' There was no need to conceal the destination of the troops. The knowledge that they were on their way would be a useful deterrent.

Iltifat found the Begum with her ladies and the boy Munna Jan (probably the boy's mother, Afzal Mahal, too, for she was seldom far away). The Begum was behind her usual purdah screen, and when Iltifat handed her the letter she said it was too dark in the room and he read it aloud to her. (It is possible that she was illiterate, but her father had been a learned man and a pushy parent, and even poor Qudsia had got herself taught to read and write.) After he read it aloud two or three times (the letter was quite short), the Begum said: 'I know well that this kingdom of Oudh is in the gift of the British government and I have no wish to act contrary to the wish of its representative. Let something be settled for my maintenance and I will do whatever he says.'

Iltifat: Please make no excuses, or the British troops will attack.

Begum: Very well, but how shall I explain all the indignity I have suffered from the King? How can I relate what I have undergone in having the vilest filth and dirt thrown into my place of prayer? I have no fear of death! All the world knows how kindly I treated the King. We were like lovers. Night and day my thoughts were intent on the preservation of his life and even now I do not wish him ill. Let him come here himself and kill me with his own hands. I am now tired of life and will kill myself.'

At which she and the boy Munna Jan burst into tears and sobbed bitterly together.[66]

There was a good deal more of this, but at the end of it the Begum agreed to pay off 3,000 of her troops and withdraw her pic- quets from their threatening positions in front of the city. As Iltifat left to return to the Resident, he saw dozens of armed men leaving the trenches. They all appeared to be strong, athletic-looking men with their arms and accoutrements in good order – an unnerving contrast to the King's troops who were in poor shape, ill-armed and in a mutinous mood, having been paid their arrears only as they were shambling into line to face the insurgents. The King had now offered her a reasonable pension and a proper place to live, but the enmity between them remained an explosive question. The Resident and the British Government had swallowed the King's lie and were secretly committed to the uncle. The Begum and the people of Lucknow were all for Munna Jan.

For a dysfunctional dynasty, the nawabs of Lucknow were hard to beat. It is embarrassing but irresistible to cast our eyes a few hundred yards up the road (still within earshot, as we have heard) on the serene acres of the Residency. Augusta had just given birth to her fourth child and first boy, William Malcolm Low (November 9, 1835), always to be known as Malcolm after Sir John Malcolm. The last weeks of her confinement were overshadowed by the death of her brother William Makepeace Shakespear at the age of 28. William had got his first good appointment, as Adjutant and Quartermaster of the 3rd Brigade, Horse Artillery, and he had come to Lucknow in high spirits, but within a few days of his arrival he caught a fever and died. John describes William Makepeace Shakespear as 'one of the most amiable and honourable young men I have ever seen.' He seems to have been a rather dreamy character and spent much of his last few days painting Augusta's portrait. Their brother John wrote to their sister Marianne: 'Barring the time that William was engaged in painting (which was considerable), he managed to keep pretty free of reverie.' The painting does not survive, and nor did William.

John Dowdeswell was an altogether brisker character. John Low had persuaded Bentinck to let him take on his brother-in-law as his Assistant at Lucknow. This piece of family patronage was not achieved without difficulty. John Dowdeswell's knowledge of Persian, Hindustani and Nagari turned out to be less fluent than the Resident had claimed. In fact, he had just flunked his Interpreter's exam, forgetting several colloquial expressions which he knew perfectly well. But he passed the second time, and had settled in nicely at the Residency.[67] He told Marianne in a typical brother's back-handed compliment that 'Augusta has grown much stouter; she would be considered anywhere a fine-looking woman.' And he adored his new boss: 'Low is a man of great ability, with the finest disposition in the world and has been a warm friend to me.'[68]

It had been hoped that John Low might be able to give the Assistant's job to his nephew Aleck Deas, the son of his beautiful sister Catherine, the one he had accompanied on her honeymoon. But Aleck was a scapegrace, had flunked the East India College at Addiscombe and was 'dreadfully careless and thoughtless to a degree about money', according to his grandmother.[69] John Low had used his influence with the Commander-in-Chief to get him posted to a regiment stationed at Lucknow, with special permission to live at the Residency and command the Escort.[70] Poor Aleck! While he might seem to have fallen on his feet, there was a price attached. He was already in debt to his uncle and his Aunt Augusta was forcing him to resume his study of the native languages which he had failed at college. Uncle John was sterner still. Colonel Low wrote to his mother:

You will be happy to hear that an evident improvement is
gradually taking place in Aleck Deas' habits, manners and ideas.
When with his regiment he used to associate *exclusively* with
three or four lads as idle as himself, and *never* went into female
society. All this had given a roughness to his manners which is
fast disappearing. I make him attend every Sunday forenoon and
join Augusta, our European nurse and myself in reading prayers
and portions of the Bible and even that seems to have had an
influence on his conversation and ways of thinking.[71]

Susan Low replied: 'Aleck is an affectionate creature and we were
great friends, but he is uncouth, and particularly at table. You may
tell him I said so and I hope he will correct it.'[72] A Scottish reproach
is seldom left undelivered.

Aleck was there for the christening of Malcolm Low. So were
Augusta's brothers, George and Richmond, with whom she had set
sail from Calcutta nearly 20 years earlier. Richmond had come with
their sister Emily Dick, and if only William Makepeace Shakespear
had survived a few weeks longer, all four Shakespear brothers would
have been together in the Residency with two of their five sisters –
a reunion never to be repeated in their vagabond lives.

Marianne, who had just married Archibald Irvine of the Bengal
Engineers at the age of 18, had also been in Lucknow the year
before, because there she is with Augusta, sharing the Residential
barouche in the corner of the gigantic picture (9ft 6ins by 5ft) by
Alexandre Dufay de Casanova, the court painter, depicting *The
Reception of Lieut-Colonel Low by His Majesty the King of Oudh on 4th
March 1834*. This vast canvas was bought on behalf of Queen
Victoria at auction and hung for many years at Buckingham Palace,
though it is now in store at Windsor. The picture is full of elephants. The King is in a gorgeous plumed and tasselled howdah on
the top of one elephant, wearing his playing-card crown, while on
another elephant stands John Low, now a colonel as befitted his station, waving his plumed hat in salutation. You would have thought

that never a cross word had passed between them. In the distance, an interminable procession of horse-drawn carriages and elephants winds its way back towards the towers and minarets of Lucknow. The picture (which is not very good) radiates the high noon of the Empire. Everything seems set fair for a harmonious and lasting collaboration between the races.

Marianne painted and drew, too – she won a silver medal from the Royal Society for a study of A Plate of Eggs and Grapes.[73] All the Shakespears could toss off a sketch or a sonnet. George Trant Shakespear, now Registrar at Dinajpur, the only non-military man of the brothers, was regarded as the dabbest versifier. His rollicking poems on family occasions are full of nicknames. Because of his roly-poly form and rolling gait, he was known as the Polar Bear; Marianne's husband was the Major; John Low, being a decade older than them all, was the Patriarch; Augusta was the Barbary Queen.[74]

His youngest sister, Selina, who had never met George until she came out to India in 1837 at the age of 17, says of him: 'George had been so much in the jungles that he was shy, but so witty and amusing when alone with us.' His cousin William Makepeace Thackeray remained devoted to him, but he did say after one of their few meetings in later life, that his 'selfishness is delightfully characteristic'.[75] The portrait of Jos Sedley in Vanity Fair – fat, lazy and overdressed – is certified by Thackeray's brother-in-law as 'an overcoloured picture of George Trant Shakespear.'[76] It is certainly a merciless one.

In the Shakespear family circle we see the early Victorian Empire at its most genial and good-hearted. Their wit, such as it is, is always kindly. They are loyal to each other and look out for each other in a life which was always precarious and often short.

The Lows and the Shakespears were essentially down-to-earth and unpretentious people. They dabbled in music, painting and poetry, but they would have thought it absurd to make a religion of art, or indeed a religion of religion. Their outlook on life was for the most part kindly and liberal, but it was essentially practical. While Nasir-ud-din was dreaming of Muharram and the Peshwa was obsessed with his pilgrimages, John Low was dreaming of water closets. All through these anxious years at Lucknow, he was writing home to his mother with detailed instructions for installing a number of these estimable inventions in or next to existing dressing-rooms:

> It is of great convenience that there should be both inside and outside doors to closets, the outside ones for servants to take water into and out of them without coming into people's bedrooms.
>
> The outside doors should be made to keep shut by means of a weight, rope and pulley. This is to prevent people ever seeing them from the public stair.
>
> Each of the new closets that I want made will be sufficiently large to have a tin (shoe) bath, or a wooden one in it. I am very partial to frequent bathing and consider it often a great preservative of health.
>
> The whole space should be raised a foot or more above the present floors, excepting a few feet near the doors to allow them to be opened, and also to admit of the servants placing pails at the edge of the stage, to carry off the water from the bathing tubs.
>
> The stage part should be completely covered with tin, well laid down and soldered in order to prevent any water finding its way into the lower rooms, and for the same purpose the tin covering of the stage should have a raised ledge of two or three inches all along the borders, having one hole and a cock (at the corner), through which the water would run into the pails.[77]

Cleanliness, discretion and advanced plumbing – these formed an important part of the Low creed.

It is not surprising that someone like John Low should have watched with horror and apprehension at the goings-on across the road. Things could not go on like this. While George was scribbling his verses and John Dowdeswell dashing off his gossipy letters to

Marianne and Emily, and little William Malcolm was cooing in his cot, heedless that in a few months he too would be packed off to Clatto via Calcutta and Leith or Dundee (he sailed in May 1837, aged 18 months), the Resident felt compelled to write yet again to Macnaghten, on September 26, the day after the Munshi had mollified the Begum and persuaded her to discharge her troops.

The letter was marked secret, and it contained the essence of what John Low had come to feel, not just about Oudh and its wretched King, but about the whole British situation in India. It was a plan of action, but it was also a deep-felt warning.

'If it shall become necessary to interfere at all in the interior management of Oudh, while the present King is on the throne, the interference must be far more complete.'

For upwards of 30 years, that reigning family had given essential aid to Britain in time of need. If ever the British took the entire management into their own hands, 'the act will be generally considered ... as nothing short of usurpation. Their natural hatred of us will be vastly increased not only in Oudh but also in some parts of our own provinces.'

For this reason, John proposed a different measure from anything proposed by Lord William. If the King should prove himself utterly unfit, then he should be 'deposed entirely', and sent off with a handsome pension to live at a considerable distance from Lucknow and 'the next heir should be placed on the Throne, without making him pay a single Rupee or give up one Acre of Land for his elevation.' [Underlined by JL in the original letter.]

This would be much better than a direct British take-over, because 'the mass of the inhabitants of this country would be better pleased at having a Ruler of their own than to be transferred to the direct Government of British officers, however pure and just they might be in their intentions and however zealous in the performance of their duties. This is in fact a common feeling which exists all over the known world, viz: a dislike of foreign masters and new usages, and I see no reason for supposing the inhabitants of Oudh to be an exception.'

With the proposed replacement ruler he had 'no personal acquaintance beyond that of giving and receiving a salaam', but Muhammad Ali Shah was known to be a man of common sense and prudence; he had no debts and he had experience of governing in his father's day. He would surely be far better than either Ghazi-ud-din or Nasir-ud-din.

But the really interesting and novel contention of this letter is that most people would rather be misgoverned a little by their own rulers than governed with unrelenting efficiency by foreigners. In fact, John Low goes further. The Indians, he says, had 'a natural hatred of us'.

This would not be the first time that the Honourable Company had turfed out a native prince they deemed unfit to rule. In 1798, Lord Wellesley had deposed Wazir Ali in favour of his uncle Sa'adat Ali Khan. But few, if any Company servants had put the basic psychological truth so bluntly. Efficiency alone would never reconcile the natives. This was something that the Efficient Baxters in Calcutta refused to accept. The 'Modernizers' in Government House (it is in India that the word 'modernizer' first came into vogue) believed passionately that first-class administration by first-class minds, evenly administered across India, would create a nation of happy peasants, whatever the cost to the pockets and the privileges of their rajas. The Supreme Government should not hesitate to do whatever it took to achieve this goal: take over every province, annex every state, instal subsidiary forces at every capital.

By contrast, the old school – and we must include among them John Low and especially his friend Sir John Kaye, the historian of the Great Mutiny – believed that reducing the Indian population to this 'dead level' would not increase the general prosperity and that such detailed interference was bound to inflame Indian resentments so badly as to threaten the future of the Empire. The argument raged throughout the middle years of the century and was echoed in the later arguments between radicals and conservatives in the emerging Indian nationalist movement. To us, it is all a bit confusing, because the liberals who claim to be putting the peasants first are also the most ardent imperialists. The trouble is that both sides of the argument tended to be swallowed up in the terrible imperial thirst for rupees. It was always difficult for the British to argue convincingly that they were taking over to help the poor *ryots* when it was so embarrassingly obvious that they were helping themselves.

Soon Macnaghten disappeared over the mountain passes to mastermind the doomed British expedition to Afghanistan. He was succeeded as the Governor-General's Political Secretary by John Russell Colvin, another Modernizer of overwhelming self-importance – he was known among the cheeky clerks as 'Lord Colvin'. And it was to Colvin that John Low wrote another snorter, on July 23, 1838:

'I fear that my opinions do not coincide with those of the Governor General, or with Macnaghten's or your own.'

Native princes would much rather have temporary aid to restore order than subsidiary forces permanently stationed on their territory. Britain should 'never propose auxiliary forces on allies who don't want them and who have not given any just cause of offence.' (John was almost as inclined to underlining in his letters as Queen Victoria was in hers.) 'The feelings engendered in their minds by these encroachments upon their dignity may at some future time excite them to such a degree as to make them combine violently against us if a tempting opportunity were to offer: whereas if we only let them alone, there is scarcely a chance of such combines being formed.' Echoing Arthur Wellesley and Thomas Munro, John Low thought that these subsidiary forces spelled ruin for a native state.

If we leave them with as much power over their own subjects as the treaties stipulated, 'we shall surely have the best chance of their not turning against us, openly or secretly, in times of difficulty.' Many of them would stand by us, if they felt 'comfortable in their own positions'. Then he adds the most chilling pay-off, based on his 30 years of service in India and his intimate acquaintance with Indians of all sorts: 'Not that any of them like us much.'

No other high official in India had, I think, faced the reality quite so coldly, or prophesied the outbreak of the Great Mutiny and its causes so sharply, and so early on.

At any rate, he did manage to persuade Lord Auckland to approve his plan, though for the moment the new Governor-General thought they should watch and wait, because 'at present, despite the King, the country is better managed and more prosperous than it was some years ago' when Lord William had first threatened to intervene. 'Personal scandal and misconduct, however gross and discreditable', did not justify interference – a gentle reproof here to Colonel Low for his horrified catalogue of the antics of the Barber of Lucknow. On the other hand, Auckland praised 'the liberal, the just and the manly spirit' in which Low had conceived and expressed his recommendations. The British Government was lucky to have him. And the other members of Council mostly agreed, especially Augusta's Uncle Henry Shakespear, the one who had lent her his horse when she first arrived in Calcutta.[78]

There the matter hovered, but not for very long. For on the night of July 7, 1837, a fortnight after the King of England died, the King of Oudh died, too. Nasir-ud-din Haidar was about 34 years old and had been ill for some weeks. His death was not so surprising, considering that outside the period of Muharram, he had been drinking himself into a stupor every night. Even so, it seems a coincidence that he should have died so soon after his chief taster, Mr Derusett, had left Lucknow just after Christmas 1836.[79] The Begum was generally assumed to have poisoned the King's mother, why should she not have finally revenged herself for her maltreatment by poisoning Nasir-ud-din himself? But there was no time for forensics to test the truth of this suspicion.

The court messenger, Ghulam Yahya, came to the Residency at 11.30pm. He told John that the King had been taken ill suddenly, and now appeared to be dead or dying. The Resident rustled up Paton, now promoted Captain, and Captain Shakespear and the ingenious Chief Munshi, Iltifat Husain Khan.[80]

Low and Paton set off to the Palace, now joined by Dr Stevenson, the Residency surgeon. They found the King lying dead on his bed. His body was still warm. Dr Stevenson opened one of the veins in his arm, and the blood gushed out, so he must have died only a short time earlier. His face was placid, without any sign of pain. His attendants had not imagined him to be in danger. He had let out a slight shriek just before he died.

John left Paton to superintend the sealing up of the Palace and the posting of sentries at the gates. He himself returned to the Residency, where he scribbled a note to Brigadier Johnstone in the cantonments about four-and-a-half miles away across the old stone bridge over the Gomti. The Brigadier was to send off five companies as an advance guard, with all disposable troops and guns to follow on to the city. John then dictated a short document in Persian which he proposed that Muhammad Ali Shah should sign. This document would commit the new King to agree to any treaty that the British Government might think proper to propose to him. In fact, granting the British whatever was the Persian equivalent of 'carte blanche'.

All this took time. It was now about 1am on the morning of July 8. The Resident then dispatched his brother-in-law, John Dowdeswell Shakespear, with the document, along with Iltifat and the court messenger who had brought the news of Nasir-ud-din's death over to the Resident's house.

Muhammad Ali Shah was elderly, not in the best of health, and fast asleep. But as soon as they shook him awake, he signed the document without a murmur. So far, so good.

Now the Resident went back to the Palace, and Paton and Shakespear brought the new King there to be received by John Low. It was about 3am when they met. After a brief chat, the debilitated new Nawab was allowed to retire to a couch in an adjoining room to lie down for an hour or two's sleep before being installed on the throne in the *Lal Baradari*, or 'the Burradurree' as the English called it. His son Amjad Ali Shah and his grandson Wajid Ali Shah – each of them in turn to succeed the trembling old man on the throne of Oudh – stayed in the side room with him.

John sat with Paton and Shakespear on the verandah facing the river, catching their breath and perhaps congratulating themselves on their speedy footwork. They took advantage of the lull to run through the order of the coronation ceremony and the list of guests who would need to be invited to make a proper show of it.

Just before the first streaks of dawn straggled over the Gomti, they heard the news they had dreaded. The Padsha Begum was on her way to the Palace, bringing with her the boy Munna Jan and a large armed force. On their way, the Begum's party passed the home of Nasir-ud-din's first consort, the beautiful Delhi princess, and the Begum press-ganged her to join the party and lend a touch of class to her coup.

John had expected just such a move and had already, at about midnight, sent a messenger to her instructing her on no account to leave her house, which was at the Almas Gardens, four or five miles away. The messenger found her entourage already on high alert and ready to set off to the Palace. The Begum sent a message back to John, imploring that she be allowed to see the corpse of her beloved Nasir-ud-din, whom she had not been allowed to see for so long while he was still alive.

In fact, the Begum's force was already closing in on the main north-west gate, and John's messenger to tell the advance guard to hurry up was pushed back by a disorderly crowd only 500 yards from the Palace. He scurried back to tell the Resident, and Paton ran to the outer gate, where he found only a tiny guard, commanded by two black slaves.

Now he could hear the Begum's mob hammering at the gates. Paton shouted out that the British Government had directed the Resident to put Muhammad Ali Shah on the throne, and the gates had been shut on the orders of the Resident.

The rebels paid no attention and brought up two elephants to force the gate. The first elephant charged in vain and reared back in pain, but the second elephant smashed open one leaf of the gate, half-crushing Paton who managed to hide behind the other leaf, bruised and bleeding, while the mob swept on past him, waving swords and muskets, until they filled most of the Palace.

Low, Shakespear and Iltifat on the outer verandah were now separated from the cowering King and his family, while the rebels, 2,000 or more of them, roared through the Burradurree and occupied the long intervening space between the Throne Room and the rest of the Palace. At this moment the Begum and the boy arrived. Things were going badly wrong. In a few minutes, the boy would be clambering up the steps of the *gaddi*, the royal throne, and seating himself on the *musnud*, the Cushion of State, before the spiky crown was placed on his head. And once crowned, it would be fearsomely difficult to uncrown him.

Until the British troops arrived, all that John Low could think of doing was to insist that he must speak to the Begum alone. After all, she needed him if the crowning was to be credible. He reasoned afterwards: 'I was utterly useless as a prisoner on the verandah. If I could once reach the Begum, I might perhaps be able to persuade her of the impossibility of her ultimately succeeding in keeping the boy on the throne. Above all, I thought it advantageous to get so much nearer the place where I knew our troops must arrive, also to do anything that might gain a little time.'

They managed to push their way through the dense screaming mass and succeeded in reaching the Burradurree, where at that moment the assailants were pushing the boy up the steps of the throne and firing ecstatic salutes from their blunderbusses. The Padsha Begum was seated in a covered palanquin just below the throne. The band was playing 'God Save the King' – as bands in Lucknow did at the annual re-crownings – to the booming of a double royal salute from the big guns out in the courtyard.

A party of dancing girls – belonging to the dead king or to the live Begum, nobody was sure which – began singing and swaying, though it was hard to hear them against the noise of the guns and the smashing of the chandeliers, which were taking heavy punishment from the blunderbusses. The wild crashing and banging would have been agonizingly audible to Augusta in bed at Residency no more than 300 yards away across the road. For all she knew, her husband and her brother had already been killed by the Begum's troops. Soon, perhaps any moment, they would come for her and torch the Residency.

The rebels pressed forward in John Low's face, poking him in the chest with their bayonets and firing matchlocks within inches, demanding that he salaam and pay tribute to the boy who was now sitting on the throne, looking down anxiously on the wild and threatening scene.

The Resident refused. He demanded to be allowed to leave, and eventually got out into the courtyard. Thank God, five companies of the 35th had at last arrived and were drawn up a few paces outside the Burradurree.

Now there was a stand-off. The Resident was outside waiting for the big guns. Munna Jan was sitting on the throne. The Begum was sitting in her palanquin below him. For the next few minutes, messages passed to and fro at a bewildering rate, threatening from the Resident, evasive from the Begum.

JL: You can never succeed. I am acting under the orders of my government, which has declared the right to the throne to be another's. Even if I and all my assistants are killed, my Government would soon send others to carry out their orders.

Begum: I am in my right place, and so is the young King, my grandson, and so are you. Why do you talk to me or to anybody else of leaving the throne and the Burradurree?

Not everyone was made of stuff as stern as Low and Shakespear. As the Resident went out into the courtyard, a Colonel Roberts, who commanded a brigade in the Oudh army, presented Munna Jan his ritual offering of gold mohurs, then went and hid himself to see how things turned out. The embarrassment of this officer on the morning after can easily be imagined. Captain Magness, who commanded the

Palace guard, told John that he did not feel quite sure of his sepoys and he had stationed a line of British troops to keep them steady. The hearts of his men, he said, were with Munna Jan and the Begum. Several parties of the King's troops had already deserted their posts and were swelling the wild crowd in the Throne Room. Mustafa Khan, who commanded a King's regiment of 1,000 horse, now paid homage to the young would-be King and presented his offering of gold, too. Mustafa was the most high-profile defector to the Begum's cause, and he was accordingly appointed her final envoy to the Resident.

He came out to the courtyard with a message that Colonel Low must return to the Throne Room and talk directly to the Begum. John repeated what he had already said: she had no hope of winning, the boy must get down off the throne which he had no right to occupy.

Then he took out his watch.

'Unless my orders are obeyed within fifteen minutes, my guns will open fire upon the throne room. Once they open fire, neither the Begum nor her followers can expect favour or even mercy. And unless you, Mustafa Khan, separate yourself from her party, you shall be hanged as a traitor if you are still alive.'

Nobody paid him the slightest attention. The nautch girls went on singing and dancing. The rebels, both inside the Palace and now out in the streets of Lucknow, went on blazing away. All over the city, there was plundering and jubilation. The city was with the boy. But the Brigadier had arrived, and so had the big guns.

John Low was still looking at his watch.

'Now five minutes are left ... now only three minutes ... please note there is less than one minute left.'

Boom! The guns now stationed all around the Palace, wherever there was a usable line of fire, opened up with grapeshot upon the Burradurree. After six or seven crushing discharges, a party of the 35th stormed the Palace, through a narrow passage, up a steep staircase and into the Burradurree, where they kept up a running fire and chivvied the rebels out at the point of the bayonet. The fire and smoke and screams were compounded by a great splintering of glass. When the men of the 35th came into the Throne Room, in the acrid haze they mistook for the enemy their own reflections in the enormous mirror behind the throne, and they poured their first volley into it.

Thirty or 40 rebels were killed inside the Palace, according to John Shakespear's report, 60-plus according to other estimates. One count from the Indian side reckoned that no less than 500 of the insurgents, inside and outside the Palace, had tasted the sherbet of death.[81]

The Begum had been carried into an adjoining room, still maintaining a precarious state of purdah amid the chaos and uproar. The sobbing Munna Jan was found concealed under the throne he had so briefly occupied. Both were arrested. Mustafa Khan did not survive to feel the rope that John Low had promised him. The beautiful Delhi princess who had been roped into the Begum's coup was roped out of it. She had been carried into a side-room as soon as the firing started. Her two female attendants, one of them with a shattered arm, tied some clothes together and let her down from a height of 24 feet into a courtyard, from where she escaped, relieved to be seeing the back of her late husband's Palace for the second time.

It was 9am before the Palace was finally cleared of the insurgents. The Resident was now desperate to get on with the coronation. A huge mop-up began to remove the bodies of the killed and wounded from the Throne Room and to sweep away the blood and the shattered glass.

When the Burradurree was more or less presentable again, the Resident proceeded there from the adjacent Palace with the Brigadier and all the British officers, their uniforms still reeking of cordite, to be greeted by an immense concourse of the nobility and gentry of Lucknow. John Low placed the crown on the trembling head of Muhammad Ali Shah, as he sat upon the same throne that his putative great-nephew, the boy king/pretender, had just vacated.

That throne, and the spiky crown too, are now preserved in the Husainabad Imamabara, which was to be built by Muhammad Ali

Shah during his short reign and where he now lies buried. Few
pieces of royal furniture can ever have had such an eventful night.[82]
The King was dead. Long live the King. No more 'Boppery bop', no
more 'Hip, Hip, Hoora'. The bean-counters had taken over. The
canny old Hakim Mehdi was recalled as Chief Minister (although he
was to die a few months later). In no time, the State's finances were
back in shape. The new King spent his time, not with barbers and
dancing girls but with State papers and revenue accounts. Nasir-ud-
din had been more popular with his people than he deserved to be –
there was, after all, a certain gaiety about him. The childishness
which upset the British was beguiling in small doses. But across the
road at the Residency there was no mourning, only the satisfaction
of a ticklish mission accomplished in the small hours and, though it
was not to be boasted of, brought off with considerable coolness.[83]

John Low accompanied the Begum and the boy back to the
Residency and put them up under armed guard. At first they were
kept separately, but then John heard the boy crying and let him go
into the Begum. After this, he looked in on both of them now and
then. The Begum was reading the Koran and appeared unper-
turbed.[84]

The new King was much relieved to see her go. He told the
Resident that 'the Begum was the most wicked and unscrupulous
woman he had ever known, and that he could expect no peace at
Lucknow while she remained.'[85]

Unrest was still bubbling in the city, though. There was talk of an
insurrection to murder the Resident and rescue the Begum and the
boy. A rumour, too, that the British Government might change its
mind and overturn the Resident's coup.[86] Low realized that his prisoners could not remain at the Residency, or in the city at all. At
midnight on July 11, the Begum and Munna Jan were sent off in
covered palanquins from the Residency under a strong escort of
infantry and artillery with John Shakespear in attendance. They
marched all day without resting, throughout one of the hottest days
of the year. The closely guarded party reached the boundary of

Oudh at Cawnpore at 9.30 on the evening of July 12, where they crossed the Ganges.

John sent on after them the boy's mother, Afsal Mahal, together with 18 slave girls and ten suits of cloth, both male and female, plus 18 cartloads of garments, gold and furniture from the Begum's house, also the Begum's favourite parrot, which she badly missed.

The prisoners were eventually taken on to Chunar Fort, near Benares, where they remained locked up for the rest of their lives. Their swift removal from the scene had halted the unrest in Lucknow. The new King was at least a familiar figure, being not only the old King's uncle but a former Chief Minister.

Despite the enduring love of his mother, Munna Jan grew up to be an unappetizing adult, resembling his father both in face and figure as well as in his hot temper and wilful nature. Anyone who saw him in later life, as Colonel Sleeman did, had little doubt that he really was the son of Nasir-ud-din and so the legitimate heir to the throne.[87]

I wonder if John Low reflected on the day 20 years earlier when he himself had escorted a royal prisoner to Cawnpore. First the Peshwa, now the boy-king of Oudh ... How odd it was that he, who believed so strongly in keeping native princes on their thrones, should now have toppled two of them.

Still, the Court of Directors was well pleased with the night's work and congratulated Colonel Low on his coolness and daring. They ordered Monsieur Dufay de Casanova, the Court Painter, to commemorate the scene in the Burradurree.[88] This sepia drawing, entitled *The Begum's Attempt to Usurp the Throne of Oudh for Moona Jan, 7th July 1837*, is a murky production, although it does convey the darkling chaos with the heroic Resident standing firm and his brother-in-law John Shakespear with his huge black moustachios being manhandled by the supporters of the Begum, who is just visible in her palanquin below the throne.

Lord Auckland too was grateful – up to a point. Officially, he wrote a week later to record 'his high sense of the judgment and promptitude displayed by you on this occasion; and while he regrets the loss of life which has been sustained among the infatuated adherents of the Begum, he feels satisfied that nothing short of the most vigorous and decisive measures could have put a stop to the disaffection and anarchy which was rapidly spreading throughout the city.'

But he felt compelled to add that 'I should undoubtedly have been better pleased if Col. Low had not in this moment of exigency accepted the unconditional engagement of submissiveness which the new King has signed.'[89] He did not wish it to look as if the British Government was twisting the arm of the trembling old uncle. This disapproval was strictly for the record. Auckland's real view can be judged by the speed with which he set about exploiting this 'submissiveness'.[90]

Within days, Auckland had sent John Low his draft of a new treaty. The draft compelled the new King to pay for a new auxiliary force, freeing the existing subsidiary force for military operations outside Oudh. Auckland completely ignored the fact that Oudh had already ceded more than half her territory to pay for the first force.

Low was appalled. He was hostile to a treaty so flagrantly designed 'more for our own purposes and interests than for the King's or for the direct advantage of his subjects'. Such a treaty was 'of a nature that would be very grating to the feelings of a native sovereign of respectable character, and must be peculiarly painful to the present King'.[91] The Kings of Oudh were being asked to pay twice for the same service. The whole premise of Low's original plan to instal the new King was that he 'should be placed on the throne <u>without making him pay a single rupee or give up one acre of land for his elevation</u>' – a condition which he had underlined in his original plan, and now he underlined it again in his horrified letter to Auckland of August 3. If it had been right 'to adhere to a liberal and really disinterested line of policy when they were actively deposing the King, was it not still more incumbent upon the British government when the new King was succeeding by his own lawful right to the throne'? The letter was phrased with exquisite, even painful courtesy – John confessed to 'feelings of deep regret which have oppressed me during the last few days at finding myself differing in opinion from my own government to which I owe so much'. But he stuck to his guns.

Auckland refused to budge. In his tortuously phrased letter of August 11, he told Colonel Low that it was his job to obey orders and not to question the morality or legality of measures deemed necessary for the good of his country. He ended with a veiled threat:

> I am well aware that you share with me in an anxious desire to support the honour and consolidate the power of our country; and if I had not the most perfect confidence in the zeal and ability with which you will pursue those objects, I should look upon your residence at Lucknow with different feelings from those of the satisfaction with which I have been accustomed to view it.[92]

But John was not alone in his disgust. On the Supreme Council, both Mr Ross and Uncle Henry Shakespear pointed out that the Treaty of 1801 released 'the Nawab of Oudh from the obligation of defraying the expences of any *additional* troops'. His Majesty really could not be expected to pay twice when his predecessor had already surrendered half his kingdom. Lord Auckland still did not budge. But the Court of Directors were strongly of the same view, that the proposed deal would reflect very badly on Britain.

In the end, and with the greatest reluctance, Lord Auckland withdrew the clause about the new auxiliary force and kissed goodbye to another £160,000 a year to pay for his Afghan War. But the King still had his arm twisted to make a massive loan of £460,000 for the same purpose.[93]

Even then, Lord Auckland – who had seemed like a shy but honourable sort of bachelor before he was over-promoted to Calcutta – was incapable of playing straight. He gave the King to understand that he had dropped the auxiliary force as 'an act of grace'. He never informed Muhammad Ali Shah that the whole treaty which he had signed had been rejected *in toto* by London. Because of this double-dealing, 20 years later people were still referring to the Treaty of 1837 as though it was still operative. Only John Low himself, by now a member of the Supreme Council, was able to put the record straight. He had told the King officially on July 8, 1839 (nearly two years after the extortionate demand had been made), that he would be permanently relieved of the expense of the auxiliary force, but the King was not told that the whole Treaty of 1837 was now dead, 'and no official intimation to that effect has ever been made up to this date, to any one at Lucknow, European or native.'[94]

We have seen the fierce rapacity of Lord Wellesley in screwing the Nawab out of half his dominion. We have seen the deviousness of Lord Hastings in tempting the Nawab to declare himself a King and then extracting loan after loan from him. Now we see the double-dealing of Lord Auckland, first in demanding an unjust treaty from the new King, and then concealing the truth about it to cover up his personal humiliation, while forcing him to stump up another giant loan.

British historians over the years have liked to rank one Governor-General as superior or inferior to another. But if you were a nawab or even an ordinary citizen of Lucknow, you could be forgiven for thinking that they were all much of a muchness: equally unrelenting in their desire for acres and rupees, and equally unscrupulous in their methods of extracting either, or preferably both. When the Raja's Treasury was brimming, the Governor-General would pester him for loans: Hastings in the 1810s, Amherst in the 1820s, Auckland in the 1830s. When the Raja's Treasury was empty and he was in hock to the Honourable Company – often because of the expense of maintaining the Company's auxiliary force – then the Governor-General would insist that he cede enormous tracts of land to pay off the debt: Wellesley in Oudh in 1801, Dalhousie in Hyderabad in 1854. Archbishop Morton's Fork had nothing on the Governor-General's pincers.

But John Low was an old soldier, used to taking things in his stride. And he and Augusta gave Lord Auckland's sisters their usual genial welcome when the three Edens sailed up the Ganges at the end of 1837 (the Governor-General himself felt himself unable to come to Lucknow, because protocol forbade him to pay obeisance to the Kings of Oudh, although it was the British who had egged them on to proclaim themselves as such). After everything that had come before, Lord Auckland's outrageous plan had been quietly shelved, Muhammad Ali Shah was quietly setting the kingdom straight, and for once Oudh was fulfilling its role as 'the Garden of India'.

Emily Eden enthuses over her breakfast in the Palace, 'which was quite as Arabian-Nightish as I meant it to be'. She sums up recent political events in Lucknow in her usual, breezy, clipped manner: 'The late king drank himself to death about six months ago; and then there was a sort of revolution conducted by Colonel L. (who was nearly killed in this palace), by which the present king was placed on the throne; so these are early days for acting royalty.'[95]

The Edens' party toured the royal yacht, the royal gardens and the royal stud. In the evening there were fireworks on the river: 'On the opposite bank there was an illumination in immense letters, "God save George Lord Auckland, Governor-General of India", "God save the King of Oude," and then there was a full stop, and "Colonel L., Resident of Lucknow," stood alone. Whether he was to be *saved* or not was not mentioned; it was not very correctly spelt, but well-meant ... The river was covered with rafts full of fireworks, and the boats in front were loaded with nautch girls, who dance on, whether they are looked at or not.'[96]

Were these perhaps the same party of nautch-girls who had danced on regardless when Colonel L. was tussling with the Begum in the Throne Room? Who can tell? As Miss Eden points out, nobody was looking at them.

X

RICHMOND THE RESCUER

Colonel Low was on top of his world. Never before and never again was he so entirely in command of all he surveyed. He had placed the playing-card crown on the King of his choice. And his choice turned out to be the right choice for the people's welfare. He had taken the high moral ground and held on to it, slapping down the attempts of the Governor-General to fleece the new King. As Resident, he was earning 66,000 rupees a year. And his family was swelling with his fortunes.

Augusta had just given birth to their second son, Robert Cunliffe Low, born January 28, 1838. The baby sprawled on the dimpled lawns of the Residency until the weather warmed and the ayah took him below to the delicious cool of the underground rooms where Augusta, now grown decidedly plump after her fifth pregnancy, sat fanning herself. From Clatto, Granny Low wrote to report that the two elder children were blooming. 'Malcolm is a very handsome child and nobody more ready to show off his accomplishments than dear little Charlotte. She is quite enchanted with him.'[1]

And her grandmother was enchanted with her:

Darling Charlotte is in high health & spirits, just gone out to walk and the day delightful. Her frock is a very pretty one which came with her, & never was peacock more proud of its radiant tail. She turned herself round to shew it when she came into my room this morning. I asked her in French if she was going to walk today. Her answer was – "J'irai s'il fait beau"; you must not imagine from this that she knows a great deal of French, she merely answers questions she has been taught, but she has a great collection of words which she uses of herself. She prays for you both every night before leaving my room. She really is not spoiled. I shall give you an instance; she has a little fork which she uses sometimes when she comes into the dining-room after dinner. The other day she thought proper to scratch the table with it, & when she was forbid, did it again, so I took it from her. When she went to the nursery, she addressed a doll she calls Grania: 'Now, Grania, you behaved very ill about the fork, if you had been quiet you would have got it again, but instead of that you roared.'[2]

The little girl had a beguiling self-confidence which entranced maiden aunts and visiting elderly generals. 'Darling Charlotte is at present the centre of attraction to a numerous train, which does not spoil her for she walks off with her maid whenever she is bid, telling them she will be back bye & bye.'[3] On Sundays she drank a toast in sugar and water to all her friends in India. Her education seems to have been focused on French and Bible studies, no doubt egged on by her pious Aunt Georgina: 'Little darling can repeat the first chapter of Genesis but has gone no further in book learning than the alphabet ... When she hears a word that is new to her, she immediately asks *the French of it*, in English she is a bit of a cockney, for she frequently uses W. for V ... she told Georgina that a *wariety* of people thought she was clever. Georgina told her not to believe all she was told on that subject.'[4]

A friend from England had just brought out to Lucknow a water-colour of Susan Elizabeth Low in her frilly white bonnet and a miniature of Charlotte, both by the same artist, Frederick Cruickshank. John wrote to thank for these long-awaited reminders of the two people who meant most to him. In his letter, he also said he hoped that the building part of the improvements at Clatto would be finished, and reminded his mother to plant a good mixture of trees around the house. You can see that he is dreaming of home ever more urgently now – of the fairways at St Andrews, of the water closets at Clatto, above all, of the children. His mother's letters, carefully treasured all the years he was in India, are a whispered allurement to come home: to the peaches ripening on the south wall, to the carriage rides along the tumbling burns of Dura Den, and the pawky gossip of Fifeshire neighbours.[5]

At last, after seven years at Lucknow, there was a realistic chance that he could afford to leave India. He was becoming something of a nabob:

> I am now come to an interesting, I might say exciting period of my career, for I am remitting home all I have saved, & purchasing India stock, & the possession of it will give me some votes in the Court of Proprietors for the election of Directors etc.
>
> I can now also be here only two more hot seasons, possibly only one, yet ... the great advantage of staying here till 1840 is not merely the addition of £3,000 to my purse, but that I should in all probability reach the rank of colonel without coming out at all.[6]

This was as near jubilation as a canny Lowlander could permit himself. His spirits were undimmed by the fact that he had just had to meet another call for £1,000 from the creditors of the Fife Bank, which had collapsed 13 years earlier, for then as now a bank failure leaves as long a trail of debris as a medium-sized comet.[7]

As though seeing the frown beginning to form on his mother's alert, apprehensive features (so like his own), he hastened to reassure her that 'I hope & think, however, that I don't think about money too much ... but there is something very comfortable to my feelings to think that, by staying only a little more than two years, I should secure the means of educating & providing for my children (when I say providing for them I only mean furnishing them with *the means of exerting themselves successfully in life*).' Even that carefully hedged sentiment he felt he needed to qualify by adding that nobody was 'more fully aware than myself of the *extreme uncertainty of all human schemes*.'[8]

The only downside to his life was his own health. Fifteen Indian summers since his last excursion to more temperate climes had left his lungs and liver frazzled. His doctor had warned him that unless he took 'a cooling and complete relaxation from business for 12 or 15 months', he would become dangerously ill. He and Augusta and baby Robert set off for Calcutta to take ship for the Cape of Good Hope, the recuperation resort for all Anglo-Indians. Augusta's brother John Shakespear was entitled to a long leave and he came with them, but at Calcutta he fell in love and came on board ship in a gloom.[9]

When they reached the Cape, it was not only John Shakespear who was in poor spirits. Augusta, too, was depressed after a bad bout of fever. The doctors suggested that she and baby Robert should go on to Scotland. But after a few weeks she perked up and resolved to stay at the Cape with her husband, while little Robert was sent on to Clatto with the William Lows, John's brother and sister-in-law, who had turned up at the Cape on their way home. Whenever Augusta had to choose between staying with her babies or with her husband, she usually chose John.

She did not remain childless for long. Six months after parting with Robert, she gave birth to a third son, who was christened John Alwes. We shall hear a great deal of Robert but very little of John Alwes – except for one memorable appearance at the age of 17 on his return to India after all hell had broken loose.

Braced by the mild breezes of the Cape, the Lows returned to Calcutta with a different son from the one that they had sailed down the Hooghly with 18 months earlier. With unnerving rapidity and regularity, Augusta, now fully recovered, was soon pregnant again. This was to be the last baby they would have in India. By the end of 1841, John would have completed ten years' service at Lucknow, not to mention 36 years in India. He was 53 years old – many of his brother officers had retired when they were younger than that. It was time to go home, at least for a long furlough, perhaps for good, to see Charlotte and Malcolm and Robert while they were still children, and to see his mother while she was still alive.

Then something happened which knocked the whole British Empire in India off its perch, and sent John Low spinning off his. It was a national humiliation and a personal disaster. Afterwards, as with all disasters, the obloquy was flung in every conceivable direction, but everyone knew that there was only one man to blame: the Governor-General, George Eden, Lord Auckland. In his sisters' diaries (for Fanny wrote a journal as well as Emily), George or 'G.' figures as a querulous, awkward, rather impatient bachelor, who is not entirely unsympathetic. At any rate, you can see why his sisters might be fond of him. But on the imperial stage, his weaknesses had consequences which were as calamitous as they were foreseeable and foreseen.

Auckland had taken it into his head to launch an army across the Indus into Afghanistan, with the aim of restoring the old King Shah Shuja and ejecting the brutal but forceful warlord Dost Mohammad. The purpose was to secure that alarming northern kingdom against the Russians, or any other potential hostile ally of the Afghan regime, such as the Persians, perhaps even the French.

It was not Auckland himself who had dreamed up the idea, and he was at first reluctant to look at it. He was worked on by his three aides, Macnaghten, Colvin and Henry Torrens, the zealots of the 'modernizing' school, ridiculed by Emily Eden in her letters as Mr A., Mr B. and Mr C. Later apologists, such as Colvin's son (named Auckland after his father's old chief), made out that Auckland was essentially acting under orders from London. That was not what people in India thought at the time. True, letters from the India House and from the British Government often expressed anxieties about the North-West Frontier and how it might be secured. But the 'forward policy' and the decision to invade were Auckland's responsibility and Auckland's alone.

Originally, his plan had been only that the British should encourage an alliance between Shah Shuja and Ranjit Singh, the great Sikh chief, to recover the domains that Shuja had lost and had already made several abortive efforts to get back. 'England was to remain in the back ground jingling the money-bags.' But as the spring of 1838 hotted up, His Lordship became increasingly attracted by the idea that Britain should join the alliance and contribute some of her own troops. Ranjit Singh purred with delight at the prospect: 'This would be adding sugar to milk.' It was a classic case of mission creep.

In the view of Sir John Kaye, the intoxicating air of Simla was partly to blame. 'Unfortunately, at this time, Lord Auckland was separated from his Council. He was on his way to that pleasant hill sanitarium, at Simlah, where our Governors-General, surrounded by irresponsible advisers, settle the destinies of empires without the aid of their legitimate fellow-counsellors, and which has been the cradle of more political insanity than any place within the limits of Hindostan.'[10] Simla's record for disastrous decision-making continued long after Kaye's death. There, Curzon dreamed up the calamitous partition of Bengal; there, Younghusband's invasion of Tibet was planned; and, most disastrous of all, it was in Simla that all parties met to discuss the partition of India.

Even on this Magic Mountain, Lord Auckland wobbled. Captain Alexander Burnes, the devil-may-care British agent at Kabul who saw nothing wrong with leaving Dost Mohammad in power, gives a piquant description of arriving at Simla after the decision for British troops to cross the Indus had already been taken: 'when he arrived, Torrens and Colvin came running to him, and prayed him to say nothing to unsettle his Lordship; they had all the trouble in the world to get him into the business, and even now he would be glad of any pretext to retire from it.'[11]

Certainly the Court of Directors in Leadenhall Street were dead against the project. So were the members of the Supreme Council in Calcutta, who were furious to have been left out of the loop.

Military men from the Duke of Wellington downwards thought the expedition a flagrant folly. The Commander-in-Chief, Sir Henry Fane, thought that any advance to the west, across the River Sutlej, let alone the Indus beyond it, weakened the Empire rather than strengthening it: 'Make your self complete sovereigns of all within your bounds. *But let alone the Far West.*'[12]

We have already seen John Low repeatedly express his strong disagreement with Macnaghten and Colvin over how to deal with native states. The idea of invading Afghanistan looked to him too like an equally doom-laden folly. He had written to his old friend, Sir James Lushington, the reformed mutineer of Madras who had just become chairman of the East India Company, on October 15, 1838, just as the huge Army of the Indus was gathering for its march to Kandahar through the snow and the high passes:

> The only thing that I fear (& enough too) is the dreadful expense of sending so large an army to such a distance, and the future inconvenience that must follow extending our position so enormously as to take military occupation of Candahar, Cabool, etc., on the other side of the Indus, for I suspect that we shall *never* be able to withdraw our troops from those countries.[13]

But in November 1838, for anyone who sought military glory or who just wanted to do his bit, there was only one place to be: in the Army of the Indus. John's unreliable nephew, Aleck Deas, was already in cantonments with his regiment, the 5th Bengal Native Infantry, on the plains of Ferozepur beside the River Sutlej, which marked the boundary of the British territories.

Augusta's youngest brother, Richmond, was still stuck in the Survey Department. The Great Arc survey was by now in its final stretches, pushing north towards Sir George Everest's eyrie in the Himalayas (which was, as it happens, at Mussoorie, where John and Augusta had been married). But this was no time for trigonometry. Richmond applied to be posted to a company, received no reply, and resigned from the Survey Department. His resignation was ignored and he was ordered to rejoin the Army.[14]

Since we saw him going off to Charterhouse School with his cousin William Makepeace Thackeray, Richmond had grown up. His eldest brother John wrote to their baby sister Selina: 'He must be much altered from what he was when you knew him; he is now six feet two inches in height and stout in proportion, sports large whiskers, is very intelligent and has a great flow of spirits.'[15]

Richmond really was a force of nature: unfailingly exuberant, optimistic, resourceful. Not academic by nature, he had failed in his first attempt at Addiscombe College, though he eventually passed into the Bengal Artillery.[16] But like many of the Shakespears, he was mechanically minded. His great-uncle Colin invented a collapsible bridge of ropes and bamboos which could span rivers of 300 feet and more, known as the Shakespearean Pont Roulant Militaire.[17] Another cousin, John Davenport Shakespear, invented a safety lamp for use in mines.[18] Later in life, en poste at Gwalior and Jodhpur, Richmond spent much of his leisure in his workshop engaged in electrical experiments and devising pumps and windmills. He delighted the Maharajah of Jodhpur by rigging up a circuit which enabled His Highness to fire a toy cannon at the end of the garden by pressing a bell at the side of his throne.[19] But he was a gunner first and foremost, and whenever there was a gunner's battle to be fought in India, he was in the thick of it.

He was to need all these qualities, both mechanical and moral, in Afghanistan. In October, he had written with his usual incurable high spirits to his eldest sister Emily: 'I am posted to the experimental Camel Battery, from which great things are expected ... My marching establishment is *quite* complete, as I have a good horse, Coverley [his soldier servant], tent, gun, five camels, and, as Dogberry says, "everything handsome about me." Add to which I have not one rupee of debt, and shall start to the wars with 1,000 rupees in hand.'[20] On his way to join the Army, he calls in at Lucknow to say hello to his sister Augusta and his brother John

Dowdeswell, as ever teasing both of them: Augusta about her embonpoint and John about his unmarried condition. He himself was liable to be teased back. John had written of Richmond to his sister some years earlier: 'The young man is in love, I suspect, with whom I know not, but it is a susceptible youth.'[21] Then Richmond passes gaily on his way, promising to spend his next leave there when he comes back.

It was Richmond's Camel Battery which fired the salute to Auckland's ally Ranjit Singh, the ruler of the Punjabi Sikhs, when the two potentates met at Ferozepur. Nothing had been seen like their meeting since the Field of the Cloth of Gold (a parallel which did occur to one of Auckland's more cynical ADCs). Ranjit had sent 600 of his gardeners to arrange gardens of potted roses around the officers' tents.[22] Even Emily Eden was impressed: 'Behind us there was a large amphitheatre of elephants belonging to our own camp, or to the Sikhs, and thousands of Runjeet's followers all dressed in yellow or red satin, with quantities of their led horses *trapped* in gold and silver tissues, and all of them sparkling with jewels. I really never saw so dazzling a sight. Three or four Sikhs would look like Astley's [Circus] broke loose, but this immense body of them saves their splendour from being melodramatic.'[23] Ranjit was presented with the picture that Emily had done of the young Queen Victoria. Up close, he looked 'exactly like an old mouse, with grey whiskers and one eye'[24], and a drunken old mouse at that. But he had created a great empire, and at dinner Fanny, at least, thought he showed a certain style, being dressed in plain white pyjamas and wearing only a single jewel, which happened to be the Koh-i-Noor.

By the time this splendiferous cavalcade set off, news had already reached Lord Auckland that the reasons for the whole expedition had already sharply diminished if not disappeared. Both the Russians and the Persians had backed down from their forward moves. Palmerston, then Foreign Secretary, had persuaded his opposite number in St Petersburg, Count Nesselrode, to remove his aggressive ambassador to the Persian court and to recall his agent who was stirring up trouble in Kandahar. The Persians themselves, alarmed by the news of British war preparations, had abandoned their siege of Herat. As Sir John Kaye pointed out: 'The legitimate object of the expedition was gone. All that remained was usurpation and aggression.'[25] Lord Auckland's Simla Manifesto had put the siege of Herat as the prime justification for invading Afghanistan. The logical thing now was for him to break up the great Army or, better still, slim it down to constitute what would still be a formidable protective force along the North-West Frontier. He would have needed to pay off Ranjit Singh and do a deal with Dost Mohammed, but then both chiefs were themselves veterans of the volte-face. All this would have cost a few million rupees, but nothing like the cost of a full-scale invasion and occupation.

Even the enthusiastic Richmond wrote a few months later to Emily and her husband: 'Had we made a treaty with Dost Mahomed and the Kandahar Chiefs many years back, we might now have avoided sending this force across the Indus. Dost Mahomed tried to make a treaty with us, our guaranteeing him against aggressions of Runjeet Singh, but this was refused and he then applied to Persia, and thus the Russians found an opportunity of opening communications with him and his brothers.'[26] Every old India hand could see it (and Richmond was only 27 at the time). Only Auckland, egged on by Messrs A. B. and C., was blind to the plain truth. This was the classic case of a weak man made fatally stubborn by fear of being thought weak. And so off the Army of the Indus went to war: 15,000 Europeans and native sepoys, 6,000 irregulars laid on by Shah Shuja, followed by no less than 38,000 Indian camp followers and 30,000 camels.[27]

Ah, the camels. General Sir Willoughby Cotton, the headstrong army commander, needed 260 of the beasts to carry his kit over the passes. Even a mere brigadier required 50. The Army's wine cellar took up 300 camels. One regiment had two camels carrying nothing but the best Manila cigars.[28] Sir Henry Fane had exhorted his army to travel as light as possible but, as Sir John Kaye remarked, 'there is a natural disposition on the part of Englishmen, in all quarters of the globe, to carry their comforts with them.' And there was a feeling in the officers' messes that this was not so much a mission of life and death but rather 'a grand military promenade'.

Richmond fancied his battery decidedly under-camelled: 'if they will give us six instead of four camels to each gun, we may act with Cavalry, provided there are no puddles on the road. We were detained the other day three hours by a water-course not four feet in width. You have no idea of the floundering, splashing, etc., roaring of the poor oonts. ['Unt' is the Hindi word for camel.] One comes down and the others drag him on, and, in a moment, the poor beast is doubled up into the smallest possible space, head along neck to one side, hind legs to the front and forelegs to the rear ... but the most surprising thing is that, on being unharnessed and extricated, our fallen friend is found to be uninjured and, if anything, refreshed by his roll in the sand and water.'[29]

All this was at least on the flat, as they crossed the tributaries of the Indus and then the deserts beyond. Getting over the Bolan Pass, which led to Quetta, then only a miserable village, was grimmer work.[30]

In the foothills, the camels managed to trudge along, slowly but tirelessly, over stretches where even the horse artillery had been obliged to use drag ropes. But the high pass was too much for many of Richmond's baggage camels. 'The road was literally strewed with them. The poor beasts went on to the last moment, then stopped and sat down. They make no struggle or noise, but wait patiently till death puts an end to their sufferings.'[31] Many an officer had to burn his tent and jettison his cherished goods for want of a camel to carry them, and the thieves came down from the hills to haul away all the parcels of cheroots and pickles and Madeira and eau de cologne. The next pass, the Khojak Pass which gave access to Kandahar, was more arduous still. Already dozens of the cavalry horses were too exhausted to go on and had to be shot. The Experimental Camel Battery had to use drag ropes both ascending and descending, which took a whole day. Richmond was knocked down by a wagon which had broken loose from the ropes. 'Both wheels passed over me very lightly. The ground was soft, and after two or three hours I was able to walk about and in two or three days as well as ever again.'[32] The water was putrid from the dead animals that had fallen in, and anyone who drank from it was immediately racked by stomach cramps and diarrhoea. Food had almost run out among the camp followers. One officer saw the body of a man who had died while gnawing gristle from the carcass of a bullock. All this before they had caught sight of a single enemy soldier.

The Grand Army that staggered out into the plain of Kandahar was already a moral and physical wreck. But at Kandahar they were in luck. Instead of the fierce resistance they might have expected, they were met by a trickle of local nobles offering allegiance to Shah Shuja. Macnaghten, now Auckland's envoy to Afghanistan, believed that this showed he had been right all along. The Afghans respected the principle of legitimacy and were glad to see their true sovereign restored. To us, it may seem more likely that the nobles who 'came in' were simply backing what they thought was the winning side. At any rate, Macnaghten wrote in jubilation to Auckland from the palace of Kandahar, that it was as if the Army had suddenly dropped into paradise: 'We have, I think, been most fortunate in every way. The Shah made a grand public entry in the city this morning and was received with feelings nearly amounting to adoration.'[33] Already Macnaghten was seeing only what he wanted to see. Another observer, the young teetotal Baptist, Captain Henry Havelock, wrote that: 'Unless I have been deceived, all the national enthusiasm of the scene was entirely confined to His Majesty's immediate retainers. The people of Candahar are said to have viewed the whole affair with the utmost mortifying indifference.'[34]

The Army of the Indus were right to enjoy their respite, for there was to be hard fighting ahead on the road to Kabul, especially at the fort of Ghazni. But Richmond Shakespear was to have no part in it, for he was detached as one of six officers to accompany Major D'Arcy Todd on a special mission to the north of the country, to Herat. Also in the party were a fellow Bengal artilleryman, Captain James Abbott, and Captain Sanders, a battle-hardened engineer who was the acknowledged beau of Richmond's youngest sister, Selina, 'dear Selinthus'.

The Persians had only just abandoned a long and furious siege of Herat, in which the British spy, Lieutenant Eldred Pottinger, originally disguised as a horse-trader, had played a gallant part. However, the victorious Wazir was not showing much gratitude. He threatened to have Pottinger killed, had his men cut off the hand of one of Pottinger's servants, and opened secret negotiations with his besiegers, declaring that 'I swear to God that I prefer the fury of the Shah to the kindliness of a million of the English' – a maxim that continues to resound in our ears today.[35]

Major Todd's mission was to conciliate the Wazir and settle the frontier with Shah Shuja's domain, so that there would be a pro-British ally in the northern buffer zone – a classic move in what was to be known as the Great Game. Like most moves in that game, it was a provocative and expensive undertaking. The Wazir turned out to be a brute, who boiled, baked and roasted his enemies.[36] Richmond's task was to train the Heratis in gunnery. But as there was neither a foundry nor a powder mill there, he found it hard to get going. There were, however, compensations: 'at the River Farrah we halted three days and caught some fine fish and ate the most delicious grapes, each grape as large as a greengage and of the most exquisite flavour.'[37] The country was beautiful and the climate lovely, and there were plenty of pigs to stick.

The new threat, though, was not from the Persians but from the Russians. The British invasion had, like most moves in the Great Game, provoked a counter-move. For several years, Count Perovsky, Governor of the Russian border town of Orenburg, had been lobbying to revive Russian power in the region by annexing the Turkoman Khanate of Khiva. The pretext was the rescue of the hundreds of Russian serfs who had been kidnapped and sold into slavery by the Khivans. But it was the British invasion that prodded St Petersburg into reaction. The Czar's ministers decided that an expedition to Khiva would 'consolidate the influence of Russia in Central Asia, weaken the long-standing impunity of the Khivans, and especially that constancy with which the English government, to the detriment of our industry and trade, strives to spread its supremacy in those parts'.[38] A wish list which pretty much mirrored the motives of the British in pushing up in the opposite direction.

Major Todd, acting on his own initiative, thought that he might frustrate this move by himself getting the Russian captives released before the Russian army reached Khiva. So on Christmas Eve 1839, he sent off a small party, led by Captain James Abbott, bearing a friendly letter to the Khan. Stage One of the mission worked a treat. Abbott, togged up in Afghan costume, reached Khiva, where he discovered that an outbreak of disease in the Russian ranks had already forced their army to retire. Perovsky had lost half his camels and nearly half his men in the terrible weather. The Khan was now happy to release all the Russian captives, if the Russian government would send back in exchange to Khiva the hundreds of Khivan subjects it held. Abbott set off to St Petersburg to deliver this message. Unfortunately, he was captured by Turkoman brigands on the way and disappeared from view. Major Todd had no clue what had happened to him. The Russians were still captives, and still presented a standing *casus belli* any time the Russians were ready to invade again. The danger of war was only postponed.

Undeterred, Major Todd decided to send out another mission, consisting of handpicked Heratis commanded by the next officer in line, Lieutenant R. Shakespear. If Richmond did not manage to free the Russian slaves, at least he might find out what had happened to poor Abbott. Besides, on May 9, 1840 – more than four months after Abbott had left Herat – Todd received dispatches from Macnaghten authorizing Abbott to act on behalf of the Government of India at Khiva. So he had to send somebody. The next day,

Richmond, up for it as always, wrote to his sister Emily: 'Never man yet had a fairer chance of an opening.'[39]

Richmond had no idea whether Abbott was dead or alive, whether the Russians were retreating or advancing. He himself might be murdered by the Russians, by the Khivans, even by the Persians. He was as happy as any man alive. 'In short, the chances of distinction are so great, and the hazard so slight, that the heart of even a wren would be gladdened by the prospect,' he wrote in his journal on the morning of May 15.[40]

Like Abbott before him, he set off dressed in Afghan style: a turban of white muslin with large folds, bright red trousers 'so preposterously wide as to be inconvenient', shirt 'of the same blushing hue', and a long, collarless surtout of a light blue chintz, trimmed with cashmere shawl. And, to fend off the dust of the desert, a full, brown cloak with long sleeves. Under his shirt he had nearly 300 ducats concealed in his purse; so had the four leading Afghans in the party, making a total treasury of 1,500 ducats, about £900. There were about 30 of them all told, with 35 horses and mules. 'The first seventeen miles of the road are truly beautiful; you cross over the crest of the hills which must be, I should say, at an elevation of 7,000 feet. There are hundreds of hills sloping off in all directions, and covered with the most luxurious grass; every variety of colour was to be found in the weeds and every little valley had its own peculiar stream of the purest water.'[41]

Then they came into dry and barren country. 'Our place of rest during the heat of the day was ill chosen; heat great, flies troublesome, grass indifferent and water distant.' They still travelled 30 miles that day, as they did most days. At the banks of the Moorghaub, a muddy, fast stream fringed with tamarisk jungle: 'Here we found a kafilah of grain bound for Heraut, and a man with a note from the Cazee [Qazi, judge] of Yellatoon to Major Todd, in which I found it written that Captain Abbott had not only succeeded in stopping the advance of the Russian army, but had reached St Petersburg, and procured an order for the return of the force and the destruction of the forts. I don't believe this, though what on earth could make the Cazee of Yellatoon write such a falsehood, is difficult to imagine.'[42] Richmond was right to be sceptical. In any case, his orders were to press on to Khiva.

Now they were in bandit country, roamed by gangs of Turkoman slavers. 'Before starting yesterday, the Cazee came to my tent and said that three Turkomans were carrying away some natives of Heraut as slaves. On coming out, I found young Daood had seized the bridle of the leading Turkoman, and was bringing the party to our camp. There were ten slaves, two females, and the rest boys – mere children. I am ashamed to say that I was silly enough to let my anger lead me into the absurdity of expressing the disgust and horror which I felt, and was guilty of the folly of lecturing Turkomans on the evil of their ways. The poor children seemed thin and harassed, but not the least frightened, nor very anxious for their release ... I had no power to release these poor creatures, and had I taken upon myself to do so, I should most probably have defeated the object of my mission, which will amongst other things, I hope, lead to the cessation in toto of this most detestable traffic. Had I turned the poor children loose, they would soon have been retaken.'[43]

At Yellatoon, he was received by the Governor and fed with raisins and bread. In the Governor's tent he learned how the more intelligent tribesmen were alarmed by the advance of the Great Powers: 'Do you think we are such dolts as not to perceive what will be the end of all this? You and the Russians will meet and shake hands, and we shall be crushed in the operation.' The Governor insisted on giving Richmond two superb hawks, each of them said to be worth at least four slaves.[44]

Beyond the Moorghaub they relied on a young Turkoman guide through the trackless wastes. 'When the first dawn of day appeared, it was fine to see the young Turkoman gazing like a startled antelope from side to side, scampering up to every mound and peering over every sand-hill.' Even with the aid of Richmond's telescope, the road was hard to find, and fresh water even harder. 'By daylight even, it was difficult to trace the road, the soil being nothing but loose sand which drifts with every breeze. The only good marks are the bones of dead camels and other animals, of which there are great quantities. Some public-spirited people have been at the trouble of occasionally putting the skeleton of a camel's head on a bush near the road; and this is considered an infallible sign.'[45] Richmond curled up in the sand for a nap, and dreamed of drowning Turkomans, telescopes, streams of water, and the horrors of dying of thirst.

Even when the Turkoman guide finally found a well, the water was so impregnated with saltpetre and had such an unpleasant flavour that Richmond refused to drink and waited until the sturdy irregular horseman Fazil Khan came back with two leather bags of water which tasted like nectar and made a capital cup of tea. After travelling two hundred miles under these testing conditions, they finally reached the banks of the Oxus:

> which is a magnificent stream, with rather high banks. I should estimate the distance between the high banks at three miles. Through this channel the body of the water takes a serpentine course, now on one side, and now on the other, leaving large portions of dry ground, which are invariably covered with the most luxuriant jungle. Immediately you ascend the high bank you are on the desert, and, I think, the same would be found on the other side. This noble stream flows on its stately course without deigning to hold any connexion with the barren wilderness on its banks; a fine image for one poetically disposed – vanity of vanities ... God grant that my wanderings may bring me to old England![46]

They reached Khiva on June 12, having covered a distance of 697 miles in 25 days. And here at last they had reliable news of Captain Abbott, from another son of the Qazi's who had been sent on to look for him several months earlier. Abbott had indeed reached Khiva, reached agreement with the Khan and gone on towards the

Caspian Sea, intending to get the Russians to agree to their side of the deal. But on his way he had been attacked at night by a party of 50 Cossacks, had been beaten senseless and had two fingers of his right hand slashed off by their sabre cuts. He was taken into captivity, near starvation and alone, his servants having been distributed as slaves. But the Qazi's son and the cavalrymen, whom the Khan had sent with him, managed to overawe the Cossacks, and they allowed him to escort poor Abbott to Novopetrovskoye (later Fort Alexandrovsk, today Fort Shevchenko), where the Russian authorities put him on a ship to carry him across the Caspian.

Khiva town consisted of a few streets of mud houses. The water lay so near the surface of the soil that the mosques and the bazaar had no stable foundation and the minarets all sloped from the perpendicular. But the gardens were beautiful, sheltered by mud walls 20 or 30 feet high, with poplars shading a pool in the middle and a pavilion built into the corner of the walls. There, Richmond gorged himself on the numberless varieties of melon 'as delicate as new-fallen snow' and raisins, apples, plums and sugarloaves, and listened to the mullahs debating tricky points in the Koran. The Russian slaves were still captive in Khiva, hundreds of them, and the pressure was off the Khan to deliver them, as the Russian army was no longer pressing up against the mud walls of his fort. Richmond realized that the only way to be sure that the Russian captives reached their fatherland was to take them there himself. For this onward expedition he had no authority at all. Even his blithe nature faltered at the responsibility he was assuming. In a letter to Emily, he wrote, 'This is all very fine, but perhaps the poor politico will be well wigged for his officiousness instead of receiving thanks . . . I would give all I possess to know what is the opinion of the Powers-that-be on a letter I wrote just a month ago. It is very painful waiting two or three months for a letter by which you must live or die.'[47]

Richmond spent 52 days at Khiva, gradually gaining the confidence of the Khan as they sat together in the garden pavilion almost every day. The Khan was a good-natured man of about 45, eager for news of the outside world and especially of England. Little by little, Richmond gathered in the Russian slaves at a camp he had pitched in another royal garden five miles outside the city. By August 4, he had assembled 325 men, 18 women and 11 children, the children having been born in captivity. They were all Greek Orthodox. The women had been kidnapped in Russian territory around Orenburg, the men either captured while fishing on the eastern shores of the Caspian, or bought or recaptured from the Persians.

From Richmond's account of the negotiations, you derive a powerful sense of how inbuilt slavery had become in these remote kingdoms. The official charged with assembling the slaves to be freed was himself a slaveholder, and two of his slaves escaped from his house with chains on their feet and threw themselves on Richmond's mercy.

One woman refused to leave Khiva without her daughter who was in the hands of a lady in the Khan's own palace. Richmond rode into town and demanded that the Khan hand her over. 'The khan urged that she did not wish to go; I pleaded her not being of age. He was silent for some time; at length, turning to the minister, he muttered, "Give him the child". Shortly afterwards, a beautiful little girl was brought to me. It was very dark, so, taking a lamp, I advanced to have a closer view of my hard-earned prize, when the little puss screamed out lustily, vowing nothing should make her go to "that Russian slave-dealer!"'[48] The little girl had mistaken Richmond with his black beard and his Persian robes for one of the bandits who had torn her from her mother. Eventually she was persuaded to jump up on the back of another man's pony and rejoin her mother to the cheers of the other prisoners. Even now, the Khivan authorities continued to drag their feet, and Richmond had a list of those still in detention. Again, he went to the Khan, and this time he said that unless the Khan released all the prisoners, he would call off the whole deal. The Khan was startled by this plain speaking and issued an order threatening death to anyone who obstructed the work.

By the time they set off across the barren steppe which separated

Khiva from the Caspian, they had 416 Russians in tow, many of them old men, women and children, compared with his earlier party of 30 fit men. Together with the escort provided by the Khan, he was now leading a considerable cavalcade across another 700 miles of terrain little more hospitable than the country they had already passed through. Yet, Richmond tells us, 'thanks be to God! Not a man, woman, nor child was lost during the whole of this most fatiguing march ... Not a horse or camel was lost. When crossing one of the stages over this steppe, the whole of the prisoners were together – it was a glorious sight to pass them. They spoke no European language but their own [Russian], and our only mode of salutation was the "Az salam Alliekoum". This they shouted to me as I rode by them; and thus the salutation which a true Mussulman will not exchange with an infidel, became the only greeting between Christians. The plain was so open that the camels crowded together, and marched ever en masse, the children and women riding on panniers, singing and laughing, and the men trudging along sturdily; all counting the few days which remained ere they should rejoin their countrymen, and escape from what they must have considered a life of hopeless slavery.'[49]

It was a remarkable achievement, and the generous Captain Abbott declares in his own personal account that 'I am still of the opinion that had any officer of less genius, prudence and engaging manners than Captain Shakespear been sent after me to Khiva, the negotiations might have had a different result from the brilliant conclusion to which his prompt and judicious mediation brought it.'[50]

As they approached the fortress of Novopetrovskoye on the eastern Caspian, the male prisoners marched in a line, with the camels carrying the women and children close behind them. The Russian commandant 'was overpowered with gratitude; his receiving charge of the prisoners would make a fine picture and was a scene which I can never forget.' But just as Richmond had been punctilious about making sure that every last slave had been tracked down in Khiva, so now he was eager to make sure that the other side of the bargain was

kept. He was accompanied on the boat across the Caspian by some
of the Russian prisoners, then they bumped along in post carts to
Orenburg. There the natives of Khiva, who been taken prisoner by
the Russians along the Caspian shores, were released and allowed to
go home. There were 640 of them, 'which added to the 416
Russians brought with me, makes a very satisfactory little total in our
favour; to say nothing of the numbers which the prohibitory orders
may be hoped to save from a life of slavery.'[51] For the Khan had issued
a decree prohibiting, under penalty of death, the seizure of Russian
subjects or the purchase of natives from Herat – a prohibition entirely
novel in Turkestan.

As Richmond jolted along on an agonizingly springless carriage
all the way to Moscow, he was feted by grateful Russians. By
November he had reached St Petersburg, where the numerous
English community was ecstatic. He was presented to the Czar and
the Czarina and a Grand Duke or two. He was offered the hand of
the Grand Duchess Helen to kiss, but missed his target and 'only
managed to rub my nose against Her Highness's knuckles'. The
Russian government, by contrast, gave him a grumpy reception,
and conspicuously refrained from offering him a medal. He had, after
all, destroyed their excuse for going to war. Richmond wrote to his
sister Emily: 'the Russians are much annoyed, but have formed
friendly relations with Khiva, at least have commenced doing so, and
no army advances this year on Khiva. *This* is all that was wanted. And
who did it? Eh! Not a Lieutenant of Artillery, surely! Excuse this
boasting, but my head reels with delight that I have been successful.'[52]

I think you can excuse him. He was not yet 29 and he had just
stopped a war, ended the slave trade in a large tract of Central Asia,
and liberated over a thousand captives and restored them to their various homelands.[53]

After a few weeks enjoying the delights of St Petersburg,
Richmond was sent on to London, as he had hoped, carrying dis-
patches from the Ambassador to Lord Palmerston, congratulating
Richmond on his 'remarkable zeal, steadiness and judgment'.[54] Back

in England, he charged around visiting all his relations. His double cousin the Rev Francis Thackeray[55] remembered this great black-whiskered fellow bursting into the vicarage at Broxbourne, followed by the faithful Fazil Khan carrying a long rifle, crying out to his mother: 'What! Don't you remember Richmond?' William Makepeace Thackeray recalls in the *Roundabout Papers*: 'When he came to London the cousins and playfellows of early Indian days met again and shook hands. "Can I do anything for you?" I remember the kind fellow asking.' In London, at any rate, the Government was eager to do something for him. And on August 31, 1841, he was knighted by the young Queen at the Palace. Here, too, as with the Grand Duchess Helen, he muffed the ceremony and stumbled as he rose from his kneeling position. It is not known who drew 'Rise Up, Sir Richmond!' I suspect Marianne. She had, after all, won a silver medal for her study of a Plate of Eggs and Grapes , which she was to have received from the Queen's uncle, the Duke of Sussex, except he failed to turn up.

The fount of honours had been gushing for the Afghan heroes. After the relatively painless taking of Kabul on July 23, 1839, and the restoration of Shah Shuja, Auckland had been made an earl in December 1839, the new C-in-C Sir John Keane a baron and Macnaghten a baronet a month later. The fortress of Ghazni, which had been successfully besieged on the way to Kabul, gave its name to a new gallop, 'the Ghazni', danced at fashionable balls. In the Afghan capital, the English started up their usual sports – cricket, horse racing, skating and amateur theatricals. Senior officers began import-ing their wives; Sir William brought in the formidable Fanny Macnaghten, described as a cross between Rosamond Vincy in *Middlemarch* and Lady Catherine de Bourgh in *Pride and Prejudice*; and General 'Fighting Bob' Sale brought in the even more formidable Florentia, Lady Sale, together with their youngest daughter Alexandrina. There was talk of annexing Afghanistan permanently, perhaps even of moving the Empire's summer capital from Simla, that inaccessible saddleland, to the pleasant Kabul valley. Had not the

Mughals once migrated every May from Delhi and Agra to Kashmir and Jalalabad?[56]

But by the time that Sir Richmond was so awkwardly arising, the occupation had turned sour and ominous. By the terms of the treaty with Shah Shuja, Macnaghten was, as Lord Melbourne caustically observed, 'the real king of Afghanistan'. And that was just the trouble. That stubborn, bookish Ulsterman might be incredibly learned (Emily Eden waspishly remarked that he 'speaks Persian rather more fluently than English; Arabic better than Persian; but, for familiar conversation, rather prefers Sanscrit.')[57] But his famous blue-tinted spectacles did not seem to take in much of the human world. In particular, he failed to grasp that fewer and fewer Afghans shared his conviction that Shah Shuja was the legitimate sovereign of all Afghanistan. It was embarrassingly obvious that he was the puppet of the English; it was Macnaghten who called the shots and paid the bribes. Macnaghten, like many political leaders seeking to control Afghanistan before and since, never quite grasped how utterly the territory lacked any serious sense of nationhood, riven as it was and is by so many differences of clan and language. Afghanistan was not so much 'a failed state', as a never-was state. Such a place required overwhelming force and huge resources of men and money to hold it together. Neither was forthcoming.

By September 1840, even the ever-optimistic Macnaghten had woken up to the horror of his situation. 'We are in a stew here,' he wrote to Major Rawlinson at Kandahar.[58] The whole of the country this side of the Oxus was reported to be in favour of the exiled Dost Mohammad. Kabul itself was in a feverish state. Shops were shutting up, people were sending their families away. The irrepressible Dost was biding his time: 'I am like a wooden spoon. You may throw me hither and thither, but I shall not be hurt.'[59] On the last day of 1840, the Secret Committee of the Board of Control had explicitly pronounced that it would be hopeless to try and maintain Shah Shuja in power by a mixture of British influence and a small British force: 'we should prefer the entire abandonment of the country, and a frank confession of failure to any such policy.'[60]

From the start, Auckland had made it clear to Macnaghten and to the Commander-in-Chief that this was to be an 'invasion-lite'. He turned down requests to build a new citadel in Kabul and a new fort at Kandahar. Shah Shuja was to build up his own efficient national army, as 'our regular troops cannot remain there beyond the present season'. Only a month after Macnaghten had settled in Kabul, he received orders from Simla that the Bombay troops were to be withdrawn en masse by the Bolan Pass, and a large portion of the Bengal Army was also to leave for India via Jalalabad and the Khyber. Relatively small detachments of the remaining troops were to be dispersed to the major towns – Kabul and Kandahar, Ghazni, Quetta and Jalalabad.[61]

Payments to the local chiefs were to be cut sharply, most fatally those made to the eastern Ghilzai tribes who policed the passes between Kabul and the Khyber. These, like other tribal leaders, had naturally expected that the arrival of the fabulously rich feringhees would mean larger subsidies, not savage cuts. Nor could Macnaghten expect to be buoyed up by any sort of 'surge' if trouble flared in the newly conquered country. Auckland had taken the conquest so much for granted that he had simultaneously embarked on what was to become known as the First Opium War against the Chinese. Already large parts of the Bombay Army were being drafted for service overseas. The Army of the Indus could expect no reinforcements.[62]

Even after these withdrawals the expense of the whole thing was damnable. 'Money, money, money is our first, our second, and our last want,' Auckland wrote to Macnaghten in March 1841. 'How long we can continue to feed you at your present rate of expenditure I cannot tell. To add to the weight would break us utterly.' Anyone doing the maths could see the shape of coming things. Henry Tucker, formerly Accountant-General of Bengal and now a Director of the Company, wrote to the new Foreign Secretary, Lord Aberdeen, in March 1842 that 'ere six months elapse, the treasures of

India will be completely exhausted.'[63] The C-in-C, Sir John Keane, drew the inescapable conclusion: 'That country drains us of a million a year or more [in reality, more than two million at least] – and we only, in truth, are certain of the allegiance of the people within range of our guns and cavalry ... The whole thing will break down.' And break down it did. By the end of August 1841, just as Richmond was being knighted, Auckland told Macnaghten that the Company had been forced to take out a £5 million loan from Indian merchants at crippling rates of interest just to continue paying salaries.[64] However much Macnaghten might splutter that it would be a 'cheat of the first magnitude' to abandon Shah Shuja now, the mission had to be aborted.[65]

The terrible story of the retreat from Afghanistan has been told many times, most brilliantly by Sir John Kaye in 1851 and by William Dalrymple in 2013. The horror and the humiliation bit into the British soul, and stayed there, imprinted even more indelibly by Lady Butler's great oil painting, 'The Remnants of an Army', of the supposedly lone survivor Dr Brydon staggering towards the walls of Jalalabad on his expiring horse. When Dr Brydon's story reached Calcutta on January 30, 1842, 'poor George aged ten years in as many hours', according to his sister Emily. He screamed and raged, took to his bed, emerged partially paralysed, lay prostrate on the lawns of Government House at night, pressing his face against the turf for comfort. To John Cam Hobhouse, the President of the Board of Control, he wrote that 'the plans of public good and public security upon which I had staked so much have all broken down under circumstances of horror and disaster of which history has few parallels'.[66]

John Low's nephew, Aleck Deas, marched out of Kabul with the 5th Native Infantry on January 6, 1842. They were guarding the baggage; the 37th were with them, guarding the treasure. As soon as they came under attack, the whole army of 4,500 troops and 12,000 camp followers degenerated into a chaotic rabble, unprotected from flank attack by the tribesmen on the escarpments, often aware of their presence only when they heard the rattle of the *jezails* being loaded. From the first day, the ill-equipped sepoys began to collapse in the unbroken glittering snow. Two days later, Akbar Khan, Dost Mohammad's forceful, mercurial son, demanded hostages to ensure that the British keep their agreement to evacuate Jalalabad on the far side of the pass. Among others, Eldred Pottinger, George Lawrence and Colin Mackenzie were taken. They at least were spared the slaughter that then ensued as the British trudged into the opening of the Khord-Kabul pass.

This was the nightmare that echoes in every Kipling ballad: the dark defile, the slithering to and fro across icy torrents, and the tribesmen pouring down from the hillsides. Three thousand men died; shot down by the ten-rupee *jezails*, knived by whooping villagers, or simply frozen to death. The little party of women, headed by Lady Sale and the now-widowed Fanny Macnaghten (Sir William's head was being carried round the streets of Kabul in triumph), almost all survived. Akbar offered to take them under his protection, a day's march behind the army. And so the women and children joined the growing number of hostages left behind but alive. Not that their journey back towards Kabul spared them any of the horrors. Lady Sale wrote in her diary:

> We passed some 200 dead bodies, many of them Europeans, the whole naked, and covered with large gaping wounds ... Numbers of camp followers, we found still alive, frostbitten and starving; some perfectly out of their senses and idiotic ... The sight was dreadful; the smell of blood sickening; and the corpses lay so thick that it was impossible to look upon them as it required care to guide my horse so as not to tread upon the bodies ... Subsequently we heard that scarcely any of these poor wretches escaped from this defile; and that driven to the extreme of hunger they had sustained life by feeding upon their dead comrades.[67]

By the evening of January 10, the fourth day of the retreat, 12,000 men were dead. Among them was Aleck Deas, wiped out along with nearly all his comrades of the Bengal Infantry. John and Augusta grieved greatly when they heard. Beyond the debts, the drinking and the bad table manners, there was something lovable about Aleck.

The blame for the chaos of the retreat, the lack of patrols sweeping the hillside, the shortage of supplies and the breakdown of discipline fell, rightly, upon the indecisive and doddering general, William Elphinstone, a cousin of the far abler and sharper Mountstuart. An averagely alert and active general would have suppressed the uprising at Kabul on November 2 and would have managed the retreat with discipline and dispatch. There would have been lives lost in the snow, sepoys shot by the *jezails*; but an entire army of 15,000 would not have perished. Elphinstone was pitifully bad.

But who appointed this useless commander? The Governor-General. Nor did Lord Auckland have the excuse of not knowing his man. For only a few months earlier, in February 1840, the Edens had bumped into Elphinstone on their way down from Simla; he was clearly paralysed by gout and unable to walk without being supported. He was such a cripple that Emily failed to recognize him as the 'Elphy Bey' she had met striding across the Scottish moors. Even when in health, according to the sharp-tongued General Nott, who should have had the job, he was 'the most incompetent soldier that was to be found among all the officers of requisite rank'. Among other defects, Elphinstone had not seen action since Waterloo, and had returned to full pay at the age of 55 only to pay off his debts. Emily also notes that he 'cannot, of course, speak a word of Hindoostanee, neither can his aide-de-camp. "My groom is the best of us, but somehow we never can make the bearers understand us. I have a *negro* who speaks Hindoostanee but I could not bring him."' To which Emily comments tartly, 'I suppose he means a native. He can hardly have picked up a woolly black negro who speaks Hindoostanee.'[68]

Auckland himself was doomed anyway, even if a change of government in London had not already meant a change of

Governor-General. Lord Ellenborough, the tough, unpleasant, conceited former President of the India Board, had been appointed by Peel in October 1841 and was already on his way before the disaster shattered Britain's prestige across India.

Richmond was on his way back to India, too. He had only a few weeks in Calcutta before he was appointed military secretary to Sir George Pollock, who was commanding the force assembled at Peshawar to relieve Sir Robert Sale at Jalalabad. Pollock could not have been less like Elphinstone; he was ruthless, sensible and hard as rock. If you were looking for a commander for an Army of Retribution, he was your man. Richmond was hard pressed to get his army ready for him, but his exuberance was undiminished. He was, after all, one of the few men in India who had been left untouched by the disaster. On March 30, he wrote to his sister Marianne: 'Packing up! Hurrah for the Khyber! You can't think how delighted I am to get away from the desk to which I have been nailed for the last six weeks.'[69]

Even during these frantic preparations, Richmond kept up a stream of letters to his siblings, especially his youngest sister Selina, whom he had only met for the first time on his return to Calcutta and instantly adored. Nearly a century later, browsing through his letters to Selina, his son John came across two blank sheets in an envelope with 'invisible' written upon it in Selina's handwriting. John, who himself served in India for many years, applied the standard mixture of iodine and water and immediately the words written in rice-water ink sprang into view:

Camp Jelalabad 31st May 1842

My dearest Selinthus,
    Your dear, kind letter of the 14th instant reached me today ... I cannot without compromising my dignity write to you, and I have hit upon the expedient of writing in invisible ink, to save my 'Purdah' as the Persians say ... I am fond of you, my little sister, and proud of your affection for me. Elise, please

God, shall one of these days make my happiness complete, and
then with such sisters and such a wife, why! Old Time shall
smile as he passes.[70]

Richmond's letters are full of allusions to his beloved Elise. In fact
he eventually married someone called Sophy. Invisible ink was not
the only clandestine method of corresponding in desperate circumstances. French or Greek characters, or a simple code, might be used
to get the message through unread by the enemy. General Sale
resorted to fractured French. Others dotted individual letters in old
newspapers to compose their messages. General Pollock, using
Richmond as his amanuensis, had sent a typical coded letter to Sale
from Peshawar two months earlier, on March 12. (General Sale preferred fractured French to cipher.) Here is the first paragraph.
Training at Bletchley not required for decoding:

YK PQMD SQZQDMX ——U my ea eufgmfqp ftmf uf tme
nqoayq m oazeupqdmfuaz ar ftq gfyaef uybadfmzoq ftmf metap
dqoquhq yk dquzradoqyqzfe ar Pdmsaze mzp T. Mdfk nqradq U
yahq fa kagd dqkuqr.[71]

The letter that Richmond had encoded contained grim news for
General Sale. Pollock wanted to wait until another regiment of
Dragoons and more horse artillery had arrived from Ferozepur, and
he was still short of camels and ammunition. 'Pray therefore tell me,
without the least reserve, the latest day you can hold out.' Sale
replied, in invisible ink, that his last supplies of salt meat would run
out on April 4.[72]

For once, things were not as bad as they seemed. The cavalry and
the artillery, and the camels, too, arrived on March 29. And within
a week, Pollock's sepoys were filing up the Khyber. Richmond
dashed off a note to his sister: 'My dearest Selina, I seize upon a spare
half-hour to write to you, my dear little lady.' And he outlines the
operations which are to begin the next day. This time, the British

sent out flanking parties to clear the hillsides, while the guns on the road shelled any enemy sighted within range. Richmond led 200 *jezailchees* (native riflemen) on the right flank, and they swept on through the pass to retake Ali Masjid.

Almost the same day, 'Fighting Bob' Sale led a daring and superbly organized break-out from Jalalabad. Akbar Khan and his besieging army had only just finished celebrating the death of Shah Shuja, murdered in a ditch by his godson, when, as the sun rose over the mountains, they saw almost the entire garrison marching out towards them, preceded by a sustained cannonade from the fortress walls. It was a brilliant victory, notable especially for the sangfroid of the young Henry Havelock, who was to play such a part in the Great Mutiny and who now showed himself 'as calm under fire as if he stood in a drawing room full of ladies'.[73]

When the Army of Retribution limped up to the walls of Jalalabad, instead of the long beards, haggard faces and tattered garments they expected to see, they found the defenders 'all fat and rosy, in the highest health'.[74] Sale's garrison had liberated themselves, but at any rate the first part of Pollock's mission had been achieved.

Now they were all itching to go on to Kabul. But to their amazement they discovered that the supposedly implacable Lord Ellenborough was getting cold feet. He began sending messages to Pollock and Nott, arguing that now that Jalalabad had been relieved and Akbar Khan defeated, they should begin to wind down operations and prepare to return to India, but at the same time he left the operational decisions to Pollock.

Richmond was as aggrieved and dumbfounded as anyone. He wrote to Marianne on May 31: 'The Government has ordered us back, but a remonstrance has been sent which will, I trust, save us from this disgrace, for surely it would be nothing else were we to quit this country, leaving the prisoners without an effort.' He could not make Ellenborough out: 'The Governor-General appears very arbitrary; I wish he would order me back to my regiment, for really I don't see how anyone is to gain honour by serving such a

Government.'[75] John Low wrote later to Mountstuart Elphinstone that, although he got on remarkably well with Ellenborough, he was glad that he did not have to serve long under his direction, for he was 'a hasty, inconsistent "shuks"'.[76]

This was an understatement. Ellenborough's instructions were baffling and infuriating. In Sir John Kaye's words, 'he betook himself to an expedient unparalleled, perhaps, in the political history of the world. He instigated Pollock and Nott to advance, but insisted that they should regard the forward movement solely in the light of a retirement from Afghanistan.'[77] The instruction were so tortuously couched, as Kaye puts it, 'as to cast upon the Generals all the onus of failure, and to confer upon the Governor-General, or at least to divide with him, all the honour of success.'[78]

Anyway, General Pollock cheerfully took up the challenge. Richmond wrote to Thomas Herbert Maddock, Ellenborough's sec-retary, who was equally infuriated by his boss's in-and-out running, 'I don't know any circumstance which has before so much delighted me. Please God will now burn the fathers of these rascals!'[79]

Nott at Kandahar was at first inclined to retire, but then he too decided to advance on Kabul. Three days later, Richmond wrote: 'My dearest and gentlest Selina, with a heart overflowing with joy I sit down to write to you that we have just heard that General Nott has decided on advancing on Kabul, and we, of course, move up to support him ... How old Jonathan [their brother John] will exult at this chance of retrieving our lost fame, Augusta too and Low, it is a national source of enjoyment ... Maiden, be I remembered in thy prayers.'[80] All over India, entire families like the Lows and the Shakespears were exulting that vengeance would in the end be theirs.

But first there was a ferocious rematch in the Khord-Kabul pass. 'The Dragoons and all our troops were in no humour to show mercy, for all along the route they had come on skeletons of our poor men who had been massacred ... We passed the skeletons of at least five hundred men to-day in the Khoord-Kabul pass. The sight of these objects has driven our men nearly frantic and it will be very difficult to save Kabul from destruction, but it is of the greatest importance to protect it, for we are dependent on it for supplies.'[81] At the holly barrier near Jagdalak Fort, they came across hundreds of corpses impaled on the hedge, where they had been shot trying to claw their way over the thorns in the darkness.

In retribution, the British burnt every village they passed through, every orchard, every tree (sometimes ringing the trees with deep cuts, the quickest way of killing them). Nott's troops coming up from Kandahar took an even more terrible revenge, bayoneting every male past puberty and raping every available woman. The vengeance culminated in Pollock's systematic dynamiting of the great bazaar in Kabul, where Macnaghten's body had been displayed on a butcher's hook. As Dalrymple points out, this was a hideous final irony, for the original impulse for Britain's venturing into Afghanistan had been to promote trade between the two countries.[82]

The Muslims had mostly fled the city; it was the Hindu shop-keepers who stayed behind and who had had no part in the war. In his last letter from the city to his sister Augusta, Richmond wrote: 'A subject which gives me much annoyance is, what is to become of those chiefs who have taken our part in the disturbances. I heard it said the other day: "Your government is a great one, but it cannot afford to sacrifice its character. You come into this country and split the people in two parties, those who opposed you and those who were friends to you, and now you are about to leave those who have befriended you to certain destruction." We may in time recover our military fame, but we must for ever be detested in this country.'[83]

But what about the British prisoners? In the frenzy of murder and destruction their plight seemed almost forgotten. There were now 120 of them in captivity up at Bamiyan, 140 miles north-west of Kabul, where the two great Buddhas stare out over the valley, or did until the Taliban dynamited them in 2001. They were under the control of Akbar's father-in-law, Mahomed Shah Khan, who showed little willingness to enter into a bargain for their release. The

Qizilbash horsemen who had remained in the city – they were Persian colonists who were pro-British – offered to send a party up to recover the prisoners.

Richmond jumped at the idea. As he wrote to 'old Jonathan':

> The day before we arrived at Kabul I begged and prayed the General to let me go on and see what could be done to send off the Kuzzilbash horsemen. When he found he could not answer my arguments he gave grumpy answers, and when the next day it appeared that the horsemen were not off and that they still made excuses, he let me go with 10,000 rupees, more to get rid of my remonstrances than anything else. Just as I was leaving his tent I said, 'It may be necessary, General, to go on to Bamian', to which he replied, 'Nonsense, don't run any risk.'
>
> Well, off I went and wrote to him from the Kuzzilbash quarters that I saw that unless I went myself they would not start that night and might delay on the road, and hoped he would excuse my going with them.[84]

General Nott, on the opposite side of the city, was nearer to Bamiyan, but he was even less enthusiastic. When asked by Pollock, twice and in writing, to send a detachment from the Kandahar division to support the rescue mission, he refused, adding a gloomy forecast that:

> I sincerely think that sending a small detachment will and must be followed by deep disaster. No doubt Mahomed Akbar, Shumshoodeen and the other chiefs, are uniting their forces, and I hourly expect to hear that Sir R. Shakespear is added to the number of British prisoners.[85]

In any case, 'he considered from the tenor of Lord Ellenborough's dispatches the recovery of the prisoners to be a matter of indifference to government.'[86]

The prisoners had recently heard that, on the orders of Akbar Khan, they were to be conveyed to Bukhara and there sold, by twos and threes, to Turkestan chiefs. Any hope of a civilized exchange of prisoners now seemed remote. In desperation, they collected all the cash they could muster and began to bribe their guards, several of whom they recognized as former troopers of theirs. Their chief gaoler, a greedy and biddable old soldier of fortune, handed over the fort on the promises of a pension of 1,000 rupees a month from General Pollock. The prisoners hoisted their own flag and even began receiving salaams from local chiefs who had got wind of the British advance.[87] They then set out to march to meet Pollock's army at Kabul. Vincent Eyre, who along with Florentia Sale and several other prisoners left a vivid account of their long ordeals, describes them sitting in the shade of a fort near the Kalu mountain:

> We had only rested a couple of hours when a body of horse were descried descending into the valley down the distant pass of Hajeejuk. In an instant all were on the alert. The nearer approach of the party enabled us to recognize the friendly banner of the Kuzzilbash streaming in the air. A few minutes more of eager suspense elapsed when Sir Richmond Shakespear, galloping up to where we stood, dissipated every doubt. Our gallant countryman was greeted on our side with no boisterous cheers of triumph – our joy was too great, too overwhelming for the tongue to utter.[88]

Even with Richmond's escort, the small party was still in pressing danger. Nott, as we have seen, thought that the whole lot of them would be taken prisoner. Pollock himself, in forwarding Major Pottinger's account of their captivity and release, declared that: 'Had Sir R. Shakespear arrived with his party a few hours later, it is probable we should not have recovered the prisoners, as Sooltan Jan arrived soon after the prisoners from Bamian with one thousand horse, and would, no doubt, have followed them had he not heard of the force sent to protect them.'[89]

So, once again, Richmond had brought off a rescue mission. At Khiva, he had rescued 416 Russians; at Orenburg, he had arranged the release of 640 Khivans. Now, disregarding the discouragement of the generals, he had brought in to Kabul more than 100 British troops, women and children. In a ghastly saga of folly, brutality and vengeance scarcely rivalled in British history, he stands out, the lone survivor of a moral earthquake.

Those he had rescued were properly grateful. On September 24, 1842, just before Pollock torched the bazaar, 37 of them wrote Richmond a joint letter from Kabul, which began:

> Dear Sir,
>
> Rescued as we have so lately been from a cheerless captivity, which threatened soon to terminate in hopeless slavery, in a land where the laws of humanity are unknown or unacknowledged, restored by a wonderful interposition of Providence, to country, friends & all that renders life desirable, it will ill become us, in the midst of our rejoicings, to forget those through whom the happy change has been effected. To you we are bound to utter our heartfelt thanks for the promptitude with which you marched a party of Kuzzilbash horsemen to our assistance at a most critical period, to whose timely arrival amongst us at Kaloo, it may be attributed that our flight from Bamian was not intercepted . . .

The letter is signed by, among others, Florentia Sale and her daughter Alexandrina Sturt (who had been married and widowed during her time in Afghanistan), Fanny Macnaghten, Vincent and Emily Eyre, Eldred Pottinger (who had fought so bravely to keep the Persians out of Herat), George Lawrence, Colin Mackenzie, the appalling peppery General Shelton, and by no means least, John Nicholson, who was to become the fiercest of all British commanders in India.

Eight children and 56 NCOs also owed their escape from slavery, in part at least, to Richmond. Richmond had already been mentioned in dispatches four times for his services in the battles on the way to Kabul. General Pollock said he ought also to have been awarded the CB for the rescue. But he wasn't. Richmond told his brother John only that he was perfectly and entirely contented with the letter of thanks from the rescuees, 'which will be a good match for the Russian receipt for Khivan prisoners.'[90]

Yet even Richmond had not escaped unscathed. He still had all his exuberance, but he had lost his innocence. His respect for the British Empire in India and the men who ran it could never be the same again. Nothing could be sharper than his contempt for the absurd over-the-top celebrations that Lord Ellenborough staged to welcome the returning troops: hundreds of elephants with trunks painted, one or two by the Governor-General's own hand, triumphal arches, bands playing 'See the Conquering Hero Comes'. What was there to celebrate in such a sequence of humiliations, disasters and atrocities?

Most ridiculous of all were the supposed Somnath Gates, now garlanded with marigolds for the 'victory' parade. Ellenborough had ordered the gates removed from the tomb of Sultan Mahmud outside Ghazni and brought to India, in the mistaken belief that these were the legendary sandalwood gates that the Sultan had looted from the great Hindu temple of Somnath in Gujarat. Ellenborough's illusion came from his reading of James Mill's *History of India*. Mill famously had never visited India, knew no Indians and no Indian languages.

By chance, the officer in charge of the removal of the gates was Major Henry Rawlinson, possibly the foremost archaeologist in India. Rawlinson saw at a glance that the inscriptions on the sarcophagus and on the gates were Islamic work, of a piece with Mahmud's tomb, both being of a much later date. However, his was not to argue with the Governor-General, and with that worldly coolth which was eventually to loft him to the House of Lords, he commented in his journal, 'I call them [the gates] trophies, although

assured they are spurious, for the belief in their genuineness is, polit-
ically considered, the same as if they really were so.'[91]

The gates were tenderly lifted from their hinges, under the super-
vision of Colonel Sanders, Selinthus's beloved, who had blasted
Ghazni into ruins for Nott. The gates were then taken from Ghazni
and paraded round India, accompanied by a high-flown proclamation from Ellenborough that he had avenged centuries of Hindu
humiliation. As it turned out, Rawlinson was wrong about it being
the same as if they really were the lost gates. Ellenborough became a
laughing stock. John Low commented that 'the whole proceeding
appears *quite preposterous* and I have never known a public measure of
Government regarding which there was so little diversity of opinion
in India.'[92]

XI

A SHORT OPIUM WAR

E llenborough had at least brought Auckland's wars to an end, but only to make room to start two more wars of his own. From youth, his heart had been set on military glory. He had not come to India merely to clear up other men's messes. He intended to rule India 'as if I were its sovereign, having nothing to look to but India'. In his eyes, the Court of Directors were timorous tradesmen, the old political hands in India no better than the tools of moth-eaten and corrupt rajas and amirs. 'I must act like Akbar, and not like Auckland.' And in Charles Napier he found a proconsul in his own image.

Napier, a stunted, villainous-looking paranoiac, combined cynicism and megalomania. He prided himself on having no illusions about what the British were up to. 'Our object in conquering India, the object of all our cruelties, was money.' Every shilling had been picked out of blood. 'We shall yet suffer for the crime as sure as there is a God in heaven.' In the same breath, he accepted a military command at Poona solely 'to catch the rupees for my girls', his two illegitimate daughters by his Greek mistress Anastasia, whom he had lived with when he was Military Resident in Cephalonia.[1] He was as avid for military glory as Lord Ellenborough; to command an army was 'a longing not to be described'.

In August 1842, he was appointed military commander in the far north-west country of Sind, in what is now Pakistan, and he lost no time in making extortionate demands of the local amirs; if they refused to accept his new treaty, he would smash them. His assistant, Major James Outram, who knew how chaotic the amirs' armies were, warned Napier about this ultimatum: 'every life which may hereafter be lost in consequence will be murder'.[2] Napier was unmoved. He famously wrote in his diary: 'We have no right to seize Sind. Yet we shall do so and a very advantageous, useful, humane piece of rascality it will be.'

Napier was vastly outnumbered in the final battle on March 24, 1843. He had 5,000 men against 25,000, but his opponents were a tribal gathering rather than a trained army, and they were slaughtered in their thousands. This spectacular victory, coming so soon after the humiliations of Afghanistan, restored British nerves and made Napier a hero, especially to common soldiers, whose interests he always put first. His statue at the bottom of Trafalgar Square bears the inscription which used to move me, until I came to know a little more about the man: 'Erected by public subscription, the most numerous subscribers being private soldiers.' In October 2000, the mayor of London, Ken Livingstone, demanded its removal from the square, as he hadn't a clue who Napier was. So soon are the villains as well as the heroes of Empire forgotten.

At least the annexation of Sind survives faintly in our memories, if only for the joke that *Punch* made about it, imagining that Napier had sent a one-word message 'Peccavi' – I have sinned. Posterity, literal-minded as ever, assumed that Napier really had sent such a message.

Totally forgotten, though, is the other war that Lord Ellenborough launched in 1843, the Gwalior Campaign against the Sindia's army. He took advantage of a quarrel within the ruling elite in Sindia's domains (nothing to do with Sind which is several hundred miles to the west). The Sindia in question was Jiyaji Rao, a boy of nine years old, who was torn between two powerful ministers, his pro-British maternal uncle Mama Sahib, and the anti-British Dada Sahib who had become Prime Minister after the expulsion of that formidable Begum-Regent, the Baiza Bai, who was still clocking up her millions in her various banking houses from Ujjain, the commercial capital of the state, to faraway Benares. The tussle between the Mama and the Dada factions could have been quietened with a little patience and goodwill – qualities in which Lord Ellenborough was utterly deficient.

In any case, he regarded the Sindia state as an artificial entity with 'its many scattered territories in Hindoostan, bound together by no common interest or feeling amongst the people'. The state had no reason to exist and continued entirely because the East India Company legitimized it. The ruler ruled 'only by our sufferance'.[3]

Ellenborough set about demolishing Gwalior's pretensions to independence. He sacked the emollient Resident and replaced him with a man more to his own taste, William Sleeman, who had already opined that 'As a citizen of the world I could not help thinking that it would have been a great blessing upon a large portion of our species if an earthquake were to swallow up this Court of Gwalior and the army that surrounds it.'[4] Sleeman had already earned a national reputation for putting down the Thugs. Surely he could do the business in Gwalior.

Ellenborough then appointed the rising star Sir Richmond Shakespear as Sleeman's assistant. He had already proved himself the sort of forceful soldier and negotiator that the Governor-General needed to carry out his plan. This was a great leg-up for Richmond. His cousin William Ritchie claimed that 'It is, perhaps, the first instance of a subaltern holding so distinguished a situation, except in days of emergency ... No other man in the Army, perhaps, could have been so elevated without exciting much dissatisfaction, but his merit is so generally admitted that even the envious are compelled to be silent.'[5] It is hard to tell how much of an idea Richmond had of what he was getting himself into, but the whirl of promotion turns many a head.

Anyway, he was soon to find out. Ellenborough's first move was to accuse the Minister of the State, the Dada Khasgiwala, of the 'high crime' of intercepting a letter from His Lordship to the Maharani. As the Maharani was a child of 13, unable to read or write any language, the Minister would have had to read the letter to her anyway. The accusation was absurd, as was the Governor-General's demand that the Dada be given over to the British for punishment. No self-respecting state would accept such a demand. But anxious to avoid trouble, the Court banished the Dada and sent him under guard to Agra, there to have his name blackened by the British propagandists. But that wasn't enough for His Lordship. He told the new Minister, a pliable figure called Ram Rao Phalke, that he had found a clause in the Treaty of Berhampur, signed back in 1804, which 'obliges the British Government, if at any time Scindea should be unable to cope with his enemies, to afford him military assistance.' Because of the instability in the neighbouring Punjab after the death of Ranjit Singh, his duty was to assure the British a quiet frontier in the northwest. Accordingly, he intended to march his army to Gwalior.

Phalke had been around for years, but he had never heard of any such clause. The clause in the treaty had been devised to deal with local bandits, and the British had in any case abrogated the treaty a year later. He protested that 'the invasion of a friendly state on such a pretext was quite a strange anomaly in the conduct of the Honourable Company.' The whole thing was 'a barefaced sham', in the words of John Hope, the acerbic British surgeon at the court of Gwalior. Phalke pleaded with Ellenborough to reconsider, but General Gough was already on the march, with Richmond as his ADC, and Lord Ellenborough trotting alongside to share in the glory. Nothing was going to stand in the way of this power grab.

At the Battle of Maharajpur on December 29, 1843, Ellenborough had the satisfaction of exposing himself to harm's way. It was a decisive victory. After the battle, General Gough paid generous tribute to the courage and fighting abilities of Sindia's troops. The patriotic spirit they had shown demolished Ellenborough's claim that Gwalior had no national identity. Losses on both sides were severe, far worse for the British than their casualties in Napier's

battles, more than 1,000 being killed or wounded in the campaign.
Among the dead was Lieutenant-Colonel Sanders, who had been
Ellenborough's Military Secretary. He volunteered to lead a charge
against the enemy's guns and fell instantly, shot through the heart. His
understanding with Richmond's youngest sister, 'dearest Selinthus',
was never to be fulfilled. She was heartbroken and never married.

After the victory, Ellenborough received the young Maharaja at an
improvised durbar, designed to demonstrate the boy's complete
impotence. Ellenborough blasted on about the gallantry of his troops
and the generosity of the British in restoring the Maharaja, while the
little boy burst into tears and quietened his nerves by chewing *pan*.
Neither he nor the nobles standing around him understood a word
of His Lordship's oration, which had to be translated for them by
Colonel Sleeman, who offered a milder version of Ellenborough's
hot-tempered bluster. Ellenborough, who was many things but not
stupid, detected this alteration of tone and stopped Sleeman and
rudely ordered him to 'to speak out as *he* did'.

The treaty that was signed on January 13, 1844, was brutal.
Gwalior's great army was disbanded and replaced by a much smaller
contingent under British control, designed to overawe the people of
Gwalior rather than to protect them. To pay for the troops, the
British took over a good slice of the Gwalior country, bringing in at
least two million rupees a year. Then there was the bill for the costs
of the late war, 260,000 rupees, which the durbar was ordered to pay
within a fortnight, and did. Apart from the 100 guns taken in battle,
the British also confiscated many splendid pieces of cannon and
took them off to Agra.

The British then commandeered the great fort of Gwalior whose
walls command the surrounding country in such superb style. Most
ridiculous of all the humiliations visited upon the citizens of Gwalior
was the inversion of the indigenous custom of removing shoes in the
presence of royalty, so that now, as Colonel Sleeman informed his
masters with childish glee, 'we all sat on chairs with our boots on'.[6]
One wonders what Richmond, who had always been so instinctively

courteous to Indians and so respectful of their sensibilities, can have thought.

Almost Lord Ellenborough's last act before leaving India was to order a triumphal monument to the Gwalior dead to be constructed on Strand Road, Calcutta. The memorial, now half-hidden by trees, still stands. Once known as the Pepper Pot, it is in fact a handsome structure based on the traditional Indian *chatri*. Unkind critics said that Lord Ellenborough had the monument erected because it was the only battle at which he was present.

But the subjugation of Gwalior was not a trivial matter. Nor were the reasons for embarking on such a ruthless campaign. Those reasons can be summed up in a single word: opium. Behind the flannel about Britain's need for a 'tranquil frontier' lay a hard commercial imperative.

Sindia's territories, and Malwa in particular, constituted one of the two largest opium-producing areas in India. As Britain was the world's largest organized supplier of narcotics, and the exclusive supplier of opium to East and South Asia, above all to China, Malwa was crucial. Not only did opium supply a huge fraction of Britain's Indian revenues, it paid for the imports of Chinese tea and it financed the whole commercial apparatus which sent dividends back to London. Bengal opium, from Benares and Patna, had been a Company monopoly since the end of the eighteenth century, but the Company had no control over the Malwa poppy fields. Native merchants were making huge fortunes. Sindia derived vast revenues from the traffic through customs duties, sales taxes and land taxes. The durbar at Gwalior at times seemed like a chamber of opium entrepreneurs. And the shipments were increasing all the time: in 1818/19 Malwa sent 977 chests of opium to China; in 1823/4, 5,535 chests; in 1830/31, 12,856 chests. Sindia's peasant proprietors prospered. Sindia's soldiers were paid well and paid on time. Worse still for the British, much of the opium was smuggled through to Karachi, in distant Sind, where it was shipped on to China. It wasn't only the British state but also the Far Eastern opium dealers, such as

Jardine Matheson, who were in a constant state of indignation about the Malwa 'interlopers'.[7]

The truth is, then, that the Gwalior war, and to a lesser extent Napier's war against the amirs of Sind, were opium wars, fought to protect the British monopoly of the supply of the drug, whereas the wars against China were to protect the monopoly of the Far Eastern market for Britain. Ellenborough might well have gone on formally to annex Gwalior if he had not run into public indignation at home. The invective in Parliament against him began as a trickle and soon became a flood. Leading MPs of all parties inveighed against Ellenborough's high-handed and extravagant behaviour. Lord John Russell declared that 'Lord Ellenborough was not a man in whose hands such an Empire as that of India could safely be left.' The Court of Directors, for which Ellenborough had shown such open contempt, needed little encouragement to get rid of him. And in 1844, he was recalled, the first Governor-General since Wellesley to suffer this humiliation.

And Richmond? There he was, as Number 2 to Sleeman for the next four years, knocking around in the great fortress at Gwalior. But he was no longer alone in his quarters. Three months after the Battle of Maharajpur, he married Sophy Powney Thompson. She was only 21, 12 years younger than Richmond, as the inevitable Shakespear ode on such occasions made plain:

> Sophy is young, Sophy is gay,
> Richmond is grave, Richmond is grey.

In the ode, the character of Dan Cupid declares:

> I confess I'm doubtful whether
> A better match I e'er did tether.

It was a happy one, producing nine children. They always hated being apart, and Richmond was stricken with loneliness after they decided that Sophy should go with the elder children to England, ironically to prevent them having the lonely, unsettled childhood that Richmond himself had suffered. In her absence, he busied himself in his workshop with his scientific experiments and rode around the Sindia country, collecting taxes and flushing out the occasional gang of local bandits. There were quarrels with his boss, Colonel Sleeman, who had a difficult, paranoid side.

Behind this bickering we can, I think, catch a deeper sadness; an echo of that melancholy which had afflicted John Malcolm when he revisited the Nizam's palace at Hyderabad, or Mountstuart Elphinstone when he sat in the Peshwa's old palace, or John Low when he was the Peshwa's gaoler at Bithur. There was something empty, something inauthentic about the British occupation of these ancient quarters, something which could only be described as a sense of usurpation. And in Richmond Shakespear's situation there was a darker over-hanging, the shadow of the opium trade which was driving events.

It is sad to watch someone who really was so noble-natured caught up in such a shoddy enterprise. Let us rather leave him riding out gaily over the Chorasmian waste, Richmond the irresistible rescuer. When he died of bronchitis in October 1861, he was mourned all over India, from begum to washerman. One of his assistants wrote 'He made me love him as I never expected to love anyone again after my father's death.'[8]

Thackeray wrote a joint tribute to his two first cousins, Richmond Shakespear and William Ritchie, who had just become the legal member of the Supreme Council in Calcutta and who died a few months after Richmond:

> I saw a young officer yesterday to whom the first words Sir Richmond Shakespear wrote on his arrival in India were, 'Can I do anything for you?' His purse was at the command of all. His kind hand was always open. It was a gracious fate that sent him to rescue widows and captives. Where could they have had a champion more chivalrous, a protector more loving and tender?

I write down his name in my little book, among those of others dearly loved, who, too, have been summoned hence. And so we meet and part; we struggle and succeed; or we fail and drop unknown on the way. As we leave the fond mother's knee, the rough trials of childhood and boyhood begin; and then manhood is upon us, and the battle of life, with its chances, perils, wounds, defeats, distinctions. And Fort William guns are saluting in one man's honour, while the troops are firing the last volleys over the other's grave – over the grave of the brave, the gentle, the faithful Christian soldier.[9]

The Battle of Maharajpur had another curious aftermath. Two months after it, just before Richmond's wedding, 3,000 boys aged between 10 and 12 got together on the outskirts of Gwalior town and played out the battle between the British army and the Sindia army. The boys followed the facts in that the Sindia forces were defeated, but the boy playing Lord Ellenborough was 'slain' and the quisling Phalke was taken prisoner and given a severe drubbing with shoes. Thousands of the townspeople flocked out to see the show, which went on for three days until forcibly dispersed by the authorities. The tableau was regularly repeated among the poorer families, especially those who had been reduced to beggary by the disbanding of the army. Sleeman reported to government that 'since the Artillery and Infantry Brigades have been disbanded, great numbers of the people of the city who provided them with food and clothing have of course suffered in circumstances from the diminished demand for their services, and all who so suffer naturally regret the change that has taken place ... at present they have manifested themselves only in this little affray between the boys.'[10]

In the name of economy, the British had steadily disbanded the armies of the Indian states in the Ganges region since the beginning of the century. C.A. Bayly calculates that as many as 200,000 may have been demobbed.[11] Sleeman puts the consequences with brutal clarity: 'We do the soldiers' work with one-tenth of the soldiers that had before been employed in it over the territories we acquire, and turn the other nine-tenths adrift. They all sink into the lowest class of religious mendicants, or retainers; or live amongst their friends as drones upon the land.'[12] This 'colonial squeeze' had dire effects upon the general level of demand. Richard Jenkins, the long-standing Resident at Nagpur, pointed out that the disbanding of the local courts and their regiments had caused a 'sudden reduction in the amount of population of the city and environs'; 'the dispersion of these hordes on the introduction by us of order and good govern-ment, necessarily diminishes the consumption of produce of the land as of the loom.'[13]

The little boys of 1844 would have been in their early twenties by 1857–8. Many of them would have belonged to the Gwalior con-tingent which was to revolt with such passion against its pro-British ruler, the same little weeping gum-chewing Maharaja of 1844, who was forced to take refuge in the British camp. Nothing about the Great Mutiny came quite out of the blue.

XII

CRASH CITY

Augusta rejoiced in her brother's glory, John mourned the death of his lovable, hopeless nephew in the Khord-Kabul pass but, for John, the whole disastrous Afghanistan venture had another impact. With a thump, his dreams were grounded. 'The extreme uncertainty of all human schemes' was putting it mildly. Once more his finances collapsed. This time, John had been destroyed by a malign combination of two of the greatest bunglers he had ever tangled with: Lord Auckland, the Governor-General, and his own brother Henry, the serial bankrupt. Auckland's Army of the Indus and Ellenborough's Army of Retribution had between them run up a bill of £15 million, billions in today's money.[1] 'All this enormous burden fell upon the revenues of India, and the country for long years afterwards groaned under the weight.'

The injustice of it was flagrant. For the Afghan War was neither initiated by the East India Company nor approved at any stage by its Court. The ministers of the Crown were responsible, but resisted any suggestion that the British taxpayer should contribute towards its expense. As early as March 1841, the Accountant-General at Calcutta reported that the Treasury was already £3.75 million lighter and Lord Auckland had been forced to advertise a 5 per cent loan, but progress was sticky, for as the ever-sceptical Commander-in-Chief Sir

Jasper Nicolls recorded in his journal: 'Money is not rapidly sub-scribed to the loan, because it gains twelve to eighteen per cent for short periods elsewhere – amongst natives, twenty-four per cent or more.'[2]

The Afghanistan fiasco wrecked the financial credit of the East India Company just as it shattered Britain's reputation for invincibil-ity. One by one, the agency houses of Calcutta tumbled, just as they had in the last slow-motion crash of 1830–33, when Cruttenden & Co. was the final domino to fall, removing what remained of the for-tune that William Makepeace Thackeray had inherited from his father. Richmond Thackeray had been the chief Collector of Revenue for the Calcutta District. His only son was more of a dis-sipator of revenue.

In *Vanity Fair*, Thackeray attributes the collapse of the agency houses to 'Messrs Fogle, Fake and Cracksman of Calcutta'.[3] In truth, criminality was not the driving cause of this or any of the other col-lapses. Calcutta, like any thriving honeypot, certainly attracted fly-by-night characters from all over the world, but the crash of 1840–2 was really a systemic one, as the crash of 1830–33 had been and the crash of 1846–7 would be too. What triggered these serial crashes were the huge debts that the British Government ran up vir-tually overnight when they raised armies to defend or expand territory for the Company: Burma in 1826–7, Afghanistan in 1838–41, the Punjab in 1845–6. Each time, in order to attract lenders, the Company was forced to offer ruinously high rates of interest. The agency houses had to follow suit if they were to deter their customers from taking their money elsewhere. These interest bills had to be paid out of their profits on their other business, their vast speculations in commodities – opium, indigo, sugar, tin, coffee, tea. Those markets, too, suffered in the general crisis of confidence. In desperation, the houses would borrow millions of rupees from each other, until these wholesale markets dried up as well. Then the whole house of cards went down.

Sir George Larpent, the biggest noise in Calcutta banking, put his finger on the weakness in the system: what was wrong was that the agency houses practised 'a combination in their operations of banking and commercial speculation, an arrangement which meant that they were tempted far too frequently into the investment of monies entrusted to them into imprudent and unprofitable schemes.'[4] In other words, they were gambling with their customers' money, customers like the Thackerays and the Lows.

Does all this sound a little familiar? It was pretty much how things went wrong in 1929, and in 2008, too. Sir George wanted this toxic combination of savings bank and casino bank to be outlawed. But then, as now, the bankers came up with all sorts of ingenious reasons why it shouldn't be.

The crucial enabling factor had been the East India Act of 1813, which had removed the Honourable Company's monopoly on the East India trade. The merchants who had clamoured for free trade and who were powerfully represented in the House of Commons poured into the opening. In no time, there were 20, 30, 40 agency houses in Calcutta, Bombay and London competing for contracts and wooing the savers of the subcontinent, both native and European. The 1813 Act was the equivalent of the Big Bang Act of 1986 in the UK, liberating, intoxicating and full of danger. And those who had benefited from it were not going to surrender their new freedoms without a fight.

Among the many houses that failed was one called Cantor & Co., of No 3 Fairlie Place, Calcutta. The list of those adjudged to be insolvent in the *Calcutta Gazette* of November 20, 1841, included 'Henry Malcolm Low and William Marcus Westermann, late of Calcutta, and now residing at Chundernagore, heretofore trading in co-partnership, at Calcutta, together with one Charles Augustus Cantor, who is now residing in England, as merchants and agents, under the style or form of Cantor & Company.' Charles Cantor and Henry were friends. The Cantors' first child was christened William Low (he survived only five months and lies buried in South Park Street). Henry decamped further east, into darkest Burma, while

Charles returned to London, where he was registered as insolvent – thus going broke in two continents, while Henry was now bust in three.

Henry's elder brother was broke along with him. For all the splendours of his position at Lucknow, John Low had lost every farthing he possessed. The money he had squirrelled away for the education of his children and the improvements that were going ahead at Clatto – all of it was gone. It may seem bizarre that a cautious character like John should have banked all his hard-scrabbled cash with someone whose flaws he knew as well as he knew Henry's, but in the India of the 1830s a safe place to put your money was hard to find. Even the most respectable and solid-seeming houses like Sir George's own firm of Cockerell, Larpent and Co. fell into desperate difficulties, which dragged in his partner Dwarkanath Tagore, founder of the great Tagore dynasty and grandfather of the poet. Native and European financiers alike were brought down in these debacles. Larpent argued, to no avail, that there ought to be a State bank to offer a safe haven for savings, but the tycoons of Calcutta and London united in opposing this 'unfair competition'. The British Empire went on expanding to the background noise of serial crashes which engulfed the savings of its loyal servants.

Once again John Low had to write to a Governor-General, pleading to be allowed to stay where he was because he was too broke to move. The request was even more embarrassing this time than it had been in 1833, because Lord Auckland had already appointed a replacement for him at Lucknow, none other than William Sleeman. In the most gentlemanly way, Sleeman offered to stand aside and give Colonel Low time to get his finances in order. Sleeman was sent off to Gwalior instead.[5] At the very moment that Henry and Charles Cantor were going belly-up, Augusta was giving birth to yet another child, her seventh birth and her fourth son, Irvine, born at Calcutta in December 1841, where they had been making preparations, now aborted, to go to Europe. Banks might fail, but Augusta never did.

So they returned to Lucknow in the spring of 1842 for one last stretch. They arrived at the Residency just in time for the death of the King, on May 17, 1842. The reign of Muhammad Ali Shah had been short, just under five years, but, for a sickly and shy man who seemed old before his time, he had achieved a lot.

John Low wrote in his final dispatch from Lucknow, addressed to Thomas Herbert Maddock, himself formerly Resident there and now Political Secretary to the Governor-General, that 'a gradual and steady improving state of things was manifestly going on up to the date of the late King's death.'[6]

The troops had all been paid, the excesses of the court had been slashed, there were no arrears of revenue, no insurrection in any part of the country. Darshan Singh, the brutal but effective collector of taxes, had been brought back and, within a few months, had reduced all the rebellious landholders to obedience and captured all their forts and guns. Darshan had been harsher than was necessary, John admitted, but he had been 'far more beneficial than his imbecile predecessor'. The late King had left behind seven million rupees in gold and silver, along with a collection of jewels 'with detailed amounts of everything carefully recorded in a clear intelligible manner'. Muhammad Ali Shah had been an accountant's dream.

'In short, very few sovereigns ever succeeded in India in so tranquil a manner, in such comfortable circumstances and with such prospects before him for the happiness of his subjects as did the present King of Oudh.' And for that, an unspoken subtext might run, the new King, like the old one, had the coolness and quick reactions of John Low to thank.

The only blot on the horizon was the new King, whom John now crowned. Amjad Ali Shah was a corpulent Shia bigot, who had read nothing much but the Koran, from which he liked to recite large chunks, and who was dreaded by the Sunnis of Lucknow. On the other hand, like his father he was frugal and a kindly family man.

Muhammad Ali Shah was laid to rest in the charming, frivolous Husainabad Imambara which he had built in memory of the martyred Imam. There to this day amid the glitter of the chandeliers and mirrors and the shimmer of the silk hangings, you can see his stepped velvet throne and canopy and, in a glass case nearby, the spiky crown that John had placed upon his head after that terrifying night of July 7 five years earlier.

Muhammad Ali Shah and John Low enjoyed a relationship of mutual respect, and the Resident's tribute to the man he had made King was a warm and genuine one. Yet what a lot it leaves out. For all his great economizing, Muhammad Ali Shah was also a great builder. It is to him we owe not only the Husainabad Imambara but also the Jama Masjid, the Friday Mosque, with its giant honey-combed gateways, its three domes and its elegant octagonal corner towers. I find no mention at all in John's correspondence, public or private, of these or any other of the towers and mosques that the King was building all through John and Augusta's last years at Lucknow. Yet they must have seen these amazing structures rising as they trotted along the banks of the Gomti to and from the Dilkusha on their evening rides, often accompanied by one of Augusta's sisters or poor Aleck Deas. It is as though the British Resident had bound himself like Odysseus to remain blind and deaf to the siren call of nawabi culture.

By contrast, the building projects of the Honourable Company were strictly utilitarian. As Bayly wryly puts it, 'the Company in its time was celebrated only for the construction of jails and court-houses' – though a few bridges, roads and barracks could be added to the list, not to mention churches for their own worship.[7] The vast building programmes of the nawabs fulfilled a social as well as a spir-itual function. Asaf-ud-daula is said to have employed 40,000 men on the building of the Great Imambara, to relieve the terrible famine of 1783. The building of the Kaiserbagh 60 years later by Wajid Ali Shah was also a rich source of employment.[8]

Yet John was certainly a cultured man. He could speak Persian as well as Urdu and Hindustani (as it was then called). He played the cello and the flute. The Russian artist Prince Soltykoff, who visited Lucknow shortly before the death of Muhammad Ali Shah, recorded that the Resident 'did not look at all like an Englishman but had much more the air of an amiable Frenchman'. Low spoke French admirably, to the delight of Soltykoff, knowledge of French at that time being possessed by very few Englishmen in India. He lived in great state. The howdah of his elephant was a wonderful affair, shaped like a pair of swans, cut in silver gilt, set off by imitation diamonds, rubies & emeralds, which hung loosely on it, and jingled as the great animal moved.[9]

John was a prince in Lucknow. Yet he was never really *of* Lucknow. We hear not a word from him about the great flowering of art and literature there, with all its elegance, melancholy and wit; nothing either about the character of Lucknow life, the courteous, cynical, flirtatious quality for which the city was then celebrated – and often resented – throughout India. The different genres of Lucknow poetry – the tear-jerking *marsiyas,* elegies for the martyrdom of Husain and his followers at Karbala, the lyrical, erotic *ghazals,* the sardonic, parodic *rekhtis* – all reached their zenith in the 1830s, much to the annoyance of poor, declining Delhi.[10]

Nothing of this seems to have percolated to John and Augusta. The great Lucknow poet Khwaja Haidar Ali Atish wrote:

> I worry about the nightingales
> Now that spring has come.

As far as we can tell, John did not worry about the nightingales, in Lucknow anyway. His head was full of Shakespeare, the Bible and Burns. Augusta's youngest sister, Selina, recalled that he never stopped spouting poetry when he took her out in his buggy. But unlike his mentor Elphinstone, the poets of Persia and India remained closed books to him.

After the horrors of the Great Mutiny, the British denounced everything about Lucknow. Its art and architecture were as effete and decadent as its rulers. The most entrancing of the city's *imambaras,* the most delicate of her poetry and music were dismissed as bastardized and kitsch. Only a few honest observers like W.H. Russell were prepared to say how beautiful the city was. With all its dreadful faults, in those years Lucknow presented one of the most entrancing *anciens régimes* on earth, of a sort to be found nowhere else in India, perhaps nowhere else since.

Before he left the city for the last time for his long delayed and eagerly awaited home leave, John was asked by the British community to sit for a full-length portrait by George Beechey, Sir William's son, who had migrated to India and had succeeded Dufay de Casanova as Court Painter to the King of Oudh. The portrait was hung in the banqueting hall of the Residency, where it was shelled to smithereens in 1857. A more lasting memorial to John's Residency was presented by the Lucknow expats in the form of an address praising 'the extreme liberality of your contributions to all objects of public utility', which is 'generally known. But none but those who have benefited by them are aware of the extent of your private charities. No one ever appealed to you in vain, and according to the circumstances you either gave advice as a friend or afforded relief as a prince.'[11]

This 'liberality of a prince' was mentioned by William Ritchie, Aunt Ritchie's son, who had fetched up in Calcutta, from where he wrote home to his fiancée Augusta Trimmer, declaring that Colonel Low's generosity 'will prevent, I fear, the carrying home of the large fortune which he might have accumulated'. This was, as we have seen, quite an understatement. Flattery in paint and prose would do nothing to repair the gash in the Colonel's finances.

Years earlier, the young Shakespear siblings had met William in Bloomsbury at Aunt Ritchie's. Then he had been a spoilt and insufferable brat, but he had grown into a well-meaning young man, and nobody he met in India impressed him more than John and Augusta. He wrote to his fiancée, 'She is your namesake, Augusta, and somewhat resembles you in sweetness of disposition. They have long held one of the finest appointments in India ... and have been used to quite a royal residence & state ... Never were people less spoilt by high position, they are both the most warm-hearted, unaffected persons you can imagine. No man in India is more esteemed than he is . . . for he combines the soundest judgment & finest determination with the mildest manners & unbounded courtesy and benevolence.'[12] Even making allowances for William being young and impressionable, I think the tribute is quite convincing: John and Augusta clearly did have an unspoiled quality, which they never lost.

In Calcutta, William Ritchie also met Augusta's brother George Trant Shakespear, who was travelling home with the Lows, and his judgement of George is memorable, too: 'a fat, shy, eccentric but most entertaining old fellow'.[13] George was in fact 33 years old, but already seemed a lot older.

Brother and sister were travelling together to England, just as they had done so tearfully 26 years earlier. Now, instead of the long sail round the Cape, George and John and Augusta and baby Irvine took the *India*, one of the new wooden paddle steamers that carried passengers and mail to Suez. Once there they could take the overland route and make the whole trip in just over two months instead of more than five. It was George's first home leave since he had come out to India. The journal that Augusta kept of the trip for their sister Marianne provides the only extended glimpse we shall ever have of him.

The first entry in Augusta's crimson leather diary is a romantic farewell to the city which had dictated their fate for so many years:

February 9, 1843
We embarked on board the *India* late in the evening; the moon
shone clear and bright, and as the boat carried us slowly to the
ship, showed us the whole city of palaces laid out before us.

Whenever they go inshore, the steamer develops an alarming tendency to run aground. The Lows' cabin is on the same side as the coal hatch, and when the boat takes on coal they are covered with smuts. The *India* is also overbooked, so that some of the gentlemen

have to eat and sleep on deck. Little Irvine mewls as he does not care
for the cramped quarters after the cool great chambers of Calcutta.

But very soon the journal is dominated by the misfortunes of
George, who is failing to live up to the genial, waggish role expected
of him. 'George has been suffering from seasickness, & I have therefore no good saying of his to relate.'

At Madras, George goes ashore with John to drive to the club, but
he is ejected because he is not a member of the corresponding clubs
at Madras and Bombay. He drives off with his servant, looking
piteously at his brother-in-law and moaning, 'I am rejected.' But he
makes himself 'very comfortable at a Punch house where he played
billiards at a very old table, full of holes, with a little black boy who
he says gave him ten and beat him'. Then John goes to call on the
Governor, Lord Tweeddale, at his pretty country house. George
does not go.

Back on board, George has a bad fall which prevents him from
going ashore when they reach Ceylon. 'He has been a good deal
pulled down by his fall, and declares he thinks wherever he is put on
shore, there he will remain, & never go on board another vessel. He
says also he will leave off cheroots and beer.'[14]

When they are rounding the tip of Ceylon, they see the Great
Comet of 1843. The first night it appeared 'so very faint, the star or
nucleus being below the horizon. The moon rose immediately and
the comet became invisible. The next night about eight o'clock the
Comet appeared most brilliant, like a feather of fire with a small star
at the end of it. It sank below the horizon as the moon rose.'

They all go ashore at Suez and set off overland in carriages to cross
the 90 miles of desert to Cairo. George does not enjoy the journey
on land either. He detests bumping across the sand from one flea-
blown station-house to the next. At the fourth station-house, John
calls out to Augusta to come and look at the pretty Arab woman
waiting on the passengers. She turns out to be an Englishwoman
from Kent, married to an Arab. 'She was most civil and tripped
about in a light and airy way. George, however, was quite put out by

her politeness, and said, as we drove off: "Sooner than have that pretty damsel flitting about him, he would have fled across the desert on foot."[15]

You begin to get a strong sense of George's morose alter ego, which in company he managed to hide behind his bachelor joker's façade.

At Cairo, they visit the citadel of the notorious Pasha, Mehemet Ali, and an old friend of John's wangles him an invitation to dine with the Pasha. George is not included and has to stay outside the banqueting hall, peeping through the door at the scene. At the Pyramids, George does go down the shaft with John to visit the King's and Queen's Chambers, while Augusta sits outside. She is only 36, but after seven children, she has grown plump and rather lethargic. Marianne's children have nicknamed her 'Enormous Aunty'.[16] During John and Augusta's voyage up the Ganges on one of the Company's river steamers, when they disembarked at Benares, the gangplank had given way under her weight and she plunged into the sacred river. She was fished out, as ever none the worse.[17] Now she sits contentedly by the Great Pyramid, and she laughs as they emerge. 'You should have seen George come out of the King's Chamber! He was covered with dust and scarcely able to speak.'[18]

In Cairo, they also pay a visit to the slave market. John and Augusta seem unfazed at the spectacle of this traffic in human flesh (although John has outlawed it in Lucknow, in accordance with British law), but George is ill at ease:

We saw several Abyssinian women exposed for sale. There was a Turk evidently bargaining for one, feeling her arms and examining her. The slaves seemed fat and in good spirits: they were seated in a kind of open court with a small piece of sail extended over them to protect them from the sun and wind. Their food, which we saw, was a kind of pulse. On one of the women saying something, they all laughed, and they told us it was because she said she would like to be bought by that 'young man'. This was George! George said her selection was 'a great trial'.[19]

You cannot help feeling that in her robust, imperturbable way Augusta is missing signs of real distress in her brother. He seems so detached from the party, wandering off on private excursions and only returning to play his part as the family wag, increasingly the butt of the group. Poor George. Where does he go off on his own? Why does he bridle so, whenever they meet a woman outside his own family?

After ten days in the French hotel at Alexandria, the Lows board a French steamer which is to take them on to Athens, to continue their leisurely tour of ancient remains. 'George came on board with us and we took leave of him at 9 o'clock.'

That is all. No word of where he is going or what his plans might be.

We do know that he eventually went on to London, because he joined the Oriental Club there at the end of the year. The following June, his first cousin William Makepeace Thackeray mentions to an aunt that he has seen George twice, adding that 'we have besides exchanged cards genteelly'. In July, Thackeray reports having had tea with his childhood friend and finds him as selfish as ever.[20] They were born in Calcutta within a few months of each other. Their friendship dates back to their sailing to England together at the age of six and lasted all through their schooldays. Yet you get the feeling that these attempts to pick up the threads have not been a total success.

The next we hear, and the last, is that George Trant Shakespear died at Geneva three months later on October 4, 1844, by his own hand.

What made him take his own life? Was he in debt, or a semi-alcoholic, or partly gay, or just dreadfully lonely? We'll never know. Perhaps Augusta didn't know either. For her he was always the frolicsome Polar Bear. George was not the only servant of the

Honourable Company to come to a dead end. It is easy to imagine how hard he might have found it to settle in London, cut loose from his old Indian associations. Perhaps, too, though he might not admit it, he was a little oppressed by the shadow of his younger brother Richmond, a celebrity in London as he was in India and now blissfully married. The solitude of his own life might suddenly come to him, as it had not when he was dealing justice and collecting taxes in the backwoods of Dinajpur, Murshidabad and the Sunderbunds. How cruelly Thackeray senses George's defencelessness and transforms him into the dislikable Jos Sedley, who has none of George's warm and affectionate side.

Vanity Fair was published in 1847–8, three years after George's death, and it has a rather strange ending. The last few pages are taken up with the death of Jos at Aix-la-Chapelle. He is virtually bankrupt and physically decrepit. His only discoverable asset is a life insurance policy for £2,000, which he had bequeathed in equal shares to his sister Amelia (now Mrs Dobbin) and 'his friend and invaluable attendant during sickness, Rebecca, wife of Lieutenant-Colonel Rawdon Crawley CB' – alias Becky Sharp, who is also appointed Jos's administratrix.

Does Thackeray mean us to think that Becky has murdered him? That is certainly a popular interpretation, but I think that Thackeray's intentions are, typically, not so simple. Jos is already in very poor health. The faithful Dobbin found him in Brussels 'in a condition of pitiable infirmity' and 'dreadfully afraid of Rebecca, though eager in his praises of her'. The solicitor of the insurance company eventually pays out, though he 'swore it was the blackest case that ever had come before him'. But is it murder that he suspects, or suicide, both being bars to paying out on the policy? The author, in his usually teasing way, leaves us to play with the possibilities. What is clear, I think, is that George's lonely death played upon Thackeray's own imagination, and came to stand in his mind for the sad ends of other 'Indian civilians' who had no real life to come home to.

Which could not be said of John and Augusta. By July 1843,

they were at Clatto, overjoyed to see Charlotte and Malcolm and Robert and John Junior – who all now met little Irvine for the first time. Overjoyed, too, to see the newly installed water closets and the other internal improvements that had brought modern comfort to the draughty old house. At Lucknow, Augusta had become accustomed to princely splendour. Clatto was no comedown.

For John, though, the immediate sadness was to see his mother going downhill so quickly. Her decline was not slowed by two of her daughters, Maria and Georgina, who insisted on preaching the stern doctrines of the new Free Church of Scotland around her bed. Georgina was the worst. A visiting minister reported that 'Miss Low was a faithful witness for Christ before all, especially by placing the *truths of the Gospel* before her mother with great earnestness and affection.' If she had been up to it, I am sure that Susan Elizabeth Low would have retorted that she was already perfectly well acquainted with the truths of the Gospel. As it was, she soon drifted out of reach of the pious clamour, and she died on September 20, 1843, at the age of 83. She was buried beside her husband in the little churchyard next to the older, ruined church at Kemback, overlooking the braes of Dura Den. After 38 years absence, John had at least caught a fading glimpse of her.[21]

Apart from this sadness, John and Augusta might seem to have escaped into that rare serene, a Fifeshire retirement. They watched the older children grow into their teens, they visited the Foulises and the Bethunes and the Cleghorns. John pruned the roses on the high south-facing wall of the garden and played golf on the Old Course, where he once fainted after having fallen off a ladder a couple of days before – the sort of mishap that happens to retired military men.

But how retired was he? Could he afford to stay at Clatto when his well-deserved home leave ran out? He had been angling to be the Military Member on the Supreme Council in Calcutta, but General Pollock had outranked him. Undeterred, he wrote to Elphinstone a year after he had come back to Scotland, 'from what I see of expences in this country I think it highly probable I may return to

India some 15 or 16 months hence, merely as an *omeedwar*.'[22] *Hobson-Jobson*, the legendary glossary of Anglo-Indian terms, translates *omeedwar* as 'an expectant, a candidate for employment, one who awaits a favourable answer to some representation or request'.

If he was already running out of cash, some of his Fifeshire neighbours thought he might have only himself to blame, for John Low was by no means finished with improving Clatto. Peter Cleghorn wrote in 1845: 'Col. Low has come into St. Andrews for the summer, as great alterations are going on, the house filled with wrights & masons. Gen. Bethune thinks his alterations will cost £2,000 or £2,500, which, begging my friend's pardon, is very foolish. The old house was very comfortable & quite sufficient for the property.'[23] The additions in the Scotch Baronial style, by the fashionable Edinburgh firm of Bryce & Burn, were indeed quite something: round turrets with spires and weathercocks at the corners, high-stepped gables and great bay windows and gateposts with pillars and stone balls, like Mrs Ludlam's establishment in the North End Road.

Charlotte had been taken down to a boarding school in England. Soon the four boys were also sent off to schools in the north of England. So school fees were being piled on to the bills for battlements and bay windows. The Colonel wanted to live like a nabob, but on a half-Colonel's half-pay. Or was there a reckless part of him that was almost deliberately engineering yet another decline into the financial depths? Was he secretly a little bored already with shooting grouse and paying calls on county neighbours, and the gossip in The Royal & Ancient clubhouse? Did he hanker just a little for the heat and the dust and the danger?

In *The Newcomes*, Thackeray offers a poignant illustration of John Low's dilemma. Colonel Newcome tells his old mistress, the Comtesse de Florac: 'I shall very probably have to go back to India. My furlough is expired. I am now taking my extra leave. If I can get up my promotion, I need not return. Without that I cannot afford to live in Europe.'[24]

Colonel Newcome's spendthrift dilettante son Clive is amazed. He had thought his father's pockets bottomless, but 'he is not near so rich as we had thought. Since he has been at home, he says he has spent greatly more than his income and he is quite angry at his own extravagance' – though half the money has gone on indulging his beloved son.[25] Colonel Newcome is overdrawn both at the Newcome family bank and at his agents in Calcutta, and unless one or two senior officers die, he is done for.

There is, though, another angle to the Colonel's unhappiness. In a touching confession, he tells young Arthur Pendennis: 'You young fellows are too clever for me. I haven't learned your ideas or read your books. I feel myself very often an old damper in your company. I will go back, sir, where I have some friends, and where I am some-body still. I know an honest face or two, white & brown, that will light up in the old regiment when they see Tom Newcome again. God bless you Arthur. You young fellows in this country have such cold ways that we old ones hardly know how to like you at first.'[26]

It is the same complaint that John Blakiston made a generation earlier on returning to England after 12 years serving abroad. He found 'a coldness and reserve' among his fellow countrymen, a lack of the easy fellowship that existed between Europeans thrown together in India. This had 'a very chilling effect' on the returning Anglo-Indian, and would, 'I am sure, drive many a man back to lay his bones in a foreign land, who would gladly have spent the evening of his days among his kindred'.[27]

Nor was this disappointment confined to men. Thackeray's mother Anne felt the same when she returned to England. She wrote to her mother who was still in India, 'England is very delight-ful, the climate fine, the Country Paradise, but the people! The people are not Indians, they live for themselves, we live for our friends & I don't think in a whole life I should ever make such a friend as a few months in your kinder land has given me.'[28]

The character of Colonel Newcome is reliably said to be based on Anne's husband and Thackeray's stepfather, Major Henry

Carmichael-Smyth. Thackeray himself said as much to an American woman he met in Paris when he was writing the last chapters of his book.[29] The Major was a simple soldier who lost a good part of his savings along with Thackeray's fortune in the 1833 crash. He then put most of what he had left into a new newspaper, *The Constitutional*, for which Thackeray acted as Paris correspondent, and which folded after five months.[30] The Major also had Colonel Newcome's combination of unfailing kindness and inability to see any point of view but his own, which made him both lovable and infuriating. But other families too claimed their own patriarch as the original, because the character of old Tom Newcome had such resonance for those early Victorians who, like him, were buffeted and bewildered by the modern age.[31]

The truth is, as with most memorable characters in fiction, Colonel Newcome was a composite. John Low has a good claim to be part of the mix. On his frequent visits to London, he bumped into Thackeray several times and he, like Colonel Newcome, was an arresting figure, tall and erect, with a genial, approachable manner and a considerable store of knowledge, combined with a certain innocence which seemed unbruised by all his experience of life. He was also the world's worst investor, and would not have hesitated to plunge, as Colonel Newcome did, into the Bank of Bundelcund, which was obviously doomed from the first. Most relevant of all, unlike Major Carmichael-Smyth, he did actually return to India to recoup his fortune, only a few years before his wife's cousin started writing the book. So I feel entitled to take Richard Doyle's illustration of Colonel Newcome waving farewell,[32] as a fair approximation of John Low going aboard the *Vernon* at Southampton in November 1847.

The difference is that Colonel Newcome sailed alone, while John had not only his wife with him, as ever, but also the two daughters that the inexhaustible Augusta had given birth to while they were at Clatto, little Augusta and Selina, now aged three and two respectively. It sounds like a relaxed family party. But John's situation was

unsettled, to put it mildly. He had no job to go to, and no immediate prospect of one. He was joining the queue of field officers
loitering at Bombay, Madras and Calcutta in the hope that an epidemic or a battle would carry off enough of their seniors to leave a
gap. John told Mountstuart that 'I can perfectly well afford to remain
at Madras for a considerable time if necessary merely on my
Colonel's pay & allowances without any specific employment. I
should live in perfect good humour "waiting events" as old Sir Barry
[Close] used to say', though he admitted he did not fancy being sent
off to Vellore or Trichinopoly merely to command a garrison, 'probably under the orders of someone originally junior to me'.[33]

After he had lost out to Pollock for the Supreme Council, he had
written to George Clerk, the Governor of Bombay, asking if there
were any on the first-class roll of Residents likely to come home and
was told 'only Aden', which he understandably called 'an odd hole
to find myself stuck into'. What was clear was that he had no chance
of anything as long as he stayed in Britain. Anyway, there was no
prospect of a military post at Bombay being offered to a Madras officer. The old pecking order lingered on: Bengal first, then Bombay,
and last the 'Muls' of Madras.

It is painful to watch a man in his late fifties scrabbling for a job.
Could Elphinstone put in a word for him with Sir Henry Pottinger,
the new Governor of Madras, who might be joining the Lows' ship?
He had had a cordial talk with Pottinger at an East India dinner at
Douglas's Hotel in Edinburgh and had also met him once in
Chaplin's house at Poona in 1824. He is poignantly pleased to report
that his 'somewhat dreaded' interview with the Chairman at India
House had gone well.[34] Most poignant of all is the way that John
ends this letter to his old friend:

> If I had not been a miserably bad manager of my own affairs, I
> might have been as well off <u>now</u>, as I shall be after five years of
> Council if ever I get the post and live to go through those five
> long years of stewing in Bengal.

Once again, Calcutta was Crash City, and once again it was not only the financial innocents, the Colonel Newcomes and the John Lows, who were going under. In the crash of 1846–7, the originating cause was, as usual, the huge debts of the British Government, now engaged in the first great war to subdue and secure the North-West Frontier. Sir George Larpent had diagnosed the disease, but he could not keep his own house safe from contamination. Once again, the agency houses had to offer exorbitant rates of interest to hold on to their depositors and then had to embark on a frenzied concatenation of inter-bank loans to keep paying that interest. James Wilson, founder of the *Economist*, who had seen it all before by the time he became Financial Secretary to the Treasury in 1853, describes the process in terms which, once again, evoke our own dear bank crashes:

> Houses in Calcutta drew upon their own houses in London and the houses in London to cover themselves drew upon their houses in India, or the India houses drew new sets of bills, and with the proceeds of such bills purchased other bills upon other houses ... and transmitted them to London to pay former bills of their own drawings. And thus an enormous amount of cross bills became current, representing no transactions, and what was even worse, drawn without any regard to the state of the exchange, whether profitable or ever so much the reverse, under the dire necessity at all hazards to meet their obligations.[35]

All this is again familiar. The money whirls round and round until the banks have no reliable picture of how much they ultimately owe, and to whom. 'Turbo-capitalism' is not, it seems, an invention of the late twentieth century. One can forgive John Low for being baffled and enraged.

XIII

COTTON-PICKING

The Lows were an unusual family to be returning to India, as they stepped off the harbour boat on to the ghat in the second week of January 1848: the grizzled elderly man now in his sixtieth year, clearly not in the best of health, his plump, much younger wife, and their two little daughters, Augusta junior not yet four and Selina still only two. At that age, children were usually being sent to England rather than coming out to Calcutta. As for John, many officers junior to him were already retired to Bournemouth or Cheltenham. Yet he here he was, hanging around for employment, with only his Colonel's pay to keep them, not to mention the debts he had left behind in Scotland.

Then, not for the first time in his long career, he had a bit of luck. It was a coincidence which seemed heaven-sent at the time. In the same week that the Lows docked at Diamond Harbour there landed also the incoming Governor-General, and Calcutta was junketing to greet him. James Andrew Broun Ramsay was already the tenth Earl of Dalhousie and the chief of clan Ramsay. At the age of 35, he now became the youngest Governor-General that India ever had. He was to turn out to be the most remarkable of them all. By the time he left seven years later, a widower broken in health, he had transformed the country. Of all the modernizers who wanted to 'make something' of India, he was the indefatigable chief. And in that transformation John Low played a part that was by turns exhilarating, head-spinning and humiliating. If Lord Dalhousie had never come to India, John Low might well have glided on into retirement and old age with a serene mind and a clear conscience.

The two men clicked instantly. For one thing, they came from the same part of the world. If you stood on Clatto Hill and looked across the Firth of Forth, you could see the hills on the other side which sheltered Dalhousie Castle where the Governor-General was born. Much later, when they were disagreeing strongly, and not for the first time, Dalhousie wrote looking forward to the days when 'we shall return to our far happier position as two Scottish gentlemen on the banks of Forth.'[1] And though in their social position they were far apart, both liked to drop into Lowland Scots. Trying to persuade John to come up to Simla, Dalhousie implores him to 'gie a thocht to't'.[2] And when John is bowed down by his ailments, Dalhousie replies that 'I am grieved to see you writing in so *dowie* a tone' and beseeches him to 'cock up your bonnet'.[3]

Besides, Dalhousie really had charm. There was not much of him. But his being so small and slight only added to the power of his bright eye and the surprising resonance of his voice. He had a good conceit of himself and was aware of the fact. In his diary when he was at Christ Church, Oxford, he wrote, 'we certainly are immensely cocky, but then, hang it, we have reason.' He was auto-cratic by design, but autocratic with style. His turn of phrase could be caustic. He wrote of the brothers Charles and James Napier: 'The two Napiers were vineyards on a volcano. They would have been gay and genial but for the perpetual flames bursting out and scorching and blasting all that was good in them' – a summing-up which didn't fit Dalhousie himself too badly.[4]

In all his abundant correspondence with John, Dalhousie was good-humoured and solicitous. They gossiped about their colleagues, about the situation in the Punjab, about current events in Europe. Often Dalhousie would ask for advice from the Indian veteran who was old enough to be his father.[5]

Like John Low, Dalhousie was broke, but on a far grander scale. When he sailed for India, the estate he had inherited was encumbered with a debt of £48,000. Like many other Governors-General before him, he had accepted the post partly with the aim of remaking his fortune. He succeeded. When he was briefing his successor Lord Canning eight years later, he 'said that he came here a poor man, with a small property and a large debt; that now he had paid off the debt; bought an old cotton mill which intruded on his estate, and should find himself with about £7000 of savings in hand.'[6] Lord Ellenborough had thought the Governor-General ought to be able to send home £1,000 a month, but Dalhousie had not had his expenditure at Government House properly controlled. He was eager to help John Low remake his fortune, too, and made it one of his first tasks at Government House to find him something.

What Dalhousie came up with was only a temporary post, but it had lasting and fateful consequences. General James Stuart Fraser of the Madras Army had been Resident in Hyderabad for ten years. Now he applied for leave to take his sick daughter on a voyage to Singapore to restore her health. 'Sea and the Straits' was a standard remedy for afflictions of the lungs. John Low was drafted to stand in for him at the Nizam's court. It was his first prolonged visit to Hyderabad since he had been there as John Malcolm's Assistant 30 years earlier. The Residency was as glorious a palace as ever, although John Low had no need of the Rang Mahal, the Oriental pavilion where James Kirkpatrick had placed his lovely *bibi*, by then his wife, and her entourage.

But conditions in Hyderabad distressed John almost as much as they had distressed Malcolm on his return visit. This great state enjoyed rich soil and great natural resources, but its ruler was wretchedly, hopelessly in debt to the British Government, to the tune of 7 million rupees and rising all the time. True, the State was poorly managed. The Nizam and his Ministers were prone to the usual extravagance, negligence and corruption. But the real culprit was not the Nizam but the British Government.

In Low's view, Britain had been guilty of nothing less than 'cruelty' in compelling the Nizam to pay four million rupees a year to support the British so-called Contingent Force, 'in other words, for purposes of our own, not of the Nizam!'[7] Most of these troops had not fired a shot in 30 years, for there had been unbroken peace in the Nizam's dominions. Internal security required a force of half the size, if that. 'In short, it is a melancholy fact that the only people who have gained by what I call the *unnecessary* half of the Nizam's Contingent are the officers and men who have composed that half.'[8] Those five British brigadiers and 90 British officers and 9,000 men were simply lolling about at the Nizam's expense.

Low's friend on the Court of Directors, Sir James Lushington, the ex-White Mutineer made good, was well aware of all this, as he was of the fact that there was no legal obligation on the Nizam under the Treaty of 1800 to pay a single rupee in time of peace for any such force. His Highness (and his father and grandfather before him) had been conned into it, and the arrangement was beggaring him.

In a second letter, John set out for Lushington's benefit a scheme for gradually reducing the size of the force and absorbing the men elsewhere.[9] Very sensible the plan was, too. And in a PS he added a stinging warning against taking over the country, as the 'annexationists' hankered to do for the supposed welfare of the natives:

If they [our native allies] shall ever hear of our reducing the Nizam and his Minister to ciphers, and of our managing the whole country and collecting its revenues by instruments of our own selection, made responsible exclusively to English officers, our allies will most assuredly ascribe the whole proceeding to our ambition and our supposed innate aversion to all Native Sovereigns in India.

And hence there will be no trifling increase to their suspicion, and fear and dislike of us that now exist in the minds of a great many Chiefs in other Native States, while the Nizam, and almost all the families of high rank in his country, and most of the military classes among his subjects, will, of course, most cordially detest us.

Even some of those classes who will really and truly be relieved from oppression by our assumption of the Government will, after a short time, feel no sort of gratitude to us for that relief. They will forget their former miseries, and remember only the vexations they will be subject to under our rule; for the Natives of this country are, after all, not different in one respect from the inhabitants of all parts of the known world, in that they like their own ways better than those of foreigners.[10]

He had said a good deal of this ten years earlier, to John Russell Colvin in relation to Lucknow, and he was to say it again. But what John adds here is that it is not simply the rajas and the high-ups who will loathe British interference but the peasants and the common soldiers will in the end come to resent foreign dictation, too. The 'Levellers' who hoped to flatten out class inequalities in India could never hope to flatten that overwhelming obstacle.

Lushington sitting in Leadenhall Street was in no position to put any sort of plan into operation. Nor was John Low, at least not off his own bat. He had to persuade Dalhousie.

It was at this moment that General Fraser returned with his daughter, her health much improved (he resumed the Residency on July 22), and the Lows went back to Calcutta.

To his surprise, his noble friend was non-committal, in fact decidedly unreceptive. Yes, the Contingent was costing too much. The staff, with those five brigadiers, was 'preposterously large'. But at the same time, Dalhousie refused to agree that there was any cruelty to the Nizam involved:

I cannot perceive or acknowledge that the British Government commits any injustice or practices any extortion whatever on the Nizam's Government in requiring that this force, fully manned, equipped and disciplined, shall be maintained in His Highness's territories, and at his expense.[11]

Ominously, when John Low apologized for raising the 'vexatious' subject, Dalhousie said, No, no, every public man should give his opinions honestly, whatever they were, but adding 'besides, I feel sure we shall have opinions very different from yours before us on that subject, so that we shall have full opportunity of judging correctly at last.'[12] He was not going to lift a finger in the direction suggested by John Low. His Lordship had a quite different policy in mind, though he did not come clean about its nature then.

Poor old General Fraser also fretted and badgered the Governor-General to allow him to do something to help the Nizam sort out his affairs. Lord Dalhousie did nothing, sanctioned nothing. 'The Nizam must go to the dogs his own way, for the Government of India has no time just now to take care of him.'[13]

Dalhousie now began to accuse the Nizam of making trouble. 'If the Nizam chooses to ruin himself in spite of aid and advice, he shall not disturb the peace of British territory, or either injure or play with British interests.' In fact, the Nizam had been a dutiful and affectionate ally of the British and had shown no sign whatever of attempting anything of the sort. The Governor-General declared that 'I will not contravene the Treaty on the pretence of protecting the Nizam.'[14]

Quite simply, Dalhousie wanted the money, and 'if the Nizam can't repay it, he must raise a loan in the ordinary way from capitalists. This demand will probably either cause or enable me to make a crisis which will afford me an opportunity of putting our relations on a different footing by a new treaty.'[15] 'His large debt enables us to put the thumbscrews on, and he deserves to get a squeeze.'[16] Seldom in the history of the British Empire can a proconsul have laid out his plans with more cynical clarity.

Augusta Shakespear, just before
going to India, by Adam Buck,
1825 or 1826.

Jos Sedley, alias George Trant
Shakespear. Illustration by
Thackeray himself to *Vanity Fair.*

The British
Residency,
Lucknow, at the
time of John Low's
arrival.

'Public Reception of Lt-Col Low by HM the King of Oudh on the 4th of March 1834', by Alexandre Dufay de Casanova. Formerly hung at Buckingham Palace, now in store at Windsor.

'The Begum's Attempt to Usurp the Throne of Oudh for Moona Jan, 7th July 1837', by Alexandre Dufay de Casanova, presented to John Low by the Court of Directors.

Susan Elizabeth Low, by Frederick Cruickshank, 1836.

Charlotte Low, 'darling little Charlotte', a miniature by Frederick Cruickshank. This and the preceding picture were sent to John and Augusta in Lucknow by his mother in 1836.

Richmond Shakespear, engraved from a drawing by Prince A. Soltykoff.

'Rise Up! Sir Richmond.' Ink drawing by one of the Lows depicting Richmond's stumble when being knighted by Queen Victoria on August 31, 1841, aged twenty-nine.

The Husainabad Imambara, Lucknow, burial place of Muhammad Ali Shah, who built it.

Portrait of Muhammad Ali Shah in the Husainabad Imambara.

Charlotte Low, by Kenneth McLeay, RSA, 1836. She stands in front of Clatto House as it was before John Low's baronial embellishments, which helped to bankrupt him.

Clatto after the embellishments, the house as the later Lows knew it.

'Farewell!' Colonel Newcome returns to India to repair his fortune. Illustration by Richard Doyle from *The Newcomes*.

Lord Dalhousie, by George Richmond.

The Nizam of Hyderabad, Asaf Jah IV, who reigned from 1829 to 1857, for the last four years over a sadly shrunken kingdom.

The Dilkusha, Delhi, with the Qutb Minar pillar in the distance, from the *Delhi Book* of Sir Thomas Metcalfe.

The Dilkusha as it is today, a Mughal tomb once more, shorn of its British encasings.

Theo Metcalfe after the Mutiny. Photograph by Felice Beato, 1858.

Emily Anne Metcalfe, 'Annie', Charlotte Low's best friend in India.

ord Canning.

Robert Low in his teens at Clatto, shortly before he left for India.

The Santal Rebellion, as seen by the *Illustrated London News*, quite accurately.

Storming the batteries at Badle-ki-Serai. The commander on the white horse is the unstoppable Brigadier Showers.

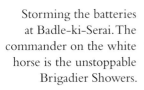

The advance of the siege train from Amballa to relieve Delhi. Its slow progress was agonizing for the besieged/ besieging British.

Blowing up the Kashmir Gate.

Brigadier Showers, photograph by Felice Beato after the Mutiny.

Ruins of the Kashmir Gate. Felice Beato photograph.

In the meantime, he had a war in the Punjab to win, and he did not care to have his hands full with the affairs of these 'booby potentates'. If the Nizam dared to interfere in the business of the British Government, he wrote from the battlefront, 'I will make his knuckles so smart as never Nizam's knuckles smarted before.'[17]

By January 1851, the Nizam's debt to the British Government stood at 70 lakhs of rupees. There was no sign of the debt being cleared, despite early promises from the Nizam to do so by yearly instalments of 12 lakhs.[18] General Fraser recommended a new instalment plan. Dalhousie rejected it. Fraser at last began to cotton on to what the Governor-General was up to. 'Cotton' would turn out to be the *mot juste*.[19]

The General was beginning to see that Dalhousie actually wanted the Nizam to go to the devil. Then, when the debt had grown too mountainous to be paid off in money, he could grab the Nizam's superb cotton fields to clear it. The Governor-General's language grew more menacing still. Unless the Nizam kept up the Contingent Force at full strength *and* paid off the debt by giving up the equivalent acres to the British, then he would feel the full force of 'the Government of India whose power can make you as the dust under foot, and leave you neither a name nor a trace.' The terrifying language of this *kharita* (the ornamental bag in which letters to princes were delivered) was confined to the Persian version. For English consumption, rather milder words were used.

The Nizam hurriedly set out to raise a loan on the security of his jewels. The leading merchants of Hyderabad agreed to open a new bank in the city to arrange this loan. Henry Dighton, an experienced and respected local banker who had had amicable dealings with Dalhousie, was willing to lead the new bank. Dalhousie, ignoring his own previous demand that the Nizam should raise a loan from 'the capitalists', forbade the formation of any such bank. He even threatened to have the blameless Mr Dighton deported. The proposed bank might well have raised most, if not all, of the sum required. But what Dalhousie wanted now (perhaps had wanted all along) was not money but land.

Poor General Fraser was deputed to nominate some juicy districts to be handed over in the last resort by compulsion. For if the Nizam refused, 'the British government will not submit to such an outrage upon all justice, and will take temporary possession of the territories by force.'[20]

The distraught Fraser replied that 'as regards the Nizam, I consider it [the proposed arrangement] to involve his certain ruin, and the utter extinction of his power as an independent Sovereign.'[21] After further acrimonious exchanges on this and other subjects, Fraser resigned on November 12, 1852, fed up and forced out.[22]

So a huge tract of the Nizam's territories, equivalent to one third of the whole, was lined up to be transferred to Queen Victoria. These lands included, in the inventory colourfully laid out by Sir Edwin Arnold, Principal of the Government Sanskrit School at Poona and later editor of the London *Daily Telegraph*, 'the rich red and black soil about Omrawattee, the metropolis of the cotton fields which have since rescued Manchester from her shameful partnership with the slave-drivers [because Britain thereafter no longer had to rely on the southern states of America for supplies of raw cotton]. It included Berar, and Pal Ghaut, the fattest and most fertile tract, perhaps, in Central Hindoostan, where poppy-heads and cotton-pods may be grown bigger than anywhere in the world. It included, too, the Raichore Doab, between the Tombudra and Upper Krishna Rivers – a country almost as fruitful as the Berar district, and admirably irrigated by tanks and wells.'[23] A doab is a stretch of land between two rivers, and usually highly fertile and desirable for that reason. In selecting these districts, Fraser had described them as 'without exception the richest and most fertile part of the Nizam's dominions', which 'hold out great prospect of improvement in regard to revenue and commerce, from an extended culture of the two articles of cotton and opium.'[24] And who was to give the screw the final turn? Who was to do the dirty work that General Fraser refused to do?

Just as the Lows were quitting Hyderabad in 1848 after John's temporary posting there, Dalhousie had written to say that he had been looking out for a suitable permanent post for his friend, but 'your reputation and your rank, both high, make it difficult to find for you the employment you desire.'[25] The death of Colonel Sutherland had created a vacancy in Rajputana, but Dalhousie felt unable to advance John 'at the expence of other officers of considerable standing who have been serving continuously in India since your return to England.' Returning officers could not expect to jump the queue over the heads of those who had endured the heat and dust. There was Major Thoresby who had long acted in Rajputana in Sutherland's absence; the admirable Colonel Sleeman had put in a claim, too. All he could offer Colonel Low was the Residency in Nepal. 'I know Katmandu is not Lucknow, but still it is better than nothing; and I can do no more than offer you the best thing at my disposal, bound as I feel I am to attend to the just claims of officers on the spot.'[26]

John was packing his palanquins when he got the offer, and he broke off to explode into eight pages of indignation. Were his 38 years of previous service in India to count for nothing? He would accept Nepal, of course, but 'I was *particularly* desirous of being Governor-General's Agent in Rajpootana, chiefly owing to my long experience among Rajpoots.' Thoresby, he conceded, might have a decent claim, but as for Sleeman, 'I remember that it is only about seven years ago since he for the *first* time in his life, held *any* substantive office in that line & has never served at all as a political officer in Rajpootana whereas I have been three times longer in *continuous* employment in various political duties than he has been' – and so on.[27] John always splutters and underlines when he feels hard done by, and never more so than in this *cri de coeur* from an affronted Buggins who has not had his turn.

But his aggrieved protest worked. With a flick of his lordly wrist, the Governor-General replied, in a dozen words:

My dear Col. Low,
   If you have a mind to be a Rajpoot chief, you shall be.
   Yours sincerely
   Dalhousie[28]

For the next four years, the Lows settled in Ajmer, 75 miles south-
west of Jaipur, with its ancient mosques and charming Mughal
pavilions along the artificial lake that the town girdles. The British
Residency is a delightful stucco villa, today a government guest
house, on a small hill overlooking the lake. Best of all, the Rajput
chiefs were mostly content with British rule. Rajputana was, in
short, as cushy a billet as there was in India. John Low was in
Dalhousie's debt.

Only once in four years was the amiable tenor of John's life there
interrupted, and then only briefly. On July 10, 1852, Narsing Pal,
the Maharaja of the small Rajput state of Karauli, 150 miles east of
Ajmer, died while still a minor, leaving no direct heir. He had himself been adopted as ruler and the question now was whether the old
Hindu principle of adoption should be followed again – or whether
the succession should be deemed to have lapsed and Karauli be
annexed to the British Crown. Lord Dalhousie was to become notorious for his fondness for this principle of 'Lapse'. But in the case of
Karauli, his bid to annex the little state was rather half-hearted. John
Low was firmly in favour of allowing the ancient ruling house to
choose a new maharaja, both because this was morally right and
because it was a sensible policy, to keep the state friendly.

Dalhousie wrote back, quite good-humouredly: 'Although the
question of *right* does not appear to me in the same light in which
you view it, the question of *policy* regarding Kerowlee is fairly open
for discussion.'[29] He also believed that the Court of Directors would
recognize the adoption, and he had passed John's views on to the
Court: 'Col. Low is a temperate and safe man, and his views will
probably incline you still more to the liberal view which I have
anticipated that the Court would take.'[30]

The Court did indeed take that liberal view and recognized the adoption of one of the two candidates who was endorsed by the Governor-General, Madan Pal Sing, who showed steadfast loyalty to the British throughout the Great Mutiny – justifying John's argument.

A newcomer to this debate of Adoption versus Lapse, which vexed British statesmen throughout the nineteenth century, might think that they all made rather heavy weather of it. In many if not most cases, the person adopted as the heir was a near, if not the nearest kinsman of the deceased ruler. The system did not differ that much in its essentials from inheritance practices elsewhere, even in England, except that the heir was often adopted *after* the old ruler's death, by the choice of the widowed begum or of some other local potentates. In any case, Karauli was small potatoes. The state was only about 30 miles wide. Dalhousie was not to be so easy-going when bigger and juicier targets for annexation came up. We may also detect here a secondary motive: to keep the useful Colonel Low on side.

Certainly when General Fraser resigned from Hyderabad in exasperation and despair, Dalhousie did not hesitate in choosing his successor. 'You are the fittest man in India by far to fill the office,' he wrote to John on November 30, 1852. He was to be sent to Hyderabad again, this time as the permanent Resident. And so, for the third time, John Low was in Lord Dalhousie's debt.

The Governor-General lost little time, too, in telling the new Resident what was expected of him when he got to Hyderabad. On February 17, 1853, he wrote from on board the *Serapeion* with long and detailed instructions for handling the Nizam, confirming the verbal briefing he had given John the day before.

The instructions were simple and brutal. The British Government would continue to offer His Highness full protection, both externally and internally; the Contingent Force would be maintained at full strength; the demand for immediate repayment of the debt would be withdrawn. In return, 'His Highness will engage to make over to the

British Government in perpetual possession the districts mentioned in the schedule to the Treaty.' Colonel Low was to point out to the Nizam all the advantages he would derive from this excellent deal, not least the 9 lakhs he would save each year (though Dalhousie had the grace to add 'I am not quite sure of the figures', which indeed turned out to be inaccurate).

John Low, for 40 years the defender of native princes and native rights, was being sent back to Hyderabad to rip off the richest parts of the Nizam's territory for the British. It was a blatant offence to his instincts and a reversal of all he had stood for. Yet he swallowed it. There was, after all, another mounting debt, his personal debt of gratitude to Dalhousie.

The interviews that lay ahead were to be painful and humiliating for the Nizam, but they must have been distasteful for John Low, too. Perhaps we can catch a hint of just how distasteful by the remarkably full and scrupulous way he reported the conversations for the records.

Every few days from the middle of March 1853 to the middle of May, John Low would come out under the great classical portico of the Residency and trot down the handsome staircase guarded by its stone lions, and take his carriage across the river to the Chowmahalla Palace. There in the delicious pavilions of the Nizam's private quarters, to the sound of plashing fountains, he would attempt to persuade the distraught Nizam of all the advantages he would gain from signing on the dotted line. Nasir-ud-daula was a tall and corpulent man, of amiable and kindly temper, inclined to avoid trouble wherever possible, self-indulgent but also indulgent to others, in both cases to a fault. On April 30, for the first time, he expressed his true feelings and expressed them with passion. They talked for three hours together, most of the time just the two of them alone. It was a remarkable conversation which John reports with a novelist's sympathy and eye for detail.

'I found the Nizam in a state of considerable excitement; his face was much flushed and his eyes appeared somewhat inflamed.' At first he thought that His Highness must be under the influence of wine or opium, but in the talk that followed, 'I have never known him more acute in argument nor more fluent in conversation.' John was later told that the Nizam had been sitting up all night engaged in angry argument with his aides about the proposed treaty.

His eyes were red because he had been weeping. Like the other rajas who had been on the receiving end of British policy, like the Peshwa and the boy-kings of Oudh and Gwalior, when he realized his fate, he could do nothing but cry his eyes out.

'God forbid that I should suffer such a disgrace. I don't want any new treaty at all, how much soever you or any other person or persons may fancy it to be advantageous to my interests.'[31]

'You are aware, are you not, that the Treaty is already on its way from Calcutta.'

'Yes, you told me that you were going to propose a Treaty, but you never told me that such a Treaty as this was to be proposed to me. You never told me that you were going to ask me to give up a large portion of my dominions in perpetuity.'

Col. Low adds here that 'His Highness dwelt particularly on the word "perpetuity".'

'Did I ever make war against the English Government or intrigue against it? Or do anything but co-operate with it, and be obedient to its wishes, that I should be so disgraced.'

John persisted in arguing that there would be no disgrace in signing the treaty. The Nizam was having none of it.

'Two acts on the part of a sovereign prince are always reckoned disgraceful; one is to give away unnecessarily any portion of his hereditary territories, and the other is to disband troops who have been brave and faithful in his service.'

The Nizam pleaded with John to tell the Governor-General that he would personally make sure that the debt was cleared and that the troops' arrears were paid off. But John had no authority except to repeat woodenly that the treaty must be signed.

'I could answer in a minute, but what is the use of answering? If

you are determined to take districts, you can take them without my
either making a new treaty, or giving any answer at all.'

'Would Your Highness consent to sign the Treaty?'

At this renewed demand, the Nizam broke into an eloquent and
anguished lament, aimed directly at John Low himself and hitting
home in no mean fashion, as I think we can guess from the faithful
reporting of his words:

> Gentlemen like you, who are sometimes in Europe and at other
> times in India; sometimes employed in Government business, at
> other times soldiers; sometimes sailors, and at other times even
> engaged in commerce – at least I have heard that some great men
> of your tribe have been merchants – you cannot understand my
> feelings in this matter. I am a sovereign prince, born to live and die
> in this kingdom, which has belonged to my family for seven gen-
> erations; you think I could be happy if I were to give up a portion
> of my kingdom to your Government in perpetuity; it is totally
> impossible that I could be happy; I should feel that I was disgraced.
> I have heard that one gentleman of your tribe considered that I
> ought to be quite contented and happy if I were put upon the
> same footing as the Nawab of Arcot; to have a pension paid to me
> like an old servant, and have nothing to do but to eat, and sleep
> and say my prayers.

Here the Nizam broke off and swore loudly in Arabic to express
his anger and disgust, before resuming:

> You are not quite so preposterous in your way of judging me as
> that, but you too do not comprehend the nature of my feelings as
> a sovereign prince; for instance, you talked of my saving eight lacs
> of rupees per annum by making this Treaty as something that
> I ought to like! Now I tell you, that if it were quite certain that I
> should save four times eights lac, I should not be satisfied, because
> I should lose my honour by parting with my territory.

Seldom can a native prince have defended his honour more elo-
quently to a here-today-gone-tomorrow colonial servant. The
nizams of Hyderabad could claim to have shown unbroken fidelity to
the British Crown and, besides, to have maintained a regime which
for all its imperfections possessed the great virtue of stability. Between
1762 and 1911 there were only five nizams, each reigning for an
average of 30 years. But this splendid lament was all to no avail, mere
spitting in the Imperial wind.

John had reported back to Dalhousie that the Nizams was passionately resisting the treaty.[32] Dalhousie retorted sharply: 'The
conduct of the Nizam causes me no surprise, though I regret the
folly of his course. I shall certainly not consent to have our relations
on any such indefinite footing as he is aiming at.'[33]

Still no sign of a breakthrough. To John's next report, Dalhousie
replied that 'the proceedings of the Nizam are very discreditable to
him, and the more he has shown greater capacity than he has hitherto got credit for, the more inexcusable is his present dishonest
shuffling. I am not disposed to be trifled with; nor shall I permit
myself to be so.'[34]

The self-righteousness of a Governor-General on the warpath is a
wonderful thing to behold.

It was time to tighten the screw one final turn. This work was
deputed to John's Assistant at Hyderabad, Major Cuthbert Davidson.
On May 14, Davidson wrote an 'informal' letter to Siraj-ul-Mulk,
the Nizam's chief minister:

My dear Nawab,
    I believe the Resident requires your attendance this evening,
to inform you that his negotiations with the Nizam are at an
end, and he applies to the Governor-General to move troops by
today's post . . .
    Indeed, I have a letter from my nephew at Poona, mentioning
that the 78th Highlanders and H.M.'s 86th Regiment have
received orders to be in readiness to march on Hyderabad. Don't

suppose military operations will be confined to the Districts; and
if you are a friend of His Highness, beg of him to save himself
and his dignity by complying at once with what the Governor-
General will most assuredly compel him to accede to.

    Cuth. Davidson.[35]

The clear meaning of military operations not being 'confined to
the Districts' was that the whole city of Hyderabad would be occupied by British troops. This was the most grotesque kind of
'protection', of the type practised in our own day so effectively by
the Mob.[36] The game was up. The Nizam surrendered. He signed
the so-called Treaty of Berar on May 21.

When Dalhousie eventually got the news, he was overjoyed. 'My
eyes opened this morning on your Treaty which arrived during the
night, and a most welcome daystar it is. I congratulate you with all
my heart on your speedy and great success.'[37]

To the world, the Governor-General declared that 'the conduct of
the Government of India towards the Nizam, in respect of the
Contingent and of all his other affairs, has been characterized by
unvarying good faith, liberality and forbearance, and by a sincere
desire to maintain the stability of the State of Hyderabad and to
uphold the personal independence of His Highness the Nizam.'[38]

Effrontery is too mild a word for it.[39]

The Court of Directors congratulated Colonel Low on 'the skill,
judgment and firmness, which enabled him to overcome all difficulties and bring the discussion to a successful issue.' The Court
regarded the settlement with the greatest satisfaction. The Governor-
General and the officers employed by him 'are entitled to our cordial
thanks.'[40] Any trace of the earlier misgivings of a substantial minority of the Directors seemed to have been erased.

The original draft of the Court's letter had been rather different.
No less than three passages were stricken through and suppressed
from the final public version, the Blue Book.[41] Originally, the letter
had referred to the milder alternative of helping the Nizam to sort

out his financial difficulties – which would have drawn attention to the harshness of the line actually taken. The second suppressed passage referred to the fact (agreed by both the Court and the Governor-General) that Article 12 of the 1800 Treaty gave Britain no right to require the Nizam to maintain this huge standing army, which existed 'only by sufferance'. And the third suppressed passage noted that, after the assigned districts were tidied up, 'the ultimate surplus is likely to be considerable'. In short, the Court was well aware that this was a piece of strong-arm tactics with no legal backing undertaken for reasons of financial gain. So the Court was not an innocent player either. The more wide-awake directors were well aware that what had been done to the Nizam was wrong, but as John Bruce Norton, the Advocate-General of Madras, commented sourly in *The Rebellion in India*, 'Cotton stuffed the ears of justice, and made her deaf as well as blind.'[42]

The sanitized wording of the Court's dispatch to Dalhousie was typical. The Court – and indeed the Board of Control behind it – often professed to have no desire for further territorial acquisitions, which might turn out to involve ruinous extra expense. But popular feeling and the difficulty of undoing fait accomplis thousands of miles away usually led the authorities at home to accept new territory with a semblance of grace, and to offer a leg-up in the peerage to the Governor-General of the day.[43] But Dalhousie had already got his marquessate after annexing the Punjab. This time, the juiciest reward was to go to the man who had actually landed the deal.

On July 4, 1853, Dalhousie informed John that he was to be nominated for the vacant military seat on the Supreme Council of India. This had always been John's ultimate ambition, for financial no less than for military reasons, for the seat carried with it a splendiferous salary, 96,000 rupees per annum no less, nearly half as much again as he had earned as a Resident. If he could hold out on the Council for the allotted five years, all his financial troubles would be at an end. A few months later, he was promoted Major-General as the dignity of the seat demanded.

There is no getting away from it. John Low had profited mightily from the Nizam's impoverishment. It is hard not to feel too that he had been led astray by Dalhousie's driving will. The younger man had corrupted the older.

There was another question too. Was he really right to go on to Calcutta to assume the military oversight of the entire subcontinent? He was 64 years old and his health was shakier than it had ever been. In letter after letter to Dalhousie and Mountstuart Elphinstone, he rehearses his various ailments: Sometimes he can hardly walk, sometimes he can hardly breathe, sometimes it is his liver that it is playing up again, sometimes his lungs. Only a year earlier, Dalhousie had written to him: 'I am concerned to see you have been ailing, though Mrs Low's improvement will help to cure you. The truth is my good friend we are none of us so young as we were ten years ago [Dalhousie himself was only just forty, though ill most of the time, as was his wife] – and you are no exception to the very general rule. You know very well I have no desire to part with you but still beware of the "one year more".'[44] Everyone knew of officers who had stayed on that extra year to gain a step in rank or a few more rupees and who had not survived to go home.

And now John had contracted for not one, but five years more. The consequences, for his own reputation and for India, would be considerable.

XIV

CHARLOTTE RETURNS
TO INDIA

harlotte was only seven months old when they put her on
board the *Hungerford* to sail to England. They did not see her
for ten years. All they had of her were the glowing reports from her
grandmother and the miniature done by Frederick Cruickshank
when she was not quite four years old and which was not received in
Lucknow until more than a year later. When John and Augusta went
back to Clatto in July 1843, they found that every word her grandmother had said of her was true. Charlotte was as bright as she was
pretty and as wise as she was charming. John fell besottedly in love
with her. After the deaths of his first two children, Charlotte's survival seemed a miraculous gift.

Yet they only kept her with them for little over a year during their
time at Clatto. In September 1844, they took her down to school in
London. As with the four boys, only an English education would do.
This second separation was not quite so total. There were the
summer holidays at Clatto to look forward to, and John went down
to India House at least once a year to brush up his contacts, and he
could look in on his 'dear little pet'.

When John and Augusta had taken the steamer from
Southampton to go back to India on November 20, 1847, there was

a consolation for Charlotte. Augusta's sister Marianne Irvine had come back to London with her brood a year earlier, and all at once Charlotte had a new home as warm as the one that had broken up again.

Marianne was the sparkler of the family. She was four years younger than the rather more stately Augusta, and she had always been the centre of attention. Adorably roly-poly as a child, lively and imaginative when grown up, she was the preferred correspondent of her brothers and sisters. It was for Marianne that Richmond had written his graphic dispatches from Afghanistan, for Marianne that Augusta had written the diary of her journey home by the overland route, peppered with quotations from the Bible when they were passing through Egypt and interrupted by stanzas from Lord Byron as they gawped at the wonders of ancient Greece.

William Makepeace Thackeray adored Marianne. By now he was living apart from his poor wife Isabella, who was by turns manic, autistic and suicidal. He was leading an erratic bachelor life and in his wanderings would drop in on Marianne at the various houses she took, starting with Little Holland House, the rustic dower house which Lord Holland's sister, Lady Caroline Fox, had dubbed the 'Paradisino'.[1]

Eighteen months later, when Marianne had left the Paradisino and moved to Highgate, Thackeray wrote to his beloved Aunt Ritchie in Paris to describe another visit:

We went yesterday and atchieved [sic] the ascent of Highgate Hill, with a broken winded horse I have got who suffered woefully in the journey, and lighted upon all the little Irvines at their dinner of wh. we ate ravenously (I am eating all day now), but the ladies were away on a shopping excursion into London, and we lost them. Charlotte Low showed us the new baby with great pride: a sweet little thing it was too and waxen-faced; and there is one of the other children, Augusta, the very image of what her mother was when we were all young folks in Southampton Row – I think

that Southampton Row was the only part of my youth wh[ich]
was decently cheerful, all the rest strikes me to have been as glum
as an English Sunday.[2]

It was one of the bonds between Thackeray and Marianne that
they both had such acute memories of Southampton Row: the
bustle of Uncle Ritchie's Baltimore merchant's business on the
ground floor, the L-shaped drawing room where they staged plays
and William acted Dr Pangloss in a huge wig, the fig tree in the long
London garden.[3]

Now, 25 years later, Marianne recreated that loving, tumbling,
knockabout home for a new generation of 'Indian children'. Soon
they were joined by her husband, the genial Major Archibald Irvine
of the Bengal Engineers, widely regarded as the finest sapper of his
day. Twenty years earlier, he had blown open the gates of Bhurtpore
(now Bharatpur), supposedly the most impregnable fortress in India,
by a new technique devised at Chatham of digging long ventilated
mineshafts under the target. The 10,000 tons of gunpowder in
Irvine's three tunnels exploded according to plan and caused
appalling havoc. All told, 6,000 natives died in the ending of the
siege. Irvine had been just about to leave for England with his family,
when the first war against the Sikhs broke out. Irvine sent Marianne
and the children on ahead, volunteered for service and performed
brilliantly at the decisive Battle of Sobraon in February 1846 which
ended the war and, among other things, tossed the Koh-i-Noor
diamond into Queen Victoria's lap. Arriving back in England with
the Governor-General's praises ringing in his ears, he was immediately appointed Director of Works at the Admiralty by the First
Lord, none other than our old friend the Earl of Auckland (minist-
erial talent in the House of Lords was not so plentiful as to disqualify
the author of one of the worst disasters in British military history).

Irvine's sweet and noble nature made him yet another candidate for
the original Colonel Newcome. 'The Major' was a hero to George
Shakespear, too. Augusta recorded in her red leather notebook that

'G. told me this evening in speaking of I. that M. ought to "salaam" to God twenty times a day for having such a husband.'

Alas, the Major was not destined to enjoy the retirement he deserved, for on a tour of inspection of the Admiralty docks at Portsmouth he had a bad fall, and he died before 1849 was out, leaving Marianne a widow at the age of 33 (there was the usual age gap between them – he was 53 when he died) with eight children ranging from 12 years to three months, the last being the placid, waxen-faced infant that WMT had seen on his surprise visit to Highgate. What all the rebellious sepoys in Rajasthan and Sikhs in the Punjab could not manage was brought about by a slippery cobblestone on a Portsmouth quay.

It is a testament to Thackeray's gift for friendship with the young that it seemed natural for Charlotte, then aged 16, to write to tell him the sad news. And it is typical of him that he should have broken off from writing *Pendennis* and instantly written back to her with such overflowing sympathy:

My dear Charlotte,

There is no answer to such an afflicting letter as yours – for who can offer any consolation to a tender and devoted wife bereaved of her greatest earthly treasure? I think we have scarce a right even to offer condolence. May God Almighty help and comfort yr dear aunt under her calamity. The pang which makes the parting with such a man, so upright, so honest, so pure-minded, so tender-hearted, inexpressibly bitter to the woman who has possessed his entire confidence & affection (and knows his goodness infinitely better than we) must yet after the first keenness yield to thoughts more comforting. Where can a good and pious man be better than in the presence of God? away from ill and temptation and care, and secure of reward. What a comfort to think that he, who was so good & faithful here, must be called away to dwell among the good and just for ever?

There never seems to me to be any cause for grief beyond the sorrow of those who survive him and trusting in God's mercy and wisdom, infinite here and everywhere, await the day when they too shall be called away.

Goodbye, my dear Charlotte, write to me if I can be of any service, and believe me always,

Affectionately yours

W.M.Thackeray[4]

The Goodbye at the end suggests that Charlotte must have said in her letter to Thackeray that in the New Year she was being dispatched to India, 'returning to the land of her birth', just as her mother had at the same age. When she reached India, she travelled straight to Ajmer, to the villa by the lake, to see her parents and her two little sisters. She found John and Augusta in poor shape. In his letter to Dalhousie dated January 17, 1851, John apologized for not answering the Governor-General sooner. He had begun a reply several times, 'but I was then *compelled* to leave off by the sharp attacks of fever and ague which for many weeks in succession knocked me down every weekday; and although many young people at the same place who caught that sort of fever were quite well again apparently in the intervening days, it was very different with me who am old. What with my poor wife's continued ailments (which now compel me to send her to Simla), my own illness for two months and more, the absence from my camp of *all* my assistants during the whole month of December and the sickness still of some of my writers and moonshees ... I have of late been more oppressed with low spirits and unpleasant forebodings than I have been at any time during the last 25 years.'[5]

The cold weather had restored both of them to tolerable health in a week or two, and Augusta was not sent up to Simla after all, but Charlotte was. Where else was a girl of 17 to go if she was to find a husband? Mooning in the Mughal pavilions by the lake at Ajmer would not conjure up a well-born lieutenant or a rising star in the Governor-General's Foreign Office.

By 1851, Simla was very different from the wild wooded ridge on which Charles Pratt Kennedy had built his *cottage orné* in the 1820s. All along the precipitous slopes, bungalows had sprung up with long verandahs, deep eaves to let the snow run off and names that spoke of home – Fairlawn, Annandale, Rookwood, Strawberry Hill. Lady Canning wrote, a few years later, 'Here if one sees ten yards level, one screams out "what a site for a house".'[6] There were hotels now, the Central, the Titla, the Glenarm. There were dances at the Assembly Rooms, where Captain Kennedy was still the presiding Beau, and at Auckland House, where the legendary 'Lola Montez' first caught the eye of the Miss Edens when she was not-so-plain Mrs Thomas James. There were cricket and horse racing on the flat ground at Annandale, not to mention the obligatory racquet court next to the Assembly Rooms. Relentless amateur dramatics filled the stage at the Jubilee Theatre.

The 41-mile zigzag up to Simla, accessible only by mules and ponies, still took 20 hours. Ladies were carried up in a *jampan*, a curtained sedan chair carried by four coolies, though the coolies were often hard to round up, many of them preferring to stay down in the plains. By now there was, though, a native town of several thousand at Simla, with a fair-sized bazaar, and about 400 European houses scattered along the girths of the saddle-hills. William Hodson, the daredevil founder of Hodson's Horse, wrote in October 1850: 'The change to the utter comfort and civilization of this house [a Mr Thomason's] was quite "stunning", and I have not yet become quite reconciled to dressing three times a day, black hat and patent leather boots.'[7]

Almost everyone loved the delicious air, the elegant society, the views of the glistening peaks. Lady Dalhousie declared herself 'charmed with her house, the place and everything about it'.[8] The notable exception to this chorus of delight was the Governor-General himself. He disliked Auckland House and decamped to Strawberry Hill and later to Captain Kennedy's old house, now much enlarged. He thought Simla 'greatly overrated in climate and everything else'.[9] The place was, he conceded, 'a suitable eyrie from which to watch the newly-annexed plains that stretch below'.[10] But the social life was, quite frankly, unendurable:

> We have had a terrible fortnight of festivities – balls without number, fancy fairs, plays, concerts, investitures – and every blank day, almost, filled up with a large dinner-party. You may judge what this 'Hill Station' has grown to when I tell you that 460 invitations were issued for the last ball at Government House, and most of them came too.[11]

After an encouraging start, the fabled climate did little for the health of either of the Dalhousies, which, after all, was the prime reason for going to the hills: 'Lady D. had, as I told you, picked up wonderfully when she came here. The weather has been very oppressive for Simla, and then the rains came on with constant and heavy thunderstorms, producing great variations of temperature. These causes have affected her and she has fallen off very much of late, and has again grown thin and weak. I also am not right. I do not suffer from dysentery or from the dreadful exhaustion of Bengal, but I am very weak somehow, and suffer many inconveniences arising, they say, from general debility of system. For months too, I have had a lameness in the joint of my right heel, which comes and goes, which they don't understand the cause of, and which for some time has so lamed me that I can neither walk nor ride.'[12]

Even the self-confidence of the little Governor-General was being eroded: 'All this is depressing, and although I fight against it, yet this, and the anxiety in which I feel myself (in spite of all I can do) until I hear what the decision on my acts at home has been, combine to keep me low in strength.'[13] The huge distance from Leadenhall Street left the Governor-General deliciously free to pursue his own line. But at the same time, he was perpetually gnawed by a fear that his decisions would ultimately be reversed by the Court, and that he would be reprimanded or even recalled as Lord Ellenborough had been.

Dalhousie sought a refuge from the rains in the high mountains beyond Simla. In June 1850, he set out for Chini, a legendary valley 145 miles further towards the Himalayas (today the village of Kalpa), where the upper waters of the River Sutlej run directly under the peaks. He called it 'a province near the snow, where the rains do not come, and where the climate is described as better than anything since Eden.'

At Chini, and on the journey to Chini, this strange, driven little great man was happy. The mixture of danger and beauty calmed his unquiet spirit. But he certainly put poor Lady Dalhousie through it.

> We arrived here yesterday, after a fortnight's travel. The track, for it hardly could be called a path, was desperate, and for women terrific. It is simply the native track, neither engineered nor formed. Flights of stairs formed of loose stones are the chief ascents, and sometimes stairs of trunks of trees. In rounding the corners of the precipices I have seen the track not 3 feet wide, and the Sutlej 3000 feet or so sheer below you! My lady was carried in a thing they call a dandy, like a hammock slung on a single pole. It is carried on two men's shoulders, and long rope-traces are attached by which they pull up the ascents where the zigzags are long enough to allow it, and lower you down the steep descents on the other side. Near to this place you cross a face of rock several hundred yards long, and as many high, by continuous flights of these steps, and rude wooden platforms supported on pegs of wood driven into the clefts of the cliffs. The descent is direct to the river, I should say nearly 5000 feet below! It was very grand but *really* funky.[14]

The great man sounds as excited as a schoolgirl – 'funky' being used not in its modern sense, but to mean 'inspiring funk'.

But the trip was worth it. 'We passed from thence into the valley situated between the ranges of the snowy mountains, but filled with luxuriant vineyards of the finest grapes, with orchards of apricots, and with pears, peaches, walnuts and chestnuts. The Raldung, one of the eternal snows, rises to 23,000 feet in height opposite to us – the avalanches are daily audible, roaring down its sides, and yet the valley is covered with rich green crops, and adorned with forests of deodars high up, and green hardwood trees below. It is a strange mixture of beautiful contradictions.'[15]

The expenses of moving the Governor-General across the mountains were as terrific as the drop into the Sutlej. He had an advance bodyguard of 25 sepoys and a rearguard of six men under a *havildar*, and his young under-secretary Edward Bayley and his newly wed wife, Emily Anne Metcalfe. Messages back to Simla, and thence on to the plains, were carried by a ceaseless chain of mountain runners. Later, Lord Dalhousie had a road built, the forerunner he intended of a grand trunk road linking Hindustan and Tibet. Even in his quest for a primeval paradise, the modernizing itch never ceased to nag at him.

What also nagged at him were the complaints heard as far away as Leadenhall Street that the Governor-General was neglecting his duties:

'I am surprised Mr Melvill should tell you my sojourn in Chini last year had excited a good deal of observation at the court. Neither the court nor any member of it ever made any observation to me upon it publicly or privately but seemed to regard it as a matter of course.'[16] He had asserted at the outset that 'the mail will be only 46 hours from Simla, and I can get there in four days, so that I am ready if wanted.'[17] Chini lay not in Tartary, whatever the ignorant might think, but in a protected hill state. He could be back inside British territory within 60 hours.

All these optimistic calculations, and the relays of runners scrambling up and down the funky paths, could not entirely remove the whispered objections to Dalhousie's long sojourn at Chini. The complaint was not that he was holidaying outside British territory but that he was so far from events at a dangerous time – and when was there not a dangerous time in India?

In retrospect, one cannot help thinking that this urge to get as far away as possible from the people of India was symptom of an alienation which was not confined to Dalhousie and not caused by health reasons alone. The vision of a pure kingdom in the mountains – so different from the hot and smelly reality of the plains – was ingrained in the psyche of the British overseas, recurring in the fiction of Kipling and Rider Haggard and later John Buchan. In military terms, that physical isolation was to play a significant part in the catastrophe of 1857.

But even in overrated Simla, Dalhousie found compensations. One of them was the appearance in the hills of his old friend's daughter. In July 1851, he wrote to John Low beseeching him and Augusta to come up to Simla to see him one last time before he left India (in fact he was to stay on for four years more): 'It would do Mrs Low good, do you good, please, I am sure, your charming daughter, and give me pleasure also.'[18]

Flushed with fatherly pride, John replied that they would be delighted to come as soon as he could arrange a stand-in in Ajmer:

> I feel flattered and obliged and so does Mrs Low at the very kind attention which Lady Dalhousie and your Lordship have paid my daughter. I hope she will not be spoilt by it, and I really don't apprehend it will have any such effect upon her, because in addition to having from infancy been blessed with a grateful and happy sort of disposition, I cannot help believing that there was much truth in a little speech made about her by an old lady neighbour of mine in Fife, who said to me: 'Your dochter, Sir, has a lairge portion of gude sense for her years.'[19]

A month later, John and Augusta and the little girls did indeed go up to the hills, and not only to see Charlotte and the Dalhousies or even to repair their health.

THEO AND CHARLOTTE

The Simla whirl was a small one. Everyone who was anyone soon met everyone else. Friendships and courtships sprouted overnight in the sparkling air. In no time, Charlotte had become best friends, not only with the Dalhousies, but with the irresistible Metcalfe sisters: Emily Anne ('Emmie' to her father, Sir Thomas Theophilus Metcalfe, 'Annie' to her siblings), Georgiana ('GG') and Eliza ('Eli'). The Metcalfe clan was the nearest thing to a hereditary aristocracy that British India could offer. Thomas Metcalfe senior came out as a cadet, rose to Major, then deflected into civilian life, made a fortune and became a director of the Company for 24 years, an MP and a baronet. From these sturdy foundations, his second son Charles rose even further to become Acting Governor-General of India, Governor-General of Canada and a lord.

Charles Metcalfe was one of the great proconsuls – scholarly, chilly, unflappable – to be ranked with Elphinstone, Malcolm and the Lawrence brothers. Officially, he remained unmarried, but during his embassy to the court of Ranjit Singh, he had 'married by Indian rites' a lovely Sikh woman, by whom he had three sons, Henry, Frank and James. They were brought up in England alongside their Metcalfe cousins, like them sent to the East India College at Addiscombe and returned to India when they were grown up.

Metcalfe fretted anxiously after their welfare and was grateful to his sister Georgiana who took them under her wing in England. Henry got into business difficulties in Calcutta and shot himself in 1840. Frank disappeared from view, but James prospered in the Bengal Army and later became ADC to Lord Dalhousie. Charles was a generous donor to Eurasian charities and left James £50,000 in his will, half his personal estate.

The sons' existence was not mentioned in Sir John Kaye's two-volume biography of Charles Metcalfe and only came to the surface in Edward Thompson's *Life* in the 1930s. Their mother is not referred to at all. Was she alive or dead? Had she returned to her family? No effort was made to suggest that James was the legitimate heir – liberal views had their limits – and on Charles's death his peerage expired and the baronetcy passed to his younger brother, Thomas Theophilus, every bit as scholarly and chilly a man as Charles, though less easy to admire. Charles had taken Thomas junior on as his assistant when he was Resident at Delhi between 1811 and 1819. There Thomas remained for 40 years, after 1835 as Resident himself.

Between them, Charles and Thomas the younger little by little extinguished first the power and then the dignity of the Emperor of Delhi. Under their reproving eyes, the Great Mughul dwindled to a pathetic figure. Charles was a whiggish improving sort, who yearned to expropriate the landlords in favour of the true proprietors, the peasants who actually tilled the soil. Like many other modernizers, and there were plenty of them in India in the 1830s and 1840s, he would not have dreamed of applying these radical nostrums to England. He believed in 'socialism in one country', as long as it wasn't his own. Accordingly, he was diligent in supporting the annexation of princely states and the removal of all marks of subservience by the East India Company to their princes. 'I have renounced my former allegiance to the House of Timur', he proclaimed jocosely in 1832, before recommending that Lord William Bentinck put an end to the giving of ceremonial gifts to the Emperor as homage.[1] 'I think it is our best policy to let him sink into insignificance instead of upholding his dignity as we have done.'

It was the younger Metcalfe brother who inflicted the final indignity. The Emperor had passed over his eldest son, Mirza Fakhru. Spotting an opportunity, in 1852 Sir Thomas signed a secret understanding with the disinherited one, by which the British would formally recognize him as the heir. In return, Mirza Fakhru agreed to move his court to the suburb of Mehrauli and hand over the Red Fort, which was at once the glory and the strategic centre of Delhi, to the British for use as a barracks and powder magazine. When he became Emperor, Mirza Fakhru was also to drop the Emperor's claim to be superior to the Governor-General. In future, they would meet on terms of equality.[2] As always, the British showed themselves to be as obsessed with protocol and status as any petty princeling.

Sir Thomas had his personal dream, too. Most Residents at Indian courts seem to have regarded themselves as only temporary kings, but not Thomas Theophilus Metcalfe. As William Dalrymple says in his brilliant account of the Metcalfes' life at the court of the Emperor Zafar (or Bahadar Shah II, as he was also known), 'In his letters, Metcalfe sometimes envisaged himself as an English country squire. In reality, however, he seems to have had slightly more exalted ambitions, and to some extent he set up his establishment as a rival court to that of Zafar's, with the Metcalfes as a parallel dynasty to the Mughals.'[3] From the battlements of the Red Fort, looking upriver you would see Sir Thomas's great white Palladian palace, built to his own specifications the year he became Resident, 1835, with its lawns and marble pillars and its swimming pool, its library of 25,000 books and its Napoleon Gallery filled with memorabilia of another Emperor, including Bonaparte's diamond ring and a Canova bust (an obsession with *l'Empéreur* is always a worrying sign).

Even more remarkable was the other Metcalfe House in Delhi, Thomas's weekend retreat to the south of the city, at Mehrauli where the Emperor had his summer palace, Zafar Mahal. There, Sir Thomas occupied an octagonal Mughal tomb which had been converted into an English country house by Mr Blake, an official in the Bengal Civil Service, among the amazing complex of tombs and mosques which fan out from Delhi's most famous ancient monument, the Qutb Minar, once said to be the tallest tower in the world. Blake had tossed out the tomb slab to make way for his dining-room table and was later murdered at Jaipur in revenge, it is said, for this careless profanation. Metcalfe carried on the impious work, laying out gardens in the Mughal style stretching to the monument, thus converting the Qutb Minar into his personal eye-catcher. He christened his tomb-house 'Dilkusha' – 'heart's delight' – a name often given to Mughal pleasure domes, at Lucknow for example. He surrounded it with follies – a toy fort, a lighthouse, a miniature ziggurat, a boating pond.

In person, this would-be Emperor was unimpressive, as even his devoted eldest daughter Annie had to admit: slight and smallish, about five foot eight, baldish and grey, with a face much marked from boyhood by the smallpox. But, Annie declares, 'a perfect gentleman, every inch of him'. Not aping the Mughal dress, as so many Residents liked to do, but beautifully turned out by Mr Pulford of St James's Street, who sent him out fresh suits of clothes every year.

As a young man, he had frittered his £10,000 inheritance and left old Sir Thomas and his brother Charles to pay his bills. His early life in Delhi had not been happy. His two sons had died in infancy, and his first wife Grace died, too, in 1824. Two years later, he married Félicité Anne Browne, whose brother Sam was to become a famous fighting man (we shall hear more of Sam). They had four daughters and two sons, and Thomas was as blissful as this prickly, buttoned-up man could hope to be. Then the children were sent to England to be schooled and in 1842 Félicité died, at Simla, on September 26 – a date which ever after held a mournful significance for him, so that he could not bear to be at Simla on that date and would wait in the plains until the day had passed.

He was haunted by the memory of Félicité and their shared felicity. He commissioned the finest artist in Delhi, Mazhar Ali Khan (also patronized by the Emperor), to paint the monuments, ruins and mosques of the city and had the pictures bound into an album which he called *The Delhie Book* and sent off to Annie just as she was coming back to India. This wonderful album, now in the British Library, is the finest surviving record of Delhi before the Great Mutiny, and it is accompanied by a commentary in Sir Thomas's hand. Metcalfe House is prominently featured. There is even a floor plan, on which he has inked an asterisk with a note in the margin: 'The door by which your lamented mother left the House for the last time at 9 o'clock of the evening of 2nd May 1842.'[4] Under the picture of the underground billiard room at Metcalfe House, Sir Thomas has written: 'Strive my beloved girls, during your Pilgrimage on earth, to imitate the example of your sainted Parent that you may hereafter be deemed worthy, through the Intercession of our Saviour, of being reunited to her, for all eternity in the many mansions of our Father's House' – to which their own father's mansions were the nearest approximation on this earth.

While the children were in England, Sir Thomas had been knocking about the huge halls of Metcalfe House on his own, browsing on the latest parcel of books sent out from Piccadilly, smoking his beautiful silver hookah and becoming set in some rather odd ways, as the girls discovered on their return. Annie gives a vivid account of his unvarying morning routine: breakfast on the verandah at 5am, his morning swim in the pool below the verandah – today the standard plunge for plutocrats but then a novelty – then prayers in his book-lined oratory, followed by half an hour's gurgle on the hookah.

If the servant failed to prepare the hookah to his liking, Sir Thomas would call for a pair of white kid gloves. These were brought on a silver salver. He would slowly pull them on over his delicate white fingers (one of his best points, according to Annie). Then, having given the servant a talking-to, he would gently but firmly pinch the ear of the culprit and let him go, 'a reprimand that was entirely efficacious'.[5] In his eating habits, he was no less fastidious. He could not bear to see ladies eat cheese or mangoes or oranges. Annie recalled that she and an ADC used to take a basket of oranges up to the top of Qutb Minar to guzzle them, taking care to bring down all the peel, because Sir Thomas was equally fussy about litter. After his smoke, he would retire to his study to write letters. Then at ten o'clock sharp he would walk across to the portico to board his carriage, passing through a row of servants on his way – one holding his hat, another his gloves, another his handkerchief, another his gold-headed cane, and another his dispatch box. Then his *jemadar* would mount the box beside the coachman and they drove off with two grooms standing behind. He kept two pairs of carriage horses, the chestnuts for the day, and the bays for the evening drive.[6]

Bundle of affectations though he might be, he was unaffectedly delighted to see his daughters again and to discover how much they remembered of their childhood in Delhi. In their company, he recovered some fraction of his former happiness. Not surprisingly, he became desperately possessive of the girls, and soon showed himself choosy about whom they should marry.

GG was already over 21, but he tried everything he knew to prevent her from marrying an unsuitable baronet, Sir Edward Campbell, who was not only penniless but a former ADC to Sir Charles Napier, with whom Sir Thomas had quarrelled in his usual peevish fashion. He forbade the couple to meet and confiscated Edward's letters, so that for months he had to enclose his love messages to her in letters to Annie. It was a year before he relented and gave his consent to the match.

The love letters GG wrote over those miserable months were mostly never sent. Today they fill a large box in the South Asia Library in Cambridge. For page after page she goes back over the slender incidents of their courtship: how they first met one morning in Delhi when GG had gone to Dr Grant's house to tune his pianoforte and they had finished up singing parlour songs together under the chaperonage of Captain Douglas, the Commandant of the Palace Guard.[7] Then how they had met again at someone else's wedding:

That wedding! And though I was so miserable I was happy, for our eyes met for the first time for so many months and I knew you still loved me. Do you remember the last time at Simla, my hand was within yours at that Flower Show in the Assembly Rooms when you were on duty and I came down with Lady D., just by the little temple, you stopped her Jaunpaun where we were all standing and shortly afterwards we all went down to the Flowers and the Band had been playing *some rot*. That was on a Saturday, the day after Lady G's second At Home.

Lady D was of course Lady Dalhousie. Lady G was Lady Gomm, the wife of the indolent C-in-C who spent as much time as he could up in the hills. Love in the summer capital of the Empire was distinguished from courtship in Cheltenham or Torquay only by the dizzying view of the Himalayas.[8]

Annie herself had had an easier run. Her suitor, Edward Clive Bayley, was the nephew of Butterworth Bayley, who had briefly acted as Governor-General, and Edward himself was a proper man of 27 who shared Sir Thomas's antiquarian enthusiasms, especially for Indian art and Oriental languages. He was also just about to be made under-secretary in Lord Dalhousie's Foreign Office. They were married in no time and had 13 children. When Annie was pregnant for the first time, they were accompanying the Dalhousies on their funky journey to Chini, and she wrote an ecstatic travelogue about her experiences, expressing surprise that the serious symptoms which afflicted her, and for which she was going to be sent back to England, turned out to be nothing more than the imminent arrival of her first child, little Annie. The elementary facts of gynaecology had not yet reached the hill country.

Sir Thomas's relations with his daughters were always affectionate, if sometimes exasperated. Not so his fractious, edgy dealings with his elder son Theo, also just back from England. Theo was bouncy, loud and sociable, fond of horses, dogs and parties – all the things his father was not, although they shared an imperious will. They rubbed each other the wrong way at every turn. Where Sir Thomas was feline and cautious, Theo was blustering and reckless to the point of criminality. The further they were kept apart, the better for everyone.

Then Theo managed to do something which did please his father. He fell in love with Charlotte Low. And so did everyone else in the Metcalfe family. GG could not get enough of her. 'Charlie is such a dear,' she wrote to Edward, 'and every day I love her better.'[9] For Annie, she was always 'my sweet Charlie', only a little lower than the angels.

It was not the least of her virtues that she exercised a calming influence on Theo. Nobody appreciated this more than Sir Thomas, who was alarmed that his son and heir planned to come and live on top of him in Delhi, at Metcalfe House. He wrote to GG, 'I tell you candidly that I fear our reunion, especially if Charlotte does not accompany him. At my time of life I do not wish to be put out of my way and play second fiddle in my own house. Your brother I know from experience: all must give way to his wishes. My temper is hasty too, and I keep it always under control.'[10]

Even as his father wrote, Theo was already in trouble over 'an illegal act of a civil nature', for which Sir Thomas thought he might well be prosecuted in the Supreme Court and have to pay 10,000 or 12,000 rupees in damages – or rather Sir Thomas would pay to keep Theo out of jail. This illegal act may well have been the wrongful imprisonment of an influential moneylender, an event referred to elsewhere in the correspondence and the sort of intemperate conduct for which Theo was later to become notorious. 'How frightening it is that Theo could not act with discretion and judgment. His extravagance is bad enough,' but this was folly in the extreme.[11]

We must presume that John and Augusta knew none of this, for Sir Thomas would have been careful not to say a word about it. When Charlotte's parents arrived in Simla in September 1851 with the two little girls, they found that they were not only in for a family reunion but for a family wedding. Theo and Charlotte were to be married in the not-quite-finished Christ Church at the end of Simla Mall. John and Augusta might be reluctant to see their daughter go so soon after being reunited with her, but Charles Metcalfe had been an old friend, and this alliance was hard to improve on. Between them, John and the Metcalfe brothers had governed most of northern and central India. And on October 14, when they sat on either side of the aisle, both families must have congratulated themselves. For little Selina Low, then aged six, her obstreperous behaviour on the lawn of Charlotte's new home was her earliest and happiest memory.

Eleven months later, Lord Dalhousie wrote to John: 'I was grieved to learn from Metcalfe of your daughter's disappointment. Poor soul – it is a sad business for young mothers and shakes their health. However, in that climate, she will soon be restored.'[12] The Metcalfe who had let him know about Charlotte's miscarriage was, I think, not Theo but James, Charles's half-Sikh son, now Dalhousie's ADC. It may seem like a liberal gesture that James should have been appointed to such a key post in a government which was increasingly for whites only, but the Metcalfes were an exception to every rule. Besides, a good ADC would also be an adept interpreter and while other ADCs might have learnt their halting Hindustani at Addiscombe or Haileybury, James would have learnt it on his mother's lap.

It was not an easy time for Charlotte. Theo was down in Delhi, having insisted that his wife should stay in the hills for the sake of her health. Nor did she have her own mother to comfort and advise her. Augusta had set off to Calcutta with the two little girls to take them back to England, along with her cousin William Ritchie's children, Gussie and Blanche, who were a couple of years younger. Gussie Ritchie always remembered her father standing over her in her berth with tears in his eyes as he took the long farewell.[13] The migrations were now continuing into the third generation, as pitiless and pitiable as ever.

Charlotte's loneliness was relieved by a stay at Delhi over Christmas, 1852. Sir Thomas had implored them all to come – Annie and Edward Bayley with little Annie, Theo and Charlotte, and the lovesick GG who had gone on hunger strike and had persuaded her father to allow her to correspond directly with the absent Edward. It was a glorious month's holiday with log fires crackling in the grates of Metcalfe House and rides down to Dilkusha and picnics in the Mughal gardens and billiards in the evenings after Sir Thomas had gone to bed.

Charlotte wrote from Delhi to Edward Campbell describing 'the large and merry party' and congratulating him on his engagement to GG, which had finally got the go-ahead: 'I am so very glad that everything is now happily settled and dear Georgie now looks quite bright and happy and is I hope gaining strength by degrees although she still looks rather pale. She is so sweet and nice and I can fancy your being very proud of her when she is your wife. I wish so much we could have her at Simla for a few months.'[14]

Amid the merriment at Metcalfe House, Charlotte became pregnant again. Her happiness that spring was clouded by the thought of a fresh separation from Theo. Sir Thomas, charmed by his new daughter-in-law, had warmed towards Theo, too, and appointed him joint magistrate in Delhi. On April 19, she wrote to GG from Simla:

> My darling Georgie,
>   The only doubt now is whether I shall accompany him or not. I am myself very anxious to do so, although he is very much against it and I am afraid the doctor is also but I cannot bear the thought of being left alone for that many months and if I do not go to the plains *now* I cannot hope to do so until the end of October. I have no great dread of the heat but I want you dear Georgie to write quickly please and tell me the general average of temperature in your father's house during the hot weather . . . Anything under 84 degrees I think I could bear very well, and if you can tell me the heat in your father's house is not

greater than this in general, I think I might contract to go down with Theo. The Doctor is very much afraid of my getting fever but I should not think this was very likely to happen. You never had it last year, had you? And I am a particularly *chilly* person . . .

Excuse these few hurried lines Dearest and let me hear from you as soon as possible.

Your very affectionate sister

C.H. Metcalfe.

Even in her anxiety, her warmth and openness shine through, qualities she shared with her sisters-in-law. She might have known the Metcalfe girls all her life.

Theo won, of course. Charlotte stayed at Simla. As the birth came nearer, she was more and more anxious not to be on her own. And she persuaded Annie to come across the hills from Dharamsala, where the Bayleys were stationed. Everyone was looking forward to GG's wedding in October as well as to the birth of Charlotte's baby. Even Sir Thomas had promised to make the trip.

Then in the summer, he began to feel violently unwell. He always took great care of himself, finicky about his food, never staying up late, keeping fit. But now at the beginning of the monsoon, he began to vomit the whole time. Other high officials – Sir Henry Elliot, Mr Thomason – were reporting similar symptoms. Sir Thomas began to suspect that he was being poisoned. The obvious perpetrator would be the Begum, who was vindictive at the best of times and was now in a fury when she got to hear of the terms of the secret agreement with Mirza Fakhru. Nevertheless, Sir Thomas promised to make it to the rendezvous in Simla, though on the usual condition that he must stay at the foot of the hills, at Kalka, until the anniversary of his wife's death had passed.

Annie takes up the story:

I arrived at Simla on August 31, 1853, and was lovingly welcomed by Charlotte. Theo was not there, as he could not leave his work at Delhi till the middle of September, so we were very quietly happy expecting the event, which took place on September 8th. She was overjoyed when she was told she had a dear little son ... The infant was a fine child and all seemed full of promise and hope for a speedy recovery for her. She was kept perfectly quiet, only Mrs Mountain and I seeing her – when Theo arrived unexpectedly on the eighth day after the baby's birth. It was a surprise to her – but a great pleasure and both were intensely happy over their boy.

On the ninth day she was moved onto a sofa and I went out for an hour, leaving Theo sitting by her side. When I returned home, I was told she had had a shivering fit and Dr Cannon had been sent for and ordered her back to bed immediately. She did not seem ill, & was quite cheerful, but from that evening ... every hour was full of anxiety, as more and more symptoms supervened. Her restlessness increased, and though she did not complain of pain, she seemed to become less and less conscious of what was going on – apparently dozing a great deal, and didn't appear to be awake even when taking food. The Doctors looked graver and graver each day, & were both shocked as I was to hear her constantly harping on one thought – '*What day is it? Your Mother died on 26th September, did she not Annie?*'

Even in her delirium, Sir Thomas's obsession filled her brain – a tribute to the force of his personality, if nothing else. Theo too shared the belief that September was a fatal month in their family.

It was the only idea that seemed to fill her thoughts & though in accordance with the Doctors' orders we tried to reassure that that date was passed, it would not do. "No," she said, "Your Mother died on that day, and I too shall die on 26th September."

On September 22, Holy Communion was administered to the little group by the bedside. By now Charlotte seemed far away in thought most of the time. At the doctors' suggestion, Theo asked her, 'Darling, do you not know who I am?' She looked at him with the sweetest smile and said, 'Yes I know – you are little Baby's Papa.' Theo broke down completely and had to be taken out of the room, wild with grief. She slept much of the time, but by 6pm on September 25, 'there began a series of convulsions which lasted through several hours and were terrible to witness by those who loved her so dearly.

'At last when she was quieter, she suddenly turned round to me and said – "Annie, don't you hear them?" And I said – "What is it you hear, Darling?" "Oh," she said, "the angels singing and the harps. I can hear them all so plainly. Hark! Hark!" And her face seemed in an attitude of listening with rapt attention.'

She asked those round her bedside to sing for her, and she uttered 'a bitter bitter cry of despair at having to tread that dark valley alone'. One last time she turned to them and 'entreated Theo to accompany her "forward – across the deep dark track to that beautiful country"'.

'After a little while in the dead of night, she turned to me and said – "Annie, when will be September 26th?" I tried to persuade her by the Doctors' orders that the date was passed, for they said this idea fixed in her mind was killing her. But though dead to all else, her mind was clear on this point. After midnight the convulsions began again and to us, watching by her, they were awful hours.

'Just as the sun was rising and shining on her bed, she suddenly rose up in her bed and poured forth a song so wild and unearthly – not a word in it – only music, with her face in a rapturous glow, that we could only look on in silence and wonder. She had not moved for days, and yet with supernatural strength, she raised herself thus suddenly. Theo rushed to support her with his arm – she took no notice of him, but when her song ceased, she fell back in her bed and never moved again – and died at 3pm September 26th!!'[15]

Annie closed her eyes and mouth and decked her with flowers, and put her in her coffin and gave her waxen face one last long kiss. Charlotte was buried two days later in Simla's second cemetery down by the Old Bullock Station.[16] She was buried next to Félicité, the mother-in-law whom she never knew but whose death-day she shared. There was nobody much at the funeral except Theo and Annie and a couple of the doctors; none of Charlotte's family, and neither GG nor Edward had arrived yet. Theo leant on Dr Douglas's shoulder all the way down the Mall to the graveyard and sobbed bitterly the whole time. The baby was christened Charles Edward Theophilus, 'as he is the Young Pretender' and his mother was Charlie, too, to all the Metcalfes. On her deathbed Charlie had asked Annie to be a mother to him. But Theo was having none of that, and insisted on looking after the child himself.

It was suggested that Charlotte, too, might have been poisoned, though this seems fanciful, as does the doctors' own suggestion that the obsession with September 26 was killing her. Her doctors also spoke to Annie of the possibility of an internal abscess. What seems most likely is the fever was brought on by the sort of infection then so common in childbirth, as often as not caused by the doctors themselves not washing their hands properly. Knowledge of basic hygiene as of elementary gynaecology seems to have been scarce in nineteenth-century India.

Sir Thomas heard the news down at Kalka and slowly made his way up to Simla. Annie was horrified when she saw him on October 1: 'I found him looking very thin and ill – so white – and he continually suffered from sickness – irritating vomiting of a watery stuff. The small pox on his face, generally very slight, became most pronounced – and quite black. It was easy to see he was ill though he suffered no pain whatever.'[17]

He was dying. There could be no question of a grand Simla wedding for GG and Edward. They were married quietly in Theo's sitting room. The newlyweds headed off for a honeymoon in the hills. Theo took his father back down to Delhi, where Sir Thomas died in Metcalfe House on November 3. Again, there are perfectly adequate alternative explanations for his death. Several types of intestinal cancer exhibit much the same symptoms in their final stages.

But as the princely hakims were famed for their mastery of poisons that left no trace, poison was always the explanation of first resort.

Theo was broken. Years later, Annie wrote that the loss of Charlie 'wrecked poor Theo's life'. And he did not know how best to look after little Charlie. He told GG that 'I never can part with him altho' I feel the great disadvantage of leaving him so many hours alone every day without the company of a Lady but I long to show him an affection which I never experienced when a child but for the loss of which I always mourned.'[18] A year later, he wrote to Edward Campbell, 'I cannot account for this numbness of feeling that weighs me down and makes me helpless. I think without a relief from all work, without a long and perfect holiday, I will never rise.'[19]

Part of the trouble was a pain and weakness in his left eye. At the age of 17, while he was at Addiscombe College preparing to go into the Indian Army, he had been struck by an eye infection which had left him blind in the right eye and destroyed his hopes of a military career. Now he feared he might be left completely blind. He had to give up work and lie in a darkened room. He wrote plaintively to GG, 'Do you know any widow who wants to take care of a single gentleman, for I am comparatively helpless and am forbidden all reading or writing.'[20]

He said it was because the boy had grown so tall, but it may have been partly because his eyes were so bad that Theo did not recognize his son when he came down to Metcalfe House after recuperating in the hills. But the little boy – probably then just three – recognized his father and pulled him round the great empty house, pointing with his finger from room to room until they reached the great Bow Room where he brought Theo up in front of the two portraits of Charlotte which hung there. Theo, clearly moved, tells us he did so quite unprompted by his nurse Mrs Baxter. Alas, the two portraits were smashed to bits in the Mutiny, along with Sir Thomas's superb collections, and so we have no idea what Charlotte looked like in her brief grown-up life.[21]

The dreaded task that now haunted Theo was to follow his father's

instructions and arrange for the sale of all Sir Thomas's moveable
property both at Metcalfe House and at the Dilkusha. The task was
repugnant to him because it betokened the end of the Metcalfe
dynasty in Delhi, but also because there were so few buyers for such
priceless items. Delhi was still a smallish town with an even smaller
European population. His agent, Mr Brown, was an honest and
painstaking man, but Theo was no help at all. Annie complained that
'as he was at that time living in the house being joint magistrate of
Delhi, he could interfere with Mr Brown's arrangements in a most
annoying way.'[22] As a result, although the sell–off began in January
1854, three years later it was nowhere near finished. When the
Mutiny hit Delhi in May 1857, the rebels had a rich choice of plate,
furniture and pictures to smash or loot. To add to this total disaster,
Mr Brown and his family were killed in the uprising and all the
money standing at the bank to the Metcalfes' credit from the sales
that had been made was looted, too. Nothing was left for Theo or
for his exasperated sisters, whose tolerance of Theo's conduct was
wearing thin anyway.

He was as extravagant and inconsiderate as ever, but now he had
become bitter and ill–humoured, too, as he himself admitted. Even
loyalty to Charlotte's memory did not prevent the financially
strapped Edward Campbell from losing his temper when they looked
after the little boy and his nanny and Theo failed to contribute a
rupee towards their keep: 'about the rent, I think there is no use
asking him, and not the slightest in giving hints for he *will not* take
them. I think we might just make out a little memo, showing him
the actual expense we were put to by having Mrs Baxter and Charlie
boarded on us, and then ask him to pay.'[23]

Charlotte's death had broken John Low, too. He received the news
less than a fortnight after he had docked at Calcutta to step ashore as
a member of the Council of India, the almost unthinkable summit of
his ambition. Outwardly he remained the imperturbable proconsul,
but he was tortured by grief, which he expressed only in the letters

that he exchanged with Theo. It was as though only the two of them really knew how terrible the loss was. Among the letters of condolence he received, he kept only one in the papers at Clatto. It was a little note folded into a tiny black-edged envelope, no more than two-and-a-half inches by four:

What can I say to you, my dear friend, but that my heart, sore with the worst agony that the spirit of man can suffer, aches for you again in this afflicting loss of your most sweet child, and can enter into all the depths of your sorrow with you.

May the great God comfort you with the thought that her spirit is now in bliss before his throne, waiting for that re-union wh. we all look and long for. Do not think of Council. You have no occasion either to ask leave or to give any cause for it to anybody. All will know and all will deeply lament the cause, none more so than
Your sincere friend,
Dalhousie

The letter was drenched in Dalhousie's own raw grief for his wife. After years of remorseless ill health, the doctors had finally ordered Lady Dalhousie home in January 1853. The plan was that she should recover her health with her daughters in Scotland and then return to India in the autumn. On June 13, a telegraph reached Calcutta with the news that she had died at sea within sight of England. For two days, Dalhousie shut himself in his room. When he emerged, he said that the light of his life had gone out. He called for work and more work, but was too stunned to speak of his loss to anyone around him. A week later, though, he wrote to his 'private correspondent' to spill it all out:

The severance of two souls bound together 'till death shall them part' is the bitterest drop in this cup of mortality. But to be called upon to drink it suddenly when comforting my loneliness by anticipations of the joy of mother and children reunited, to see her who had battled with and conquered so many perils sink under no distemper, but from the very sea that all thought was to be her restoration – to hear of her children looking upon her face again, but dead – to hear of her return to her home but only to the grave – surely, surely, God will pardon me if for a time I feel it almost too hard to bear.[24]

So there they were, two Scottish gentlemen, not happily reminiscing by the banks of Forth but slaughtered by grief and near-paralysed by ill health, both longing to go home but condemned by pride (and avarice, too) to see out their time in India. Yet these two physical and emotional cripples were between them to decide the political direction and the military strength of the British Empire at its tipping point.

XVI

THE CHERRY RIPENS

L ord Dalhousie was in a hurry. He had promised that he would
stay in India until April 1854. Ten days after his wife died, he
wrote to the Court: 'The Almighty has stricken me sorely, and I try
to submit myself to the severity of His will. If my health does not disable me, I will redeem the pledge I gave last year. When that has
been done and things are settled, I must go without hindrance.'[1] His
health did disable him. His leg was so swollen that he could hardly
walk, and in Calcutta he was so beset by fever that he had to retreat
to the southern hills near the growing resort of Ootacamund. But
things were not settled. His Lordship had so little time, and so much
to do.

The railways, for one thing. The first section of the Bombay line
had opened to traffic in April 1853. The lines to Madras and Nagpur
were still being surveyed; so was the great line projected from
Calcutta to Allahabad and then on to Delhi. His Lordship had his
own views about everything: the route, the locomotives, the gradi-
ent on the ghats, the quality of the track. When the contractors
pushed for lighter rails, he retorted: 'You may rely upon it that
knocking up a corduroy railway is a short-sighted policy. I am all for
making them here as cheap and as quick as possible, but they must be
solid, or the money may as well be dropped into the Bay of Bengal.'[2]

The Ganges Canal had just opened in April, too, exceeding in its length 'all the irrigation lines of Lombardy and Egypt', as Dalhousie was to boast in his farewell dispatch.[3] The reform of the postal service was under way. There were now 753 post offices across the country, offering a uniform rate of postage, not only within India but between India and England. The Governor-General trumpeted: 'A Scotch recruit who joins his regiment at Peshawar may write to his mother at John O'Groats House and may send it for sixpence, which three years ago would not have carried his letter beyond Lahore.'[4]

Then there was the electric telegraph, nearly 4,000 miles of cable connecting Calcutta with Peshawar, Madras and Bombay, an amazing achievement – some of the river crossings were two miles wide. On March 24, 1854, the first telegram from Agra reached the Governor-General 800 miles away in Calcutta less than two hours later.[5]

The whole subcontinent was opening for business, parcelled, surveyed and criss-crossed by modern communications, all of them either begun, completed or hustled on by the unstoppable little Governor-General. All achieved in eight years against worsening ill health and desolating bereavement. Nowhere before or since, I think, has a British proconsul driven on the modernization of so great a country with such dynamism and panache.

There was one exception, one enormous blot on the map now being drawn with such scientific precision. Across the path of these vital modern communications there still lay a wodge of native principalities, as much a barrier to the spread of British justice as to the British spirit of modernity. The petty princes of Bundelkhand, the greater rajas of Nagpur and Jhansi and above all the King of Oudh were an offence to His Lordship's pious and impatient eye. With their eunuchs and their dancing girls, they stood, or rather lolled, in the way of progress. The millions of rupees they frittered on their trivial and squalid amusements could have done so much good to their people – and to the East India Company. It was to be the work of Dalhousie's last two full years in India, 1854 and 1855, to expunge these blots and to bequeath a gratifying expanse of pink on the map, stretching from Rangoon to the Punjab and interrupted only by the hold-over domains of a few tame 'booby potentates'.

In the winter of 1853, he was in Burma, surveying his latest acquisition, when the first juicy opportunity turned up. Raghoji Bhonsle, the Raja of Nagpur (or Berar as the state was formally known), the ruler over four million people and 80,000 square miles – including some of the richest cotton fields in India – had died, leaving no male heir. He was only 46 years old, and his death had been quite sudden, which might help to explain why he had adopted no heir.[6]

Raghoji was a good-natured, backslapping sort of fellow, amiable to everyone he met. Charles Mansel, the Resident at Nagpur, thought that, as a Maratha, Raghoji seemed to feel that he had sprung from the people. He behaved more like the president of a modern republic than an arbitrary monarch. Unfortunately, Mr Mansel sighed, 'a distaste for business and low habits seem the distinguishing features of his temperament.' The Resident had great trouble in tearing him away from his preferred pastimes of wrestling, kite-flying and card-playing. He would dismiss his staff with the words, 'Now go away and study the provisions of the Treaty, so that they are enforced to protect me in the enjoyment of those pleasures of dancing and singing that I have loved from my boyhood.' Over the past eight years, his concubine Janee had led him into drinking at least a bottle of brandy a day. No wonder things had rather gone downhill in Nagpur. Senior officers of the state were chosen by caprice or the influence of the *zenana*, justice was for sale to the highest bidder, and the Raja had been plundering the country to fill his own coffers.

On the other hand, Mansel fair-mindedly reported that 'if a traveller passing through the country stops but to look at the luxuriant cultivation in the cotton soil, the absence of crimes by open violence, the civil, simple people, or the bustle of the main street of the capital, he will form a judgment favourable to the character of the

Raja, and to the action, if not the principles of his rule.' The country might have degenerated since the golden days when Richard Jenkins had been Resident, but even in the absence of 'the Jenkins System' there were worse places. Nagpur was quiet, and the regime was unfailingly loyal to the British.

Mr Mansel suggested, therefore, that the country now be entrusted to the Banka Bai, the widow of an earlier ruler, now 75 years old but still sharp: 'she is really a superior woman of good feeling and good sense.' Meanwhile, the nearest plausible heir to the late Raja, Yashwant Rao, a well educated boy of 18, could be trained up to succeed her in due course. With a prudent Resident to guide her, Mansel thought that 'an experiment like that I have shadowed out would best satisfy the people, placing them effectually under the shield of British protection, and leaving them to partial self-government.'[7]

Dalhousie was having none of it. Within days of his return to Calcutta, he composed the most enormous Minute, about 14,000 words long.[8] Its burden was brutally simple. Raghoji had left no male heir of his body. He had not adopted an heir. Nor had his widow. In fact, he had shied away from discussing the problem with Mr Mansel, because he did not like to advertise the 'impuissance' brought on by his drinking.

In any case, it was the British Government which had placed the Raja on his throne, and the British Government had never recognized any right to adopt. Nagpur was ours to dispose of, and the way to dispose of it was to resume the sovereignty we had given away. How could we guarantee that Raghoji's successor would not also turn out to be 'a seller of justice, a miser, a drunkard and a debauchee'? It was in the interests of the people of Nagpur that the British Government should take over the province.

It was also – and here Lord Dalhousie's argument shed its high-minded wrapper – in 'the essential interest of England'. For 'it is well known that the great field of supply of the best and cheapest cotton grown in India lies in the Valley of Berar.' Evidence had been given

to the House of Commons that the area 'would afford cotton sufficient to supply the whole of England'.[9] As if all this was not enough,
Dalhousie took the opportunity to refer back to his mission statement at the outset of his Governor-Generalship, that naked statement
of intent which stuck in everybody's mind, to the effect that, one
way or another, Britain should never pass up a chance to incorporate
those 'petty intervening principalities'.[10] Taking over Nagpur would
give Britain a territory with an annual revenue of four million
rupees. It would extinguish 'a separate military power, out of which
there must always be a possibility that embarrassment, if not anxiety,
might some day arise.'[11] 'It would completely surround with British
territory the dominions of his Highness the Nizam in a manner
highly beneficial for the purposes of internal administration', and 'It
would place the only direct line of communication which exists
between Calcutta and Bombay almost entirely within British territory.'[12] When the railways came into their full glory, troops would
take hours, instead of months, to cross India, and the cotton and the
opium could be on the quayside in no time.

His Lordship's natural desire would be to submit the whole question to the Court of Directors and await its decision. But Nagpur
could not wait. The country might be tranquil now, but prolonged
uncertainty might unsettle the minds of the people and weaken the
authority of local officers. He therefore proposed to proclaim the
take-over straightaway. An area larger than England and a population
of more than four million souls were to be wafted into the arms of
the British Government before the British Government had been
given the chance to say yes or no to the idea.

So the other members of Lord Dalhousie's Council were wasting
their breath. The senior member was Mr Joseph Dorin. He had
risen through the Finance Department, and even his friends admitted that during his 30 years in India he had never ventured more
than 16 miles from Calcutta. He kept his place by writing short and
emphatic Minutes in support of whatever the Governor-General
said. Mr Dorin was a Yes Man of Olympic class, and he did not fail

on this occasion. He backed Lord Dalhousie all the way. 'The gradual extension of European principle, and science, and literature in India must inevitably have the effect, sooner or later, of overpowering all purely Asiatic systems.' Taking over Nagpur was simply 'a link in the inevitable chain of progress'.[13] In this ineffably smug judgement, Mr Dorin epitomized half a century of progressive preaching from British functionaries, fuelled in equal measure by Evangelical zealots and Utilitarian prigs. In Lord William Bentinck's day, a generation earlier, this tendency still had the remnants of an earlier tolerance and willingness to leave other people's cultures alone. Not any more.

Next up was John Low. He was under no illusions. Writing this Minute, 'practically speaking, will have no effect whatsoever on the majority of the public functionaries in London, who will have to consider and decide this question.' The Board of Control would pay no attention to the views of an officer who was entirely unknown to them, when opposed to 'the deliberately-formed opinion of a statesman like the Marquis of Dalhousie'.[14]

But oppose it he did, and at a length scarcely less than His Lordship's. In fact, he fired off two Minutes one after the other, like two barrels of a shotgun, as soon as he read Dalhousie's. Nobody else on Council, including the Governor-General, had one tenth of his experience of the other India outside Calcutta, the India of bullocks wading in the shallows, of camps in rocky nullahs under a silver moon, of angry men in the bazaars clamouring at the sahib's elbow, of leisurely talks under the trees with holy men and village headmen, of the Raja's hookah bubbling beside the plashing fountain, and the fluted whisperings from the *zenana* screen. His friend John Kaye wrote of him in his great *History of the Indian Mutiny*: 'No man had so large an acquaintance with the Native Courts of India; no man knew the temper of the people better than John Low. He could see with their eyes, and speak with their tongues, and read with their understanding.'[15]

That was why, Kaye said, Colonel Low looked with some dismay

at the widespread Englishism of the Dalhousie school, and sorrow-
fully regarded the gradual dying out of the principles in which he
had been nurtured and trained, and to which, heedless of their
unpopularity, he still clung. And now he was going to speak up for
those principles, whatever the cost to his friendship with Dalhousie
and despite the very real debt he owed him.

He was under no illusions about the way the wind was blowing.
It was highly probable that 'the whole of India will, in due course,
become one British province'.[16] But all the great statesmen of India
whom he had known and loved – men like John Malcolm and
Mountstuart Elphinstone – agreed that 'we ought most carefully to
avoid unnecessarily accelerating the arrival of that great change.'

No country 'governed as India is, by a few foreigners' could hope
to be prosperous or even safe until its native subjects were much
more attached to their rulers than they were in British India.
Annexing native states which had not broken their word to Britain –
as Nagpur had not – further alienated the people. So did 'remitting
large portions of the revenue for pensions and salaries in England
(which bring no return to India), instead of spending such revenues
within the countries which produce them.' Again, 'our not employ-
ing natives in high military commands, or in very important civil
offices, must also have the same general tendency; and so must the
fact of our being foreigners, who never associate with, or make personal friends of natives of India.'[17]

There had been a time when British officers lived with their
Indian sweethearts and slept under canvas among their sepoys. They
went hunting together and sat side by side at the nautch shows. But
the coming of the bungalow and the memsahib had put an end to
such easy fraternizing.[18]

All this might be inevitable, Low thought. And the only remedy
for it was education and the distribution of land leases to build up a
prosperous Indian middle class. But we should be in no doubt about
the evil effects. Low could recall from his own experience cases, both
in the Deccan and the North-West Provinces, 'of our having suffered

heavy losses in revenue, and very extensive losses in human lives, owing to the want of wealth among our native subjects; while in the neighbouring native states, which had experienced exactly the same drought, they did not suffer nearly so much, either by the death of their subjects, or in revenue, solely because the men of property made large advances of money from their private funds, whereby great numbers of men, by digging new wells, were enabled to raise sufficient grain to keep them alive for the season.'[19]

In other words, British rule was not always more effective or humane, an indictment which was still echoing a hundred years later after the terrible Bengal famine of 1943. John Low did not pretend that the native squires lent the money out of the goodness of their hearts, but rather to protect themselves against heavy money losses in the following year. For all the inequality and oppression, peasants and landowners were 'all in it together' in a way the British could never be.

Low asked the question which had been asked a dozen times since the days of Pitt the Younger, the question which acquisitive governors-general usually affected not to hear: 'Ought we not to be contented with the territories already in our possession?' 'Would it not be wiser, over the next twenty years, to avoid rather than to seek opportunities of annexing more native states?' Some chance, with men like Lord Dalhousie in Government House.

What had Nagpur done wrong? The place was so quiet that no British soldier had fired a shot there in 30 years. Britain already had ample supplies of cotton, not least from the fields that John Low had just winkled out of the Nizam – though he did not put it quite like that.

Already the notorious events of recent years – Napier's grabbing of Sind, Ellenborough's attack on Gwalior, and especially Dalhousie's annexation of Satara – had shaken 'the confidence of our native allies in our good faith'. John records how, on a recent visit to Malwa where he had held his first command nearly 40 years ago, he had met many old acquaintances whom he had known when he was a very young man. It was remarkable, he thought, that every native who ever spoke to him about the annexation of Satara asked precisely the same question: 'What crime did the late Raja commit that his country should be seized by the Company?' As soon as the annexation of Nagpur became known, the same question would be anxiously asked all over India. Britain might gain a few lakhs of rupees and save a good many families from occasional over-taxation. But the downside was likely to be 'a deep-rooted hatred of our supremacy'.

We would deceive ourselves if we thought that our future rule would be as popular as Sir Richard Jenkins's had been. 'He did not send away to a distant country a single rupee of the revenues.' The money, which came in on a very moderate tax assessment, was all spent within Nagpur for the benefit of the people. Jenkins had left most things much as they were, whereas the new British rulers would be itching to make major reforms, which were bound to be unpopular. For 'the natives of India are in one respect exactly like the inhabitants of all other parts of the known world, they like their own habits and customs better than those of foreigners.'[20]

John had said exactly the same thing to the Modernizers when he was at Lucknow (and again in Hyderabad). Now he said it once more in the heart of the citadel of the Modernizers. Colvin and Macnaghten had not listened in 1837. Dalhousie and Dorin were not likely to listen now.

The Modernizers believed that the courtiers and landowners might lose out under British rule. Some of them – the Levellers as they were dubbed – actively wanted India to be a more equal country. But they all agreed that the great mass of the people would be happier under the Dalhousie system. John Low drew again on his early experience with the Marathas to question this comfortable assumption:

I fear that a large proportion of the people will be too likely to do, as I know they did in the Poona territory, namely, to forget the injustice and the oppression which they often suffered under their native rulers, and to magnify the annoyances to which they will occasionally be subjected from the strictness of our general system, and from the arrogance and petty tyranny of native official servants under our officers, which last is a species of evil that no exertions on our part can prevent.[21]

The common people of Poona had regretted the turfing-out of the Peshwa with all his debaucheries and religious extravagances. The people of Napgur, too, would look back with nostalgia on their days under the Rajas.

In any case, the Governor-General had no right, legal or moral, to annex Nagpur. By conferring independence on Raghoji, Britain had conferred on him and his widow the full right to adopt according to Hindu tradition. John could have added, but did not, that Lord Dalhousie had no male heir of his body either, but nobody in England would have dreamed of contesting the right of his cousin Fox Maule to succeed to his Earldom.

John Low was certainly right about one thing. Nobody, either in Calcutta or London, paid any notice to his critique. Lord Dalhousie thanked him warmly for his candour, assured him that their differences would not injure their friendship, and proceeded without delay to inform the four million inhabitants of the Nagpur that they were now British subjects. In due course, the Court of Directors limply acquiesced. As for Colonel Low, they condescended to mention only that bit of his argument which conceded that the inhabitants would in future be governed with more justice than they had been under the Raja.

Mr Mansel was removed from his office for daring to propose an alternative solution; he left the service in disgrace and dudgeon. The old Queen Mother threatened to set fire to the Palace if their furniture was removed. But the furniture was removed, and, along with half their jewels and their elephants and camels and bullocks, auctioned off at knock-down prices. Banka Bai and her daughters-in-law spunkily sent agents to London to plead their cause, with no better luck. In fact, the agents ran out of money, and their passage back to India had to be paid by the Honourable Company to avoid embarrassment. Nothing was left of the house of Bhonsle, and Lord Dalhousie moved on.

In quick time, too. The Raja of Jhansi had actually died three weeks before the Raja of Nagpur, but this rocky little state was only a fraction the size of Nagpur, and so it took second place in the queue for Lord Dalhousie's attention when he returned from Burma at the end of January 1854.

Jhansi's superb rose-red fortress topped by its memorable round keep – India's answer to Pembroke or Windsor – stood at the crossroads of the subcontinent. Today the tourist board calls Jhansi 'the Gateway to Bundelkhand', but it is much more than that. It is at Jhansi that the official north-south corridor connecting Kashmir and Cape Comorin crosses the east-west highway between Calcutta and Bombay. At Jhansi Junction too meet the railroads from the four corners of India. Lord Dalhousie had only to look at the map to see that he must have Jhansi.

There was, however, a difficulty. The Raja, Ganghadar Rao, was a popular and cultivated man who had added to the architecture of the city and built up a fine collection of Sanskrit manuscripts. He had done his best to repair the finances of the State. Colonel Sleeman, not an easy man to please, as we shall see, remarked that 'I have always considered Jhansi among the native states of Bundelkand as a kind of oasis in the desert, the only one in which a man accumulated property with the confidence of being permitted by its rulers freely to display and enjoy it.'[22]

True, Ganghadar Rao had his eccentricities. He liked to go up on to the roof of his palace and dress up as a woman in a resplendent sari with pearls and bangles. He would also observe four days of segregation each month as would a menstruating woman (shades of Nasir-ud-din Haidar at Lucknow). When quizzed about this by the British Commissioner, he replied that his loss of independence and subservience to the British had made him feel timid and inadequate like a woman.[23]

The Commissioner left it at that. After all, the Rajas of Jhansi were passionately loyal to the British. Ganghadar Rao's predecessor had even requested permission to adopt the Union Jack as the flag of Jhansi.[24] But Ganghadar Rao too had no living male heir of his body. The day before he finally succumbed to dysentery, he sent for a five-year-old boy cousin of his, Anand Rao, and adopted him according to the Hindu rites laid down in the *shastras*. The pundit performed the *sangkalpa* – Anand Rao's father poured water on the Raja's hands. No ceremony could have been more authentic. And the old Raja wrote to the Resident, reporting his actions and hoping that 'in consideration of the fidelity I have evinced towards government, favour may be shown to this child, and that my widow during her lifetime may be considered the Regent of the State and mother of this child, and that she may not be molested in any way.'[25]

That widow was Lakshmi Bai, who was to become one of the most famous heroines in Indian history, compared by her many British admirers to Boadicea or Joan of Arc. Now 25 years old or thereabouts, she was the daughter of an official at the court of the ex-Peshwa at Bithur, where John Low had once been the chief gaoler. From childhood she had heard all about the downfall of the Maratha Empire and the pains of exile. She was a playmate of the ex-Peshwa's adopted son, Nana Sahib, and of the son of another court official, Tantia Topi. Like them, she learnt to ride and shoot and fence, accomplishments bound to win her British fans. She was also beautiful, spirited, literate and highly religious. She had been married off to Ganghadar Rao at the age of 14 by her ambitious father. Other fathers acquainted with the Raja's habits declared that they would rather have pushed their daughters down a dark well. The marriage had not turned out happily.

But now Lakshmi Bai came into her own. Immediately she requested that the Raja's dying wishes be honoured and that she be recognized as Regent while Anand Rao was a minor. Like everyone who met her, Major Malcolm, the Political Agent for the region, was dazzled by Lakshmi Bai. He told Dalhousie that she was 'a woman highly respected and esteemed and I believe fully capable of doing justice to such a charge.'[26]

Major Malcolm knew Lord Dalhousie's inclinations – who in India did not? He assumed that the Government would take back the state. This, he said, would not be difficult, because Jhansi was a tranquil place and had continued to be managed much as it had been when the British were last in control. Malcolm's Political Assistant, Major R.R.W. Ellis, was less resigned. He had burrowed back in the history books, and he could not discover any difference in the Treaties which would justify their withholding the privilege of adoption from one state and allowing it to the other. It would damage the spirit of enlightened liberalism if they now refused the right to ruling families who had rendered loyal service to the British Government.[27]

Lord Dalhousie paid no attention to political pipsqueaks. He heard the news about Jhansi as he was being rowed down the Irrawaddy. He did not hesitate. Jhansi must be British. We had every right to resume the sovereignty which we had ourselves conferred. For the British Government was the heir of the Maratha Empire, which had been Jhansi's overlord. It was a subordinate state, and we were now its overlord. In his mind's eye as he listened to the songs of the Burmese boatmen, His Lordship already saw the trains chuffing through Jhansi Junction, carrying cotton and opium to distant ports and soldiers to far-off battlefields.

This was an outrageous argument, a dishonest attempt to smother the past. While the Peshwa was still on his throne, it had been British policy to deny at every opportunity that the Maratha Empire existed at all. At that period, Britain was eagerly building up the independence of other states and denying that they owed any sort of loyalty to the Peshwa. The British Government had refused to recognize the ex-Peshwa's son, the so-called Nana Sahib, as his heir. When Baji Rao eventually died in 1851 – having survived far longer than any man of his habits had any right to expect – Lord Dalhousie not only refused to acknowledge Nana Sahib as the new Peshwa but refused to continue the handsome pension which Sir John Malcolm had awarded Baji Rao all those years ago when Lieutenant Low had led the deposed king into exile.

Yet now when it suited him, Lord Dalhousie was arguing that Jhansi had always been a Maratha dependency and never an independent state at all. 'I have no hesitation,' he declared, 'in concluding that the right of the British government to retain Jhansi as a lapse or escheat is clear.'[28]

Two days later, John Low threw up his hands. 'I should have preferred it,' he said in his response, 'if the Governor-General had pursued a similar course towards Jhansi to that which we lately adopted towards Chuttercote and Kerowlee' – viz, allow the Raja to adopt, with safeguards against future misrule – but 'I concede that the Government of India has now a full right, if it chooses to exercise that right, to annex the lands of Jhansi and therefore I have nothing more to say on the subject.'[29]

Easy to say that he should have fought on. But he was as racked by ill health as the Governor-General. He too was grieving and on his own, for Augusta was still in England visiting her sisters and keeping an eye on her younger daughters. He was in much the same plight as the man to whom he owed all his preferment and prosperity – although Dalhousie could at least look forward to the arrival of his 17-year-old daughter, called Susan Georgina just like her mother, who was coming out to keep him company. Anyway, John Low had placed his views on record. He did not see it as his duty to keep nagging.

Lakshmi Bai protested with all her flashing eloquence. Jhansi had always been loyal. She listed all the services it had willingly poured out to the British while other states were plotting or shirking. She argued, and with some brilliance, that the terms of the treaty did not bar succession in accordance with the customs of her country, and those customs had been properly observed down to the last *shastra*.

She had a visiting British barrister to help her. John Lang describes the tantalizing glimpses he caught of her behind the purdah screen in her palace. The Rani was 'rather stout, but not too stout. Her face must have been very handsome when she was younger and even now it had many charms ... though according to my idea of beauty it was too round. The expression was also very good and very intelligent. The eyes were particularly fine and the nose very delicately shaped. She was not very fair, though she was far from black. She had no ornaments, strange to say, upon her person, except a pair of gold earrings. Her dress was in a plain white muslin, so fine in texture and drawn about her in such a way, and so tightly, that the outline of her figure was plainly discernible ... and a remarkably fine figure she had.'[30]

Lord Dalhousie was implacable. In the voice of the Supreme Tidy-minded Bureaucrat, he pronounced that 'As Jhansi lies in the midst of other British districts, the possession of it as our own will tend to the improvement of the general internal administration of our possessions in Bundelkhand. That this incorporation with the British territories will be greatly for the benefit of the people of Jhansi ... the results of experience will suffice to show.'[31] As Sir John Kaye commented wryly, 'the results of that experience have since shown to what extent the people of Jhansi appreciated the benefits of the experience.'[32]

There was a further twist to Lord Dalhousie's harsh verdict. He *did* recognize the adoption of Anand Rao for private purposes, and so all the old Raja's personal property went not to his widow but to his adopted son.[33] For the Rani, private injury was added to public insult. Worse followed. The Lieutenant-Governor of the North-West Provinces, John Low's old adversary, John Colvin, supported the Superintendent of Jhansi, Captain Alexander Skene, in ruling that the Raja's outstanding debts should be paid out of the Rani's pension, and not out of state funds. Many of her lands and gardens were confiscated and re-settled with other tenants. Captain Skene had reintroduced the slaughter of cows to Jhansi, and he refused the Rani's complaints about this, privately minuting that if he gave in, it would look as if the Rani was about to be restored. He even refused leave for her to go to Benares to carry out the widow's rituals at that holy city.

430 THE TEARS OF THE RAJAS

All the British attempts to erase the Rani from the picture only drew more attention to her fascinating figure. The truth was that the British were in two minds. They wanted to strip Lakshmi Bai of all the trappings of sovereignty. Yet they recognized that her presence helped to keep Jhansi tranquil, so they were reluctant see her leave the city. She moved out of the Royal Palace into her own mansion, but in all other respects she behaved like a queen. Before dawn, she exercised in the gymnasium or went for a horse ride. Then she prayed to the sound of sacred music and holy stories. Sometimes, she would be dressed as a man in pyjamas, cummerbund, and topi, with the sword of the Peshwas stuck in her belt; sometimes she would appear as a prayerful widowed queen in white, shorn of ornament, as John Lang had glimpsed her. The British admired her cross-dressing as much as they had deplored her late husband's. When she dispensed justice from her dais, from behind a screen, when she visited the temple every Tuesday and Friday with her adopted son, there could be no doubt in the minds of the crowd who was their legitimate sovereign. In her frequent letters to the British Government, she continued to protest her loyalty to the British Crown, but who knew what lay in her heart?

Thus, within a couple of years Lord Dalhousie had stored up two potential enemies. He lost no time in moving on to create a third. There is no doubt that he had always had it in mind to acquire control of the richest prize of all, the Kingdom of Oudh. Only a few months after first arriving in India, he was confiding to his friend in Scotland Sir George Couper that 'I have got two other kingdoms to dispose of – Oude and Hyderabad. Both are on the high-road to be taken under our management – not into our possession; and before two years are out I have no doubt they will be managed by us.'[34] It was to take rather longer than two years. But having sucked the juice out of Hyderabad, he was not going to leave Oudh hanging. Three years later, he had described Oudh as 'a cherry which had long been ripening'.[35] Now at last it was ready to drop off the branch.

He was still doubtful whether he could get away with it. Once again, the trouble with these native princes was that they were so infernally loyal: 'I should not mind doing it as a parting *coup*. But I doubt the people at home having the pluck to sanction it, and I can't find a pretext for doing it without sanction. The King won't offend or quarrel with us, and will take any amount of kicking without being rebellious.'[36]

Yet barely six weeks later, he was writing excitedly from the southern hills where he was convalescing: 'Lately I have been trussing up the Kingdom of Oudh preparatory to putting it on the spit.'[37]

How was he going to bring off this parting coup, his final and most fateful action in India? This was no last-minute business. Dalhousie had begun, rather stealthily, to prepare the ground quite soon after he arrived in India. It was as early as September 1848 that the Governor-General wrote to Colonel William Sleeman offering him the Residency at Lucknow. As we saw, Sleeman had first been selected for that plum post back in 1838, but had generously let John Low stay on at Lucknow to give him time to pay off his debts. Now he was to have a second go, but on conditions. The previous Governor-General, Lord Hardinge, had already warned the King a year earlier that if His Majesty did not mend his ways within two years, the British Government would take over the management of the Kingdom. There was little hope, Dalhousie claimed, that any improvement whatever would have happened by the deadline of October 1949. So Sleeman was being offered the job 'with especial reference to the great changes which, in all probability, will take place' – i.e. the take-over.[38] He was, as the Bristol journalist Samuel Lucas put it in his famous pamphlet, *Dacoitee in Excelsis*, or 'Robbery in High Places', 'the emissary of a foregone conclusion'.[39] To help the process along, Colonel Sleeman was to make a personal tour of all parts of the kingdom, in order 'to acquaint the Honourable Company with the actual condition of the Kingdom', in other words to prove what a disgusting and degraded state the country was in. It was a set-up, and Sleeman was the patsy.

Dalhousie had never actually met Colonel Sleeman. He knew him only as the implacable enemy of the Thugs. It is estimated that, during Sleeman's campaign against the murderous bandits of Upper India, more than 14,000 Thugs were hanged, transported or imprisoned for life. The DNB entry for Sir William Sleeman, as he later became, says that the report derived from his three-month tour of Oudh 'largely influenced Dalhousie in his resolve to annex the Kingdom'. But Dalhousie had long ago made his mind up. It was the queasy Court of Directors that the report was supposed to influence. And it did.

His Lordship was cunning, but he was also lucky. For Sleeman was even more suitable for the task than Dalhousie could have hoped. To start with, he detested the court of Lucknow even more than Dalhousie did: 'Such a scene of intrigue, corruption, depravity and neglect of duty and abuse of authority I have never before been placed in and I hope never again to undergo.'[40]

The worst thing about the court was the King himself. Wajid Ali Shah (1822–87), now in his early thirties, was a corpulent, good-humoured fellow. Like the nawabs before him, he was a Shia, but he had reacted against his father's bigotry: 'Of my two eyes,' he said, 'one is Shia and the other is Sunni', and he surrounded himself with Sunni advisers – his vizier, his zookeeper, his paymaster were all Sunni.[41] He was teetotal and he was devout, praying the statutory five times a day and observing Muharram with great solemnity. Alas, though, for Colonel Sleeman he committed the cardinal sin: Wajid Ali Shah paid little or no attention to public business:

He is entirely taken up with the pursuit of his personal gratifications ... He lives, exclusively, in the society of fiddlers, eunuchs and women: he has done so since childhood, and is likely to do so to the last. His disrelish for any other society has become inveterate: he cannot keep awake in any other ... He sometimes admits a few poets or poetasters to hear and praise his verses, and commands the unwilling attendance of some of his relations, to witness and applaud the acting of some of his own silly comedies, on the penalty of forfeiting their stipends; but anyone who presumes to approach him, even in his rides or drives, with a petition for justice, is instantly clapped into prison . . .[42]

When the Colonel set off in December 1849 on his journey of inspection, sometimes carried in a *tonjon*, a sort of sedan chair, sometimes on the back of an elephant (he could not ride a horse, because he had broken his thigh falling from one before he set out), he found exactly what he wanted to find: a cheerful and industrious peasantry and a country which, if it were not so horribly misgoverned, could easily become 'the beautiful garden which the parts well cultivated and peopled now are'.[43]

Everything in the garden of India was lovely, except the King and his officers. As Sleeman jogged along with local peasants and landowners walking beside him, he listened to endless tales of extortion, banditry or neglect. Mixed in with these stories of crimes going unpunished, of brutal tax-gatherers and corrupt officials, Sleeman included tales of the infanticide of daughters among the Rajputs, of wolf-children in the jungle, of a balloon ascent in Dilkusha Park, indeed of anything that caught his fancy. Some of his horror stories were 20 years old. Sleeman tells the story of Emma Walters, the white Begum, of the death of Nasir-ud-din Haidar and how John Low stopped the Begum from usurping the throne for her boy. It is a weird compendium, inconsequential but still highly readable.[44] What it is not is a systematic and exact description of a state which has been so mismanaged as to cry out for annexation to the British Crown.

There were doubts about Sleeman's mental state and they extended as far as Calcutta. When a sentry fell asleep and his gun went off, Sleeman immediately declared that it was an attempt on his life. He appeared to quarrel with everybody: with Dr Bell the Residency Surgeon, for example, whom he denounced for mixing with the unsavoury Mr Brandon, an old drinking partner of the

Barber of Lucknow. He claimed that Bell and Brandon were trying to persuade His Majesty that 'all my advice and suggestions might be disregarded'.[45] He was even more at odds with his own Assistant, Captain Robert Bird, who he thought was plotting with the courtiers to get rid of him. When his efforts to get Bird transferred failed, he demanded that the Captain should stop mixing with the eunuchs at Lucknow Races and that the King should ban the races, because they encouraged gambling. The sporting Captain merely transferred his patronage to Cawnpore, where he ran his horses under the alias of Mr Hope. The Council was disturbed by Sleeman's 'apparent animus' against his colleagues. Colonel Low thought that Sleeman 'has shown a proneness not only to listen to, but to believe, the wretched tittle-tattle of the place'.[46]

In short, Sleeman was both a puritan and a paranoiac. Not exactly the ideal person to convey an impartial and perceptive picture of the province. But then that was not what Dalhousie wanted. The more scandalous and hysterical Sleeman's tales of the iniquities he had found, the better for His Lordship's purposes.

By the time Dalhousie was ready to launch his 'parting coup' at the end of 1854, ill health had forced poor Sleeman to leave Lucknow, first on sick leave to the hills and then, when he got no better, back to England. Like many another long-serving officer, William Sleeman died on the voyage home.

Pending his hoped-for return, Colonel James Outram, another veteran, was to act as Resident, and it fell to him to draw up the final indictment to send to London. As he had only a couple of months to complete the task, he had to rely almost entirely on Sleeman's material.[47] So the report submitted by Outram was pretty much Sleeman's work, and exhibits his characteristic mixture of hearsay and flamboyant denunciation among genuine examples of violence and misgovernment. Its appendices are filled with long lists of muggings, punch-ups, kidnappings and murders – rather as though the most lurid crime stories published in the *Daily Mail* over five years had been collected by the Government and then published in a White Paper to prove that law and order had collapsed in Britain.

The sheer volume of stuff impressed everyone in England – the Court of Directors, Parliament, the press and the public. How could Britain honourably tolerate such misgovernment a moment longer? It was Dalhousie's wonderful luck that as his report was winging its way home, everyone there was lapping up the scandalous *Private Life of an Eastern King*, which had been published in the spring of 1855. Reliable or not (John Low's dispatches suggest that the book is more reliable than some historians have thought), that luscious account was the perfect colour supplement to Sleeman. The events it described might be 20 years old, but who was to say that the Lucknow Court was not still as appalling as that – or possibly even worse?

Britain had to take over, somehow or other. No lesser remedy would cure those appalling evils. In his enormous Minute of June 18, 1855,[48] perhaps 30,000 words long, Dalhousie reviews the whole unhappy history of Britain's relations with Oudh, picks out the juiciest bits from the Sleeman/Outram report and concludes that the best option is to tell the King that the Treaty of 1801 is now dead and he must sign a new treaty handing over the administration of his kingdom entirely and for ever.

This time, he has the backing of his old friend and companion in grief. John Low almost trumpets his opinion in not one, but three forceful Minutes (March 28, July 21 and August 18, 1855):

> I accordingly beg to declare it to be my deliberate opinion that the disorders of Oude are of such long standing, and are so deeply rooted, and the corruption of the native Government officers, from the Prime Minister down to the meanest Chuprassee, is so general, and so inveterate, that there is now no other efficient remedy available for effecting and maintaining a just government over the people of Oude than that of placing the whole of its territory, *exclusively*, and *permanently*, under the direct management of the East India Company.[49]

Lord Dalhousie was effusive in his gratitude, both publicly and privately. In his compendious Minute, he brings it in as a clincher that 'My honorable colleague, General Low who was himself for many years the Resident at Lucknow, who ... has shown himself an earnest supporter of native states, and who many years ago wrote of himself at Lucknow, "No man can be more anxious than I am to avoid interference as long as such policy is justified" ... has now expressed his entire concurrence ... in the immediate necessity for our direct interference in the affairs of Oude.'[50]

From the southern hills, where he was waiting for the Court's decision, he wrote to John: 'The expressions of feeling & opinions contained in a Minute by you, whose personal sentiments & whose long local experience are so well known to the Court, will have great weight.'[51]

The great defender of native rights had caved in. The onrush of the imperial imperative was too much for him. John Low had voted to depose his third King (three-and-a-half if you include the emasculation of the Nizam).

He was quite prepared to face the logical consequence of that decision. The Governor-General was not yet prepared to say what should happen if the King refused to sign the new treaty. John Low was.

'If the King would not sign,' he wrote in his third Minute, 'I would alter the tone towards the King entirely. I would announce to him, openly, that we should take possession of his country, and keep it.'[52]

Is there a touch of bravado, even unease about the brutality of the language? Deep down, was he unhappy about this volte-face, this huge deviation from principles he had held so passionately all his life? He tacked on a note, which certainly suggests some compunction about the whole business. The belligerent language of his civilian colleagues sparked him into recalling all the services which the last five kings of Oudh had performed to the British; how 'attentive, courteous and friendly' they had been; how they had sent elephants, cattle, camels and heaps of grain whenever the British needed them; how they had lent millions of rupees to meet Britain's debts when she was broke during the wars in Nepal and Burma; how the King had lent another three million rupees to enable Lord Ellenborough 'to push on and equip General Pollock's Army, to retrieve our disasters in Afghanistan.' The Kings of Oudh had always co-operated wholeheartedly in capturing criminals and bandits who had escaped into their territory; they had settled frontier disputes with alacrity and kept up an efficient frontier police. In triumph and disaster alike, the British had had no more faithful friend than the Kings of Oudh. In external relations with the British, their conduct had been 'remarkably irreproachable'.[53]

It was only 'the sad mismanagement of their own affairs' which left the British Government with no alternative but to intervene. But what exactly did this mismanagement amount to? Clearly there was plenty of crime, banditry and extortion in Oudh. But had the situation got any worse in recent years, and was it so much worse than in the British provinces? T.R. Davidson, Sleeman's predecessor at Lucknow, had been doubtful: 'On comparing the past with the present, I cannot say that robberies, dacoities and plunderings have sensibly decreased; still, from having been employed in our own provinces as a magistrate, superintendent of police, and criminal judge, the mass of mischief here has not perhaps struck me to be so enormous as it has officers whose experience of crime has been confined to Oudh alone.'[54]

None of the witnesses found any evidence that despairing farmers were migrating over the border into the British provinces. Sleeman himself was candid that nobody much in Oudh was crying out for the British system of government, mostly because the British courts were reputed to be so implacable.

Even in the official detailed narrative, the Blue Book, the evidence was contradictory: Major Troop stated that crime had gone up in Sultanpur; Captain Bunbury said it had gone down; four other British officers said that crime in their districts had gone neither up nor down. In any case, terrible things went on in the British provinces, not least in Bengal, as attested by the Lieutenant-Governor there, Mr Halliday, soon to be a member of the Supreme Council.[55]

Sleeman claimed that the revenue in Oudh had declined sharply. The King in his petition (which was still lying before the House of Commons when the Mutiny broke out) claimed that the state's revenues had hardly budged over 50 years; all that had changed was that the sum deducted to pay for the King's troops was no longer included in the figures.[56] Outside observers, ranging from Bishop Heber to the British troops who had come to seize the province, remarked how prosperous the countryside looked.

Far from making no improvements, the King pointed out in his hasty letter to Outram of February 1 that he had transferred the whole country to the fashionable *amani* system of revenue collection, as urged on him by the British. So far the new system had actually produced less revenue, because the system specified no fixed amount to be collected, and depended on the honesty of the collectors, but that was scarcely the King's fault.

In his agitation, he failed to mention two other cogent points in his favour. After Lord Hardinge's dressing-down, he had started to reform the Army, but had been sternly discouraged by the Resident from meddling in military matters. Then, in the spring of 1848, he had drawn up with Captain Bird a plan to introduce the British system of administration in portions of his domain adjoining the British territories. Captain Bird had taken these pilot experiments to Mr Thomason, the Lieutenant-Governor of the North-West Provinces. That high priest of the Modernizers was delighted and tinkered with the scheme to improve it. But when the improved scheme was sent to the newly arrived Lord Dalhousie, what did he reply? 'If His Majesty the King of Oude would give up the whole of his dominions, the East India Government would think of it, but it was not worth while to take so much trouble about a portion.'[57]

This contemptuous snub showed that, right from the start, the last thing Dalhousie wanted was that the King should succeed in his reforms. What he wanted was Oudh. The scheme was shelved. But Captain Bird, still boiling over his treatment by Sleeman, kept the documents. Thus we have a paper trail, stretching from His Lordship's first actions in India to his last, which reveal what he was really up to.

There was one crucial question to be settled. What was to happen to the money? Where would the surplus revenues of this rich province go after the British had taken control? Most of those old India hands who wanted the British Government to 'interfere' were clear about this. Back in 1845, Sir Henry Lawrence, the Pacifier of the Punjab, had put it in italics: '*Let not a rupee come into the Company's coffers.*'[58] Sleeman, who was an honourable if unbalanced man, wrote to Sir James Hogg, the Chairman of the Court of Directors: 'We must, in order to stand well with the rest of India, honestly and distinctly claim all interested motives, and appropriate the whole of the revenues for the benefit of the people and royal family of Oudh ...'[59] He wrote to Dalhousie, too, hazarding that 'I believe that it is your Lordship's wish ... that the British Government should disclaim any wish to derive any pecuniary advantages from assuming to itself the administration.'[60]

It wasn't His Lordship's wish at all. On the contrary, Dalhousie needed every rupee that was going. In the eight years of his administration, £8,354,000 had been added to the public debt. And things were not improving. There had been a deficit of £2,044,000 in 1853–4, and of £1,850,000 in 1854–5.[61]

His Lordship was unashamed: 'The Government of India would not be justified in making over such a surplus to the reigning Sovereign of Oude, only that it might be unprofitably wasted by him, and squandered upon the follies and excesses which are the usual characteristics of a native Prince. In such circumstances, it would surely be far more wise, and at the same time reasonable and right, that any surplus so accruing should be placed at the disposal of the British Government.'[62]

Seldom has covetousness posed so nakedly as statesmanship. One or two of the civilians on Council, such as the brilliant, caustic John Peter Grant, wanted to go further. Instead of granting generous pensions in perpetuity to the royal family, we should cut the pensions off at the King's death, as Dalhousie had done in the case of Nana Sahib. Otherwise, we would have 'palaces filled with idle profligates' to the end of time.[63]

Here we hear John Low's voice for the last time in the matter of Oudh. With gentle irony, he points out that the princes of Oudh do not, 'unlike European gentlemen', save more than they spend and send their savings off to a distant country. 'The money paid in those pensions will not be lost to the public; it will be extensively circulated, and many industrious men of the working class will be benefited.'[64] Those rupees would go, not to the purchase of a villa in Cheltenham or an apartment in Bayswater but to the builders and plasterers working on the King's vast new palace, the Kaiserbagh, to the butchers and jewellers and pastry cooks of Lucknow, yes, and to the courtesans, eunuchs and fiddlers, too. John Maynard Keynes would surely have applauded this early exposition of his doctrines.

The Court of Directors was overjoyed by the dispatches from Calcutta. Feeling in London was running hot in favour of annexation. Lord Dalhousie was making the King an offer he could not refuse, and if he did refuse, then the Court was prepared to endorse the only alternative: 'that of assuming authoritatively the powers necessary for the permanent establishment of good government throughout the country.'[65]

The Court was especially pleased to have the support of Major-General Low, whose testimony was 'entitled to particular weight on account of his long experience as Resident in Oude'. They quoted his thumping conclusion verbatim. If General Low thought it was all right, then it was all right.

But what exactly was 'it'? The Court did not use the A-word. They did not get into ticklish questions of detail which might have forced them to use it. They left those to the Governor-General.

They wanted that great nobleman to do the deed. Which meant doing it sharpish, because His Lordship was due to leave India on March 1, 1856, and the Court's decision would reach Calcutta only at the beginning of January.

What about the money? The Court said nothing about the disposal of the surplus revenue. Which was odd, because Dalhousie had raised the question quite explicitly. But, as H.C. Irwin points out in *The Garden of India*, 'answer came there none'.[66]

If we have a look at the original draft of the Court's dispatch of November 21, though, we find three rather interesting paragraphs. There, the Directors state that 'the pecuniary resources which under a good government will in time be afforded by so fine and so improvable a country as Oude, so closely connected by geographical position with all the northern provinces of India, should be made available for the benefit of India generally, and not of Oude alone.' If Wajid Ali Shah should 'express a decided repugnance to this', then he should be offered a fixed proportion of the surplus revenues. This sweetener would 'enable you to obtain his assent to the employment of the remaining surplus for the general benefit of India' – i.e. for the benefit of the Company. The King was to be bribed to allow the British to pocket the cash.

When the Government in London came to re-examine these three paragraphs, it decided they stank too badly to be published, so they were expunged and never appeared in the Blue Book. Not for the first time, I echo Sir John Kaye's contempt for the bowdlerizing of State papers: 'I cannot, indeed, suppress the utterance of my abhorrence of this system of garbling the official correspondence of public men – sending the letters of a statesman or diplomat into the world mutilated, emasculated – the very pith and substance cut out of them by the unsparing hand of the state-anatomist.'[67]

Kaye was talking about the doctoring of Captain Alexander Burnes's dispatches from Kabul, which had cogently argued the case for sticking with Dost Mohammad. He could just as well have been referring to the bits left out of the Blue Book on the take-over of the

Nizam's territory, which would have showed how queasy some of the Directors were about plundering a faithful ally. As long as Blue Books and White Papers are published, dossiers will be dodgy.

The Court's go-ahead was received on January 2, 1856. Lord Dalhousie went into overdrive, his habitual impatience exacerbated by his fevers and his imminent departure for England. Outram had come to Calcutta to be ready for his orders. When he set off again for Lucknow on January 24, he had in his satchel his detailed instructions, plus Dalhousie's message to the King, the draft treaty, Proclamation A if the King agreed to sign, and Proclamation B if the King refused to sign. At the same time, Brigadier Wheeler was ordered, via the newly upgraded electric telegraph, to rendezvous at Cawnpore with an enhanced brigade of troops – the force totalled a terrifying 13,000 men – and then to advance on Lucknow.

On January 30, Outram reached Lucknow and presented the treaty to the King's Minister, Ali Naqi Khan. The Minister was startled by the ultimatum and distressed by the impending presence of so many troops. The next day, Outram saw him again, and told him that if the King did not sign the treaty within three days of it being presented to him, then Outram would assume the government of the country. Then Outram saw the Queen Mother. With the usual forcefulness of begums under fire, she implored the Resident to reflect on the utter ruin facing the King and assured him that they would adopt any measures which might satisfy the British Government. Nothing doing. The Government's resolution was final and irrevocable. 'His Lordship was unable to alter in one title the orders he had received from the Home Government' – for all the world as though His Lordship had not composed those orders himself. All that Outram was empowered to do was to offer the Queen Mother a bribe: 100,000 rupees a year if she could persuade the King to sign within the three days.[68] The Queen Mother pleaded for time. There was no time. Wheeler's advance guard was now only eight miles from Lucknow.

Outram's meeting with the King was a memorable occasion, as

theatrical as it was poignant, for Wajid Ali Shah was both a stage manager and a poet.

As the Colonel arrived at 8am on the morning of February 4, he found the Palace precincts strangely deserted. Then he noticed that all the guns in the courtyard were dismounted from their carriages. The foot guards carried no weapons. When they saluted Outram, they saluted with their hands alone. The court officials wore no swords or pistols. The King was advertising his helplessness.

Wajid Ali Shah read Dalhousie's letter with great attentiveness (although Ali Naqi Khan had already told him what was in it). Then he looked up and said: 'Why have I deserved this? What have I committed?'

Colonel Outram explained what the British thought he had done, or not done. If the suffering of his subjects was to be relieved, he must sign the new treaty.

The King replied in a burst of grief: 'Treaties are necessary between equals only: who am I, now, that the British Government should enter into Treaties with? For a hundred years this dynasty has flourished in Oude. It has ever received the favour, the support, and protection, of the British Government. It had ever attempted faithfully and fully to perform its duties to the British Government. The kingdom is a creation of the British, who are able to make and to unmake, to promote and to degrade. It has merely to issue its commands to ensure their fulfillment; not the slightest attempt will be made to oppose the wishes of the British Government; myself and my subjects are its servants.'[69]

Then he wept and took off his turban and placed it in the hands of Colonel Outram as a sign of his utter impotence. Wajid Ali Shah was the last of the weeping Rajas to discover how much British friendship was worth. Every native prince's dealings with John Low and his clan seemed to end in tears.

The British did not think much of this 'exaggerated display of helplessness', as Sir John Kaye called it.[70] It was unmanly and too, well, Oriental. But the King *was* helpless. Brigadier Wheeler's troops were within two miles of Lucknow. There was no disguising the fact: this was a heavily armed invasion of a faithful ally.

Three days passed. The King still refused to sign the treaty. Outram issued Proclamation B. And so the Garden of India passed into British hands. Dalhousie was thrilled. The moment he received the telegraph from Outram with the news, he wrote off to Couper: 'So our Gracious Queen has 5,000,000 more subjects and £1,300,000 more revenue than she had yesterday.'[71] It would have looked best if the King had signed. But, as for the future, the outcome was better, for the British Government would now have to shell out less and would have a free hand in the province.

It is a scurvy tale, in which avarice skulked behind compassion, and British misunderstanding combined with Indian miscalculation to produce the extreme outcome which only the out-and-out Modernizers admitted to wanting. Certainly Sleeman didn't want it, and Low had not wanted it before he swung into line behind his friend and patron. And the people of Oudh, and far beyond, were not so slow to see the whole transaction for what it was. Annie Bayley spoke for many, British and Indian alike, when she declared that 'the humanity of the act was soiled by the profit we derived from it, and to the comprehension of the multitude the good of the people we had vaunted while serving ourselves was nothing more than pretext and sham.'[72]

Ghalib, the great poet of Delhi, who was rather pro-English and never cared much for Lucknow, wrote to a friend a year later, 'Although I am a stranger to Oudh and its affairs, the destruction of the State depressed me all the more, and I maintain that no Indian who was not devoid of all sense of justice could have felt otherwise.'[73] You could find in all classes the reaction of a landowner, again pro-English, who asked H.C. Irwin, 'Why had the British Government deposed Nawab Wajid Ali? He was a poor meek creature, a humble servant and follower of the British. What had he done to be so summarily wiped out?'[74]

A delegation, led by the forceful Queen Mother (chief wife and

now widow of Amjad Ali Shah), set off for London on the SS *Bengal*
to lobby the British Government and, if possible, Queen Victoria
herself. In her numerous entourage she had the dubious John Rose
Brandon, landscape gardener to Nasir-ud-din and formerly crony to
the Barber of Lucknow, and also the aggrieved Captain Bird who
churned out pamphlets and delivered an impromptu harangue from
the balcony of the Royal York Hotel, Southampton, in defence of
the deposed Royal Family. Such a deputation was not unprecedented. There had already been thirty such missions by disgruntled
groups of Indians. Some had obtained redress or the promise of
redress. Not this one. The mysterious veiled Queen Mother drew
huge crowds wherever she went, but the British Government was
offhand and dismissive. The Mission ran out of money and had to
beg for a loan from its oppressors, the East India Company. The
Queen Mother died in Paris on the way home and is buried in
Père-Lachaise cemetery.

At Lucknow, people recited dirges, and many followed the King
all the way to the border at Cawnpore as he went off into exile at
Calcutta. The city, it was said, was lifeless without its nawab – a condition described by Colonel Outram as 'tranquil', that habitual
British epithet.

Wajid Ali Shah's favourite wife, Khas Mahal, wrote from her
Calcutta exile that 'we departed from Lucknow like a nightingale
from a garden, like Joseph from Egypt, like fragrance from flowers.'
Nowhere is the gulf between the mid-Victorian British mindset and
the mindset of nawabi Lucknow more painful and unbridgeable than
in their respective estimates of Wajid Ali. Even a sympathetic
observer such as the civil servant Henry Irwin dismissed him as a tri-
fler: 'He was a poetaster in a small way, and dabbled, in his loftier
moments, in music and painting, and if he had had to earn his living
by these accomplishments he might have passed muster in a crowd as
a decent member of society.'[75] Kaye equates Wajid Ali's dabblings
with his effeminacy: 'Stimulated to the utmost by unnatural excite-
ments, his appetites were satiated by the debaucheries of the *zenana*,

and with an understanding emasculated to the point of childishness, he turned to the more harmless delights of dancing and drumming, and drawing, and manufacturing small rhymes.'[76]

Wajid Ali's dilettantism and his neglect of his official duties drove some British officials to paroxysms of disgust. Mr Dorin insisted on affixing to one of his own Minutes some extracts from the Resident's diary which mingled incidents of violence and misrule with some of the King's more frivolous engagements, such as:

> February 15. The Eunuch Basheer made a present of a pair of cameleopards to the King. This morning the King received the obeisance of his physicians, and gave twelve suits of clothes to his fairies.[77]

Fairies! This does indeed sound like an infantile pastime. But we must beware of the Resident's distorting lens. Wajid Ali Shah's *Parikhana* or 'Abode of Fairies' was in fact a sort of Royal Ballet School, where talented girls were taught music and dancing, and performed in music dramas often composed or choreographed by the King. The *paris* could rise to heights. Wajid Ali's first wife, Hazrat Mahal, a courtesan taken into the royal harem, was selected as a *pari,* and was officially promoted to Begum after she bore a son to the King, known as Birjis Qadr. It was Hazrat Mahal who led the revolt in Lucknow in the name of Birjis Qadr and took charge of the state – a revolution led by an ex-fairy!

Wajid Ali Shah composed a sort of erotic autobiography under the title of *Pari Khana*, in Urdu, or, in Persian, *Ishqnamah*, or 'Chronicle of Passion'. This remarkable Manuscript, with its 103 painted miniatures of the King's loves, now sits incongruously in Windsor Castle (it was looted from the Qaisarbagh during the Mutiny and presented to Queen Victoria). One by one, the Fairies parade before the King, sometimes hiding their faces behind fans or even shown from behind, sometimes entertaining the King to dinner in their own quarters. There is no indecency about the catalogue. The only

nakedness is in the way the King records his own oscillating feelings – passion, irritation, coldness, regret.

Wajid Ali was a prolific author in many genres. More than 40
works are attributed to his pen name, 'Akhtar' or 'Star': *thumris*,
romantic love songs usually in Oudh dialect, *ghazals*, traditional
amorous rhymed couplets, *masnavis*, long narrative poems, and *rindis*,
combination of the erotic and the mystical. At Muharram, not only
did he spend freely on alms and food for the poor, he also led the
recitation of mourning songs, *marsiyas*, with his own troupe. Some of
his *marsiyas* are still sung in Muharram ceremonies today. The King
was especially fond of *rahas*, ballets based on the myth of Krishna
dancing to a flute accompanied by milkmaids. Wajid Ali would himself take the part of Krishna with the ladies of the palace as the
milkmaids. During the great fairs, these performances were thrown
open to everyone who came dressed in red-ochre garments. 'Even
old men of eighty would put on red garments and became young
sparks, filling the cups of their old age with the joyous wine of the
King's youthfulness,' Abdul Halim Sharar recalled in *Lucknow: the last
Phase of an Oriental Culture*.[78]

The King's most famous *thumri* took the form of a *babul*, a term
now used in Bollywood movies to denote a song about a newly married daughter leaving home, but here obviously referring to the poet
himself going into exile:

My father! I'm leaving home:
The four bearers lift my palanquin, I'm leaving those who were
    my own;
Your courtyard is now like a mountain,
And the threshold a foreign country;
I leave your house, father, I am going to my beloved.

That song featured in the 1930s movie *Street Singer*, but today
Wajid Ali is perhaps best remembered for his revival of *kathak*, the
ancient school of dramatic dance, which dates back to before the

Mughal conquest of India. It was at Lucknow and under Wajid Ali's energetic patronage that *kathak* was at its most graceful and sinuous. The effect is apparently not unlike flamenco, which may well have been imported to Spain from India by the Romany.

Not surprisingly, the British of Wajid Ali's day did not care for the *kathak*. They associated it with courtesans and lumped all such displays under the contemptuous name of 'nautch', ignoring its refinements described, for example, in the novel *Umrao Jan Ada (Courtesan of Lucknow)*, where the heroine prides herself on her repertoire of song and dance, much of her own composing. In the old days, sahibs and sepoys had attended nautch displays together, but now the padres denounced it.

The genres in which Wajid Ali wrote or sang or drummed or fluted were essentially popular, and this too was repugnant to the sahibs and the padres, who were accustomed to admire art that was reserved for the higher echelons. Even those Residents who were fond of the natives of Lucknow, such as Low and Sleeman, could not really abide the endless festivals and ceremonies and processions, nor the way the religious and the secular were so unnervingly intertwined. They could not get their heads round that mixture of faith and frivolity, of joyful abandon and tearful mourning, of marigolds and sweets and ashes all jumbled up together. The worst was when His Majesty himself appeared in the midst of these ambiguous frolics dressed as a yogi, in saffron robes smeared with ashes and swathed in pearls. It was especially remarkable for a Muslim nawab to be posing as a yogi or Krishna. One of Wajid Ali Shah's legacies to the region was a rich and easy mingling of religious traditions.

It was a relief for British officials to apply themselves to the more seemly task of collecting the taxes now due to them. No longer would the honest *ryot*'s rupees stick to the paws of the Nawab's officers. At last the common people of Oudh would learn to appreciate the virtues of British rule.

Unfortunately, the Summary Settlement of 1856–7 did not work out quite as intended, not to begin with anyway. The first thing that went wrong was that the revenue was always collected in instalments, and the new British collectors began by insisting on collecting the arrears as well as the tax due for the current period. The next snag was inherent in the Modernizers' long-held dream of collecting direct from the individual cultivators and getting rid of the *taluqdars*, the landowners and village-owners, who in their view were grasping parasites. Dealing direct would not only be more socially just and help to level out the inequalities of rural India, it would surely also raise more revenue.[79] Cut out the middleman and how could you fail? Most *taluqdars* lost dozens of villages under the Summary Settlement, and so the natural supporters of the British became a disgruntled class of the expropriated. But even the peasants found that they were now being screwed for more than they could afford. The assessments might be lower in many places than under the Nawab, but the amounts due were now remorselessly extracted down to the last rupee.

The new British officers needed to hit their revenue targets to have any hope of promotion. Every newly acquired province was expected to 'pay'. In times of drought or crop failure, or illness or family bereavement, the British officers had no scope for flexibility, whereas a *taluqdar* could always stretch a point and relax or postpone his full demand. So the one great benefit of annexation – that the people would prefer it – began to look somewhat tarnished. The old methods of collecting taxes – sometimes sleepy, often corrupt and occasionally violent – began to seem in retrospect rather more desirable. Wajid Ali might be away with his fairies, but his negligence had its upside.

Lord Dalhousie went back to Scotland, and Wajid Ali went off to exile outside Calcutta. John Low had seen him first as a 15-year-old boy in the palace at Lucknow, cowering in a side-room with his father and grandfather, while John went off to unseat the Begum's boy from the throne. Now he was to have the bloated ex-King as a neighbour at Garden Reach, only a couple of miles down the Hooghly from Fort William.

Wajid Ali set up his new royal compound at Matiya Burj, or 'Earthen Dome', called after a modest tumulus near the river. There was nothing modest about his establishment. We have a glowing account of it by Abdul Halim Sharar, whose mother's father was one of the King's secretaries and accompanied him into exile. Sharar himself spent his teenage years at Matiya Burj, and all his life he thrilled at the memory of this glittering little 'Lucknow in Bengal'.

Hoping to keep the royal exiles quiet, Dalhousie had awarded them pensions totalling 1.5 million rupees a year. Immediately the King began spending. He built himself a fine classical mansion, the Sultan Khana, on the lines of Metcalfe Hall further up the banks of the Hooghly. He collected musical instruments and musicians, singers and dancers from all over. Soon there were more musicians at Matiya Burj than anywhere else in India. And more animals, too. Wajid Ali was an obsessive zoo-maker. His vast estate – six or seven miles round – was full of lions, tigers, cheetahs, giraffes, herons and flamingos. There was a huge tank full of snakes – claimed to be the first of its kind. Wajid Ali paid sky-high prices for rarities – 24,000 rupees for a pair of silk-winged pigeons, 11,000 rupees for a pair of white peacocks. The zoo had 800 keepers, but then his little town soon had 40,000 exiles in it.

> The real Lucknow had ended and was replaced by Matiya Burj. There was the same bustle and activity, the same style of poetry, conversation and wit, the same learned and pious men, the same aristocrats, nobles and common people. No one thought he was in Bengal: there was the same kite-flying, cock-fighting, quail-fighting, the same opium addicts reciting the same tales, the same observance of Muharram, the same lamentations of *marsiya* and *nauha* as in former Lucknow.[80]

The same easy-going marital arrangements, too. Wajid Ali developed a great taste for the Shia custom of *muta*, temporary but legal marriage. He made it a rule not to look at a woman who was not his temporary wife, so that he felt compelled to marry the young water-carrier who passed him on her way to the women's quarters; she was given the title of Her Highness the Water-Carrier. The same with a girl sweeper he bumped into; she became the Begum Purifier. He formed these temporary wives into a group and had them taught music and dancing. He built houses for them all; the ones who bore children were dubbed Mahal and received separate apartments and extra allowances.

What seemed to Sharar like a transplanted Garden of Eden looked to the British an endless source of trouble – a smelly, overcrowded, lawless enclave where mothers refused to vaccinate their children against smallpox, where the tradesmen – the animal dealers in particular – were never paid, where marauding tigers escaped from their rickety cages, and the King treated his teeming wives and children with coldness and neglect. Wajid Ali Shah did not dispute the last charge. When twitted with spending too much on his menagerie, he conceded that 'I am attached to it with a degree of fondness which far exceeds that I entertain towards my sons, daughters, etc.' As for his steepling debts, the King could and did point out that he had never been repaid the millions of rupees he and his predecessors had lent the Honourable Company to pay for their wars.

The truth was that the mere existence of Wajid Ali Shah's time-warp mini-kingdom was an anomaly and an affront to the tidy-minded, clean-living British, just the sort of thing that made Joseph Dorin sick. (It turned out that Mr Dorin himself had left his wife in Chepstow and, when he returned to England, he brought with him the widow he had been living with and their two sons, who went under the not very brilliant alias of Dorington). The sanctity of marriage seemed even more precious to the British after the Mutiny, when so many of their own wives had undergone such ordeals and death had indeed parted them from their husbands in such horrific circumstances. As for Wajid Ali's *muta* wives, who can say whether their lot was much worse than that of Lord Bath's wifelets or of White House interns under President Kennedy or President Clinton?

Wajid Ali's court survived the Mutiny, though the King himself was confined in nearby Fort William for its duration. After his release, he went on to hold court at Matiya Burj for another 30 years until his death. When he died, the British took the opportunity to throw out the Nawab's followers, who mostly returned to Lucknow in great poverty. Some of the buildings at Matiya Burj (today called Metia Bruz) were demolished, others auctioned off. There was to be no rallying point for another revolt. Only the mosque and the *imambara* were spared, for fear of offending the Muslims.[81]

Another irony is that, of the three personages we have been following through the downfall of the royal house of Oudh, Wajid Ali was the only one left in Calcutta after the annexation had been completed. Lord Dalhousie was already limping home, and General Low followed in his footsteps a month later. As the hot weather of 1856 approached, John set off to England to restore his health and see his family again. He had been separated from Augusta for three years – their longest separation ever – and from the little girls, too, who were now 12 and 11.

After being reunited, the Lows traipsed from Fifeshire to St Leonards and Cheltenham – all of them haunts of old 'Indians' – but John never got any better. He apologized to old Mountstuart Elphinstone, nearly 80 now, for not coming to see him before he returned to India, but 'I did not like to sleep out of my own abode owing to the horrid noise that I make every early morning from my very obstinate cough and I dread the fatigue of going so far as Hookwood [Elphinstone's house was only at Limpsfield, Surrey, barely 20 miles from London] and returning to town the same day – for bodily fatigue aggravates my ailments.'[82]

Was a man in John's condition really fit to carry on as the Military Member of the Supreme Council? Lord Canning, the incoming Governor-General, had been reluctant to grant him the leave: 'One great trouble I foresee will come from Gen Low being about to go home for a time; there will then be no Military Member of Council ... so that all Military details will fall upon me.'[83] Lady

Canning wrote to a friend that 'A number of notabilities go home invalided by this steamer ... the chief being a good old member of Council: General Low, who has six months leave but whom no one expects can return.' John's handwriting was now so quavery, his loops and scrawls so wayward that they even attracted the attention of Canning's biographer.[84]

How could such an old crock think of going back to India at all? He acknowledged that his friends thought the idea very imprudent, but 'my medical friends say that a voyage to Calcutta at this time of year is *better* for my ailments than a sojourn in the winter or spring would be in any part of Great Britain.'[85] Well, expensive doctors will often say what their patients want them to say, and John Low could not resist the 'one year more' of that splendid salary.

But we cannot pretend that he was leaving the military affairs of India in safe hands. For the past five years, the Commander-in-Chief had been Sir William Gomm. Like his predecessor, Lord Gough, General Gomm had preferred to spend much of his time in the hills. He had even put in an application to spend part of his time at Dalhousie's old Shangri-La of Chini. The Governor-General did at least veto that: he knew from experience how long it took to get to and from Chini, and in any case the place lay outside Gomm's command.

It had been a dreadful appointment. The best that Gomm's own Quartermaster-General could say of him was that he was 'quite content to sit inside the coach, and let another drive it'. Even the Chairman of the Court, Sir James Hogg, admitted that, though Gomm was a gentleman, 'he ought not to have been selected for such a command at the age of seventy, and with no recent experience'.[86] Again and again, Dalhousie complained that the Government kept on sending him these very old commanders who knew nothing of India.

Gomm's replacement, George Anson, might be a mere 59 years old, but he had not held a military command since Waterloo, having spent the intervening years as an MP and an agreeable man about town. He had won the Derby in 1842 with a horse called Attila which he had bought for a song, and he was reputed to be the best whist player in Europe. Disraeli quipped that Anson 'had seen the Great Mogul so often on the ace of spades that he would know how to deal with him' (high-quality packs of playing cards then had pictures of the Great Mughal stamped on them).[87] When Anson came out in early 1856, he too headed for the hills, ensuring that like both his predecessors he was a thousand miles away from the Supreme Council which was supposed to take the strategic decisions.

Canning was just as much of a novice in army matters. For most of 1856, the only Military Member of his council was wheezing and coughing in England. General Low was the only man in India both who knew where and how the troops ought to be deployed (he had sent Dalhousie letter after letter on the subject when he was in Ajmer and Hyderabad) and who had the authority to move for their better deployment. But General Low was not there.

What made matters so much worse was that the Supreme Council was not supreme at all. For its supplies of troops, it was dependent on the Court of Directors and the Government. The real danger lay in the chronic imbalance between the numbers of European regiments and the native regiments of the Company. When Dalhousie arrived in India, he had at his disposal a Company army of 247,000; he had only 26,000 European troops and cavalry – a ratio not far short of ten to one.[88] The trouble was that European regiments cost so much more to keep up. A regiment of Royal cavalry cost 712,000 rupees a year; native cavalry only 372,800. Royal infantry and the Company's European infantry both cost about 550,000 rupees per annum to maintain; native infantry cost half that.[89] The Company could not contemplate the expense; the Government could not spare the troops; and the sepoys never ceased to resent their inferior pay and conditions as compared to the Royal troops (it had been one of the grievances that caused the mutiny at Vellore).

Posterity has often accused Dalhousie of complacency. In his part-ing dispatch, he notoriously claimed that he was 'guilty of no presumption in saying that I shall leave the Indian empire at peace without and within.'[90] But he was not an idiot. He was well aware that 'The Government of India has no element of national strength to fall back on in a country where the entire English community is but a handful of scattered strangers . . . amidst distances so vast, amidst multitudes so innumerable, amidst people and sects various in many things, but all alike in this that they are the lately conquered subjects of our race, alien to them in religion, in language, in colour, in habits, in all feelings and interests.' He was only echoing what Lord William Bentinck had written from Madras after the Vellore Mutiny 50 years earlier: 'We are in fact strangers in the land.' Even the Resident was only a temporary resident. They were all camping in another's country.[91]

Dalhousie pleaded again and again with London that European troops should not be withdrawn from India to fight European wars: 'We have not like the Colonies, anything to fall back upon. We must be strong, not against the enemy only, but against our popula-tion, and even against possible contingencies connected with our own Native Army. Again I adjure you not to allow us to be weak-ened in European infantry.'[92]

It is unfair to criticize Dalhousie, as Sir John Kaye does, for doing nothing to correct the imbalance. He sent no less than ten Minutes pleading for more European troops between 1854 and his very last days at Calcutta in February 1856. Between them, Lord Canning and the India House contrived to mislay or at any rate not to publish most of these Minutes, so that in this respect the pile of official post-mortems on the Mutiny did Dalhousie an injustice. Once again, the Blue Books lied by omission.[93]

But in a more important sense, Dalhousie *was* complacent, or at any rate culpably reckless. Because he did not get the extra troops. In fact, the number of the crack Royal troops had actually gone down, from 28,000 in 1852 to 23,000 in 1856, many of them drawn off for service in the Crimea. Worse still, the troops were concentrated in the wrong places. Part of the Army was sailing off to fight in China. The rest of it was deployed everywhere but in Oudh. You did not need to be a military genius to see what was wrong. Mrs Harris, the chaplain's wife at Lucknow, saw it instantly: 'can you conceive the folly of having no European troops at Cawnpore, and only one regiment in Oude – a country of which we have so lately taken unjust possession, and where a rebellion might have been expected any day? Again, at Delhi, not a single European soldier within thirty miles.'[94]

Was this really the moment to embark on all the unnerving changes that Dalhousie had set in train, affecting almost every aspect of Indian economic, social and political life? It was surely a time for caution and small steps. But Dalhousie believed in giant strides. He would not, could not, leave without making a bigger splash than any other Governor-General had ever made.

It was exactly 50 years since the Mutiny at Vellore. The lessons of that terrible massacre and counter-massacre were as pressing as ever. Who had learnt them?

There was no adequate supply of European troops near any of the potential centres of disaffection. There were now half a dozen deposed or mutilated ruling dynasties, whose bitterness could be harnessed to the disaffection of their subjects. Native customs of every sort were being extinguished or threatened (General Anson had already ordered his Muslim sepoys to shave their beards – shades of General Cradock at Vellore).[95] The command structure was the worst possible for rapid deployment. Above all, every warning of trouble was brushed aside. The worst offender of all was Dalhousie, who disregarded his own warnings. As his successor Lord Canning put it sharply a week after the outbreak of the Mutiny: 'We have been blind and stupid to go on annexing Pegu, Nagpore and Oude without adding a single English soldier to our strength. Indeed, we are weaker by two regiments than we were before the Russian War.'[96]

The truth was that Dalhousie wanted to believe that nothing

could ever go seriously wrong. Back in 1850, when Sir Charles Napier, newly appointed Commander-in-Chief, told the Governor-General that the country was in a position of 'great peril' – 24 native regiments were reported to be on the verge of mutiny – Dalhousie pooh-poohed. 'There is no justification for the cry that India was in danger. Free from all threat of hostilities from without, and secure, through the submission of its new subjects, from insurrection within, the safety of India has never for one moment been imperilled by the partial insubordination in the ranks of its army.'[97] Two such imperious spirits could not coexist. Napier resigned, muttering that Dalhousie was 'a poor, petulant man, cunning and sly'.[98] Dalhousie's confidence had been misplaced then, and it was even more misplaced now, as his successor was shortly to find out.

There only needed to be one more little thing, one tiny spark which could be fanned into flame by those who wanted to.

One day in January 1857, at the place the British called Dum-Dum, eight miles outside Calcutta, a low-caste labourer meeting a high-caste sepoy asked him for a drink of water from his brass pot. The Brahmin refused, saying that this would defile the pot. 'You will soon lose your caste altogether,' the labourer retorted, 'for the Europeans are going to make you bite cartridges soaked in cow and pork fat. And then where will your caste be?'[99]

The firearms of the period were loaded through the muzzle with a cartridge composed of a ball and enough powder for a single shot wrapped together in a tube of paper. The sepoy had to bite off the tip, pour the powder down the barrel, then force the rest of the cartridge in with a ramrod. The new Enfield rifle had a grooved bore, which meant that the cartridge paper needed to be greased to go in smoothly. Four years earlier, when the first Enfield cartridges had been sent out to India, old Gomm had been alert enough to warn that the grease must not offend the prejudices of caste. But the Military Board was fatally negligent and failed to specify what type of tallow the sepoys would be biting.

It was never proved that either beef or pork fat had been used in a single cartridge issued to the men at Dum-Dum or anywhere else, but the suspicions refused to die. Even Lord Canning admitted that the grievance about the grease had 'turned out to be well founded'. General Anson mulishly denied it. The cartridge question was 'more a pretext than reality'. He complained that the sepoys had been 'pampered and given way to and had grown insolent beyond bearing'. But Anson did at least cancel target practice until the question was sorted out. Other commanding officers lacked even this much sense.

XVII

1857: THEO, EDWARD, ROBERT, MALCOLM

Theo at Delhi

Theo's eyes were hurting, not for the first time. The pain stayed with him and kept him angry. In Delhi, he had taken to wearing an eyepatch. The natives called him One-eyed Metcalfe to distinguish him from his father. Now the inflammation had flared up and he had applied for three months' leave to go to Kashmir, while little Charlie and the nurse went up to Simla to stay with his sister GG.

At 7am on the morning of May 11 he went down to his office to tidy up and hand over to his assistant. It was not a long trek from Metcalfe House. The courthouse was only just inside the Kashmir Gate. The moment he came in, his assistant told him that the sepoys had mutinied at Meerut the day before. Hundreds of them were marching towards the city.

Theo rushed to the window overlooking the river and the Bridge of Boats, the only way in from the Meerut side. He saw a huge crowd crossing the bridge, mostly native cavalry or *sowars*, their lances glinting in the sun. He jumped into his buggy – a two-wheeled gig with a hood, like the London cabs then – and he galloped to the Calcutta Gate. He stopped for a minute at the Magazine to see if they could bring up a couple of guns to keep the rebels off the bridge, but they looked out of the bastion and they could see it was too late, the cavalry had already crossed the bridge and were too close for the field guns to depress their sights.

At the Calcutta Gate, he found a huddle of the other British officials: his fellow magistrates and the Commissioner, the corpulent Mr Simon Fraser. Theo did not know it then, but Fraser had had an early alarm of trouble. The night before, a mounted police sergeant had ridden like the devil from Meerut with a warning letter, but Fraser had already fallen asleep in his chair after dinner. Even after the sergeant called to him several times, he merely grunted, put the letter in his pocket and went back to sleep.[1] Now Fraser and the others had managed to close the gates and put up the barricades, only just in time. They could hear the tramp of the Meerut men on the bridge, and then their battering at the gates. They can't have had any battering rams, because they turned off down to the left, and Theo could hear the shuffle of their hooves on the dry sand of the riverbed under the walls of the Red Fort, where the King was.

'You had better drive round and secure the little water gate,' Fraser said, now wide awake and full of belated decision. It was the last thing he ever said to Theo.

When Theo was only halfway along the great red walls of the Palace, he met hundreds of mutineers galloping towards him out of the Lahore Gate, flourishing their swords and shouting hoarse, delirious cries. Half a dozen of them caught sight of One-eyed Metcalfe, recognized him perhaps or saw only another European, and they rushed towards him, slashing at the buggy, but all they cut was the leather hood.

In front of him Theo saw an enormous mob already collected on the open ground in front of the Lahore Gate. 'They were all dressed in white,' he said, 'as if in expectation of a gala day.' There, in that one glance, the scale of the mutiny became horribly clear. Somehow the *sowars* had already got into the Palace from the river side and charged through its gorgeous courts, its gates flung open by ecstatic Palace guards, and now they were coming out the other side towards the main street, Chandni Chowk, where a festive crowd was waiting to greet them and cheer them on. Everyone *knew*, everyone but the British.

The Mutiny brought home to the British just how little they really knew about the people they were governing. Captain E.M. Martineau, the Depot Commander at Ambala, reflected: 'I see them on parade for say two hours daily, but what do I know of them for the other 22? What do they talk about in their lines, what do they plot … For all I can tell I might as well be in Siberia.'[2] Roderick Edwards, the bold magistrate at Saharanpur, wrote on hearing the bad news, 'Our very servants might be plotting our death and anni-hilation with every description of atrocity and we be in perfect ignorance of it. Not until now had we ever really felt how utterly we were excluded from the "inner life" of the people. Not until now had I ever felt what *real intense* fear was.'[3] At once Theo could see that this was not simply a few disgruntled sepoys on the rampage. He was seeing the beginnings of a national revolt.

Sir Theophilus Metcalfe was the last Englishman in India to be surprised. He had been pessimistic about the future for a long time, probably since the terrible days of Charlotte's dying at Simla. Only a month earlier, he had said to his friend Osborn Wilkinson, who was returning to England, 'Goodbye old fellow, you are lucky in going home, for we shall soon be kicked out of India, or we shall have to fight to the death for our existence.'[4] On March 18, he had seen a dirty sheet of paper stuck up on the back wall of the great mosque, the Jama Masjid, purporting to be a message from the Shah of Iran, proclaiming that the Persian Army was coming to liberate Delhi from the infidels. With typical ferocity, Theo tore it down and tram-pled it underfoot in front of an awestruck crowd.

Before that, in February, there had been the mysterious distribu-tion of the chupattis. One watchman would bring one of those little pancakes to the watchman of the next village, instructing him to make five more and distribute those to watchmen in five more villages, so that the message would spread across the country like a chain letter. But what was the message? Theo had asked their family friend, Mainodin Hassan Khan, the Police Superintendent at the south-west suburb of Paharganj, what it meant. Mainodin said that his father had told him that, just before the downfall of the Maratha Empire, sprigs of millet and morsels of bread had passed from village to village in the same way and that the chupattis too must presage some great impending disturbance.[5] There was the rumour, too, in the bazaars that the Empire of the Feringhee was destined to fall exactly one hundred years after it had begun, and the centenary of the Battle of Plassey was on June 23.

If you were looking for harder evidence, you had only to look at the Calcutta money markets, like markets anywhere the first to pick up vibrations of trouble. At the end of 1856, Captain Rawlins, Adjutant of the 44th Native Infantry, noticed that all his native officers had cashed in their Company bonds in favour of gold mohurs. He got only evasive answers from the officers and reported the mysterious trend to his Colonel, who passed it on to the Lieutenant-Governor, John Low's old adversary John Russell Colvin, who was much agitated by the news and said he would put his secret agents on the case. But whatever information they dredged up was lost in the swirl of events.[6]

Nor was Meerut the first station to erupt. Over to the east, at Berhampur, the 19th Native Infantry, and at Barrackpore, ominously near Calcutta, the 34th had protested in February against the new cartridges. After elaborate but fruitless negotiations, both regiments had been disbanded, and the sepoys returned to their villages weeping and humiliated. The two regiments had, it seemed, conspired to inflame one another. And they had sent a signal to the whole of northern India. A few days after the story of the greased cartridges had first surfaced at nearby Dum-Dum, the telegraph station at Barrackpore was burnt down. Soon fires were breaking out along the line as far as Raniganj, the terminus of the new railway from Calcutta which Lord Dalhousie had opened two years earlier. In no time, the news from Barrackpore was zinging along the line all the way to the Punjab. The sepoys were using the feringhee's own technology to spread the word. Theo felt as if he was the only Englishman who was really listening to events. He passed on all the warnings to the proper quarters, and the proper quarters nodded and ignored them and, like Mr Simon Fraser, resumed their slumbers.

Why did the outbreak which turned out to be catastrophic happen at Meerut, 800 miles to the west, at a big military centre where not one but two of those scarce British regiments were garrisoned, the 60th Rifles and the 6th Dragoon Guards? As W.W. Ireland, the Assistant Surgeon, pointed out, Meerut was 'the only cantonment in India where European force was stronger than the native'.[7] Any outbreak in that British stronghold ought to have been relatively easy to contain and suppress.

Hundreds of miles further to the west in the Punjab, there was far more reason to be anxious. At Peshawar, there were 8,000 native troops and no more than 2,000 Europeans. But there, the Chief Commissioner, Sir John Lawrence, the fiercest of the three famous Lawrence brothers, acted with ruthless rapidity. The moment they heard on May 12 that Meerut was ablaze, he and his equally ruthless assistants, Herbert Edwardes and John Nicholson, knew what they must do. The only way to be sure of keeping control was to disarm and disband the sepoys before they had time to organize. Surprise was crucial. To allay any suspicion, the regimental ball must go ahead. Lieutenant Arthur Lang of the Engineers described the evening as 'a perfect sham of smiles over tears. Half the Ladies were not present and those who were there could scarcely disguise their anxiety.'[8] The next morning was agonizingly tense.

'We were riding within a few yards of the line and could see every face and hear every murmur, but not a sound. Then came the critical moment. "Order the 16th to pile arms." I looked at the unfortunate Native Infantry officers amongst their men. We could have escaped with but one volley, for we were on horseback, and could have joined the Horse Artillery, but what would they have done? "Grenadiers, shoulder arms." Done. "Ground arms." Done. "Pile arms." A moment's hesitation, a few men began to pile: a look at the black Artillery muzzles must have been decisive: all piled arms. "Stand from your arms ... Quick march." Away they went unarmed, the clusters of bayonets glittering under the morning sun, marking where they had stood and showing their obedience.'[9]

As the piles of arms grew higher on the parade ground, and the sobbing sepoys shuffled away, some of their English officers were so moved by the spectacle of degradation that they threw their own swords and spurs upon the discarded muskets and sabres to show their sympathy with the sepoys. Edwardes reported that this shocking insubordination would have incurred serious punishment, 'had it been prudent to exhibit such a division in the European element in the eyes of the Native troops and the people of this country.'[10]

Lawrence and Nicholson were two of the hardest men who ever lived. Disarmed and disbanded sepoys might be full of rancour and vengeance, but they had no weapons and no officers. All his time in India (he was still only 34), the newly promoted Brigadier Nicholson had doubted the loyalty of the sepoy. In his view, 'neither greased cartridges, the annexation of Oudh nor the paucity of European officers were the causes. For years, I have watched the army and felt sure they only wanted their opportunity to test their strength with us.'[11]

To his fellow officers, Nicholson was the most memorable man they ever met. He had been the youngest British officer in the Afghan War, at the end of which he had been among the prisoners who were shepherded to safety by Richmond Shakespear. Now in physical terms alone, he had grown into an imposing figure: a massive Ulster Protestant, 6ft 2ins tall, with a long, black beard and a wonderful sonorous voice and 'dark grey eyes with black pupils which under excitement would dilate like a tiger's, a colourless face over which no smile ever passed'. His language was rough and sarcastic, but he inspired unbreakable loyalty on closer acquaintance, not least from his native troops who adored him, literally, to the point of idolatry, for there grew up a mysterious cult of 'Nickalsain' among the natives which lasted long after his death. His stern sense of duty had expunged the word 'mercy' from his vocabulary, according to the awestruck Ensign Wilberforce of the 52nd Light Infantry.[12] In Nicholson's view, hanging was too good for those who had murdered women and children: 'If I had them in my power, I would inflict the most excruciating tortures I could think of on them with a perfectly easy conscience.'[13]

Those who had begun to mutiny in the Punjab could expect no mercy. After the disarming parade of May 24 came the punishment parade of June 10. Forty selected mutineers of the 55th were blown away from guns – a spectacle so horrific that neither Edwardes nor the men's Commanding Officer, Sydney Cotton, says a word about it in their reports. But it did the trick. The other troops on the parade ground remained 'steady'. In Sir John Kaye's words, 'to our newly raised levies and to the curious onlookers from the country, the whole spectacle was a marvel and a mystery. It was a wonderful display of moral force, and it made a deep and abiding impression.'[14] The Punjab was cowed and stayed cowed, and Nicholson was free to lead a mobile column of troops down the Grand Trunk Road to rescue Delhi. The word of his merciless brutality went before him, as a grateful Lord Canning put it, 'sweeping the country like the incarnation of vengeance' and striking terror into wavering hearts.

But at Meerut there had been no such ferocity, no dash, no decision. The Colonel of the 3rd Light Cavalry was George Carmichael-Smyth, the youngest brother of Thackeray's stepfather. He was a standoffish, contentious type, not much liked by his officers or his men. When he heard there had been disturbances at other stations over the new cartridges, he decided to hold a parade to give the sepoys what he thought was the good news, that they would not be forced to bite off the ends of the cartridges but instead could tear them off with their fingers. Even an 18-year-old cornet in the regiment, John Macnabb, could see what a silly idea this was. He wrote to his mother: 'There was no necessity to have a parade at all or to make any fuss of the sort just now. No other Colonel thought of doing such a thing, as they knew at this unsettled time their men would refuse to be the first to fire the cartridges.'[15]

The men did refuse, or 85 of them did. So under the inflexible logic of the Army they had to be court-martialled and sentenced to imprisonment with hard labour for ten years. At a terrible parade in front of all the troops stationed at Meerut, the men were stripped of their uniforms, their boots removed, their ankles shackled in leg-irons before they were led off to gaol. When Lieutenant Hugh Gough visited them to settle up their pay, at first they seemed sullen or impassive, but 'once they began to realize all they were losing, and the terrible future before them, they broke down completely. Old soldiers, with many medals gained in desperately fought battles for their English masters, wept bitterly, lamenting their sad fate, and imploring their officers to save them from their future; young soldiers, too, joined in, and I have seldom, if ever, in all my life, experienced a more touching scene.'[16]

Hugh Gough went back to sit on the verandah of his bungalow. A native officer came up to him and, under pretext of discussing the accounts, told him that the native troops at Meerut were going to mutiny tomorrow. Gough rushed to tell Carmichael-Smyth, who treated him with contempt. That same evening, he told the Brigadier, Archdale Wilson, but he was incredulous too. He even told the Major-General commanding the Meerut Division, 'Bloody Bill' Hewitt, a hugely fat sluggard, whom even Archdale Wilson condemned as 'a fearful old dolt'. None of Gough's superior officers dreamed of taking any preventive action, let alone of disarming the men.

The next day was Sunday and in the early morning they all drove off to church. Gough remembered young Macnabb's frock coat 'of alpaca, but with the wrong lace'. He told him he must correct it, or Carmichael-Smyth would find fault. It was by the frock coat and the wrong lace that Gough identified Macnabb's body that same evening.

At five o'clock that evening, Gough's servants came running to tell him that the bungalows were on fire and the Europeans were all being murdered. Major-General Hewitt, having utterly failed to forestall the mutiny, now utterly failed to suppress it. In Gough's words, he seemed completely unmanned to the point of paralysis. It took him an age to grasp the simple fact that, having torched the bungalows and murdered all the white men, women and children they could lay their hands on, the sepoys had all left Meerut and were now on their way to Delhi to pay homage to their King. He did not think of sending a single squadron after them. All he could think of was protecting the station. He gathered the whole of his force on the European parade ground and there they bivouacked for the night, surrounded by the smoking ruins and the corpses of their fellow countrymen. By the morning, 2,000 native cavalrymen were crossing the Bridge of Boats into Delhi.

It was weeks before Hewitt was sacked, and not until July 16 that he passed through Muzaffarnagar on his way to leave in the hills. The General made a deplorable impression on Roderick Edwards, the feisty magistrate now posted there: 'Old Hewitt is nervous and useless and past all work ... He had been sitting for a long time with his head resting upon his hand and I had been internally pitying him thinking his being superseded was preying on his mind, when all of a sudden he jumped up, struck his hand vehemently on the table while his eyes were lighted up with an expression of delighted surprise as he called out, "By Jove, that's capital, I forgot there's the ham sandwiches"!!! I was able to give him a bottle of beer and he was happy.'[17]

It was as clear as anything could be in that smoking chaos that if the Meerut cantonment had not been commanded by three such superannuated fools as Carmichael-Smyth, Archdale Wilson and Hewitt, the 3rd Light Cavalry would have never have got as far as mutinying and even if they had, they would never have got as far as Delhi. Was there no one, Lord Canning wailed, to do with the Carabineers and the Horse Artillery what Gillespie, half a century

before, had done with his Dragoons and galloper guns? If this was
what happened at stations where English officers had English cavalry
and artillery to help them, what would happen at stations where they
had none?[18]

From Calcutta 800 miles away, there came a stream of good
advice. Lord Canning declared himself in favour of disbanding any
regiment that showed signs of disaffection. Mr Dorin, the one who
had never been more than 16 miles outside Calcutta, pronounced
that 'the sooner this epidemic of mutiny is put a stop to, the better.'
Put a stop to with what? Lord Canning pleaded for reinforcements
from Lord Elgin, whose punitive expedition to China was still within
hailing distance:

> Our hold of Bengal and the Upper Provinces depends upon the
> turn of a word – a look. An indiscreet act or irritating phrase from
> a foolish commanding officer at the head of a mutinous or disaf-
> fected company, may, whilst the present condition of things at
> Delhi lasts, lead to a general rising of the Native troops in the
> Lower Provinces, where we have no European strength, and
> where an army in rebellion would have everything its own way for
> weeks and months to come.[19]

It was true, and it was pitiful. Not often can the Governor-
General of a vast Empire have made such an admission of impotence.

John Low agreed for disbandment, but as for the cartridges, 'probably the main body of this regiment in refusing to bite the cartridges
did so refuse, not from any feeling of disloyalty or disaffection
towards the government or their officers but from an unfeigned and
sincere dread . . . that the act of biting them would involve a serious
injury to their caste and to their future respectability of character . . .
If they were to bite those cartridges, they would be guilty of a
heinous sin.'[20]

Which might be true enough, but it was too late. While Canning
and Low were composing their Minutes, the bungalows at Meerut

were ablaze and the bodies of the women and children already lay
bleeding on the verandahs. As the office boxes were passing from
house to house in Calcutta, in amongst those thoughtful Minutes
there was a slip of a telegraph message from Agra giving the awful
news from Meerut. The last message to get through before the wires
were cut was from the postmaster's sister to her aunt in Agra, warning her not to come for her visit because the cavalry had risen. Even
the communications now hung by a thread.

The news of the outbreak at Meerut had reached Canning on
May 12. Over the next two days, cables from Agra added more terrifying detail. Delhi was in the hands of the rebels, Bahadur Shah II
was proclaimed Emperor, many Europeans had been killed. What
was to be done? Canning's Council was split, although this demoralizing fact did not leak into the public domain: the Civil Members
thought that the attack on Delhi should be delayed until substantial
reinforcements could be brought up; it would be folly to lock up all
the pitifully thin European forces under the walls of Delhi, while the
rest of the country was left exposed to the rampages of the rebels.

General Low thought differently: Delhi must come first. And he
drew up a Minute 'full of sound arguments in favour of an immediate effort to recover the lost position'.[21] But Canning needed no
convincing. The Governor-General saw instantly that the imperial
Mughal capital had become the heart of the rebellion. And he fired
off messages to Colvin in Agra and fat old General Hewitt in
Meerut, impressing on them that 'it is of the utmost importance that
Delhi should not remain an hour longer in the hands of the insurgents than can possibly be avoided.'[22]

Theo rode full tilt into the mob, then jumped out of the buggy and
elbowed his way through the crowd into the lanes, where he pulled
off his dark coat and trousers which marked him out from the white-
robed crowd, and ran on in his white shirt and under-drawers. He
saw a group of mounted police waiting under some trees and he
ordered them to charge the pursuing mutineers. The police refused

to budge. Theo seized their captain, threw him out of the saddle, grabbed the reins and jumped on the horse himself, a one-eyed giant as strong as Polyphemus. He kicked off in the direction of the bazaar but was blocked that way, so he turned off towards the Ajmer Gate and the refuge of Mainodin's police station outside the walls.[23]

Somewhere near the great mosque, a large stone or brick thrown from an upper window hit him on the shoulder near the spine and knocked him off the horse. He rolled into a ditch and lay unconscious there, for how long, he could not be sure. When he woke up, he saw his horse still grazing a few yards away. He clambered back on, and horse and rider staggered on through the back ways to the Ajmer Gate.[24] As he stumbled through the gate, he saw the body of his friend Dr Topping lying in a pool of blood.

Mainodin's police station was not that far away, and soon the loyal superintendent was saluting the herculean figure of the Joint Magistrate, noticing in the same moment that he was clad only in his shirt and drawers. Mainodin togged him out in a suit of native civilian clothes and gave him a fine sword.[25] Theo's first thought was to go back to Metcalfe House and collect the 13,000 rupees in notes and gold which he had hidden in his bedroom. Mainodin said this would be madness, Sir Theophilus would be better off sheltering in his brother's house where his tribesmen would protect him. Theo said, 'My duty is with the troops. It may be that by this time I am the only civil officer alive. It is not fitting that I should think of personal safety, while there is a military force near at hand to restore order.'[26] If nothing else, this mutiny would make a soldier of him at last.

Theo's estimate was not far from the truth. All the officers who had huddled at the Calcutta Gate now lay murdered in the streets. All the Europeans inside the Palace had been killed: Captain Douglas, the Commandant of the Palace Guard (the Captain Douglas who had chaperoned Edward and GG while they sang parlour songs at Dr Grant's piano), the egregious Padre Jennings and his family, and with them the dozy Commissioner Fraser, who had lumbered along to the Red Fort to attempt to rouse the guard. By

10am that terrible morning, the massacre of the leading British officials in the city was complete, though there were still Europeans hiding in cellars or in the tall grass beyond the city walls. The last figure of authority left standing was now fleeing through the suburbs disguised as a native.

Mainodin took Theo on to the house of a local landowner called Bhura Khan Mewati. Mainodin didn't even know the man, but he was said to be fearless and upright. As soon as he recognized 'Mutculub Saheb' – the local corruption of Metcalfe – he offered to help him, saying to Mainodin, 'Your friends are my friends.' A bed was arranged for Theo on the roof of Bhura Khan's *zenana*. For three days he lay there, recovering from his bruises. In the evening, he and Bhura Khan walked out towards the city, which was about three miles away, to watch the fireworks lighting up the sky to celebrate the destruction of British power. Each day, Theo expected to hear news that the British troops from Meerut were on their way, but all that happened was that on the fourth day Bhura Khan told him that he had been tracked down and would have to move to a new hiding place.

At dusk, Bhura Khan took him to a limestone pit where they quarried material for road-making. There was a small cave in the quarry with an even smaller entrance. In this miserable lair, Theo crouched for a couple of days, Polyphemus in his cave, gigantic and boiling for revenge. Even here he was not safe. The second night he heard footsteps outside the cave. There was enough light to see the outline of the figure in the entrance and Theo cut him down with his *tulwar*, and then slashed again at a second figure, or perhaps it was the first one coming back for more.[27]

Again Bhura Khan came to help him and brought him a fresh disguise. This time Theo was to be a *sowar*, a native cavalryman riding on a native saddle, with his feet naked and stained the colour of native feet and his face tied up in a *sowar* headcloth. If he wanted to get a message to Mainodin, he was to say it came from 'Shere Khan' – the Lion King, a piquant alias for an abject fugitive. In this rig, on the fine pony that Bhura Khan had given him, he managed to reach the Palace of the Nawab of Jhajjar, like Mainodin an old friend of the Metcalfe family and a fellow patron with Sir Thomas of the Company School of Artists who had painted the lovely *Delhie Book*.[28]

This civilized potentate turned out to be a false friend. Like many another merchant and raja and native official (including Mainodin himself), he was hoping to keep in with both sides, positioning himself for any turn of events. At first he said that Theo could shelter in his palace but that he himself could not possibly see him or he would be attacked by the King of Delhi for sheltering Europeans. Finally, when Theo persisted, he offered him a horse and a guard of two soldiers to show him the way back to Delhi. As the Nawab was aware that Theo knew the way back to Delhi as well as his soldiers did, sending the escort was obviously not a friendly act. Their secret orders may well have been to hand him over to the King's men and claim credit for the Nawab for bringing him in.

Theo made the two soldiers ride in front of him, and then after night had fallen, he turned off into the sandy jungle and rode as fast as he could away from Delhi, towards Hansi 70 miles away, where he hoped to find refuge with Alec Skinner, youngest son of Colonel James Skinner.

The wretched pony the Nawab had given him was not a patch on Bhura Khan's, and it soon collapsed, leaving Theo to walk day and night, sleep in the jungle and beg milk and chupattis off the villagers he met. As he was thankfully gobbling up whatever they could spare him, he listened to the villagers talking among themselves. For the first time in his frantic escape, he heard the natives' view. They were discussing, with equanimity if not exhilaration, how the Europeans – the *saheb-log* – had all been killed and how the King of Delhi had taken over the government.

Mark Thornhill, the magistrate at Mathura, an ancient holy city between Delhi and Agra, describes a similar moment in his wonderful account, *The Personal Adventures and Experiences of a Magistrate during the Rise, Progress and Suppression of the Indian Mutiny* (1884). He had just heard the news of the rising at Meerut. The main body of sepoys was now said to be advancing towards Mathura. Thornhill immediately decided to send the women and children away to the great fort at Agra. After they had gone, he went down to his office and told his native staff the news which he had hitherto kept from them: 'they expressed great astonishment; but ere long I perceived from the remarks they let fall that they had heard it all before, and, indeed, as regarded what had occurred at Delhi that they were much better informed than I was.'[29] Just as Theo had when he saw the crowd in white robes already assembled outside the King's Palace, Thornhill had the eerie realization that the natives all *knew*.

The papers had all been tidied up, and there was nothing left for Thornhill to do. 'However, to while away the time, I continued to chat with them about the events at Delhi. They soon got so interested in the subject as partly to forget my presence. Their talk was all about the ceremonial of the Palace, and how it would be revived. They speculated as to who would be the Grand Chamberlain, which of the chiefs of Rajpootana would guard the different gates, and who were the fifty-two Rajahs who would assemble to place the Emperor on the throne.'

This casual talk was a revelation to the British magistrate. 'As I listened, I realized, as I had never done before, the deep impression that the splendour of the ancient court had made on the popular imagination, how dear to them were its traditions, and how faithfully all unknown to us they had preserved them. There was something weird in the Mogul Empire thus starting into a sort of phantom life after the slumber of a hundred years.'[30]

That exhilaration is blocked out from most European accounts, which are understandably preoccupied with massacre and retribution. The exhilaration was mixed with apprehension, though. In Delhi, the fear of the licentious roving sepoys – unpredictable easterners from Oudh – led people of all classes to hide their valuables and keep to their houses. The shops shut and the fleeter-footed merchants fled the city. But out in the country, the mutineers often received a real welcome. When the rebel troops swept into Mathura after the bankers and the police had quit the place, Thornhill recorded that 'the inhabitants, left to themselves, went out in a body to meet the army. They carried an offering of flowers and sweetmeats, and were preceded by a troop of Brahmins singing hymns. On reaching the mutineers they welcomed them as their deliverers, and conducted them into the city with every demonstration of delight.'[31] At Meerut, the butchers and vegetable sellers, the weavers, the grooms and the grasscutters had gleefully joined in the havoc.[32]

After Nana Sahib's troops had chased the British out of Cawnpore, he led a grand procession back the short distance to his palace at Bithur at an auspicious hour chosen for him by the royal astrologer. Hundreds of clay lamps illuminated the road. Bithur itself was gay with flags and floral arches as the caparisoned elephants entered to the sound of drums and flutes. The site of the Peshwa's long exile had become the place of his return, the counterpart to Baji Rao's ignominious exit from Poona 40 years earlier. A wandering young Brahmin priest up from the Peshwa's old dominions was awestruck by the splendour of the spectacle, not least by the lavish feasts laid on for the Brahmins who performed the holy rites. This Te Deum celebrated a victory which was as much religious as it was national.[33]

According to Thornhill, 'no one regretted the loss of our rule; and, with the exception of the Bunniahs [moneylenders], who suffered by it, all classes enjoyed the confusion.'[34] A large landholder told him that 'the last three months had been the happiest of his life'. But the real surprise was that 'very similar sentiments were expressed by the peasant cultivators, and by that still lower class who, of all others, had especially benefited from our rule.' They liked the freedom and the excitement and paying no land taxes. John Low's prophesy 20 years earlier that even the peasants would not be grateful for the British reforms was now being fulfilled.

Even a spectator like Thornhill found the change in the appearance of the country very agreeable. 'From the monotony of modern civilization it had reverted to the wildness, the picturesqueness that we associate with the feudal ages.' In every village, fortifications sprang up, the grandees resumed their ancient state, and sallied forth at the head of colourful cavalcades, followed by crowds carrying swords and spears. 'Life was now for them full of poetry, full of romance.'[35]

In order to press on towards Hansi, it was necessary for Theo to return to the high road. Behind him he heard the sound of galloping hooves, and he turned round to see two horsemen in the Nawab's livery approaching. His only hope was to go into the village just ahead, otherwise a risky option, as most of the local villagers had been far from friendly. It was high noon and hellish hot. Theo saw a group of recumbent sleepers at the roadside wrapped in their robes from head to toe to keep off the dust and the sun. He lay down amongst them and pretended to be asleep. A few minutes later, the two cavalrymen clattered up, shouting, where was the Englishman hiding. One of them prodded the man next to Theo with his lance and asked again. The indignant sleeper swore at him, and said no sahib had passed that way. The two horsemen galloped off, and Theo had survived once again, saved by the Indian siesta. It is a piquant scene: the arrogant Magistrate, accustomed to towering above the natives and shouting orders at them, now relieved to prostrate himself amongst them on a dusty roadside.

Even at Hansi, Theo was not safe. He borrowed a horse from Alec Skinner and set off at dawn the next day, riding non-stop another 70 miles to the British camp at Karnal. The week after, the troops in Hansi mutinied, too, and Alec and his old Muslim mother had to flee to the Raja of Bikaner on the back of a single camel. Colonel Skinner was himself half-Indian and is said to have had 16 native wives and mistresses.

The morning after he reached Karnal, Theo wrote to Mark Thornhill's brother, who was Secretary to the Lieutenant-Governor at Agra: 'although my health is not very good, I write to beg that the Lieutenant Governor will allow me to accompany the force and the

Commander-in-Chief to Delhi in some official capacity; and I trust what local information I possess of the Delhi town and district may be of service to government.'[36] He could claim to be 'the only European who has escaped from Delhi and who was present at the taking of the town by the troopers of the Third Cavalry'. His knowledge of the lanes and villages in and around the city was precious and now unique.

He brought something else with him: a volcanic rage against the natives and against India as a whole. His wife had died in this vile country, the natives had poisoned his father, his beautiful house had been smashed and looted, his friends and colleagues murdered in the streets, their wives and children cut down on their verandahs, and he himself had suffered the humiliation and betrayal of a refugee. Vengeance was not going to be left to the Lord, let alone the law. Theophilus Metcalfe would repay.

He had joined the right outfit. The mobile column had now been given the grandiose title of the Delhi Field Force. It had only 600 cavalry and 2,400 infantry, plus a siege train of 50 guns, but it made up in ferocity what it lacked in numbers. As it lumbered down the Grand Trunk Road towards Delhi, it was already 'hanging niggers' (all delicacy of language had fled) from the nearest tree, or shooting them as they fled into the jungle or tried to swim out of range across the rivers. This had the hearty approval of their mesmerizing commander. John Nicholson had no patience with the flummery of trials or evidence. The penalty for mutiny was death, instantly administered. Theo joined the lynching with, well, a vengeance is the only word. Richard Barter, a lieutenant with the 75th Gordon Highlanders, though himself an Irishman from Cooldaniel, Co. Cork, describes how the foot of a little white child, cut off at the ankle and still in its shoe, was brought into camp in the heat of the afternoon as he lay asleep in his tent:

Immediately after, there arose the hum of voices like the sound of some huge bee-hive disturbed, there was a rush of many feet, and in an incredibly short space of time every village within reach of the camp was in a blaze; several officers joined in the perform-ance.[37]

Nine villagers were hanged from a tree by the road after parade that evening. The retribution had begun.

The first regiment selected to move down to recapture Delhi were the famous Guides under their exuberant commander, Captain Henry Daly, who was delighted with this honour. He wrote on June 1, 'I am making and mean to make the best march that has been heard of in the land!' The Guides belted on down the Grand Trunk Road from Ludhiana to Ambala. By June 6 they were in Karnal. There Daly met Theo, who was panting for revenge and insisted that the Guides should turn aside to punish the neighbouring villages, which he claimed were swarming with insurgents. Daly at first said no, their mission was to push on and take Delhi. Theo persisted in his forceful, high-handed way, and Daly gave in. 'The villagers fled in dismay; some were killed on the retreat, others were made pris-oners; and soon the blaze of their burning houses could be seen for many a mile.'[38] Daly refused to kill the women and children. The day's delay meant that the Guides missed the Battle of Badli-ki-Serai, where they would have come in handy. This was the first occasion on which Theo's thirst for revenge trumped everything else. It was not to be the last.

Edward: a sapper's war

Edward Thackeray had only arrived in India in January 1857 on the *SS Ripon,* fresh out of Addiscombe and Chatham. He was just 20, a tall and reserved boy, whose manner seemed as lofty as his physical stature. His nickname at Addiscombe had been Lord Tallboot – his second name was Talbot. But he was by temperament a good-natured gentle soul, like his father the Reverend Francis Thackeray. His brother, Francis St John, was also a clergyman, both of them classical scholars. Edward was Augusta's first cousin twice over – his mother had been John Talbot Shakespear's sister Mary Anne. So he was first cousin, too, to William Makepeace Thackeray, who was fond of the boy and helped get him into Addiscombe College. To the Lows, Edward was known as The Silent Friend, but on paper he was open-hearted and capable of eloquence – the Thackerays were, after all, a literary clan.

His first posting was to the Bengal Sappers and Miners at Roorkee, the depot at the head of the Ganges Canal, which now stretched hundreds of miles southwards between the Ganges and the Yamuna, irrigating the wonderfully fertile tongue of land known as the Doab.

At 8am on the morning of May 13, Edward was gossiping with a couple of fellow lieutenants outside their bungalows, idly inspecting a pony which someone was trying to sell them, when another lieutenant rode up and called out: 'Have you heard the news? We are to march to Meerut this afternoon.' By 6pm that evening, 500 native

sappers and nine British officers were marched down to the landing
stage and embarked on whatever boats could be patched up in time.
None of them had a clue what had happened. Some sort of local
riot, Edward had the impression.[39]

The canal was mostly used by construction traffic, and it was an
agreeably novel sensation to be part of this impromptu flotilla, the
men rowing with the current, the white peaks of the Himalayas
behind them and the sappers chanting '*Gunga Jee Ka Jai*' (victory to
holy Ganges) for good luck every time they passed under a bridge. In
the morning of the second day, they passed a European driving furiously along the left side of the canal in a buggy, an Irishman whom
they recognized as an overseer in the Irrigation Department. The
sappers hailed him, but he wouldn't stop, shouting as he whipped his
horse on towards Roorkee, 'they're cottin' throats in Meerut like
mad, and burnin' 'ouses.' Then the boats began to overtake the
corpses floating in the canal. Most of the bodies had gashes in the
head, suggesting that they had been whacked by lathis, the iron-
bound sticks that were the local weapon of choice.

When they got to Meerut, Edward wrote to his brother, the
Reverend St John:

> My dear brother, I congratulate you extremely on your success
> in getting a fellowship [at Lincoln College, Oxford]. I assure you
> I was so pleased to hear it, especially just starting on the march.
> We knew nothing till we got here. We were astounded by the
> dreadful news we got on arriving. We marched in between
> European regiments, the Carabineers (Queens) and 60th Rifles.
> The men were standing ready at their guns.

He told his brother about the slaughter and the burning of the
bungalows.

> We never stir without revolvers and swords. I hope, dear St
> John, you will not be alarmed about me. I am very happy and

put my trust in a good Providence. The sappers, I do not think, will ever mutiny.

Thank William Thackeray for his very useful present to me of a revolver.

The novelist had sent him £10 'to buy a saddle or a telescope or a revolver'. Edward's choice of the fine Tranter revolver with its dual-action trigger was going to come in useful sooner than expected (it was a lucky weapon – he had it stolen twice during the Mutiny but got it back again both times). His next letter to St John begins:

I am sorry to tell you that the day after I wrote to you, the Sappers and Miners, natives, mutinied. They shot poor Captain Fraser, our Commanding Officer, and fled. The Adjutant ran the gauntlet of the whole line. The Carabineers and Artillery pursued them and cut down fifty or sixty.

Like many another subaltern, Edward had been convinced until the last moment that *his* sepoys would never desert. And he was flabbergasted by the casual way they did it, without any visible warning at all. He had been sent out on the morning of May 16 to take a party of 90 sappers to demolish some old walls along the side of the road, which might offer cover to any rebel party making a sortie back from Delhi.

The sun beat down fiercely on our little party, and the hot wind felt like the air from a furnace as we passed through the deserted and blackened remains of the bungalows. As we passed through the streets of the bazaar, the natives peered over the walls at us, and I remarked to the sergeant on their furtive and scowling looks.

The sappers set about knocking down the walls willingly enough. Then about 3pm, Edward heard bugles blowing at the cantonment

behind them. At the same moment, a trooper of the 3rd Light
Cavalry (the original mutineers) came galloping past, his horse's
mouth and flanks lathered with foam. The trooper waved in the
direction of Delhi with his sword, and in the instant that Edward
turned from this frantic horseman to look at his diggers, he saw
them laying down their picks and shovels and running to the piles
of muskets and grabbing their arms. Before he could say a word,
they were pelting off after the trooper in the Delhi direction.
Edward managed to get the bugler to blow and with the help of his
European sergeants he persuaded 36 of the men to fall in by bran-
dishing the novelist's pistol. By then, the rest of them were a cloud
of dust on the Delhi road. Later that afternoon they were followed
by most of the other 500 sappers in the cantonment. Was it a pre-
arranged signal, or had they scarpered on impulse? There seemed
such a random divide between the sappers who rebelled and those
who stayed behind. The loyal handful stuck with the British
throughout the worst days of the siege of Delhi. By the end of it,
they were the only Hindus from Lower India still serving with the
British Army.

Edward's confidence in the loyalty of his sappers and his astonishment when they mutinied were typical. As Adelaide Case, the wife
of the colonel of the 32nd at Lucknow, reflected: 'the extraordinary
infatuation of officers in native corps never choosing to believe it
possible that their regiments could prove faithless, is one of the most
remarkable features in the whole of this mutiny.'[40]

After the sappers had gone, the British regiments made no effort
to go after them and dallied in the smouldering ruins of Meerut, on
a 24-hour alert for an attack from Delhi which never came. Brigadier
Archdale Wilson sat tight in the Horse Artillery Barracks, while the
rest of the garrison was safely tucked up in the Field Magazine, the
so-called Dum-Dumma, an enclosure about 200 yards square with
walls eight-feet high, four bastions and a ditch. So completely
deserted was the rest of the cantonment that many of the natives
believed that the Europeans had been exterminated.[41]

It was not until ten days later that the inert Brigadier finally led his column – the only European troops available for miles around – out of Meerut and down the road to Delhi. By which time, the mutineers were ready for them and came out in strength to forestall their joining up with the other troops who were marching down from Ambala. The two forces met on the banks of the Hindon River about ten miles north of Delhi. It was Edward's first battle.

> We ran two miles in the heat of the day. The grape were tearing the trees all around us. Such a whistle they make, knocking up the dust all round us. We were a very small body to which I suppose we owe our escape. I thank God for his mercy in having saved us. We got up to the heights and drove the enemy back . . . Twelve of the Rifles were struck down by the sun, four of them died. The heat was fearful. When the water-carriers came up, the rush was tremendous. I suffered very much from thirst. I always wear white clothes, and a hat made of pith, a sort of helmet, as a protection. I think it was owing to their small cloth caps the Rifles suffered so. I saw one man sun-struck, he was raving. I saw a good many of the enemy dead. Round shot had hit some of them and knocked them to pieces . . .
>
> I never was better in my life than I am now, and we are all very jolly and have great fun . . .
>
> I am so glad you have a fellowship . . .
>
> PS Am very lucky in getting into action so soon.[42]

The British success at the Hindon River enabled Archdale Wilson's column to join up with the main column from the Punjab under the Commander-in-Chief, General Anson. By the time the forces had joined up, on Trinity Sunday, June 7 at Alipore on the Grand Trunk Road, a mere eight miles from Delhi, that popular boulevardier had played his last hand. The General had succumbed to cholera before seeing a shot fired. The new C-in-C was General Sir Henry Barnard, a decent old sort who had even less experience of

India than General Anson. At Alipore, too, Theo met his new boss, Hervey Greathed, formerly the Commissioner of Meerut and the senior British civilian with the Field Force. 'Metcalfe says he is well enough to work and his knowledge of Delhi will prove very useful to me,' Greathed reported. 'He is a most cheerful, merry fellow – nothing puts him out.'[43] Theo was always able to project his sunny side when he needed to.

At 1am the next morning, the combined forces marched out of Alipore and ran smack into the enemy in front of the old Mughal caravanserai of Badli-ki-Serai. This was the first great pitched battle of the Mutiny. The King's most forceful son, Mirza Mughal, had not only pressed hundreds of workmen into repairing the walls of Delhi, he had also constructed a strong forward defensive position at this old staging inn on the Grand Trunk Road. The position was ideal: marshland on either side and a hillock in the middle to provide a commanding field of fire for his guns. At Badli-ki-Serai, the British for the first time realized how well they had taught their native troops the arts of war (although the sepoys had also learned much from motley European soldiers of fortune in the service of native princes). Another of the King's sons, Mirza Khizr Sultan, com-manded a large and disciplined infantry spread between the guns with reinforcements waiting behind. They aimed well.

Lieutenant Kendall Coghill said, 'I have never seen such splendid artillery practice as theirs was. They had the range to a yard and every shot told.'[44] General Barnard said he had not experienced a hotter fire in the Crimea. He ordered the front line to lie down. Richard Barter remembered: 'I was not at all sorry to dismount and make myself as small as I possibly could, while the shot went shriek-ing over our heads with the peculiar sound which once heard is never forgotten. After a few minutes the order came, "The 75th will advance and take that battery". In an instant the line was up. Soon our fellows were dropping fast ... their shot striking the line with every discharge. I remember one in particular taking a man's head off, or rather smashing it to pieces and covering my old Colour

Sergeant Walsh with blood and brains so that it was some time before he could see again.'[45]

Edward was in the thick and loving it. He wrote to his aunt Henrietta Shakespear, who was also one of his guardians after the early death of both his parents, her sister Mary Anne and the Reverend Francis Thackeray:

> I never knew anything more exciting than getting closer and closer, and then the round shot and shell began to whistle past us, and tear up the ground all around. The Ghurka Regiment and 75th Queen's were with us. Men were carried past in palanqueens – poor fellows, many dead and badly wounded. We passed one of our light batteries which had met the brunt of the enemy fire. One tumbril had blown up, and two or three Artillery men were lying dreadfully scorched and dying in the road. I never saw such a ruin . . .
>
> We had orders to destroy all the villages on the way which had harboured the rebels. No quarter is given to them. I daresay you will think this cruel, but if you think of the horrible massacres of our women and children and of the mutinies where six or seven European officers were shot down in front of their native regiments, without a man trying to help them, you will see it could not be otherwise . . .

Aunt Henrietta had at least a dozen nephews and cousins fighting in the Mutiny, so she was destined to hear a good deal more of this sort of thing.

> Who do you think I met in the middle of the fight on the 8th, just after we had taken the heights – Robert Low. He is orderly officer to General Barnard. His regiment has not yet mutinied but I suppose will, as about 30 regiments have now.[46]

Robert and the Santals

There was never much doubt that Robert Low would be a soldier like his father. The first photo of him, the first I have seen of any member of the family, shows him looking sharp and confident with a double-barrelled shotgun tucked under his arm. He has probably been out rabbiting on Clatto Hill. He cannot have been more than 14 or 15. By the time he was 16, he had a cornet's commission on the Bengal Cavalry. When his kit arrived at Clatto, he began prancing around the dining-room table in a menacing fashion, causing an ancient maid to shriek, 'Tak' awa' Maister Robert's sword.'[47] Nobody ever did.

He went to school in England, to Mr Day's academy on Brixton Hill, where he learnt enough of maths, classics, French and fortifications to satisfy the professors in those subjects at the East India Company's College at Addiscombe. While he was at Mr Day's, Augusta had been lodging with her widowed sister Marianne at Tunbridge Wells, and was able to see something of her second son before he set off for India. He seemed so painfully young to her, not nearly mature enough to be a soldier. She wrote to her husband in Calcutta:

If you are writing to Lord Dalhousie, will you say how grateful I am for his kindness in allowing Robert to do duty with the Bodyguard which allows him to remain with you for some 3

months & which is of such importance when he is so young &
his character so unformed.[48]

Dalhousie had taken Robert under his wing. When his father
wrote to assure the Governor-General of Robert's attention to his
duties, Dalhousie pshawed the notion: 'As for "working very hard",
it would be too much to expect it of a gay lad of seventeen in the
first year he mounts the cockade and spurs.'[49] Without a son himself,
he warmed to the vigorous insouciance of a young man enjoying the
health he no longer had any hope of recovering. So at the beginning
of January, 1855, Robert had been seconded to the Bodyguard in
Calcutta, instead of being sent up to the Punjab to join his destined
regiment, the 9th Bengal Light Cavalry.

By a bizarre turn of events, Robert was not to have too many
months to sample the balls and race meetings of Calcutta. Far from
being sheltered under the wing of the Governor-General, he was
immediately swept up in one of the weirdest and most embarrassing
campaigns ever fought by British troops in India.

Less than a hundred miles up the rivers that debouched in the
Calcutta Delta there began the country of the Santals. The anthro-
pologists who delighted in the songs and legends of this primeval
tribe described them as 'Proto-Australoid'. They were indeed similar in appearance to the Australian aborigines, very dark, with short
flat noses and a sunken nose-ridge and curly hair. They were a
numerous tribe, in fact the largest in India to be still speaking an abo-
riginal language. They possessed no script. It was not until the
beginning of the twentieth century that one was invented for them.
They had no guns and no money, either. Not surprisingly, they were
adrift in the modern world, living deep in the wooded valleys that
opened into the great rivers.

All the same, the British forced them to pay cash rents for their
land, which meant that they had to go to market immediately after
harvest to sell a fair slice of their crops. The Bengali merchants
easily got the better of these spirit-worshipping innocents who

soon found themselves having to take out loans at usurious rates from 50 to 500 per cent. If his Bengali creditor sued him, the only evidence that the Santal farmer could produce was a knotted string, in which the knots represented the number of rupees he had received and the spaces between the knots the years that had elapsed since he took out the loan. The creditor had his ledger and day-book ready, not to mention a mortgage deed, which might well be forged.

When a Santal defaulted, the merchant would use British law to pursue him, taking care that the Santal should know nothing of the proceedings, which would be taking place in a court a hundred miles away. Without warning, the Santal's buffaloes and his home-stead would be sold, not to mention his wife's brass vessels and iron armlets.

The surprise is not that the Santals rose in rebellion but that they had not risen sooner. At the end of June, 1855, four Santal brothers announced to a gathering of 10,000 tribesmen that the Bongas (their spirit deities) had instructed them to cast off the foreign yoke. Moneylenders were seized and killed. European bungalows, tele-graph and railway stations were burnt. Santal insurgents chopped off the legs of the *zemindar* of Narainpur at the knees, crying 'four annas', meaning that a quarter of the debt had now been paid off; then cutting off his legs at the thigh, they cried 'eight annas'; then his arms, 'twelve annas'; finally they cut off his head, exclaiming tri-umphantly 'Pharkati!' (Full settlement!)

British troops in the area were scanty. The Santals easily routed a small detachment of 150 men under Major Burroughs on the banks of the Ganges near Pirpainti. The local Commissioner reported to Major-General Lloyd at Dinapur that the rebels had stood their ground firmly and fought with handbows and a kind of battle-axe.[50] There were thousands of them now, perhaps as many as 30,000, wielding these primitive arms rather effectively and terrorizing the country. Although they lived mostly in the woods, their territory spanned all the main arteries out of Calcutta: the great rivers, the Grand Trunk Road, and now the line of the electric telegraph and the new railway which operated as far as Raniganj in the heart of Santal country. All post and railway operations had to be closed down during the emergency.

The Santal leaders boasted that the Company's rule was at an end and that the era of their Bongas had begun.[51] The local indigo farmers were in a panic. So was the *Calcutta Review*, which wailed: 'The confidence of our subjects in our rule is shaken and in many parts they have undergone great suffering. A portion of the public is audibly grumbling at the apparent want of union and concert in the Government. Public money is melting away. Public works are at a standstill. Especially it is to be feared that the pet scheme of the day, the Railway, has received a serious check.'

The Stone Age was inflicting an intolerable humiliation on the nineteenth century, and all within a few dozen miles of the great metropolis of Empire. Lord Dalhousie, still recuperating in the southern hills, scratched together a combined force to sally up the river. He even had to sacrifice his own Bodyguard to make the numbers presentable. Which is how Robert Cunliffe Low's first military encounter came to be against half-naked tribesmen armed only with bows and arrows and axes.

The Governor-General wrote from faraway Kotagiri to John Low in Calcutta: 'I should have been very glad to have heard more of your views regarding this Santhal outbreak. It is a very distressing occurrence in its effects and has given me, sitting here at a distance, a good deal of anxiety and annoyance.

'I hope your laddie will not be taken prisoner by fever – our worst enemy just now.'[52]

The trouble to begin with was that the Santals ran away into the jungles at the approach of the troops, so that very few of them were even wounded. Major Shuckburgh boasted that he had made 'another successful raid against the Santhals and destroyed a good deal of property, but as the insurgents fled at the approach of the Troops, instead of standing their ground, he could not (in the absence of cavalry) get near enough to attack these persons with any effect.'[53] It was ignominious enough to be bringing modern fire-power to bear on little men with bows and arrows but more ignominious still to be unable to hit them. All they could do was burn their villages, which was not exactly showing 'that true mod-eration and humanity' that Mr F.J. Halliday, the Lieutenant-Governor of Bengal, claimed was the British policy. Worse still, the British were uncomfortably aware that they were intervening on the side of the exploiters, in contradiction to their avowed mission to protect vulnerable tribes.

Little by little, the British troops began to kill off the insurgents. Soon the operation became a hideous turkey shoot. Major Vincent Jervis, of the 56th Native Infantry, which played a leading role in the suppression, ruefully observed:

> It was not war; they did not understand yielding. As long as their national drum beat, the whole party would stand and allow them-selves to be shot down. Their arrows often killed our men, and so we had to fire on them as long as they stood. When their drum ceased, they would move off for a quarter of a mile; then their drums beat again, and they calmly stood till we came up and poured a few volleys into them. There was not a sepoy in the war who did not feel ashamed of himself.[54]

Why did the Santals stop running away? They might not possess any guns themselves, but they had seen what terrible damage the rifles of the Ingrez could inflict, both on wild game and in punish-ing malefactors. Why on earth did they now come out of their jungles and stand so patiently until they were mown down? No explanation for this curious change of behaviour appears in the offi-cial accounts or in the judicial proceedings at which large numbers of Santals were sentenced to death or imprisonment.

In the account of the *Hool*, as the Santals called their rebellion, writ-ten by Digambar Chakraborti, a local schoolteacher who qualified as a lawyer and became the first lawyer to offer professional representation to the Santals, a curious story emerges.

The Santals *were* fearful of the British rifles. To persuade them to take up arms, Chando Manjhi, a Santal wizard/hypnotist, explained that the Bongas had appeared to him in a vision and had promised that they would be immune to the British rifles, which would spew forth only water instead of deadly bullets. A few days later, the Santals had a scuffle with a local indigo planter on an elephant. After the planter's *mahout* had been killed with a rusty iron bar, the planter fired blanks at the Santals to frighten them off. When they saw that nobody had been hurt, they began to believe in Chando Manjhi's vision.

Still they were not fully convinced of their immunity. When, later on in August, thousands of them faced the British task force under Major Jervis across the banks of the Torai Nadi, they remained reluctant to wade across the river. Instead, they sent up a shower of arrows at the British, taking care to stay out of range of the rifles.

To encourage them to come forward, Major Jervis instructed his men to fire a volley of blanks. When the smoke had cleared away, the Santals looked around and saw that not a man was hurt. Then at last they began to cross the river, with Sidhu, one of the four brothers who led the rebellion, making magic gestures and uttering incantations to keep the water level low, because the skies were darkening to the west and a deluge was coming from the hills.

Having reached the other bank, the Santals began to fire their arrows. Contrary to British fears, the arrows were not poisoned, for in their chivalrous way they coated the tips only when they were hunting, not when they were making war. Three or four soldiers were slightly wounded. In response to the clamour from his men, the Major gave the order to fire two or three live rounds. In a moment, 50 Santals were dead, hundreds more badly wounded. The Santals threw away their bows and arrows and ran back to the river. Now the storm had broken, and the river was too high for them to cross. The British kept on firing, and the Santals kept on falling, hundreds of them drowning in the Torai Nadi as the muddy torrent carried them away.[55]

None of this found its way into Major Jervis's official report. Even if it is only half-true, it would help to explain the extraordinary inconsistency between the Santals' prudent timidity at the start of the uprising and their foolhardy stoicism at the end. Chakraborti (1849–1913) wrote his account in about 1895, but it was not published, as *History of the Santal Hool of 1855*, until 1988, so it played no part in nationalist propaganda, although the story of the blank cartridges did remain current. Nor were the Santals unique in their illusion. The Tibetans in 1904 went into battle thinking that the amulets blessed by the Dalai Lama rendered them immune to the British Maxim guns.

In the course of mopping-up operations, the British confiscated the Santals' drums and flutes, which they had beaten and blown to summon their war bands and warn of enemy approach. Just as the Santals had cut the railway and the telegraph wires, so now their own communications were cruelly severed.

Even before the rebellion had been finally crushed, at the beginning of 1856, the conscience-stricken British authorities began to make amends. The Santals were put under the protection of British district commissioners, given effective legal rights and some protection from racketeering. Even so, it may be no accident that the Santal heartland is the area of west Bengal where the Maoist Naxalite movement was born a century later and today continues to plague the Indian Government.

After this dubious introduction to war, Robert Low was promoted to lieutenant (September 29, 1855) and posted to his regiment, the 9th Bengal Light Cavalry, up in the Punjab. The fate of the 9th Cavalry was to be every bit as horrific as that of the Santals.

Up at the top of the Punjab just before the foothills began, there lay the old town of Sialkot. Napier had chosen it for its area HQ, and it had become a considerable military station. It was one of the three stations selected for the testing of the new cartridges – Dum-Dum outside Calcutta and Ambala were the others. In all three stations, the thousands of native troops garrisoned there were in a ferment – the 9th Cavalry included. Older officers shook their heads when they heard that John Nicholson was drawing off hundreds of these discontented sepoys for his Movable Column, including one wing of the 9th Cavalry. Why had he not disarmed them, as he had disarmed the 16th at Peshawar? Surely it was crazy to take trouble with you.

But John Nicholson was as cunning as he was ruthless. He marched his column off southwards in the direction of Delhi. Then, three days later, as they were coming into the fort of Phillaur, he lined up his European troops either side of the road and, without any advance warning, suddenly ordered the native infantry to halt and pile their arms and ammunition pouches. Taken by surprise and iso-lated from the rest of their brigade, they sullenly obeyed just as the 16th had obeyed. Having neutralized half the brigade, Nicholson turned north again. He had not yet disarmed his wing of the 9th Cavalry, fearing that if he did the other half left behind at Sialkot would be provoked into mutiny.

When he got to Amritsar, the local telegraph wires brought the news, which didn't surprise him much, that all the sepoys at Sialkot had already mutinied and were murdering and plundering their way though the cantonment. So now Nicholson disarmed the 9th Cavalry, too, commandeered all their horses, and ordered the infantry privates, most of whom had never been on a horse before, to ride them instead and he led this impromptu cavalry off at a cruel gallop to intercept the Sialkot mutineers who were now heading south, high on *bhang* and laden with loot, to join the rebels at Delhi.

He caught sight of the French-grey uniforms of the 9th just after they had crossed the River Ravi, at a ford called the Trimu Ghat.[56] The smooth-bored muskets of the rebels were as toys against the new Enfield rifles of the British troops. For artillery, the rebels had dragged along with them only the old Sialkot station gun which boomed at sunrise and sunset, while Nicholson had nine field guns which set about spraying the startled insurgents with shrapnel and grapeshot.

One half of the old brigade was now fighting against the other half, and Nicholson feared that the native drivers of the gun cattle might run off. So might the mounted police, who certainly 'seemed undesirous of engaging', Nicholson reported with atypical under-statement, and were ordered to the rear. The mutineers fell back upon the river, leaving three or four hundred dead and wounded behind them, not to mention the entire spoils of the Sialkot canton-ment. The few who were not shot in the water crawled on to an island in the river. Nicholson's column then pursued them in boats which he had hustled up from somewhere, and bayoneted them in the long grass.

Nicholson himself rushed the battery. His biographer reports that 'his keen sword, impelled by a singularly nervous arm, crashed down with Cut No 1 upon the shoulder of the man who worked the gun, and clove him literally in two. "Not a bad sliver, that", he remarked to his ADC.'[57] Not that the station gun was much of a threat, because its elevating screw was too rusty to be depressed and it boomed harmlessly over their heads. In the end, all that remained were the French-grey uniforms floating in the water. The 9th Bengal Light Cavalry ceased to exist.

The Battle of Trimu Ghat was not unlike dozens of similar engagements which were to be fought across northern India in the next few months. It is remarkable for the foresight and rapidity of John Nicholson, still only 34, in splitting the mutineers to make it more manageable to disarm them, and then in cutting them off and annihilating them; and for the fact that Robert Low's first regiment, like his father's, had disappeared from the earth. The men whom he had drilled had murdered the officers he had messed with, and most of both were dead.

It is a further coincidence that Robert Low, like his father, was not actually with his regiment when it mutinied. If he had been, he too would probably have been murdered when the sepoys went berserk in the cantonment. With that streak of luck which seemed to stick to the Lows, he had been seconded to the staff of the new Commander of the Field Force, Sir Henry Barnard. And it was as Barnard's orderly officer that he greeted his cousin Edward Thackeray on the high ground of Badli-ki-Serai.

The Ridge and the Siege

That same evening, the Field Force took possession of the long ridge that arched like an eyebrow above the walled city of the Emperor, as he had now again proclaimed himself. The Siege of Delhi had begun.

It was not a siege in the ordinary sense. From three-quarters of the city the rebels were free to come and go, to gather fresh food and beckon in floods of fresh recruits. If anyone was hemmed in, it was the so-called besiegers. In front of them were the formidable walls and bastions of Delhi. To their left, the River Yamuna cut off access to Allahabad and Calcutta. Behind them they had the Najafgarh Canal. Only to their right had they a way out, which was the way they had come, along the Grand Trunk Road from the north-west, and even that route was fiercely, if intermittently, contested. Everyone from the Brigadier to the Chaplain recognized the unpleasant reality. As the Reverend John Edward Rotton put it: 'We came to besiege Delhi, but we very soon learnt that, in reality, we were the besieged, and the mutineers the besiegers.'[58]

Theo had come up to the Ridge (in no time, it had an iconic capital 'R') with the Field Force and so began for all three of them, Theo and Edward and Robert, as weird a three months as any of them ever spent. Life on the Ridge was a hectic mixture of plague, gaiety and danger. The old cantonment behind the ridge road had been gutted by the mutineers. General Barnard's makeshift new camp was out of range of the guns on the Delhi bastions, but it was exposed to frontal attack through the no-man's-land between the Ridge and the city walls, a sniper's paradise of swamp, ditches, disused mosques, ruins, tangled scrub and walled gardens.

Arthur Lang, who had joined his fellow Engineers on the Ridge, told his mother that 'although the smell from the carcases of camels, horses and Pandies is most offensive, the camp looks exceptionally pretty, the lines of white tents, beyond the green swampy meadows, stretching along the top of the Ridge, which is a long line of hill ground covered with grass, low trees and boulders, on which stand conspicuously the various points: the Flagstaff Tower, the Mosque, Hindu Rao's house, all of which are now posts of our army.' Riding along the canal bank in the evening with a party of Hodson's 'Plungers', Arthur felt he could have been in an English meadow: 'this illusion would be occasionally dispelled as we saw the troops of monkeys cross the path and scampering up the trees, or peacocks strutting proudly along, and parrots flying screaming about and smelt the strong scent of the bubul blossoms [babul tree, gum arabic in English usage]: still more so if we looked over our shoulders and at the khaki-coated, crimson-turbaned horsemen at our backs.'[59]

Like his fellow Engineer Edward Thackeray, Arthur Lang had already found it thrilling rather than alarming to be in action. 'I don't know how it is that I can't feel the danger as it ought to be felt; I'm either apathetic or stupid about it – tho' not apathetic, for I feel occasionally the *pleasure* of the excitement.'[60] Now more than ever, he had come to feel that 'I really chose aright when I thought a soldier's life was the life for me. Exposure and fatigue, the music of ball and bullet, marching and roughing it, all that makes up a soldier's life, I enjoy.'[61] He wrote every day to his fiancée back in Lahore, Sarah Boileau. She was, he said, 'an awful stunner', but he had a war to win before he could think of settling down.

From the top of the Ridge, the British soldiers could see the minarets of the Red Fort and the Great Mosque, the Jama Masjid. They could also hear the rebels' buglers playing the British calls and the rebel bands blaring out the old favourites they had learnt from their masters – 'Cheer, boys, cheer', 'The British Grenadiers' and 'The Girls We Left Behind Us'. On the walls, they could see the rebels still wearing their scarlet British uniforms. When they came upon the rebel corpses after the daily skirmishes on the slopes, they collected the numbers of their old regiments from their caps. Edward wrote to Aunt Henrietta: 'Is it not a dreadful thing, fighting against, as it were, our own men whom we have educated and made soldiers and armed? They are fighting us with our own guns and everything.'[62]

Edward, like any other sane observer who stumbled upon this strange scene, was also struck by the folly of the British: 'Fancy us leaving a place like Delhi with all our stores and guns in it, with nothing but native troops.'[63]

Survival in the forward line was a simple matter. 'A man sits on the parapet: when he sees the flash from the enemy's batteries, he says "Down", and down we all bob beneath the parapet. The worst is getting up there, as the shot come crashing about in the most unpleasant way.' The handful of native sappers who had stayed with Edward were behaving beautifully. One of them had his leg taken off and Edward had to tie it up himself as there was no doctor. A Carabineer next to him was hit, and said in a most matter-of-fact way, 'Oh there goes my arm and leg. Give me a glass of water.'

The Bengal Engineers were lucky in getting hold of one of the few bungalows still standing in the cantonment (it had belonged to a European officer who had been killed in the first days of the Uprising). Its main room still had a billiard table in it. The officers sawed off the edges of the table and slept on it side by side like sardines.[64] The entire mess dined off the table, too.

The 20 Engineer officers were a remarkable lot: 14 of them became generals, three of them won VCs. Their high spirits were relentless, so was their nicknaming: Edward was Lord Tallboot; the Consulting Engineer, Wilberforce Greathed, was The Insulting Engineer; the mathematician-astronomer James Tennant was The

Objector-General; and the Highlander Charles Thomason was dubbed Robinson Crusoe from the peculiar bleached rags he went around in. Thomason was an unstoppable piper, insisting on performing 'Wi' a Hundred Pipers' as the monsoon drenched them all. His collection of bagpipe music, *Coel Mor*, was later to become a classic. In between being drenched and shot at, they swam and fished in the canal and wrote letters to their families insisting how snug and jolly they were. Arthur Lang thanked his mother for the last number of *Little Dorrit*, which completed the set: 'when Thackeray's new serial commences, please send it out to me.'[65] In the evenings, they played loo for high stakes. One sapper subaltern staked his entire Engineers' allowance until he should reach the rank of major. He lost, and the winner, a VC from another regiment, drew several hundred pounds per annum for years to come, apparently without a qualm. Edward was the youngest of them at 20. His cousin Robert, the veteran of the Santal campaign and now of Badli-ki-Serai, often dined at the billiard table. He was a year younger still, just 19.

Theo took little share in the gay camaraderie of the sappers' mess. He mooched about the Ridge, his eyes painful and swollen again from the dust and the flies, and his mind enraged by the sight of the ruins of Metcalfe House immediately below them, its pleasant verandahs now obliterated by sandbags and rubble piled up to shelter the Field Force's forward picquets. His only entertainment was to lead raiding parties to disarm and burn villages behind the Ridge. His brother-in-law Edward Campbell, now posted there, wrote to his sister GG: 'I cannot see the use of his being here, except for the information he gives of the country, which they do not seem to care much about.'[66]

Twice a day, at noon and sunset, native servants in spotless linen processed slowly along the road that crested the rocks, carrying trays laden with dishes and glasses for their masters' tiffin, silhouetted against the sky, an excellent target for the first-rate rebel snipers but quite unruffled by the plague of flies and bullets. The British were so short of ammunition that they paid their servants to pick up the

THE RIDGE AND THE SIEGE

roundshot fired by the enemy. The competition to collect the red-hot shot before they rolled back down the hill was so sharp that the servants often burnt their fingers.

The stench from the corpses lying out in no-man's-land was horrible. The water from the canal tasted like pea soup. The fearsome William Hodson recorded that 'everything is stagnant save the hand of the destroying Angel of Sickness: we have at this moment 2,500 in hospital of whom 1,100 are Europeans – out of a force of 5,000 Europeans. Delhi in September is proverbial and this year we seem likely to realize its full horror.' By comparison, the enemy was reckoned to be 30,000 strong. Almost every day, they could see through their glasses fresh regiments of mutineers crossing the Bridge of Boats into the city.

Hodson contracted cholera. Dear old General Barnard came to see him and covered him with a blanket to protect him from the draughty night.[67] Hodson recovered, but Barnard himself was not so lucky. In the early morning of July 5, he was mulling over a plan for an immediate assault on the city, as recommended by the newly arrived Chief Engineer, Richard Baird-Smith, and his brilliant young assistant Captain Alex Taylor. They talked for three hours, and Baird-Smith noticed only 'a worn and anxious expression of face, with a certain heaviness and dimness of eye, not at all natural to him', and even these disappeared as the discussion grew animated.[68] But by 11am, the General was stricken with cholera and he died that afternoon. The next morning, Robert Low was escorting his body on the gun carriage down to the cemetery at the back of the Ridge.

For the Field Force to lose two elderly commanders in a row to cholera might seem like rotten luck. But British soldiers of all ranks and ages succumbed to the disease just as rapidly and unpredictably. One minute they would be playing whist in the mess or dodging bullets in the scrub and the orange groves, and the next morning they would be dead. In the Crimea two years earlier, there had been four deaths from disease to every death in action, and cholera had been the biggest killer. The tragedy was that the cure was so simple:

rehydrate the patient in time and all he would suffer would be a bad go of diarrhoea. Bad water carried the bacillus; pure water flushed it away.

The doctors and public health officials stuck obstinately to the theory that cholera was carried by foul air. The stench of the corpses on the Ridge or at Sebastopol gave credence to the theory, just as the stench of the London slums did. Young Lieutenant Richard Barter was as convinced as any that the disease was carried by a 'miasma' in the air, and in his siege memoir frequently mentions the stench as the cause. Yet his own uncle, another Richard Barter, had discovered back in the 1830s that rehydration would cure almost all his cholera patients and had written a pamphlet to prove it.[69]

Barnard's successor, Major-General Reed, lasted less than a fortnight, before he invalided himself out to the hills, struck by a sense of his inadequacy for the task. He in turn was succeeded by Brigadier Archdale Wilson, whom we have already seen playing a less than dynamic role at Meerut. Wilson was in wretched health and spent much of the day lying on his cot with a wet cloth round his head. He was the fourth commander the Field Force had had in a month, and not the least feeble.

By contrast, the Engineer officers were going from strength to strength. Barnard's first Chief Engineer had been an old major who arrived at the war accompanied by his Persian wife and 20 or 30 camel-loads of luggage. When he went sick, Major Baird-Smith succeeded. Like the rest of them, he was in miserable health, being in constant pain from a wound which kept him away from dinner at the billiard table, but he was unsparing and forceful in argument. Barnard had twice already been on the point of ordering an all-out assault but let the moment slip. Now Baird-Smith managed to kindle something resembling a fire in Archdale Wilson.

Far away from the horror and tedium of the Ridge, the British public, both in London and Calcutta, were fretting. They had expected to hear within a week, a month at most, that Delhi had fallen and the national humiliation had been avenged. In the backwoods of Oudh and the North-West Provinces, the expectation was no less feverish. The little huddle of British officers waiting for the mutineers at Saharanpur had held a sweepstake on the exact date. Roderick Edwards, the Joint Magistrate, drew the ticket for June 27, and hoped he wouldn't win because the city ought to be back in British hands before then.[70] Now it was already August and, according to the newspapers, the British were still lolling on the Ridge, gorging themselves on port and brandy and six-course meals. The Press asked impatiently why they didn't just 'jump over the garden wall'. In fact, the walls of Delhi were seven miles round and 24-feet high, surrounded by a deep ditch, and within them were four times the number of troops that the British had, even if you included the hospital cases.

At least, those had been the odds in the first weeks of the siege. As the British numbers were strengthening, though, the rebels were deserting in considerable numbers, as they realized that the Emperor lacked the funds to pay them properly. Colonel Keith Young, the Adjutant-General, estimated that by the time the British eventually attacked on September 14, the rebels inside the city were no more than 12,000, though their defensive position was still formidable.[71]

Early in the morning of August 7, a mail cart decanted on to the Ridge the huge, ominous figure of John Nicholson. That evening he cast a memorable blight on the merriment of the mess, sitting silently with his equally huge Pathan servant behind his chair. Touring the defences, he found fault with everything in his sonorous Ulster voice. Nicholson was not slow to confide his opinion of Archdale Wilson to his old boss, Sir John Lawrence, who was still guarding the Punjab after nobly contributing the bulk of his troops to Delhi: 'I have seen a lot of useless generals in my day, but such an ignorant, croaking obstructive as he is I have never hitherto met with, and nothing will induce me to serve a day under his personal command after the fall of this place.'[72]

On the August 24, the British saw through their glasses a large army setting out from the western gate. The Emperor's new General, fat old Bakht Khan, had 9,000 men and 13 guns, and he was clearly hoping to come round by the Najafgarh Canal and attack the British from behind, after taking control of the road from the north, along which the British siege train was rumbling at the pace of the slowest camel.

This was a far more serious threat than any of the previous enemy excursions from the city, and there was clearly only one man to see it off. Wilson was as pleased as Nicholson himself to see the Movable Column set off at 4am the next morning in heavy rain, with the great black-bearded Ulsterman at the head of it. Nicholson, having arrived in the mail cart accompanied only by his giant Pathan, now needed a couple of aides de camp, and Wilson gladly lent him one of his own, Robert Low.

After serving three elderly generals in failing health, for Robert to be on Nicholson's staff was something else. He was an immediate hit. Nicholson had no hesitation in declaring that Lieutenant Low was 'the smartest officer on the staff'. It was to be a gruelling day for all of them, including Theo, who had volunteered to act as guide to the back lanes.

The Movable Column was only 2,500 strong, a quarter of Bakht Khan's force, but it had 16 guns and it had Nicholson. In the first nine miles after coming off the Ridge, they stuck in two swamps, with the guns bogged up to their axles, the camels sprawling in the mud, the infantry wet to the skin, and the cavalry kicking up mud into their faces. The one piece of good advice that Wilson had given them was to stick to the roads, but Theo knew a short cut which turned out to be even more of a morass. At times, the water was waist-high, and the men had to carry their ammunition pouches on their heads. Nicholson was set on attacking before nightfall, and he sent Theo on ahead to look at the ditches in front of them. Theo found a passable place to cross. Beyond it he could just make out through the pelting rain Bakht Khan's outposts, drawn up, like Mirza Khizr Sultan's forces at Badli-ki-Serai, around an old inn near the bridge.

Even the ford was waist-deep and, as they were crossing it, the enemy opened fire from the caravanserai. Nicholson rose in his stirrups to tell the troops exactly what Sir Colin Campbell had said at Chilianwala in the Punjab war, which was the same as what he had told the Highland Brigade before the Battle of the Alma: 'Hold your fire till you are within 20 or 30 yards of the enemy, then pour your volleys into them, give them a bayonet charge and the serai is yours.' In essence, don't fire until you see the whites of their eyes: the same simple frontal attack, the same *dash* that had served Wellington at Assaye and a dozen other British commanders since.[73]

In less than an hour, Nicholson had routed the rebel sepoys, captured all their guns and baggage and killed 800 of them, at a cost of two officers and 23 of his own men. At this, as at other decisive encounters in the Mutiny, the rebels fought with courage and tenacity. They were as well-trained and disciplined under fire as any European force. The difference, as British historians never ceased to point out, lay in the qualities of leadership which none of the native princes had had the opportunity to acquire – and, in this case, though not in others, in the British guns.

The news of the victory was carried back to the plague-ridden and demoralized British camp by none other than Nicholson's youngest ADC. Galloping by himself up to the Ridge ahead of the muddy and sodden victors, Robert enjoyed a genuine moment of glory. The squalid business with the Santals could be forgotten. This was an earned victory.

A week later, on September 4, the long-awaited siege train finally rolled into camp, all eight miles of it: 60 heavy howitzers and mortars, more than 600 bullock carts full of shot and shell from the Punjab munitions factories, which never stopped production throughout the Mutiny, and the huge 24-pounder siege guns which took teams of elephants to pull. There was enough *matériel* here to reduce Delhi to rubble.

Now it was a sapper's war. Lieutenant Arthur Lang exulted, 'It is grand what a position we Engineers subs have. We give our opinions more coolly and forcibly than any colonels would dare to do to generals and they all tacitly agree that we are the managing minds.'[74] Baird-Smith and Alex Taylor were calling the shots, literally, while Archdale Wilson's objections faded to a whimper. Edward Thackeray's task was to build No 2 Battery, just in front of the battlemented mock castle which Sir Thomas Metcalfe had taken for the Residency offices and which was known as Ludlow Castle after Dr Ludlow who built it for himself. No 2 Battery was only 500 yards from the Kashmir Gate, which had been chosen as the focal point for the main attack. The plan was to silence the guns on the bastion next to the gate and to smash the parapet walls which gave cover to the defenders, then blow open the gate itself.

On the evening of September 7, Edward led a procession of no less than 1,400 camels carrying the fascines (the bundles of faggots to firm up the battery walls). He was struck by the brilliance of the fireflies which sparkled among the trees and bushes as they marched silently along beside the long train of camels. For the previous fortnight, working parties had been stumbling about in the jungle from dusk to dawn soaked to the skin and under constant fire, cutting down the trees and bushes to clear sites for the huge guns. No 2 Battery was to comprise nine 24-pounders, seven big howitzers and six 9-pounders. This was to be bombardment on an industrial scale, a foretaste of twentieth-century war.

All morning on September 11, the guns of No 2 Battery pounded away at the walls of the Kashmir Gate. 'It was an exhilarating sight to watch the stone-work crumbling under the storm of shot and shell, the breach getting larger and larger, and the 8-inch shells made to burst just as they touched the parapet, bringing down whole yards of it at a time.'[75] On the starlit night of September 12, Baird-Smith sent out four of his lieutenants to inspect if the breaches were large enough yet: Medley and Lang to the Kashmir bastion, Greathed and Home to the Water Bastion. These intrepid subalterns slid down the ditch, up the other side and put up their ladders to the breach. They ran back to their batteries, breathless but untouched, to give the news that the breaches were wide enough and there were no guns at the sides of them. Baird-Smith seized the moment. Archdale Wilson could only accept his advice. They would attack at dawn the next day, and they would stake everything.

The day before the assault, they made their wills and entrusted them to the Adjutant. Arthur Lang told his mother, 'We have been sharpening our swords, kukris and dirks, and tried cutting silk handkerchiefs after breakfast. My favourite fighting sword, Excalibur, one of Aunt Mary's presents, has now an edge like a razor and a surface like a mirror.'[76] Richard Barter remembered, 'There was not much sleep that night in our Camp. I dropped off now and then but never for long and whenever I woke I could see that there was a light in more than one of the officer's tents and talking was going on in a low tone amongst the men, the snapping of a lock or springing of a ramrod sounding far in the still air telling of the preparation for the approaching strife. A little after midnight we fell in as quietly as possible on the left of our tents; by the light of a lantern the orders for the assault were then read to the men.'[77] Leave the wounded where they fell. No plundering. Take no prisoners. Take care not to injure the women and children. The men answered at once: 'No fear, sir.' The officers then swore on their swords, and the men swore to follow them.

A little after 3am the big guns fell silent, and the five storming columns, each with two or three Engineer officers attached, stole down from the Ridge and through the Mughal gardens, named after Qudsia, a dancer who had caught the fancy of an old Emperor. In the silence, Richard Barter, with Nicholson's column, could hear the birds twittering in the trees. Despite the brooding odour of gunpowder, he could smell the orange blossom and the roses.[78]

Not with them was Major Cobbe of the 87th Royal Irish Fusiliers, who had been ordered to keep a look-out at the Flagstaff Tower and fell asleep in the hot morning sunshine, woke up, and seeing nobody about, concluded that the attack had been called off, had his bath and breakfast and asked the mess sergeant where the rest of the officers were. 'Why sir, they are in Delhi. They stormed the city last night.' This no-show did not prevent Cobbe from rising to the rank of lieutenant-general.[79]

Medley and Lang, together again, were first into the breach with the ladder men. They met a terrific and unceasing fire. For ten minutes it was impossible to let down the ladders for the storming party. 'Man after man was struck down, and the enemy, with yells and curses, kept up a terrific fire, even catching up stones from the breach in their fury, and, dashing them down, dared the assailants to come on.'[80] Lang told his mother, 'the bullets seemed to pass like a hissing sheet of lead, and the noise of the cheering was so great that I nearly lost my men ... It was exciting to madness and I felt no feeling except to rush on and hit; I only wondered how much longer I could possibly go on unhit, when the whole air seemed full of bullets.'[81]

Theo was with the third column, the one that was to blow up the Kashmir Gate. He had last come this way in the early morning four months earlier, trotting across from Metcalfe House to tidy up his office before his holiday. Now he watched as the five sappers advanced to the gate. Each of them carried a 25-pound bag of powder. They strolled up to the heavy wooden gates as calmly as men laying wreaths at a memorial. For a moment the audacity of it nonplussed the defenders, which gave the five men half a second to lay their bags. Then a terrible fire opened up, and one after the other the sappers were shot or rolled away into the ditch before they had time to light the fuse. Only the fifth of them, Sergeant Smith, managed to get the lighted fuse to the bags. There was a huge explosion. The bugler, Hawthorne of the 52nd, sounded the call, but in the uproar half the men didn't hear, and Hawthorne blew twice more. Then the rest of the column poured in, with Theo leading the way through the lanes to the Jama Masjid. It was one of the most famous feats of daring in British military history. Three of the five were killed; three of them plus the bugler received the Victoria Cross.

Close behind came Edward Thackeray with the reserve column:

The Cashmere Gate presented a terrible sight. Several sepoys had been blown up by the explosion, and others, bayoneted or shot by the assailants, were lying all about. I noticed that the men on guard at the gateway were for the most part men of the Haryana Light Infantry. I remember also noticing that they were a villain-ous-looking lot. The same scene of carnage was visible along the walls and bastions. No quarter was asked or given. I went into the Cashmere Bastion, and such a scene of destruction has seldom been witnessed. Almost every gun was dismounted and smashed by the fire from our guns, large pieces of iron being in many cases knocked out of the guns. Dead Sepoys lay about in all imaginable positions. The troops took up positions in the College and Church, but the enemy fired at us during the whole of the night of the 14th. I saw hundreds of wounded men carried by on doolies; I also saw the dooly carried by that contained General Nicholson, who had been shot.

Nicholson had been shot in the chest, just below the armpit, while leading a suicidal attack through the heavily guarded lanes in an attempt to reach the Lahore Gate at the end of Chandni Chowk, the main street of the city. The wound was mortal and it was not the only bad news.

Theo had guided the third column through the back lanes where there was little resistance, though he was soon losing men to snipers on the rooftops. They crept along a deserted Chandni Chowk to the north gate of the Great Mosque. It was only then that they realized that they had brought no powder charges with them to blow the gates. They stood there for a moment at a loss. Then to their amaze-ment the gates of the Mosque opened slowly, seemingly of their own accord, and the massed jihadis poured down the steep steps shriek-ing the war cries of the faithful. With their swords and axes, they left 40 of Theo's men dead in front of the Mosque. What was left of the third column fled back down Chandni Chowk, still fighting as they stumbled all the way back to the Kashmir Gate.[82] The fourth column was to attack the suburbs to the right and pour in through the Kabul Gate after Nicholson's troops had secured it, but its commander, too, had been struck down. As a result, the western half of the town was still in the hands of the defenders. And the British losses were grievous: in less than six hours, 66 officers and 1,100 men had been killed or wounded, a fifth of the entire Field Force.

Archdale Wilson had been watching the storming with Robert and the rest of his staff from the roof of Ludlow Castle, and they had a fine view of the dawn and the fighting. When things looked encouraging, he moved his HQ down to Skinner's old mansion by Skinner's church, just inside the walls. But there, as the bad news started to come in, he began to lose his nerve all over again. Perhaps with so few troops and only half the city captured, and that not securely, he ought to withdraw the assaulting columns back to the Ridge. Could they really hang on to the ground they had won at such a cost? Baird–Smith answered in four words: 'We *must* do so.'[83] And they did.

By now, Nicholson had been carried up to the field hospital on the Ridge. When he heard about Wilson's wavering, he reached for his revolver, saying, 'Thank God that I still have the strength to shoot him, if necessary.'[84] Robert Low must have wished that he had not been obliged to return to his previous boss.

Inside the city, the sappers were burrowing on from house to house, 'first getting on the roof, firing on any inside the next yard; then the sappers would pick a doorway through a wall and in we would go, turn out the old men, women and children, and make that house safe, and so on to the next ... Some of the houses in Canal Street are very pretty: courts in the centre of them with little canals and fountains, shrubs, flowers and creepers, balconied rooms, gorgeous in barbaric style of gilding and glass; immense mirrors with rich carpets & comfortable chairs, elegant furniture and a scent of attar all about. Strange it seemed to see these rooms full of rough soldiers.'[85] This tactic, of bashing through from house to house, was the sapper's way of avoiding the perilous streets which were bristling with rebel muskets at every window and on every rooftop. The tactic was to come in handy at the recapture of Lucknow, too.

Edward writes to his brother St John: 'On the 15th we attacked and took the Magazine. But in the afternoon they returned and attacked the Magazine and set the roof on fire. We had to get up on the roof with leather bags of water and put it out, while they threw large stones at us. They were fanatics, I afterwards heard.'[86] As the street fighting hotted up, the fanatical ghazis, the nineteenth-century Awabite ancestors of Al-Qaeda, became more prominent. If the magazine exploded, not only would anyone within several hundred yards be killed, it would be a desperate setback for the British, who were already running low on ammunition and coveted the 171 large-calibre guns and howitzers, not to mention the ammunition of every kind, which they had found in the magazine.

While Edward was sloshing water all over the burning thatch, the ghazis started popping their heads over the wall and firing at him from ten yards away. Lieutenant Renny of the Artillery clambered up on to the roof beside Edward with a bag of ten-inch shells. He lighted their fuses and dropped them on the heads of the ghazis. After he had let off five or six shells, the ghazis fled, leaving the magazine intact and piles of corpses under the smouldering eaves.

Edward's account of how the magazine was saved earned Lieutenant Renny the VC, his own part in the exploit being rather soft-pedalled. But then there were many others who had deserved it, not least the Indian water-carrier who handed up the bags while under terrifying close-range fire. Similarly medals could have been dished out to the eight native sappers under Havildar Madho who helped to lay the powder bags at the Kashmir Gate. Although Indians might be Victoria's subjects, it was not until the First World War that they became entitled to receive her highest award for valour. Even in battle, there was a sense in which they were invisible.

After two days of unbelievable bravery and extravagant slaughter, it was all over. Largely unseen by the British, the rebels had been fleeing through the far gates in their thousands, and the streets were suddenly filled with British troops, many of them reeling drunk, scarcely able to carry their liquor or their plunder. The British poured a torrent of fire into the Red Fort, and the victorious sappers made for the Great Mosque. 'Taylor rode his horse up the steps of the Jama Masjid and we danced about, drank beer and brandy, and the Sikhs lit fires in the sacred mosque.'[87] Of the 25 Engineer officers who had taken part in the storming, only Taylor, Lang, Thackeray and Ward were not dead or wounded.

The Emperor and the Princes, who had been the generals in the fight, fled to Humayun's Tomb, the beautiful Mughal mausoleum just outside the city. With only tepid encouragement from Archdale Wilson, Hodson went out to the Tomb and brought Bahadur Shah in for trial. Then he went back again and captured the Princes, Mirza Mughal, Khizr Sultan and Abu Bakr. Entirely on his own initiative, he shot them himself with his Colt revolver at the Delhi Gate, not forgetting to strip the corpses of their signet rings and turquoise armlets and to appropriate their jewelled swords. Their bodies were left naked outside the city walls, for the vultures and the gawpers to feast on.

Edward stayed in the conquered city for a couple of weeks. Then along with Theo and Robert, he was sent out in a column under Brigadier Showers to clear the country to the west of Delhi. The semi-desert here was peopled by the Mewatis, unthrifty, drought-ridden farmers who had broken into an orgy of violence and plunder in May and took weeks to pacify.[88] Showers was a renowned fighting man, but he was also a merciful one. Edward took a harsher view. 'Brigadier Showers is very lenient to them. I think every village that ever harboured a mutineer ought to be burned, but they have all been spared. These natives don't understand kindness, as this mutiny has shown.'[89] In fact, Showers's column did burn perhaps as many as 50 villages, destroyed four forts and captured 70 guns without firing one; it also brought back three rebel princes as prisoners, and coin to the value of £70–80,000.

It was a strange excursion, though. They marched through rough, broken country, mostly during the nights, which were cold, so they were huddled in rugs as they marched. Many of the column, including Edward, were suffering from recurring fevers and had not recovered from the strain of the siege. But service with Showers's column soon restored their health. Edward attributed their better health to the fresh air and the marching after being cooped up on the Ridge, but the fresh water to be had out in the country may have had more to do with it. They were no more than 50 to 100 miles from Delhi, but these grimy, muffled soldiers were the first Europeans most of the natives had ever seen. Not for the first time, it is brought home to us how thinly spread the British had been all this time. This was the country of Theo's wanderings when he was on the run. And he took a fierce satisfaction in personally arresting the Nawab of Jhajjar, the one who had refused to see him and had sent him off with a couple of *sowars* who were probably under instructions to deliver him up to the Emperor. The Nawab was sent for trial in Delhi, where he was hanged.[90]

Delhi was a miserable place now, full of stagnant water and charred rubble, with worn-out soldiers shuffling through the desolate streets. Mrs Coopland had not been in Delhi long before she heard about Theo. He was the talk of the shattered town: 'Sir Theophilus Metcalfe is a wonderful man in the eyes of the natives, who have a wholesome dread of him. When I was at Delhi, he was busy hunting out, trying and hanging mutineers and murderers: he has a lynx eye for detecting culprits. One day when passing General Penny's house, amongst a guard of *sowars*, he detected a murderer, and instantly singled him out, tried, and condemned him: he also found out poor Mr Frazer's murderer and had him hanged. One day, a native jeweler came to offer his wares for sale to Mrs Garstone, who, thinking he charged too much, said, "I will send you to Metcalfe *sahib*"; on hearing which, the man bolted in such a hurry that he left his treasures behind, and never again showed his face.'[91]

Theo erected a gallows in the grounds of Metcalfe House, made out of the blackened timbers of his beloved home. There he strung up any Indian he suspected of having taken part in the Mutiny. He did not restrict himself to the gallows. The *Delhi Gazetteer* reported that he shot 21 villagers in a place that had given up one of his servants to the insurgents.[92] Refugees sheltering in mosques and temples would be plucked out and executed by the terrifying figure of the Magistrate, now promoted to Special Commissioner by virtue not only of his status as the sole surviving authority in the city but also of his heroic exploits in the storming. His post-siege exploits now reached the columns of the London *Times*. A correspondent in January 1858 reported that Metcalfe was 'every day trying and hanging all he can catch . . . he is held in great dread by the natives.'[93]

Theo was not in the least ashamed. There was another letter published in *The Times* from 'A Civil Servant of the East India Company', dated November 17 and published on January 9, 1858. The writer complained that 'the king of Delhi has been spared. His son is allowed to ride about the streets of Delhi on an elephant with an English Colonel behind him.' The city too had been spared, and the authorities were doing their best to re-people its deserted streets. 'The Nawab of Jugghur, whose men and money helped the rebels at Delhi has been allowed to live and even his protestations of loyalty are believed.' As we have seen, none of this came true – and it was on Theo's evidence that the Nawab was hanged.

Worst of all in this Civil Servant's view was that 'Lord Canning published some time ago a mischievous order that all sepoys apprehended, except those who had killed their officers, were not to be hanged but sent in irons to Allahabad. I, for one, have dared to disobey, and have hanged men who did not imbue their hands in the blood of their own officers but who fought like fiends against us . . . I, for one, will not spare or show leniency to any Sepoy or Mahomedan, but for this I am liable to be at any moment disgraced and removed.' Right from the commencement of the outbreak when 'highway robbery and dacoiteries were of daily occurrence, I apprehended and hanged from the nearest tree the offenders, and at once all violent crime ceased. Surely the *Times* newspaper will listen to the statement of one, like myself, who has watched the present crisis from its earliest commencement, and has had to bear the brunt of the toil and danger.'

The author of this letter could be none other than Sir Theophilus Metcalfe. Nobody else was in a position to exercise such relentless retribution. Nobody else had been there from the start. Who else took such a fierce pleasure in hanging? Who else was so frantic and paranoid? Seldom can a hangman have had so much to say for himself.

Theo was right at least about being 'liable to be at any moment disgraced and removed'. His superior, Sir John Lawrence, had heard all the rumours and sent agents to Delhi who reported that 'Metcalfe was *maddened* with revenge against the Mahomedans, that he seemed to have a personal animus fomented by the sight of what he had suffered and the defection of those whom he had trusted and befriended'. Lawrence's agents felt strongly that 'this *furor* is opposed to the just deliberation required in a Special Commissioner and the sooner the power of life and death is taken from him the better for the interests both of the people and of our administration.'[94]

Lawrence, no slouch himself when it came to ruthless on-the-spot punishment of mutineers, had to agree. Theo's parents had been his oldest friends and he wanted to do all he could to help him, but for all the soldierly qualities Theo had displayed at the storming, he was 'wrong-headed and injudicious', and he had to be neutralized.[95] Lawrence reported to Canning that Theo had been guilty of 'wholesale slaughters'.[96] By the end of April, Lawrence had stopped individual civil officers from hanging at their own pleasure. Theo had been sent home. But he was not, of course, prosecuted.

Palmerston, along with many others, wanted Delhi levelled to the ground, mosques, palaces and all, but Lawrence persuaded Canning that this would be counter-productive, for military rather than aesthetic reasons (the Red Fort was, after all, a fort and a formidable one). Gradually he began to convince the Governor-General that the only way forward was for a general amnesty, which was eventually enshrined in Queen Victoria's Proclamation of November 1858.

But the recapture of Delhi was far from the end of the Uprising. There remained, above all, Lucknow.

Robert and Edward at Lucknow

In his own way, Henry Montgomery Lawrence was as charismatic as his younger brother John, and as unforgettable as John Nicholson. Another hot-tempered Ulsterman of intense religious feeling, he had a sweetness of nature that Nicholson had not a hint of. 'Above the middle height, of a spare, gaunt frame, and a worn face bearing upon it the traces of mental toil and bodily suffering, he impressed you, at first sight, rather with a sense of masculine energy and resolution than of any milder and more endearing qualities. But when you came to know him, you saw at once that beneath that rugged exterior there was a heart as gentle as a woman's.'[97]

Like John Low, he had come out to India as a cadet in the Company Army when he was 16. Like John, he got in on the recommendation of John Hudleston MP, a Director, and, also like John, he quickly developed an instinct for the apprehensions and antipathies of the natives. In the farsighted articles he wrote for the *Calcutta Review* in the 1840s, he warned that the disasters of Afghanistan could well be repeated in India itself: 'How unmindful we have been that what occurred in the city of Kabul may some day occur at Delhi, Mirath [Meerut] or Bareli ... What the European officers have repeatedly done [i.e. mutinied] may surely be expected from Natives. We shall be unwise to wait for such occasion. *Come it will, unless anticipated.*'[98] If 300 rebels were to rise tomorrow and seize Delhi, 'does any sane man doubt that 24 hours would swell the hundreds of rebels into thousands.' It would take a month to bring sufficient European troops from the hills: 'We should then be liter- ally striking for our existence, at the most inclement season of the year, with the prestige of our name vanished, and the fact before the eyes of imperial Delhi that the British forces, placed not only to pro- tect but to overawe the city, were afraid to enter it.'[99]

All this had pretty much come to pass. And the haggard Cassandra with the straggly beard had been right about other things, too: about the dangers of annexing the Punjab, and the still greater dangers of seizing great tracts of land from their long-standing owners. For voicing these unfashionable opinions, he had been 'cavalierly elbowed' out of the Punjab and replaced by his less imaginative younger brother, who was readier to jump to Lord Dalhousie's bid- ding.

Sir Henry Lawrence was now sent to take over another huge dis- contented province. As if it had not been bad enough that Oudh should be annexed so abruptly and on such a thin pretext, Lucknow had been burdened by the ill-humoured and incompetent Coverley Jackson as its first Chief Commissioner. Pensions went unpaid, the local landowners had been ousted from their villages, three-quarters of the King's Army were now unemployed and even the peasants, whom the land reforms were supposed to benefit, found the new tax regime intolerable.

Alas, it was only at the end of March 1857 that Henry Lawrence was dispatched to restore Britain's reputation for fairness. The new Chief Commissioner did his best. He spoke to everybody in their own language (he was competent in Hindi, Urdu and Persian), he listened to everybody, he held durbars for all classes of society. But Lucknow was already in an irretrievable ferment, and the native troops outnumbered the Europeans by nearly ten to one, 7,000 as against 750.[100] As always, Lawrence was a stranger to false optimism. He was well aware that he had come too late.

Within a couple of weeks, Lawrence had thrown up earthworks round the 33 acres of the Residency compound, laid in sizeable

Lord Hardinge meets Wajid Ali Shah, Lucknow, November 1847, Company School painting. Despite the embrace, the Governor-General had come to warn the King to put his house in order.

Wajid Ali Shah and his wife Hazrat Mahal, later to become the titular leader of the rebel government in Lucknow, after her husband had been exiled to Calcutta. From the *Ishqnamah*, now at Windsor Castle.

The Ganges Canal, with the Himalayas in the distance, watercolour by William Simpson.

'The first Relief of Lucknow', by Sir Henry Havelock, September 25, 1857.

'The Flight from Lucknow', by Abraham Solomon. The women and children evacuate the Residency on November 19, 1857.

Sir Colin Campbell, later Lord Clyde, alias Sir Crawling Camel.

The second Relief of Lucknow, by Sir Colin Campbell, November 17, 1857, by Thomas Jones Barker.

Ruins of the defences at the Begum Kothi, Lucknow. Felice Beato's photograph shows the damage done by Edward Thackeray and his sappers.

Ruins of Metcalfe House, by Felice Beato. A terrible sight for Theo Metcalfe's very sore eyes.

Looting of the Qaisarbagh, witnessed by W.H. Russell of *The Times*. An early example of the war reporter taking centre stage.

Malcolm Low at the time of his marriage, by E.K. Tayler, 1872.

'Our Magistrate', by George Francklin Atkinson, from *Curry and Rice*, first published 1859.

'Our Bath', from *Curry and Rice*.

Lieutenant-Colonel Samuel Browne, wearing his VC and his famous belt.

Ruins of the
Residency, by
Felice Beato.

Death of Major
Alexander Skene,
as described by
Christina Rossetti
but not as it actually
happened.

Lakshmi Bai, the Rani of
Jhansi, on the warpath.

Minnie Thackeray, by her family's friend, Julia Margaret Cameron.

Annie Thackeray, by Julia Margaret Cameron.

Edward Thackeray in middle age, with his VC.

General Low on his pony,
playing the Old Course,
St Andrews, in the 1860s.

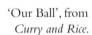'Our Ball', from
Curry and Rice.

Robert Low, when
Commander-in-Chief of
the Bombay Army, at a fancy
dress ball, Government
House, Poona, 1903.

Robert Low (seated, second from right) with his staff at Chitral after the Relief. The heroic Surgeon-Major Robertson is on his right, with arm in sling. Ian Hamilton, Quartermaster-General to the Expeditionary Force and later the ill-starred commander at Gallipoli, is seated on the ground at the left.

Maxim Gun detachment of the King's Royal Rifle Corps, Chitral, 1895.

Lieutenant-General Sir Robert Low, the careworn hero of Chitral.

stores of grain, powder and bullets, and brought in the treasure from outlying stations. By the end of April he had turned the Residency into a citadel as best he could. For this rolling English country park with its neo-classical banqueting hall, its little Gothic church, its delicious miniature mosque and *imambara* built for the White Begum Emma Walters, and the rambling Residency building itself, which bore more of a resemblance to a banker's villa in Tunbridge Wells than anything Indian – none of it was designed with defensive purposes in mind. Yet 'the Residency', as the whole estate was shorthanded, was about to become the legendary site of the whole Mutiny, the most resonant Residence in Victorian history.

The 'Siege of Lucknow' was as much a misnomer as the 'Siege of Delhi' had been. Henry Lawrence could see at a glance that any attempt to defend the great sprawling city of half a million hostile Indians would be ridiculous. Lucknow, having become a metropolis only recently, had no walls. The best he could hope to do was defend the Residency compound and the picturesque, long-disused old fortress, the Macchi Bhawan (which he quickly abandoned and blew up, seeing that it would dissipate what strength he had to try to defend two separate positions at once).

So the place that had been home to John and Augusta for longer than any other in their married life was converted into a fortress. The lawns where, one after the other but never together, Charlotte, Malcolm and Robert had played as babies before each of them was sent 'home', were now covered with tents and ringed with sandbags and field guns. The pleasant views over the city were blocked off by earth banks firmed up by wooden palisades. The cool underground rooms – the *tykhana* – in the Residency and in Mr Gubbins's and Surgeon Fayrer's no less palatial villas were filled with pale mothers sitting beside the cots of their ailing children. The lovely banqueting hall where the Lows had toasted the cream of Lucknow was now divided between a hospital and a small prison for several members of the Oudh royal family who had not gone to Calcutta with Wajid Ali Shah. St Mary's Church, where Malcolm had been christened at the only family reunion that the vagrant Shakespear clan ever had in India, was turned into a storehouse and granary, and its little grave-yard was soon full of pits for the dead, hurriedly dug under incessant fire.

The siege was not long in coming. On May 4, the men of the 7th Oudh Irregulars refused to bite the new cartridges. The next evening, Lawrence paraded them in front of the rifles of the 32nd Foot and the guns of the European artillery. The mutinous sepoys could see the artillery port fires already flickering in the moonlight. Sir Henry ordered them to lay down their arms. Terrified in the darkness, the sepoys mostly fled, then came back and in trembling obedience piled their muskets. Sir Henry then assembled all the native notables of the city and wooed them in his fluent Hindi, reminding them of the English Government's long traditions of toleration and the genuine friendship between the sepoys and their officers. Above all, he warned his audience how ultimately futile any crusade against the British would be. Look at their mighty Navy, look at what they had achieved in the Crimea. It was, by all accounts, a brilliant speech, warm and menacing at the same time. But he knew it was too late.

Everyone who was half awake could see it. Roderick Edwards, the Assistant Magistrate at Saharanpur, saw Lawrence's speech reported in the *Mofussilite* (the 'Provincial' or 'Backwoodsman') while he was having breakfast at Heseltine's Hotel in Dehra Dun, and wrote in his diary: 'excellent and well timed. It appeals to the sense and experi-ence of the troops, but I doubt its being of any permanent effect. There is a feeling, universal throughout the native army, that we have attempted to tamper with their religion, and not the "winged words" of the most heavenborn orator will convince them to the contrary.'[101] Edwards himself had already taken his wife and children up to Mussoorie to keep them safe.

Lawrence now brought most of the troops into the Residency compound, and he urged Canning to bring in European troops wherever he could find them – Nepal, Ceylon, China. 'Time is everything just now. Time, firmness, promptness, conciliation, prudence ... A firm and cheerful aspect must be maintained; there must be no bustle; no appearance of alarm, still of panic; but at the same time there must be the utmost watchfulness and promptness; everywhere the first germ of insurrection must be put down promptly.'[102] He brought the women and children in from the cantonments the other side of the river and he began to drill the clerks and copyists to swell his slender numbers of Europeans and Eurasians. Nobody could say that Sir Henry was not ready. At the most, he expected to have to hold out for 30 days.

On the night of May 30, while Lawrence was dining in his bungalow at the cantonments, the native troops began burning the bungalows and murdering their officers. Regiment by regiment, infantry scampered and cavalry galloped across the parade ground to join the first insurgents. Nor was the outbreak confined to the sepoys at Lucknow. Within two days, Lawrence received word that the entire province was up in arms against British rule. By June 12, the British had lost control of every station in Oudh. The great majority of landowners were arming their villagers and repossessing the villages which the British Commissioners had taken away from them. Now there was a great mass of rebels only eight miles from Lucknow, at Chinhat, out on the Faizabad road.

Lawrence went out to meet them with most of the force he could muster – 700 men, ten guns and a howitzer drawn by an elephant. They ran into a fierce cannonade from the 12–15,000 rebels drawn up around the village of Chinhat. The grapeshot was so heavy that almost all the Europeans who were hit were killed – 115 out of 154 in the 32nd alone. Sir Henry sat calmly on his horse at the Kukrail Bridge, waving his hat to encourage his men to rally for a final stand. But the Battle of Chinhat on June 30 was a disaster that Lawrence could ill afford with his shrunken numbers. Among the dead was the Commanding Officer of the 32nd, Colonel William Case, shot through the heart while rallying his men.

At first the wives had been relieved to move from the dreary cantonments to the fresher air and safety of the Residency on its gentle eminence. Adelaide Case wrote on June 9: 'The view from the top of the Residency is truly beyond description beautiful, and in the early morning, when the sun begins to shine on the gilded mosques and minarets, and towers, it is like a fairy scene. The whole of this vast city spread out before one, and on all sides surrounded by beautiful parks and magnificent trees, forms a panorama which it would be difficult to see equalled in any other part of the world.'[103]

William Case was still across the river in the cantonments: 'I always long for four o'clock, when the messenger arrives every day with a letter from the camp for me. I write without fail every night to William; Agaib, the bearer, coming in for my letter before I am awake in the morning.'[104] In one of his notes, William wrote: 'Who would have thought we should have been within four miles of each other, and yet not see each other for a whole week? I fancy that I am the only one who has not been down, but I dare not leave even for a few minutes. Still, I leave in hopes that ere long I shall be able to pay you a visit. Truly these are sad times, and I think no nation was ever in such a fix as we are in just now; but don't despair, you'll see we will pull through with the Almighty's aid. The Psalm of this morning ought to give you every encouragement. I derive much every morning from one verse or another that I read.'[105] After the battle, William's successor as CO, John Inglis, brought Adelaide his Bible, prayer book and the copy of Bishop Comber's *Companion to the Altar*, which she had given him. The *Companion* was shot right through.

Now the rebels had complete control of the city, and the siege began. It was to last four and a half months. But Sir Henry Lawrence was not destined to see much of it. Only two days after Chinhat, just after 8am on July 2, he was lying on his bed in the Residency dictating to Captain Wilson, the Assistant Adjutant-General, with his nephew George lying on another cot beside him. 'I read what I had written. It was not quite in accordance with his wishes, and he was in the act of explaining what he desired altered, when the fatal shot came; a sheet of flame, a terrific report and shock, and dense darkness, is all I can describe. I then got up, but could see nothing for the smoke and dust. Neither Sir Henry nor his nephew made any noise, and, in alarm, I cried out, "Sir Henry, are you hurt?" Twice I thus called out without any answer. The third time, he said, in a low tone, "I am killed."'[106]

The chaplain's wife, Mrs Harris, looked after him for the two days he lived on: 'I was upstairs all day, nursing Sir Henry, who still lingers in extreme suffering; his screams are so terrible, I think the sound will never leave my ears; when not under the influence of chloroform, he is quite conscious, and James has been reading to him all day psalms and prayers as he was able to bear them. He several times repeated them after him in quite a strong voice.'[107] The Reverend James Harris now had five or six funerals to conduct every night, and risked his life every time he went down to the churchyard. He was the only officer present at Sir Henry's burial because none of the others could be spared from the batteries.

Three weeks later, the Court of Directors, ignorant of Lawrence's death, appointed him to succeed Lord Canning as Governor-General in case of misadventure. At the grisly auction of his things which followed every officer's death, even the most modest items fetched absurd prices: a tin of soup, sufficient for one dinner, went for 25 shillings, four small cakes of chocolate two pounds ten shillings, a ham seven pounds. At another auction, Mrs Harris records that 'a very old flannel shirt of poor Captain Fulton's which had seen service in all the mines about the place and was covered with mud and dust sold for forty-five rupees.'[108]

Inside the Residency, there were now 153 male civilians, 500 women and children, 776 European troops and 765 natives. Apart from the relentless shelling from all directions, and the cholera and smallpox, there were flies everywhere, swarming in horrible clusters and festoons. The privations were not quite as bad as they had been at the siege of Cawnpore a month earlier. Martin Gubbins, the Deputy Commissioner, still managed to serve the guests crammed into his house a glass of sherry and two glasses of champagne or claret at dinner. There were still a few hens, goats and cattle in the native outhouses, and the compound possessed several decent wells.

Outside the fortifications that Lawrence had flung together, there were at the height of the siege more than 53,000 rebels. Of these, nearly 8,000 were rebel sepoys from all over northern India, 5,600 were identified as soldiers in Oudh native regiments, another 7,720 were cavalrymen, but the majority, over 30,000 of them, were 'Talukdar's men'.[109] That is, they were not professional soldiers but peasants and tenant farmers who had come to fight, more or less willingly, under the leadership of their local landowners. If ever evidence was needed that the rebellion was no longer 'a mere military revolt', it was to be found at Lucknow that summer.

As the attackers found their range and their targets, shells began to penetrate places that had been thought quite safe. Mrs Dorin was killed in an inner room at Gubbins's house. A young apothecary was killed by a round-shot while asleep in his bed in the hospital.[110] Miss Palmer, the daughter of Colonel Palmer of the 48th Native Infantry, had her leg taken off by a round-shot as she was going into her bedroom at the Residency.[111] A plaque still marks the spot. Bullets would skid across the floor in the ladies' quarters as they were sewing or doing their own washing for the first time in their lives, because so many of the dhobis had fled.

At night, there were shattering explosions as the enemy's mines blew up beneath them. One of the ladies heard the rebels tunnelling beneath her as she was taking her bath.[112] The mining and counter-mining never stopped. The insurgents would sink a four-foot-square shaft between 12 and 20 feet below the surface and dig through under the fortifications to the spot calculated to have the maximum impact. Outram later reported that 'I am aware of no parallel to our series of mines in modern war. Twenty-one shafts, aggregating two hundred feet in depth and three thousand two hundred and ninety-one feet of gallery, have been executed. The enemy advanced twenty mines against the palaces and outposts; of these they exploded three which caused us loss of life, and two which did no injury; seven had been blown in, and out of seven others the enemy have been driven and their galleries taken possession of by our miners.'[113]

Both underground and above ground, the battle was fought at unnerving close quarters. At many points, the rebels were only the width of a street away, and when the rainy season came in September, the grass grew so tall that they could crawl unnoticed right up to the British defences.

Three weeks into the siege, on July 22, Gubbins's trusty spy Angad arrived with his latest message, carried as usual rolled up in a quill pen secreted in his rectum (his reward was stupendous – £500 a trip). His news was doubly encouraging: General Havelock had arrived at Cawnpore and smashed Nana Sahib in three battles. No longer did it seem likely that the Nana would bring his large force to join the besiegers at Lucknow. And there was now the promise of relief, within five or six days perhaps.

But Havelock's force was pitifully small for such a task: 1,500 men, with ten second-rate guns and not enough gunners to man them. And he was still being harried by the Nana's troops. With the usual appalling rate of sickness in the hot season, by July 30 he had no more than 850 men to put into battle.[114] He had managed to eject the advance guard of the rebels from the little town of Unnao, but he could not hope to force his way through one and a half miles of Lucknow streets bristling with guns and snipers. So he fell back and informed his number two, Brigadier James Neill, whom he had left in command at Cawnpore, that he could not advance on Lucknow without 1,000 more European troops and another artillery battery.

His retreat provoked one of the rudest replies in British military history from the ferocious Neill: 'I deeply regret you have fallen back one foot. The effect on our prestige is very bad indeed ... The belief amongst all is that you have been defeated and forced back. It has been most unfortunate your not bringing any guns captured from the enemy. The natives will not believe that you have captured one. The effect of your retrograde movement will be very injurious to our cause everywhere, and bring down upon us many who would otherwise have held off, or even sided with us.'[115] Havelock, with some reason, described this as 'the most extraordinary letter he had ever perused' and retorted: 'Understand this distinctly, and that a consideration of the obstruction that would arise to the public service at this moment alone prevents me from taking the stronger step of placing you under arrest. You now stand warned.'[116]

Pricked on by Neill's insolence, on August 3 with only a few modest reinforcements Havelock advanced again. Once again he mowed down the rebels at Unnao. But now cholera had broken out in his camp. The River Sai, which lay between him and Lucknow, was in spate and the line of fortresses beyond it were said to be held by 30,000 men. For the second time, Havelock fell back.

On August 11, for the third time he advanced and pushed the enemy out of Unnao, but, still unconvinced that he had enough men to attack the great city, he fell back yet again, this time the whole way to Canwpore, where he had an uncomfortable meeting with Neill and, worse still, discovered, only by reading the *Calcutta Gazette*, that he had been superseded in his command by Major-General Sir James Outram.

In a remarkable gesture, which proved that he had not been wrongly dubbed 'the Bayard of India' by Sir Charles Napier back in 1842, Outram waived his rank and gave back to Brigadier-General Havelock the honour of relieving Lucknow. This rare and noble act of self-denial was greeted with astonishment by everyone in the army from Sir Colin Campbell downwards. In practice, according to Havelock's son and ADC Harry, Outram continued to issue orders as though he had never set aside his command, which meant that no one knew who was actually in charge. Havelock never regained his self-confidence and, when asked for orders, would mumble, 'You had better go to Sir James first.'[117] At least the relieving force was now up to 3,000 men, most of them European troops.

Which was just as well because by now the defenders were desperate. Gunfire, disease and hunger were carrying off more than 20 of them a day. Their spirits had been lowered by Havelock's repeated retreats. Nor were they much raised by his advice to Colonel Inglis that the garrison should try to cut its way out. Havelock's next exhortation, on August 29, was even less appetizing: 'I can only say do not *negotiate*, but rather perish sword in hand.'[118]

Then, at long last, on Thursday September 24, Adelaide Case heard distant guns during the day. On Friday, she wrote: 'What a day is this to be remembered for life with gratitude towards our Heavenly Father, for his great mercies by all those who have lived through this siege! Our relief has arrived!'[119]

Havelock's men had suffered terrible loss on the way, 700 men killed and wounded. Brigadier Neill was killed by one of the last shots fired. The fiercest man in the army after John Nicholson, he had died, like Nicholson, trying to retrieve men who had gone the wrong way in the narrow streets of a strange city. His courage and piety had equalled Nicholson's, and so had his brutality.

By Sunday the bitter truth had dawned. 'After all, this has been a very painful day,' Adelaide wrote. 'Everyone is depressed, and all feel that we are in fact *not relieved*. The fighting men we have are too few for our emergency and too many for the provisions we have in the garrison.'[120] Or, as her friend Mrs Harris put it rather more sharply, 'The "reinforcement" – for, alas "relief" is the wrong word – turns out to be very much smaller than we were led to expect.'[121] The hospitals were now overflowing with Outram's wounded. Their horses, a waste of space in a fortified enclosure, had no grass to feed on and died in great numbers, adding to the stench. They all had to stay put until they should be genuinely relieved by the larger army being assembled by Sir Colin Campbell at Cawnpore.

After the first 'Relief of Lucknow', there followed a second siege, which lasted another six weeks. It was not until sunrise on November 12 that Sir Colin Campbell swept in from the east of the city with 4,700 men and 49 guns. He took the Dilkusha, the King's hunting lodge in its bosky park, and then the extraordinary pleasure palace built by General Claude Martin, the so-called Martinière. There Sir Colin, in his habitual deliberate fashion, paused: to give his troops a breather; to bring up the stores; to get the field guns into position. Sir 'Crawling Camel' was criticized by young subalterns like Arthur Lang and Richard Barter for his lack of dash, but later historians have learnt to appreciate his methodical diligence and his unwilling-ness to risk unnecessary casualties. So far everything was going nicely.

On the morning of November 16, the cavalry trotted out along the banks of the Gomti through thick mango groves and low mud houses, with the infantry and the Engineers close behind them along the slushy narrow paths. In front of them lay the Sikandar Bagh ('Alexander's Garden'), a high-walled enclosure about 150 yards square with towers at the corners. It was known to be swarming with sepoys. It had to be taken. First Lang and the sappers had to knock down a high mud wall in front of the Sikandar Bagh, so that the big guns could begin to play on Alexander's Garden.

> While I was working hard at getting one of these guns dragged close up, I saw Lt Paul rush ahead waving his sword, and the 4th Punjabs yelling and shouting, as they charged along behind him straight at the building. The effect was electrical; down we dropped the ropes and rushed along too; up sprung 93rd and 53rd and, cheering and shouting 'Remember Cawnpore', on we went, some at a breach in one of the corner towers and some (with whom I was) over a loopholed mud wall straight at the gate; axes and muskets soon smashed in the gate, and then didn't we get revenge – the first good revenge I have seen![122]

The first men in had to jump through a small hole in a bricked-up doorway, about three feet square and the same distance from the ground. The first two men through, a Sikh and a Highlander, were shot dead instantly. The jump made by Lieutenant Richard Cooper of the 93rd reminded a fellow lieutenant of 'the headlong leap which Harlequin in pantomime makes through a shop window'.

'Such a sight of slaughter I never saw,' Arthur Lang recorded. 'In the open rooms right and left of the archway, Pandies were shot down and bayoneted in heaps, three or four feet deep; in the centre Bara Dari they made but little stand, but at the house in the middle of the rear wall and in the semicircular court beyond it they shut the many thin doors and thousands of bullets were poured in, into the masses. It was a glorious sight to see the mass of bodies, dead and wounded, when we did get in. The bodies have now been buried and counted – 1,840 Pandies. The mass of bodies were set fire to, and to hear the living as they caught fire calling out in agony to be shot was horrible even in that scene where all men's worst passions were excited.'[123]

The rebels had inflicted their casualties, too. In the inner court, Captain Dawson of the 93rd found a heap of his men lying dead under a large peepul tree. Inspecting the bodies, he discovered that they had all been shot from above. He summoned 'Quaker' Wallace, an educated oddball so-called because of his taciturnity not his fear-fulness. In battle, Quaker was given to singing Scottish metrical psalms. He had gone into the Sikandar Bagh singing Psalm 116, 'I love the Lord, because my voice/ And prayers he did hear' and had already killed 20 men single-handed. He fired into the bushy tree and down fell a body dressed in a tight-fitting red jacket and pink silk trousers. With the fall, the jacket burst open revealing a woman's breasts. Her heavy old cavalry pistols were still loaded in her belt and her ammo pouch was half-full, but Quaker Wallace burst into tears: 'If I had known it was a woman, I would rather have died a thousand deaths than have harmed her.'[124]

This was the fiercest fighting of the battle, perhaps of the whole Mutiny. The assault on the Sikandar Bagh still holds the record for the most VCs won in a single action – 18 – just as that day, November 16, 1857, holds the record for the most VCs awarded in a single day, 24.

For the rest of the day, the gunfire was relentless and the slaugh-ter unceasing. Even by the end of it, as the invaders lay down to sleep with their weapons in their hands, they were still several buildings away from the Residency. They had yet to carry the clunking mass of the so-called Mess House, the large nawabi mansion which had been taken over by the officers of the 32nd before they were with-drawn into the Residency, and the Moti Mahal, the Pearl Palace, Wajid Ali Shah's old summer retreat. Campbell's men were awakened on November 17, not by their own bugles but by the bells of the city and the beating of the enemy's drums. The great superiority of the British lay in their heavy guns which bombarded from the early morning until 3pm when they stormed the last obstacles and at last Campbell's vanguard was within touching distance of Outram and Havelock.

The meeting of the most famous generals of the war was an iconic event at the time, and the heroic painting by Thomas Jones Barker, now in the National Portrait Gallery, has enshrined it in the national memory. As the smoke of battle clears, Christian soldiers shake hands in the restrained British way and Britannia resumes her reign. Sir Colin walks forward, raises his cap to Outram and says, 'How do you do, Sir James.' Then turning to Havelock, 'How do you do, *Sir Henry*' – which is the first that Havelock, incommunicado for six weeks, knows of his knighthood. Just behind Havelock there is an officer in a white helmet, with a quizzical smile on his bearded face. This is James Metcalfe, Lord Metcalfe's mixed-race son, who is now interpreter and ADC to the Commander-in-Chief and is accompanying Sir Colin through most of the campaign, before being promoted Major and commanding a wing of the 4th Bengal European infantry in the final assault on Lucknow. Quite a career for someone who had such an unpromising start in life.

The reality was not quite so dignified as Barker's picture, nor the resuming so uncontested. There was still half a mile of open ground between the two forces, a no-man's-land sprayed by relentless fire from the high walls of the Kaiserbagh, the enormous royal palace, Wajid Ali Shah's most conspicuous bequest to the city, completed only five years earlier.

The eight officers who stepped out to meet Sir Colin had not gone a few yards before the enemy spotted them and the dust was kicked up with bullets, and the generals had to run for it. Napier, later Lord Napier of Magdala, Havelock's son Henry, who had won the VC two months earlier, and a couple more senior officers were struck down. Outram, Havelock and Vincent Eyre reached the Moti Mahal uninjured and had a few minutes of talk with the Commander-in-Chief, relieved in every sense of the word. They then had to run back across the terrible space. General Havelock, already weakened by dysentery, could not make it on his own. He gasped to the Deputy Adjutant General, 'Dodgson, I can do no more', and had to be dragged to safety. He died at the Dilkusha a week later.

Outram and Havelock tried to persuade Campbell to attack the Kaiserbagh and take the whole city. Colonel Inglis insisted that he could hold on to the Residency with only 600 men. But Campbell could see how fragile his hold was. He looked at the casualties he had already incurred – over 500 of them. He looked at the women and children. And he decided, in that mulish, deliberate way of his, that he would have to evacuate them first and leave Lucknow to the rebels until he could return with a large enough army to recapture it once for all.

So once more the British retreated from Lucknow. And this time, they were leaving the Residency empty. Adelaide Case recorded her amazement the next day: 'When Colonel Inglis came to dinner he told us that Sir Colin Campbell's orders are that we are all to leave Lucknow tomorrow evening! Our consternation may be more easily imagined than described, and I think our faces when we looked at each other wore an expression of the most complete bewilderment. How all the wounded and sick people and women and children are to be got off in such a hurried manner, at only a few hours' notice, I cannot imagine.'[125]

They were to take with them almost nothing except the clothes they stood up in. The solution was to stand up in as many clothes as possible. Maria Germon wrote in her journal: 'I put on four flannel waistcoats, three pairs of stockings, three chemises, three drawers, one flannel and four white petticoats, my pink flannel dressing gown, skirt, plaid jacket, and over all my cloth dress and jacket that I had made out of my habit ... I forgot to say I had sewed dear mother's fish-knife and fork in my pink skirt.'[126]

On the evening of November 19. the British walked in silence through the dusk to the Dilkusha, the ladies borne along beside them in doolies. The only sounds were the tramp, tramp of the dooly-bearers and the screaming of the jackals in the jungle.[127] They left behind in the ruined Residency all their crockery and glass, their musical instruments and books (except their treasured Bibles and prayer books).

But they had survived. Only 66 of the 500 women and children died during the siege and 51 of those were children. The children mostly died of malnutrition and disease rather than enemy fire. The highest casualties were among the men manning the batteries who were within range of the enemy 24 hours a day.

They also left behind Captain Waterman of the 13th Native Infantry, who had fallen asleep in the Residency and woke suddenly in the middle of the night, startled to find everything so quiet around him. He had to run as fast as he could to catch up the bedraggled British convoy. The shock was said to have disturbed his brain, although unkind comrades wondered whether there was much to disturb. Another oversleeper was Sergeant Alex Macpherson of the 93rd, spotted by his mates in the distance scurrying across the plain after having snored away in the barracks until after daybreak. He was known thereafter as Sleepy Sandy.[128] Once again we are reminded how utterly fagged out British soldiers on campaign were. Waterman and Sleepy Sandy at Lucknow, Major Cobbe at Delhi, Blakiston in the night attack on Fort Cornelis – oversleeping was an occupational hazard.

The evacuation was a spur to the rebels, perhaps a surprising one. They can scarcely have expected that, after fighting his way through such carnage, Campbell would immediately retrace his steps to the Alambagh. According to a report received by the Secret Branch of the British Foreign Department on November 25, 'It was then proclaimed in the city that the Europeans had abandoned the place, and addresses to the same purport were sent to the district authorities and to the king of Delhie.' The Begum had given instructions to occupy Benares and Allahabad. The Nana Sahib with the Gwalior troops were surrounding Cawnpore. 'The war is now believed throughout Lucknow to be a religious crusade, and crowds of people are flocking into the capital from the districts to take part in the struggle.' By the end of January, Outram, who had been left behind with a holding garrison at the Alambagh, reckoned that there were 96,000 rebel troops in Lucknow, including more than 27,000 trained sepoys, and there might be another 20,000 *taluqdar*'s men on top of that figure.[129]

No less than 15,000 men were employed in building three gigantic earth walls, barring the eastern approaches which the British had favoured. Every street had been barricaded and loopholed, a deep moat dug round the Kaiserbagh. Outram's little garrison at the Alambagh, the big country palace four miles out of Lucknow on the Cawnpore Road, was vulnerable not only to military assault (he was attacked half a dozen times by forces of up to 30,000 men) but also to being starved out. The surrounding villages refused to supply any provisions at all. Forays had to be made to distant settlements and extravagant prices paid for a few bags of grain. By the beginning of 1858, and for most of that year, the people of Oudh were more or less solidly in revolt.

Only the decisive recapture of Lucknow would show who was master. It was not until the end of February that Sir Colin began to march again on the city – the fifth time in seven months that a British force had set out to take it. This was said to be the most powerful British army ever concentrated in one place in India: 20,000 cavalry and infantry, 137 guns and mortars, 22 siege guns.

Sir Crawling Camel might be derided for his caution, but his plan this time showed a certain daring. He divided his army into two, with an unfordable river in between, and all the dangers of the two halves getting irreparably separated. Outram with the cavalry and half the heavy guns were to cross the Gomti by two pontoon bridges and make a big loop the far side, via the racecourse, and bombard the palaces across the river. Campbell was to come in from the east, as before, by way of the Dilkusha and the Martinière, with most of the infantry and the sappers, who would then bash their way through the heart of the city.

It was 4am on the morning of the March 6 when the 2nd Punjab Cavalry – led by Brigadier James Hope Grant and the famous Captain Sam Browne, of whom we shall hear more, and Lieutenant Robert Low, who by now had as much combat experience as almost anyone – led the way across the hasty pontoons, with Sir Colin himself chivvying them on, anxious to get the whole lot across before dawn. Outram sat placidly on the ground, puffing at a cigar. Lieutenant Vivian Majendie, fresh from the Crimea, leaves a vivid account of the nervous gallop through the dawn, then the waiting in the mango groves before they attacked the Chakar Kothi, or Yellow House, which was the racecourse pavilion: the horses with their heads in nosebags, officers handing round cigar cases and brandy flasks, the men carving hunks of bread and meat for their last breakfast with the same knives they carved their tobacco, then the canter through the jungle, with the white-robed rebels fleeing through the trees. At first they went so quietly that they came upon a party of sepoys finishing their breakfasts who were bayoneted with their mouths full as they got up to flee. Outram's force included the first of the reinforcements from overseas. Many had never seen action before, but they showed the instant retributive ferocity of old hands. Sepoys were stripped, tied to the ground, branded and roasted: 'Sepoy or Oude villager, it mattered not – no questions were asked. His skin was black and did not that suffice? A piece of rope and the branch of a tree, or a rifle bullet through his brain, soon terminated the poor devil's existence.'[130]

Soon the backmarkers were galloping over a morass of corpses. Then they turned sharp left and galloped on along the river with mosques and palaces glittering in the morning light. When they had come up to the two bridges into the city, one of iron, built by the British, the other of stone, the cavalry reined in, and the bombardment began. For four days Outram's guns battered all the great buildings of Lucknow: the Begum Kothi, the Kaiserbagh, the Chatter Manzil, the two *imambaras*, the Machi Bhawan. All the glories of nawabi architecture were pounded without let-up.

So was the Residency. Robert Low found himself part of an army that was doing its best to destroy the place that had briefly been his childhood home. He, if anyone, could say like the narrator in *Brideshead Revisited*, 'I have been here before.' The final act of Outram's force, on March 16, was to assault the Residency compound. Now the roles were reversed: the English the attackers, the Indians the defenders. Colonel Malleson's account is exultant: 'The difference showed itself in a remarkable manner. For, whereas in the former case the Englishmen defended themselves unassisted, for eighty-four days, in the latter the Asiatics were disposed of in less than half an hour. One charge of Outram's division, and the enemy fled, panic-stricken and panting, from the classic ground.'[131] That charming overgrown villa, which Asaf-ud-daula had built for the British Resident to cement the 'friendship and perfect union' between them, had been mercilessly bombarded by both sides. Now it was left in ruins, a monument to human endurance and human folly.

On the other side of the river, Campbell's Engineers had to cut their way through the new 30-foot bank the far side of the canal. Arthur Lang and Edward Thackeray and their Punjab sappers were digging all through the night of March 11 and then throwing a causeway across the canal to make a nice road for the guns. Sir Crawling Camel made it his rule never to hazard the infantry until the engineers had told him that the artillery and the sappers between them had made a passable way through. This time, instead of sticking close to the river on their way to the Residency, they would fight their way through the eastern end of the town, but avoiding the streets, which were bristling with snipers at every loopholed window and guns at the end of the street. Instead, they would burrow along the south side of the Hazratganj, then as now the main street, artillery smashing a way first, then sappers with pickaxes and crow-bars. For this, like the first hours of the siege of Delhi, was the sappers' moment.

'Fancy getting into a house in Park Lane,' Edward wrote to his brother, 'only twice the size, with gardens and courtyards, and knocking a hole in the next with 68-pounders, then bringing up the gun and knocking a hole in the next, and rushing in, and so on. The rebels did not understand it, they had prepared the streets with bat-teries, loopholes &c, while we went into the houses themselves and broke through from house to house.'[132]

The Begum's house came first and it was the toughest nut: 600 rebels were killed in the hand-to-hand fighting but only a small number of British, though they included the irrepressible William Hodson, who kicked open a door with the words, 'I wonder if there is anyone in this house' and was shot by a musket-ball through his liver. Archdale Wilson commented to his wife, 'He had no right to be at the Begum Kothi. He should have been five miles off with his Horse.' Like Nicholson and Neill, he died in the wrong place because he insisted on being in the thick of it.

'I was not on duty in that assault,' Edward reported, 'but had to go down in the evening and build a battery in the road, at the side of the Begum's house. Such a sight as it was. Imagine a splendid house and garden with lamps all over it, with enormous rooms and mirrors and dead sepoys everywhere. I never saw such a sight either as the engine house, bodies lying in and out of the machinery. Half the room had caught fire. At night a great part of Lucknow seemed in a blaze, fires and mines exploding in all directions, while our shells continued to pour into the city.

'The duty was nothing like as arduous or dangerous as Delhi. And I would rather go through *four or five Lucknows* than another Delhi.'[133]

Then began the looting, and on a spectacular scale, equalled per-haps but probably never surpassed in British military history.

'The plunder got by some of the regiments is enormous,' Edward reported. 'Privates have got diamond bracelets and jewels worth hundreds of pounds, and which they have sometimes been selling for a few rupees.'[134] 'I was *knee*-deep in valuables,' wrote Arthur Lang, 'and yet did not improve my chance. Seeing that I did not help myself, a man held up a bag full of jewels – a bag as big as his head – and said: "Take a share, sir. Take this." Like a fool I came the magnanimous and rejected everything! I took some handsome *tulwars* which I stuck in my belt. One officer in the tent next to mine has upwards of 500,000 rupees worth of diamonds, pearls and rubies! I never saw such precious stones as I have here.'[135]

After the battle, Campbell was widely criticized for not cutting off the thousands of rebels fleeing out the other end of the city across the Gomti. He had told Outram not to advance if it would cost him the life of one single man – misguided compunction in the eyes of military experts. This lack of ruthless pursuit meant that thousands of rebels survived to plague the British for months. But there were tens of thousands of rebels already out in the countryside. In any case, as Eric Stokes points out, 'It was inevitable that the blows aimed by the British at Lucknow would have something of the effect of punching a pillow in the middle. While giving at the centre, the pillow threatened to burst out at the extremities.'[136] The immediate priority was to wrap up the recapture of the city. Then the pacification of the province could begin in earnest.

Campbell did not dawdle. A week later, he sent out Brigadier James Hope Grant (the laconic younger brother of Francis Grant RA, who painted a grim but splendid portrait of him) with the 2nd Punjab Cavalry to attack 4,000 rebels gathered at Kursi, a small town 25 miles to the north. As soon as Hope Grant caught sight of the rebels, he sent on two squadrons of the 2nd Punjab under Captain Sam Browne to dash at them.

At the age of 33, Sam Browne was already a legend for his exploits in the Punjab. Henry Lawrence had chosen him to lead the new Punjab Frontier Force, for which he raised the 2nd Punjab Irregular

Cavalry, later to be renamed Sam Browne's Cavalry. Sam's sister Félicité, who was 16 years older, had married the pernickety Sir Thomas Metcalfe. So he was Theo's uncle, although they were almost the same age. It is hard to say which of them was the more pugnacious. Certainly, Robert Low, who had been posted to the 2nd Punjab, was now serving under perhaps the only man in the Indian Army who could rival his former boss John Nicholson in that department.

He did not disappoint on this occasion. Hope Grant wrote in his diary: 'Captain Browne, who commanded, seeing some guns moving off, charged the rebels in the most magnificent style. Five times he rode clean through them, killing about two hundred, and taking thirteen guns and a mortar.'[137] By the time they had ridden over the rebels for the fifth time, their hooves must have been cutting up a steaming mush.

Robert was then sent off to join the ubiquitous Brigadier Showers, this time to subdue Tantia Topi and the Maratha rebels in central India. This was a military experience of a different kind, though, oddly enough, again one that his father had experienced 40 years earlier. For months, Tantia Topi proved as elusive as the Peshwa had been in the same region, endlessly doubling back across the wild terrain, sometimes with a tiny band of followers, sometimes with a sizeable army. Time and again it seemed impossible that he could escape. By January 1859, he was hemmed in by Showers on the north-west, by Napier on the north-east, Somerset on the east, Smith on the south-west, Benson and Michel on the south and Honner on the west. Yet somehow he managed to slip away. Some of his associates escaped into the northern hills disguised as pilgrims, but Tantia Topi never abandoned the struggle. Eventually he was betrayed by his long-time ally Man Singh and captured while asleep. On April 18, 1859, he was hanged for the crime of rebellion against the British, although even British historians questioned the verdict, for he had been born a servant of the Peshwa at a time when that dubious figure ruled large parts of western India, so he owed no allegiance to the British.[138] Like the Rani of Jhansi, he lives on in the Indian imagination.

In his short military career, Robert Low had already taken part in two great sieges and confronted two opposing types of guerrilla fighters: the Santals who never ran away and Tantia Topi who did little else. These were not to be his last experiences of facing resourceful rebels. By the end of his career in the Indian Army he could have written a manual on the subject. But he did not, for alone of all his clan Robert seldom put pen to paper except to write a military dispatch. His life story, though, is itself abundant confirmation of Sir John Kaye's assertion that 'India had been won by the sword and must be retained by the sword.'

Malcolm in the mofussil

I t was the horror of Cawnpore, the drama of Delhi, the serial agony of Lucknow that gripped the public. But everywhere in northern India, in those terrible summer months, the British were holding their breath or already fighting to the last gasp. In the *mofussil* – as the backwoods outside the three Presidencies were called – District Officers with a handful of loyal native police were hanging on, with small hope of reinforcements, except of dubious Native Infantry and Cavalry who were just as likely to swell the rebellion as to suppress it.

Malcolm Low was the only civilian among John and Augusta's sons. He was three years older than Robert, and he was better at his books. John and Augusta sent him to the East India College at Haileybury, while Mr Day's Academy on Brixton Hill was thought good enough for Robert. The two boys slotted into their allotted destinies – Robert a cavalryman with a doomed native regiment in Bengal, while Malcolm passed into the elite Imperial Civil Service. This corps was the ambition of every Anglo-Indian mother, but the life its officers led was anything but rarefied.

John Lawrence, their boss in the Punjab, reckoned that 'the ideal district officer was a hard active man in boots and breeches, who almost lived in the saddle, worked all day and nearly all night, ate and drank when and where he could, had no family ties to hamper him, and whose whole establishment consisted of a camp bed, an odd table and chair or so and a small box of clothes such as could be slung on a camel.' He would be deciding cases either on horseback in the village gateway or under a tree outside the walls. He was to spare no time for the refinements of life, as one officer who took his piano with him to the Punjab famously discovered. Sir John declared, 'I'll smash his piano for him', and had the poor fellow moved four times in two years, the piano's transport costing a small fortune.[139]

The brilliant George Otto Trevelyan, who went out to India a few years after Malcolm, declared that the life of a young Collector in the *mofussil* was infinitely preferable to the dreary grind of a junior lawyer in London or a classics master at Eton or Westminster:

He rises at daybreak and goes straight from his bed to the saddle. Then off he gallops across fields bright with dew to visit the scene of the late dacoit robbery; or to see with his own eyes whether the crops of the *zemindar* who is so unpunctual with his assessment have really failed; or to watch with fond parent care the progress of his pet embankment. Perhaps he has a run with the bobbery pack of the station, consisting of a superannuated foxhound, four beagles, a greyhound, the doctor's retriever and a Skye terrier belonging to the assistant magistrate ... They probably start a jackal, who gives them a sharp run of ten minutes, and takes refuge in a patch of sugarcane ... On their return the whole party adjourn to the subscription swimming bath, where they find their servants ready with clothes, razors and brushes. After a few headers, and "chota hasree" or "little breakfast" of tea and toast, flavoured with the daily papers and scandal about the Commissioner, the Collector returns to his bungalow, and settles down to the hard business of the day. Seated under a punkah in his verandah, he works through the contents of one despatch-box after another ... Noon finds him quite ready for a *déjeuner à la fourchette*, the favourite meal in the Mofussil, where the tea-tray is lost amidst a crowd of dishes – fried fish, curried fowl, roast kid and mint sauce, and mango-fool. Then he sets off in his buggy to

Cutcherry [courthouse], where he spends the afternoon in hearing and deciding questions connected with land and revenue. If the cases are few, and easy to be disposed of, he may get away in time for three or four games at rackets in the new court of glaring white plaster, which a rich native has built, partly as a speculation, and partly to please the sahibs. Otherwise, he drives with his wife on the race-course, or plays at billiards with the inspector of police ... Then follows dinner, and an hour of reading or music. By ten o'clock he is in bed, with his little ones asleep in cribs enclosed by the same mosquito curtain as their parents.[140]

In a curious way, this hyperactive life was both responsible and carefree. Malcolm was well suited to it. He had passed out of Haileybury in December 1855, and by May 1857 he was Assistant Commissioner of Revenue at Meerut. With the Lows' knack of not being actually present at the outbreak of mutinies, he was on sick leave up in the hills at Dehra Dun when the sepoys at Meerut began to murder their officers. As soon as he heard the news, he applied for his leave to be cancelled and headed for the action.

When he reached the first town on the plains, Saharanpur, the old Mughal city 40 miles to the south, the chief magistrate there, a redoubtable, peppery, hard-drinking character called Robert Spankie, immediately gave him an elephant and told him to take the treasure up to Mussoorie, just beyond Dehra Dun, the remote hill station where Malcolm's parents had been married. Only these inaccessible British enclaves now seemed safe. Already roving bands of sepoys, bandits and local *badmashes*, or bad characters, had smashed open the treasuries in half a dozen towns in the country between Delhi and the hills.

When the treasury was threatened at the sizeable town of Bijnor, 40 miles north of Meerut, the magistrate there, Alexander Shakespear, one of Malcolm's innumerable cousins, removed the cash from the *cutchery* and hid it in a well, until Hugh Gough arrived from Meerut with 25 cavalrymen to escort it to a safer place: 'having

quickly annexed some of the Raja's elephants, we with much difficulty fished up the treasure, in one thousand rupee bags, and having
laden our elephants with as much as we could carry, I prepared to
return. But before starting I most earnestly begged Mr Shakespear to
return to Meerut with me, together with his wife and young Palmer,
but nothing would induce this brave man to leave his post, nor
would his wife leave him.'[141] The Shakespears eventually managed to
escape to another hill station, Naini Tal, and thence to Mussoorie.

Not everyone was so impressed with Alexander's conduct.
Roderick Edwards, sweating out the hot mutinous season down at
Muzaffarnagar, regarded him as a 'muff' who had bolted when there
was no real trouble. Edwards thought that 'the general impression is
that after seeing his wife and the other ladies safe ... Shakespear
should at once have returned to his post', and he could not forgive
him for filling Mrs Edwards's ears with alarmist rumours.[142] In fact,
Alexander did eventually return to Bijnor and restore order there,
and was congratulated by Lord Canning for his 'energy and sound
judgment'.[143]

Hugh Gough had a gruelling ride back to Meerut with his richly
laden elephants. The mutineers were everywhere – 'a sore temptation to men like mine. They were in no way bound to me by any
personal feeling, they barely knew me by name, their *bhaibunds* (or
comrades) were mutineers and marching in close proximity to us,
and they had the temptation of the loot in their very hands. All they
had to do was to kill the English lad, their commander and make
their way unmolested to Delhi to join their friends. But not a man
wavered in his loyalty or murmured one word of discontent.'[144] On
the contrary, they got milk for him, made him chupattis and rubbed
down his horse.

When they reached Meerut, to a warm welcome from his friends
who had not expected to see him again, Gough was bowled over by
a sharp attack of fever. When he recovered, he learnt to his chagrin
that his whole detachment had finally mutinied and decamped to the
enemy, without even waiting for their arrears of pay. The bemused

Gough still could not work out why they had refrained from killing him and making off with the 250,000 rupees while they had the chance. The episode, like so many others, suggests that many sepoy units brooded on their choice for quite a time and then finally made up their mind to mutiny on an impulse rather than as part of any pre-arranged, co-ordinated plan.

After Malcolm had come back down from Mussoorie, Mr Spankie sent him off to collect revenue in the district, which it would be an understatement to describe as disturbed. For this task he was given an escort of Punjab Irregular Cavalry, and he seems to have brought in the rupees, for Spankie wrote him a letter of congratulation and advice:

> I am highly pleased with what you do, & the discretion you exhibit . . . I must trust very much to your own judgment. I think that by soothing rather than by irritating, & at the same time keeping up a bold front, you will fulfil your task. Only remember, there is no pledge against punishment for old misdeeds; only consideration for repentance to be shown. You are a good man, Sir,
>   R.Spankie.[145]

In other words, the British could only hope to go on extracting the essential revenue by a mixture of bluff and cajolery. Experienced British officials often hankered for the old native methods of collection. Thomas Fortescue, Delhi Commissioner in 1821, after clumsy efforts to reform the town duties, noted of the old system: 'I found in short that an astonishingly large revenue continued to be realised by a process which was extremely delicate and refined and yet easily conducted and in a manner free from irritation and discontent.'[146] The task had been ticklish enough in peacetime. In the middle of a national revolt, the British hold on these fortified towns and villages was as fragile financially as it was militarily. On the one hand, the huge quantities of rupees in the *cutcheries* had to be whisked away out of the reach of the sepoys. On the other hand, the loyal troops and policemen still had to be paid, and the usual land rents extracted from a surly peasantry. With the contents of his Treasury salted away in the hills, the hot-tempered Spankie found himself short of running expenses and was compelled to send his agent Sadr Amin down to the moneylenders in the town to borrow 14,000 rupees. Spankie was furious when Sadr Amin made a public show of the transaction.[147] Any hint that the sahibs were in trouble was liable to encourage rebellion. In their extremity, the British were as dependent on native bankers as they were on native policemen.

Revenue collectors were in the front line, and were among the first to be killed. Mr Thompson, the Collector at Hansi, had been murdered by his own messenger. Eric Stokes points out in *The Peasant Armed*, that 'It is noticeable that the most formidable anti-British combinations in the Western parts of Meerut and Muzaffarnagar districts occurred not on the immediate outbreak of sepoy revolt but two or three months later when the agents were dispatched to collect the revenue instalments.'[148] Like the English Civil War and the American and French Revolutions, the Indian Mutiny was as much a rebellion against unfair taxation as it was anything else. After all, as C.A. Bayly reminds us, 'the vast majority of historical revolts have involved issues of taxation.'[149]

Malcolm wrote to his father in Calcutta, sending his 'best love to dearest mama and yourself' and enclosing a memorandum which he said was 'an unvarnished statement of facts, hardly looked over a second time, & only intended for yourself.' He gives a vivid personal account of the frantic helter-skelter efforts of the British to put down the rebellion as it broke out in town after town. Sometimes he would be facing a detachment of mutinous sepoys from Delhi, sometimes the tenantry of a resentful local landowner who had lost half his villages in Coverley Jackson's resettlement, sometimes simply a mob of villagers whose mood was quite unpredictable.

In the big cities, the major battles might be fought mostly by disaffected sepoys, but out in the country the revolt began to attract support from all sections of the population. Sergeant-Major William

Forbes-Mitchell of the old 93rd (later to become the Argyll and Sutherland Highlanders) recorded that in Oudh, 'it was clear as noonday to the meanest capacity that we were now in an enemy's country ... none of the villages along the route were inhabited, the only visible signs of life about them being a few pariah dogs ... it needed no great powers of observation to fully understand that the whole population of Oudh was against us.'[150] Another District Officer, Dundas Robertson, revisiting villages to the east of Deoband which he knew well, was amazed: 'Troops might mutiny, but I could hardly realize this rapid change among peaceful villagers ... the *zemindars* were one with the lower orders ... rebellion, not plunder alone, actuated the mass of the population.'[151] Roderick Edwards, now posted as Magistrate at Muzaffarnagar, also noticed this common front: 'The whole of this district is "up" and the villains no longer war against each other as at the commencement of the disturbances but have agreed to let their private feuds remain in abeyance and war against the government and its servants and all who assist and shelter them.'[152]

Some modern historians, preferring to concentrate on the cities, have argued that there was never much of a revolt in the countryside.[153] This was certainly not the view of those who had to deal with the outbreaks. In mid-September, Edwards lamented that 'the risings are increasing in number almost hourly. No sooner do we suppress them in one place than they appear in another some 20 miles distant. They remind me of wildfowl diving at one shot to come up again almost immediately at another spot.' Outram, protesting against Canning's threat to expropriate any *taluqdar*, or landowner, who had taken part in the Mutiny, told him that there were not a dozen landowners in Oudh who had not assisted the rebels in some way or other.[154] Rudrangshu Mukherjee's detailed analysis supports this: out of 126 *taluqdars* he found that 82 had joined the rebels or given them aid.[155]

The motives for joining the rebellion were varied. Muslims felt the threat to their faith, Hindus the threat to their caste. In many villages, the moneylenders had bankrupted the peasants and taken over the land. Perhaps worst of all, the diverse pattern of Indian landholdings had bewildered Gubbins and his officers, and, with the best of intentions, their revenue assessments had turned out to be too stiff. The ingenious Mountstuart Elphinstone had made similar mistakes in the Maratha country 40 years earlier, and Gubbins was no Elphinstone. Even the good deeds of the British could turn sour, literally so along parts of the Ganges Canal where the need to build up the banks had left the surrounding terrain a salty bog in which the only crop was malaria.

The peasants were not in any sort of uniform, but then nor was Malcolm. He was simply a district officer with a sword in his hand.[156]

On Saturday September 5, he rode into Muzaffarnagar to meet Edwards who had just been posted there as Chief Magistrate to restore order.[157] The whole district was in a frightful state. To the west, Gujjar bandits were plundering the country for the hell of it. More seriously, to the south, 'Large bodies of fanatic mussulmans assisted by sepoys in considerable numbers ... were assembled, not so much for purposes of plunder, as to bear their part in what they vainly imagined was to be the total destruction of the English govt. and the English in that part of the country.' To the east, the large walled cities, mostly belonging to the King of Delhi, were under the sway of a local warlord, the Khazi of Kanakkoum, whose grandson had just been hanged for the murder of poor Sam Fisher, a young officer in the 15th Irregular Cavalry.

By soothing rather than irritating, just as Mr Spankie had recommended, Malcolm managed to get in the revenue in the northern part of the country. But further south, there was uproar. Mr Grant, the Joint Magistrate, was at Shamli with the remaining loyal fraction of the 3rd Light Cavalry. He hurried off, not waiting for Edwards's permission, to quell a nearby village called Parasauli, where he hoped to seize another local warlord, Khairati Khan, a fearless old Maratha bandit who was also a leper and a shareholder in the village. This turned out to be a big mistake. The place was swarming with armed rebels. Grant retreated in a hurry. The news of the British humiliation was all over the country within hours.

Edwards, furious at Grant's rash sortie, rushed to Shamli, accompanied by Malcolm and a full troop of the 1st Punjab Cavalry. He collected a satisfactory haul of 275,000 rupees from the cowed citizens of Shamli to send to HQ at Meerut. All was quiet at Shamli, and the trusty police chief Ibrahim Khan had everything under control.[158] But then they heard that a village to the north called Hurhar had been taken over by rustlers who seized 40 carts of supplies containing sugar, gum, bark and dyes destined for Shamli and they were now levying tolls on travellers, and murdering those who refused to stump up.

Malcolm and Mr Edwards galloped off to Hurhar with their little band of cavalry. 'The stir and commotion inside the village was plainly discernable, but not a shot was fired by the villagers. They had by this time seen the company of goorkas advancing and deemed resistance useless. The village was entered and given up to plunder; various govt. stores were discovered. The ringleaders were put to death and many others flogged at the carts tail.'

A reasonable morning's work (there was no talk of anything resembling a trial), and Malcolm sat down to breakfast under a tree. It was interrupted by a native policeman who had ridden over from Thana Bhawan, where the Raja was in open revolt with a huge mixed force of 8,000 men. 'This was not very satisfactory,' writes Malcolm with proper British understatement, 'but a little more was yet to be told.' The Raja's men had ambushed the magazine party on its way to Malcolm, which gave the rebels 2,000 rounds more and the British 2,000 rounds less.

Clearly it would have been madness to attack Thana Bhawan against such odds, so they decided to go back to Shamli. The next morning, the alarm was sounded and they jumped to their horses, but they were pleasantly surprised to find that the cloud of dust approaching was not the Raja's army but Captain Smith, late of the 24th Native Infantry (late, because his regiment had mutinied) on his way from Peshawar to Meerut with a fine troop of Afghan horse and 50 Sikhs armed with *tulwars*. Would Captain Smith stay and take command of their combined forces? There was no time to refer back to HQ for guidance. Like the rebels, the British had to improvise.

So off they go to subdue the royal towns of Burhana and Jaula, currently in the hands of the ferocious old leper, Khairati Khan. They leave only a small police guard at Shamli under the command of Ibrahim Khan, who insists that he can hold the place without extra help – which turns out to be another mistake.

At daybreak, they are outside Jaula. They hear the drums beating in the town, then they see crowds of armed men streaming out of the town towards them. Captain Smith halts the column. Malcolm gallops up from the rear for orders. Smith tells him to stay at the rear and guard the baggage. There is a distinct impression that he would rather not be saddled with a mere civilian when they go into action. Malcolm persists. He and his Punjabi cavalrymen are likely to prove far more reliable than the remnants of the 3rd Light Cavalry (the original mutineers at Meerut). Smith relents and allows him to charge the enemy on the right flank, while he takes the left with his Afghan horse.

'We charged accordingly, and a fine sight it was; the rebel infantry stood, but almost all their cavalry bolted. The result was that they were thoroughly beaten and dispersed, that upwards of 100 dead bodies were left on the field, while we lost but 9 killed and wounded, 2 horses killed and 7 wounded, my own horse got a nasty sword cut.'

The dispirited rebels fled to the high ravines, but many of them were cut down by Malcolm's cavalry. '*All* the great men of the town were captured and hung,' he reported gleefully. 'What would burn was then set on fire, and we left Jowlah in a fearfully different state from what it had been in the morning. Altogether it was a fearful lesson to the rebels in that part of the country (in all more than 400 men were killed at Jowlah) and most beneficial in its results.'

On they went to Burhana under a cruelly hot sun, and they reached the fort at about 2.30pm. Through their telescopes they could see armed men running along the ramparts. It would have been hard to guess the mood of those inside. Malcolm volunteered to ride up to the town and speak to some of the head-men in his best Hindi. As he cantered in, he was greeted 'with profound salaams but unequivocal looks of mistrust'. With difficulty, he persuaded one of the head-men to come forward. Apparently the old leper had been in the town with 50 mutinous sepoys:

but who, O sahib, can stand before your invincible 'ikbal' [iqbal = good fortune, success] and he is now escaping on the other side.

Malcolm galloped back and gave the reassuring news. They blow open the gates and there is no resistance. The rebels have fled, leaving behind their baggage and cooking utensils. Mr Edwards imposes a stonking fine on the town for being so unhelpful. And after 21 hours in the saddle without anything to eat, they sleep like heroes. The old leper never shows his face in the district again and is later captured and hanged at Meerut.

When he fled the hopes of the rebels fled with him; what our appearance at Shamlee commenced the victory at Jowlah continued; the final discomfiture of Khyratee Khan at Bourhanah completed; the people saw that the British Lion was roused and vigilant and the rebellion of southern Moozuffurnuggur was at an end.

But these little victories are by no means the end of the story. The Raja of Thana Bhawan got wind that the British force had marched south, and he took advantage of this to send 3,000 men and a couple of guns to Shamli, which was then only defended by the gallant revenue chief officer Ibrahim Khan and his 60 policemen. As soon as rebellion is squashed in one place, it squirts out in another.

Ibrahim Khan, taken entirely by surprise, gathers his little force inside the walls of his office, barricades the gates and declares that he will never surrender. But his little force is outnumbered by 30 to one.

Out of 73 defenders, 'but one trooper, frightfully wounded and some few police lived to tell the tale ... A more horrible tragedy than the massacre at Shamlee will I believe hardly be found in the annals of this great rebellion.'

Back Malcolm marches to Shamli to avenge this atrocity. But by the time he gets there, the rebels have left the town and have moved back to their home town of Thana Bhawan, which is a tougher nut than any of the places they have assaulted so far: walled and loop-holed with muskets poking out of every loophole. The gates are massive and closed. The trees and undergrowth around the town are so dense it is impossible to bring up the guns.

After throwing in shells for an hour, Captain Smith, of whom Malcolm has already formed a poor opinion, gives the command to advance in skirmishing order.

> Now although I am not a military man yet I cannot help express-ing my opinion that this was a great mistake – we never could see more than a few heads of the rebel artillery men above the walls and our men were killed in the most pitiable manner by the dis-charge of musketry from the loopholes ... I shall not soon forget the first curious sensation on having round shot whistling over my head; presently I heard a sort of cracking noise and looking round saw that a three pounder shell had buried itself in one of my troopers horses entering at the chest; we were now in fact under a smart cannonade, and the first shot over I found myself perfectly cool, and I fear very indifferent to the horrid wounds I saw; the skirmishers had by this time lost over 20 men killed and wounded, and Johnstone was carried to the rear severely wounded and bleeding profusely.

The headstrong Smith now gives the order to storm the city, and the storming party manages briefly to get hold of the enemy's two big guns, 'but alas our infantry, at first only 200, was now too fear-fully thinned to compete against such large numbers and after very heavy loss Smith was obliged to come to conclusion that with our little party of infantry it would be madness to continue; Cayler was accordingly ordered to retreat, but not before some 70 corpses of the enemy in that bastion together with some 15 of ours had attested the enormity of the contest.'

Captain Smith, now realizing the folly of his attack, tells his shattered troops to regroup 500 yards to the rear of the town. 'Just as the last word was out of his mouth, I saw him throw up his hands; and I rushed up just in time to save him from falling, and saw that his right arm was shattered, holding him on with difficulty we got him into a doolie; and Fraser took the command; a retreat upon Moozuffurnuggur was now determined upon, and we fell into the order of march.'

But their ordeal was not yet over. After marching four miles, they were attacked by 1,500 cavalry and infantry who had followed them from Thana Bhawan. Out in the open, Malcolm tells us, the rebel hordes are no match for the disciplined cavalry he is leading. The enemy is broken and dispersed and then pursued up to the walls of Lohari, the next town beyond Thana Bhawan. 'The behaviour of my men was splendid, and tho' I had now only 40, yet 60 dead bodies of the enemy were counted on the ground over which they had charged. The rebels lost altogether upwards of 150 men many of whom I am glad to say were men of power and influence amongst whom was the great man of Loharee, Ahmed Ali Khan, a noted rebel.'

They have now been 20 hours in the saddle non-stop. Both horses and men are thoroughly knackered, but Malcolm has enough puff left for one final caper, and so does his horse.

'My dear old Arab (bought in Calcutta with the money my father gave me for the purpose) was still fresh and in wind in spite of the bullet he got at Thanahbhown; The consequence was that when I found myself at Loharee, not one of my men was up with me.'

He chases an irregular cavalryman right into Lohari. 'Before I could touch him he had cut my reins through and my situation was truly critical, as I could not wheel about my horse; the noble animal tho' now wounded by two sabres cuts, one on the head and the other on the shoulder, stood firm as a rock, and let me fight off his back as if I had been sitting in a chair. But to make a long story short I received three severe wounds, one through my solar topi, through the ear almost dividing it, and slightly into the head, and one on the left arm into the bone and the last and least one on the left thigh, before I succeeded in cutting him down; meanwhile my men appeared, some wounded, some dismounted ... I now slowly and with some difficulty rejoined the force, my wounds were looked to, I was put into Mr Edwards buggy.'

The journey home was slow and painful and haunted by mixed feelings: they had suffered a humiliating exit from Thana Bhawan, but followed it with an exhilarating counter-charge under the walls of Lohari. They had left behind 33 men killed, with many more brought in wounded. The much heavier losses of the rebels were poor consolation for the failure of an attack which should never have been embarked on against a far stronger force holed up in such a formidable citadel. Colonel Malleson describes the Battle of Thana Bhawan as 'strangely mismanaged', which is an understatement.[159]

Then as they limped back to Muzaffarnagar, the great news came in that Delhi had at last fallen. At once the odds changed utterly and with it the mood of the rebels. A few days later, a stronger British force was sent out to regain control of Thana Bhawan. It was led by the already legendary Robert Wallace Dunlop. He found the city abandoned. Dunlop's famous 'Khaki Risala' were volunteer cavalrymen without any military experience who had only fired guns for sport before they put on the dirt-coloured uniform. This makeshift corps had quickly acquired as fearsome a reputation as any regular unit. In the Muslim village of Basaud, they had shot or put to the sword all 180 adult males; Dunlop explained that 'a severe example was essential, and the slightest mawkish pusillanimity in such a case would have spread the flame of revolt throughout the district.'[160] They did the same at the village of Akalpura where the handsome young chief Nirput Singh had refused to pay the taxes. No wonder the Raja of Thana Bhawan had fled when he heard the men in khaki were coming.

Malcolm's self-confidence is no less breathtaking than his courage. He had had a sword in his hand for only a matter of weeks, but he had no hesitation in criticizing Captain Smith for his tactics. Yet what this Assistant Commissioner of Revenue had seen – several thousand men killed in three battles, one massacre of loyalist natives for which he and Edwards could be held responsible after leaving Shamli so lightly guarded, and two mass executions, at Hurhar and Jaula – would have attracted the attention of any war crimes tribunal today.

The Magistrate was not inclined to accept blame for any of this. First, Roderick Edwards blamed his predecessor at Muzaffarnagar, Mr Berford.[161] Colonel Malleson agreed. As soon as he had heard the news of the mutiny at Meerut, Berford, 'with a precipitancy as unworthy as it was rare', had closed down all the public offices in the town, and holed up in a small house, for his own protection having drawn off the guard from the jail, which led to a general break-out and the looting of the Treasury.[162] Berford's health had collapsed. He had left Muzaffaranagar ignominiously in a *bhylee*, or native ox cart, hoping to be taken for a native if he encountered any mutineers on his way to Saharanpur – 'he was a sad sight', according to his unforgiving successor. Edwards had been rushed to Muzaffarnagar to take his place.[163] Rather than shoulder the blame for leaving Shamli unguarded, Edwards blamed Ibrahim Khan for the massacre. He had left Shamli with an adequate garrison and 500 rounds of ball cartridges. If Ibrahim had not cooped up everyone in the town offices, 'the result would have been very different'.[164] For the fiasco at Thana Bhawan, Edwards blamed Captain Smith: 'the question of sufficient strength was one for the military to determine.' Edwards himself had merely been obeying his previous instructions 'to proceed at once and crush the rebels.' It was only when they were retreating from the town that he had received 'a letter from the Commissioner telling me on no account to attack Thanahbhowan, as it was far too strong for our small force.' So the Commissioner had blood on his hands, too. Everyone was to blame except Roderick Mackenzie Edwards.[165]

All over northern India there was a desperate blame game going on. There is a curious divergence between Malcolm's narrative and Mr Edwards's two official reports of the engagements in which they rode side by side. At Hurhar, Edwards mentions the plundered property they discovered, but he says nothing in either of his accounts about putting the ringleaders to death or the 'many others flogged at the carts tail'. At Jaula, he describes a fierce little battle, in which they 'killed great numbers dead calculated at 150' and 'entered the village at the point of the bayonet', but he says nothing about burning the village, and he does not say, as Malcolm does, that '*all* the great men of the town were captured and hung'. In other words, he blanks out any actions which were not legitimate acts of war. He sanitizes his account, just as 50 years earlier Rollo Gillespie had sanitized his account of how he had suppressed the mutiny at Vellore. This is not out of personal squeamishness. Edwards does not shrink from recording in his diary when he hangs half a dozen bandits – 'horrible work'. Nor is he one to skip details: we hear much of a passing subaltern's stutter and of his own children's coughs and colds up in the hills. It is thus only in Malcolm's uninhibited account of what they did in Hurhar and Jaula that we find any mention of the murder of the prisoners at both places. And it is his account which, first resurrected by Ursula Low, came back to embarrass David Cameron's visit to India 150 years later. Malcolm, being younger and more impulsive, had not yet learnt the discretion which really was the better half of valour, if you were interested in promotion in the service. I wonder if he ever regretted sending his 'unvarnished statement of facts' to John and Augusta.

As for himself, Malcolm told his father: 'the loss of the use of two or three fingers of the left hand will I fear be permanent, at least so say the doctors. The cut was just above the wrist, severing all the tendons and cutting well into the bone; however, I shall be able to hold my reins, and thank God it is the left hand.'

After the final recapture of Lucknow, the thousands of rebels whom Campbell had allowed to flee the city lent muscle to the revolts across the countryside. Russell of *The Times* was emphatic that the war was far from over. He wrote in his diary on April 3, 1858: 'At present all Oudh may be regarded as an enemy's country, for there are very few chiefs who do not still hold out, and defy the threats of the Proclamation. The capture of Lucknow has dispersed the rebels all over the country, and reinforced the bands which the rajas and *zemindars* have collected around their forts . . . All our machinery of government is broken and destroyed. Our revenue is collected by rebels. Our police has disappeared utterly.'[166]

The rebels had now explicitly adopted guerrilla tactics, as recommended by Khan Bahadur Khan, the warlord of Rohilkhand, who had set up his government in Bareilly: 'Do not attempt to meet the regular columns of the infidels, because they are superior to you in discipline and firepower, and have big guns; but watch their movements, guard all the ghats on the rivers, intercept their communications, stop their supplies, cut up their *daks* and posts, and keep them constantly hanging about their camps; give them no rest.'[167]

By the hot season of 1858, Malcolm, having recovered from his wounds, was stationed in Pilibhit, near the Nepal border, within the country that Khan Bahadur Khan claimed to rule in the name of the Emperor of Delhi. At the age of 23, Mr Low was the chief civil officer of the region. His station was threatened by a considerable band of rebels led by two notorious chiefs, Nazim Ali Khan and Ali Khan Mewati. These were swiftly reinforced by the pseudo-viceroy Khan Bahadur Khan and a couple of other local nawabs. Between them they could put 12,000 men into the field, and they were only about 12 miles away, at the edge of the jungle three miles from a village called Nuria.

On August 28, 1858, Malcolm set out with a threadbare collection of 200 local policemen and roadmenders scratched together by the intensely loyal Superintendent of Roads – Malcolm freely confessed that he himself could not persuade the local landowners to find him ten men. The idea was to fortify the police station at Nuria

and reopen it. They dug all day until, at 10pm, their pickets came
running in to report that the enemy was advancing from Sirpura, the
neighbouring village. At this monsoon season, except for the roads,
the whole country was under water, and quite impassable for cavalry.
It was impossible to sally out and engage the rebels. All they could
hope to do was to keep them at bay until reinforcements arrived
from Pilibhit. There followed one of those pointless but not bloodless skirmishes which pepper the history of the Mutiny: scrambling
through mango topes, splashing through the rice fields; 30 enemy
killed and the rebels withdrawing to fight again.

The reinforcements were commanded by none other than
Captain Sam Browne, who now found himself fighting alongside a
Low brother for the second time. Typically, the moment Sam
arrived, he agreed with Malcolm that 'this was an opportunity not to
be missed'. The British spies returned at 11pm with the news that
the enemy had dug in at Sirpura and showed no signs of going anywhere.

Sirpura was a ruined village on a hard, dry mound, almost surrounded by swampland, which at this season was one huge sheet of
water interrupted only by a tongue of land a hundred yards wide,
leading back into thick jungle. Malcolm, or 'the energetic magistrate'
as Colonel Malleson calls him,[168] found a couple of guides, an old
woman and a small boy (perhaps they were the only locals who
would talk to the infidels). These incongruous sherpas led them out
at midnight to work round the back through the jungle, a detour of
about eight miles. 'At 3am on the 30th the column silently fell into
the order of march. A long and toilsome secret march through Jungle
and water followed and at 7am we emerged from the jungle 800
yards from the rebel camp.'

At first they crept forward through the high, wet grass without
being detected, but then a musket was accidentally discharged, and
the enemy were quick in bringing round their guns from the front to
the rear of the ruined hamlet and opened fire. Sam Browne takes up
the story:

Accompanied by Mr Malcolm Low, C.S., with my two orderlies and the Police cavalry following Mr Low, I rode up the road towards the mound, on the right of Skirmishers. When about 100 yards or so from the mound, a 9lb gun on the side of the road had been playing on the squadron on the right under Craigie, and I had sent off an orderly to order them to push on and then wheel to the left and charge into the left of enemy's position; this nine-pounder now opened on us with grape, and its first round bowled over 5 men behind us on the road.

I then, followed by my orderly, galloped on to the gun, which was being re-loaded, and had a hand to hand business with the Gun's crew. Their leader attacked me with his Tulwar, after emptying his musket and missing. He was on my left between me and the Gun. I gave him a whack over the left side of his head, but as it was protected by a cloth hanging from his head my sword only cut him slightly. He now gave me 3 or 4 cuts in succession, all of which I parried. But one cut slipped down from my sword and caught the top of my knee, which it sliced. Some others of the Gun's crew now again fired at me and hit my horse, just stinging him on the bit, I believe, and made him swerve round to the right leaving my first opponent on my left rear who then rushed in and before I could cover myself or get out of his reach gave me a slash thro' my left shoulder. As I wheeled round my horse reared and fell back on me. Just then the Woordie Major of my Regt. [Native Adjutant] and my orderly, who had charged in with the Squadron from the right, came up to where I was. The Woordie Major got badly wounded also by a Tulwar cut, but all the gun's crew were slain.

In the mean time the Infantry had rushed in also and the enemy were cleared out of the position. They were followed by the cavalry into the jungle. Some 300 were killed and their Camp, Elephants and 4 guns fell into our hands.

On rising from my fall I got a kummarbund from one of the men and strapped it round my shoulder, and then moved off to meet my Doctor, T. Maxwell. I had not gone very far when, feeling very faint, I threw myself down under a Cart, just as Maxwell arrived. When I came to myself again I found myself in a Dooly minus my arm.[169]

This is close fighting not very different from how Homer describes it. Colonel Malleson wrote that 'few more gallant deeds than this were performed during the war.'[170] And Sam Browne received the VC for it. Malcolm Low, being a civilian, was not entitled to any such award, though he was officially thanked by Queen Victoria for his services. When General Sir Sam Browne died in 1901, Malcolm received a further accolade, but a misplaced one. The obit in *The Times* recorded that 'as Captain Browne fell, he exclaimed "that brute Sheriff" (referring to his swerving horse) and the next instant Mr Low had killed the sepoy. Fortunately Mr Low had a tourniquet in his pocket, which he promptly applied to the injured limb, and thus undoubtedly prevented Browne from bleeding to death.'[171] It was a fine example of military myth. On March 19, Malcolm wrote from 22 Roland Gardens, Kensington, to deny any consciousness of having grappled with Sam's assailant, let alone of having killed him, and even more emphatically to deny that he had anything to do with the tourniquet, which had been applied by Dr Maxwell, who had been close on their heels.

The incident achieved immortality for another reason. Sam Browne's lost arm was to become the most famous in military history after Nelson's. Desperate above all to continue his military career, he had designed for him a special leather belt with an extra belt passing diagonally over the right shoulder to stop the scabbard from sliding around and to keep the pistol pouch steady, so that there was no danger of an accidental discharge. These features turned out to be very useful for two-armed officers as well. Even when swords were no longer worn in battle, in the early years of the twentieth century the Sam Browne belt was brilliant for holding steady the heavy pistols of the day. By the time of the Boer War, it was becoming standard issue, and later on, became fashionable across the world, being regularly worn by Hitler, Mussolini and other men of destiny. Its inventor maintained a close interest in the details of its design. Among the papers found after Sam Browne's death was a note of the exact specifications, which stated that 'Mr R. Garden, Saddler, 200 Piccadilly (who retired from business in 1891) was the only maker who used to make my belts properly.'[172]

After two years under canvas, Malcolm Low retired back into civilian life from which he had been so abruptly torn. He never lifted a sabre again. He very rarely spoke to his daughters of the Mutiny years, and never of his experiences in the fighting line. Many of the memories were too painful, he said.[173] All the same, he preserved among his papers the narrative which records his bloody deeds in that awful September.

He was not alone in this reluctance. Even Theo Metcalfe sometimes found himself at a loss in recalling what he did in the Great Mutiny. Many years later, when she was staying in Scotland with Theo and his second wife Kate, his sister GG persuaded him to dictate the story of his adventures. 'The remembrance of those days of horror, however, the recollection of the awful sights he had witnessed, and of the Devils he had encountered roused such violent emotion, that Aunt Kate stopped the recital for fear it would bring on a stroke.'[174]

'Thank God it is all over,' Edward Thackeray wrote after the siege of Delhi. 'I am sick of bloodshed and seeing men killed. You necessarily get callous, but I am very glad it is all over. I never felt so much seeing a European killed as a poor private of HM 61st. I was in a turret with him in the magazine making some loopholes of sandbags. The sepoys were firing from houses all round and he was firing at them with his rifle and asked me to take a shot. I took his rifle and was aiming at a man, and he was looking through a loophole, when a bullet sang through the turret and killed him by my side.'[175]

For Arthur Lang, it was the death of his best friend that turned him. Elliot Brownlow, a fellow sapper, had been blown up in a stupid accident after the fighting was over at Lucknow. A chain of sappers had been removing the huge store of gunpowder packed in tin cases which had been discovered in the Jama Masjid and throwing it down a well. One of the tin cases struck the side of the well, and the whole chain ignited, killing 32 men. 'Elliot was so scorched I should not have known him: his face was black, and I thought he was blind, but he said he could see with one eye. He said he knew he should die, but was quite prepared and did not fear . . . God grant that I may meet my end as hopefully as he did his. He died about midnight.'[176]

From that moment the music of ball and bullet lost its charms for him. 'The death of my dear friend Elliot has of course cast a gloom over the campaign as far as it concerns me, and has rendered it distasteful to me, and spoiled all my pleasure in war and victory and Lucknow.'[177] Lang asked to be sent back to the Public Works Department. There for the rest of his career, he laboured on building roads and cantonments, studiously avoiding the front line. After the Mutiny, he married his 'awful stunner', Sarah 'Pussy' Boileau, and they had eight children.

XVIII

POST MORTEM

How did it start? What was the immediate cause? Who was to blame? What ultimately was it all about? As soon as the awful news broke, these questions troubled the startled and frightened British public, both in India and in England. The same questions troubled them for years afterwards. Even today, the answers to them are far from settled.

The mutineers at Meerut on May 10, 1857, were not the first, and they were certainly not the last. Kaye and Malleson list over 80 separate mutinies as breaking out between May and the end of November and early December when the last eruptions reached far-away cities such as Chittagong and Dacca in what is now Bangladesh. Nor do Kaye and Malleson's figures include all the rural outbreaks of disaffection, which may not have involved sepoys at all but rather consisted of disgruntled landowners and overtaxed peasants armed with sticks and axes. Malcolm Low was under canvas for two years fighting these jacqueries until the beginning of 1859.[1] There were also the important centres where sepoys began to mutiny, or at least to exhibit signs of disaffection, but were swiftly disarmed (and usually disbanded) by vigilant British officers and civil commissioners before they could make havoc. Up in the Punjab, Henry Lawrence's brother John, aided by the merciless Herbert Edwardes and John

Nicholson, had disarmed the mutinous regiments and freed up British regiments to rescue Delhi. And from the Punjab, too, came the siege guns and the ammunition from its factories. No less crucially, in the huge state of Hyderabad, the Resident, Major Cuthbert Davidson (whom we last saw threatening the Nizam with British troops if he refused to sign John Low's treaty), had his guns ready on the bastions and suppressed the rebellion with a barrage of grapeshot.[2] He had the enthusiastic support of the pro-British First Minister Salar Jung and of the new Nizam, who had just succeeded his father in the midst of it all, on May 18. Similarly, at Nagpur, another metropolis with a grievance occupying a crucial location in central India, the Commissioner, George Plowden, and Colonel Cumberlege disarmed the local troopers without spilling a drop of blood and with the aid of only a company of European gunners.[3] Plowden even managed the delicate and dangerous task of restoring the arms to the local troopers after the furore had died down.

When we draw the true map of the Great Mutiny, we need to include these thwarted outbreaks. On this fuller map, the rebellion can be shown to have stretched all the way from Peshawar in the west to Dacca in the east and as far down as Nagpur and Hyderabad. Bombay, too, suffered serious trouble, not least because the Governor, Lord Elphinstone (Mountstuart's nephew), had selflessly denuded the city of troops and sent them off to help crush the mutinies beyond the borders of his own Presidency. The city of Bombay was saved from large-scale violence by the energy of little Mr Forjett, the Chief Superintendent of Police. Forjett was everywhere, always ahead of events. He even disguised himself as a lovesick native in order to find out what the sepoys were saying.[4]

Only the south of the subcontinent was mostly free from any trouble (as was Ceylon). Perhaps some people there still remembered what Gillespie had done to the rebel sepoys at Vellore 50 years earlier. Even so, there were stray outbreaks as far south as Madras, and the authorities in all the major stations, while expressing satisfaction that all seemed quiet, were desperate that the mutiny should be contained higher up, above the line of the Nerbudda River.[5] No sensible British official could be confident that his sepoys could resist the contagion if they came into contact with it.

We must not forget either the hundreds of smaller outbreaks, which seldom made it into the history books. For example, at Hansi, the crumbly old city on the edge of the desert where Theo had hoped to find sanctuary with Alec Skinner. At 11am on May 29, the detachments of the Haryana Light Infantry and the 14th Irregular Cavalry stationed at Hansi both rose. Major Stafford, the Commanding Officer at nearby Hissar, had been warned by one of his native officers, and he managed to escape. But the rest of the Europeans were massacred, including the Magistrate/Collector Mr Wedderburn, and their bungalows torched. The convicts were released from the town jail and some of the women and children were murdered by their servants, others by the rebel *sowars*. In all, 23 Europeans and Christians were murdered in the two places. Fighting continued throughout June, until the Haryana Field Force finally managed to restore order. As so often, the victims of the retribution were more numerous than the victims of the mutiny. A total of 133 men in the district were hanged. Many of the rebels had come home to their villages from native regiments which had been disbanded elsewhere – reminding us that disbandment was not a problem-free solution. A small mutiny in a medium-size town, not many dead at least by the standard of Cawnpore, Lucknow and Delhi. But even at Hansi, the revolt exhibited most of the characteristics which typified outbreaks all across India.

The immediate reaction to these terrible events which had rocked the Empire – it was the single worst revolt in Britain's imperial history – was to look for a conspiracy. There must have been a central ring of conspirators planning and directing operations, with an evil mastermind behind it all. One popular explanation was that the blundering of Carmichael-Smyth had caused a premature detonation of this nationwide conspiracy. Mary Amelia Vansittart, wife of a Bengal civil servant, offered an account that was popular both in India and Britain:

This mutiny has been planned since the taking of Oudh. It was settled about 20 May that every cantonment all down the country was to rise and murder all the Europeans, seize forts, magazines, treasure. But the confining of the 80 troopers of the 3rd Cavalry at Meerut, and putting them under the guard of their own brethren in arms, caused the plot to explode ten days too soon.[6]

Others, like Roderick Edwards, thought that the general rising had been planned for a week or two later, the end of May or the first week in June. But all were uncomfortably aware that 'Had the people risen en masse against us, not a white man would now be living.'[7]

When Colonel Malleson came to complete Sir John Kaye's great history of the Mutiny, he too grasped at the idea of a mega conspiracy: 'With Oudh disaffected, the chiefs and the territorial interest doubting and trembling, with the Sipahis alienated and mistrustful, there needed but one other element to produce insurrection. The country, the army, the newly-annexed provinces were alike ready for the machinations of conspirators.'[8]

Who exactly were these conspirators? Surely it must be possible to name at least some members of the inner circle, the general staff of this enormous war against the infidels. Not so, says the Colonel. 'Who all these conspirators were may never certainly be known. Most of them died and made no sign.'

If they made no sign, how can we know for sure that they ever existed? Malleson mentions only one by name, the *maulvi* Ahmadullah of Faizabad, a remarkable roving holy man, the friend and adviser of the deposed royal family of Oudh. This tall, beetle-browed, lantern-jawed charismatic was certainly a fine military leader: 'no other man could boast that he had twice foiled Sir Colin Campbell in the field.' He had been wandering through Oudh in the spring of 1857 circulating seditious pamphlets for which he was tried and sentenced to death (the revolt broke out before he could be executed).[9] But Malleson offers no evidence that he or any other named person had co-ordinated a national plot.

In the first volume, Sir John Kaye offers another candidate for mastermind: Nana Sahib, the adopted son of the deposed Peshwa, Baji Rao II. Still aggrieved by Lord Dalhousie's refusal to continue his father's pension, Nana Sahib is supposed to have been at the root of it all. For months, years even, he and his Muslim consigliere Azimullah Khan 'had been quietly spreading their network of intrigue all over the country. From one Native Court to another Native Court, from one extremity to another of the great continent of India, the agents of the Nana Sahib had passed with overtures, invitations, discreetly, perhaps mysteriously worded, to Princes and Chiefs of different races and religions, but most hopefully of all to the Marathas.'[10]

Again, it's hard to see much evidence for this pre-planning. Apart from one visit to Lucknow in the spring of 1857, Nana Sahib seems to have been idling at Bithur in his English-style country house with its handsome park and menagerie, playing billiards with his European guests and allowing them to win. Nobody thought that he possessed any great skills, except at billiards. None of the British spies had any subversive material on him; nor was there any among the documents the British captured when they demolished the Nana's palace. The best guess must be that, like the other disgruntled rulers who joined the uprising, he was reactive rather than proactive: a case of 'I am their leader, I must follow them.' Even the disputed accounts of his joining the rebels suggest that he did so under duress. One version says that a deputation from the rebels told him, 'Maharaj, a kingdom awaits you if you join our cause, but death if you do not.' To which the Nana speedily replied, 'What have I to do with the British? I am altogether yours.' And he placed his hands on their heads and swore to join them.[11]

There is no shortage of documents, both in English and in the native languages. Every Resident or Commissioner ran a sizeable secret service with native agents in the cantonments and the bazaars. Many native officers had divided loyalties and would have reported at least the rumours of a national plot to their European superior officers. They often did report when a local outbreak was imminent, for example to Hugh Gough on his verandah at Meerut, or to Major Stafford at Hansi. Of a plot on a larger scale we hear nothing.

In any case, as Philip Mason, the historian of the Indian Army, concludes after reviewing all the contributory grievances that were agitating the sepoys, 'the plot seems an unnecessary supposition; and the firmest adherents to the theory of a plot have to suppose that it broke down.'[12]

British observers on the spot were divided on the question. James Cracraft Wilson, a judge who was appointed a Special Commissioner after the Mutiny to pick out the guilty and reward the deserving, was convinced that 'Sunday, 31st of May, 1857, was the day fixed for the mutiny to commence throughout the Bengal Army, that there were committees of about three men in each regiment, which conducted the duties of the mutiny; that the sepoys, as a body, knew nothing of the plans arranged.'[13]

But Major G.W. Williams, his fellow Special Commissioner, claimed that it was only after the outbreak at Meerut, that 'corps after corps caught the infection, excited and encouraged by the uncontradicted boast of the extermination of all Europeans, and the overthrow of the British rule.'[14]

Even if there was such a plot and it had been prematurely detonated, would not the outbreaks have been bunched closer together? The rebels' capture of Delhi was clearly an inspiration which sparked other outbreaks like those at Cawnpore and Lucknow three weeks later. But it was still over a month before the Little Boys of Gwalior rose in revolt, nearly two months before Agra rose, six months before trouble reached east Bengal.

What all this looks like is *contagion* rather than co-ordination; more like the spread of an epidemic or an evangelical movement than a planned national strategy. That spread might be encouraged by wandering *maulvis,* just as the open-air meetings of Wesley and Whitfield had brought Methodism to distant towns and villages in England. Rudrangshu Mukherjee argues that we can see the rebellion spreading down the Ganges valley through May, branching out up to Lucknow at the end of the month and then down south to Agra and Jhansi – by natural diffusion rather than central direction.

Just as well for the British that the outbreaks were serial and not simultaneous, or their thinly stretched troops would not have had a hope. We have seen how a small number of subalterns were present at virtually all the major engagements of the Mutiny: Robert Low was at Badli-ki-Serai, Najafgarh Canal, the storming of Delhi, Showers's mopping-up operations to the west, and the recapture of Lucknow, as well as Showers's pursuit of Tantia Topi down into central India. Theo Metcalfe, Edward Thackeray, Richard Barter and Arthur Lang covered almost as much ground during those hectic months. The British Army was another stage army, the same small body of troops desperately crossing and recrossing the stage. Arthur Lang boasted, with some justification, that 'Not a soldier sent from England for the saving of India will arrive before all the great deeds have been completely done, without their assistance.'[15] What might a co-ordinated rebellion, under an energetic unified command, have achieved? As John Lawrence said at the end of it all, 'the mutineers seemed to act as if a curse rested on their cause. Had a single leader of ability arisen among them, nay, had they followed any other course than that they did pursue in many instances, we must have been lost beyond redemption.'[16]

. What about the causes? Those who had been most closely involved with events did not like to examine the causes too closely. John Lawrence, after an exhaustive argument, arrived at the conclusion that the Mutiny was caused by the greased cartridges and the greased cartridges only.[17] Sir James Outram spluttered: 'What amazing statements and opinions one hears both in India and in England. What can be more ridiculous than the cry that the rebellion was caused by the annexation of Oudh, or that it was solely a military mutiny?'[18] It is a disagreeable thought that one's own actions may have triggered the most terrible mutiny in British history, but to assert that the outbreak had nothing to do with the annexation of Oudh at all is equally amazing.

What the British public wanted to hear was that the whole business was a sudden if terrifying flare-up, provoked by British bad handling and Indian bad faith. Nobody wanted to confront the thought that it might be a full-blooded national revolt born out of popular revulsion against British rule. The most plausible way of limiting the recriminations was to argue that it was, quite simply, a sepoy revolt. The sepoy's grievances – poor pay as compared to the rewards enjoyed by European troops (the monthly rate of seven rupees had not increased for half a century), the threat of overseas service following the General Service Order of 1856, the diminishing opportunities for promotion as the insolent young English subalterns flooded in, the threats to their caste culminating in the cartridges – all these were genuine, and substantial enough to provoke a rebellion, and a rebellion which had every prospect of success with the native troops outnumbering the Europeans by nine to one.

This explanation continues to have its supporters today, for example, in the formidable work of the most recent British historian of the Mutiny, Saul David. On this analysis, the religious grievances, notably the cartridges, were little more than a pretext by the conspirators to fire up the sepoys. The real underlying motive was a strictly material one, to better their pay and conditions by seeking a more generous employer, as had always been the way in the military market of India. Now that the British had come to exert a monopoly on that market, the only way for the sepoys to improve their lot was to make a colossal concerted effort to throw them out.[19]

Clearly the rebel leaders and those they recruited to their cause did hope for this, but was this all they hoped for? Do material motives alone suffice to explain the violence, duration and peculiar nature of the events? We need to look more closely at what actually happened. As Rudrangshu Mukherjee points out, the grievances of the sepoy have been enumerated ad infinitum: 'what is not often, if ever, enquired into is whether the mutinies followed any kind of pattern in types of action and in their spread from station to station.'[20] If we simply plough through a disjointed narrative of wild and terrible atrocities, we will most likely conclude that what we are seeing is just random mob violence, as senseless as it is frightening.

There *is* a pattern, though. It is marked, explicit and deliberate: in the actions of the mutineers, in the proclamations of their leaders, and in the repetition of the same happenings in smallish places like Hansi as in major regional centres like Lucknow, Delhi or Allahabad. What did the mutineers actually do? And what did their leaders say they were doing it for? These are the simple questions we must ask.

First of all, who did they kill? They began everywhere by murdering their officers and every representative of British power they could get their hands on – collectors, magistrates, jailors, commissioners. At Hansi and Hissar, they murdered David Thompson, the *tehsildar* or District Revenue Officer, Mr Wedderburn the Magistrate, and Lieutenant Barwell, the Commanding Officer.

Then they went for the two places they needed to commandeer if the revolt was to have legs: the treasury and the magazine. You cannot run a rebellion without guns and rupees. In some places, the local civil and military officers were too quick for them. The magazine would be stoutly defended or the treasury spirited away to a safer place, as Mr Wedderburn tried to do at Hansi before he was cut down. In northern districts, alert collectors would load up their treasure on whatever beast they could find and lug it up to the safety of the nearest hill station. Malcolm Low removed the Saharanpur treasure on elephants and ponies up to Mussoorie. But in Jhansi, for example, the rebels got in first, getting hold of the Star Fort which contained both the magazine and the treasure of nearly 4.7 million rupees.[21] Sometimes, the British authorities were criminally negligent. At Cawnpore, Brigadier Wheeler had not only failed to secure the magazine, which would have been the best place for the garrison to defend itself, but he also withdrew to an indefensible entrenchment. It was alleged that the General had not even bothered to inspect the magazine and was under the illusion that it was virtually empty. As for the entrenchment, which the garrison held out in so gallantly amid appalling suffering for three weeks, the chaplain's wife from Lucknow, when taken to see it later, was amazed: 'The entrenchments by way of a defence are quite laughable: a very narrow ditch, not knee-deep, and a low bank of earth, over which we stepped with the greatest ease, was all that divided them from the enemy, and yet the cowards never attempted to come over.'[22]

All these actions by the mutineers do have a military rationale, and they fit well enough the military-revolt theory. But other actions by the mutineers do not.

At Hansi, as at Meerut, Agra, Jhansi, Allahabad, Delhi and a dozen other places, the jail was broken open and the convicts released. In some cases, of course, the sepoys would be releasing other sepoys who had been banged up unjustly. But far more often, they would be releasing *badmashes* to create mayhem and terrorize the ordinary citizens. Not exactly the sort of action that came naturally to sepoys, many of whom were military policemen. It is hard to avoid the conviction that the liberation of the prisoners had a more symbolic meaning: that the harsh rules of British justice no longer applied and that from now on, the Indians would make their own laws.

Each squalid local jail was a little Bastille, and its fall betokened a new dawn. Soon the countryside was full of marauding bands of convicts. Mark Thornhill gives a hair-raising description of riding through the night towards what he hoped would be the safety of Agra. They hear a muffled, clanking sound: 'We had ridden about a quarter of a mile when the same sounds again caught our ear. This time there was no mistaking them. From the side of the road came a clear, low clanking of chains, just like that which in stories of haunted houses accompanies the appearance of the ghost. We stopped our horses, and turned to the side of the road from whence the sounds proceeded. The trees just there were thinner; there came through them a faint glimmer of light. We saw a row of dark figures passing slowly along under the shadow of the avenue. They were proceeding in single file, each behind the other. The ground was soft, their footsteps made no noise, but at each movement came the clanking of a chain. The truth flashed upon us: the Agra gaol had broken loose – these were the escaped prisoners.'[23]

At Hansi, and everywhere else, the rebels lost no time too in murdering every Christian they could lay hands on. This was not an accidental circumstance, arising from the obvious fact that most of the Europeans were Christian. It was an explicit part of the mission. The letter that the doomed and drowsy Simon Fraser finally read at breakfast the next morning warned not only that the sepoys at Meerut intended to mutiny that day but that they intended to massacre the entire *Christian* population. When the 3rd Cavalry got to Delhi, they did indeed hack down every Christian they could find, including all Indian converts to Christianity, whether of Hindu or Muslim origin. Conversely, British men or women who had converted to Islam were spared. Mrs Aldwell, an Anglo-Indian Christian, managed to save herself because she knew the *kalima*, the Islamic profession of faith. Her captors told her that if they were to kill a Muslim, 'they would be as bad as the infidels; but that they were determined on killing all the Christians'.[24]

Christian churches were smashed up, too. Monsignor Persico, the Vicar Apostolic of Agra, said that in his area alone, the rebels had destroyed a cathedral, 25 churches and five seminaries. This was, after all, only tit for tat. British regiments frequently looted mosques and temples and afterwards used them as arsenals or barracks. The beautiful Jalantesvara Temple in Vellore Fort had been commandeered for an arsenal 50 years earlier (and had suffered the indignity of having a fives court tacked on to it). Edward Campbell wrote from Delhi to the pregnant GG in Simla, reporting that Metcalfe House was a wreck but that the Kootub (Qutb) was intact, not looted and still with their servants in place: 'Is it not strange?' It did not occur to him that the rebels were unlikely to smash up a house which had at its core a sacred Mughal tomb.[25]

Appeals from one sepoy regiment to another were couched in passionate religious terms. The troops who had captured Delhi informed their brethren cantoned at Lahore that 'the Hindu and Mussulman soldiers have without any notion of worldly gain fought for their religion, destroyed the tyrants and enemies of their faith and are prepared to fight to uphold for ever the religion of the Hindus and Mussulmans. May God banish the tyrants!'[26] A similar letter from Delhi to Jhansi asserted that the whole of the Bengali army had risen and if the men of Jhansi failed to join them they would be regarded as outcasts and infidels.[27] Another letter, sent out in the name of the King of Delhi, Bahadur Shah II, and probably the work of his son, the vigorous and ambitious Mirza Mughal, appeals to all princes and rajas of India, arguing that the English were out to over-throw all religions, and were the common enemy of Hindus and Muslims and that 'we should unite in their slaughter . . . for by this alone will the lives and faiths of both be saved.'[28]

Hindus and Muslims did unite in the shared struggle. The old Muslim battle-cry of '*Din! Din!*' resounded from Hindu sepoys, too. The rebel soldiers forced open the gates of Jhansi, a Hindu Maratha city, to yells of '*Din ka jai!*' – victory to the faith. Any hopes the British had of setting one faith against the other were repeatedly dashed during the course of the Mutiny.[29]

Queen Victoria had declared in her famous Proclamation of November 1, 1858, (it was composed by Lord Derby with input from Victoria and Albert) that:

> Firmly relying ourselves on the truth of Christianity, and acknowl-edging with gratitude the solace of religion, we disclaim alike the right and the desire to impose our convictions on any of our sub-jects.

No one was to be favoured, molested or disquieted by reason of their religious faith, and those in authority under Her Majesty were to abstain from any interference with religious belief or worship.

Another Queen, the Begum of Oudh, the ex-courtesan, ex-Fairy, Hazrat Mahal, riposted with a magnificent counter-proclamation:

In the Proclamation [of Queen Victoria] it is written, that the Christian religion is true, but no other creed will suffer oppression, and the laws will be observed towards all. What has the administration of justice to do with the truth or falsehood of a religion? That religion is true which acknowledges one God, and knows no other. Where there are three Gods in a religion, neither Mussulmans nor Hindoos – nay, not even Jews, Sun-worshippers, or Fire-worshippers – can believe it is true.

Having made short work of the doctrine of the Trinity, the Begum moved on to the recent record of the British in India:

To eat pigs and drink wine, to bite greased cartridges, and to mix pigs fat with flour and sweetmeats, to destroy Hindoo and Mussulman temples on pretence of making roads, to build churches, to send clergymen into the streets and alleys to preach the Christian religion, to institute English schools and to pay people a monthly stipend for learning the English sciences, while the places of worship of Hindoos and Mussulmans are to this day entirely neglected; with all this, how can the people believe that religion will not be interfered with? The rebellion began with religion, and for it, millions of men have been killed.[30]

Nor could it be denied that English culture *was* making inroads – partly through the advance of Western education, partly through the repression of those Indian customs which the British found odious, but also partly through direct preaching of the Gospel. Most embarrassing of all the events leading up to the Mutiny was the evidence freely given by Colonel Steven Wheler, the Commanding Officer of the 34th Native Infantry, at the Court of Inquiry into the violent events at Barrackpore on March 29. What had happened was that a

sepoy named Mangal Pande, high on *bhang* and opium, went berserk
on the parade ground, inciting his fellow sepoys to mutiny and eventually shot himself – thereby achieving a backhanded immortality, all
rebellious sepoys thereafter being dubbed Pandies. Colonel Wheler's
part in the affair had been inglorious. He had failed to arrest Mangal
Pande and had then left the parade ground.

The evidence he gave to the Court of Inquiry was far worse. He
said he was not ashamed to admit that he freely sought Christian
converts wherever he could find them: 'It has been my invariable
plan to act on the broad line which Scripture enforces . . . to speak to
all alike as sinners in the sight of God . . . I have told them plainly that
they are all lost and ruined sinners . . . As to the question whether I
have endeavoured to convert sepoys and others to Christianity, I
would humbly reply that this has been my object, and I conceive is
the aim and end of every Christian who speaks the word of God to
another, namely, that the Lord would make him the happy instrument of converting his neighbour to God, or in other words, to
rescue him from everlasting destruction.'[31]

John Low declared, on reading this evidence, that 'Having regard
only to Colonel Wheler's habitual and persevering personal endeavours to convert Hindoo and Mahomedan sepoys in our army to the
Christian religion, it was my decided opinion that the dictates of a
sound policy require that this officer shall be removed from the
command of the 34th Regiment and prevented from commanding
any other regiment composed of natives of India.'[32]

Lord Canning thought exactly the same. But it was no good
denying that Christians in India were on the hunt for converts. The
natives could hear the sound of hymns rising from the cantonments.
Judge Tucker at Fatehpur had erected huge stone columns either side
of the high road inscribed with the Ten Commandments in Hindi,
Urdu, English and Persian.

The new chairman of the East India Company, Mr Ross Mangles,
was an ardent Evangelical. Frustrated by the slow progress of the
Gospel in India, back in 1834 he had proposed that an elite seminary

should be set up at Calcutta to train Indian clergymen. Now when Disraeli twitted him in the House of Commons that 'his mission was to convert the whole of India to Christianity',[33] Mangles had replied that, no, he had not said that, what he had said was that 'the Government of India should scrupulously abstain from all interference with religion but had added that he thought that country had been placed by Providence in our hands in order that we might be instruments in His hands for ultimately spreading Christianity throughout the millions by whom it was inhabited'[34] – which sounded pretty much the same thing. So it was not paranoid or irrational to suspect that more Christianization was on the way.

The secular grievances were real enough: for the sepoys, the lagging of their pay and the loss of their status; for the princes and landowners, the annexation of their domains and the confiscation of their villages; for the peasants, the inflexible new tax regime. But what united all classes and all faiths was the threat they perceived to the core of their social being. Only by fully appreciating the religious apprehensions can we account for the systematic ferocity of the Great Mutiny. Both British and Indian historians, many if not most being of a secular tendency, have shied away from confronting those apprehensions. Moreover, it is only natural that military historians should tend to look for military answers.

Both British and Indian historians have also been slow to grasp that the rebels had any systematic purpose and practice at all. The sources on the British side were so abundant, and the behaviour of the British could be so minutely scrutinized: the dash of a teenage lieutenant, the hesitation of an overweight colonel, the promptness of an alert Resident. By contrast, the papers in native languages languished in dusty provincial archives, unread and untranslated.

Only recently have historians begun to appreciate the way in which sepoy units kept their shape and their chain of command after coming out in revolt; how they passed instructions and appeals to other units in the same regiment and to other regiments they had campaigned with or shared stations with. Mahmood Farooqui's herculean labours

in the National Archives of Delhi[35] have demonstrated how quickly
the Emperor, or rather his two most energetic sons, Mirza Mughal and
Khizr Sultan, managed to exert some sort of control over the incoming rebel hordes, to arrange for their billeting and provisioning, and to
restore order and arrest looters. Within a fortnight, the royal mint had
been reopened and coins bearing the King's name issued. If the new
authorities never solved their inherent problems – the lack of immediate access to land revenue and to an ongoing supply of munitions –
they did enough to indicate that, in easier times, the royal family
could have governed reasonably well.

In Jhansi, the sepoys devolved power to a council of ministers,
reserving the right to intervene when they felt the need. Lakshmi Bai
appointed many of the same officials the British had used since
annexation three years earlier: the same superintendent of jails, magistrates and tax collectors. This regime ran Jhansi between July 1857
and March 1858, until Sir Hugh Rose besieged the city and captured
it. The Rani fled on horseback, supposedly jumping over the walls of
the city, to die a hero's death outside the walls of Gwalior.

In Lucknow at the outbreak of the rebellion, there was no King.
Wajid Ali Shah was locked up in Fort William for the duration. But
his forceful wife, Hazrat Mahal, presided over a huge fighting force,
which by December 1857 was estimated at 53,000. More than 60
per cent of this force was drawn, not from the professional soldiery
but from the general rural population, landowners and peasants combining to form territorial forces. At Lucknow, as elsewhere as the
rebellion went on, civilians joined up and fought in their thousands.

Like Jhansi, the city of Lucknow was ruled by an executive committee of well-known bureaucrats and court officials. There was a
separate military command consisting of sepoy captains and police
chiefs. The Raja Jailal Singh, who had been elected as the sepoys'
spokesman at the outset of the rebellion in June, was the key figure
in both bodies, reporting direct to the Begum, who seems to have
been a semi-ceremonial head of state, acting on behalf of her son
Birjis Qadr, whom Jailal Singh had insisted on having crowned King.

The whole governing structure looks rather like that of a modern Western constitutional monarchy at war.

The reality was that power lay ultimately with the sepoy leaders. They agreed to the coronation of Birjis Qadr only on the condition that orders from Delhi (that is, from the army leaders there) were to override the new King's; the army was to have the deciding voice in choosing the new chief minister; the sepoys were to receive double pay; and they were to have a free hand in dealing with the lackeys of the English.[36]

There was plenty of disorder and plundering and misrule, but these rebel regimes all had a relatively coherent and organized character. I emphasize this, not just to suggest that they were capable of governing under difficult circumstances – though the evidence does suggest that – but to draw attention to the neglect of this side of the story by most historians.

The centenary of the Great Mutiny in 1957 was celebrated rather uneasily. Yes, this was a National Uprising, but it was so embarrassingly 'reactionary'. Percival Spear called its leaders 'backward-looking men whose aims were incompatible' and whose followers had 'no ideas of creating anything new'.[37] Christopher Hibbert calls the Mutiny 'the swansong of the old India'.[38] Rather regretfully, Indian historians mostly agreed. R.C. Majumdar was particularly severe: 'The miseries and bloodshed of 1857–58 were not the birthpangs of a freedom movement in India, but the dying groans of an obsolete aristocracy and centrifugal feudalism of the mediaeval age.'[39] In his history of the freedom movement in India, Tarachand was equally contemptuous: the rebellion was merely 'the last attempt of the medieval order to hold the process of dissolution and to recover its lost status'.[40]

More recent historians, such as Tapti Roy, Mahmood Farooqui and Rudrangshu Mukherjee, have been less dismissive. To them, 1857 does look more like a national revolt as well as a military mutiny; one which attempted, in a spontaneous fashion which was not pre-planned, to set up an alternative regime to the British Raj (widely called such only after 1857). C.A. Bayly agrees that 'over the last generation the conviction of the Bengal military that the Mutiny was in large part a civil rebellion has been borne out by detailed research'.[41] In areas where the rebellion lasted a year or more, such as parts of Oudh and Rohilkhand, peasants of all faiths joined the rebels along with their landlords, burying their tribal differences for the duration of the Uprising.

Everywhere the rebellion began with the sepoys. That was a matter of rational calculation. Peasants, armed only with axes, sticks and a few old blunderbusses, would have been mad to take the initiative in charging the Ingrez with their rifles and artillery. The time to join in was when the British were on the run. The American scholar Thomas Metcalf argues that, yes, without the sepoy discontent the popular outburst would never have taken place. 'But once the sepoys had risen, the Mutiny derived its real strength from the adherence of the civil population. The sepoy uprising was in fact little more than the spark which touched off a smouldering mass of combustible material.'[42]

The fact that most of the major outbreaks began with an appeal to the old rulers looks more like a search for popular legitimacy than a longing to re-establish the old regime in unchanged form.

Here we must note two unmistakable facts. First, the old rulers were reluctant to take the lead in the rebellion, even when pressed by flattery or threats. They mostly preferred to recline under the British umbrella, even after being deprived of power and status. The heirs to the Maratha kingdoms – Holkar at Indore, Sindia at Gwalior – dodged and weaved to avoid being signed up by the rebels. Sindia stuck to the British so loyally that at the end he had to flee from his own people and take refuge in the British camp. At Jhansi, the northernmost Maratha principality, as late as January and February 1858 the Rani was still pleading to be allowed to govern the province on behalf of the British. She became the heroine on horseback only after the British attacked her beloved city.

As for the King of Delhi, when the *sowars* of the 3rd Light Cavalry from Meerut first appeared under the walls of his palace, Bahadur Shah immediately informed Captain Douglas. When the soldiers marched into the Hall of Audience, Bahadur told them, 'I did not call for you; you have acted very wickedly.' He may have been playing for time, for he did accept the role of Emperor as soon as it was offered to him. But there is no evidence that he himself, as distinct from his courtiers, had anything to do with the pre-plotting of rebellion. He turned out to be a fretful war leader, constantly threatening to give up his crown and go on a pilgrimage to Mecca. Nana Sahib, in British eyes the arch-traitor, seems to have been decidedly equivocal until threatened by the rebels. He too was probably waiting to see whether the rebellion was going anywhere before he openly joined it.

Second, even when restored, these reluctant or semi-reluctant rulers did not enjoy unchallenged power. In the council of war at Cawnpore, the Nana's court had to share power with the committee of sepoys. At Delhi, the troopers showed little respect for the person of the Emperor, jostling him and addressing him in a familiar style. His Majesty's orders were often disregarded or disobeyed.

These sepoy councils resemble those juntas of young officers who seize power in modern states. This is what a national revolt often looks like. Just because the uprising is led by soldiers rather than by progressive intellectuals lately returned from the LSE or the London Inns of Court, it does not mean that it does not have the seeds of modernity in it. It certainly cannot be written off as a cry of rage against the modern world.

The one feature of the Great Mutiny that indicates its nature and scale as a national revolt is a feature that few historians have been willing to confront directly: the relentless and systematic slaughter of European women and children. This assertion may sound odd. Surely the history books, not to mention the newspapers, both at the time and in subsequent flashbacks, have been soaked in the blood of the innocent. Did not the avenging British troops shout 'Remember Cawnpore' as they stuck their cold steel in Indian guts? How can we talk of there being any neglect of this most terrible aspect of events?

Yet, intellectually, neglect there has been: neglect by Indian historians who, out of a sense of shame, have preferred to soft-pedal the horrors; and by British historians, who have depicted the massacres as the evil excesses of intoxicated sepoys urged on by fiends like the Nana. In other words, they are represented as the extreme examples of a collective mania, without examining whether they might have a purpose behind them.[43]

If we consider the actual facts, the massacres do seem to have not only a consistency but a terrifying logic to them. To return to the modest towns of Hansi and its neighbour Hissar: within hours of the first outbreak at 11am, every European woman and child who had failed to escape had been murdered: Mrs Barwell and Mrs Wedderburn and their children at the Cattle Farm, Mrs Jefferies and Mrs Smith and their children at their homes. The Barwells and the Wedderburns were murdered by the troops, but the Jefferieses and the Smiths were murdered by their own servants. Mr Thompson, the Collector, was murdered by his *chuprassie*, his personal messenger. It was not merely that no European was to be spared by reason of age or sex, but any Indian felt licensed to take part in the killing, not just the sepoys. This pattern was repeated at every mutiny in every city. Sometimes the women and children were butchered in their own bungalows, on the verandah or in the bedroom. We find few cases where a woman or child was spared by reason of personal fondness or loyalty – there were a couple at Meerut at the outset of the Mutiny before the pattern was fully established, and later on at Gwalior, but not many others.

Sometimes all the Europeans were herded together, supposedly for their safety. The 52 Europeans at Delhi had been kept under the personal protection of the Emperor. But then they were bound together and led out into a yard where, despite the pleas of the Emperor, they were slaughtered by the sepoys, first by a volley of gunshots, then finished off by the sword.[44]

At Jhansi, after murdering several officers who were trying to flee from the fort to get help or to enlist the support of the Rani – her

palace was down in the town – the sepoys agreed with Captain
Skene that the remaining Europeans should be allowed to leave and
be escorted to another station, on condition that they yielded the
fort to the Rani. But as soon as the 56 Europeans came out from the
fort, the rebels fell upon them, bound them and carried them to an
orchard called the Jokan Bagh. Near a cluster of trees, they were
drawn up in three lines as if for a group photograph, children in
front, women in the middle and men at the back. Then the captain
of the jail guard announced that 'the orders of the Risaldar [the
senior native officer] are that they shall be put to death.' At which he
raised his sword and cut down Captain Skene with a single stroke –
a feat of which he later boasted. This was the signal for the rest of the
group to be murdered.

A more romantic version of these terrible events became current in
the British illustrated papers, in which Captain Skene and his wife and
two daughters were besieged by screaming fanatics in the Round
Tower and he put a pistol to her head to save her the horrors of what
was to come, before killing himself. Christina Rossetti wrote a poem
called 'In the Round Tower at Jhansi', which describes this scene:

> A hundred, a thousand to one; even so;
> Not a hope in the world remained:
> The swarming howling wretches below
> Gained and gained and gained.
>
> Skene looked at his pale young wife:-
> 'Is the time come?' – 'The time is come!' –
> Young, strong, and so full of life:
> The agony struck them dumb.
>
> Close his arm about her now,
> Close her cheek to his,
> Close the pistol to her brow –
> God forgive them this!

'Will it hurt much?' – 'No, mine own:
I wish I could bear the pang for both.'
'I wish I could bear the pang alone:
Courage, dear, I am not loth.'

Kiss and kiss: 'It is not pain
Thus to kiss and die.
One kiss more.' – 'And yet one again.' –
'Good-bye.' – 'Good-bye.'[45]

This desperate resort certainly did occur to the minds of some panic-stricken British officers. On the evening of May 11, 1857, Mr Colledge, the Assistant Magistrate at Saharanpur, came rushing into the office of his boss, Roderick Edwards, bringing news of the mutiny at Meerut: 'His state of alarm and excitement was painful to witness. He seemed to think that the game was up ... and talked of shooting his wife and family and then himself to prevent them from falling into the hands of the sepoys.'[46] But this did not happen to the Skenes (nor to the Colledges, after Edwards had calmed the Assistant down). There was no opportunity for them to make a suicide pact. They were not even in the Round Tower, but in the orchard below outside the city walls.

The confusion about the exact circumstances of the massacre was so great that Charles Ball, in his instant history of the Mutiny (published in 1859–60), recounts both versions and includes dramatic steel engravings of both reported scenes. Robert Montgomery Martin in his *History of the Indian Empire*, published at much the same time, tells both stories too.[47] This might seem to indicate a carefree, almost post-modern attitude to the truth, but it is more likely a reflection of the newsflow which was still painfully slow and unreliable.

There is a subtext to the romantic version: that Captain Skene was saving his wife from a fate worse than death. Sexual violation by a native was the nightmare of the British, but the most exhaustive enquiries failed to turn up any evidence of rape at this or any other massacre in 1857. Sir William Muir's report, drawn up for Lord Canning, was emphatic: 'nothing has come to my knowledge which would in the smallest degree support any of the tales of dishonour current in our public prints.'[48] There seems to have been a hideous purity of purpose rather than random savagery and the slaking of long pent-up lust, or even the wish to defile. Muir, later renowned as one of the foremost Islamic scholars in India, certainly thought so: 'the object of the mutineers was, I believe, not so much to disgrace our name, as to wipe out all trace of Europeans, and of everything connected with foreign rule ... There was cold and heartless blood thirstiness at the farthest remove from the lust of desire.'[49]

Sir John Kaye says of the Jhansi massacre, 'A doubt has been raised as to the complicity of the Rani in the atrocious deed ... but it was she who profited by the slaughter. She wished to be rid of the English that she might seize the principality which she considered to be rightfully her own, and she hesitated not at the means by which they were moved from her path. Her conduct after the massacre disclosed the passion of her soul.'[50] But the Rani claimed at this moment to be the helpless prisoner of the sepoys and to have had nothing to do with the massacre, which she passionately deplored. We may never know the truth for sure, but even the official account, by Sir Robert Hamilton, the Agent at Indore, says that the killing was ordered in the name of the Cavalry Commander, Risaldar Faiz Ali, rather than of the Rani. It is true, though, that she had plenty of reason to dislike Captain Skene, who had interpreted his orders in the harshest spirit.

The sepoys who carried out the massacre at Jhansi were attempting to recreate the formality of a firing squad or a blowing-away from guns. Like the other notorious massacres, it was done on open ground, in front of a crowd, purporting to carry out the sentence of a court. At Cawnpore, the Nana sat on a specially constructed platform to watch the killing, with his lieutenants, notably Tantia Topi, his childhood playmate and the Elusive Pimpernel of the last stages of the campaign. The sacred mark was put on the Nana's forehead in front of a large crowd, estimated at 10,000 to 12,000. The massacre had been decided on by a full council of the Nana's advisers, and sanctioned as right and proper by the *maulvi* Liaqat Ali and the local judge, Waziuddin.[51] The city was illuminated to celebrate the victory over the British garrison and their extermination. A proclamation was issued, declaring that it was the duty of all subjects to be as obedient to the present government as they had been to the former one, and that 'it is the incumbent duty of all the peasants and landed proprietors of every district to rejoice at the thought that the Christians have been sent to hell.' Every effort was made to demonstrate that the proceedings were the legitimate expression of rebel power.

The first massacre at Cawnpore was a very public business: the prisoners who had been promised safe passage down the Ganges were slaughtered as they scrambled into the boats before the eyes of the Nana and his entourage. By contrast, the second massacre, of the 120 women and children who had survived the first, the even more horrible massacre of Bibighar, the so-called House of the Ladies, was a desperate hole-and-corner business, carried out when the British relief force was already approaching and there were no crowds to watch. This massacre, too, was carried out by the Nana's orders, there is no doubt of that, but it had to be done by professional executioners after the sepoys had refused to obey. The balance of legitimacy was swinging round again. Killing defenceless women and children and throwing their bodies down a well no longer seemed such a hallowed action.[52]

Not all the massacres were as formal and public as those at Jhansi, Delhi and Cawnpore. But they were still systematic, thorough and authorized, for example at Allahabad, at Indore, at Gwalior (where one or two women were allowed to escape – the formidable Mrs Coopland survived to tell her story).[53]

These horrible killings were not a sadistic add-on. Getting rid of the next generation of Europeans was at the core of the project. The coming of the memsahib and her brood had coincided with the tightening of the grip of British culture and religion. Until they were got rid of, India would never be free. Saul David argues that the mutineers had decided in advance to kill all the Europeans, including women and children, only in order to tar whole regiments with the same brush. The less enthusiastic sepoys, being dipped so deep in blood, would be forced to join the rebellion because they no longer had anything to lose.[54] But this compulsory 'blooding' might be just as likely to deter the half-hearted, unless there existed a more powerful, overarching motive for such hideous crimes.

To use terms which had not yet been invented, the aim was surely genocidal; ethnic cleansing was intrinsic to the programme of the Mutiny. It was a genocide whose victims were to be counted in hundreds rather than millions, because the number of Europeans in India was still relatively small. But it was a genocide none the less. There is no point in pretending otherwise.

William Howard Russell, that unblinking observer of war, was in no doubt: 'Here ... we had a war of religion, a war of race and a war of revenge, of hope, of national promptings, to shake off the yoke of a stranger and to re-establish the full power of native chiefs, and the full sway of native religions ... Whatever the causes of the mutiny and the revolt, it is clear enough that one of the modes by which the leaders, as if by common instinct, determined to effect their end was the destruction of every white man, woman and child who fell into their hands.'[55]

In retaliation, the British committed a great number of what we would now call war crimes, whose victims were to be counted in thousands. There is no point in denying that either.

To mention but one: at Ajnala, near Amritsar, 282 sepoys of the 26th Native Infantry who had mutinied at Lahore surrendered to the Deputy Commissioner, Frederic Cooper, in the belief that they would be given a fair trial. Instead, Cooper, a proud Christian, had the first 200-odd brought out of the revenue office in batches of ten and shot by his Sikh troops. After the first 150 had been shot, one of the firing party fainted, and they took a breather before shooting another 87. Meanwhile, the remainder were kept locked up in one of the bastions. When the bastion doors were opened, to quote Cooper's own exultant words in his *Crisis in the Punjab*, 'Behold! They were nearly all dead! Unconsciously the tragedy of Holwell's Black Hole [of Calcutta – it was the account of John Zephaniah Holwell, a British surgeon who had survived the Black Hole, that outraged the British public] had been re-enacted ... forty-five bodies, dead from fright, exhaustion, fatigue, heat and partial suffocation were dragged out.'[56] These bodies were tipped down a dry well on top of their executed colleagues. T. Rice Holmes in his *History of the Mutiny* comments that 'for this splendid assumption of responsibility ... Cooper was assailed by the vulgar cries of ignorant humanitarians.'[57] Robert Montgomery, the deeply religious Judicial Commissioner for the Punjab and grandfather of the Field-Marshal, wrote to Mr Cooper, 'All honour to you for what you have done, and right well you did it ... It will be a feather to your cap as long as you live.'[58] Malcolm Low's boss, Roderick Edwards, thought that 'every European in Upper India is indebted to him for not having shrunk from the awful responsibility.'[59]

Today, we might be more inclined to side with the surgeon W. W. Ireland, who thought that Cooper recounts the story 'in so flippant and heartless a manner ... No man ever more thoroughly murdered his own reputation'.[60] The victims of the 'Black Hole of Ajnala' were tipped down the well a fortnight after the women and children had been thrown in the well at Cawnpore. Nor did Cooper omit to mention this horrific parallel when he came to write his account: 'There is a well at Cawnpore; but there is also one at Ajnala!'[61]

At Benares and Allahabad in early June, even before the Nana's massacres at Cawnpore, Colonel James Neill had hanged hundreds of natives with or without proof of criminality. 'Every day ten or a dozen niggers are hanged. Their corpses hung by twos and threes from branch and signpost all over town ... For three months eight dead-carts daily went their rounds from sunrise to sunset, to take down corpses which hung at the cross-roads and the market-places, poisoning the air of the city, and to throw their loathsome burdens into the Ganges.'[62] It was on Neill's orders that Major Renaud set off to Cawnpore with a column of Madras Fusiliers and Sikhs, leaving a trail of blackened bodies dangling by the road, their lower parts already eaten by the village pigs. Guilty villages were to be burnt, and their inhabitants slaughtered to the last man. Neill, like Frederic Cooper, had God on his side: 'God grant I may have acted with justice. I know I have with severity, but under all the circumstances I trust for forgiveness.'[63] When he reached Cawnpore and found out what had happened at the House of the Ladies, he made the murderers lick the blood off the floor before they were hanged.

We have seen how the mopping-up operations of Robert Dunlop and his Khaki Risala were marked by 'no mawkish pusillanimity'. On a larger and even more horrific scale, the total extermination of the adult male population of Jhansi after Sir Hugh Rose's siege continued for three days and left 5,000 dead.[64] Dr Thomas Lowe of the Bombay Engineers was proud that 'no maudlin clemency was to mark the fall of the city'.[65] The revengers were not at a loss for words. They trumpeted their deeds at the time and in the memoirs they published as soon as the presses could print them.

Accounts of the British retributions reached the Governor-General very quickly. Before the end of July, Lord Canning was preparing the Resolution (not a Proclamation) which was to earn him the derisive name, coined by *The Times* and *Punch*, of 'Clemency' Canning. It is in fact a remarkably even-handed document, insisting on proper punishment of the guilty as firmly as it warns against 'measures of extreme severity being unnecessarily resorted to, or carried to excess, or applied without due discrimination, in regard to acts of rebellion committed by persons not mutineers', and also against 'the general burning of villages', which might well lead to famine. But the public was not in the mood for even-handedness. It wanted blood for blood, and by large that was what it got. In all the controversy over the 'Clemency Proclamation', it is often forgotten how little effect it had on the conduct of British troops. As we have seen, the slaughter at Lucknow the following year and the wholesale burning of villages, not least by Showers's columns, were well up to the standard of Neill and Nicholson in June and July 1857.

'National revolt' is a descriptive term. It is not necessarily a pretty sight. In fact, the deeper the passions engaged in a national cause, the uglier the actions that men are capable of. The Turkish massacres of Greeks and Armenians, the Nazi massacres of Jews and gypsies were undoubtedly expressions of national feeling. So were the massacres of 1857.

There remains to this day a curious and probably unique thing about the Great Mutiny: nobody has the faintest reliable idea of how many people died in it. There are firm estimates for the horrific numbers who died on both sides in the other two great slaughters of the time: the Crimean War and the American Civil War. But no serious historian of the Mutiny has attempted to offer a figure for the numbers who died over the whole period from May 1857 to April 1859. I.T. Tavender's *Casualty Roll for the Indian Mutiny* (1983) gives a list of the British soldiers who died at the hands of the enemy: approximately 2,875 of them, over 350 of whom were massacred in cold blood by the mutineers. Three times as many British troops are estimated to have died from cholera, malaria and heatstroke – roughly the same terrible proportion as died from disease in the Crimea. Another 1,000–1,500 European civilians are thought to have been murdered. So probably about 13,000 Europeans died in the conflict, one way or another. But as for the Indians? Nobody knows, or much bothers to know. A hundred times as many possibly, or even more, perhaps a lot more.

For certain specific campaigns within the Uprising, estimates have been drawn up. The Archaeological Survey of India's guide to the Lucknow Residency tells us that there were 20,265 Martyrs during the Freedom Struggle of 1857–58.[66]

But these figures are based on suspiciously round numbers supplied by the regiments and communities which fought on the rebel side at Lucknow. Even the body counts made by the victorious British are quite unreliable. Were 5,000 Indians massacred at Jhansi, as computed by Kaye and Malleson,[67] or 3,000 or 4,000, as other accounts of Sir Hugh Rose's victory maintain? In the little battle at Jaula, did 150 or 200 men die, as Roderick Edwards says in his various self-serving accounts, or 400 as Malcolm Low tells us? One conspicuously level-headed witness, the Mathura Magistrate Mark Thornhill, who was present at the rout of the enemy in the grassy plain outside Agra, tells us that the official estimate of the rebel losses in that engagement was over 1,000. But he and a friend took the trouble to go out from the city the morning after the battle and count the corpses, which had not yet been removed, and found that they amounted to no more than 56.[68] The British figures for their own dead do not tot up the large numbers of Sikhs, Gurkhas, Pathans and Beluchis who were fighting on their side. Nor do they begin to compute the thousands of Indians cut down in the punitive expeditions into the country led by men like Sam Browne and Brigadier Showers, or the nameless thousands who perished from starvation and disease in the dismal ruins of Delhi and Lucknow. These will remain known only to their various Gods.

News from India now took little more than a month to reach England, via the electric telegraph and the overland route. The first intimation of the Mutiny hit the columns of *The Times* on June 9. Our Bombay Correspondent opens his dispatch of May 11 in reassuring style: 'I have nothing of any moment to communicate ... somnolent tranquility, characteristic of this hot season, broods over India.' But then, while he is still in mid-dispatch: 'As I write there arrives from Meerut, in the North-West Provinces, or rather from Agra, a telegraphic message containing intelligence which rather mars that profound tranquility to which I have alluded as pervading the whole of India. It runs thus:– "The 3d (bengal) Cavalry are in open mutiny. They have burnt down the lines and the officers' bungalows. Several officers and men are killed and wounded.'"

From then on, the full scale of the calamity begins to trickle, then to flood into the columns. But because of the time-lag, reassuring dispatches and editorials continue to appear, many referring to the earlier events at Barrackpore. On June 15, Our Calcutta Correspondent writes: 'The news of the recent mutinies in the Bengal Army has been received in England with a feeling of perhaps unnecessary alarm ... The Sepoy Army is not in revolt; it does not even appear that it is discontented ... The mutiny is not instigated by any religious feeling.' The causes of mutiny in India were always a reduction in pay or some outrage on caste prejudice. There could be no question of a national revolt among these credulous, childlike Asiatics: 'they have no patriotism, for during 600 years they had no country.'

When the news of the massacres was confirmed, and the British public learned that many women and children had been hacked down alongside their men, they were incandescent and inconsolable. The thirst for vengeance was more unappeasable than after any other such grim news in British history. There is no denying that the peculiar vengefulness was fuelled by an indignation that was essentially racist: black savages had dared to assault their white masters and to commit 'unspeakable' atrocities against white women. Such a nightmare had always haunted the British. The reality was even worse than the nightmare.

All this is accurately attested by post-colonial historians. What is less often described in detail is how quickly the horrors of the British retaliation were reported back to England, and what an impact these too made on anguished British minds. As early as January 1858, while the fighting was still going on, readers of *The Times* were informed that Theo Metcalfe had gone berserk and was 'every day trying and hanging all he can get' – a story confirmed a few months later by Mrs Coopland in her memoirs and by Robert Montgomery Martin in his *History of the Indian Empire*, where he complains that 'It is contrary to English ideas of justice, that a man should be suffered to carry out his notions of retribution by hanging as many victims as he pleases on the beams and angles of his ruined mansion.'[69]

Frederic Cooper had destroyed his own reputation by publishing, also in 1858, his jubilant account of how he had suffocated hundreds of sepoys and then thrown their bodies down the well at Ajnala. Martin quotes extensively from Cooper's narrative and leaves his readers to draw their own horrified conclusions. William Hodson's murder of the three princes of Delhi, his unarmed prisoners, was also condemned by Martin as the act of an unchivalrous freebooter.

Charles Ball, in his two-volume history of the Mutiny, probably published the following year, not only condemns the cruelty of the British retribution but offers, as does Martin, an extensive critique of the greed and oppression of British rule before the Mutiny: the deceit behind Dalhousie's annexations of Jhansi and Oudh, the brusque land reforms and excessive revenue demands, the blowing from guns. Ball even includes a fine steel engraving to adorn the gruesome account of the punishment scene, reported by a Bombay medical officer: 'all you see at the time is a cloud like a dust-storm, composed of shreds of clothing, burning muscle, and frizzing fat, with lumps of coagulated blood. Here and there a stomach or a liver comes falling down in a stinking shower.'[70] The burnings of villages and the looting and flogging that accompanied them are given as many pages as the heroic accounts of sieges and battles.

William Howard Russell adds to his eyewitness report of the unbridled looting at Lucknow several accounts of the casual and brutish racism which he had observed among the British in India: 'The habit of speaking of all natives as niggers has recently become quite common.'[71] George Otto Trevelyan is often criticized for his excessively patriotic and melodramatic account of the Cawnpore massacres, but he also draws attention to the contempt that the new generation of British officers showed towards their native soldiers: 'And so it came to pass ... that the sepoys were niggers ... That hateful word, which is now constantly on the tongue of all Anglo-Indians ... made its first appearance in decent society during the years which immediately preceded the mutiny.'[72] It is a modern illusion that decent people did not recoil from the word until the latter half of the twentieth century.

At the same time, most of these instant historians were at pains to rebut the more lurid atrocity stories, especially those about the rape and sexual mutilation of women. By the early 1860s, therefore, any reasonably alert reader in Britain would have been driven to the conclusion that, morally, there was not much to choose between the two sides and that if the Mutiny was not justified, it was certainly not surprising. That verdict was echoed by the leaders of elite society up to and including the Queen and Disraeli. Ball quotes at length Disraeli's famous speech at Aylesbury, delivered as early as September 30, 1857, only a couple of months after the first news of the Mutiny had reached Britain: 'I protest against meeting atrocities with atrocities. I have heard things said, and seen them written of late, which would make me almost suppose that the religious opinions of the people of England had undergone some sudden change; that instead of bowing before the name of Jesus, we were preparing to revive the worship of Moloch.'[73]

Nor, contrary to later myth, were the accounts of actual combat relentlessly gung-ho and jingoistic. There were plenty of stories of incredible heroism, self-sacrifice and grace under pressure, but there were also unstinting accounts of the horrors of close combat. It is not in accounts from the trenches of Flanders but in those from Lucknow and Delhi that the British public was first exposed to what war was really like; nowhere more so than in Lieutenant Vivian Majendie's *Up Among the Pandies,* published in 1859:

See that soldier plunging down his bayonet into some object at his feet – see, is it not red as he uplifts it for another blow? Raise yourself in your stirrups and look down and behold that living thing, above which the steel is flashing so mercilessly: is it a dog, or some venomous and loathsome reptile? No, but a human being: it is a man who lies at that soldier's feet – a man disguised with wounds and dust and mortal agony, with blood gurgling from his lips, and with half-uttered curses upon his tongue, who is dying there; and the reeking bayonet is wiped hurriedly upon the grass, and the killer passes on, to drain, in the wild excitement of his triumph, every drop of that cup of blood which this day the God of War holds out to him and which he sees foaming and brimming over before him. Ugh! It is horrid work at best.[74]

These narratives are painfully unstable and conflicted, mingling patriotism and revulsion, war-pride and war-guilt, communicating a lasting unease. (See Christopher Herbert for a fine discussion.) That is why the Mutiny remained the single most traumatic event in Victorian history, though it was not so large in terms of manpower deployed and British casualties suffered as the Crimean War or the Boer War. The British could never again think of themselves as wholly innocent. Nor could they ever again think of their Empire as something that had grown up more or less naturally, and was destined and deserving to endure for the foreseeable future.

Authority did its best to buttress public confidence. Even when the full scale of the calamity had burst upon the nation, the first instinct of the President of the Board of Control, Mr Vernon Smith, was to tell the House of Commons that 'there are not the slightest symptoms of the mutiny being a national revolt.'[75]

Instead, Government spokesmen described the revolt as 'a sudden impulse, occasioned by superstitious feeling'; it was 'a mere military mutiny'. And to repress it, stern action would be taken: extra troops would be sent from everywhere possible – Europe, South Africa, Persia, the high seas (Lord Elgin's punitive expedition to China was being recalled). It was, Mr Vernon Smith was compelled to admit, 'one of the most awful events which have happened in our history'. But at the same time, it posed no larger questions for British dominion.

Beneath the panic, there was a bedrock of complacency. And it was this complacency that Disraeli set out to fracture in his great Commons speech of July 27. The question was: 'is it a military mutiny or is it a national revolt?'[76] We had to examine the underlying causes. 'The decline and fall of empires are not affairs of greased cartridges.'[77]

The British Empire in India had been based on 'respect for nationality'. Britain had conquered India 'only in the same sense in which William of Orange conquered England' – a rather fanciful analogy, for William had not had to fight his way up from Land's End to John O'Groats, as the British had had to do in India. Dizzy argued that 'our occupation of any country has been preceded by a solemn proclamation and concluded by a sacred treaty, in which we undertook to respect and maintain inviolate the rights and privileges, the laws and customs, the property and religion of the people, whose affairs we were about to administer.'[78] Ours had been an Empire based on non-interference in internal affairs.

But recently, especially in the past eight years, 'our government in India has alienated or alarmed almost every influential class in the country.'[79] We had confiscated the property of traditional landholders, we had annexed state after state and, worst of all, 'the legislative council of India have, under the new system, been constantly nibbling at the religious system of the natives.'[80] As a result, the mutual suspicions of the rival religions and the different races and classes had dissolved; there was 'communication between classes who have never communicated before'. This was not a mere military mutiny; 'the conduct of the Bengal Army in revolting against our authority was the conduct of men who were not so much the avengers of professional grievances as the exponents of general discontent.'[81]

It is a stirring and cogent attack on the improvers and interferers, the whiggish school of Bentinck and Mill and Macaulay. Disraeli had put in plenty of hours on the Select Committee on India; he had read the Blue Books and the dispatches. And although on that night of July 27 he was doing the first duty of a Leader of the Opposition, to destroy the credibility of the Government, he was also stating or re-stating a traditional minimalist doctrine of Empire: that the domination of one race over another was tolerable only if the cultures of the subjected were scrupulously respected, and not defaced and deprived by the greed or religious prejudice of the conquerors. It was the same doctrine which Burke had immortally expounded in the affair of Warren Hastings and the Begum of Oudh. Now Disraeli saw before him a new Hastings (and would soon see a new Begum of Oudh, in the shape of Hazrat Mahal).

The new Hastings was, of course, Lord Dalhousie. Disraeli gleefully picks out the most obnoxious boasts from Dalhousie's farewell dispatch: that 'the position of the native soldier in India has long been such as to leave hardly any circumstances of his condition in need of improvement';[82] that the Maharajah Duleep Singh, the last ruler of the Punjab, had been converted to Christianity; and that Queen Victoria's dominions had so splendidly sprouted while Lord Dalhousie was in charge.

If Lord Dalhousie was the villain of Disraeli's piece, there was also a hero in it; there was one just man in India who could see what was going wrong and who had the courage to say so. And his name was John Low.

For the central thrust of his attack on Dalhousie – and on the Government both of India and Britain – Dizzy relies hugely on the testimony of General Low.

I have no personal acquaintance with him; I can only form my opinion of him from public report, and by reading that which shows the ability and integrity of the man – the Minutes made by him in Council. But I may say that he has always been considered as one of our first Indian statesmen. He is a man who has risen by his own energies and merits. He has passed fifty years as the representative of the Indian Government at various Courts of India – with Mahomedan Sultans, Hindoo Rajahs, and Mahratta Princes – and he is supposed to be more familiar with the wants of

India and the life of India than any other Indian statesman of the day.[83]

After this elaborate introduction, Disraeli asks us to listen to the General, 'for all agree that when we get the opinions of a mature and experienced intellect among Indian statesmen, delivered confidentially, that it is above all price. What says General Low?' And then Disraeli, who has never been to India in his life, reads out the words of a man who has spent 50 years there. What he reads out is a large portion of John's Minute opposing Dalhousie on the annexation of Nagpur.

Hard to tell at this distance in time what sort of impression John's easy, conversational, personal style made on a restive late-night Chamber full of fury and recrimination, but I cannot help believing that some mark was left when Disraeli quoted the plaintive question addressed to the General by old Indian friends who had known him when he was young: 'What crime did the late Rajah commit that his country should be seized by the Company?'[84]

What needs to be noted is Disraeli's extraordinary acuity in grasping what sort of a man John Low was: 'The House must not for a moment suppose that General Low is a man overconfident in his own opinions, or of a temper which listens with impatience to the suggestions of others. On the contrary, it is clear, from the tone of these Minutes, that, if he has a fault, it is that of too easily yielding up his own convictions to the predominant practice of the moment. These Minutes are full of evidence that it was with the greatest pain, and with the utmost desire to avoid the irksome duty, that he felt it necessary to come forward and oppose this policy. They are full of expressions of admiration and devotion to the Governor-General. But invariably as the proceedings advance you find that General Low gives up the struggle in despair.'[85]

Disraeli had put his finger on John's amiable weakness. He did not go on to point out (for it would have spoilt his case) where that amiable weakness had ultimately led him: to cave in and concur with Lord Dalhousie in his last great hubristic act, the seizure of Oudh.

It is a piquant moment. Right at the tail-end of his career, in fact quite a few years after he ought to have declared a dignified end to it, John Low is identified as the one man who understands what the British Empire ought to be like (and once had been like) – and identified by the British politician who goes on to become the great artificer of Empire, the jeweller who places the jewel in Victoria's crown. Disraeli's rare accolade must have made bittersweet reading when the text of it finally reached Low in Calcutta. For in the end he had become Dalhousie's accomplice, and if Dalhousie was to blame for the catastrophe, then so was he.

There was worse in store for General Low.

XIX

HOMECOMING

J ohn Low finally staggered back home in the middle of April 1858. Staggered is the word. He wrote to Lord Canning, thanking the Governor-General for his warm letter of farewell: 'It reached me at a time when it was in a peculiar degree soothing to my feelings, for I had just then reached my cabin on board the "Bengal" steamer at Garden Reach in bad spirits and so weak from illness, that I (literally speaking) could not walk three paces without assistance.'[1] Canning had said he had been 'greatly grieved to hear of your having been an invalid during your last few weeks in India'.[2] But the truth was that John had been an invalid for a long time. He had sweated out those last five years on the Supreme Council, and he had earned half a million rupees in that time – £50,000, or £3–4 million in today's money. But he had paid heavily for it, and not just in the cost to his health.

As the news reaching England had worsened during the high summer of 1857, so the recriminations became sharper and more personal. It was no good shovelling all the blame on Lord Dalhousie – he too was a sick man, dragging his swollen leg from one spa to the next, and he was out of the game. The public needed a scapegoat who was still active. The Opposition wanted a fresh angle of attack. And Disraeli, the most brutal, unscrupulous and brilliant leader of any parliamentary opposition, was not slow to identify the juiciest target.

Barely three weeks after Disraeli had praised his wisdom to the skies, John Low found himself on the receiving end of Dizzy's matchless vituperation. On August 11, in the Commons debate on sending fresh troops to India, the Tory leader turned his attention to the incumbent Governor-General. There was a difficulty in attacking Lord Canning himself: 'he has had little experience in India, and is little responsible for the present state of that country.' Besides, he was now displaying energy in coping with the dreadful situation. He deserved credit for that, and the support of the House. 'But no one can deny that Lord Canning was caught napping, and that his first measures showed vacillation and irresolution.' Whose fault was that?

'He is surrounded by men who have created that state of affairs which has resulted in such disaster; they are the very men who have been the prime councillors during the last ten years, and they are the very men whose conceit and arrogance have endangered the Indian empire. We must not repose, then, with confidence on Lord Canning, when the Council of India is composed of individuals who are the chief criminals and who ought to be called to account for the present state of affairs.'[3]

On that Council, who could be more to blame than the Military Member, General Low, when the troops were so woefully insufficient, ill-prepared and stationed in the wrong places?

There was no doubt either about what was wrong with General Low. In *The Sepoy Revolt: Its Causes and Consequences*, an instant polemic rushed out by the famous London house of John Murray before 1857 was out, Henry Mead, the firebreathing editor of *The Friend of India,* declared:

> Of General Low it is almost sufficient to say, that he had been fifty-three years in the service. He was known throughout India as a kind-hearted honourable man, ripe in knowledge of the native character, and friendly to the support of Asiatic dynasties ... His

heart was with the memories of the past, and his mind too feeble to sustain the anxieties of state policy. Had his faculties answered to his will, a vast amount of evil would have been averted.[4]

John Low was past it, if not certifiably gaga. He should have gone years ago. In desperation, John wrote to the Chairman of the East India Company, Mr Ross Mangles, begging to be reassured that the Court did not think he was clinging on when he should have retired. Mangles had his own troubles: he had been accused by Disraeli of planning to convert the whole of India to Christianity; and in a recent speech to the cadets' passing-out parade at Addiscombe, he had criticized the attitude of European officers towards their native colleagues,[5] not exactly a morale-booster at a time of national peril. Mr Mangles did not want any more problems, so he wrote back to John from India House 'to assure you that you needed not to have taken so much trouble to convince me or any other member of the court that you were not capable of clinging to your high and respon- sible office when you were incapacitated by illness from effectively fulfilling the duties of it.' On the contrary, the Court 'rejoiced . . . that you have not been driven from your post a day earlier than you would, of your own accord, desire to retire from it.'[6] I doubt whether he meant a word. The sooner General Low went, the better.

The sniping went on and on. The next fusillade came from the other side of the House, from Sir Charles Wood. This was especially wounding, as the high-minded Wood had only recently been President of the Board of Control at a time when Low and the others were already on the Council, so he might be presumed to know something about how they had performed. Wood said that he admired Lord Canning, and they should treat him with confidence for a while longer, because he alone had preserved his judgement and acted with firmness and discretion, 'when surrounded by mutinous soldiers, and there was nought but vacillation and pusillanimity on the part of his Councillors'.[7]

'Vacillation' – that word again, the quality which among all other military vices John Low most deplored. And this accusation now coupled with 'pusillanimity' – which was, if anything, worse. How could anyone say such things about a man who had dashed with Gibbs and Gillespie at the walls of Fort Cornelis, who had cut short the Peshwa's wrigglings, who had charged with John Malcolm at Mehidpur, who had reacted within minutes to turf the boy-usurper off the throne of Oudh, who had not hesitated to bring up the guns to make the Nizam sign, and who in this present calamity had been the first of Lord Canning's Council to recommend that the sepoys at Barrackpore be disarmed and the first, if not the only one, to demand that Delhi must be recaptured without delay? There were the Minutes on the record to prove it. Yet such things had been said and said several times.

There was a flurry of umbrage. Mr John Peter Grant, the most excitable and voluble member of the Council, fired off letters in every direction. On being prodded, Sir Charles wrote a letter which was published in *The Times*,[8] admitting that 'on looking at the words as they stand, they could bear the construction of "the Members of the Council of India"', but he wasn't referring to them at all but to unnamed 'persons in Calcutta and elsewhere with whom Lord Canning must have been more or less in communication' – a vague get-out which fooled nobody.

Canning himself wrote a public letter to the Court of Directors, declaring that it caused him much regret and pain to hear allegations in Parliament, on more than one occasion, that he had not received from the members of the Council of India the decided and effective support he might have expected. He wanted to place on record his distinct denial of the allegations. His colleagues had been first-rate, zealous, supportive and independent-minded. It was particularly important that no injustice should be done to the past valuable services of Mr Dorin and General Low who had just retired to England.[9]

But the mud stuck. Now the larger histories were coming out. In one of the first, Robert Montgomery Martin tells us that 'General Low's experience of native character was second to that of no man in

India.' But why had General Low not deployed that experience, and his equally far-reaching military experience, too? Why had he not, for example, as Military Member of the Governor-General's Council, insisted that a strong European regiment be stationed at Delhi, to frighten the mutineers away from their Emperor? Alas, Martin sighed: 'Had the energy of the general been equal to his judgment and integrity, a much wiser course would probably have long before been adopted by the council: but fifty-seven years' service in India [in fact, 52] can hardly be expected to leave a man the physical strength needful to the lucid exposition of his views, and to the maintenance and vindication of his own ripened convictions in antagonism to the prejudices of his younger colleagues.'[10]

In August 1860, Canning was still hosing down the deeply affronted Low. Like all Indian public servants, 'even the most distinguished', the General was unduly sensitive to the attacks of Press and of Party, Canning said. He should not attach such importance to that speech of Mr Disraeli's. 'Such flippancies' were constantly vented in debate to give point to a sentence. Politicians generally let these 'little pertnesses pass unheeded'. As for Henry Mead's book, he had not looked at it since it came out, but if he remembered rightly, 'there are others than yourself against whom the Author is virulent'. There certainly were. Mead said of Lord Canning himself, 'he had been more than twenty years in the House of Peers, and had never exhibited a sign of the capacity for empire. The impression which he left on the minds of men who transacted business with him was that of plaintive imbecility.'[11] His Lordship did not think that people were reading or quoting the book nearly as much as John imagined. It was 'a flea-bite, at the most'.[12]

Lord Canning's life had not begun and ended with India, as John Low's had. His Lordship was a hardened politician, not a serious-minded, perhaps literal-minded, public servant. Lord Canning could move on and forget. John Low could not.

Nor could Lord Dalhousie. When he first heard the news from India, he told his oldest friend, 'the Indian tidings haunt me day and night, and harass me in sleep which no difficulties or responsibilities or dangers in my own eight years were ever able to do. I know I could do nothing to prevent or to remedy all these miseries even if I were in health, but it depresses me to feel myself rotting, and likely to rot on, in inaction and uselessness.'[13]

He would admit no blame, though. He bristled when attacked. It was not his fault that the European troops had been taken away. Again and again, he had told London that he must have more of them – he had asked for 20 European battalions for Bengal alone. As for his not foreseeing the Mutiny, 'everybody can say, as "The Times" does, that, after all, I did not foresee the mutiny. Well, honestly, I did *not* foresee the mutiny; and I boldly aver that no other human being at that time foresaw it any more than I did.'[14]

Sunk in despair though he might be, Dalhousie remained cocky to the last. He still boasted of not having taken his boots off in the shrine at Amritsar.[15] He was proud too of having refused to demean himself by paying a call on the King of Delhi and of having shredded the last pretensions of the Mughals.[16] In discussing Havelock's tactics for relieving the siege of Lucknow, he admits, *en passant*, that 'I never was in Oude and do not know the ground.'[17] It is in his wretched retirement that we really see what a blanket of ignorance and arrogance had enfolded Lord Dalhousie during his eight amazing years in India.

He spent the winter of 1857–8 in Malta. John Low docked at Valletta on his way home, but Dalhousie had left the island a couple of weeks earlier. In Scotland, too, they kept on missing each other, first when Low had returned for his four months health break in 1856. At that time, Dalhousie had written from Arrochar on the west coast, to save his old friend from 'a bootless march to the South tomorrow', because the builders were in at Dalhousie Castle and he was wandering west in search of health. A reasonable excuse, but one cannot help sensing that, far from choosing to spend their retirement reminiscing together, 'as two Scottish gentlemen on the banks of Forth', Low and Dalhousie were actually avoiding each other. They continued to correspond with every appearance of warmth, but I can find no record of them meeting again before Dalhousie died of Bright's Disease on December 19, 1860.[18] For all their mutual courtesies, in the light of later events their shared history was too fraught to be recalled with comfort.

The changes to the governance of India were speedily agreed by Palmerston's government after the final suppression of the Mutiny. The East India Company was abolished – although a good case could be made that it was the financial and imperialist pressures from the British Government and the British public rather than the miscalculations of the Honourable Company that had been primarily responsible for the catastrophe. India was to be directly governed by the Crown. Victoria did not become the Empress of it until Dizzy, with his gift for the theatrical gesture, had her proclaimed as such in time for the Delhi Durbar of 1877.

By bringing India directly under the Crown, Palmerston shored up the financial standing of her Government. A sovereign nation issuing its own currency, rather than the incurably shaky East India Company, now stood behind her and enabled her to weather the recurring shocks of war and slump. Even more important was the rebuilding of that Government's internal finances. As significant as the posting of any noble proconsul was the arrival in Calcutta at the end of 1859 of Mr James Wilson, the dynamic Scot who had founded the *Economist* and had recently served as Financial Secretary to the British Treasury. Wilson took one look at the books and saw that India was heading for disaster: there had been a deficit of nearly £8 million in 1857–8; after the horrendous expense of suppressing the Mutiny, the deficit had risen to over £13 million for the following financial year. Over the whole period of the Mutiny, the accumulated debt in London and India had gone up from £59 million to £98 million and the annual interest bill from £2.5 million to £4.5 million. This was unsustainable.

The real trouble, Wilson saw as a good Treasury man, was that India was the most lightly taxed nation on earth. Most of what revenue did come in was really land rent. What the Government of India needed to balance the books was to tap the great wealth of her merchants and bankers. What she needed was a thumping income tax, plus a few imposts such as customs duties and traders' licences. In no time, India would be solvent again. And she was.

After less than a year in India, Wilson died of dysentery, in August 1860. Almost his last words are said to have been 'Take care of my income tax.' His funeral was reputedly the largest ever held in Calcutta, which must be a unique tribute to a man famous for inventing a new tax. But he deserved his cortege, for James Wilson was as much the saviour of British India as Nicholson or Havelock.

The Budget had been balanced. As Sir George Otto Trevelyan trilled triumphantly in 1863, in his parody of the old Scots ballad:

> John Company, my Jo, John,
> When we were first acquent,
> You borrowed, like the Yankees,
> At eight or ten per cent.
> Our fours are now at par, John,
> Our cash requirements low . . .
> Those tight tight days are past,
> The English Budget system
> A surplus shows at last.[19]

As a result of the fresh revenue, Britain was able to rebalance the Indian Army. By 1863, when the reorganization of the army was complete, there were 62,000 British and 125,000 native troops, just about one to two, as opposed to one to nine in 1856.[20] Almost every gun battery in India was now worked exclusively by European gunners. Never again would British rule have to rely entirely on the fidelity of her native soldiers. Never again was the Indian Army to be plagued by anything more than minor outbreaks of discontent. There was no longer any pretence or illusion of ruling by goodwill. India was henceforth held down by unashamed and unbeatable force.

Most brutal of all, at least in theory, was Canning's Proclamation of March 1858 that confiscated the rights in the soil of the entire province of Oudh. Any landowner who wanted to regain his estate had not only to surrender his arms and his person to the Chief Commissioner but also to prove that 'his hands were unstained with English blood murderously shed'. In practice, as it was pointed out to His Lordship that virtually every *taluqdar* had been more or less part of the rebellion, this bit of the Proclamation was quietly buried. The influx of British soldiery, with their huge appetites and their fistfuls of rupees, filled a gap in demand which had plagued most of the country since the old native armies were demobbed.

There were to be no more annexations. The remaining native rulers were to enjoy the explicit right to adopt their heirs. Religious liberty was to be scrupulously respected. Provided that they paid their taxes and did not make trouble, Indians of all classes were to be left free to live their lives, unfree but unhassled. Those parts of the settlement at least were in line with the principles that John Low had believed in all his career and had only strayed from at the end of it, under the imperious, irresistible Dalhousie.

General Low's political legacy might be ambiguous, but he certainly bequeathed quite a personal legacy to India. As he staggered down the gangway of the *Bengal*, he left behind no less than four sons serving the Empire in India.

It is easy to imagine Augusta's feelings as she lent her formidable weight to her tottering husband. All through the Mutiny she had lived on little scraps of information about the wellbeing of Malcolm, Robert, John Alwes and now Irvine. Lord Canning had passed on the news that Malcolm was safe – he had marked the relevant passage in Mr Muir's letter from Agra with a little red mark.[21] Soon Mr Muir had another enquiry: 'Mrs Low of Calcutta is anxious to hear particulars regarding her son [Robert] General Wilson's ADC and has written to Colonel Fraser on the subject. Can you help us?'[22] At least General Low's wife could get a message through. But now she was leaving all four of them in this huge country which had turned so dark and hostile. Which of them would she ever see again?

The third Low son, John Alwes, had arrived in the Governor-General's camp at Allahabad a few days after his eighteenth birthday. In the course of a long letter about the terms of his Proclamation to the nation, Canning finds space to report to John Low: 'Your son has been announced ... as I am writing; and I have lost no time in seeing him. He looks so fresh & happy & English, as to be almost out of place amongst the dried-up careworn faces that daily present themselves. He is delighted to hear that he is sure to be in time for Lucknow. I am going to give him a bad dinner – which is all I have to offer.'[23]

It is a pitiful irony that the fresh-faced youth who was so delighted to be in time for Lucknow was to be incapacitated by illness for most of his time in India and was eventually invalided out of the service on the grounds of sunstroke. He recovered in body but never in mind, though he lived to the age of 92. His younger brother Irvine had a different kind of ill-fortune. He rose to become Deputy Commissioner of Oudh, but died of dysentery at Lucknow at the age of 39, leaving a wife and four children. John Alwes and Irvine were two of the countless casualties of the war between the British and the Indian climate, a war which the British never looked like winning. Lucknow had made John Low's career; it destroyed two of his sons.

Then, not overnight, but within a remarkably brief time, everything changed. The spirit of recrimination melted away. The search for scapegoats was abandoned. All at once, the British people and their leaders hoisted in the marvellous outcome, an outcome scarcely to be hoped for and for months nearly despaired of: they had won, and won against huge numerical superiority, 10,000 miles from home, in the heat and dust and the barely more endurable monsoon. They had avenged the terrible atrocities committed by the enemy. Cawnpore had been remembered, and the sacrifice of British blood had been honoured and repaid several times over.

The victory was glorious. 'No other nation in the world can show a defence equal in its resoluteness and in its result to that of Lakhnao,' wrote Colonel Malleson.[24] 'The sons of Great Britain have, during the building up of their vast and magnificent empire, accomplished wonders. But of all the marvels they have achieved there is not one that can compare with the re-conquest, by small means, of the great inheritance which had suddenly, as if by the wave of a magician's wand, slipped from their grasp ... Not for a second did they flinch from the seemingly unequal struggle. They held out, they persevered, they pressed forward, they wore down their enemies, and they won. It was the greatest achievement the world has ever seen.'[25]

How was it achieved? General Havelock, in his Field Force Order of July 13, 1857, thanked his soldiers after the Battle of Fatehpur 'for their arduous exertions of yesterday, which produced in four hours the strange result of a rebel army driven from a strong position, 11 guns captured and their whole force scattered to the wind without the loss of a single British soldier. To what is this magical effect to be attributed? To the fire of British artillery, exceeding in rapidity and precision all that the British general has ever witnessed in his not short career; to the power of the Enfield rifle in British hands, to the British pluck.'[26]

Training, technology and pluck: that was the invincible combination – skills and qualities that had been honed and toned, not on the playing fields of Eton, for not many of the victors belonged to the aristocracy, but in the middle-class masterclasses of Haileybury and Addiscombe and Woolwich. Time and again, the British wondered with palpitating hearts why the sepoys did not simply clamber over their knee-high mud walls and hop over their pitiful ditches. According to Malleson, the inferior moral nature of the Asiatic, shrinking involuntarily from actual contact with the European behind defences, neutralized the superiority of numbers. Leadership was the key: 'it is a remarkable fact that the mutiny produced amongst the mutineers no real general – not one man who understood the importance of time, of opportunity, of dash, in war.'[27]

General John Jacob was the most influential military thinker in the years after the Mutiny and was largely responsible for the way the British Army in India was reorganized. He had no doubts about the underlying reality: 'We hold India, then, by being in reality, as in reputation, a superior race to the Asiatic; and if this natural superiority did not exist, we should not, and could not retain the country for one week ... Away, then, with the assumption of equality: and let us accept our true position of a dominant race.'[28]

It was not simply the generals and historians who set out to remind the British how superior they were. The poets, too, hymned the incomparable qualities of the British race, from Christina Rossetti in the 1860s to Sir Henry Newbolt in the 1890s. The heaviest guns were carried by the Poet Laureate. 'The Defence of Lucknow' celebrates the way the Union Jack flew over the Residency throughout the siege:

> Shot thro' the staff or the halyard, but ever we raised thee anew,
> And ever upon the topmost roof our banner of England blew.

It is perhaps the most unashamedly patriotic of all Tennyson's patriotic verse. It is remarkable also in that, unlike, say, 'The Charge of the Light Brigade', it was not dashed off immediately on reading the newspaper reports but carefully composed more than 20 years later, after talking to survivors and consulting written accounts of the siege. As a result, it contains a good deal of accurate detail about the mining, the loyalty of the native soldiers, the stinking corpses, the hopeless amputations, and about the course of events:

> Hold it we might – and for fifteen days or for twenty at most.
> 'Never surrender, I charge you, but every man die at his post!'
> Voice of the dead whom we loved, our Lawrence the best of the
>   brave:
> Cold were his brows when we kiss'd him – We laid him that
>   night in his grave.

Historians argue that the rise of Social Darwinism helped to drive the growth of this sense of racial superiority in late Victorian Britain. But, as far as India went, no scientific back-up was needed. It was a moral truth, earned and demonstrated in battle. According to the hard-nosed James Fitzjames Stephen, who served as Law Member of the Viceroy's Council between 1869 and 1872, England's conquest of India was the result of an equitable 'competitive examination which lasted for just a hundred years, and of which the first paper was set upon the field of Plassey, and the last (for the present) under the walls of Delhi and Lucknow.'[29] This sportive analogy, characteristically contained in a letter to *The Times*, combined the twin late-Victorian enthusiasms: competitive examinations and colonial warfare.

There followed an unavoidable conclusion. Having shown our superiority, it was our duty to stay in India for the foreseeable future. To borrow General Colin Powell's 'Pottery Barn' analogy after the Iraq war: we broke it, now we owned it. As Francis Hutchins puts it in his brilliant essay, *The Illusion of Permanence*, Britain had now 'psychologically annexed' India. Stephen argued that 'But for the restless, dissatisfied, officious interference of English theorists, there is no reason why the present state of things should not continue indefinitely.'[30]

Gone were the intimations of earlier proconsuls, such as Mountstuart Elphinstone, that the British Empire like other empires would have its day and would pass, and that there would come a time when Indians would run their own affairs. Gone too were the gloomy prognoses of generals like Charles Napier who had forecast that 'The system will not last fifty years. The moment these brave and able natives know how to combine, they will rush on us simultaneously and the game is up.'[31] The rising had come, and the rising had been seen off. 'India belongs to us,' the social reformer Harriet Martineau told her readers.

The Mutiny had another effect. It had left a poisonous aftertaste, a racial distrust that could not be rinsed away by polite proclamations and splendid durbars. Sir George Otto Trevelyan witnessed the change: 'The distrust and dislike engendered by such an experience are too deeply rooted to be plucked up by an act of volition.'[32] All through the 1830s and 1840s John Low had warned his masters against presuming that 'the natives actually *like* us.' On the contrary, the average Indian had a natural dislike of his conquerors, and that dislike had to be understood and coped with.

But now the feeling was the other way round. The conquerors had been infected by an abiding dislike of those they had conquered. In the old days, British feelings about the Indians had been a muddle of condescension and fear, but occasionally there was affection, too. Now there was contempt, and worse. 'Dislike appeared by the side of disdain . . . At the period of the Mutiny the feeling of aversion was intensified into deadly hatred. For a season this hatred was shared by the entire mass of our countrymen. Invectives against the treacherous, blood-thirsty Mussulman, ironical sneers about the "mild Hindoo" were nuts alike to the civilian and the planter.'[33] The Raj, as it had come to be known, might show a more glittering façade than the ramshackle old East India Company, but there was not much love about it.

Nobody expressed the new state of things more bluntly than James Fitzjames Stephen in his memorable account of the funeral of Lord Mayo, the only Viceroy to be assassinated:

When Lord Mayo was stabbed, I think every man in the country felt as if he had been more or less stabbed himself . . . There was a dead silence nearly all the way . . . all that was to be heard was the rattle of the gun-carriage, and the tramping of the horses, and the minute-guns from the fort and ships . . . Troops and cannon and gun-carriage seem out of place in England . . . but it is a very different matter in India where everything rests upon military force . . . it is pleasant to think that Lord Mayo is not to lie here in a country which we can govern and where we can work and make money and lead laborious lives; but for which no Englishman ever did, or ever will, or can feel one tender or genial feeling. The work that is done here is great and wonderful; but the Country is hateful.[34]

Service in India was a duty, an honourable profession, but the British no longer pretended that it was much of a pleasure. Nor did the new breed of civil and military officers feel much respect for the cultures of the natives. Their religions, their festivals, their princely courts seemed irretrievably barbaric and benighted. The old 'Orientalists', such as Sir William Jones, had been genuinely respectful of the antiquity of Indian art and thought, and were conscious of what Burke called 'our insect origins of yesterday'. Now there arose a new generation of Orientalists who often seemed patronizing rather than reverent – the word 'primitive' seemed to hover on their lips.

Luckily, the greater the number of the British in India, the less call to mix with the Indians, to wander in the bazaar, to watch the nautch girls, to frolic in the marigold garlands of the great festivals. India was reduced to the club, the polo field and evensong.

Rather than continue to try to modernize Indian society, the British authorities now felt compelled to support the native princes and to make much of caste distinctions in the Indian Army. Rather to their surprise, the old landowners were restored to their lands, with the extra confirmation of an official *sanad*, or certificate of ownership. No longer were the *taluqdars* of Oudh, the *zemindars* of Begal, the *malguzars* of the Central Provinces seen as indolent parasites to be ejected wherever possible. From now on, they were to be the bulwarks of British rule. No longer was India to be a laboratory for the sort of socialist experiment that nobody would have dreamed of attempting back home. Sir Charles Wood, a typical mid-Victorian liberal, wrote to Sir Bartle Frere that 'the dead level of nothing between our officers and the people is an unnatural state of things.'[35] In the interests of peace and quiet, what India needed was a prosperous native aristocracy not unlike Britain's.

While Britain juddered towards democracy, India was quietly but deliberately nudged backwards. There was a 'tilt to the landlords'.

On the subcontinent there was no answering echo of Disraeli's 1867 Reform Act pushing Britain in the direction of adult male suffrage. On the contrary, the new Viceroy, John Lawrence, who might have been expected to be sympathetic to the native cause, reduced rather than expanded the few avenues for Indian advancement.

Yet there soon occurred, only a handful of years later, another bouleversement, a quiet upheaval in the politics of India, which nobody could have prophesied and few understood at the time. In December 1885, the first meeting of the Indian National Congress was held at Bombay. Only 72 delegates turned up, and many of those had to be badgered to come. But for posterity, more significant than the thin turn-out was the sympathy of the Viceroy of the day, Lord Dufferin, who looked benignly on the Congress proposals to introduce elected members into the Legislative Councils, to discuss the budgets, and to work on other ideas which would clearly lead in the long run to parliamentary self-government. These demands represented the most startling departure from subservience since the Mutiny, and were potentially far more coherent than the resentments which had triggered that furious cataclysm. Yet Dufferin described the Congress's plans as 'neither very dangerous, nor very extravagant', and said he was inclined 'to give quickly and with a good grace whatever it may be possible or desirable to accord'.[36] The next Congress was held in Calcutta, and he held a garden party in its honour at Government House.

While in theory British rule was destined to last for ever, in practice its high representative was preparing the ground for a gradual slipping away. Dufferin and his colleagues in London disclaimed any such intention. So did Lord Minto and John Morley 20 years later when, as Viceroy and Secretary of State for India, they carried the process a stage further. Burke had thought that the Bloodless Revolution had shown the British genius for carrying out a revolution while pretending that nothing had really changed. A succession of British Viceroys, mostly mild and benign noblemen – Ripon, Lansdowne, Minto, Chelmsford, Reading, Irwin – continued the quiet retreat from Empire. Only Curzon trumpeted against the tide: 'We have not the smallest intention of abandoning our Indian possessions and . . . it is highly improbable that any such intention will be entertained by our posterity.'[37] But less than two decades later, in the last months of the Great War, Lord Chelmsford and Edwin Montagu openly abandoned the principle of autocracy in India and announced that their policy was now 'to guide the steps of India along the road that in the fullness of time would lead to complete self-government within the Empire.'[38]

India had volunteered more than a million troops for the war effort. She had earned in battle the right to govern herself. There could be no going back. Over the next generation, there would be acts of repression, press censorship and atrocities on both sides. Gandhi and the Nehrus were in and out of jail. But the overall direction of travel was in one direction only. The Great War had famously unhorsed three Emperors in Continental Europe. It helped to unhorse a fourth on the subcontinent.

Impatient commentators have criticized the British for letting several decades more slip by before independence finally arrived. Did not the painful foot-dragging allow the Muslim-Hindu divide to become toxic and contribute towards the hideous slaughter in the Punjab at the time of Partition? Perhaps, but the long gestation period also left time for the Army to train 15,000 Indian officers, for the police and the civil service to be thoroughly Indianized and for the Provincial Councils to gain deep experience of governing. Few liberated colonies have had a fuller preparation. Mountstuart Elphinstone's long-term vision a century before had more or less come true. The mulish resistance of Curzon and Churchill may have slowed progress, but that slowing was perhaps no bad thing.

It remains an odd story. Why ever did British proconsuls at the high noon of Empire set in train a process that would eventually bring about that Empire's end? And why did politicians in London acquiesce, though often grudgingly, in defiance of strong pro-Empire feelings among the public? Sir Penderel Moon, as the brightest spark in the Indian Civil Service, spent his life observing and contributing to this remarkable train of events. He was driven to the conclusion that it was because 'no one had thought out or was able to suggest any clear alternative'.[39]

Parliamentary democracy was the only language the British spoke. When they were under pressure from the 1890s onwards to dilute their benevolent despotism in India, all they could do was set up embryonic replicas of their own home-grown institutions. If they were not always conscious of what they were doing, then the same could be said of the manner in which they had acquired India in the first place. To borrow the famous remark of the historian Sir John Seely, the British let their Empire go rather as they had conquered it, 'in a fit of absence of mind'.

There was underlying the debates of the later nineteenth century a certain disappointment. For the British, India had not lived up to its golden promise. Except for the tea and coffee plantations of Assam, there were few British settlers. European cotton plantations had not worked. India seemed to lack the sturdy pioneer spirit of the white dominions. Despite the spread of Western education, the Indians themselves remained stubbornly alien, their commercial life as impenetrable as ever, continuing to bear little resemblance to capitalism as the British understood it.

The British had ruled India, often brutally and graspingly, but they had seldom actively sought to penetrate Indian culture. To that extent, 'non-interference' was a genuine principle, adhered to in practice on and off throughout the Raj. When modern anti-colonial scholars such as Ranajit Guha describe British rule as 'domination without hegemony', they are really pointing to something of which the British themselves were well aware and often prided themselves on. If Western capitalism, Western rationalism, and Western religion were to seep into Indian minds and hearts, they would have to do so by natural growth, not by forcible implanting. Only those abuses which were most intolerable in British eyes, such as widow-burning, could legitimately be interfered with.

The optimistic British liberals of the 1830s and 1840s, the Bentincks, Macaulays and Trevelyans, had indeed looked forward to the decline of Hinduism with all its intolerable superstitions and to the gradual spread of Christianity. Nothing much like that seemed to be happening. On the contrary, a revived Hinduism seemed to be a key part of the nascent Indian nationalism. The trouble was that India had never been a *terra nullius*, a land empty except for small numbers of nomadic tribes. The Indians were there, and in enormous numbers, 200 million of them. The antiquity of their civilizations, which had once fascinated Western scholars, now presented itself as an insuperable obstacle to 'making something' of the country. As early as 1813, Indian nationalists had been complaining about the 'drain of wealth' from India to Britain.[40] Now one or two British sceptics had begun to wonder whether the drain might not be operating in the opposite direction. The huge Indian market for British goods had to be set against the no less huge costs of the Indian Army and bureaucracy. Who could be sure which way the balance now tilted?

The long-drawn-out, surreptitious retreat did have a respectable pedigree and a moral logic to it. James Wilson's son-in-law Walter Bagehot, who succeeded him as editor of the *Economist* and as a leader of elite opinion, was sharply conscious of the history of the whole enterprise: 'is it not the almost unanimous declaration of every Anglo-Indian statesman we have ever had that our rule in India is not and never ought to be regarded as political *ownership*, or as anything but the administration of a trust? "Let us recollect," they say with one voice, "that we are trustees for the natives – that if we cannot keep India consistently with promoting their progress, we ought not to keep it at all".'[41] This had been argued again and again by men like Munro, Bentinck and Metcalfe. This was why 'it has been the persistent purpose of all this class of statesmen to introduce natives more and more into the government of India, in order that eventually they may become the real rulers of India, when we who have trained them to their work have completed our task.'[42]

Anyway, the British were not making the hoped-for impact on Indian life. 'The experience of the English in India shows – if it shows anything – that a highly civilized race may fail in producing a rapidly excellent effect on a less civilized race, because it is too good and too different.'[43] We were exhausting our national energies and sacrificing our finest young men in a hopeless cause. In private, Bagehot drew the logical conclusion, as reported by his friend R.H. Hutton, editor of the *Spectator*, in a memorial tribute after Bagehot died in 1877: 'He would have been glad to find a fair excuse for giving up India, for throwing the Colonies on their own resources and for persuading the English people to accept deliberately the place of a fourth- or fifth-rate European power – which was not, in his estimation, a cynical or unpatriotic wish, but quite the reverse, for he thought that such a course would result in generally raising the calibre of the national mind, conscience and taste.'[44] It was too early to voice such heretical thoughts in the public prints, but they were already brewing in the minds of the elite.

Still, the spirit of the later 1860s and 1870s had this much to be said for it, from John Low's point of view: as the arguments about who to blame for the Mutiny faded from public debate, so the respect grew for the men who had made India what it now was. In the polemics of 1857 and the years immediately after the Mutiny, Dalhousie had been condemned as an overweening and reckless bully. By the end of the century, his biographers were carving a marmoreal figure of vision and sagacity. If the Empire was to survive as a creditable enterprise, it had to have a make-over. The 'New Imperialism' needed its heroes at all levels.[45] Far from being thought spineless, men who had weathered the Mutiny like John Low were now regarded as the backbone of Empire.

He was knighted in 1862. Five years later, he was promoted to full general. And in 1873, he was appointed Grand Commander of the Star of India. This was a brand-new order of chivalry, minted after the Mutiny to reward and cement the loyalty of the great native princes. It was Queen Victoria, with her often surprising sensitivity, who pointed out that the native princes would be even more flattered to wear the Star of India on their bosoms if they knew that the great potentates of Britain were wearing it too. So when the first list came out in 1861, it included not only the Nizam of Hyderabad, the Sindia, the Holkar and the Maharajahs of Nepal and Kashmir, but also the Prince of Wales, Lord Canning, Lord Clyde (as Sir Crawling Camel had now become), Sir John Lawrence, Sir James Outram and Sir Hugh Rose. It was into this crème de la crème that John Low was ladled at the age of 85.

All was forgiven and, publicly at any rate, forgotten. Even Sir Theophilus Metcalfe was awarded a CB in 1864 for his services at the Siege of Delhi. Of his services *after* the Siege of Delhi, no more was said. And Theo was a welcome guest at Clatto, when he brought little Charlie with him, John and Augusta's adored first grandchild, all they had to remind them of Charlotte, of whom they never spoke but who was never out of their thoughts.

Charlie was an engaging boy and developed into a brilliant mimic. Malcolm's wife Ida remembered, on her first visit to Clatto as a bride, how Charlie, coming down early one morning and seeing the chairs set out for family prayers, sat in each chair in turn and imitated the posture and facial expression of every member of the household.

What should he do with his life, this bright young spark? When he left Harrow for University College, Oxford, there was a family conclave at Clatto round the dining room table. Theo, as ever overdoing it, suggested, half joking, that with his charms Charlie could probably manage pretty well without a profession – with luck he might pick up an heiress. At which the frail old general at the head of the table rose painfully to his feet and said with all the severity of a Lowland patriarch: '*My daughter's son shall not be an idler.*'[46]

Nor was he. Charlie Metcalfe became an empire-builder in the most literal sense. As a consulting engineer, he helped to build all the railway lines of Rhodesia, in fact pretty much every line from the Cape to the Congo. Coal from Wankie, copper from Katanga, zinc and lead from the Broken Hill mines – all were carried along the tracks which Charlie had surveyed and constructed, walking huge distances across the veld and through the jungle. He was two months younger than Cecil Rhodes. They had been at neighbouring colleges at Oxford and became lifelong mates. Charlie was one of the two or three friends standing by the grave when Rhodes was buried in the Matopos Hills. Like Theo, he was a great raconteur and ladies' man. He never did pick up an heiress, but Theo did, which was just as well, because he remained as extravagant in his last years in Paris as he had been as a young man in Delhi, to his father's despair.

The Thackeray girls, Minnie and Annie, went to Clatto too, and often wrote to their cousin Augusta. It is Minnie who writes long gossipy letters to her sister describing her first visit there in 1863:

> My Dear Gal. I have just been into a large empty spare bedroom to steal a bit of paper to write to you, which is a gt. deal more than you would do for me in the dark. It is a very long time since I heard from you but as there is no post & no turnpike here on Sundays, I couldn't expect to – I came here yesterday morning. Robert crossed over the Firth with me wh. was very kind of him as there was a Scotch mist – now I thought a Scotch mist was a mist, but it is nothing but a very heaving shower of rain, however Robert says that he has been wet through for 3 weeks at a time and I was very glad that he came because he got me a place to lie down on or I shd. have been sea sick, & the boat is a thing like a dirty Lord Mayors barge with no sort of accommodation for being unwell.[47]

Minnie took to Clatto and to her Low cousins the moment she got there:

> Clatto is such a nice pretty place on the top of a hill cut into terraces with lots of yellow dalias [sic] and there is a beautiful view from it across fields & meadows to the Perth hills & on one

side a bit of the sea the house is covered with dear little turrets
wh lead out of almost all the bedrooms and just hold a round
bath.[48]

The plumbing arrangements which John Low had dreamed of in
the heat of Bengal were now fully on stream. In old age, he had
finally achieved the nabob's dream with all mod cons. Apart from
Robert home on leave, John and Augusta had the two girls with
them, Augusta junior now aged 19 and her sister Selina a year
younger. But that was only the home team. The fearsome Aunt
Georgina and John's four other sisters, all now bereft of their much
older husbands, had taken up residence in Edinburgh. Each of them
hopped across the Firth to Clatto for a summer visit which was to
be measured in months not weeks. The most conspicuous of them
was Catherine, as always the centre of attention. For years she had
worn a heavy black wig, which she suddenly discarded, emerging as
a beautiful silver-haired old lady. At intervals, she announced that
she was dying and summoned John to her bedside, but she always
recovered, even on the occasion when she insisted on ordering her
coffin and laying in swathes of mourning crepe for her nearest and
dearest.[49]

I forgot to tell that there were two old Scotch aunts one is a dear
smiling old lady who is very lame & rides on a sort of wooden
spring horse in the passage it gives her horrible pain to move but
she always smiles & nods kindly when she does move, so that
you may not see that she is in pain – The other one I do not like
so much, but she is not a bad old lady. Only she has been a
beauty in her youth & the other hasn't which makes a great
difference between the two – The old beauty bothered me today
by asking me if my Papa was a handsome man. I said I did not
know & she thought it very stupid of me so I described him as
well as I could & and then she looked at me finally & said, but
would he be a handsome man if it wasnt for his nose.[50]

The novelist was now in terminally poor health – he died the following year – and he resented it when either of his daughters left his side. But he saw a lot of General and Mrs (now Lady) Low in London, and he really could not complain, for Minnie had her father's bright eye and warm curiosity, and her letters were worth waiting for. She even managed to squeeze some sport from the relentless churchgoing which punctuated life at Clatto.

St Andrews is such a pretty old town with the ruins of a
Cathedral bigger than St Pauls wh. the wicked Scotch pulled
down. The general drove me to church in his little sort of gig, &
we had a sweet sermon about Dives from an Irish-man with a
Scotch brogue.'[51]

Sir John preferred the easy-going Episcopalian rite at St Andrews, but Minnie was also subjected to the austere service of the local church at Kemback:

Augusta & I have had a long windy walk to a little Scotch
church in a pretty valley with such a nice German looking
manse with holly hocks & a church yard all complete. All the
Scotch people gathered together in little knots to talk long
before the service began. One old man had an immense bow of
crepe on the back of his hat the 2 swells of the church are not
lively looking people the pews have little tables in them, the
Service was not so bad – no worse I think than the Episcopalian
service at St Andrews – but no sooner was one long sermon
over than we had another one by the same man – the general
expression of the country people seemed to me rather like those
casts which hang round the chamber of horrors a sort of dogged
shrewdness – there was a little boy behind me who made me
uncomfortable by expectorating throughout the whole service,
however poor child one could hardly grudge him that little
amusement with those 2 long sermons to sit out.[52]

Churchgoing was not the end of it. 'They dine at half past 5 on Sundays and as the evening after wd have been rather long (for it is not etiquette in Scotland to do anything on Sundays except read sermons or sing hymns without a piano) we put on a great many cloaks & took a long walk until it grew quite dark ... It makes me feel rather like a serpent when I am alone with the girls & they say that it seems to them very dreadful to go to a place like Little Holland House on Sundays & play at Croquet. I am so afraid of putting my wicked notions into their heads, for they are as innocent as little sucking pigs.'[53]

The other religion of St Andrews was golf, a game with which Minnie seems unfamiliar:

I am very glad that I brought thick boots & winter clothes for we went yesterday to play at Golf on a boggy hill & it is so cold & brisk and windy just like the top of the Righi. I like it very much, especially as the house is full of fires when one comes in, & like a nice comfortable oven. Golf is a game of little holes in the ground as much as four and a half miles apart & balls are sent into them with sticks called Putters and clinks & when the balls are lost little boys called Coddys go & find them. General Low cannot walk so many miles so he goes on a yellow pony he is the only person allowed to ride, but then he is much respected in the county.[54]

This privilege was unique in the history of The Royal & Ancient Golf Club. It was mentioned in the speeches at the annual golf ball which was the social highlight of Minnie's stay:

The Ball was really rather fun – There were such heaps of old gentlemen dancing & capering – for there is gt dearth of young men in this neighbourhood – I begin to think that we know an unusual number at home. All the Captains of Golf had red coats on & the Gen had his tail, there was a speech about him at

supper – the 2 girls & I went into supper with 3 old Colonels &
it is a sort of rule that I didn't know, that you are to dance a sort
of scotch country dance with the man who brings you back
from dinner. You may fancy my alarm when I found myself
flying & spinning with my old Colonel.[55]

That year's ball was a special occasion, for the new Captain of the
Club was the Prince of Wales, later Edward VII, who had just married the Danish princess Alexandra. The Town Hall was elaborately
decorated with crossed golf clubs and Prince of Wales feathers and
Danish stars. The caterer Mr Hunter of St Andrews had performed
wonders, the music was provided by Wallace's celebrated Quadrille
Band from Edinburgh, and so many members, wives and guests
attended that supper had to be taken in two sittings. The only let-
down was that the Royal Captain was unable to be present. In his
absence, the evening's star was the oldest member of the club,
General Sir John Low, who, in the words of Mr Whyte Melville, the
chairman, 'although unable to walk could yet be seen every day
upon the links as keen at the golf as ever and it was not everyone
they would permit to ride over their golfing course on a pony as they
allowed their trusty friend to do ... the gallant General acknowledged the compliment.'[56]

John was to follow the Prince of Wales, and his own father, as
Captain of The Royal & Ancient two years later. He might never
have been away from Fife. How little life at Clatto had changed
since he had first left home more than half a century before. Here
he was back among his ain folk, who loved dancing as much as they
loved golf. But then a soldier's life had always included plenty of
dancing, nowhere more so than in British India. Every Governor
and every Resident was expected to pay host to innumerable balls.
Every cantonment had its regular hops. The accomplished young
officer was expected to master the schottische, the lancers and all the
other variants of the quadrille. The ball was of course an opportunity for young men and women to meet and get acquainted. It was

the first port of call for the 'Fishing Fleet' of girls just out from England.

But in India the ball was also the visible expression of British solidarity. And it was a deeply British occasion, more muscular than erotic. After the polka and the gallop, the lieutenants in their tight-waisted uniforms would be visibly perspiring, and the nipped-in young ladies would be glowing. The gradual acceptance of the waltz had introduced one-on-one encounters, but even the waltz was danced at arm's length, for the matrons and the commanding officers had a quick eye for those who overstepped the mark.

What a lot of dancing John had seen in his 50 years in India. There were those lavish masqued balls that the Thackerays and the Shakespears had given in Park Street and Alipore, with the guests togged out as Punch and Judy, emperors and dwarves, sailors and babies. There was that peculiar ball Lord Minto had given for his invasion fleet at Malacca to celebrate mad King George's birthday, where the subalterns danced with the 'intensely brown and beautiful' Malay-Dutch women – a rare racial mingling on the dance floor. There were the 'philandering' entertainments that Mountstuart Elphinstone had hosted at Bombay, which he would slip away from to curl up with Aeschylus or Anacreon. Then there were the endless balls at Simla, which Lord Dalhousie never stopped groaning about while Lady Dalhousie grew paler and thinner – but those were memories too painful to be dwelled on, for those were John's last memories of Charlotte, so bright and happy, dancing with Theo when they were engaged. There was the ghastly dance at Lahore the night before the sepoys were disarmed when the ladies were shivering with fright. But the dancing had to go ahead or the mutineers would guess that they had been rumbled. And a fortnight later, Lord Canning had insisted that the grand ball at Government House to celebrate the Queen's Birthday should go ahead too, although by now the mutiny had broken out. John Low had been there and hobbled round the floor, but his head was whirling more with the movements of British troops up the Ganges than with those of the quadrille. At all costs, the sahibs, and the memsahibs, too, had to show that they were not afraid.

The feminine was not entirely excluded from these routs. The cotillion was, after all, named from the French word for the petticoats which flashed as the girls swirled. But there was about these occasions something essentially 'manly', to use the word which sprang so readily to Victorian lips. The British sort of dancing was, implicitly and sometimes explicitly, contrasted to the sort of dancing the natives went in for: sinuous, erotic, suggestive, and, well, effeminate. Nothing had shocked John Low more than the reports of his 'silly king', Nasir-ud-din Haidar, dancing with Mr Derusett. It is hard to say which was the most deplorable aspect of it: a King dancing with a barber, an Indian dancing with a European, or a man dancing with a man. It was one of the principal charges against Wajid Ali Shah, too, that he was in the habit of dancing with his Fairies, most of them well under the Western age of consent. The Nawab's supporters protested that he didn't actually dance at all. On the contrary, the strictest propriety was observed: the girls danced on one side of a curtain, while Wajid Ali Shah played the sitar on the other. The British were no more sympathetic to the religious elements in Indian dance. The rituals of the Muharram had been gingerly treated by British Residents, for fear of provoking violence if they were interfered with. But the weird ceremonies with which Nasir-ud-din had embroidered the processions were too much for John Low. The interweaving of the sensuous and the religious was repugnant to him, as to most British officials.

As for the more secular entertainments provided by the nautch girls, they simply bored the British. The days when they would accompany their native officers to nautch evenings had long gone. In his trip round India in the winter of 1875, the Prince of Wales was forced to sit through nautch after nautch. A journalist on the royal tour reported that 'long before he reached Madras, His Royal Highness, like everyone else with the expedition, seems to have become thoroughly tired of the stupid spectacle.'[57] The prevailing attitude was that of Emily Eden who noted the inevitable appearance at the fireworks display held in their honour at Lucknow: 'The boats in front were loaded with nautch-girls who dance on, whether they are looked at or not.' Only six months earlier in the Red Throne Room, the girls had danced on through whistling bullets and smashing chandeliers, as Colonel Low brought up the troops to turf the boy-king off the throne. As General Low watched Minnie and his daughters being whirled round by the old colonels in St Andrews Town Hall, I doubt whether he reflected that he must be the only officer there who had ordered his men to open fire on a room full of dancing girls.

The Prince of Wales may have failed to show up at the ball, but a few years later, according to Indian legend, he paid an impromptu visit to a rather more surprising venue. It was to acclimatize the natives to the idea of a Queen-Empress that Disraeli had sent Bertie on his comprehensive tour of India in the winter of 1875–6. All the native princes came to Calcutta to pay him homage – Sindia, Holkar, the Rajas of Benares, Patiala and Jodhpur and Kashmir, the little Begum of Bhopal, to name but a few. But what was to be done about the only local royal resident, the ex-King of Oudh? At Matiya Burj, Wajid Ali Shah could hear the guns boom the salute from Fort William as the Royal Yacht *Serapis* glided up the Hooghly past his ghat. Wajid Ali Shah's Indian biographer tells us that His Royal Highness was keen to meet him and Wajid Ali Shah was sent an invitation to the great durbar. But he refused, saying with the self-pity which we have seen so frequently in native princes: 'If you consider me a king, then it is below my status to go to you. But if in your eyes I am a homeless beggar, then how dare I face you?'

The Prince, in that easy, unstuffy way with which he defused awkward situations, decided to go to Matiya Burj instead. It was a piquant meeting between these two plump potentates, both addicted to women and the stage, particularly to women on the stage, both easy-going, tolerant sensualists: the one kicked off his throne for these qualities, the other despaired of by his mother but loved by his people for precisely the same qualities. As Bertie left, Wajid Ali Shah, despite his protestation of poverty, presented him with a walking stick studded with diamonds and pearls.

Alas, there is no reliable evidence for this enchanting meeting. It is mere wishful thinking by those who yearned to see Wajid Ali Shah restored to his former dignity. For one thing, it is unlikely that the British authorities would have sent out a royal invitation that would have enhanced the pretensions of a king they had dethroned.[58]

At the beginning of October, Minnie left Clatto and went south, back to her ailing father in his new house at Palace Green, Kensington. The Lows were leaving Clatto, too, as they did every autumn. They packed away all the spoons and things, Minnie reports, and the girls were very dismal. This had become the annual ritual: a night at the hotel in Edinburgh on the way down, then a rented house, in South Kensington perhaps – they were thinking of Thurloe Square. Some winters they went to the south of France, with a long stop-off at Paris to see Theo and Charlie.

For so long, Clatto had been the focus of John's hopes and ambitions. It had also been the leading cause of his horrendous debts. Now it had become merely a holiday home. Quite soon, he became too tottery, his lungs too creaky, to come up even in the summer. He and Augusta settled on Brixton Hill, next door to Robert's old dame school, at a house called Strathallan, where he died on January 10, 1880, at the age of 91. Augusta lived on until 1893 (she was, after all, 20 years younger) and died at Torquay. They were both buried beside the church wall in the wooded dell at Kemback, but like many 'old Indians' they had remained essentially vagrant in their retirement, drifting to the south-coast promenades where they could raise their hat to their own kind.

John Low was mourned as the last of the old school, as a proconsul who had known the natives and their princes better than any other British officer in India. The obituary engraving of him in the *Illustrated London News* depicts him as a mixture of Karl Marx and Elijah, full of fire and certainty.

Yet for all his speed and decisiveness in situations of conflict, about the ultimate purpose and justification of British rule in India he remained uncertain to the last. He never lost his instinctive willingness to admit that he might be mistaken, nor his recurring fear that the British Empire might be heading in a disastrous direction. His fierce aspect was no less misleading, for in all his ups and downs you cannot help noticing a natural tenderness, especially towards the browbeaten and bewildered people he was supposed to be ruling.

Edward Thackeray came home, too. His mother and father were long dead, and he drifted into the family circle of his cousin William Makepeace Thackeray who greeted him with great affection. Because of the difference in age, Edward had always regarded him as 'more like a revered father than a cousin'. The novelist's daughters were just about Edward's age and were more quizzical about this lanky taciturn Engineer captain. Edward's eyes were soon fixed on another member of the household, Amy Crowe, sister of Thackeray's hard-up gopher, Eyre Crowe, who was also employed as drawing master to the girls. Kindly as ever, Thackeray had taken in the motherless Amy and developed a tendresse for her. He took the whole household on delightful outings to eat duck and peas at the Old Ship Hotel in Greenwich and the Star and Garter at Richmond. On the pleasant drives back to Kensington by moonlight, Edward drew ever closer to Amy.

In her usual laconic style, Annie described the denouement in her Journal:

> Came home on the 24th to find Papa ill & to hear from Amy that she had refused Edward.
>
> 25th Very anxious telegraphed to Edward to come back. 'We hope tho' we don't expect that you will return.'
>
> 28th. Edward arrived & everything was settled. He had cared for Amy for a year.[59]

Which did not mean that Annie greeted the engagement with unmixed joy. Candid as ever, she wrote to Amy: 'I was rather surprised to hear of things going on smoothly – but don't let your sister Eugenie make fun of him. He isn't a bit clever but we should be dull enough if we had to build a fortification or put out a gunpowder magazine. And I think it was very clever of him to fall in love with you.'[60]

Thackeray himself admired Edward wholeheartedly for his courage and read out to the girls the letter from Colonel Baird-Smith recommending him for a VC: 'Colonel Smith says he is one of the bravest of the Engineers, and after all, as Papa says, bravery is the best thing in the world & makes everyone more friendly & enthusiastic than cleverness or wisdom, or learning or rank or whatnot, & so it is no wonder that we all feel proud to have a VC come into the family.'[61]

As a result of Baird-Smith's tireless campaigning, Edward's VC was gazetted at the end of April 1862, four-and-a-half years after it was earned – then a record for the longest interval between exploit and honour.

All the same, Thackeray, ailing and wifeless, was desolate to be losing Amy. He gave the couple a beautiful 18-place cutlery service, laid on the wedding breakfast at Palace Green and made a short funny speech in their honour, but afterwards he went off to the studio of his friend John Everett Millais in South Kensington and spent most of the afternoon in tears on Millais' sofa. Annie went to see Amy and Edward off: 'I remember her back getting into the cab in the mist. Good speed to them. Knocked at Papa's door he wouldn't let me in.'[62]

The Thackerays never saw Amy again. She and Edward went to India where she bore three daughters in quick succession and died in childbirth with the third (who also died). Thackeray himself died a few months after the departure of his beloved Amy, so he never knew what happened to her. Within three years Edward returned with the surviving babies, Margie and little Annie. The Thackeray sisters, who like their father had a warm heart as well as a sharp pen, took them in and brought them up, two more casualties of what Henry James called the 'wheel that ground the dust for a million early graves'. Even after his death, Thackeray's household continued to be a refuge for homeless Indians, just as Aunt Ritchie's and Marianne Irvine's had been to earlier generations.

Edward married again and had four sons, but in London seemed a forlorn figure, ill at ease with his daughters, able only to unburden himself to Annie: 'Edward only began to say something really a little bit last night first about Papa and then about the children. He is rather miserable because they never utter in his presence he says it is such a strange sort of life with his children in England, strangers almost, & his wife in the hills & all his days at work in a little office.'[63]

Like many another old Indian, Edward eventually found it easier to settle abroad. He spent the last 30 years of his long life at Bordighera, where he became a much respected citizen. When he died in 1927, a guard of honour of the local *fascisti* fired a salute over his grave.

Malcolm too declined to live full-time at Clatto when he was invalided home in 1874. He developed a successful second career as a mining investor and so he could have afforded to play the laird, but he settled firmly at 22 Roland Gardens, South Kensington, briefly sat in Parliament as MP for Grantham, and only took his two daughters to Scotland for the summer holidays. Clatto was finally sold a week before Malcolm's death in 1923. It had been let for 40 years and in the 80 years since its rebuilding the Lows had properly lived in it for no more than half a dozen. The nabob's dream had never quite lived up to its expectations. Now it had finally evaporated.

Looking back over this vast sprawl of experience, what strikes one with a poignant force is how little it all impacted on the souls of the British soldiers who gave their lives to India. The inner life of the British in India appeared hermetically sealed, preserved intact so that they eventually returned to the 'home' they barely knew as though they had never left it. Deliberately dunked in British culture as soon as they were weaned (or by the age of six at the latest), they came instinctively to think of their Britishness as something precious and hard-won, an integral asset which must be guarded with every fibre of their being.

Only Robert stayed on in India. He went on soldiering there into the twentieth century. His missions were very different from those his father had undertaken. John Low had spent his 50 years cementing British control over the territory of imperial India. That was not what he had set out to accomplish. His instincts had always been to try to assist the old India to live on undisturbed as far as humanly possible. But time and again, he had been instrumental in sweeping away the old regimes. 'Each man kills the thing he loves.' I don't imagine that John Low and Oscar Wilde would have been soulmates, but it is undeniable that his career was soaked in the tears of native princes who had thought him their best friend.

By contrast, Robert Low spent the next 50 years protecting the frontiers of what was now, internally, a solidly held domain. Year after year, he was sent off to fight now-forgotten border campaigns against forgotten enemies: in the Yusufzai Expedition of 1863, against the Afridis of the Bazar Valley in 1879, against the Zaimukhts on the Zava Heights in 1880, then back marching with Lord Roberts from Kabul to Kandahar in the Second Afghan War after the Russians had occupied Kabul, then in 1887–9 two arduous years of guerrilla warfare in Upper Burma. Finally in 1895 he commanded the expedition that stormed the heights of the Malakand Pass and relieved Chitral, high in the foothills of the Hindu Kush.

This was the last great relief expedition of the nineteenth century, almost the last set to be played in the Great Game before it was revived again in our own time. The Russians had been pushing down through the Pamirs towards the unclaimed mountains north of British India. The old British fears of invasion from the north sprang up, as lurid as ever. To us who have seen the agonies the Soviet Union went through in its efforts to subdue Afghanistan, the thought of an invasion over the watershed of the Hindu Kush, where the mountains rise to 20,000 feet and more, may seem fanciful. But paranoia is a secondary symptom of imperialism. Even the most

daunting natural barriers come to seem incurably fragile. Besides,
there were five British officers and 343 British troops, mostly Sikhs,
marooned in the little mud and stone fort, which was only 60 yards
square. So a relief force of no less than 15,000 men was sent out from
Peshawar under the command of Major-General Sir Robert Low.
With its 20,000 camp followers and the same number of pack animals, this disproportionate expedition was clearly intended as a
demonstration of power and intent to the Russians, no less than to
the tribesmen of the Hindu Kush.

The expedition caught the public imagination, and its progress
was anxiously followed by the emerging mass media. Already the
military had learnt how important it was to feed the *Daily Beast*. The
expedition was accompanied by the photographic section of the
Bengal Sappers and Miners under Sergeant Mayo.[64] Robert also had
with him Captain Francis Younghusband, formerly Agent at Gilgit,
who was covering the war for *The Times*, and the well-known
sportsman Major Roddy Owen, who was there for the Lucknow
Pioneer. As Robert was setting out from the south, up the precipitous
river valleys, another column was coming to the rescue from the east,
on the even tougher route across the mountains from Gilgit. This
much smaller relief mission, under Colonel J.G. Kelly, had with it
Francis's brother, Captain George Younghusband (the two were
always being mistaken for each other), who was also reporting for
The Times – a classic early example of the newsdesk having every
angle covered.

In one of the dozen books about the Relief of Chitral, the
Younghusband brothers, themselves to become legendary figures on
the North-West Frontier, wrote: 'Since Lord Roberts made his
famous march from Kabul to Kandahar, the Indian Army has perhaps taken part in no campaign so rapid, brilliant, and successful as
the operations which resulted in the relief of the sorely pressed garrison of Chitral.' The British public had 'watched with breathless
suspense the keen struggle, as the columns pushed forward over
high mountain passes, girth deep in snow, across rivers broad and

deep, swollen with rain and melting snow, and fiercely opposed by the desperate bravery of mountain warriors born and bred to the sword.'[65]

The horrors of siege and rescue in the mountains had changed little since the First Afghan War. The Pathans still came whooping down from the heights, the guns still got bogged down to their axles, the fighting strengths of both the besieged garrison and the relieving columns were decimated by desertion, dysentery and cholera. In the high passes, the gunners were disabled by snow blindness, and the most valued accessory was dark glasses, which Kelly's column were desperately short of.

Both the British columns staggered on, constantly harassed on all sides, and eventually reached Chitral. They found the fort abandoned by Sher Afzul's men, who had fled when they heard how vast Robert Low's army was. The first of Low's men into Chitral were Francis Younghusband and Roddy Owen, who had ridden on far ahead of the main column, setting a journalistic precedent to be followed by Max Hastings in the Falklands and John Simpson in his burqa at Kabul. Owen and Younghusband had carefully avoided seeking Low's permission, knowing that it would be refused.[66] In fact, though, it turned out that Kelly's column had already got there a week earlier, to find that the five British soldiers had all amazingly survived, though they were 'like walking skeletons' and down to their last bottle of brandy.

Training, technology and pluck had triumphed once again. Especially technology, for this was the first time that the Maxim machine gun had sprayed an Indian hillside (it had had its very first outing a year earlier, in the Matabele Wars). Already this portable, rapid-firing weapon had become a legend in the Hindu Kush. In Munda Fort, Lowforce discovered letters from a Scottish firm in Bombay to Sher Afzul's ally Umra Khan offering him Maxim guns at 3,700 rupees each.[67] The tribesmen were painfully aware of the truth to be enunciated only three years later by Hilaire Belloc in *The Modern Traveller*:

Whatever happens, we have got
The Maxim Gun, and they have not.[68]

In his first engagement 40 years earlier, Robert's men had deployed Enfield rifles against the bows and arrows of the Santals. Now they were firing machine guns against those same Enfields – always a jump ahead in the technology of war.

The public reaction at home mattered as much as the display of British power to its target audiences in Kabul and Moscow. The Younghusbands declared: 'When therefore within three short weeks the welcome news was flashed down the wire that Chitral was relieved, and that the British Agent and his escort had been snatched from a horrible fate, there was perhaps hardly a corner of the British Empire which did not feel proud of the hardy leaders and brave men who had so signally upheld the proud standard of British resource, pluck, and endurance.'[69] The age of global news had dawned, and the Relief of Chitral conformed perfectly to Lord Copper's insistence that the British victory should be decisive, heroic and, above all, quick.

Sergeant Mayo had been hard at work throughout the campaign. His photo of 'Sir R. Low and staff on the Janbattai Pass' gives an idea of the hard yomping at altitude demanded even of elderly force commanders. When they reached Chitral, he lined up Robert and Surgeon-Major Robertson, the unflappable commander of the garrison, for a group photograph. It is hard to say who look the more exhausted, the relieved or the relievers. Mayo also rounded up the defeated Sher Afzul and his followers, who look rather more at home in their native environment. These team photos are not unlike those taken after a cup final, which for both sides in the Great Game perhaps it was.

There also survives a portrait of Robert taken just after Chitral, at the height of his brief fame. It is hard to recognize in this battle-worn anguished face the fresh, perky boy with his gun under his arm. Forty years of displaying pluck under pressure had left their mark.

Chitral had been relieved. But was it worth retaining? High-ups like the Duke of Cambridge and Lord Roberts were convinced that the place was of the greatest strategic importance. But the legendary fighting soldier, Sir Neville Bowles Chamberlain, wrote to *The Times* that a Russian onslaught via Chitral was 'extremely improbable, if not impracticable', because there was no food in the valleys. The dandyish diplomat Sir Lepel Griffin thought that 'a small Russian detachment might occupy Chitral, but the British Empire would not collapse because a few hundred Cossacks foolishly immured themselves in a death-trap.'[70] Lord Salisbury did decide to garrison Chitral, and it stayed garrisoned until it became part of Pakistan in 1947, the northernmost outpost of British power in India. Least impressed by the whole affair was the hero of it all, the surgeon turned garrison commander, George Robertson, who subtitled his account 'the story of a minor siege'.

Sir George Scott Robertson, as he later became, is today better remembered as the founding anthropologist of the Kalash tribes of Chitral. His seminal work, *The Kafirs of the Hindu Kush*, was published only a year after the siege. It was Robertson who implanted the belief among the Kalash that they were the descendants of the army of Alexander the Great. And it was Robertson's comrades in arms who brought back from Chitral the carved effigies of the dead, the *gandaus*, which are among the glories of the British Museum. Not for the first time in the Empire's history, ethnography followed the siege train.

Robert Low retired in 1905 as a full general and Commander-in-Chief of the Bombay Army. The last picture I have of any Low in India is of Robert presiding over a fancy dress ball at Government House, Poona, in 1903. The C-in-C is got up as a lawyer with his daughters costumed as grim shepherdesses. It is a melancholy coda to a century of such masquerades. Four years later, he was appointed Keeper of the Crown Jewels. After only two years at the Tower of London, he died, not there but at his home, 20 Cornwall Road, Dorchester. He was buried in Dorchester. For him, too, Scotland had become as distant a memory as India.

Among the diadems he had custody of in his last post was Queen Alexandra's Crown. This rather squat little crown, newly artificed for her Coronation, contained as its centrepiece the Koh-i-Noor diamond, which had endured even more of a battering in life than its keeper. The stone had originally been mined in southern India, probably somewhere in Andhra Pradesh, perhaps as early as the thirteenth century. Centuries later, it had been inset in the Peacock Throne in Agra, and was then filched along with the Throne by the Shah of Persia, from where it passed to the rulers of Afghanistan. The exiled Shah Shuja then gave the Koh-i-Noor to Ranjit Singh in return for his help in being restored to his throne. Emily Eden saw it glittering on the breast of the old whiskered mouse and sketched it. Ranjit in turn was forced to disgorge it by Lord Dalhousie after the British conquest of the Punjab. It was then shipped to Windsor, where Queen Victoria used to wear it as a brooch. Today, it has been reset as part of Queen Elizabeth's Crown. For most of its long life above ground and through its several re-cuttings, the Koh-i-Noor has remained the ultimate badge of conquest. Now it sits in the Tower as the reminder of a gone glory. The only part of the 'brightest jewel in the crown' that is still in British hands is the jewel in the Crown. And the Indians want it back.[71]

Sometimes, strolling through the ruins of earlier civilizations, we idly wonder what it must have been like to live through the end of one of them. Now we know for ourselves.

NOTES

Introduction

1 Lieutenant John Blakiston, who fought alongside Arthur Wellesley in his hottest fights, describes in his *Twelve Years Military Adventure in Three Quarters of the Globe* (1829) the gentler uses of the elephant: 'I have myself seen the wife of a *mahout* (for the followers often take their families with them to camp) give a baby in charge to the elephant, while she went on some business, and have been highly amused on observing the sagacity and care of the unwieldy nurse.' (Chapter vi)

2 As usual, Kipling struck a nerve when he chose the head of an elephant as the emblem to be embossed on the front of his collected works. It was bad luck for his reputation with posterity that he placed alongside the elephant the ancient Sanskrit emblem meaning good luck. In 1933, Kipling required his publishers to remove the swastika from his book covers, because it was now 'defiled beyond redemption'. (Jan Montefiore, letter to *Times Literary Supplement*, January 31, 2014)

3 Low, *Fifty Years with John Company: from the letters of General Sir John Low of Clatto*, Fife, 1822–1858, p 37.

Chapter I: Low Country

1 Hunter, *Thackerays in India*, p 71.

2 Hunter calculates that the annual salaries and allowances drawn by the first William Makepeace Thackeray over his ten years of residence in the wilds of Sylhet in north-east Bengal would add up to only 16,230

rupees, less than a single year's pay of the lowest grade of Bengal tax collector in Hunter's own time. (Hunter, ibid., p 99.)

3 Bayly, *Indian Society*, pp 59–60 and 69–71.

4 Bayly, *Rulers, Townsmen*, p 262.

5 Aunt Georgina takes her place in the formidable ranks of the aunts who ruled the childhood of so many colonial children – of P.G. Wodehouse (whose father was a judge in Hong Kong), of Saki (whose father Charles Augustus Munro was an Inspector-General of Police in Burma), of Rudyard Kipling (father an artist/museum curator in Lahore), of William Makepeace Thackeray (father a judge and tax collector in Calcutta). For Kipling and Thackeray, the aunts offered a loving refuge from the ghastly schools and boarding houses they were dispatched to. For Saki and Wodehouse, the aunts were worse than the schools. I'm afraid that Georgina belonged in the latter category.

6 Quoted Ferdinand Mount, *The Subversive Family*, p 254.

7 Low, p 42.

8 Professor David Stevenson of St Andrews points out in his fascinating book on the Beggar's Benison that 'most of the evidence identifying recruits was probably not normally issued to local members, the men who actually met in Anstruther annually.' The diplomas were issued as a sort of honorary membership to celebrities who might never attend the meetings. So any local gallant could well have frolicked in 'Merryland', as the members called their domain, without there being any documentary record of his belonging to the club. (Stevenson, *The Beggar's Benison*, pp 152–3.)

9 Low, pp 148–51.

10 Bentinck Papers, Low to Bentinck, December 16, 1833.

11 Behrend, p 88.

12 Low, p 150.

13 Low, pp 343–4.

14 Undergraduates were supposedly compelled to wear this flaming costume around town so that the authorities could spot them in the taverns more easily, though what was there to stop them stripping off as soon as they got to the bar?

15 Low, pp xvi–xvii. The three portraits are reproduced in *Burlington Magazine*, April 1938, pp189–91, 'Three Early Portraits by Wilkie'.

16 Wilson, *Madras Army*, iii, p 79.

17 Wilson, iii, pp 80–82.

18 IOR/F/4/226/4957.

19 Letter from Fort St George to the East India Company, February 12, 1806.

Chapter II: Massacre in a fives court

1 Hoover, *Men Without Hats*, p 73.
2 The total figures for the Madras Army in 1806 were: 7,900 British troops as against 55,050 sepoys. (Cameron, p 2.)
3 Wilson, iii, pp 169–70.
4 Wilson, iii, p 171. Bentinck had already had occasion to complain of Fancourt's 'want of temper and judgment', in particular his failure to co-operate with Marriott. Could he not be moved elsewhere? Ironically, it was Cradock who had said that this would be unfair without a court-martial, for which they did not have enough evidence. Which is why Fancourt was still in command at Vellore on the night of July 9. (Cameron, pp 163–4.)
5 Cameron, p 59.
6 Cameron, p 201.
7 Cameron, p 258.
8 Chapter XVI.
9 The natives saw so little religious observance among their new masters that one of them once asked an English gentleman taking his morning walk up and down the verandah whether these were his times of prayer.
10 Cameron, p 80.
11 Wilson, iii, p 175.
12 Wilson, iii, p 174.
13 Cameron, p 84.
14 It may have been as late as July 8. The date is unclear.
15 Wakeham, *The Bravest Soldier*, pp 98–99; Wilson, iii, pp 175–6.
16 To be fair, such warnings were not unknown. After the mutiny, there were to be many more such warnings, causing panics all over southern India, and most of them turned out to be nothing more than the ravings of fakirs high on *bhang* or arrack.
17 Hoover, p 104.
18 Dean, *United Service Magazine*, January 1841, p 24.
19 Add MS 29181, f233. There was originally a third sheet. That sheet is now available only in an obscure collection of reprinted articles, *The Plain Englishman*, edited by C. Knight and E.H. Locker, 1820–3, vol ii, chap xx, p 437.
20 Wilson, iii, p 178.
21 Kaye, *Mutiny*, i, p 166.
22 Kaye, pp 166–7.
23 Wilson, iii, p 182.
24 Wilson, iii, pp 183–4.

25 Wilson, iii, pp 184–5. How did Ewing and his stragglers get out of the
    fort? Wilson says that they must have left the fort by the sally port or
    Amboor Gate on the south side of the fort which was still held by the
    Colonel's own men. But Lieutenant Blakiston says with unconcealed
    disgust that they found a rope hanging over the wall which had been
    used to let in some of the mutineers, and they shinned up it and got
    out that way.
26 Cameron, p 20.
27 The plundering had distracted the sepoys from their prime task of
    securing the fort: pulling up the drawbridge, locking the two outer
    gates and extinguishing the remaining resistance from the 150 or so
    men of the 69th who still survived. The chests of the Paymaster had
    been broken open and 29,000 pagodas removed, large supplies of
    arrack had been looted from the godowns. By now, the sepoys, like
    the Europeans, were running out of ammunition. (Cameron, p 19.)
       As was routine, they had been issued only with six rounds of ball car-
    tridges per man (Wilson, iii, pp 180–1). These had been mostly
    expended in the planned and targeted massacre at the Main Guard.
    There was a small magazine at the bottom of the ramparts next to the
    flagstaff where the Mysore flag was now flapping in the morning sun,
    and this too had been ransacked to enable the desperate hail of bullets
    to be kept up. There were also the two 6-pounder guns which the
    sepoys had trained on the European barracks, and it was these big guns
    that had killed or wounded dozens of the sleeping 69th.
28 Wilson, iii, pp 179–81.
29 Dean, p 33.
30 Wilson, iii, p 182.
31 Dean, pp 34–5.
32 Thorn, Gillespie, p 16.
33 Wakeham, p 18.
34 Wakeham, p 49.
35 Gillespie's first biographer, Major Thorn, has the king saying less pic-
    turesquely, 'What, can it be possible that this little man is the person
    who performed so great an exploit in San Domingo?' But I prefer the
    other version. (Wakeham p 59; Thorn, pp 40–1.)
36 Thorn, pp 64–66.
37 Wilson, iii, p 177. We have already noticed the rope which had let in
    the sepoys from the huts outside – possibly the same one that was now
    letting out Lieutenant Ewing and his friends, if they did not use the
    sally port. There is no evidence that the sentries noticed any such
    comings or goings.
38 Wilson, iii, p 185.

39 Wakeham, p 106, following Blakiston, though Wilson, iii, p 185, says it was 6am, but as Wakeham says, Blakiston was there.

40 Thorn, p 102, Wakeham, p 106. Or that is what Sergeant Brady is supposed to have cried. It sounds a little too neat for an exhausted man poking his head over the battlements with every risk that it might be blown off from behind, but Irish eloquence is no respecter of danger.

41 There is a more picturesque version put about by Gillespie's comrade-in-arms Major Thorn in his life of his old friend: that the resisters on the rampart tied together their bayonet and ammunition belts to let down the men to open the gates: Thorn, p 102, Wakeham, p 106. But Gillespie says clearly in his dispatch the next day to General Cradock that he was drawn up by a rope. The original of the dispatch is in the India Office Library, next to Mrs Fancourt's narrative: Add MS 29181, f235. It is not in Gillespie's hand, for he apologizes to Cradock for using an amanuensis because the pain in his broken wrist is too bad for him to write himself.

42 Cameron casts doubt on Gillespie's claim that the fire from the sepoys had been 'tremendous' or 'well-directed', arguing that if the insurgents had really been putting up a fight, the whole thing could not have been over in ten minutes or a quarter of an hour, as Gillespie himself says that it was. (Cameron, pp 26–29.) But Blakiston confirms that 'on entering the square a smart fire was kept up on us for a short time but no sooner was a front of one squadron formed on the parade than the sepoys gave way in all directions, most of them flying towards the sally-port', which is pretty much what Gillespie reported to Cradock.

43 Kaye, *Mutiny*, i, p 168.

44 Wilson, iii, p 186.

45 Captain Charles Marriott, the Colonel's brother, who shared his house, estimates that near 700 sepoys inside and outside the fort were killed – not so far from Blakiston's estimate, which may include the European dead. The most careful modern account reaches a figure of 650 for the sepoys killed – exactly five times the 130 European officers and men who had lost their lives. (Cameron, pp 27–30.)

46 Round balls pressed into tin cans with a powder charge behind them, which gave a deadly cone-shaped spread when discharged; grapeshot, a canvas bag also filled with round iron balls, gave a spread too, but a less deadly one.

47 He was writing 20 years later.

48 Cameron, p 30.

49 Low, p 45. Jack Cavanagh, the Roger Federer of the game, was cele-brated in a famous essay by Hazlitt. The game had been taken up with enthusiasm by bored and lonely British officers all over India. Courts

had been erected, usually by public subscription, in Calcutta, Madras, Lucknow, Berhampur (where the Great Mutiny was to have its first stirring) – and Vellore. Sir Thomas Munro, the great Governor of Madras, was so partial to the game that he was frequently heard to assert that 'he would rather live upon half-pay, in a garrison which could boast of a fives court than vegetate on full batta, where there was none.' Colonel Mordaunt, the famous organizer of cockfights and other entertainments for Warren Hastings, came to a mock duel after a hotly disputed game of fives.

50 Butler, pp 44–5.

51 Butler, p 35. This did happen during the Great Mutiny of 1857, the raw memory of which clearly colours Butler's account, but it did not happen at Vellore. Yet his account of the fives court is accurate. The British Library's charming watercolour of 1816, ten years after the mutiny, shows the fives court attached to the Jalakantesvara temple, now the arsenal. In front of the court there is a viewing gallery, in which you can just make out redcoats watching the play. It is unclear whether the stand was there ten years earlier, and if so whether anyone climbed up to get a better view of the play on July 10.

52 *United Service Magazine*, January 1841, Part II, pp 24–44; a much fuller account than the one he gave to the Inquiry, Home Misc vol 508, pp 156–8, 258–9. He had felt impelled to put it all down after so long an interval because, when the thanks of the Court of Directors had been conveyed to all those who had rendered service at the time of the siege, 'the names of Mr Jones and myself had been altogether omitted', although they were the only two officers who had resisted the insurgency from first to last – a deplorable omission also noted by Lieutenant Blakiston. Later, Dean and the senior surgeon sent a memorial to London, but no answer was ever received, 'and I have often thought that it had been put on board one of the ships that was lost about this time'.

53 Hoover, p 100.

54 Hoover, pp 27, 40.

55 Kaye, i, p 168.

56 ibid.; Thorn, pp 103–4.

57 Cameron, pp 36–7.

58 Mukherjee, *Spectre of Violence*, pp 127–8, 156–9; IOR Home Misc 725, 'Memorandum containing the Result of Enquiries made by Desire of the Governor General into the Rumours of European Females having been dishonoured during the Late Mutinies'.

59 Wilson, iii, pp 186–7.

60 Wilson, iii, p 186.

61 Wilson, iii, p 188. These rewards were greeted with considerable bit-
    terness among the native officers. (Kaye, *Mutiny*, i, p 165) Far from
    being a loyal servant of the Crown, Mustapha Beg had first betrayed
    the British by joining the conspiracy and then betrayed his fellow
    Muslims by sneaking to the Colonel. That, it seemed, was the kind of
    double-dealing which the British honoured and encouraged.
62 Wilson, iii, pp 188–9.
63 Hoover, p 185.
64 Kaye, *Mutiny*, i, pp150–1; Mason, pp 106–110. Hector Munro was as
    ferocious a commander in battle as Rollo Gillespie. He was the great-
    great-grandfather of another Hector Munro, better known to us as the
    writer Saki. Though an intensely witty and cultivated character, Saki
    had himself a mystifying streak of brutality, perhaps explicable through
    this inherited gene. Any qualms provoked by the earlier Hector's mass
    execution were swept away a couple of months later when Munro
    won the decisive Battle of Buxar which cemented British power in
    Bengal, the richest region of India.
65 When his formidable network of spies told him of a plot to murder all
    the Europeans in Poona, Elphinstone had the ringleaders blown away
    from guns, although the plot had not yet come to anything. (Mason,
    107–8; Choksey, *Elphinstone*, p 136.) After John Low had stayed in
    Bombay for four months as Elphinstone's guest, he wrote home to his
    mother: 'I have watched him as narrowly as opportunities permit,
    both in his official conduct and in his behaviour as a private gentle-
    man, and I certainly consider his character to be nearer perfection than
    that of any other man I have ever met.' (Low, pp 27–8.)
        The punishment was still in vogue as late as the 1850s. Francis
    Cornwallis Maude, who was to win one of the newly instituted
    Victoria Crosses in 1857, recorded exactly what the whole experience
    was like:
        'Havelock asked me if I "knew how to blow a man from a gun?"'
    Yes, says, Maude, 'though this had not formed part of our curriculum
    at Woolwich', and that evening he is sent a sepoy who has been taken
    as a spy. 'I ordered the port-fire to be lighted, and gave the word
    "Fire!" There was a considerable recoil from the gun, and a thick
    cloud of smoke hung over us. As this cleared away, we saw two legs
    lying in front of the gun; but no other sign of what had, just before,
    been a human being and a brave man. At this moment, perhaps from
    six to eight seconds after the explosion (and the same thing happened
    on the second occasion), down fell the man's head among us, slightly
    blackened, but otherwise scarcely changed. It must have gone straight
    up into the air, probably about 200 feet. The pent-up feelings of the

bystanders found vent in a sort of gasp, like ah—h! Then many of
them came across the ditch to inspect the remains of the legs, and the
horrible affair was over.'

After performing another blowing-away, 'I became aware that I was
covered, from head to foot, at least in front, with minute blackened
particles of the man's flesh, some of it sticking in my ears and hair. My
white silk coat, puggree [the scarf wrapped round the crown of the
sun helmet], belt etc., were also spotted in this sickening manner. As
I announced the execution to Havelock, I called his attention to the
state I was in. He came through his tent door, and, striking a sort of
tragic attitude of horror, said, in a stage voice, "improving"
Shakespeare:-

> "E'en such a man, in such a plight,
> Drew Priam's curtains in the dead of night,
> And told him that a man was slain!"

Always ready-witted was the old General!' (Maude, I, pp 274–8.)
Havelock was adapting *Henry IV Part Two*, Act One, lines 124–7. It
was on Havelock's recommendation, shortly before he himself died in
the Relief of Lucknow, that Maude won his VC.

66 Wilson, iii, 199. He was to be appointed to other commands later, in
Ireland and then in Portugal, but in Wellington's words, his mind was
'soured by ill treatment' and not much softened by being appointed
Governor of the Cape and raised to the peerage, at which point he
changed his surname to the more romantic Caradoc, claiming descent
from the ancient princes of north Wales. Under any alias, he was a
fussy, tidy-minded man, at once stubborn and indecisive.

67 Wilson, iii, p 200. It was not so unusual for Commanders-in-Chief to
be sent home, and Governors, too. Perhaps because it took so long for
its orders to be transmitted, the Court of Directors could be brutal in
getting rid of its satraps. (Hoover, p 254.) Bentinck had been out of
favour for other reasons before the Vellore Mutiny. (Hoover, p 52.) It
is a symptom of the difficulty the East India Company had in finding
suitable aristocrats willing to go out and govern their domain that he
was offered the Governorship of Madras again in 1819 and finally
managed to return to India 20 years later, this time as Governor-
General (from 1828 to 1835), the post he had long dreamed of.
Wellington, who by this time was Prime Minister, said: 'Bentinck did
everything with the best intention, but he was a wrongheaded man,
and if he went wrong, he would continue in the wrong line.'
(Ellenborough, p 256.)

68 Nothing was said of Colonel Forbes's flight to the safety of the
native fort or of his failure to take active steps to summon help from
Arcot. (Home Misc Series Vol 510, f844, para 39.) But Gillespie in
his second dispatch to Cradock made his feelings rather clear, I
think: Lieutenant-Colonel Forbes 'very judiciously collected as
many of his men as he could and took possession of the largest hill
fort, his men having slept in the *pettah* without arms, but being
reinforced by about 30 Europeans who made their escape from the
fort he resolved to maintain to the last a post that would have been
of the greatest consequence had we not happily succeeded in our
coup de main. Lieutenant-Colonel Forbes was relieved in the
evening of the 10th and has been since of the greatest service to me
from his local experience and general information.' (Home Misc
510, f417 et ff.) It may perhaps be inferred from this passage that
Gillespie himself would not have behaved so 'judiciously'. He would
not have lolled in the native fort all day when he could hear the
fighting the other side of town.

But Gillespie is not above a little judicious editing of his own role in
events. In neither of his two dispatches to Cradock, on July 10 and
July 11, does Gillespie say a word about any activity in the fives court.
In none of the reports from the official enquiries can I find a word
about the massacre of 100 or more defenceless prisoners there. Yet we
have three eyewitness accounts of it, which all more or less tally. We
may also presume that there was a fourth eyewitness who gave W.F.
Butler his rather different material.

69 Dean, p 44; Hoover, p 276; Home Misc Series, vol 508, pp 103–21.
70 Cameron, p 48.
71 Bayly, *Indian Society*, pp 169–70; *Townsmen*, pp 319–30.
72 The petition from the Hyderabad native officers speaks with an eloquent anguish of their material deprivations:

'European officers in compliance with their wishes procure agreeable and beautiful women and give them the pay of 30 or 40 pagodas.
If Native Officers received pay in proportion to their just claims, they
also would be able to enjoy the pleasures desired by their hearts. At
present it is difficult for a native to obtain the slave of a handsome
woman; and we are ashamed even to show our faces to a fine woman.
Everything is dependent on gold, why should I write more; a hint is
sufficient to a wise man.

'Horses, Palinkeens, carriages, lofty houses, ample tents, couches,
pleasure and enjoyment, gratification and delight, whatever yields joy
is the portion of the European officer; rain, wind, cold and heat,
fatigue and hardship, trouble and pain, and the sacrifice of life itself in

the Company's service, these are all the portion of the sepoy.' (Cameron, pp 155–6.)

Nothing here, as Cameron tellingly points out, about threats to religious integrity.

73 Hoover, p 205.
74 Wilson, iii, p 189.
75 At Vellore, he was to see a good deal of his sister Susan, the only member of his family he was to see much of during his first 20 years in India. She, aged 20, was married to the 45–year-old Colonel David Foulis who was commandant of the cavalry barracks at Arcot. In 1822, 16 years after the mutiny at Vellore, Foulis nipped in the bud a leaflet campaign inciting the sepoys to revolt and kill every European officer. He assembled all his commanders and told them to knock sense into their native officers and sent out warnings to the commandants of all the other stations that were threatened. (Kaye, *Mutiny*, i, pp 192–3.)

Chapter III: The White Mutiny

1 Wilson, iii, p 264. There had been a mutiny of 200 officers in Bengal in 1766 over the withdrawal of the officers' double allowances, the so-called *batta*, but Robert Clive had suppressed it with typical firmness, and although quite widespread it never came to bloodshed. (Mason, pp 113–116.) There was another incipient mutiny in Bengal in 1796, but the officers thought better of it and backed down.
2 Mason, p 190.
3 Mason, ibid.
4 Kaye, *Mutiny*, i, p 184.
5 *East India Affairs (Madras Army)*, May 25, 1810, hereafter HC-1810.
6 There has only ever been one full-length monograph on the subject, *The White Mutiny*, by Sir Alexander Cardew (1929). Cardew was a retired member of the Indian Civil Service who had risen to the executive council of the Governor of Madras. He was in short a government man and, what's more, had embarked on his retirement project only at the request of Barlow's descendant, Sir Hilaro Barlow, to clear his ancestor's name. The book does provide a valuable narrative, but it steers clear of going too deeply into the minds of the mutineers. You are really not much clearer after reading it as to *why* so many young men should have leapt into such a perilous course of action which might well land them up in front of a firing squad like the ringleaders at Vellore.

I cannot help noticing that in recent years the only scholars who have done any serious work on the mutiny of the Madras officers appear to be American female academics (see Hathaway and Welsch). It is as though, even today, you need to be detached by both nationality and gender to approach the scene of the crime.

7 The Company's Army began in the 1760s. The French had been quicker to enlist Indians in their service, as early as 1674. By 1739, the redoubtable Governor Dupleix had four or five thousand Mahommedans drilled after the European fashion. (Mason, p 29.) By contrast, the Honourable Company's first troops in India were British soldiers who arrived as King's men, then were invited to ground their arms and to take them up again as servants of the Company. This tradition lasted for nearly a century, until they were transferred back to the service of the Crown, when the East India Company was abolished after 1857. (Mason, p 31.)

8 When the sepoy enlisted with the Company, he took a solemn oath: 'I do swear to serve the Honourable Company faithfully and truly against all their enemies, while I continue to receive their pay and eat their salt.' (Mason, p 66.)

   In their daily lives, these sepoys, once they had eaten the Company's salt, formed a corps that was, for most purposes, rather separate from their British commanders. They had their own native officers and NCOs: the *subadars* and *jemadars* (captains and lieutenants), the *havildars* and *naigues* (sergeants and corporals). They messed and bivouacked separately, they had their own native courts-martial. New orders and new regulations were communicated to them via the native adjutant from the European adjutant – a crucial point of contact. To start with, there had been only a couple of European officers per native battalion, but as more fresh-faced teenaged ensigns came out from England to be turned into uppity lieutenants, the native officers began to feel their importance dwindling and their pay and conditions worsening.

9 Mason, p 190.

10 Trevelyan, *The Competition Wallah*, p 12.

11 At first, King's officers took precedence over every Company officer of the same rank. A King's captain, just promoted and newly arrived in India, would be senior to a Company captain who had held the rank for ten years and had 25 years' experience of fighting small Indian wars. The young King's officer might well lead the more experienced Company man into an ambush which the old hand would have foreseen. (Mason pp 188–9.)

12 Mason, p 174.

THE TEARS OF THE RAJAS

13 Even the Court of Directors back in London had accepted that the system was unfair, but the Madras government had done little or nothing to remedy it. The Court was already noting to Bentinck that the desirable commands at Hyderabad, Poona, Mysore and Malabar were all held by King's officers; so were the commands of the regular garrisons such as Arcot and Vellore.

14 Mason, pp 187–8.

15 June 5, 1808. Kaye, *Malcolm*, i, p 460.

16 September 15, 1809. Wilson, iii, pp 238–9

17 Old India hands like Metcalfe and Malcolm might complain about 'the determined spirit of penury which is evident in this Administration'. (Cardew, p 28.) But the orders came from London, as Buchan again made brutally plain to Malcolm:

'You know that Sir G. Barlow's great object is reduction (of expenditure); but the orders which he has received from home make it quite impossible for him to do otherwise. He has been told plainly that the thing must be done; and if it is not done here, the Court of Directors will take the pruning-knife (that is the expression) into their own hands.' (May 1, 1808, Kaye, *Malcolm*, i, p 459.)

18 Wilson, iii, p 237.

19 Kaye, *Malcolm*, i, pp 394–5.

20 Wilson, iii, p 235.

21 Two versions survive, one in the Bailey Collection in the National Gallery of South Africa, Cape Town, the other in the Memorial Art Gallery, Rochester, New York.

22 Wilson, iii, pp 242–3.

23 Cardew, pp 43–4; Kaye, *Malcolm*, i, pp 457–8; Wilson, iii, pp 243–4.

24 Wilson, iii, p 244.

25 Cameron, p 253.

26 Petitions and memorials drawn up by disgruntled officers began to do the rounds. The first one had been circulated and actually got through to Leadenhall Street in 1806. A year later came another, which was more or less squashed, only to surface again in much the same form in April 1808. The Memorial came to Barlow, who sent it on to Macdowall, who said he would do with it whatever Barlow wanted him to do, but he went on to issue an extraordinary warning. Many people, he said, would view the Memorial as 'a futile and puerile attempt and as unworthy of further notice'. But he believed that 'the seeds of discontent are very widely disseminated and that almost every individual in the service is more or less dissatisfied'. He listed the causes that had led to this discontent: the abolition of the Bazaar Fund and the Tent Contract and 'the degradation of the military

character from the Commander-in-Chief to the youngest ensign.'
(Cardew, pp 40–1.)

Macdowall suppressed the Memorial in May in obedience to
Barlow's order, but he made it clear, not only to Barlow but to every
regiment he visited and at every mess he dined at, that he was totally
in sympathy with the officers. He was, as John Malcolm remarked,
waving a torch over the powder magazine.

27 Wilson, iii, p 252; Cardew, p 51.
28 Cardew, pp 63–4.
29 Wilson, iii, p 255.
30 An unfair description of the station, for Masulipatam had been the first
    British trading settlement in Bengal and had remained a significant
    port and military base after it had been wrested from the French in
    1759.
31 Kaye, *Malcolm*, i, p 464.
32 Ibid., pp 463–5; Cardew, pp 81–3; Wilson, iii, pp 261–3.
33 Innes to Adjutant-General, Fort St George, May 24 109, HC-1810,
    IIC.
34 Wilson, iii, p 262.
35 Cardew, pp 82–3.
36 Cardew, p 85.
37 Welsch, pp 20–21.
38 Davis to Falconar, July 30, 1809, HC-1810, IID, f7.
39 Barclay, Secretary-General to Col Barry Close, July 26, 1809, HC-
    1810, IIC, f43.
40 John Malcolm, Observations on the Disturbances in the Madras Army
    in 1809.
41 Malcolm thought he understood what Barlow wanted of him. But just
    before he was to sail, he had a nasty argument with a couple of Barlow's
    staff officers who accused him of being too soft and of intending to
    offer the mutineers conciliation when what was needed was a body of
    King's troops to attack and overawe them. When he cooled down,
    Malcolm realized that he had better be clear what Sir George expected
    of him. So he went back to the garden house. According to Malcolm,
    Sir George 'gave me at this second conference every assurance that
    could be given to satisfy my mind.' He was not to listen to the biffers;
    he was 'satisfied the honour of his Government was safe in my hands.'
    (Kaye, *Malcolm*, i, p 472.) In fact, he appeared to trust Malcolm so
    wholeheartedly that he asked him to draft a reply to the committee of
    158 officers stationed at Hyderabad who had just sent him an outra-
    geous ultimatum demanding that he withdraw all the suspensions of
    their fellow officers. Malcolm scribbled a memo showing these deluded

654 THE TEARS OF THE RAJAS

officers the same forbearance and conciliation as he was to show their brethren at Masulipatam. Sir George approved the draft letter, and John Malcolm set off across the surf, reassured in his mission.

42 Kaye, *Malcolm*, i, p 474.

43 Ibid., p 475.

44 HC-1810, IIC, pp 4–5.

45 Wilson, iii, p 258.

46 The same happened at Vellore, where not a man would sign, but there was no resistance to being carted off to the coast. Ditto in parts of the south, such as Tanjore and Palamcottah, where the redoubtable Colonel Wilkinson removed the more violent and abusive rebels under armed guard. The same again in the so-called Ceded Districts in the north, the parts of the Nizam's domains which he had ceded in return for British protection.

47 It turned out that Barlow never sent off John Malcolm's soothing letter (perhaps he had never intended to or had changed his mind, under the influence of those firebreathing staff officers).

48 Wilson, iii, pp 257–80.

49 Cardew, pp 233–6.

50 Wilson, iii, pp 268–70. Sometimes the mutineers turned into highwaymen. When the mutinous officers at Seringapatam were running low on cash, they sent a party out of the fort to intercept a convoy carrying 140,000 rupees from the Ceded Districts. Meanwhile, inside the fort, the acting judge and magistrate, Mr James Casamajor, was preparing to send the Government treasure to Mysore where it would be safer, but the Commandant, Lieutenant-Colonel John Bell, refused to let it go, and the next morning Captain Turner of the 15th Native Regiment came to the office and seized about 11,000 pagodas, refusing to sign a receipt. Daylight robbery.

51 HC-1810, II-E, p 23. They did allow him to leave the cantonments that same evening (August 5) and go off to Madras. Which, however, he did not do, or not immediately. Instead, determined not to give in without making a nuisance of himself, he galloped round the local outposts, and removed as many guards of the 1st/24th as he could lay his hands on, a total of 157 men, which the mutineers complained of with some chutzpah: 'the whole company is greatly endangered by his having created a false alarm, and will be the means of the villages bring totally deserted.' Robert Fletcher was, it later turned out, a man of some resource in other, more dubious ways, too. Several years later, he was still in the Northern Circars – the northernmost region of the Madras Presidency where the Bay of Bengal begins – and employed to quell the disturbances caused by the frequent misdeeds of the

zemindars, the local landholders who collected the taxes for the British.

In the forgotten hills of the frontier country, covered with impenetrable forests of bamboo and of a climate so torrid that Europeans died of heatstroke in half an hour, the *zemindars* became tribal chieftains on a large scale and enjoyed an insidious degree of independence. They became rajas, and referred to themselves as such.

Colonel Fletcher was sent up from Berhampur with a small detachment of the Madras Army to bring the obnoxious *zemindar* of Goomsoor down to Ganjam to answer charges of murdering his mother and torturing his concubines before the British magistrate, Charles Woodcock. Though the *zemindars* were mostly left to their own evil devices, this was only on condition that they stumped up the revenue and accepted the verdicts of the British courts.

A straightforward enough mission, it seemed, but then Woodcock began to receive curious messages from Robert Fletcher. Apparently the *zemindar*'s mother was not dead at all, for Fletcher's sergeant had her pointed out to him standing in a red dress at the curtain of the seraglio. The *zemindar* was an innocent man. Woodcock exploded. Colonel Fletcher's job was not to pronounce judgement on the guilt or innocence of the *zemindar*. His duty was simply to bring him in. Everyone knew that the *zemindar* was a monster. Fletcher must march off again and haul him down to Ganjam.

We then hear a litany of lame excuses from the Colonel. There is no meat in the bazaars for his men, he is short of bullocks for transport, he is anxious that the *zemindar*'s gloomy fortress of Kolaida may prove impregnable by so small a force.

Orders are orders, retorts the magistrate. Reluctantly Fletcher sets off into the bamboo forest. But somehow the *zemindar* gives them the slip. 'In the precipitation of his flight, he was seen to quit his slippers, to throw away a pike he had seized and he lost his turban.'

It is such a vivid picture: the *zemindar* bedraggled and barefoot with his turban toppling off his head, chucking away his last rough weapon. Surely the Colonel's next sentence will describe how he is taken into custody. But it doesn't. In fact, though the villain is apparently at his last gasp, they manage to lose him. How on earth? Fletcher says his men are dropping from thirst and fatigue after marching for 19 hours. And when the peasants start firing at them from two opposite hills, Fletcher fears that his forces may be scattered and cut down, and so 'I called them all in with the bugle.' Which allows the *zemindar* to make his escape.

Even a magistrate who had not already been driven mad by Colonel

Fletcher's prevarications would have smelled a rat. When the *zemindar* finally gives himself up a few weeks later, he tells a rather different story:

'Colonel Fletcher sent me a message from Berhampur stating if I concealed myself with my women in the fort of Kolaida before he came, he would merely look at the fort and return thence, saying that the Raja was not there. On this account he received from me the sum of 7,000 rupees as a bribe.'

According to the *zemindar*, this was not the end of Robert Fletcher's treachery, because he then betrayed his confederate, too. As soon as the *zemindar* fled up into the hills, Fletcher nipped in and impounded all the *zemindar's* ill-gotten property – ready cash, jewels, silks and ornaments – to the stupendous value of 250,000 rupees, which he then secretly distributed to his men, keeping the colonel's share of 20,000 rupees for himself. Colonel Fletcher was relieved of his command, and in April 1819 he was cashiered, and as plain Mr Fletcher was put on the next boat back to Europe. (Hamilton II, pp 69–71, Wilson, iii, p 359, IOR/F/4/524/ f125 et ff, IOR/E/4/922/ ff361–3, 438–9, 474, 813, 858, 878.)

In the official letter describing Robert Fletcher's actions at Ellore, he had been described as 'a zealous and spirited officer'. (HC-1810, IIB, pp 101–2.) Now it appears that he was a thief and a liar. Chicanery and embezzlement were not confined to the *zemindars*. In the bamboo forests of Goomsoor it must have seemed easy to get away with almost anything. After all, it had not been so many years earlier that such douceurs had passed between native rulers and the servants of the Honourable Company as a matter of course, and many a nabob's fortune had been built on them. The subalterns at Ellore could claim that subsequent history showed what a twister Lieutenant-Colonel Fletcher was, and how right they had been to lock him up.

52 Doveton flew into a tizzy. He forwarded the address to Macdowall's successor as C-in-C, General Francis Gowdie, and sent a copy to Captain Thomas Sydenham, the Resident at nearby Hyderabad. The next day, he followed up with a private letter to Sydenham, which must rank as the most hysterical letter ever sent by a colonel of cavalry:

'Horror on horror! My dear Sydenham, since I sent off my express to you of this date, circumstances have been made known to me that make my blood run cold ... I must either arrest the whole of the officers of the detachment or must suffer myself to be deposed from my position. The first presents immediately to the mind the horrid, horrid picture of a general massacre of the whole by the native part of the detachment, and the latter one little better. What is to be done in this dreadful extremity?' (Cardew, p 106.)

53 Cardew, p 121.
54 Davis to Falconar, July 30, 1809, HC-1810 IID, p 7.
55 Cardew, p 123.
56 HC-1810, IIF, p 23.
57 HC-1810, IIF, p 24.
58 Hazlewood was hardly one to speak himself. In the early stages of the anti-Barlow protests, he had been one of those sacked by the Governor on May 1 'for not having exerted themselves to maintain proper discipline' as well as for having circulated the infamous Memorial. (Wilson, iii, pp 254–5.) In fact, he had been giving grief to the authorities for several years. He had developed an obsession that the mutiny at Vellore was only the prelude to a vast conspiracy to subvert British power. 'I have no doubt,' he claimed, 'that a general conspiracy exists among the natives of every cast and class to expel us from the interior of India, to confine us to our factories and to reduce us to our original character of humble traders.' (Cameron, pp 307–15.) Sir John Cradock could only sigh, 'I think Major Hazlewood's letter the most curious production I have ever read. I shall endeavour to stop his tongue, though I despair of success without some stronger measures.' (Cameron, p 312.)

  Yet it was this panicky troublemaker whom the government dispatched to Ellore to bring John Low's battalion back to its senses. Nothing could reveal with more devastating clarity how short the Honourable Company was of senior officers it could rely on.
59 HC-1810, IIF, p 26.
60 MSS Eur D1082.
61 Wilson, iii, pp 282–3.
62 For example, in the case immediately after Doveton's, Dhowhul Sing, a *subadar* in the Bengal Light Infantry, was sentenced to death in 1816 by Lord Moira, along with 15 other native officers and privates, 'for having been present at one or more mutinous meetings, and taking an unlawful oath to murder their European officers and subvert the legal authorities of the State.'
63 Cardew, pp 135–41.
64 During the mutiny, Turner had written in a letter to his brother Alexander at Pondicherry (one of the many mutineers' letters intercepted by Barlow's spies): 'We shall not be the first to fire a shot, but we are solemnly pledged, if attacked, to defend the place to the last extremity.' (Cardew, pp 231–2.) Alas, it was not to be the forces of 'the Tyrant', as he called Barlow, but one of the more familiar extremities, cholera or typhus, that carried him off.
65 Wilson, iii, p 268.

66 Low, p 211.
67 Cardew, pp 143–4.
68 Wilson, iii, p 242.
69 See Christina Welsch for a fuller discussion.

Chapter IV: Lord Minto takes a trip

1 Kaye, *Malcolm*, i, p 391.
2 Minto, i, p 114.
3 Fregosi, p 76.
4 Minto, iii, p 329.
5 Kaye, *History of the War in Afghanistan*, i, p 52. The scene was further complicated by the government in London at the same time sending its own ambassador to Tehran, the pugnacious Sir Harford Jones, who disliked Malcolm as much as Malcolm disliked him. This time, Malcolm got nowhere and Jones came back in triumph waving a treaty, as did Metcalfe and Elphinstone, though only the one with the Punjab stuck for any length of time.
6 Wilson, iii, p 299.
7 The British losses in battle were trifling: one seaman, one marine and two privates killed. Not for the first time, there was a far heavier loss among the men left behind to hold the forts. Half a dozen officers and an uncounted number of men succumbed to the unhealthy climate during the five years before the islands were handed back to the Dutch.
8 Kaye, *Afghanistan*, i, p 298.
9 Minto, iii, p 249.
10 Ibid.
11 August 31, 1810, MSS Eur F148/1.
12 Hannigan, p 67.
13 Glendinning, pp 62–3.
14 Hannigan, p 62.
15 Wilson, iii, pp 323–4.
16 Thorn, *Java*, p 16.
17 Thorn, ibid., p 18.
18 Minto, iii, pp 251–2. Also taking up a fair amount of cabin space was his library. 'I have been reading "Ossian" and Crabbe's "Borough" &c. I have also with me "The Lady of the Lake" and the six volumes of Scott's works . . .' (Minto, iii, p 252.) One wonders if Lady Minto ever felt left out of his thoughts. No doubt she would have been more distressed by the persistent rumours that Gilbert had a second family

hidden away somewhere. Though they wrote regularly and with affection to each other, he certainly seemed to bear their long separations quite blithely.

Another frequent correspondent was William Taylor, who wrote often to the Mintos' eldest daughter, confusingly also called Anna Maria. He also kept a diary of the expedition which is remarkable for its laconic asides but also for his making copies which he sent her. (Glendinning, pp 78–9.) These were made on 'carbonic paper' and also on a copying machine of the sort which President Jefferson delighted in, a contraption which linked two pens together. It would have saved millions of man hours if this 'Polygraph' had been put into general operation. As it was, the penpushers of the Empire had to wait more than half a century for the typewriter.

19 Minto, iii, p 255.
20 Glendinning, p 80.
21 Minto, iii, p 262.
22 Ibid., p 268.
23 Ibid., p 264.
24 Ibid., p 265. Lord Minto had his fair share of that theatrical instinct which is such a help in public life. Indeed, he rather fancied himself as a theatre critic, taking particular delight in the plays performed every Saturday evening on the *Modeste* by the ship's company: 'I was never near so well amused at any other performance of amateurs. It is really surprising to observe the *propriety* with which these rough, uninstructed, unassisted sailors represent all the varieties of character which are found in comedy, rendering with perfect justness all that concerns nature.' (Minto, iii, p 280.) The occasional word-fumbles – 'exquisitive' for 'exquisite', 'etiquity' for 'etiquette' – did no damage at all to the performance. Such shipboard shows were no novelty. Two centuries earlier, some of the earliest recorded performances of *Hamlet* and *Richard II* were given on a slave ship off the west coast of Africa.
25 Blakiston, ch xxv.
26 Glendinning, p 87; Hannigan p 25.
27 Blakiston, ch xxvii.
28 Minto, iii, pp 285–6.
29 Glendinning, pp 87–88.
30 Thorn, p 30.
31 It was Captain William Taylor's first fight, too. Gillespie thanked him in his dispatch for 'his indefatigable assistance during the whole affair and his very zealous exertions during the whole time since we landed'. (Thorn, p 37.) Lord Minto was delighted by the successful blooding of his Military Secretary, and wrote to tell the two Anna Marias:

'Taylor, who is attached to Gillespie, distinguished himself on this
maiden occasion by the greatest activity, courage, coolness and judgment.' (Minto, iii, p 289.)

32 Fregosi, pp 319–20. Major Thorn, Gillespie's hero-worshipping biographer and brigade-major, had been injured at Weltevreden, but he
records with satisfaction the general order that Jumel circulated after that
action on August 10. Cornelis, Jumel told his field officers, was 'capable of a most desperate defence against the enemy' and could not be
carried by a frontal attack , by a *coup de main*. However, it was possible
that by some treachery or by a surprise attack at night the enemy might
somehow 'introduce himself into the place', a rather delicate choice of
phrase. 'In case of accidents,' Jumel goes on, 'four openings remain for
us to retreat by.' Then, he points out these four emergency exits.
Although he hastens to add that troops are to be given orders to fight to
the last man, the tone of his order is not exactly confidence-boosting.
(Thorn, pp 41–3.)

33 Thorn, pp 51–2.
34 Thorn, p 56.
35 Blakiston, ch xxix.
36 Minto, iii, p 292.
37 Thorn, p 86.
38 Minto, iii, p 293.
39 September 3, 1811, ibid., pp 307–09.
40 October 6, 1811, ibid., pp 313–14.
41 Ibid., p 316.
42 Ibid., p 313.
43 Glendinning, p 144.
44 Minto, iii, p 299.
45 Ibid., p 297.
46 Glendinning, p 94.
47 *Java Government Gazette*, August 29, 1812.
48 Low to Malcolm, June 23, 1817, MSS Eur D1082.

Chapter V: The Tin Men

1 Raffles to Minto, MSS Eur F148/4.
2 As if to emphasize the urgency of his advice, he wrote again five days
later: 'With respect to the Dutch, what does it signify that Your
Majesty should any longer remain attached to them and permit them
to reside in Palembang, for they are a bad nation and intend to follow
a bad course towards Your Majesty and Your Majesty's country.'

3 Glendinning, p 72.
4 Hannigan, pp 152–3.
5 Ibid., p 145.
6 Ibid., pp 154–5.
7 Ibid., p 155.
8 Ibid., p 156.
9 Thorn, p 153.
10 Hannigan, p 295.
11 Ibid., pp 294–7.
12 Ibid., p 176. The official line, swallowed whole by Captain Thorn and many another loyal soul, was that this posed a deadly menace to British rule. 'The magnitude of the threatened danger, therefore, calling for immediate action, no procrastination could possibly be admitted.' (Thorn, p 177.) But in truth there was no 'therefore' about it. The Sushunan had already been conciliated by Raffles, and the Sultan could easily be soothed back into inertia.
13 Thorn, p 180.
14 Ibid., pp 189–90.
15 A summary canto-by-canto translation is to be found in Carey, *The British in Java*.
16 Canto VI.
17 Canto VI.
18 Canto XVIII.
19 Thorn p 193.
20 Hannigan, p 217.
21 Ibid., pp 248–9.
22 Ibid., p 133.
23 Ibid., p 134.
24 Moira wrote in his journal (February 1814) that: 'Instead of the surplus revenue which, for giving importance to the conquest, was asserted to be forthcoming from that possession, it could not be maintained without the Treasury, as well as the troops of Bengal. Just now, in the height of our exigencies, we receive an intimation from the Lieutenant-Governor that he cannot pay his provincial corps unless we allow him 50,000 Spanish dollars monthly in addition to the prodigious sums which we already contribute to his establishment.' Glendinning, p 131.
25 Ibid., p 146.
26 Ibid., p 146.
27 Ibid., p 147.
28 *Guardian*, November 24, 2012.
29 Glendinning, p 151.
30 Ibid.

31 Keay, *Honourable Company*, p 447.
32 Glendinning, p 126.
33 Hannigan, pp 108, 241.
34 Wakeham, p 249.
35 Ibid., pp 253–4.
36 *Dispatches*, 6. 434.
37 Today even the Javanese remember none of it. Tim Hannigan, a British journalist living in Indonesia and author of a spirited hostile account of Raffles on Java (*Raffles and the British Invasion of Java*, 2012), records that when Indonesians complain to him about the condition of their country, they often say, 'It would have been better if we had been colonized by the British, not the Dutch.' (Hannigan, p 15.)

Chapter VI: The mutton and the baronet

 1 Blakiston, ch ix.
 2 Ibid.
 3 Cannon, p 10.
 4 Elphinstone, Journal, MSS Eur F88/368, October 26 and September 6, 1801. Dalrymple, *White Mughals*, p 119.
 5 Bayly, *Rulers, Townsmen*, pp 213–6.
 6 The whole saga is reported in IOR/F/4/528 and /529.
 7 Weatherall to Abercromby, November 26, 1813.
 8 Wilson, iii, pp 351–2.
 9 IOR/F/4/528/12689.
10 He did, however, slightly spoil this noble peroration by reminding the Court that when they were both Captains, the late lamented Colonel Dowse had been junior to him, and that being an officer in the Native Service he 'could not have had much experience in the command of European soldiers' – a double gibe, suggesting both Dowse's social inferiority and his willingness to feed any old garbage to the sepoys.
11 IOR/F/4/529.
12 The story of this claim too is to be found in the old India Office files, IOR/MIL/405 coll. 227, pp 127–59.
13 March 10, 1815.
14 February 4, 1818.
15 Cannon, p 43.

Chapter VII: The Peshwa's last sigh

1 Colonel William Dowse was dead. Sir Barry Close had gone back to England and died there. Colonel Patrick Agnew who had been Adjutant General in Java (Wilson, iii, p 327) and whom John described as 'always my warm friend' – he might have been able to help after he had been promoted General but he had gone to England and died, too.

2 June 23, 1817, MSS Eur D1082. They had met briefly seven years earlier when John was surveying at Poona and Malcolm was trying to extricate himself from blame for letting the White Mutiny get out of hand.

3 Kaye, *Malcolm*, ii, p 157.

4 Ibid., p 160.

5 Ibid., pp 162–3.

6 Ibid., p 175fn.

7 There was one last night the two Johns spent in Hyderabad which was in its way the gloomiest of all:

'On the evening of the 30th, I went to a feast at Chundoo-Lall's [Chundoo-Lall was the Dewan, or Finance Minister – really the Prime Minister of the country] which was very magnificent. Chandah was there . . . Her dress this evening was very splendid, but she looked haggard and old. Her eyes were painted overmuch, and their blackness, joined to a look of intoxication, which I fear was not feigned, made this celebrated woman an object of disgust more than of admiration.' (Kaye, *Malcolm*, ii, p 165.)

8 Kaye, *Malcolm*, i, p 202.

9 John Blakiston, who rode with him on this campaign, gives a brilliant description of the young British officers meeting the old British Resident at Sindia's court, Lieutenant-Colonel John Ulrich Collins:

'We were received by an insignificant little, old-looking man, dressed in an old-fashioned military coat, white breeches, sky-blue silk stockings, and large glaring buckles to his shoes, having his highly powdered wig, from which depended a pig-tail of no ordinary dimensions, surmounted by a small round black silk hat, ornamented with a single black ostrich feather.' But Blakiston detected a fire in the small black eyes beneath his 'shaggy penthouse brows', which more than counterbalanced his ridiculous eighteenth-century get-up, and he remembered ever afterwards Collins's last words before he and Arthur Wellesley retired into the inner tent: 'I tell you, General, as to their cavalry, you may ride over them wherever you meet them, but their infantry and guns will astonish you.' Riding home, the General and his

staff laughed themselves silly at 'little King Collins', but they little
knew how true his words would prove. (Blakiston, Chapter ix.)

10 Wilson, iii, p 109.

11 Randolf Cooper, *Anglo-Maratha Campaigns*, p 128.

12 Lieutenant-General Stuart, C-in-C of the Madras Army, reporting to
Lord Hobart, the Governor of Madras, gives a typical British ration-
alization: 'Scindiah's army consisted of a large amount of infantry
regularly constituted, composed of natives from the north of
Hindostan, the finest men in India, conducted by European officers,
and possessing all the advantages of discipline, of long experience in
war, and of the confidence inspired by numerous successes.

'His artillery had attained a degree of proficiency which was scarcely
to be surpassed by the skill of European troops, and the founderies,
which were established in his dominions under the direction of
European officers, had supplied an extensive train of ordnance of
excellent manufacture ... In all the actions which have been fought,
his troops performed evolutions with a facility and order, which
denoted a considerable progress in European tactics.' (Wilson, iii,
pp 122–3.)

Four times in that analysis Stuart refers to European training and
European officers.

13 Cooper, pp 23–32.

14 Ibid., pp 40–1.

15 Ibid., p 34.

16 Ibid., p 21.

17 I haven't even mentioned the *tulwar*, the razor-sharp Maratha swords
far superior to the British cavalry swords which were blunted by
repeated drawing from their scabbard. Blakiston saw the carnage the
tulwar wrought at Assaye: 'the wounds inflicted by the swords of the
enemy's cavalry were such as I could have no conception of. This was
the only time I ever saw heads fairly cut off.'

18 Ibid., p 251.

19 Wellesley had no scruples in attempting to buy out as many units of
Sindia's army as he could. Quite a few battalions did come over en bloc
following their British commanders. Once they had finished their
ticklish business, General Perron and his British ADC, Captain Beckett,
themselves trotted into General Lake's camp, and Perron was given safe
conducts out of the country to Calcutta where he could spend his
retirement counting the decent fortune he had piled up in Sindia's
service. Some of these partings were painful. James Skinner, the off-
spring of a Rajput princess and Lieutenant-Colonel Hercules Skinner
of the Company's Army, was unable to serve in the Company's Army

because he was a half-caste. So he took service with Sindia under Benoit de Boigne. When de Boigne retired, Skinner stayed on under that slippery former handkerchief salesman from Nantes, Pierre Cullier-Perron. When war loomed, Skinner was among those cast off by Perron. He remonstrated against his dismissal and insisted that he wanted to stay in the service and share the fate of his comrades, for he saw the Maratha horse already fleeing past him from the Battle of Aligarh.

'Ah no, no,' replied Perron, 'it is all over. These fellows have behaved ill; do not ruin yourself; go over to the British; it is all up with us!'

'By no means,' replied Skinner. 'It is not so. Let us rally yet and make a stand. You may depend upon having many yet to fight for you.' But Perron still shook his head, and after a little while said in his bad English, 'Ah no, Monsieur Skinner. I not trust. I not trust. I 'fraid you all go.' (Compton, p 301.)

20 Ibid., p 328.
21 There were exceptions: formidable warriors who were also decent administrators and who could even be relied on to keep most of their promises. Without leaders of such a calibre, after all, the Marathas would not have stretched their domains as far north as Delhi and even faraway Peshawar. After Shivaji in the seventeenth century, there was Baji Rao's grandfather, the first Baji Rao, who conquered most of what became the Maratha heartlands, and his son Nana Sahib who consolidated those conquests and made Poona into a great city. In the Sindia dynasty, there was the great Mahadji who made Gwalior not only the leading state in the Maratha Empire but one of the greatest military powers in India. Mahadji thumped most of the rival provinces in decisive battles – the Nizam of Hyderabad foremost among them – and placed the poor blinded Shah Alam II back on the throne at Delhi. Mahadji was a shrewd jovial fellow, hot-tempered but patient when he needed to be. He had nine wives and personally audited all his accounts. His biographer claimed that 'In a scene of barbarous anarchy when all bonds of society seemed to be unloosed, he was amiable, courteous and free from cruelty.' (Keene, quoted, Choksey, *A History of British Diplomacy*, p 88.) But after these great warlords there was a miserable falling off.
22 Choksey, pp 130–1.
23 He would raise cash by issuing bills of exchange called *pats*, which were immediately sold at a huge discount, and then further bills were drawn upon those bills and then issued to the troops as pay. When the troops tried to cash these drafts, they were further discounted by 20 or 30 per

cent. Thus the currency depreciated all the time and only the bankers grew fat. From time to time, Daulat Rao would think about these things, but only for an hour or so before he was distracted by 'a tiger or a pretty face, an elephant fight or a new supply of paper kites'. (Choksey, p 132.)

24 Choksey, pp 123–5.
25 Ibid., p 128.
26 Ibid., p 280.
27 Dalrymple, *White Mughals*, pp 359–60. Hutchins, *Illusion of Permanence*, p 4.
28 Choksey, *British Diplomacy*, pp 299–300.
29 Choksey, *Mountstuart Elphinstone*, p 456.
30 Bentinck Papers, Low to Bentinck, February 9, 1832.
31 Choksey, *Mountstuart Elphinstone*, p 385.
32 Ibid., p 396.
33 Ibid., pp 450–1.
34 Ibid.
35 Minute, November 7, 1830, quoted in Kaye, *Metcalfe*, ii, p 76.
36 He told his readers in the *New York Daily Tribune*, 'Indian society has no history at all, at least no known history. What we call its history is but the history of the successive intruders who founded their empires on the passive basis of that unresisting and un-changing society.' (August 8, 1853.)
37 Quoted Stokes, *The Peasant and the Raj*, p 65. The process continued over the succeeding decades. Far from being unchanging, 'in no country in the world probably do landed tenures so certainly, constantly and extensively change hands', according to an official report from the North-West Provinces in 1853. (Ibid., p 104.)
38 It was easy to blame the moneylenders. They were indeed unpopular with almost everyone, and their offices were often sacked and their banking records burnt as the first actions in the Great Mutiny. But the violence could be just as ferocious, if not more so, in areas where the moneylenders had scarcely made any inroads. In Canning's day as in Wellesley's 50 years earlier, to quote Eric Stokes, the great historian of rural India, 'one cannot but feel that the swingeing revenue assessment was the root of the matter.' There was a possible alternative: to introduce a personal income tax, and so force the merchants, shopkeepers and tradesmen of the towns to share the burden with the agriculturalists. But this was ruled out of court by the great men of the India House, such as James Mill, who had got it into their heads that by exempting India from any such personal taxes, they would be maximizing economic growth. Alas, in the long run, it turned out that all they were doing was maximizing resentment. It was only after the Great Mutiny that an

income tax became thinkable (and it worked). (Stokes, ibid.)

39 Choksey, *British Diplomacy*, p 4.

40 Colebrooke, p 40. Even the storming of the hill fortress of Gawilgarh left him unmoved. It was a desperately hard siege. The British heavy guns kept rolling back down the slope crushing the limbs of the gunmen. The iron round-shot rebounded back down from the heights, nearly reaching the muzzles from which they had been discharged. (Cooper, p 135.) Even when the British forces had scaled the perimeter wall, there was ferocious fighting inside against thousands of Marathas, many of whom threw themselves over the battlements when they saw the fort was lost. Yet Elphinstone makes it all sound like navigating his way through a crowded garden party:

'Johnson and I endeavoured to collect a party to push for the gate. This was easy; the officers were all obliging and every man you spoke to joined you and a prisoner was taken who knew the way ... When we went on into the breach, I thought I was going to a great danger; but my mind was so made up to it that I did not care for anything. The party going to the storm put me in mind of the eighth and ninth verses of the third book of Homer's Iliad' – and he quotes the couplet, in Greek, with accents. (Colebrooke, pp 42–3.)

41 Colebrooke, pp 87–88.

42 Choksey, *Mountstuart*, pp 218–220. It is worth jotting down a few samples of Grant's notes to give some idea of how deeply the Resident's network enmeshed both Palace and City.
• Cundoo Punt was awarded 1,200 rupees for 'the information about Scindia's letters'.
• Aunajee, formerly a servant of Trimbuckjee's, 100 rupees: 'he came to me two or three times in the night from 25th October to the 5th November 1817' (that is, during the build-up to the Peshwa's last break-out).
• Mahoobajee Punt Latey, 60 rupees: the lover of Gunga Baee who was in the Peshwa's confidence.
• Bulwant Rao Widh, 600 rupees. His daughter was the most beautiful girl in Poona: 'the story of this Helen is known to all the world.'
• Maru Joshee Landgay 600 rupees. 'A buffoon and a low fellow of the Peshwa. If we pension the pimps of Bajee Row, what should be done with the beauties of the Court?'

43 When in 1811 Holkar asked Elphinstone to request the Peshwa to grant his son Mulhar Rao an honorary dress, or *khilat*, as a recognition that Mulhar Rao was now the heir apparent of the Holkar family,

Elphinstone refused to pass on the request. Any gesture which might imply that the Peshwa was still titular head of a Maratha confederacy was strictly forbidden under the Treaty of Bassein. (Choksey, *British Diplomacy*, pp 346–8.)

44 Wilson, iv, pp 11–13.

45 Choksey, *British Diplomacy*, pp 333–5.

46 Choksey, ibid., p 385.

47 Though they were rivals for the great offices of India, the Governorships of Bombay and Madras (who knew, perhaps even the supreme glory of Bengal), Malcolm immediately did Elphinstone a good turn. He wrote off to William Elphinstone, Mountstuart's uncle, who was on the EIC Court, heartily backing Hastings's appeal to the Secret Committee that his nephew, who was not a rich man, should receive some extra reward for his remarkable services.

48 Kaye, *Malcolm*, ii, p 168.

49 Ibid., p 170.

50 Malcolm stayed only a week in Poona, from 5 to 12 August, and three of those days, from 7 to 9 August, were spent in hard riding to and from the Peshwa's camp at Mahanlee. At the best of times, Sir John was not a good listener, and it is clear that on this occasion Elphinstone utterly failed to persuade him of the true situation, even with all the intelligence he had shown Malcolm of the Peshwa's true intentions.

51 Wilson, iv, p 23.

52 Ibid., p 22.

53 In his *History of the Mahrattas*, Grant-Duff described the scene in memorable terms:

'Those only who have witnessed the Bore in the Gulf of Cambay, and have seen in perfection the approach of that roaring tide, can form the exact idea presented to the author at sight of the Peshwa's army. It was towards the afternoon of a very sultry day; there was a dead calm, and no sound was heard except the rushing, the trampling, and neighing of the horses, and the rumbling of the gun wheels. The effect was heightened by seeing the peaceful peasantry flying from their work in the fields, the bullocks breaking from their yokes, the wild antelopes startled from sleep bounding off, and then turning for a moment to gaze on this tremendous inundation which swept all before it, levelled the hedges and standing corn, and completely overwhelmed every ordinary barrier as it moved.' (1826, iii, p 301, quoted Choksey, *Mountstuart*, p 381.)

54 Choksey, *British Diplomacy*, p 10.

55 Choksey, ibid., p 12;

56 Choksey, *Mountstuart*, p 213.

57 Chapter IX.

58 Kaye, *Malcolm*, ii, p 174.

59 Ibid., p 229.

60 November 5, Wilson, iv, pp 10–11. Nothing could show more clearly
     that the British were longing for a scrap than the order that Hastings
     issued to his troops announcing the signature of this treaty. The
     Governor-General was concerned that 'the generous confidence and
     animated zeal of the army may experience a shade of disappointment
     in the diminished prospect of serious action.' (Kaye, *Malcolm*, ii,
     p 193.)

61 There was also the campaign against Appah Sahib, the Regent of
     Nagpur, who had murdered his incompetent cousin and seized the
     throne. This campaign consisted in two brisk battles, the first to gain
     the hills of Sitapaldi adjoining the grounds of the Residency; and the
     second to capture the city of Nagpur itself. These actions, heroic and
     victorious though they both were for the British, are relevant to our
     narrative only for the curious coincidence that they rounded off sev-
     eral earlier stories I have recounted. The decisive factor was the
     blistering charge down the hill by the 500 men of the 1st Battalion of
     the 24th Madras Native Infantry, led by Captain James Sadler (Wilson,
     iv, pp 35–39). The battalion lost 58 men killed and 102 wounded – a
     third of their strength, including Captain Sadler who was killed early
     on in the action. This was the same James Sadler who had led the
     White Mutiny at Ellore and locked up Colonel Fletcher and had
     been dismissed from the service and then restored five years later.
     And the men he commanded were the remnants of the sepoys of the
     1st Battalion who had mutinied at Vellore and been disgraced and
     renumbered. Now in their moment of victory, as they paraded before
     the grateful Resident of Nagpur, Mr Richard Jenkins, their Native
     Adjutant, pretty much the only officer left standing, pleaded in the
     name of the old 1st that their number and facings be restored. The
     Governor of Madras agreed. Captain Sadler too was restored to
     honour, if not to life.

     No less remarkable was the identity of the commander at the battle
     which captured the city of Nagpur: none other than John Doveton of
     the 7th Regiment Native Cavalry who had been court-martialled –
     and inexplicably acquitted – for marching his men out of Jalna to join
     the White Mutiny. General Sir John Doveton GCB died in Madras 30
     years later, as full of years and honours as any young ensign landing in
     that city could have dreamed of. Like all long-lived institutions, the
     British Army has always known how to bury its bodies.

Sir Thomas Hislop arrived on the banks of the river with the 1st
and 3rd Divisions, the latter being Sir John Malcolm's command.
Three of the Regent's *Vakeels* (agents) came to parley with Malcolm
by the banks of the River Sipra. Malcolm told them bluntly that the
British Government knew all about their negotiations with the
Peshwa and their plans to march on Poona. The Holkar's only hope
was to sign a treaty, not only giving up these hostile plans but promising to furnish a quota of troops for the war against the *pindaris*. If
they agreed, the British would agree to help with the crippling arrears
of pay in Holkar's army, for the regime was as usual on the verge of
bankruptcy. The *Vakeels* said they had no power to negotiate. Malcolm
sent them away but not before Holkar's horsemen had rustled a quantity of Sir Thomas's camels and bullocks. The Regent's agents returned
to her camp, where a ferocious argument brewed up that evening.

62 Kaye, *Malcolm*, ii, p 201.
63 Colonel Blacker was QMG with the Army of the Deccan, therefore
    knew what he was talking about, though Sir John Kaye in his *Life and
    Letters* of Malcolm points out that thousands of these horsemen would
    be marauding rabble, good for harassing outlying pickets and stealing
    cattle but not much use in a pitched battle. (Ibid., p 196.)
64 Ibid, p 206.
65 Wilson, ii, p 55.
66 Colonel Blacker in his history of the battle subscribes wholeheartedly
    to this up-and-at-'em approach: 'after the army had crossed the river,
    any flanking movement would have been absurd. They were within
    range of large grape from heavy guns; no situation could have been
    worse, and the shortest way out of it was by a direct attack. This suc-
    ceeded as it has always succeeded with British troops on a plain.'
    (Blacker, p 153.)
67 Wilson, iv, 64. There was another ford four miles upriver – which
    would have required a detour of ten miles – and another one below
    the village of Mehidpur three miles downstream, which would have
    taken a whole day to make it practicable to get the guns across. Blacker
    stuck to the view that the entire force should cross by the first ford.
    And as he was the QMG, and also rushed out an instant history of the
    battle, he had both the first and the last word.
68 Kaye, *Malcolm*, ii, pp 207–8.
69 Ibid.
70 Low, p 47.
71 Wilson, iv, pp 70–71.
72 There was to be another sour postscript to the battle. The Mysore
    Horse, under Captain James Grant, had captured a heap of booty,

including Holkar's sword and sword-belt. The booty was reckoned to be worth about 900,000 rupees, but the sword itself was nothing much; it had a velvet scabbard and some not very precious jewels inlaid on the hilt, and might be worth 1,000 rupees, or £100 sterling, at most. (Wilson, iv, pp 194–8; Kaye, *Malcolm*, ii, pp 219–221.) The Mysore Horse thought that the booty rightly belonged to them; Sir Thomas Hislop said that it ought to go into the general prize fund; the Governor-General decided in favour of the Mysore Horse.

The Mysore Horse had tried to present the sword to Malcolm, who declined it. The Raja of Mysore insisted that the victor of Mehidpur should have the sword, and this time Sir John gracefully accepted. But Hislop was not done yet. He protested that the sword was not the Raja's to bestow on anyone. It should have been placed at the disposal of Sir Thomas himself, who had it in mind to lay it at the feet of the Prince Regent – and no doubt earn himself a peerage or at least another ribbon. This tussle went on for more than a year, until the Governor-General approved the gift and Sir John took the sword and the belt home with him.

73 Kaye, *Malcolm*, ii, p 232.
74 Low, p 31.
75 The same family to whom E.M. Forster and J.R. Ackerley were tutors a century later and painted such delicious pictures of life at a small Hindu court in *The Hill of Devi* and *Hindoo Holiday.*
76 Wilson, iv, pp 114–116.
77 Blacker, p 280.
78 Wilson, iv, pp 120–6.
79 Kaye, *Malcolm*, ii, pp 237–38.
80 Malcolm to Low, May 18, 1818, MSS Eur D1082. If the Peshwa showed 'a disposition to procrastinate', John was to tell him that any such deal was off, and that he would immediately be attacked by the forces surrounding him: by Doveton coming up from the south, by the Russell Brigade and the 1st/14th coming down from Gogaum, by Captain Walker with eight companies of infantry coming from the east, and by the line of Malcolm's troops blocking off any escape route along the Nerbudda River.
81 Kaye, *Malcolm*, ii, 241–2.
82 Low to Malcolm, June 1, 1818, MSS Eur C961.
83 Kaye, *Malcolm*, ii, pp 244–5.
84 Ibid., p 245.
85 Ibid., pp 246–7.
86 Ibid., p 249.

87 Ibid., pp 270–2.
88 Malcolm to Low, Oct 18, 1818, Home Misc 733.
89 Low to Elphinstone, October 30, 1818, MSS Eur F88/291.
90 Low to Metcalfe, August 1819, Home Misc 733.
91 Bentinck Papers, Low to Bentinck, February 9, 1832.
92 Kaye, *Malcolm*, ii, p 265.
93 Gupta, pp 9–10.
94 November 16, 1822, Low, p 3.
95 Low, p 20.
96 Low, pp 27–8.
97 June 12, 1825, MSS Eur F88/271.
98 Low, p 37.
99 Low to Elphinstone, January 31, 1825, F88/270.
100 Low to Elphinstone, January 1, 1827, F88/274.
101 Low, p 55.
102 Low, p 21.
103 Low, pp 48, 209.
104 Susan Low to John Low, October 26, 1822, Low, pp 18–19.
105 Susan Low to John Low, November 21, 1822.
106 John Low to Elphinstone, January 1, 1827, F88/274.
107 S.G. Checkland, *Scottish Banking: A History 1865–1973*, Glasgow, 1975, p 174.
108 Low to Elphinstone, ibid.
109 Low, p 123.
110 Low to Elphinstone, ibid; see also Alistair Gibb, 'The Fife Banking Company', 2010, *banking-history.co.uk/fife*.
111 September 10, 1825, F88/271.
112 I don't know whether the nickname came from bloody deeds committed by Captain Macdonald or simply from his banging on about events at Glencoe – so reminiscent of internecine struggles among the Maratha princes.
113 R. Lewin, *The Chief*, 1980, p 201.
114 May 31, 1826, MSS Eur, F140/137a.
115 Gupta, p 18.
116 Low, p 1.

Chapter VIII: Augusta and John

1 Thackeray, *Roundabout Papers*, 'On Two Children in Black'.
2 *Roundabout Papers*, 'On Letts's Diary'.
3 Thackeray, *The Newcomes*, ch V. In his reminiscence, Thackeray speaks

of two boys waiting to be taken out to the ship, not three boys and a girl, but that is a modest selection of the facts, because what he is engaged in writing is a tribute to Richmond Shakespear, who was not only his childhood playmate but was to be his constant friend and companion when they got to England.

4 *Harper's Weekly*, March 27, 1897, p 315.
5 Low, p 67.
6 Hunter, *Thackerays in India*, pp 156–7.
7 Ibid, pp 157–8.
8 Low, pp 94–101.
9 Low, p 107.
10 John Shakespear, pp 160–1.
11 John Talbot Shakespear to Emily Dick, January 29, 1825, Low p 110.
12 Low, pp 110–111.
13 Hunter, ibid, p 172.
14 Ray, *Thackeray*, Vol I, p 58.
15 Ibid., pp 62–3.
16 Ibid.
17 Ibid.
18 For the voyage to England, she left her child in the care of James Munro MacNabb, who had been her husband's assistant in collecting the revenues of the Calcutta Districts and who was returning to England on leave. There was also amongst the 'native passengers' one Lawrence Barlow, described as 'servant to Master Thackeray', presumably a mixed-race nanny. (Ibid., p 65.) Thackeray himself remarks in *The Newcomes* on the rapid recovery time of children after parting from their parents: 'Half-an-hour after the father left the boy, and in his grief and loneliness was rowing back to shore, Clive was at play with a dozen of other children on the sunny deck of the ship. When two bells rang for their dinner, they were all hurrying to the cuddy-table, and busy over their meal. What a sad repast their parents had that day! How their hearts followed the careless young ones home across the great ocean!' (*The Newcomes*, Chapter V, p 52–3.)
19 Low, pp 104, 111.
20 Ibid., p 165.
21 Ibid., pp 103–4.
22 Ibid., p 106.
23 Ibid., p 110.
24 When she eventually returned to England, Anne Thackeray (now Carmichael-Smyth) found Aunt Ritchie rather common (her husband was a Baltimore merchant who had fallen in love with her when he glimpsed her on a stagecoach wearing deep mourning for her father)

(Low p106), but little William adored her. So did his daughter, who wrote 25 years later: 'I loved my great-aunt Ritchie, as who did not love that laughing, loving, romantic, handsome, humorous, indolent old lady? Shy, expansive in turn, she was big and sweet-looking, with a great look of my father. Though she was old when I knew her, she would still go off into peals of laughter, just as if she were a girl.' (Ray, p 68.) Laughter was not Mrs Carmichael-Smyth's forte. She was earnest and inclined to be gloomy, and given to fashionable causes like hydropathy and homeopathy. Although devoted to his mother, Thackeray once remarked, 'I would die rather than make a joke to her.' (Ray, p 109.)

25 *Roundabout Papers*, 'On Letts's Diary'.

26 Ray, p 70.

27 Low, p 114.

28 February 18, 1827, Low, pp 116–7.

29 December 14, 1825, Low to Elphinstone, F88/272.

30 Low, p 57.

31 Low, pp 37, 46.

32 Low, pp 51–2.

33 Lord Amherst was the first Governor-General to spend the hot months at Simla.

34 Low, pp 62–3.

35 Low, pp 118–9.

36 Today lived in by Victor Banerjee, famous for his roles in two great films about the British in India: Dr Aziz in David Lean's *A Passage to India*, and the Prime Minister in Satyajit Ray's *The Chess Players*. Unlike in Simla, most of the old bungalows in Mussoorie are still standing.

37 March 16, 1829, Low, p 119.

38 According to the Mussoorie website, the first church in the settlement was not built until the mid-1830s. I pictured them exchanging their vows on the verandah of Captain Townsend's bungalow. But then I came across a picture of a charming little chapel with a classical portico behind the hospital in Landour. St Peters was built the year before the marriage of John and Augusta on the top of Landour Hill – it may be the oldest church in the region. For years derelict and crumbling, it has just (2011) been refurbished as a Catholic chapel. The white pillars and cool side arches and turquoise tin roof must look much as they did on the day that John and Augusta stepped out into the porch and looked down at the whole of India spread out before them.

39 Low, p 119.

40 Ibid.

41 Ibid., p 120.

42 Ibid., p 122.

43 Ibid., p 121.

44 Ibid., p 125.

45 Farooqui, pp 44–64; Parkes, pp 252–3; Low to Bentinck, August 25, 1832, D1082.

46 Sleeman, 'The Story of Bysa Bae', *passim*.

47 Low to Bentinck, ibid.

48 Low to Bentinck, November 20, 1832, C961.

49 Low to Bentinck, August 27, 1834.

50 Low to Bentinck, August 25, 1832.

51 Rosselli, p 230.

52 Hope, *The House of Scindea*, 1863.

53 Ibid., p 26.

54 Ibid., p 29.

55 July 30, 1851, *Private Letters of the Marquess of Dalhousie*, ed. J.G.A. Baird, p 169. The title of this collection does not fully convey the unique and often startling nature of its contents. These letters were covered by Dalhousie's instruction that none of his private papers should be published until 50 years after his death. The collection consists entirely of letters to a single correspondent, his much older friend Sir George Couper, whom he deliberately used 'as a safety valve through which I have a right to blow off feelings which I can express to no one in India but my wife and do express to no one in Europe but your two selves' (p vi) – his other private correspondent was Fox Maule, later Lord Panmure, Dalhousie's cousin and heir to his earldom. In fact, he often wrote to John Low in quite unguarded terms, too, but it is only to Couper that he expresses himself with unvarnished brutality. When these letters were finally published in 1910 – Dalhousie died in 1860 – his reputation took a dive from which it has never quite recovered.

56 Low, p 128.

57 Low to Dick, Low, p 127.

58 Ibid., p 140.

59 Ibid., pp 143–4.

60 Ibid., pp 122, 148.

61 Ibid., p 151.

62 Ibid., p 152.

Chapter IX: Midnight in Lucknow

1 Emily Eden, *Up the Country*, p 62.

2 Fisher, *Indirect Rule*, p 303.

3 The heroine Umrao Jan always returns for Muharram to Khanum's house where she first practised her profession (Ruswa, 1961, and Peter Chelkowski, 'Monumental Grief: The Bara Imambara' in *Lucknow, City of Illusions*, ed. Rosie Llewelyn-Jones, 2011, pp 101–135), and when she wearies of life, she dreams of spending her last days in the sacred city of Karbala.

4 *Narrative of a Journey through the Upper Provinces of India from Calcutta to Bombay*, 1824–5, ii, p 394.

5 Five years earlier, on becoming Governor-General, he had confided to his private journal that 'our object ought to be to render the British Government paramount in effect, if not declaredly so. We should hold the other states as vassals, in substance though not in name; not precisely as they stood on the Mogul Government but possessed of perfect internal sovereignty ... The completion of such a system, which must exclude of any pretension to pre-eminence in the court of Delhi, demands time and favourable coincidences.' (*Journal*, 1858, 6 February 1814, i, 30.)

6 Fisher, 'Imperial Coronation', p 260.

7 Irwin, p 112.

8 Resident to Secretary to Government, August 28, 1823 (Bengal Political Consultations 12 September 1823, No 21).

9 IOR/F/4/1652/66001, Captain John Paton, *The British Government and the Kingdom of Oude*, 1837, p 209. In 1845, reports of the gross mismanagement of the then King became so shocking that the Governor-General 'instructed the Resident not to attend the coronation anniversary of the King as a mark of indignation.' The Acting Resident who received these orders was Augusta's brother, John Dowdeswell Shakespear, who we shall hear much of at Lucknow. (Shakespear to F. Currie September 29, 1845, see Safi Ahmad, *British Residents at the Court of Avadh*, 1764–1856, Lucknow, 1968.) Once again, no coronation took place that year.

10 The Resident was not an envoy with a specific mission, not a *Safir* – the Arabic word for peacemaker. Nor was he an *Ilchi*, the Turkish word for a plenipotentiary Ambassador. He was rather more than a *Wakil* or *Vakeel* as the English more usually spelled it, the Arabic word for 'trusted personal agent'. He was, as it were, a means of two powers getting to understand each other better, by the representative of one residing at the Court of the other. The novelty – and at the same time

the vagueness – of the post proved attractive. The Dutch and Germans and the Japanese borrowed the word for Residents in their own later-flowering colonies. And considering that Persian was the language of diplomacy in the subcontinent, it was piquant that the Persian word for 'Resident' should be 'Resident'. (Fisher, *Indirect Rule in India*, pp 47, 49.)

11 The Secret Committee of the Court reinforced the Declaration of that Act in their advice to the Governor-General a couple of years later: 'the universal principle never to be departed from, either in the present condition of the Native Powers or in any future revolutions amongst them is that we are completely satisfied with the possessions we already have and will engage in no war for the purpose of further acquisitions.' (July 21, 1786, Choksey, *British Diplomacy*, p 30.)

12 8 July 1803, K.M. Panikkar, *The Evolution of British Policy towards Indian States 1774–1858*, p 39. Charles Metcalfe, then Resident at Delhi, wrote to Richard Jenkins, the long-serving Resident at Nagpur, arguing that the arm's length policy, the so-called non-interference, was impracticable and had to be constantly deviated from: 'I want to see it openly renounced ... let us take every fair opportunity of securing and aggrandising our power.' (3 November 1814, quoted Fisher, *Indirect Rule*, p 213.) Jenkins felt the same. He looked forward to the Maratha wars as a way to break up the old, limiting treaties and carve out new states in Central India under uninhibited British control. (Fisher, op.cit., p 215.) Yet experience taught a different lesson. Twenty years later, when he had just become Acting Governor-General pending the arrival of Lord Auckland, Metcalfe looked back and concluded that 'our attempts to interfere for the better government of other states have often been wretched failures ... Interference is so likely to do evil and so little certain of doing good, that it ought, I conceive, to be avoided as much as possible.' (Minute of August 14, 1835, *The Life and Correspondence of Charles, Lord Metcalfe*, ed. J.W. Kaye, 1854, i, pp 196–7.)

13 Wellesley himself was not insensitive to his reputation. He wrote to the Resident at Sindia's court suggesting that the Resident modify his assessments which as they stood were liable 'to give his enemies in Leaden Hall Street room to found an accusation against Lord Wellesley of injustice and rapacity.' (May 1, 1804, Eur Ms Add 13602, quoted Fisher, *Indirect Rule*, p 175.)

14 Fisher, ibid.

15 Paton, *British Government*, p 85.

16 More than half the interest on this war loan was paid to the mega-rich Minister Hakim Mehdi and his family – 25,000 rupees a month out of

41,600 – because without the Hakim's persuasion the King would have refused to stump up. (Paton, pp 89–90.) Over the years between 1764 and 1856, the Company is estimated to have extracted a total of 52 million rupees at low interest from the Rulers of Oudh, not to mention grants of at least 6 million rupees to cover its 'expenses' in installing its preferred candidate as ruler. Before the Ruler ceded such huge swathes of his territory to the Company in 1801, there was also an annual subsidy of 7–8 million rupees to pay for the protection of the British troops. (Fisher, *Indirect Rule*, p 382.)

As Captain Paton, himself a loyal servant of the Honourable Company, put it in his candid history (intended only for the eyes of the Governor-General and the Court of Directors): 'These loans without having seen the secret springs of action appear a delightful proof of cordial co-operation with the British Government on the part of its Ally.' What he showed was how painfully they were screwed out of the Nawabs. (Paton, p 80.)

17 *A Journey through the Kingdom of Oudh*, 1849–50, W.H. Sleeman, 1858, i, pp 325–330.

18 Fanny Parkes, p 59.

19 Ibid., p 60.

20 This is quoted in John Low's parting dispatch ten years later to Maddock, who by then had become the Governor-General's Political Secretary; September 30, 1842, IOR/F/42002/89405.

21 Paton, *British Government*, pp 99–102.

22 November 9, 1831, IOR/F/4/1430/56539.

23 Low, p 134.

24 Pemble, p 67.

25 Ibid., April 2, 1832.

26 *The English Constitution*, 1867.

27 Paton, pp 105–108.

28 Low, p 141.

29 He had found the perfect alternative site for the Residency, at Char Bagh three and a half miles outside the city, 'a delightful place, the water and air of which is pure and near which the canal from the River Ganges will pass.' Lieutenant Paton, First Assistant at the Residency, fired back a useful Sir Humphrey-style riposte: The Resident needed a house in the city 'as his presence may often be absolutely necessary to place him within immediate communication with the government ...' (August 5, 1831, IOR/F/4/1430 56528.) The question could be reopened when Oudh was quiet again – nice use of the Doctrine of Unripe Time. Later on, the Resident thought of a different reason for not moving. If the Residency was shifted out

to Char Bagh, 'a great proportion of the inhabitants of Lucknow who were dependent of the British government would be deprived of the security which they derive from the immediate presence of the Residency in that city.' (October 7, 1832, ibid.)

When John Low arrived, the King repeated his wish to shift the Residency to Char Bagh. John introduced a fresh reason for not shifting: Dr Stevenson had advised that 'Europeans living in a situation that is lower than all the surrounding country would almost to a certainty be attacked with fever for several months after the rains of each year.' John had not forgotten the swamps of Tripassur. (Low to Bentinck, 13 February 1832.)

The King came back with two other sites. Musa Bagh, where there was already a large house, and a spot the other side of the Gomti near the King's racecourse. John was ready for him. The road to Musa Bagh was impassable after rain and even further from the Palace, five or six miles in fact, and the racecourse site was just as low-lying as Char Bagh.

Nasir-ud-din then said: Choose any site you fancy, even Dilkusha (meaning Heart's Desire), his pleasure park outside the city, though he would keep for himself the existing mansion, a free adaptation of Vanburgh's Seaton Delaval in Northumberland, which had been built for Sa'adat Ali Khan by Major Gore Ouseley, once Acting Resident in Lucknow.

John Low walked his Arab horse over to Dilkusha and found three sites near the Park wall which would do nicely, being just as elevated as the present Residency and no more than two and a half miles from the Palace. He confided to Bentinck that he could quite understand the King's wish to take over what was the most elevated and agreeable spot in the city. Bentinck agreed that the present site did bear 'an appearance of overbearing command that was almost offensive', and it might actually be an advantage that the Residency should be at some distance from the Palace and its intrigues (the corruption of Mordaunt Ricketts was still playing on his mind).

After all, the knavish Ricketts during his last three years as Resident had resided at the British cantonment across the river which was further off than the new Residency would be. John conceded that 'We should greatly gratify the harmless vanity of the King of Oudh by letting him have possession of the ground occupied by the present Residency on which he wishes to erect a very large and splendid palace and to plant an avenue of trees from it to the new Iron Bridge.' Quite clearly, too, the ulterior motive of the King was that 'the removal of the Residency from the City would by degrees, if not immediately, have the effect of leaving to the King himself both the name and reality of more complete power in his capital.'

There was, however, one possible case in which it might be desirable for the Resident to live in the city: 'that of our being compelled to depose the native sovereign entirely.' Even then, Low thought that the British would 'be so completely in possession of the Supreme Power that there would be no difficulty in resuming the present Residency if necessary.' John was prophetic in raising this cautionary note, but too complacent in brushing it aside. The geographical position of the Lucknow Residency was to be crucial for John Low himself, and later on for the destiny of India.

30 See John Keay's *The Great Arc* for this fascinating project.
31 Now and then, the cases sent up to the Resident had a more exotic tang. On November 21, 1834, John had to deal with an application for the return of a runaway slave girl. The applicant was a Mr Martin, an Indian converted to Christianity, who had been a protégé and had taken the name of General Claude Martin, the adventurer-general-nabob who had built some of the great palaces in Lucknow, including his own house, La Martinière, one of the most extraordinary buildings on earth. Mr Martin was told peremptorily that the British Government 'would never recognise property of that description, even in a foreign state.' In another case, the following year, a Mr Hunt had quarrelled with his wife, the daughter of a bandmaster in the King's service. After they had come to blows, her family had carried off all the property in Mr Hunt's house, claiming that it had been here during her first marriage. Mr Hunt appended a vast inventory, including five silver tea spoons, five silver salt spoons and a silver fish slice. All this information was sent on to Calcutta, which helps to explain why governors-general died of overwork. (IOR/F/4/1652/66003, November 21, 1834 and August 17, 1835.)
32 Low to Bentinck, November 18, 1833, MSS Eur D1082, Pemble, pp 36–7.
33 Pemble, p 43.
34 December 31, 1832, IOR/F/1456/57362.
35 Low to Macnaghten, December 4, 1834, IOR/F/4/1651/66000.
36 Llewelyn-Jones, *Engaging Scoundrels*, pp 69–70.
37 Rosie Llewelyn-Jones in *Engaging Scoundrels* unearths Derusett's account books. They are surprisingly punctilious, even if devoted solely to the pursuit of pleasure. The antics of the Barber of Lucknow were first published to the world in *The Private Life of An Eastern King*, a scandalous account of life at the court of Nasir-ud-din, which came out in 1855. The book made a huge furore, was constantly

referred to in the newspapers and in Parliament as proof of the
debauchery and corruption of native Indian courts and as justification
for taking them over and giving them honest and sober British government. The annexation of Oudh itself has been attributed in part to
this juicy report. Later historians have tended to take a disapproving
view of the book itself rather than of its contents, calling it a scandalous or notorious or 'almost certainly spurious' production.
(Pemble, p 108.) This disapproval was assisted by the book being published anonymously 'by a member of the Household of His late
Majesty'. From internal evidence, the supplier of the material was
identified as Edward Cropley, the King's librarian, not that Nasir-ud-
din seems to have been much of a reader. The compiler of the book
was identified as William Knighton, who turned out to be an eminently respectable man, headmaster of a school in Colombo and later
a professor of history and logic at the Hindu College in Calcutta.
True, as Pemble complains, there are inconsistencies in the book and
Knighton has added material from other sources. It is also true that
Knighton was himself anxious that Oudh should be annexed to the
British Crown. All the same, the essential veracity of the account is
supported by the unarguable fact that most of the material is exactly
what John Low was putting in his secret reports to Calcutta at the
time.

38 Knighton, p 88.
39 Ibid., p 47.
40 Ibid., pp 71–83.
41 December 14, 1834.
42 John Low to Macnaghten, September 30, 1836; Rabit, p 63 et ff.
43 Knighton, pp 152–6.
44 Low to Macnaghten, ibid.
45 Low to Macnaghten, September 23, 1836.
46 Ibid.
47 Rabit, pp 11–12.
48 Sharar, p 57.
49 Rabit, p 4.
50 Sleeman, ii, p 174.
51 Ibid. pp 137–67. Sleeman is uncertain whether she was a niece or a
    granddaughter.
52 Ibid., pp 181–2.
53 Ibid., p 139.
54 Edwardes, p 29; Archer, i, pp 1–27.
55 Sleeman, ii, p 172.
56 Ibid., p 149.

57 Ibid., pp 142–3.
58 Ibid., i, pp 156–61. For Knighton's different version, pp 133–47.
59 Rabit, p 63.
60 Sleeman, ii, p 141.
61 Ibid.
62 Ibid, p 115. There existed several sons of another and older uncle, and it may seem odd that these should not have been considered as next in line. But this older uncle had died, and under Islamic law the death meant that his sons went to the back of the queue to succeed. It may also seem odd to us that Nasir-ud-din was so eager to repudiate both the boys. But John Low had eventually come to the conclusion that 'His Majesty having no children of his own and hating his relations, is rather partial than otherwise to the notion of the native sovereignty of Oude terminating with himself.' (Low to Macnaghten, September 23, 1836; Irwin, p 127.)
63 Low to Macnaghten, September 24, 1836.
64 Fisher, *Indirect Rule*, pp 321, 327.
65 It was a multi-layered system of considerable sophistication. To a great extent, the system rested on a flow of credit notes, or *hundis*, which could be exchanged between parties remote from their original place of issue and could amount at times to a paper currency. The most junior dealer was expected to master double-entry book-keeping. There were schools for bankers in the major towns. Futures markets for crops like opium and cotton, so dependent on unforeseeable events in the outside world, helped to manage risk. The super-fast *dâk* postal service ensured that merchants were fully abreast of market trends, and a sophisticated insurance system minimized transport risks. Rhymes and jingles taught children that capital was best divided into four quarters: one hoarded as coin, the second invested in jewellery, the third lent out at interest and only the fourth invested in trade.

Indian merchants remained suspicious of fly-by-night Western practices such as limited liability and the joint-stock company. They were intensely family-minded and religious in their approach to business, and so dedicated to the long term that some of the older Delhi firms staged an annual ritual at which their old account books were worshipped, both as a homage to the virtuous lives of the ancestors who founded the firm and as an earnest of their own intention to maintain the family's credit for years to come. These rituals are still celebrated today, a sobering contrast to the mindsets of some Anglo-Saxon CEOs. Pilgrims and religious foundations played an active role in brokerage and wholesale business. Indian merchants lived, or aspired to live sober and pious lives, with a minimum of exterior display – not unlike the merchants of Amsterdam in its seventeenth-century heyday.

Despite their close business relations with the British, they seldom mixed socially. When Mark Thornhill, the magistrate at Mathura, returned to his post during the Mutiny, he found all the English bunga-lows burnt and decided to take up the offer of shelter from the Seths, one of the richest merchant families in India. 'I had resided many years in India, but so apart did we English live from the natives, that of their habits of life among themselves I was nearly ignorant. The prospect of entering the house of the Seths had for me all the charm of adventure.' He is astonished to find that in their immense mansion the Seths are 'destitute of what to us are the most ordinary conveniences'. They have neither plate nor china, and serve only rice and flour cakes, accompanied by water and milk which tastes of the smoke it has been simmered over.

Thus, according to Bayly, 'regardless of the steamboat, the agency houses and the joint-stock bank, Indian commercial society proved almost as impenetrable to the Westerners as its Chinese counterpart.' While a bunch of Western agency houses would go belly-up in each commercial crisis, the more conservative, durably built Indian mer-chant families tended to survive – and it was on them that everyone from the Governor-General launching a loan stock to the peasant seeking credit to buy seed and tools had ultimately to rely. Then as now, Asian capitalism was a closed book to the West, its strengths as little understood and regarded as they were during the serial crashes of Western banks between 2008 and the present day. No wonder Colonel Low was mystified by the Munshi's hanging on to his ill-paid job at the Residency. (Bayly, *Rulers, Townsmen*, pp 275–80.)

66 Low to Macnaghten, September 30, 1836.
67 Bentinck Papers, Low to Bentinck, September 17 and 29, 1834.
68 Low, pp 165–6.
69 Ibid., p 59.
70 Ibid., p 135.
71 January 1 and May 17, 1832, Low, pp 135–6.
72 Low, p 138.
73 Ibid., pp 144–5.
74 Here is a sample of George's verse, written to celebrate his brother Richmond's appointment to the Survey Branch of the Revenue Department at Gorakhpur, where he took part in 'the Great Arc', the mapping of India from tip to top:

Unwonted mats the Major's dwelling grace,
Unwonted smiles bedeck the Major's face,
The Major's wife full joyous moves about,
The house arranging, turning each thing out.

Onwards the tidings fly to gloomy Ghoruckpore,
Where witless youths the jungle's depths explore,
Stretch the long chain, or point theodolite
Going most wrong when thinking they're most right.
Richmond, the news received, ecstatic starts!
His nether garb in sunder parts,
Alas for poverty! His only pair,
His last, his nearest, dearest, parted there.

The Patriarch, in distant seat reclined,
Feels the glad notice soothe his mind,
Sepoys, or sepoy's claims no more annoy,
He waves his bony arm and shouts for joy!
Lucknow's barbaric Queen, her terrors laid aside,
Smooths her dread front and shakes her kerchief wide!
The brute creation e'en the influence share
And shuffles with his gambles rude, your *Polar Bear*.
Hail! all declare, to dust and glare and heat!
Hail to the land where palkees madly meet.

(Low, pp 199–200.)

75 Ray, *The Buried Life*, p 45.
76 Ray, ibid., pp 45–46fn.
77 Low, pp 169–70.
78 Auckland to Low, February 4, 1837.
79 Llewelyn-Jones, *Engaging Scoundrels*, p 79.
80 Sleeman, ii, p 152.
81 Pemble, p 84.
82 John Shakespear's account, IOR/F/4/1652/66003, reprinted in *Papers Relating to the Government of Oude*, House of Lords, August 15, 1838; see also Sleeman, ii, pp 152–68; Sharar p 58.
83 Lieutenant Shakespear wrote a full account the same day for the Government. John Low only added a few footnotes. It was John Shakespear too who indulged the family weakness for light verse to mark the occasion:

Despised by all, regretted by none,
To the dark silent tomb in youth thou art gone,
How unprincely thy wont to pass the night long
With low boon companions in dance and in song,
Whilst the roof of thy palace re-echoed the shout
Of their bacchanal orgies and maddening rout.

To bandy the jest, the wine cup to drain,
Forbidden to Moslem. Ah, ne'er didst thou deign,
As seated at banquet, the base crew among,
To list to the tale of oppression and wrong
By thy subjects endured.

(Low, pp 195–6.)

84 Rabit, p 87.
85 Sleeman, ii, p 175.
86 Ibid., pp 175–6.
87 Ibid., p 184.
88 Low, p 187.
89 Auckland to Low, July 19, 1837, and Minute by the Governor-General, reprinted in *Sessional Papers Relating to the Government of Oude, 1838*, Nos 10 and 6.
90 Pemble, p 83.
91 Low to Macnaghten, July 28, 1838.
92 Pemble, p 84; Home Misc 828 / MSS Eur D1082.
93 Pemble, p 85.
94 *Papers Relating to the King of Oude*, printed March 15, 1858; Minute dated August 22, 1854. See also Safi Ahmad, pp 13–20.
95 Eden, *Up the Country*, p 61.
96 Ibid., p 63.

Chapter X: Richmond the rescuer

1 S.E. Low to John Low, January, 1838, Low p 208.
2 S.E. Low to John Low, Low p 260.
3 S.E. Low to John Low, June 11, 1836, Low, p 172.
4 S.E. Low to John Low, December 15, 1836, Low, pp 181–2.
5 John Low to S.E. Low, February 8, 1838, Low pp 206–7.
6 John Low to S.E. Low, June 4, 1838, Low p 208.
7 Low p 207.
8 Ibid.
9 The woman, known in the family only as 'the Maiden of the Gully', was not thought suitable. His brother George, always on hand with a *vers d'occasion*, wrote a ballad to which the chorus was:

Her beauteous eyes, her Grecian nose
Alike contrive to pull ye,
But then, they say, I mayn't propose

For the Maiden of the Gully.
(*John Shakespear*, p 216.)

What was so unsuitable about her? Was she mixed-race, or divorced, or Irish, or what? All we know is that John Shakespear himself agreed with the verdict, as he wrote from the ship to his sister Marianne: 'I would have acted most imprudently in prosecuting my love passage with that most bewitching of young ladies.' (Low, p 216.) He was not to marry until 15 years later after he retired from India and settled in Hastings.

10 Kaye, *Afghanistan*, i. pp 320, 327, 212.
11 Ibid., p 353.
12 Ibid., pp 358–9.
13 Everyone who knew anything about Afghanistan agreed. Charles Metcalfe, who had acted as Governor-General until Auckland arrived and who should have had the job if merit and experience counted, pointed out the financial as well as the political embarrassments that would follow, even if the military operation was initially successful. Mountstuart Elphinstone made the same points in his letter to Auckland: 'If you send 27,000 men up the Bolan Pass to Candahar (as we hear is intended) and can feed them, I have no doubt you will take Candahar and Cabul and set up Shuja, but for maintaining him in a poor, cold, strong and remote country, among a turbulent people like the Afghans, I own it seems to me hopeless. If you succeed I fear you will weaken your position against Russia. The Afghans were neutral and would have received your aid against invaders with gratitude – they will now be disaffected and glad to join any invader that will drive you out.' (Dalrymple, *Return*, pp 139–40.)
14 John Shakespear, *John Shakespear of Shadwell*, p 213. This book is an invaluable family history written by Richmond's ninth and youngest child, Lieutenant-Colonel John Shakespear – he was born only a month before his father's death in 1861 – and it contains what is in essence a short biography of his remarkable father.
15 Low, p 167.
16 Ibid., p 116.
17 John Shakespear, pp 191–2.
18 Ibid., p 288.
19 Ibid., pp 258, 278.
20 Ibid., p 213.
21 Ibid., p 216.
22 Dalrymple, *Return*, p 148.
23 Eden, *Up the Country*, pp 205–6.

24 Ibid., p 198.

25 Kaye, *Afghanistan*, i, p 382.

26 John Shakespear, pp 217–8.

27 Kaye, i, pp 404–5; Dalrymple, *Return*, p 152.

28 Dalrymple, *Return*, pp 152–3.

29 John Shakespear, pp 214–5.

30 The drawbacks of the camel as a mode of transport in the hills are
    nicely expounded in Kipling's Barrack-Room Ballad, 'Oonts':

> O the oont, O the oont, O the floppin', droppin' oont!
> When 'is long legs give from under an' 'is meltin' eye is dim,
> The tribes is up be'ind us and the tribes is out in front –
> It ain't no jam for Tommy, but it's kites an' crows for 'im.

31 John Shakespear, ibid.

32 Ibid.

33 Macnaghten to Auckland, April 25, Kaye, *Afghanistan*, i, p 438.

34 Ibid., p 440.

35 Dalrymple, p 180.

36 It was something of an irony that the British should now be seeking
    to keep out the Persians, since Sir John Malcolm, as a mere Captain,
    had led a mission to Persia at the turn of the century to encourage the
    Persians to move their army into Herat, in order to keep the Afghans
    busy and discourage them from moving south to invade Hindustan –
    another illusory threat.

37 John Shakespear, p 217.

38 Dalrymple, p 204.

39 John Shakespear, p 219.

40 He later wrote up the journal and published it in *Blackwood's Edinburgh
    Magazine* for June 1842, as 'A Personal Narrative of Journey from
    Heraut to Ourenbourg on the Caspian, in 1840, by Captain
    Richmond Shakespear.'

41 'Personal Narrative', p 694.

42 Ibid., p 695.

43 Ibid.

44 Ibid., p 696.

45 Ibid., p 699.

46 Ibid., p 701. Richmond's thoughts on reaching the great river are
    reminiscent of Matthew Arnold's 'Sohrab and Rustum', which, after
    recounting how the father Rustum leading the Persians unknowingly
    murders his son who is fighting for the Tartars, finishes by describing
    the onward course of the Oxus:

But the majestic river floated on,
Out of the mist and hum of that low land,
Into the frosty starlight, and there moved,
Rejoicing, through the hushed Chorasmian waste,
Under the solitary moon . . .
A foiled circuitous wanderer – till at last
The longed-for dash of waves is heard, and wide
His luminous home of waters opens, bright
And tranquil, from whose floor the new-bathed stars
Emerge, and shine upon the Aral Sea.

Khiva is a corruption of the Iranian 'Khorasm' – hence that Chorasmian waste, which had also appealed to Shelley as the ultimate desert for the solitary Alastor to wander in. Matthew Arnold's poem was published in 1853, more than a decade after Richmond had reached the Oxus and followed it down to the Aral Sea. Alas, the Aral Sea is no longer the glittering inland ocean that Richmond saw and Arnold dreamed of. Irrigation for agriculture and industrial pollution have reduced it to a poisonous salt pan.

47 John Shakespear, p 223.
48 'Personal Narrative', p 715.
49 Ibid., p 717.
50 John Shakespear, p 221.
51 'Personal Narrative', p 720.
52 John Shakespear, p 226.
53 In the end, the imperial itch could not be restrained. Richmond's son John recalled that, 30 years later in 1873, when he was 11 years old, his mother suddenly stopped to stare at a newspaper bill at a station bookstall, which read: 'Occupation of Khiva by the Russians.' A new form of national slavery had engulfed the Chorasmian wastes, one which was not to end until the break-up of the Soviet Union more than a century later.
54 John Shakespear, p 227.
55 His parents were Mary Anne Shakespear and another Reverend Francis Thackeray.
56 Dalrymple, p 220.
57 Eden, *Up the Country*, pp 3–4.
58 Kaye, *Afghanistan*, ii, p 80.
59 Ibid., ii, p 86.
60 Ibid., ii, p 146.
61 Ibid., ii, pp 4–5.
62 Dalrymple, pp 221, 227–8.

NOTES 689

63 Yapp, pp 339–42.
64 Dalrymple, p 275.
65 In any case, the insurgency had now spread to every part of the country. Up in the north-west, Major Todd had realized that the Wazir of Herat was sidling up to the Persians and was simply pocketing the money the British were giving him to attack Persian-held fortresses. On his own initiative, Todd aborted his mission and marched back to Kandahar. Shortly afterwards, the Wazir had Shuja's cousin strangled and entered into an anti-British alliance with the Persians. Todd was not forgiven for being proved right; Auckland sacked him from the political service. (Dalrymple, p 260.) Captain James Abbott, minus his fingers, fared rather better. He rose to become a General and to have the town of Abbottabad named after him, later to become a Pakistani Sandhurst and to make the headlines as the place where Osama bin Laden was killed by the US Navy Seals.
66 Auckland to Hobhouse, February 18, 1842, BL Add MS 37707, f187.
67 Sale, p 160.
68 Eden, *Up the Country*, pp 389–90.
69 John Shakespear, p 237. Even Richmond's nonchalance was not unqualified. In another letter written three days earlier, he tells Major Outram that the brigade had not yet got over the effects of the defeat and that the Native Infantry were unlikely to be persuaded to attack a second time if their first attack failed: 'Should we fail, the whole of India is jeopardized.'
70 Ibid., p 236.
71 Ibid.
72 Dalrymple, pp 416–7.
73 Ibid., p 427.
74 Ibid., p 428.
75 John Shakespear, p 238.
76 Low to Elphinstone, January 19, 1843. The *OED* includes among the meanings of 'shuck' 'a mean or contemptible person'. It seems to have been a fairly recent slangy term, and John Low may have been uncertain of the spelling.
77 Kaye, ibid., iii, pp 285–6.
78 Ibid., p 288.
79 John Shakespear, p 238.
80 Ibid., p 240.
81 Ibid., p 242.
82 Dalrymple, p 458.
83 John Shakespear, p 245.
84 Ibid., pp 242–3.

85 Low, p 274.
86 Pottinger, p 191.
87 Kaye, ibid., pp 353–5.
88 Low, pp 272–3.
89 John Shakespear, p 244.
90 Ibid., p 247.
91 Kaye, ibid., pp 337–8. The Governor-General was keen to erase all memory of the disastrous strategies followed by himself and his pred-ecessor. At his celebration banquet, only those who had been connected with Sir Robert Sale and the heroic 13th Light Infantry, including his doughty wife Florentia, were invited. Those who had been taken prisoner and had not been officially handed over as hostages had to await clearance by courts of inquiry, including the no less heroic Eldred Pottinger, who like the other political officers had his appointment brusquely cancelled and his special allowance denied. Ellenborough also denied that the two British envoys, Charles Stoddart and Arthur Conolly, who died in Persian captivity after hor-rible sufferings, were anything but 'innocent travellers'. (Kaye, ibid., p 262.) It is not hard to see why Ellenborough made enemies wherever he went.
92 Low to Elphinstone, January 19, 1843.

Chapter XI: A short opium war

 1 Lambrick, pp 33, 36.
 2 Ibid., p 121.
 3 Amar Farooqui, *Sindias and the Raj*, p 8.
 4 'Lord Ellenborough gets rid of the Resident' in Hope, *The House of Scindea*.
 5 John Shakespear, p 255.
 6 Farooqui, p 105.
 7 Ibid., ch. vi.
 8 John Shakespear, p 350.
 9 Thackeray, *Roundabout Papers*, 'On Letts's Diary'.
10 Sleeman to Currie, February 28, 1844, quoted Farooqui, p 104.
11 Bayly, *Rulers, Townsmen*, p 282.
12 Sleeman, *Rambles*, p 365.
13 Bayly, ibid., p 268.

Chapter XII: Crash City

1 Kaye, *Afghanistan*, iii, 398–9.
2 March 29, 1841, Kaye, ibid., ii, pp 148–9.
3 In *The Newcomes*, too, Thackeray attributes the collapse of the Bundelcund Banking Company, which finally ruins Colonel Newcome, to unmitigated villainy:

> It was one of many similar cheats which have been successfully practiced upon the simple folks, civilian and military, who toil and struggle – who fight with sun and enemy – who pass years of long exile and gallant endurance in the service of our empire in India. Agency-houses after agency-houses have been established, and have flourished in splendour and magnificence, and have paid fabulous dividends – and have enormously enriched two or three wary speculators – and then have burst in bankruptcy, involving widows, orphans, and countless simple people who trusted their all to the keeping of these unworthy treasurers. (*The Newcomes*, p 719.)

4 Evidence to the House of Commons Select Committee on Commerce and Shipping, 1833.
5 He was, as it happened, to serve as Resident at Lucknow later on, between 1849 and 1856. His behaviour was crucial to the course of events, and John did not hesitate to criticize him sharply, although he was grateful to him for giving way on this occasion.
6 Low to Maddock, September 30, 1842, IOR/F/4/2002/89405.
7 Bayly, *Rulers, Townsmen*, p 59.
8 Ibid., p 102.
9 Low, p 260.
10 Carla Petievich, 'Innovations pious and impious: expressive culture in courtly Lucknow', in *The Art of Courtly Lucknow*.
11 Low, p 288.
12 Ibid.
13 Ibid.
14 Ibid., p 293.
15 Ibid., p 297.
16 John Shakespear, p 229.
17 Low, p 236.
18 Ibid., p 303.
19 Ibid, p 301.
20 Ray, *The Buried Life*, p 45.
21 Low, p 314.

22 Low to Elphinstone, May 25, 1844, F88/126/11.

23 Low, p 318.

24 *The Newcomes*, p 218. JL would not be the first Scottish Colonel to run out of money and be forced to return to India. Saki's ferocious forebear and namesake, Sir Hector Munro, the victor of Buxar, had returned to Easter Ross in the far north to beautify his estates at Novar, only to be wiped out in the Ayr Bank crash of 1772. He had gone back to India at the age of 52 and parlayed his way into the supreme command at Madras. JL was attempting to bring off the same trick as he was pushing sixty.

25 Ibid., p 219.

26 Ibid., p 265.

27 Blakiston, ch xxxiii.

28 Ray, *The Buried Life*, p 103.

29 Ray, ibid., p 98.

30 Ibid., p 105.

31 Some of the Shakespears identified Colonel Newcome with Augusta's brother, John Dowdeswell Shakespear, 'Old Jonathan' to his brothers and sisters, Low's long-time assistant at Lucknow and later Acting Resident there. Thackeray did meet Shakespear several times when he was home on leave in 1848. (*John Shakespear*, p 265.)

32 Opposite p 271 of the original edition.

33 Low to Elphinstone, September 11, 1847, F/88/134/11.

34 The Chairman was Sir James Weir Hogg, grandfather of Quintin Hogg/Hailsham, a successful lawyer who had returned to England with a large fortune. Low to Elphinstone, December 18, 1846, F88/129/77.

35 Webster, *Twilight*, p 141.

Chapter XIII: Cotton-picking

1 Dalhousie to Low, February 24, 1854, MSS Eur D1082.

2 Ibid., July 18, 1851.

3 Ibid., February 6, 1851.

4 *Private Letters of the Marquess of Dalhousie*, ed. J.G.A. Baird, p vii.

5 John said how much he would like to have half an hour's conversation on 'the late astounding change in France' – the revolution of 1848: 'The suddenness of it, the means by which it was brought about and the tranquillity that immediately followed make the event one of the most remarkable in history – but I cannot yet believe that the present state of repose can last many months and I fear that there will soon be

many desperate struggles between the two great classes of the community – those who have property and those who have not.' (Low to Dalhousie, May 10, 1848, D1082.) He was not wrong there. A month later, John was rejoicing to his pen friend on the way that, by contrast, the Chartist meeting on Kennington Common had passed off so peacefully. 'I do not think that since we first heard of the Battle of Waterloo I have ever been so delighted with news from England, as I am now with the account of the result of the threatened Monster Meeting of Chartists on the 10th April. It is truly most ratifying to find amidst such scenes of revolution and violence in most of the other capitals of Europe that so large a portion of the inhabitants of London have retained their feelings of loyalty and their love of good order, and that they will not allow the Government of the country or the industrious part of the nation to be bullied by masses of Rogues, calling themselves Patriots.' (Low to Dalhousie, June 10, 1848, ibid.) The entire English middle class shared that relief, and it is fascinating to hear it so exactly echoed from the further shores of India. Lord Palmerston called the outcome 'a glorious day, the Waterloo of peace and order'.

6 Lord Canning's Diary, March 2, 1856.
7 Low to Lushington, June 24, 1848, *Memoir and Correspondence of General James Stuart Fraser*, ed. Hastings Fraser, p 248.
8 Ibid., p 249.
9 Low to Lushington, July 14, 1848, Fraser, pp 251–4.
10 Ibid., pp 254–5.
11 Regani, p 275.
12 Low to Fraser, September 13, 1848, Fraser, p 258.
13 Dalhousie to Fraser, October 17, 1848, Fraser p 268. See also Dalhousie to Low, December 25, 1848, MSS Eur D1082, for a similar message.
14 This declaration was itself a pretence, for Dalhousie later admitted that the famous Article 12 of the 1800 Treaty imposed no obligation to maintain this huge otiose force in time of peace: 'If, however, the Nizam should turn round upon us, and deny the obligation existing by treaty, I am bound as a public man to say that I could not honestly argue that there was any other warrant than practice for upholding the Contingent.' Dalhousie to Fraser, September 16, 1852, Fraser, p 376.
15 Later defenders of Lord Dalhousie, such as his biographers Lee-Warner and Hunter, often defended his high-handed conduct on the grounds that he was motivated by concern for the Indian people as opposed to their degenerate rulers. No such defence is available in the case of Hyderabad and the Nizam. Dalhousie made it brutally clear that 'I disavow the doctrine of our having any moral or political obligation to take

the Government of his country into our own hands merely because he mismanages his own affairs; and I recognize no mission to regenerate Indian states, merely because they are misgoverned.' In a letter to John Low a month later, he registered his distaste more stridently still: 'As for the moral obligation which some assert that we are under by reason of our Paramountcy, to rescue the subjects of native powers from what we call oppression, whether they ask for rescue or not; I regard it as nothing less than an ambitious and hypocritical humbug.' (Dalhousie to Fraser, June 6, 1849, Fraser, p 291, and Dalhousie to Low, May 9, 1849.)

16 Dalhousie to Low, June 23, 1849.

17 Dalhousie to Fraser, December 26, 1848, Fraser, p 282.

18 Regani, p 284.

19 Fraser confided his fears to Major Moore, one of the several sympathetic Directors of the Court: 'I am ashamed of the weakness and irresolution of my own Government, and I would add a still meaner quality, but that it is just possible they did not speak with deliberate hypocrisy – although it has that effect – in professing a wish to maintain the Nizam's independence, while obstinately refusing to adopt or encourage measures which alone could have promoted that object.' (Fraser to Moore, May 4, 1851, Fraser pp 338–9.)

20 Dalhousie to Fraser, September 16, 1852, Fraser, p 379.

21 Fraser to Dalhousie, September 29, 1852, Fraser, p 383.

22 Fraser to Dalhousie, November 12, 1852, Fraser, p 408. Fraser was not alone in his misgivings. We would be wrong to imagine that criticism of Dalhousie has been confined to the Indian nationalist historians and anti-colonial campaigners of the twentieth century. Quite a few Directors of the Court, such as Moore, Lushington and Sir Henry Willock (see Fraser p 356), thought the same as Fraser. So did Sir Edwin Arnold, author of *The Light of Asia* and later editor of the London *Daily Telegraph*, who included a scorching analysis of the Nizam's hounding in his two-volume polemic, *The Marquis of Dalhousie's Administration of British India* (1865): 'We knew his difficulties had mainly sprung from the force we fathered upon him; we knew that no treaty sustained it, no necessity enjoined it; but he was in our power, and we served the writ upon him with merciless legal logic and punctuality. There was but one ground upon which we could do this, with the equanimity of a power calling itself just and generous, and that was that during all these years he had not objected to this slow ruin … Accordingly, the screw was gently but irresistibly turned down.' Arnold, ii, pp 136–8.

23 Arnold, ii, pp 130–1.

24 There was a knock-on benefit, too. 'The opium now grown in Berar is principally smuggled into Malwa and there undergoes further preparation

to fit it for exportation to Bombay.' (Fraser to Dalhousie, February 4, 1851.) Lord Ellenborough had already gained control of the Malwa fields. By adding Berar, Dalhousie would control all the major fields in the country and thus be able to protect the Bengal opium trade against interlopers.

25 Dalhousie to Low, July 12, 1848.
26 Ibid.
27 Low to Dalhousie, July 25, 1848.
28 Dalhousie to Low, September 14, 1848.
29 Dalhousie to Low, September 13, 1852.
30 Dalhousie to Herries, September 2, 1852.
31 The whole conversation is reported in Low's dispatch to Government of India, May 4, No 71 of 1853, and later published in *Parliamentary Papers relative to Territory Ceded by the Nizam*, HC No 418 of 1854, p 118 et ff.
32 Low to Dalhousie, April 30, May 1, May 2, 1853.
33 Dalhousie to Low, May 13, 1853.
34 Dalhousie to Low, May 26, 1853.
35 Fraser, p 414.
36 John Low does not mention this threatening message in his next dispatch to Dalhousie, of May 19. Hastings Fraser says (pp 413–14) that Low does mention 'a note' dated May 14, which was 'sent in original to the Nizam by the Minister, to impress the mind of His Highness with the belief that further unnecessary delays in settling the matter would not be tolerated'. But it is clear from the wording of Low's dispatch that this was a different note, written the same day by Low himself, demanding an immediate meeting with the Minister, but not mentioning troop movements. In any case, His Highness's mind was duly impressed. Just in case there was any lingering doubt about the intentions of the British, during those days a British officer was asked to survey the ramparts of the city in an ostentatious manner. (Regani, p 297.)
37 Dalhousie to Low, May 30, 1853.
38 Arnold, ii, pp 145–6.
39 There was, besides, an extra piece of double-dealing to add to the extortion with menaces deployed by Dalhousie and Low. In the final days, when the negotiations were near breaking point, John Low offered the Nizam an important concession. As he explained in his dispatch to Calcutta of May 4, 'Finding that the Nizam's dislike to the words "*in perpetuity*" was extreme, and fearing that the whole negotiation might fail if I insisted on that word, I announced that that was a part of the scheme which my Government had allowed me the liberty to alter if necessary; and I announced formally that if His Highness wished it, the

districts might be made over merely for a time, to maintain the Contingent as long as he might require it.'

So the words 'in perpetuity' were not included in the treaty that the Nizam signed. But as soon as they had his signature, both Dalhousie and Low took it for granted that the cotton plantations and the poppyfields would be British for ever. In a dispatch only a month later, Colonel Low remarked in passing that 'I knew that those districts are to be permanently in our hands.' (Low to Government, June 18, 1853, Fraser p 417.) And in Lord Dalhousie's dispatch to Low's successor in Hyderabad, of November 30, 1853, he said that the Assigned Districts are declared to be 'assigned in perpetuity'. (Ibid.) Nothing temporary about the arrangement at all. However, the legal uncertainty bequeathed by the treaty's wording rumbled on, so that 20 and 30 years later the next Nizam but one was still petitioning the British Government for the return of Berar. Indeed, future Nizams repeated the plea all the way through until India won her independence.

40 November 2, 1853, No 45 of 1853, IOR/E/4/822 pp 937–63.
41 *Parliamentary Papers relative to Territory Ceded by the Nizam*, No 418 of 1854, p 8.
42 Published in 1857, while the Mutiny was still in full swing, this instant book has the alluring subtitle, *How to Prevent Another One*.
43 Minto after the temporary acquisition of Java, Moira after taking Nepal, Amherst after the first Burma War, even Ellenborough after Napier had collared Sind, although he was recalled almost simultaneously.
44 Dalhousie to Low, June 9, 1852.

Chapter XIV: Charlotte returns to India

1 He dropped her letters, too, sometimes illustrated, like this one in fractured French:

Helas madame et cousine,

Je suis engagé a diner à Newgate demain avec les Chérifs de Londres – nous irons voir les prisonniers les treadmills et les jolis petits condamnes qu'on va pendre.

Apres je vais dans plusieurs soirées élegantes (surtout chez cette dame, miladi Gordon, que votre mari aime tant). Ainsi je ne serai de retour à Kensington qu'a minuit, bien trop tard pour venir frapper à votre petite porte si tranquille de votre Cottage si calme ou tout ce grand et petit monde sera couché.

Mes demoiselles sont guéries maintenant de leur chicken pox. Elles

envoient mille salutations d'amitie à la Colonie de Littl' Olland Ouse.
   Adieu madame et chère cousine
   votre affectionné
   Chevalier de Titmarsh

(February 1848, *Letters and Private Papers of William Makepeace Thackeray*, ed. Gordon N. Ray, 1945, ii, p 352.)
   Appended to the letter, Michelangelo Titmarsh, Thackeray's favourite alter ego, has drawn a smirking WMT peering in through the bars of the condemned man's cell, and then a frilled cavalier bowing and preening in high society. I like this one, too, accompanied by a sketch of the ailing WMT in bed:
   Mr Thackeray who is in bed will have great pleasure in dining with Mrs Irvine this evening. (Undated, ibid., iv, p 332.)

2 November 19, 1849, ibid., ii, p 609. The new baby was the last of the eight Irvine children. Gordon Ray identifies 'Augusta' as Augusta Georgina Low, i.e. Charlotte's younger sister. But the sense of the sentence requires that 'one of the other children' refers to a member of the Irvine family. Augusta Low junior had only arrived in India with her parents the year before. Augusta Irvine would have been much the same age as Marianne had been when she first appeared at Southampton Row. The confusion is pardonable; there were at least five Augustas in the cousinhood.
3 Marianne recalled:

When my sister Mrs Crawford and I came home from India as little girls, dear Aunt Ritchie was quite a mother to us, and to my brother Richmond and John Shakespear at school, and I don't know what we should have done without her. She was the kindest of the kind, overflowing with the milk of human kindness, and gracious to everyone. Without her our childhood would have been dreary, for there was scarcely anyone else who could receive us in the holidays, and her elastic house was always ready to open its hospitable doors and take us all in. The house was truly Holiday Hall to us & seemed at those times to be quite delivered up to us. I have walked down Southampton Row, looking, as I thought, on the house but the number is changed. (*The Ritchies in India*, ed. Gerald Ritchie, p 186.)

4 Kensington, December 31, 1849, *Letters*, ii, p 617.
5 Low to Dalhousie, January 17, 1851, MSS Eur D1082.
6 Buck, p 34.
7 Bhasin, p 31.

8 Baird, p 60.
9 Ibid., p 81.
10 Kanwar, p 27.
11 October 8, 1851, Baird, p 176.
12 June 25, 1849, Baird, p 81.
13 Ibid.
14 Baird, p 130.
15 Ibid.
16 August 11, 1851, Baird, pp 160–70.
17 Baird, p 130.
18 Dalhousie to Low, July 18, 1851.
19 Low to Dalhousie, August 20, 1851.

Chapter XV: Theo and Charlotte

1 Dalrymple, *The Last Mughal*, p 40.
2 Ibid., p 48.
3 Ibid., p 52.
4 *The Golden Calm*, p 201. The book is a fascinating compound of illustrations from *The Delhie Book*, Annie's recollections of her child-hood and later years in the city, and the recollections of the book's editor, the novelist M.M. Kaye.
5 Dalrymple, p 50.
6 *The Golden Calm*, p 126.
7 GG to Edward Campbell, October 23, 1852, Campbell-Metcalfe Papers, Box 1.
8 March 19, 1853. Ibid., Box 2.
9 January 7, 1853. Ibid., Box 1.
10 Thomas Metcalfe to GG, Kootub (Qutb), April 22, 1852. Ibid., Box 8. Dalrymple (p 462) has 1851, but Theo was not married to Charlotte by then.
11 Ibid., April 28.
12 Dalhousie to Low, September 9, 1852.
13 *The Ritchies in India*, pp 162–3 and 186.
14 Charlotte Metcalfe to Edward Campbell, January 12, 1853, Campbell-Metcalfe Papers, Box 7.
15 Emily Anne Bayley's narrative, Photo Eur 31 1B, Hardcastle Papers, pp 247–62. Also Campbell-Metcalfe Papers, Box 7, Emily Anne Bayley to Georgiana Metcalfe, September 28, 1853.
16 The cemetery is now marked only by a clump of trees near the Simla bus station. The gravestones have all disappeared.

17 Hardcastle Papers, ibid.
18 Theo to GG, n.d. but probably early 1856, Campbell-Metcalfe Papers, Box 8.
19 Ibid, 1857.
20 Theo to GG, ibid.
21 Ibid., August 12, 1856.
22 Hardcastle Papers, p 260.
23 Edward Campbell to GG, camp near Mooltan, November 27, 1856, Campbell-Metcalfe Papers, Box 6.
24 Baird, pp 257–8.

Chapter XVI: The Cherry ripens

1 June 23, 1853, Lee-Warner, ii, p 50.
2 Ibid., pp 194–7.
3 Ibid., p 203.
4 Ibid., p 205.
5 At first, messages were transmitted and received by the slow and unreliable galvanoscope, but at Dalhousie's suggestion, Professor W.B. O'Shaughnessy, the most eminent chemist in Calcutta whom he had appointed his Superintendent of Electric Telegraphs, travelled to Europe and the United States to study the Morse system, which was introduced in 1857, just in time for the Mutiny, in which it made almost as big a contribution to the British victory as Enigma did to winning World War Two. (Lee-Warner, ii, pp 192–5.) High above them all, the Surveyor-General of India, Andrew Waugh, was completing the final, Himalayan leg of the Great Arc, the mapping of India from Cape Comorin to Kashmir. In March 1856, just as Dalhousie was tottering aboard the SS Firoze to begin his homeward voyage, Waugh wrote a memo suggesting to the Asiatic Society of Calcutta that the highest peak of the great range he was surveying should be named after his former chief, Sir George Everest. (Keay, The Great Arc, p 166.) A gesture of high imperialism if ever there was one.
6 His decease cannot have been much delayed by the treatment he had from his physicians. They applied a mixture of pounded radishes to his agonizing piles, which, not surprisingly, 'caused a greater burning sensation'. For the stoppage of his urine, he was prescribed a mixture of cucumber, melon and endive seeds, sugar candy and jews' stone (the powder of the fossilized spine of sea urchins, a remedy against blockage popular far beyond India's borders). This did no good either, his entire system seized up, and a mixture of poppyseed pods

and oak-apples appeared to have dealt the *coup de grâce*. Doses of the admirable local opium eased his final hours.

7　Mansel to Government, December 14, 1853, House of Commons Paper, *Rajah of Berar*, No 416 of 1854.

8　*Berar*, pp 21–37.

9　The area he was talking about included the adjacent fields that had belonged to the Nizam before John Low's treaty which, according to Dalhousie, gave the British Government 'perpetual possession and administration'. So much for John's soothing words to the Nizam about possession being only 'for a time'.

10　'The British Government is bound not to put aside or to neglect such rightful opportunities of acquiring territory or revenue as may from time to time present themselves, whether they arise from the lapse of subordinate states, by the failure of all heirs of every description whatever, or from the failure of heirs natural, where the succession can be sustained only by the sanction of the government being given to the ceremony of adoption according to Hindoo law.' (Minute of August 30, 1848, repeated in *Berar*, p 35.)

11　*Berar*, p 35.

12　Ibid., p 36.

13　Ibid., p 38.

14　Ibid., p 39.

15　Kaye, *Mutiny*, i, p 284.

16　*Berar*, p 39.

17　Ibid., p 40.

18　Kaye Mutiny Papers, Eur MSS Home Misc 725/35.

19　*Berar*, p 40.

20　Ibid., p 45.

21　Ibid.

22　Sleeman, *Rambles*, p 221.

23　Vishnu Bhatt, pp 69–70.

24　Arnold, ii, pp 147–8.

25　House of Commons Paper, *East Asia (Annexation of Jhansi)*, No 431 of 1855, p 14.

26　Major D.A. Malcolm to Dalhousie, November 25, 1853, *Annexation of Jhansi*, p 7.

27　Ellis to Malcolm, December 24, 1853.

28　February 27, 1854.

29　Minute by Colonel Low, March 1, 1854, *Annexation of Jhansi*, p 23.

30　Lang, *Wanderings in India*, pp 84–96.

31　February 27, 1854, *Annexation of Jhansi*, p 22.

32　Kaye, *Mutiny*, i, p 66.

33 March 25, 1854, *Annexation of Jhansi*, p 31.

34 September 18, 1848, Baird, p 33.

35 July 30, 1854, Baird, p 169.

36 May 2, 1855, Baird, p 344.

37 June 17, 1855, Baird, p 348.

38 Dalhousie to Sleeman, Sleeman, *Journey*, i, pp xvii–xix.

39 1857, p 109.

40 Pemble, p 97.

41 Sherar, pp 74–5.

42 Sleeman, *Journey*, i, p 178.

43 *Journey*, ii, pp 331 and 6. The soil was 'the finest in India'. (Ibid., i, p lxiv.) He sent samples back to Calcutta, to Professor O'Shaughnessy, the wizard of the electric telegraph, who was ecstatic about its quality and who raved, too, about the admirable soap the locals made out of the *reha* earth, which they mixed with lime, fat and linseed oil. (Ibid., i, pp 191–3.)

44 Several of the tales are repeated or referred to several times. As Samuel Lucas puts it in *Dacoitee in Excelsis*: 'the managers of this impeachment deal with their allegations as the managers of a theatre, of which the resources are scanty, deal with their little army of supernumeraries. The same individual personages are passed over the stage again and again, and the result is to swell to an imaginary total and to heighten to the general eye the effect of the performance.' (Lucas, p 151.)

45 Pemble, p 100.

46 Ibid., pp 98–101. Some modern writers have even argued that Sleeman exaggerated the threat from the thugs and mythologized their rituals (see *The Strangled Traveler: Colonial Imaginings and the Thugs of India*, Martine van Woerkens, 2002; also M.J. Carter's piquant novel *The Strangler Vine*, 2014). But Mike Dash in *Thug: the true story of India's murderous cult*, 2005, argues that Sleeman's reputation was mostly well deserved and that he had rid India's roads of a genuine scourge.

47 'In the absence of any personal experience in this country, I am of course entirely dependent for my information on what I find in the Residency records, and can ascertain through the channels which supplied my predecessor.' (*Oude, Papers Relating to, 1856*, p 12.)

48 Ibid., pp 147–90.

49 July 21, 1855, ibid., p 198.

50 Minute, June 18, ibid., p 181.

51 Dalhousie to Low, August 25, 1855, Low, p 353.

52 August 18, 1855, *Oude, Papers*, p 220.

53 Ibid., pp 225–6.

54 November 21, 1846, Pemble, p 106.

55 Lucas, pp 171–2.
56 Ibid., pp 163–4.
57 Ibid., pp 101–8.
58 *Calcutta Review*, 1845, vol iii.
59 Sleeman to Hogg, October 28, 1852, *Journey*, ii, pp 377–8.
60 Sleeman to Dalhousie, September 1852, *Journey*, ii, p 372.
61 Mukherjee, *Awadh in Revolt*, p 35.
62 *Oude, Papers*, p 189.
63 Ibid., p 214.
64 Ibid., pp 224–5.
65 Court to Governor-General, November 21, 1855, ibid., p 236.
66 Ibid., p 167.
67 *War in Afghanistan*, i, p 203.
68 *Oude, Papers*, pp 285–6, 291.
69 Ibid., p 288.
70 Kaye, *Mutiny*, i, p 109.
71 February 8, 1856, Baird, p 369.
72 Lady Bayley's MS, p 274, MSS Photo Eur 031B, Hardcastle Papers.
73 Pemble, p 115.
74 Irwin, p 174.
75 Ibid., p 136.
76 Kaye, *Mutiny*, i, pp 95–6.
77 *Oude, Papers*, p 194.
78 Sharar, pp 64–5.
79 Mukherjee, *Awadh in Revolt*, p 43.
80 Sharar, p 74.
81 Ironically, these two splendid but dilapidated buildings have recently (2008 onwards) been restored by the Marxist government of Calcutta for the same reason, to conciliate the local Muslims. Satyajit Ray shot a good deal of his marvellous film *The Chess Players* (1977) in the *imambara* at Metia Bruz. The red velvet settee which was the Nawab's throne in the film is still there. The film starred Amjad Khan as Wajid Ali, Saeed Jaffrey as one of the two chess-obsessed noblemen, Victor Banerjee as the Prime Minister and Richard Attenborough as Outram. In the film, Wajid Ali Shah reproves his Prime Minister for weeping when Outram brings the bitter news. 'Only music and poetry can bring a real man to tears,' he says. In real life, though, it was the King who wept.
82 Low to Elphinstone, October 4, 1856, F88/176.
83 Diary, March 2, 1856.
84 May 2, 1856, Maclagan, p 4
85 Low to Elphinstone, ibid.

86 Lee-Warner, i, pp 113 and 361.

87 Hesketh Pearson, *Dizzy*, p 152.

88 Lee-Warner, ii, p 259.

89 Ibid., p 260.

90 Ibid., pp 342–3.

91 Minute, September 13, 1854, ibid., p 275. For Bentinck, see Rosselli, p 146. Bentinck's language had been if anything even more eloquent: 'the Europeans generally know little or nothing of the customs and manners of the Hindus ... their manner of thinking, their domestic habits and ceremonies, in which circumstances a knowledge of a people consists, is, I fear, in great part wanting to us. We understand very imperfectly their language ... We do not, we cannot associate with the natives. We cannot see them in their houses and with their families. We are necessarily very much confined to our houses by the heat; all our wants and business which could create a greater intercourse with the natives is done for us, and we are in fact strangers in the land.'

92 Dalhousie to Sir Charles Wood, August 15, 1854, ibid.

93 Ibid., pp 284–6.

94 Journal, May 22, 1857, *Ladies of Lucknow*, p 21.

95 Ireland, p 16.

96 Canning to Granville, May 19, 1857, Maclagan, p 88.

97 Kaye, *Mutiny*, i, pp 229–233.

98 Holmes, *Sir Charles Napier*, p 144.

99 Hibbert, p 63; Kaye, *Mutiny*, i, p 360.

Chapter XVII: 1857 – Theo, Edward, Robert, Malcolm

Theo at Delhi

1 Another version of the story has the warning message handed to Fraser quite a bit earlier, just after evening service at St James's by the Kashmir Gate, which would have given him more time still to barricade the city. See Dalrymple, *The Last Mughal*, pp 132–3, and Tytler, *An Englishwoman in India*, p 114. For Theo's escape, see C.T. Metcalfe, *Two Native Narratives*, pp 43–57, Lady Bayley's Account, Photo Eur 031B, pp 292–302, and MSS Eur D610/8. Also Wilberforce, pp 57–61.

2 Hibbert, p 73.

3 Edwards, Diary, May 17, 1857, MSS Eur C148. Looking back in 1863, Sir George Otto Trevelyan declared that nothing had changed: 'When but seven years have passed since such a mine lay beneath our

feet unheeded and unknown, we should be slow to affirm that we understand the feelings and character of the people of India. Their inner life still remains a sealed book to us.' (Trevelyan, *The Competition Wallah*, p 441.)

4 Wilkinson, *The Memoirs of the Gemini Generals*, p 30.
5 Metcalfe, pp 39–41.
6 Rawlins, p 152.
7 Ireland, p 23.
8 Arthur Lang, pp 30–1.
9 Lang, pp 31–2.
10 Kaye, *Mutiny*, ii, p 360.
11 Ireland, p 19.
12 Wilberforce, p 25.
13 Allen, *Soldier Sahibs*, p 280.
14 Kaye, *Mutiny*, ii, p 369.
15 Hibbert, p 77.
16 Gough, p 15.
17 Edwards, Diary, July 16, 1857. General Hewitt was by no means the only high British official who suffered a complete nervous collapse in the Mutiny. The most notorious case was that of the most senior official of all after the Governor-General, John Russell Colvin, the Lieutenant-Governor of the North-West Provinces. We first met Colvin as the joint architect of the disastrous policy that led to the First Afghan War. He never ceased to be one of the arch modernizers, eager to turf out the old landowners and introduce new rational systems of taxation. It can be argued how far he personally was responsible for the discontents that sparked off the mutinies in the countryside, but there is no doubt that he made a poor job of meeting the challenge at Agra, where he had his headquarters. The entire Christian population of the city was huddled together in the Red Fort, squabbling about precedence and living space, with an incompetent military commander and a Lieutenant-Governor who seemed to be losing touch with reality. When the Magistrate Mark Thornhill visited him, he barely raised his head from his book, lapped in a weary trance. He fired off letters in Greek and Hebrew and cipher to Calcutta, imploring aid which never came. His son, Sir Auckland Colvin, wrote a Life of him, claiming that he had been fully in control of the situation, but everyone who saw him in those dire days could see that his mind had 'irretrievably gone', to quote Roderick Edwards. He died in the fort, apparently of no identifiable complaint, except a broken heart, his dreams of modernization seemingly in ruins. (Thornhill, pp 33, 84–5, 97–99, 130–3; Coopland pp 141, 148; Colvin, pp 192–6.) The fort being encircled by mutineers,

John Colvin had to be buried in the courtyard, where to this day his Victorian-Gothic tomb brings an incongruous touch of South Kensington to the Mughal splendour.

18 Kaye, *Mutiny*, i, p 439.
19 Canning to Elgin, May 8, 1857, Kaye, *Mutiny*, i, pp 444–5.
20 Minute, May 10, 1857, Command 2252, *Mutiny of Native Regiments.*
21 Kaye, *Mutiny*, ii, 90.
22 Canning to Hewitt, May 16, 1857.
23 Metcalfe, pp 43–5.
24 Lady Bayley's account, Photo Eur O31B, pp 292–302. Also Wilberforce, pp 57–61.
25 Metcalfe, p 43.
26 Ibid., p 45.
27 Lady Bayley, ibid.
28 Dalrymple, p 214.
29 Thornhill, p 4.
30 Ibid., p 5.
31 Ibid., p 137.
32 Stokes, *The Peasant Armed*, p 146.
33 Vishnu Bhatt, pp 46–7
34 Thornhill, p 55.
35 Ibid., p 56.
36 Metcalfe to G.B. Thornhill, May 24, 1857, Eur MSS D610.
37 Barter, p 9. The story of the white child's foot still in its shoe was retold in the *Lahore Chronicle*, and it inflamed readers all over northern India, including Roderick Edwards, the joint magistrate at Saharanpur, who prophesied, correctly, that 'the massacres when our soldiers get inside [Delhi] will be terrible.' (Edwards, Mutiny Diary, June 19, 1857.)
38 Kaye, *Mutiny*, ii, p 351.

Edward: a sapper's war
39 Edward Thackeray, *Subaltern*, i, p 15.
40 *Ladies of Lucknow*, p 205.
41 Edward Thackeray, *Two Indian Campaigns*, p 8.
42 Thackeray, *Subaltern*, i, pp 10–11.
43 Dalrymple, p 230.
44 David, *Indian Mutiny*, p 158.
45 Barter, pp 12–14.
46 Edward Thackeray to Henrietta Shakespear, June 20 and July 2, 1857, *Subaltern*, i, p 12, ii, p 5.

Robert and the Santals
47 Low, p 35.
48 Augusta to John Low, May 9, 1855, MSS Eur D1082.
49 Dalhousie to John Low, Kotagiri, June 28, 1855, ibid.
50 Datta, p 39.
51 Ibid., p 24.
52 Dalhousie to John Low, August 25, 1855, ibid.
53 Datta, p 47.
54 O'Malley, *Santal Parganas*, p 53.
55 Chakraborti, pp 28–30, 40–42.
56 Kaye, *Mutiny*, ii, pp 478–85.
57 Trotter, p 249.

The Ridge and the Siege
58 Rotton, *The Chaplain's Narrative*, pp 61–2.
59 Lang, pp 56, 60. Hodson's Horse was one of the first regiments to
    sport the khaki (from the Hindi *khaki*, 'dust-coloured').
60 Lang, p 33.
61 Ibid., p 117.
62 July 2, 1857, *Subaltern*, ii, p 5.
63 Ibid., p 4.
64 Alicia Cameron, i, p 205.
65 Lang, p 62.
66 June 20, 1857, Campbell-Metcalfe Papers, Box 6.
67 Hibbert, p 282.
68 Thackeray, *Two Indian Campaigns*, p 29.
69 *On the Prevention and Cure of Cholera*, 1832. But Dr Barter was a
    young Irish quack, whose medical qualifications were dodgy, and
    nobody paid him any attention. Even 25 years later, as the Great
    Mutiny was reaching its worst, another pioneering doctor, John Snow,
    was attempting without success to convince *The Lancet* that the
    cholera in Soho was due to the infected water from the Broad Street
    pump and not to the foul air. The great panjandrums of public health,
    Edwin Chadwick and Florence Nightingale, remained 'miasmatists' to
    the last, thus condemning thousands more soldiers and civilians to a
    needless death.
70 Edwards, Mutiny Diary, June 21, 1857.
71 Stokes, *The Peasant Armed*, p 94.
72 Trotter, p 281.
73 Ibid., pp 263–7. Kaye, *Mutiny*, ii, pp 490–3.
74 Lang, p 94.
75 Kaye, ibid., iv, p 5.

76 Lang, p 82.
77 Barter, p 48.
78 Ibid., p 52. The Qudsia Bagh is as charming today as it was in that smoky dawn.
79 Ibid., p 50.
80 Medley in Kaye, ibid., iv, pp 23–4.
81 Lang, p 90.
82 Thackeray, *Two Indian Campaigns*, pp 44–5; Metcalfe, p 70; Photo Eur 31B, pp 306, 333–5; Dalrymple, *The Last Mughal*, p 325.
83 Kaye, ibid., iv, p 40.
84 Roberts, p 330.
85 Lang, p 92.
86 Thackeray, *Subaltern*, iii, p 11.
87 Lang, p 97.
88 Stokes, ibid., pp 123–4.
89 *Subaltern*, iv, p 5.
90 In fact, like many another local potentate, he had tried to avoid committing himself during the Uprising. In the last days of the siege, the Emperor had sent him a pitiful letter begging him to come and rescue him and the royal family and escort them, first to the famous Sufi shrine at Mehrauli and then on through the north-west to the shrines of Mecca and Medina. But the Nawab said, he was sorry but the times were too difficult. (Dalrymple, pp 276–7.) The Emperor's letter, produced at his trial, was one more proof of how hopelessly unsuited Bahadur Shah was to be a war leader, but it emerged too late to save the Nawab.

The redoubtable Mrs Coopland tells us: 'He was purposely put to death before Christmas Day, to show our contempt for the natives, who had threatened a rising on that day. Captain Garstone went to see the execution and said the Nawab was a long time dying. The provost-marshal, who performed this revolting duty, had put to death between 400 and 500 wretches since the siege, and was now thinking of resigning. The soldiers, inured to sights of horror, and inveterate against the sepoys, were said to have bribed the executioner to keep them a long time hanging, as they liked to see the criminals dance a "Pandie's hornpipe", as they term the dying struggles of the wretches.' (Coopland, p 190.)
91 Coopland, pp 192–3.
92 *Delhi Gazetteer*, 1883–4, p 30.
93 Dalrymple, ibid., pp 395–6.
94 Saunders to Lawrence, Agra, December 12, 1857, MSS Eur F186, No 25.

95 Dalrymple, ibid., pp 396–7.
96 March 12, 1858, MSS Eur F90, f12.

Robert and Edward at Lucknow
97 Kaye, *Mutiny*, i, p 7.
98 Lawrence, *Essays*, p 51; Kaye, ibid., i, p 332.
99 *Calcutta Gazette*, 1843; Innes, p147.
100 Kaye, ibid., iii, p 239.
101 Edwards, Mutiny Diary, May 25, 1857.
102 Kaye, ibid., iii, p 246.
103 *Ladies of Lucknow*, p 117.
104 Ibid.
105 Ibid., p 127.
106 Kaye, ibid., iii, p 293.
107 *Ladies of Lucknow*, p 48.
108 Roughly £4 10 shillings. *Ladies of Lucknow*, pp 170, 72.
109 Mukherjee, *Awadh*, p 94.
110 *Ladies of Lucknow*, p 192.
111 Ibid., p 140.
112 Ibid., p 151.
113 Kaye, ibid., iv, p 113.
114 Ibid., iii, p 334.
115 Ibid., iii, p 337n.
116 Ibid.
117 David, *Indian Mutiny*, p 310.
118 Ibid., p 312.
119 *Ladies of Lucknow*, p 179.
120 Ibid., p 182.
121 Ibid., p 65.
122 Lang, p 139.
123 Ibid.
124 Forbes-Mitchell, pp 57–81.
125 *Ladies of Lucknow*, p 206.
126 Hibbert, p 347.
127 *Ladies of Lucknow*, p 82.
128 Forbes-Mitchell, p 106.
129 Kaye, ibid., iv, p 251n.
130 Majendie, p 196.
131 Kaye, ibid., p 279.
132 *Subaltern*, March 24, 1858
133 Ibid.
134 Ibid.

135 Lang, pp 165–6. William Howard Russell, who had come out to India for *The Times* in time for Campbell's final onslaught, wrote a devastating account of the scene at the Kaiserbagh:

The soldiers had broken up several of the store-rooms, and pitched the contents into the court, which was lumbered with cases, with embroidered cloths, gold and silver brocade, silver vessels, arms, banners, drums, shawls, scarfs, musical instruments, mirrors, pictures, books, accounts, medicine bottles, gorgeous standards, shields, spears, and a heap of things which would make this sheet of paper like a catalogue of a broker's sale. Through these moved the men, wild with excitement, 'drunk with plunder'. I had often heard the phrase, but never saw the thing itself before. They smashed to pieces the fowling-pieces and pistols to get at the gold mountings, and the stones set in the stocks. They burned in a fire, which they made in the centre of the court, brocades and embroidered shawls for the sake of the gold and silver. China, glass and jade they dashed to pieces in sheer wantonness; pictures they ripped up or tossed on the flames; furniture shared the same fate.

Even worse, Russell thought, were the ravenous camp followers packed in a dense mass in the street, waiting till the soldiers had done before they scavenged what was left. (Quoted Kaye, *Mutiny,* v, pp 275–6.)

136 Stokes, *The Peasant Armed*, p 41.
137 Kaye, ibid., iv, p 287.
138 Kaye, ibid., v, pp 264–5.

Malcolm in the mofussil
139 Hutchins, p 44.
140 Trevelyan, p 139.
141 Gough, p 34.
142 Edwards, Mutiny Diary, June 19, 1857.
143 Kaye, *Mutiny*, vi, p 115. Alexander was Augusta's first cousin, the son of Henry Davenport Shakespear, John Talbot Shakespear's brother. It was Uncle Henry who had lent Augusta a horse when she first arrived in Calcutta. Alexander's granddaughter Dorothy married Ezra Pound; contrary to appearance, the child of this marriage, Omar Shakespear Pound, owed his middle name to a family rather than a literary connection. The Shakespears' brother-in-law Mordaunt Ricketts, the magistrate at Shahjahanpur over to the east, was not so lucky. Ricketts, the son of John's corrupt predecessor at Lucknow, wrote to a friend: 'I can't tell you how horrible the sensation is of hourly expecting to be massacred in cold

blood.' (Low, p 373.) On May 31, the sepoys of the 28th Native Regiment attacked the English church during service and murdered Ricketts in the porch. He and Alexander had married sisters. A third sister married General James Hope Grant, who had been Robert's commander at Lucknow. This cobweb of cousins and a few loyal native troops were all that preserved British rule out in the backwoods.

144 Gough, ibid.

145 Low, pp 373–4.

146 Bayly, *Rulers, Townsmen*, p 329.

147 Edwards, Mutiny Diary, June 18, 1857.

148 Stokes, *The Peasant Armed*, p 216.

149 Bayly, ibid., p 328.

150 Forbes-Mitchell, p 26.

151 H.D. Robertson, *District Duties*, p 43.

152 Edwards, ibid., July 20, 1857.

153 Pemble, p 238; David, *Indian Mutiny*, ch 19.

154 Kaye, *Mutiny*, v, pp 175–6.

155 Mukherjee, *Awadh*, pp 157–8 and 189–203; Chaudhuri, *Civil Rebellion*, pp 309ff.

156 This narrative of three weeks in the life of a junior civil officer in September 1857 is preserved in the Clatto Papers, but substantial extracts from it are given in Low, pp 375–83.

157 Roderick Mackenzie Edwards also wrote a published *Narrative* of these events, as well as his Mutiny Diary and two semi-official letters covering the period (MSS Eur C 148 1 and 2 and C183 respectively).

158 As Stokes remarks, 'the dependence of the British on their subordinate [native] officers was now to be shown.' (Stokes, p 180.)

159 Kaye, *Mutiny*, vi, p 124.

160 Dunlop, p 79.

161 MSS Eur C183.

162 Kaye, ibid., iii, p 201–2.

163 Kaye, ibid., vi, p 123.

164 Edwards, *Narrative*, p 14.

165 Edwards's Diary is full of the poltroonery displayed by his brother officers. When the 5th Native Infantry mutinied at Saharanpur, Colonel Guthrie of the Engineers 'did not show particularly well ... He was in a most uncomfortable frame of mind and distinguished himself by rushing into the house and blowing out all the lights, the result of which was that some of us could not find our weapons and others their ammunition.' Mr Colledge had panicked on May 11 hearing the news from Meerut and talked of shooting his wife and family and then himself. Major Palmer at Roorkee *had* shot himself, though not fatally,

claiming that he had done so because he had heard that his wife had been murdered, which Edwards dismissed as 'all "bosh", a very plausible but utterly false excuse'. Up at Mussoorie, there were more Europeans taking refuge than anywhere else north of Calcutta, and Edwards didn't think much of these 'dawdlers' either and the wild rumours they spread, when there was work to be done down in the Plains, only 30 or 40 miles to the south. Mr McClelland the missionary, who came to stay, did not escape Edwards's contempt. He was too frightened to undress or even take off his shoes for fear of an attack in the night; 'strange that the best men and those who profess the surest hope of future life should always be the most afraid of death.' (Mutiny Diary, August 5, 1857.)

166 Russell, *My Indian Mutiny Diary*, i, p 86.
167 Ibid., p 73.
168 Kaye, ibid., v, p 193.
169 Browne, pp 68–9.
170 Kaye, ibid., p 194n.
171 *The Times*, March 15, 1901.
172 Browne, pp 79–80.
173 Low, p 374.
174 MSS Eur D610/9 , 'Emily Anne Bayley's typewritten memorials of the notable connections of hers in the Mutiny.' The account was written for her daughter, hence the reference to Kate as an aunt.
175 *Subaltern*, iii, p 12.
176 Lang, p 167.
177 Lang, p 168.

Chapter XVIII: Post mortem

1 British historians such as Saul David and Christopher Hibbert tend to talk of 'the Indian (or the Great) Mutiny 1857', indicating a fleeting and concentrated flare-up. Indian writers such as S.B. Chaudhuri often refer to 'the Indian Mutiny (or Mutinies) 1857–1859', suggesting a much more prolonged and diverse resistance to British rule.
2 Kaye, *Mutiny*, v, p 82.
3 Ibid., pp 77–79.
4 Ibid., pp 30–36
5 It seems probable too that the British were keen to make little of these under-reported incidents in the south, in order to convince themselves that this was not a truly national uprising.
6 Vansittart Diaries, MSS Eur B167.

7 Edwards, Diary, June 19 and August 29, 1857.

8 Kaye, ibid., pp 291–2.

9 Kaye, ibid., iv, p 379.

10 Kaye, ibid., i, p 425.

11 Mukherjee, *Spectre*, p 60.

12 Mason, p 268. The most plausible summing up is that reached by the distinguished Indian historian R.C. Majumdar: 'It is likely that some secret negotiations were going on between the leading sepoys of different cantonments, though the exact nature of these cannot be ascertained. It is probable that the object of these was to organise a general mutiny, but for this we have no definite evidence.' (Majumdar, pp 207, 218.)

13 David, *The Devil's Wind*, ch 7.

14 Ibid.

15 Lang, p 126.

16 Minute, April 21, 1858, *Punjab Government Records*, Lahore 1911, vii, Part 2, p 391; Metcalf, *The Aftermath of Revolt*, p 55.

17 Kaye, v, pp 279–80.

18 Outram to Ross Mangles, January, 1858, Kaye, ibid., ii, p 27n.

19 David, *Indian Mutiny*, esp. Appendices 1–3, and *The Devil's Wind*, *passim*.

20 Mukherjee, *Awadh*, p 64.

21 Tapti Roy, p 29.

22 G. Harris, *Ladies of Lucknow*, p 90.

23 Thornhill, p 70.

24 Dalrymple, p 143.

25 Chaudhuri, *Civil Rebellion*, p 260; Dalrymple, pp 254–5.

26 Tapti Roy, p 51.

27 Ibid., pp 50–53.

28 Dalrymple, p 204.

29 Another Delhi prince, Feroze Shah, who fought mostly at Lucknow, argued in his proclamation of February 1858 that 'within the last few years the British continued to oppress the people in India ... and continued to eradicate Hinduism and Mahomedanism and to make all the people embrace Christianity.' (Mukherjee, *Awadh*, p 149.) The threat to faith was felt to be serious, and to be growing.

30 Mukherjee, *Awadh*, pp 151–2.

31 April 15, 1857, Command 2252, *Mutiny of Native Regiments*.

32 Minute, May 11, 1857, ibid.

33 July 27, 1857, col 537.

34 Ibid., col 541.

35 See *Besieged: Voices from Delhi*, 1857.

36 David, *The Devil's Wind*, ch 8.
37 Spear, p 269.
38 Hibbert, p 393.
39 Majumdar, *Sepoy Mutiny*, p 58.
40 Tarachand, p 11.
41 Bayly, *Indian Society*, p 188.
42 Metcalf, *Aftermath*, p 61.
43 I should add that this neglect comes within a wider neglect of the whole subject of the Mutiny, as fallow a field in 2002 as it was in the 1970s and 1980s, according to Mukherjeee. (*Awadh*, p vii.) More recently still, Farooqui says that he never met anyone at university who was specializing in 1857. (*Besieged*, p x.) The Mutiny was, it seems, as much of a disappointment to Indian nationalists as it was a humiliation to British imperialists.
44 Dalrymple, pp 207–8.
45 Rossetti wrote this poem within two days of reading the highly coloured account in the *Illustrated London News* of September 5, 1857. On discovering that the details were wrong, she added a footnote to later publications of the poem: 'I retain this little poem, not as historically accurate, but as written and published before I heard the suggested facts of the first verse contradicted.' It was, of course, not just the first verse but the whole story which was wrong.
46 Edwards, Mutiny Diary, May 11, 1857.
47 Ball, i, pp 270–5, ii, pp 294–6; Martin, ii, pp 305–6.
48 Home Misc 725, 'Memorandum containing the Result of Enquiries made by Desire of the Governor General into the Rumours of European Females having been dishonoured during the Late Mutinies'; see also Mukherjee, *Spectre*, pp 156–9.
49 Muir, ibid.
50 Kaye, *Mutiny*, iii, p 126.
51 Mukherjee, *Spectre*, pp 67–78.
52 Ibid., pp 75–77.
53 Kaye, ibid., pp 115–6.
54 David, *The Devil's Wind*, ch 8.
55 Russell, *Diary*, ed. Edwardes, 970, pp 29–30.
56 Frederic Cooper, *Crisis in the Punjab*, pp 154–6.
57 Holmes, p 373.
58 Cooper, pp 162–3.
59 Edwards, Mutiny Diary, August 5, 1857.
60 Ireland, p 218.
61 Cooper, p 167.
62 Hibbert, p 202.

63 Ibid.
64 Kaye, ibid., v, p 119.
65 Lowe, p 261.
66 Archaeological Survey of India, *The Residency, Lucknow*, 2003.
67 Kaye, ibid.
68 Thornhill, p 148.
69 Martin, ii, p 451
70 Ball, i, pp 412–13.
71 'The Sahib and the Nigger', *The Times*, October 20, 1858.
72 Trevelyan, *Cawnpore*, p 36. In fact, the hateful word had been in common use some decades earlier. See Emily Eden's account of doddery old General Elphinstone.
73 Ball, ii, p 420.
74 Majendie, pp 179–80
75 Hansard, July 27, 1857, col 482.
76 Ibid., col 442.
77 Ibid., col 475.
78 Ibid., col 446.
79 Ibid., col 444.
80 Ibid., col 463.
81 Ibid., col 444.
82 Ibid., col 445.
83 Ibid., cols 453–4.
84 Ibid., col 455.
85 Ibid.

Chapter XIX: Homecoming

1 Low to Canning, from Malta where he was recuperating, June 19, 1858, MSS Eur D1082.
2 Canning to Low, from Camp at Allahabad, April 6, 1858, ibid.
3 House of Commons, August 11, 1857, cols 1432–3.
4 Mead, p 14.
5 *The Times*, June 13, 1857.
6 Mangles to Low, November 10, 1857, D1082
7 Wood's speech in the House of Commons, May 17, 1858, as reported in Calcutta, see J.P. Grant's letter to Canning, June 28, 1858, MSS Eur F127/35. Hansard has Wood spreading the blame a bit wider, referring to 'vacillation in his Counsellors, pusillanimity on the part of the British population around him' (col. 750), which is better but not much.
8 November 4, 1858.

9 Canning to Court, July 6, 1858.

10 Martin, ii, p 141.

11 Mead, p 13.

12 Canning to Low, August 13, 1860, D1082.

13 September 1, 1857, Baird, p 385.

14 February 24, 1858, Baird, p 406.

15 Malta, January 28, 1858, Baird, p 398.

16 Malta, December 2, 1857, Baird, p 390.

17 Edinburgh, September 22, 1857, Baird, p 386.

18 What is now more often called chronic nephritis. Kidney disease had been described by Dr Richard Bright as early as 1827, and the swellings and fevers that Dalhousie complained of are common symptoms of it, but it is not clear whether his doctors ever put two and two together.

19 Trevelyan, *The Competition Wallah*, p 197.

20 Mason, p 319.

21 Canning to Low, October 13, 1857, Low, p 370.

22 Muir to Saunders, Agra, November 4, 1857, MSS Eur F/186.

23 Canning to Low, Camp, Allahabad, February 15, 1858, D1082.

24 Kaye, *Mutiny*, iii, p 369.

25 Ibid., iv, pp xi-xii.

26 Marshman, *Havelock*, p 293.

27 Kaye, ibid., iii, p 290.

28 *Views and Opinions of Brig-Gen John Jacob*, Lewis Pelly, ed., 1858, p 2.

29 Letter to the *The Times*, January 4, 1878.

30 'Foundations of the Government of India,' *The Nineteenth Century*, vol LXXX, October 1883, p 563.

31 Hutchins, p 3.

32 Trevelyan, pp 128–9.

33 Ibid., pp 304–5.

34 Leslie Stephen, *The Life of Sir James Fitzjames Stephen*, pp 293–5.

35 August 1, 1862, Metcalf, *Aftermath*, p 170.

36 Moon, p 886.

37 Ibid., p 912.

38 Ibid., p 985.

39 Ibid., p 984.

40 Bayly, *Rulers, Townsmen*, p 321.

41 *Economist*, October 13, 1860; Bagehot, *Works*, ed. Norman St John Stevas, xiv, p 234.

42 Ibid.

43 Bagehot, *Physics and Politics*, p 129.

44 Bagehot, *Works*, xv, p 119.

THE TEARS OF THE RAJAS

45 See Lucas, Bird and Arnold for the first approach; Lee-Warner and Hunter for the second. Hunter's short life of Dalhousie was published in the 'Rulers of India' series at the end of the century, which Hunter edited. By then, every proconsul had become a superman.

46 Low, p 414.

47 *The Correspondence and Journals of the Thackeray Family*, ed. John Aplin, ii, p 346.

48 Ibid.

49 Low, pp 404–5.

50 Aplin, ibid., pp 347–8.

51 Ibid.

52 Ibid., pp 350–1.

53 Ibid., pp 347, 349. The piety of the Lows was not mere social observance. They relished a good theological tussle. 'Lady Low asked me if I wd not read one of Molineuxs sermons to them, but I told her that I could not conscientiously read them with any effect but Augusta tried to convert me to Molineux by reading me an extract in wh. as they said, the repetition was very striking – but I must say for them they allow me to abuse him as much as I please, which is all that I ask.' (Ibid., p 351.) *Lent Sermons* by the Rev Capel Molyneux of St Paul's, Onslow Square, had been published in 1860.

54 Ibid., p 347.

55 Ibid., p 351.

56 Behrend, p 171.

57 George Wheeler, *The Visit of the Prince of Wales to India in 1875–6*, 1876, p 177. Sir George Otto Trevelyan sighed in his satirical excursion *The Competition Wallah*, 'I could not have believed in the existence of an entertainment so extravagantly dull as a nautch.' (pp 54–5.)

58 Mirza Ali Azhar, ii, p 417, based on Garcin de Tassy, *Lectures*, ii, p 215. Rosie Llewelyn-Jones, *Last King*, pp 296–7, can find no mention of any such visit in the official diaries of the Royal Tour, nor is the jewelled walking stick (or in some accounts, jewelled sword) included in the lists of the gifts presented to the Prince of Wales.

59 Aplin, ii, p 31.

60 *Anne Thackeray Ritchie, Letters and Journals*, ed. A. Bloom and J. Maynard, 1994, p 84.

61 *Anne Thackeray Ritchie*, ed. Hester Ritchie, 1924, p 111.

62 *Millais*, i, p 276; Aplin, ii, p 31.

63 Annie to her husband, July 1875, Aplin, iv, C544.

64 John Harris, *Much Sounding of Bugles*, p 127.

65 Younghusbands, pp 53–4.

66 Hopkirk, p 497.
67 Harris, pp 205–6.
68 Belloc, *The Modern Traveller*, p 41.
69 Younghusbands, pp 53–4.
70 Harris, pp 230–1.
71 As recently as February 2013, David Cameron refused an Indian request to return it to its original home.

BIBLIOGRAPHY

PRINCIPAL MANUSCRIPT SOURCES

British Library (India Office Records)
MSS Eur F148 Raffles–Minto Collection
MSS Eur F439 Pollock Collection (Richmond Shakespear)
MSS Eur F87–89 Elphinstone letters (John Low, Richmond Shakespear)
OIOC Photo Eur 031 1B, Hardcastle papers (Charlotte Low and Theo Metcalfe)
MSS Eur D610 Indian Mutiny papers (Theo Metcalfe)
IOR L/PS/6/455 and /493 Indian Mutiny papers (Malcolm Low)
IOR/L/MIL/17/2/492 Narratives of Events regarding the Mutiny in India of 1857–8 and the Restoration of Authority (Malcolm Low)
MSS Eur C148 and C183 Diary and letters of Roderick Edwards (Malcolm Low)
MSS Eur F108 Papers of Sir George White (Robert Low)
MSS Eur C961 Sir John Low letters
MSS Eur D1082 (formerly Home Misc 828) John Low letters
Home Misc vol 738 Charles Metcalfe letters (John Low)
Home Misc vol 733 John Malcolm letters (John Low)

National Library of Scotland
Minto papers (inc. letters and journal of Captain William Taylor)
Dalhousie papers (John Low)

Nottingham University Library
Bentinck papers (John Low)

St Andrews University Library
Cleghorn papers

Cambridge, South Asian Studies Library
Campbell-Metcalfe Letters (Charlotte Low and Theo Metcalfe)

PARLIAMENTARY PAPERS

Nos 300, 310–320 of 1810: Papers relating to East India Affairs (Madras Army)

No 369 of 1818: Hostilities with the Peishwah
No 660 of 1837–38: Succession to the Throne of Oude
No 96 of 1839: Further Correspondence Respecting the Succession to the Throne of Oude
No 131 of 1839: Afghanistan
No 9 of 1840: War in Afghanistan
No 30 of 1843: Gates of Somnath
No 31 of 1843: Afghanistan
No 416 of 1854: Rajah of Berar
No 418 of 1854: Hyderabad: Papers Relative to Territory Ceded by the Nizam
No 125 of 1857–58: The King of Oude
No 265 of 1857–58: (Oude) Proclamation
No 431 of 1855: Annexation of Jhansi
Command Paper 2086 of 1856: Oude, Papers Relating to
No 245 of 1856: Marquis of Dalhousie Minute, dated February 28, 1856
Command Papers 2252,2254, 2264, 2265, 2266, 2277 of 1857: Mutiny of Native Regiments
No 26 of 1857–8: Mutiny of Native Regiments (Proclamation and Punishment)
No 70 of 1857–8: Army: Additional Troops

A

Abbott, J., *Narrative of a Journey from Herat to Khiva*, 2 vols, 1843
Ahmad, Safi, *British Residents at the Court of Avadh, 1764–1856*, Lucknow, 1968
Ahmad, Safi, *Two Kings of Awadh: Muhammad Ali Shah and Amjad Ali Shah, 1837–1847*, Aligarh, 1971
Ali, Mrs Meer Hassan, *Observations on the Mussulmauns of India*, ed. W. Crooke, 1917
Allen, Charles, *Soldier Sahibs: The Men Who Made the Northwest Frontier*, 2000
Aplin, John, ed., *The Correspondence and Journals of the Thackeray Family*, 5 vols, 2011
Archaeological Survey of India, *The Residency, Lucknow*, 2003
Archer, Major E.C, *Tours in Upper India*, 1831
Arnold, Edwin, *Dalhousie's Administration of India*, 2 vols, 1865
Atkinson, G.F., *The Campaign in India 1857–8*, 1859
Atkinson, G.F., *Curry and Rice*, 1859
Azhar, Mirza Ali, *King Wajid Ali Shah of Awadh*, 2 vols, Karachi, 1982

B

Baird, J.G.A., ed., *Private Letters of the Marquess of Dalhousie*, 1910

Ball, Charles, *The History of the Indian Mutiny*, 2 vols, 1858, 1859

Barnett, Richard B., *North India Between Empires: Awadh, the Mughals and the British 1720–1801*, 1980

Barter, Dr Richard, *On the Prevention and Cure of Cholera*, 1832

Barter, Richard, *The Siege of Delhi*, 1984

Bayly, C.A., *Indian Society and the Making of the British Empire*, 1988

Bayly, C.A., *Rulers, Townsmen and Bazaars: North Indian Society in the Age of British Expansion 1770–1870*, 1983

Bayly, C.A., *The Raj: India and the British 1600–1947*, 1990

Behrend, John, and Lewis, Peter N., *Challenges and Championships Vol I: The R&A Golf Club 1754–1883*, 1998

Bew, John, *Castlereagh*, 2011

Bhasin, Raja, *Simla: The Summer Capital of British India*, Delhi, 1992

Bhatt, Ravi, *The Life and Times of the Nawabs of Lucknow*, Delhi, 2006

Bhatt, Vishnu Godshe Versaikar, tr. Mrinal Pande, *1857: The Real Story of the Great Uprising*, Delhi, 2011

Bird, Major Robert Wilberforce, *The Spoliation of Oudh*, 1857

Blacker, Lt-Col Valentine; *Memoir of the Operation of the British Army in India 1817, 1818, 1819*, 3 vols, 1821

Blake, Robert, *Disraeli*, 1966

Blakiston, John, *Twelve Years Military Adventure in Three Quarters of the Globe*, 1829

Boulger, Demetrius C., *Lord William Bentinck*, Oxford, 1892

Broome, Capt. Arthur, *History of the Rise and Progress of the Bengal Army*, 1851

Browne, Sam, *The Journal of Sir Sam Browne*, ed. W. Blackwood, 1937

Buck, Edward J., *Simla Past and Present*, Bombay, 1925

Butler, William F., *Narrative of the Historical Events connected with the 69th Regiment*, 1870

C

Cameron, Alan D., The Vellore Mutiny, PhD Thesis, Edinburgh 1984

Cannon, Richard, *Historical Record of the 50th, or the West Essex Regiment of Foot*, 1844

Cardew, Alexander, *The White Mutiny*, 1929

Carstairs, Robert, *The Little World of an Indian District Officer*, 1912

Case, Adelaide, *Day by Day at Lucknow*, 1858, reprinted in *Ladies of Lucknow*, 2009

Chakraborti, Digambar, *History of the Santal Hool of 1855*, 1988

Chaudhuri, S.B., *Civil Rebellion in the Indian Mutinies, 1857–1859*, Calcutta, 1957

Chaudhuri, S.B., *Theories of the Indian Mutiny 1857–1859*, Calcutta, 1965

Chaurasia, R.S., *History of the Marathas*, Delhi 2004

Chirinian, Perumal, *The Vellore Mutiny, 1806*, 1982

Choksey, R.D., Ed, *The Last Phase, selection from the Deccan Commissioner's files*, Bombay, 1948

Choksey, R.D., *Mountstuart Elphinstone, The Indian Years, 1796–1827*, Bombay, 1971

Choksey, R.D., *A History of British Diplomacy at the Court of the Peshwas (1786–1818)*, Poona, 1951

Choksey, R.D., *The Aftermath (1818–1826)*, Bombay, 1950

Choksey, R.D., *Early British Administration (1817–1836)*, Poona, 1964

Clark, Aylwin, *An Enlightened Scot: Hugh Cleghorn (1752–1832)*, Duns, 1992

Colebrooke, T.E., *Life of the Honourable Mountstuart Elphinstone*, 1884

Colvin, Sir Auckland, *John Russell Colvin*, 1895

Compton, Herbert, *A Particular Account of the European Military Adventurers of Hindustan from 1784 to 1803*, 1892

Cooper, Frederic, *Crisis in the Punjab*, 1858

Cooper, Randolf, *The Anglo-Maratha Campaigns and the Contest for India*, 2003

Coopland, R.M., *A Lady's Escape from Gwalior*, 1859, reprinted as *The Memsahib and the Mutiny*, 2009

Corfield, J. and Skinner, C., *The British Invasion of Java in 1811*, 1999

Cotton, J.S., *Elphinstone*, 1892

Culshaw, W.J., *Tribal Heritage, a study of the Santals*, 1949

D

Dalrymple, William, *The Last Mughal*, 2006

Dalrymple, William, *Return of a King*, 2013

Dalrymple, William, *White Mughals*, 2002

Datta, K.K., *Anti-British Plots and Movements Before 1857*, 1970

Datta, K.K., *The Santal Insurrection of 1855–7*, Calcutta, 1940

David, Saul, *The Indian Mutiny 1857*, 2002

David, Saul, *The Devil's Wind*, 2012

Davies, Philip, *Splendours of the Raj*, 1985

Dunlop, Robert Henry Wallace, *Service and Adventure with the Khakee Ressalah*, 1858, repub. as *The Khakee Ressalah*, 2005

Duyker, Edward, *Tribal Guerrillas: the Santals of West Bengal*, 1987

E

Eden, Emily, *Up the Country*, 1866

Eden, Emily, *Letters from India*, 1872

Eden, Fanny, *Tigers, Durbars and Kings*, ed. Janet Dunbar, 1988

Edwardes, H.B. and Merivale, H., *The Life of Sir Henry Lawrence*, 2 vols, 1872

Edwardes, Michael, *The Orchid House: Splendours and Miseries of the Kingdom of Oudh 1827–57*, 1960

Edwardes, Michael, *Red Year: The Indian Rebellion of 1857*, 1972

Ellenborough, Edward Law, Lord, *A Political Diary, 1828–30*, ed. Lord Colchester, 2 vols, 1886

F

Farooqui, Amar, *Sindias and the Raj*, Delhi, 2011

Farooqui, Mahmood, *Besieged: Voices from Delhi 1857*, 2010

Fay, Eliza, *Original Letters from India*, Calcutta 1817, reprinted Hogarth Press, 1925

Fisher, Michael H., *A Clash of Cultures: Awadh, the British and the Mughals*, 1987

Fisher, Michael H., *Indirect Rule in India: Residents and the Residency System, 1764–1858*, 1991

Fisher, Michael H., 'The Resident in Court Ritual', *Modern Asian Studies, 24:3*, 1990, pp 419–58

Fisher, Michael H., 'The Imperial Coronation of 1819', *Modern Asian Studies, 19:2*, 1985, pp 239–77

Forbes-Mitchell, William, *Reminiscences of the Great Mutiny*, 1893

Fraser, Hastings, *Memoir and Correspondence of General James Stuart Fraser*, 1885

Fraser, Hastings, *Our Faithful Ally the Nizam*, 1865

Fregosi, Paul, *Dreams of Empire: Napoleon and the First World War 1792–1815*, 1989

Fortescue, Sir John, *A Gallant Company*, 1927

G

Glendinning, Victoria, *Raffles and the Golden Opportunity*, 1781–1826, 2013

Gough, Hugh, *Under Deadly Fire*, 2011, first published as *Old Memories of the Mutiny*, 1897

Graff, Violette, ed., *Lucknow: Memories of a City*, 1999

Guha, Ranajit, *Dominance without Hegemony: History and Power in Colonial India*, 1997

Guha, Ranajit, *Elementary Aspects of Peasant Insurgency in Colonial India*, Delhi, 1983

Gupta, N., *Delhi between two Empires, 1803–1931*, 1981

Gupta, P.C., *Nana Sahib and the Rising at Cawnpore*, Oxford, 1963

Gupta, P.C., *Baji Rao and the East India Company*, 1939

Gupta, P.C., *The Last Peshwa and the English Commissioners, 1818-1851*, Calcutta, 1944

H

Haigh, R.M. and Turner, P.W., Nickalsain: *The Life and Times of John Nicholson*, 1890

Hamilton, General Sir Ian, *Listening for the Drums*, 1944

Hamilton, Walter, *A Geographical, Statistical and Historical Description of Hindustan and Adjacent Countries*, 2 vols, 1820

Hannigan, Tim, *Raffles and the British Invasion of Java*, Singapore, 2012

Harris, G., *A Lady's Diary of the Siege of Lucknow*, 1858, reprinted in *Ladies of Lucknow*, 2009

Harris, John, *Much Sounding of Bugles: The Siege of Chitral, 1895*, 1975

Hathaway, Jane, ed., *Rebellion, Repression, Reinvention*, Westport, Conn, 2011

Hathaway, Jane, 'A Tale of Two Mutinies', csas.ed.ac.uk/mutiny/conf.papers

Hay, Sidney, *Historic Lucknow*, 1939

Herbert, Christopher, *War of No Pity: The Indian Mutiny and Victorian Trauma*, 2007

Hewitt, James, ed., *Eyewitnesses to the Indian Mutiny*, 1972

Hibbert, Christopher, *The Great Mutiny: India 1857*, 1978

Hill, S.C, *The Life of Claude Martin*, Calcutta, 1901

Holmes, T.R.E., *History of the Indian Mutiny*, 1882

Holmes, T.R., *Sir Charles Napier*, 1925

Hoover, James W., *Men without Hats: Dialogue, Discipline and Discontent in the Madras Army 1805–1807*, 2007

Hope, John, *The House of Scindea: a Sketch*, 1863

Hopkirk, Peter, *The Great Game*, 1990

Hough, William, *A Casebook of European and Native General Courts Martial Held from the Years 1801 to 1821*, 1821

Hunter, Sir William, *The Annals of Rural Bengal*, 1868

Hunter, Sir William, *The Marquess of Dalhousie*, 1895

Hunter, Sir William, *The Thackerays in India and some Calcutta Graves*, 1897

Hutchins, Francis G., *The Illusion of Permanence*, 1967

I

Innes, J.J. McLeod, *Sir Henry Lawrence The Pacificator*, 1898

Ireland, W.W., *History of the Siege of Delhi by an Officer Who Served There*, 1861

Irwin, H.C., *The Garden of India, or Chapters on Oudh History and Affairs*, 1880

K

Kanwar, Pamela, *Imperial Simla*, Delhi, 1990

Kaye, John William, *The Life and Correspondence of Sir John Malcolm*, 2 vols, 1856

Kaye, J.W. and Malleson, G.B., *History of the Indian Mutiny*, 6 vols, 1897

Kaye, Sir John, *The Life and Correspondence of Charles, Lord Metcalfe*, 1854

Kaye, Sir J.W., *History of the War in Afghanistan*, 3 vols, 1874

Kaye, Sir J.W., *Lives of Indian Officers*, 2 vols, 1843

Kaye, M.M., ed., *The Golden Calm: An English Lady's Life in Moghul Delhi*, 1980

Keay, John, *The Gilgit Game*, 1979

Keay, John, *The Great Arc*, 2010

Keay, John, *Last Post: the End of Empire in the Far East*, 1997

Keay, John, *Into India*, 1973

Keay, John, *The Honourable Company*, 1991

Keene, H.G., *Fifty-Seven*, 1883

Keene, H.G., *A Servant of John Company*, 1897

Knighton, William, *The Private Life of an Eastern King*, 1855

L

Lambrick, H.T., *Sir Charles Napier and Sind*, 1952

Lang, Arthur Moffatt, *From Lahore to Lucknow*, 1992

Lang, John, *Wanderings in India*, 1859

Lee-Warner, Sir William, *The Life of the Marquis of Dalhousie KT*, 2 vols, 1904

Llewelyn-Jones, Rosie, *A Fatal Friendship; The Nawabs, the British and the City of Lucknow*, 1985

Llewelyn-Jones, Rosie, *Engaging Scoundrels: True Tales of Old Lucknow*, 2000

Llewelyn-Jones, Rosie, *The Great Uprising in India*, 2007

Llewelyn-Jones, Rosie, ed., *Lucknow, City of Illusions*, 2011

Llewelyn-Jones, Rosie, *The Last King in India: Wajid Ali Shah*, 2014

Longford, Elizabeth, *Wellington: The Years of the Sword*, 1969

Low, C.R., *Life and Correspondence of Sir George Pollock*, 1873

Low, Ursula, *Fifty Years with John Company*, 1936

Lowe, Thomas, *Central India during the Rebellion of 1857 and 1858*, 1860

Lucas, Samuel, *Dacoitee in Excelsis*, 1857

M

Maclagan, Michael, *Clemency Canning*, 1962

Maclagan, Michael, *The White Mutiny*, 1964

Majendie, Vivian D., *Up Among the Pandies*, 1859

Majumdar, R.C., *The Sepoy Mutiny and the Revolt of 1857*, Calcutta, 1963

Malleson. G.B, *The Mutiny of the Bengal Army*, 'The Red Pamphlet', pub anon 1857

Malleson, G.B., *The Decisive Battles of India*, 1883

Man, E.G., *Sonthalia and the Sonthals*, 1867

Marshman, J.C., ed., *Memoirs of Major-General Sir Henry Havelock*, 1860

Markel, Stephen, and Tushara Bindu Gude, eds., *The Art of Courtly Lucknow*, 2011

Martin, Robert Montgomery, *History of the Indian Empire*, vol II, ?1858– ? 1861

Mason, Philip (see also Philip Woodruff), *A Matter of Honour, An Account of The Indian Army, Its Officers and Men*, 1974

Masselos, Jim, and Gupta, Narayani, *Beato's Delhi 1858, 1997*, 2000

Maude, F.C., *Memories of the Mutiny*, 2 vols, 1894

Mead, Henry, *The Sepoy Revolt*, 1857

Mecham, Clifford Henry, *Sketches and Incidents of the Siege of Lucknow*, 1858

Metcalfe, Charles Theophilus (tr): *Two Native Narratives of the Mutiny in Delhi*, 1898

Metcalf, Thomas R., *The Aftermath of Revolt, India 1857–70*, 1964

Metcalf, Thomas R., *Land, Landlords and the British Raj*, 1979

Millais, John Guille, *The Life and Letters of Sir John Everett Millais*, 1899

Minto, 1st Earl of, *Life and Letters of 1st Earl of Minto*, ed E.E.E. Elliot-Murray-Kynynmound, 3 vols, 1874

Minto 1st Earl of, *Lord Minto in India*, ed. E.E.E. Elliot-Murray-Kynynmound, 1880

Mishra, Pankaj, *From the Ruins of Empire*, 2012

Misra, Amaresh, *Lucknow: Fire of Grace*, Delhi, 1998

Misra, Amaresh, *War of Civilisations: India AD 1857, Vol I The Road to Delhi*, Delhi, 1998, *Vol II, The Long Revolution*, Delhi, 2008

Misra, Anand Sarup, *Nana Sahib Peshwa and the Fight for Freedom*, Lucknow, 1961

Moon, Penderel, *The British Conquest and Dominion of India*, 1989

Moorhouse, Geoffrey, *Calcutta*, 1971

Mukherjee, Rudrangshu, *Awadh in Revolt 1857–1858: A Study of Popular Resistance*, 2002

Mukherjee, Rudrangshu, *Spectre of Violence: the 1857 Kanpur Massacre*, 2003

Mukherjee, Rudrangshu, *Mangal Pandey: Brave Martyr or Accidental Hero?*, 2005

Mukherjee, Rudrangshu, *Dateline 1857: India's First War of Independence*, 2008

Mukherjee, Rudrangshu, *The Year of Blood*, Delhi, 2014

O

Oldenburg, Veena Talwar, *The Making of Colonial Lucknow, 1856–1877*, 1984

O'Malley, L.S.S., *Bengal District Gazetteer, Santal Parganas*, Calcutta, 1910

O'Malley, L.S.S., *The Indian Civil Service 1601–1930*, 1931

P

Parkes, Fanny, *Begums, Thugs and White Mughals*, ed. William Dalrymple, 2002

Pati, Biswamoy, ed., *Issues in Modern Indian History*, 2000

Paton, John, *The British Government and the Kingdom of Oudh, 1764–1835*, ed. Bisheshwar Parasad, Allahabad, 1944

Pearson, Hesketh, *Dizzy*, 1951

Pearson, Hesketh, *The Hero of Delhi: a Life of John Nicholson*, 1939

Peers, Douglas M., *Between Mars and Mammon: colonial armies and the garrison state in India, 1819–1835*, 1995

Pelly, Lewis, ed., *The Views and Opinions of Brigadier-General John Jacob*, 1858

Pemble, John, *The Raj, the Indian Mutiny and the Kingdom of Oudh, 1801–1859*, 1977

Pottinger, George, *The Afghan Connection: The Extraordinary Adventures of Major Eldred Pottinger*, 1983

Prasad, Bisheshwar, see Paton, John

Prynne, J.T. and Bayne, A., *Memorials of the Thackeray Family*, 1879

R

Rabit, Abdu'l-Ahad, *Tarikh Badshah Begum*, tr. by Muhammad Taqi Ahmad, Allahabad, 1938

Rawlins, J.S., *Autobiography of an Old Soldier*, 1896

Ray, Gordon N., *Thackeray, vol I The Uses of Adversity*, 1955; *vol II The Age of Wisdom*, 1958

Ray, Gordon N., *The Buried Life*, 1952

Ray, Tarapada, ed., *Santal Rebellion Documents*, Calcutta, 1983

Regani, Sarojini, *Nizam-British Relations 1724–1857*, Delhi 1963

Ritchie, Anne Thackeray, *Letters and Journals*, ed. A. Bloom and J. Maynard, 1994

Ritchie, Gerald, ed., *The Ritchies in India*, 1920

Ritchie Hester, ed., *Anne Thackeray Ritchie*, 1924

Roberts, Emma, *Sketches of Hindustan*, 1837

Roberts, Frederick, Earl of Kandahar, *Forty-One Years in India*, 1897

Robertson, Sir George, *Chitral – the Story of a Minor Siege*, 1898

Robertson, H.D., *District Duties during the Revolt in the North-West Provinces in 1857*, 1859

Rosselli, John, *Lord William Bentinck: the Making of a Liberal Imperialist 1774–1839*, 1974

Rothschild, Emma, *The Inner Life of Empires, An eighteenth-century History*, 2011

Roy, Tapti, *The Politics of a Popular Uprising: Bundelkhand in 1857*, 1999

Russell, William Howard, *My Diary in India in the Year 1857–58*, 2 vols, 1860

Ruswa, Mirza Muhammad Hadi, *Umrao Jan Ada (Courtesan of Lucknow)*, 1961

S

Sale, Lady, *A Journal of the Disasters in Afghanistan*, 1840

Salmon, J.B., *The Story of the R&A*, 1956

Sen, Surendra Nath, *Eighteen Fifty-Seven*, Delhi, 1958

Shakespear, John, *John Shakespear of Shadwell and His Descendants, 1619–1931*, Newcastle, 1931

Shakespear, Richmond, 'Personal Narrative of a Journey from Heraut to Ourenbourg', *Blackwood's Edinburgh Magazine*, June, 1842

Sharar, Abdul Halim, *Lucknow: The Last Phase of an Oriental Culture*, ed. Fakhir Hussain, 1975

Sleeman, W.H., *Rambles and Recollections of an Indian Official*, 1844

Sleeman, W.H., *A Journey Through the Kingdom of Oude 1849–50*, 2 vols, 1858

Sleeman, W.H., 'The Story of Bysa Bae', unpublished, photocopy in British Library

Soltykoff, Prince A., *Voyage dans l'Inde*, Paris, 1851

Spankie, Robert, *Narrative of Events attending the Outbreak of Disturbances and the Restoration of Authority in the District of Saharunpoor in 1857–8*, 1858

Stephen, Leslie, *The Life of Sir James Fitzjames Stephen*, 1895

Stevenson, David, *The Beggar's Benison: Sex Clubs in Enlightenment Scotland and their Rituals*, 2001

Stokes, Eric, *The Peasant and the Raj*, 1978

Stokes, Eric, *The Peasant Armed*, 1986

T

Tavender, I.T., *Casualty Roll for the Indian Mutiny*, 1983

Taylor, Alicia Cameron, *Life of General Sir Alex Taylor*, 1913

Taylor, D.J., *Thackeray*, 1999

Thackeray, Sir E.T., *Two Indian Campaigns in 1857–8*, 1896

Thackeray, Sir E.T., *Reminiscences of the Indian Mutiny*, 1916

Thackeray, Sir E.T., *A Subaltern in the Indian Mutiny*, ed. C.B. Thackeray, 1930–31

Thompson, Edward, *The Life of Charles, Lord Metcalfe*, 1937

Thompson, Edward, *The Other Side of the Medal*, 1926

Thorn, W., *Memoir of the Conquest of Java*, 1815

Thorn, W., *A Memoir of Major-General Sir Rollo Gillespie*, 1816

Thornhill, Mark, *The Personal Adventures and Experience of a Magistrate During the Rise, Progress and Suppression of the Indian Mutiny*, 1884

Trevelyan, G.O., *Cawnpore*, 1886

Trevelyan, G.O., *The Competition Wallah*, 1866

Trotter, L.J., *Auckland*, 1893

Trotter, L.J., *The Life of John Nicholson*, 1898

Tytler, Harriet, ed. Anthony Sattin, *An Englishwoman in India*, 1986

V

Vaidya, S.G., *Peshwa Bajirao and the Downfall of the Maratha Power*, 1975

W

Wakeham, Eric, *The Bravest Soldier*, 1937

Webster, Anthony, *Gentlemen Capitalists: British Imperialism in South-East Asia 1779–1890*, 1998

Webster, Anthony, *The Richest East India Merchant: The Life and Business of John Palmer of Calcutta 1767–1836*, 2007

Weller, Jac, *Wellington in India*, 1972

Welsch, Christina, 'Unhappy season of delusion and disorder', Princeton Colonialism and Imperialism Workshop, February 15, 2012, princetonciw@gmail.com

Wilberforce, Reginald W., *An Unrecorded Chapter of the Indian Mutiny*, 1895, reprinted as *With Them Goes Light Bobbee*, 2011

Wilkinson, Johnson and Osborn, *The Memoirs of the Gemini Generals*, 1896

Wilson, Colonel W.J., *History of the Madras Army*, 6 vols, Madras, 1882

Wood, Peter, 'Vassal State in the Shadow of Empire: Palmer's Hyderabad 1799–1867' PhD Thesis, University of Wisconsin-Madison, 1981

Woodruff, Philip (Philip Mason), *The Men Who Ruled India*: Vol I, *The Founders*, 1953; Vol II, *The Guardians*, 1954

Y

Yapp, M.E., *Strategies of British India: Britain, Iran and Afghanistan, 1798–1859*, 1980

Young, Keith, *Delhi – 1857*, 1902

Younghusband, G. and F., *The Relief of Chitral*, 1895

Yule, Henry, and Burnell, A.C., *Hobson-Jobson*, ed. William Crooke, 1902

THE FAMILY TREES

(The leading characters are in capitals)

1. The Metcalfes

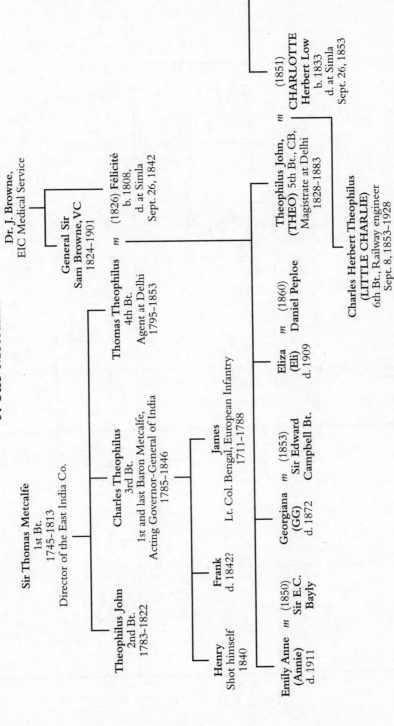

Sir Thomas Metcalfe
1st Bt.
1745–1813
Director of the East India Co.

Theophilus John
2nd Bt.
1783–1822

Charles Theophilus
3rd Bt.
1st and last Baron Metcalfe,
Acting Governor–General of India
1785–1846

Thomas Theophilus
4th Bt.
Agent at Delhi
1795–1853

m (1826) **Félicité**
b. 1808,
d. at Simla
Sept. 26, 1842

Dr. J. Browne,
EIC Medical Service

**General Sir
Sam Browne, VC**
1824–1901

Henry
Shot himself
1840

Frank
d. 1842?

James
Lt. Col. Bengal, European Infantry
1711–1788

**Emily Anne
(Annie)**
d. 1911
m (1850)
Sir E. C.
Bayly

**Georgiana
(GG)**
d. 1872
m (1853)
Sir Edward
Campbell Bt.

**Eliza
(Eli)**
d. 1909
m (1860)
Daniel Peploe

**Theophilus John,
(THEO)** 5th Bt., CB,
Magistrate at Delhi
1828–1883
m (1851)

CHARLOTTE
Herbert Low
b. 1833
d. at Simla
Sept. 26, 1853

**Charles Herbert Theophilus
(LITTLE CHARLIE)**
6th Bt., Railway engineer
Sept. 8, 1853–1928

2. The Lows

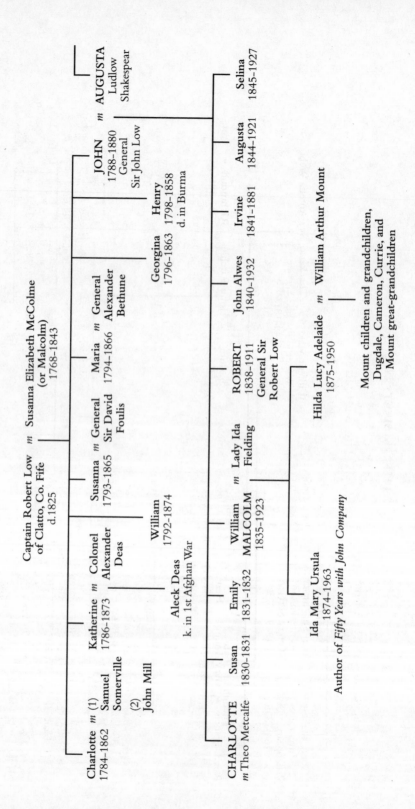

Captain Robert Low
of Clatto, Co. Fife
d.1825

m Susanna Elizabeth McColme
(or Malcolm)
1768–1843

Charlotte *m* (1)
1784–1862 Samuel
Somerville

(2)
John Mill

Katherine *m* Colonel
1786–1873 Alexander
Deas

William
1792–1874

Aleck Deas
k. in 1st Afghan War

Susanna *m* General
1793–1865 Sir David
Foulis

Maria *m* General
1794–1866 Alexander
Bethune

Georgina
1796–1863

Henry
1798–1858
d. in Burma

JOHN *m* AUGUSTA
1788–1880 Ludlow
General Shakespear
Sir John Low

Susan
1830–1831

Emily
1831–1832

CHARLOTTE
m Theo Metcalfe

Ida Mary Ursula
1874–1963
Author of *Fifty Years with John Company*

WILLIAM
MALCOLM
1835–1923

m Lady Ida
Fielding

ROBERT
1838–1911
General Sir
Robert Low

Hilda Lucy Adelaide
1875–1950

m William Arthur Mount

John Alwes
1840–1932

Irvine
1841–1881

Augusta
1844–1921

Selina
1845–1927

Mount children and grandchildren,
Dugdale, Cameron, Currie, and
Mount great-grandchildren

3. The Shakespears & the Thackerays

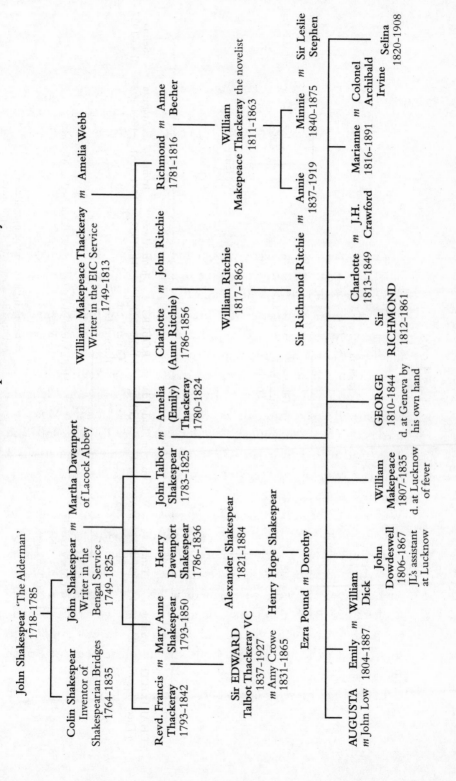

ACKNOWLEDGEMENTS

My first thanks go to Mary Mount and Pankaj Mishra who led me into India and patiently guided me to all the places I needed to see and others that I knew nothing of.

Rudrangshu Mukherjee, the great historian of the Mutiny, has directed my researches and dispelled my confusions with unfailing kindness, though he can take no blame for the outcome.

In Delhi, I have a lively sense of gratitude to William Dalrymple who on an unforgettable first day there guided us round Mehrauli and showed us the extraordinary Mughal tomb which the Metcalfes used as their weekend retreat. I did not know then that Charlotte and Theo had passed their last Christmas together there, but it was a poignant and auspicious beginning to my Indian adventure. Readers will also note how much my account of the Metcalfes owes to Willie's masterpiece, *The Last Mughal*, just as my account of Richmond in Afghanistan draws on his latest book, *Return of a King*. In Delhi, too, we had the pleasure of the company of Pankaj's parents, Ajit and Saroj, and his two entrancing sisters, Punam and Ritu. In Lucknow, we were entertained by his uncle and aunt at the Mohammad Bagh Club. In Calcutta, we were generously entertained by Amit Chaudhuri and his family. It was Amit who introduced us to the Bengal Club, that ultimate echo of British India.

In England, I owe a huge debt to my cousin Mary Cameron, who unearthed the Clatto Papers bequeathed to her by Ursula Low, our great-aunt, and showed me the portraits and miniatures which were part of the same bequest. With characteristic generosity, she and her son Alexander Cameron QC lent me the papers and allowed me to photograph the pictures, which together with Ursula Low's forgotten book make up the backbone of this book. I am also grateful to my cousin Cylla Dugdale and her son Joshua for their efforts to track down Low memorabilia.

In Scotland, my warm thanks are due to Ken Fraser and his wife Pat, former owners of Clatto and until recently living at Wester Clatto. It was Ken who drove me round Fife, showed me the Kemback churches and introduced me to the Royal & Ancient clubhouse where I was shown the portrait and mementoes of Sir John Low by the enthusiastic curator Laurie Rae. The Museum Director, Angela Howe, was also extremely helpful. At Clatto itself, I was given a welcome, the warmth of which old Sir John would have heartily approved, by the present owners, Joe and Ann Headon, who showed me round and gave me the photo of the house as it was after Sir John's baronial embellishments. In Cupar, the librarian Janice Wightman searched every corner for the memorabilia of the Lows of Clatto.

Among the research libraries of the world, there can be few to touch the Old India Office Collection now reposed in the Asia and Pacific Reading Room at the British Library, where its dedicated and friendly staff never fail to help the perplexed. As always, I am grateful to the London Library, whose holdings on British India are particularly good. I am grateful, too, to the South Asia Centre Library in Cambridge, and to the Manuscripts Department of Nottingham University, both of them so welcoming to stray visitors. For pictures, the National Army Museum, the Victoria and Albert Museum and the National Portrait Gallery have all proved invaluable and beautifully catalogued resources.

My agent David Miller has surpassed even his normal standards in the editorial care and attention he has lavished on the text, removing infelicities and inconsistencies with a kindly glee. Mike Jones, my editor at Simon and Schuster, began the final winnowing with a gentle but deadly flail, and Jo Roberts-Miller and Jo Whitford, my copy editor and project editor, completed it with an acute and vigilant eye. To all of these and to those other friends who have read and commented on the text, I owe more than I have with anything else I have written.

PICTURE CREDITS

Introduction
Aunt Ursie's elephants, author's image.

Chapter II
Tipu's Tiger, Wikimedia Commons.

Plate section 1

p. 1 Private collection.

p. 2 Original watercolour from 1911 edition of Captain G.F. Atkinson, *Curry and Rice* (top left); from Eric Wakeham, *The Bravest Soldier*, 1937 (middle right); British Library (middle left); from Charles Ball, *The History of the Indian Mutiny*, I, 1858 (bottom right).

p. 3 Frontispiece to William Thorn, *A Memoir of Major-General Sir R.R. Gillespie*, 1816 (top left); National Portrait Gallery (top right); Iziko South African National Gallery, Capetown (bottom left); National Portrait Gallery (bottom right).

p. 4 National Portrait Gallery (top left); from William Thorn, *The Conquest of Java*, 1815 (top right); British Library (bottom left); National Portrait Gallery (bottom right).

p. 5 Wikimedia Commons (top left); National Portrait Gallery (top right); from Robert Melville Grindlay, *Scenery, Costumes and Architecture Chiefly on the Western Side of India*, 1830 (middle); British Library (bottom right).

p. 6 British Library (top); author's photographs (middle and bottom).

p. 7 Provenance unknown.

p.8 British Library (top); from the illustrated edition of William Knighton, *The Private Life of an Eastern King*, 1855 (middle and bottom).

Plate section 2

p.1 From John Shakespear, *John Shakespear of Shadwell*, 1931 (top); 'Mr Joseph entangled' from 1899 edition of William Makepeace Thackeray, *Vanity Fair* (middle); from Charles Ball, *The History of the Indian Mutiny*, II, 1858 (bottom).

p. 2 By kind permission of HM the Queen (top); private collection (bottom).

p. 3 Private collection (top left, top right); from Ursula Low, *Fifty Years with John Company*, 1936 (middle, bottom).

p. 4 Wikimedia Commons (top); author's photograph (middle left, middle right); from Ursula Low, *Fifty Years with John Company*, 1936 (bottom).

p. 5 From 1898 edition of William Makepeace Thackeray, *The Newcomes* (top left); from Ursula Low, *Fifty Years with John Company*, 1936 (top right); Wikimedia Commons (bottom).

p. 6 British Library (top); author's photograph (middle); Wikimedia Commons (bottom left); frontispiece to *The Golden Calm*, ed. M.M. Kaye, copyright John Ricketts and M.M. Kaye (bottom right).

p. 7 Frontispiece to Charles Ball, *The History of the Indian Mutiny*, I, 1858, from a photograph by Mayall (top left); from John Shakespear, *John Shakespear of Shadwell*, 1931 (top right); *Illustrated London News*, 23 February, 1856 (middle); from Captain G.F. Atkinson, *The Campaign in India*, 2013 (bottom).

p.8 From Captain G.F. Atkinson, *The Campaign in India*, 2013 (top); from Charles Ball, *The History of the Indian Mutiny*, II, 1858 (middle left); Wikimedia Commons (middle right, bottom).

Plate section 3

p. 1 British Library (top); by kind permission of HM the Queen (middle); British Library (bottom).

p. 2 From Charles Ball, *The History of the Indian Mutiny*, II, 1858 (top); Bridgeman Images (middle left); frontispiece to Charles Ball, *The History of the Indian Mutiny*, II, 1858, from a photograph by Mayall (middle right); National Portrait Gallery (bottom).

p. 3 Wikimedia Commons (top, middle); from Charles Ball, *The History of the Indian Mutiny*, II, 1858 (bottom).

p. 4 Private collection (top left); original watercolours from 1911 edition of Captain G.F. Atkinson, *Curry and Rice* (top right, middle); British Library (bottom).

p. 5 Wikimedia Commons (top); from Charles Ball, *The History of the Indian Mutiny*, I, p 275 (middle); British Library (bottom).

p. 6 Photographs by Julia Margaret Cameron, dates unknown (top left, top right); from John Shakespear, *John Shakespear of Shadwell*, 1931 (bottom).

p. 7 Provenance unknown (top); original watercolour from 1911 edition of Captain G.F. Atkinson, *Curry and Rice* (middle); British Library (bottom).

p. 8 National Army Museum (top, middle); photograph by Charles Ball, late 1890s.

INDEX

Page numbers followed by n indicate a reference in the Notes section